PLAYING FOR CHANGE

The Continuing Struggle for Sport and Recreation

For more than forty years, scholars of the history and sociology of sport and recreation have studied how, no matter the time or place, sport is always more than just a game. In *Playing for Change*, leading scholars in the field of sports studies consider that legacy and forge ahead into the discipline's future. Through essays grouped around the themes of international and North American sport, including the Vancouver and Sochi Olympic Games, access to physical activity in Canadian communities, and the role of activism and the public intellectual in the delivery of sport, the contributors offer a comprehensive examination of the institutional structures of sport, physical activity, and recreation. This book provides wide-ranging examples of cutting-edge research in a vibrant and growing field.

RUSSELL FIELD is an assistant professor in the Faculty of Kinesiology and Recreation Management at the University of Manitoba.

Playing for Change

The Continuing Struggle for Sport and Recreation

EDITED BY RUSSELL FIELD

UNIVERSITY OF TORONTO PRESS
Toronto Buffalo London

© University of Toronto Press 2015
Toronto Buffalo London
www.utppublishing.com
Printed in the U.S.A.

ISBN 978-1-4426-5005-3 (cloth)   ISBN 978-1-4426-2820-5 (paper)

Printed on acid-free, 100% post-consumer recycled paper
with vegetable-based inks

Library and Archives Canada Cataloguing in Publication

Playing for change : the continuing struggle for sport and recreation / edited
by Russell Field.

Includes bibliographical references and index.
ISBN 978-1-4426-5005-3 (bound). ISBN 978-1-4426-2820-5 (paperback)

1. Sports. 2. Sports – Social aspects. 3. Sports – Canada. I. Field, Russell, editor

GV704.P53 2015   796   C2015-905232-7

This book has been published with the help of a grant from the Federation for the
Humanities and Social Sciences, through the Awards to Scholarly Publications
Program, using funds provided by the Social Sciences and Humanities Research
Council of Canada.

University of Toronto Press acknowledges the financial assistance to its publishing
program of the Canada Council for the Arts and the Ontario Arts Council, an
agency of the Government of Ontario.

Canada Council   Conseil des Arts
for the Arts   du Canada

ONTARIO ARTS COUNCIL
CONSEIL DES ARTS DE L'ONTARIO
an Ontario government agency
un organisme du gouvernement de l'Ontario

Funded by the   Financé par le
Government   gouvernement
of Canada   du Canada

Canadä

To Bruce Kidd

Contents

PLAYING FOR CHANGE

The Continuing Struggle for Sport and Recreation

Introduction: For Jets and Country, a Reminder that Sport Matters

RUSSELL FIELD

Your eyes and ears may tell you all you need to know, but if that is not enough, then use your legs. Walk through almost any city in Canada, the United States, and many other countries throughout the world. Sport matters. From ice hockey in Canada to cricket in the Caribbean and South Asia, to football (soccer) almost everywhere outside of North America, sport matters. Even beyond these stereotypical examples, in all its embodied forms – physical activity, play, dance, and other body-movement cultures, as well as codified sport competitions – sport matters. This is hardly a novel observation, but it is not as straightforward a claim as it might at first appear.

The city in which I live, Winnipeg (Manitoba), is Canada's eighth largest. To many Canadians, it is best known by its derisive nickname "Winterpeg," thanks to the Prairies' deep freeze in winter. A historical text on Siberia notes that nine of the globe's ten coldest cities are in the northern Russian region; Winnipeg is the other one.[1] When not battling the cold, the city is most renowned for its voracious summer-time mosquitoes, the frequent spring-time floods of the Red and Assiniboine rivers, and its claim to one of the highest rates of violent crime in Canada.

Nevertheless, for Winnipeggers and others in the know, the city has considerable charms. Not the least of these is a vibrant arts scene (including well-known authors, live theatre, and music). And, for a considerable number of Winnipeggers, sport matters. Many residents take to the outdoors to cycle and hike in the warm weather and to ski and snowshoe in the winter, and the city claims to be the capital of curling in Canada, boasting at least sixteen curling rinks.[2] Thanks in part to twice hosting the Pan American Games, in 1967 and 1999, the city benefits from world-class facilities in some of the Olympic sports, including the Pan Am Pool, and consequently is home to the national women's volleyball team.[3] Finally, a considerable amount of public attention is focused on the fortunes of the Blue Bombers of the Canadian Football League (CFL), who play in one of the league's newest facilities, which in the summer of 2015 also hosted three games for the Fédération Internationale de Football Association (FIFA) Women's World Cup. (Fans of the Blue Bombers' biggest rivals, the Saskatchewan Roughriders – whom Winnipeg hosts in the annual Banjo Bowl game – proudly display their "Rider pride" by wearing scooped-out watermelons on their heads. Sport, in this case Canadian football, does matter to these people; it must.)

This being Canada, however, Winnipeggers care (or, more appropriately, the impression is created that a vast majority of Winnipeggers care) about hockey. So, when we celebrated one of the warmest and driest summers in memory, one local columnist declared 2011 to be "the sweetest summer this city has ever experienced." This phantom (and perhaps needless) honour came despite "a gang war poisoning our town," "back-lane arsonists causing fear," and "a one-in-a-three-hundred-year flood." The cause for such joy was neither the summer warmth nor the thirty-year-low mosquito count. No, the source of summer happiness was a winter pastime. In the year 2011 the National Hockey League (NHL) returned to Winnipeg, bringing with it the long-departed Jets franchise. Subsequently, for the same columnist, "a feeling of pride washed over the 'Peg as we rejoined one of our country's most important national conversations"[4]: hockey.

The original Jets franchise departed for the sunnier (but less hockey-savvy, many Winnipeggers believed) climate of Phoenix, Arizona, in 1996. The reasons were various, and few had anything to do with the club's rabid local support, which culminated in a very public "Save the Jets" campaign. Although the Jets occupied a meaningful place in the fabric of the city and in the lives of many Winnipeggers, attempts to prevent their departure in 1996 were not uncontested.[5] Nevertheless, as Canadian historian and Winnipeg resident Gerald Friesen asked rhetorically, "Is the apparent mourning in Winnipeg for the death of the Jets hockey team of no consequence?"[6] Clearly not, for there was "pure, unalloyed joy" when it was announced in June 2011 that the Atlanta Thrashers NHL franchise would be relocated to Winnipeg and then that the club would begin play in the fall of the same year as the rechristened Jets. Local media briefly took to calling the club the Jets 2.0, and all prior claims to the Coyotes franchise faded from public discourse. And why not? The "Jets" were back. Four seasons later, with one, very brief play-off berth to show for their efforts, the Jets still play in front of sold-out crowds.

While conversations about the Jets, or the Briar or the Tournament of Hearts (the Canadian men's and women's curling championships, respectively), may dominate conversations at Tim Hortons doughnut shops across Winnipeg and the rest of Manitoba, similar scenes are repeated in cities and towns around the world. The relevance of sport and physical activity to the Winnipeggers' sense of themselves and their city is different only in kind from the importance that similar cultural practices play in the lives of Parisians, Nairobians, or Bangkokians. Cycling, football (soccer), or sepak takraw may replace hockey and curling in these discussions, but throughout the Western world and in the global South, sport matters. It bonds community members (although sport is not the only practice around which community forms). While sport can be a site for division and discord, it is also a place for civic identification with national or transnational commercial sporting entities – for example, the rise and prominence of Indian Premier League (IPL) cricket (certainly a more prominent example globally than the NHL's Winnipeg Jets) or the hosting of events such as the Olympics or Pan Am Games.

While sport matters to flag-waving fans and unabashed civic boosters, it is to issues such as these that an increasing body of sport scholarship – born in the political climate of the 1960s and honed with the emergence of cultural studies in the 1970s and 1980s – has also turned its attention to explore the multiplicity of ways in which sport "matters."[7] Across the humanities and social sciences, scholars continue to explore a variety of themes, including the role of the state in balancing the promotion of fitness and physical-activity opportunities with the investment in spectator facilities and the hosting of major events; the influence of material conditions on the access to opportunities for physical activity and on the ways in which sport reproduces and reconstitutes gendered, sexualized, and racialized identities as well as shaping beliefs about bodies and ability; the nature of commercialized and globalized sport, and the concomitant involvement of the sport media (especially as online resources broaden our understanding of what constitutes "media"); and the historical roots of all of these issues.

In acknowledging the cultural complexity of sport (and its relevance to cultural studies), it is important to recognize that, as Friesen notes, "games do matter to people." The announcement of the Jets' return to Winnipeg prompted a seemingly spontaneous public celebration one summer's evening in 2011 at the city's signature intersection downtown, Portage Avenue and Main Street, reaffirming Friesen's claim that a "shared sensation and shared memory creates a community." Adopting a critical perspective on sport and physical activity, therefore, is not to suggest that people's affinities, whether as participants or as spectators, are neither genuine nor well intentioned. Sport in both its contemporary and its historical forms may reflect, as well as contribute to, normative configurations of gender, race, class, and ability (among other identities), but it can also "shape one's awareness of community" as "the very lines of competition help communities to define themselves."[8] It is at the community level that sport and physical activity are experienced by many Canadians, especially as participants. But is this a community for all? Is it a community experienced in the same way by all? Or is this a community, in the case of the Jets, to which all Winnipeggers wish to (or can) belong? As Parissa Safai, Victoria Paraschak, and Robert Pitter and Glyn Bissix chronicle in this volume, sport, physical activity, and recreation matter to communities, but the ways in which the resources for these are distributed and accessed are often unequal, contested, and the subject of considerable debate.

The return of the Jets, however, was more than a local sport story. In Canada, hockey is often made to stand in for the nation; it is what Bruce Kidd and John Macfarlane have called "the Canadian universal" and "the Canadian metaphor."[9] Beyond this symbolic and oftentimes stereotypical attachment, professional hockey – and the cartel (NHL) to which the Jets were (re-)admitted – is a continental business. The NHL, headquartered in New York, may embody the dreams of many Canadian boys (and, increasingly, girls), but the league itself is a business that has been dominated by U.S. capital since the mid-1920s. This was a troubling state of affairs for Kidd and Macfarlane – "We may still call it our national game, but like nearly everything else in this country we have sold it to the Americans"[10] – which, four decades ago, when they wrote this in *The Death of Hockey*, symbolized American dominance of Canadian industry and culture. It was telling, of both the commercial nature and the continental scope of what is often perceived in Winnipeg as a community property, that the original Jets' logo that was proudly displayed by some Winnipeggers during the team's fifteen-year absence had remained the property of the NHL and that, through purchasing this apparel, these fans were contributing financially to the very institution against which many of them believed they were protesting.[11]

Kidd and Macfarlane gave voice to a perceived Canadian regret over "the changes commodification has wrought in hockey."[12] In arguing that Kidd and Macfarlane deploy a "practical nostalgia" to interpret the past and suggest an alternative future, Philip Moore contends that for the authors the "Americanisation of the game, more than anything else, alienated the game from its 'rightful' owners."[13] A prime contributor to the commodification and subsequent continentalization of Canadian sport is the media, which privileges men's commercial sports, primarily those based in the United States – for example, NFL football, NBA basketball, Major League Baseball, men's professional golf, and NASCAR auto racing; the increasing television presence of European men's soccer leagues is the only challenge to this American dominance, and the difference is geographic, not ideological. Each March the annual NHL "trade deadline" feeds a media machine that devotes a full day's worth of live television coverage across both of Canada's 24-hour sports television networks, and in February the annual Super Bowl, the football championship of the United States, regularly draws a greater Canadian television audience than does its counterpart north of the forty-ninth parallel, the Grey Cup game. (This gap varies depending upon the teams involved in the Grey Cup match, but the 2013 Grey Cup between the Hamilton Tiger-Cats and the Saskatchewan Roughriders attracted an average audience of 4.5 million, which peaked at 5.5 million viewers late in the second quarter. By contrast, the February 2014 Super Bowl attracted 7.3 million Canadian viewers on English-language television and an additional 610,000 on French-language television.)[14] The popularity of "American" sports in the Canadian media market is often cited as an indication of how the commodification of sport has changed the experience of sport in Canada. However, as Moore argues, "commodification is often a contested process as local understandings of the game are negotiated through time."[15] Similarly, the chapters by Stephen Hardy and Colin Howell in this volume revisit the historical record to assert that continental cultural dominance, especially where sport is concerned, is neither straightforward nor uncontested.

February is not just Super Bowl month, though. It is also the time of year in which the world's elite winter-sport athletes gather quadrennially for the Winter Olympic Games. In the same week that over eight million Canadians watched the Super Bowl, the national sports media (especially those outlets that had paid for broadcasting rights) blanketed screens with coverage of the 2014 Winter Olympics from Sochi, Russia. The media coverage of the Sochi Olympics was dominated initially by stories of international reaction to Russia's anti-gay-rights stance and rumours of graft and corruption in the Games' financing, before shifting to the usual human-interest stories and the inspiring medal-winning performances that followed the Opening Ceremonies.[16] Olympic Games are, as Alan Tomlinson and Christopher Young note, a "platform for national pride and prestige."[17] (They are also a vehicle of civic boosterism, as David Whitson and Donald Macintosh, John Hannigan, and others have argued.[18]) Tomlinson and Young's argument was borne out in the national pride that circulated around Canada's success at the 2010 Vancouver Olympics, topped off by Sidney Crosby's gold-medal-winning overtime goal in the men's hockey final, the last event of the Games. This was "the most-watched television broadcast in Canadian history, with a final audience of 16.7 million viewers," as "nearly half the Canadian population watched the entire game on average."[19] The Olympic Games are an international event, one of many that, as Tomlinson and Young note with irony, "purport to be spheres of neutrality and embodiments of universalist and idealist principles."[20] Yet, as journalist Stephen Brunt noted on the one-year anniversary of the 2010 Vancouver Olympic Games, the event was for Canada "a watershed moment, not just in terms of sport but the larger culture, setting off the greatest mass display of patriotic fervour since the end of the Second World War."[21]

Ten months prior to Sochi, Winnipeg (or, at least, some political leaders and members of the city's sport community) was celebrating the opportunity to host Canada's future Olympians. In April 2013 the city won the right to host the Canada Summer Games in 2017, the year of the country's sesquicentennial, and fifty years after Winnipeg had first hosted the Pan Am Games.[22] An event born in the 1960s as the federal government began to play a prominent role in promoting and supporting sport development, the Canada Games, which alternates between summer and winter incarnations, is a national competition for young athletes with international aspirations. As a developmental opportunity, the Canada Games were not far removed from the "original aspirations of the Olympic Movement," which Bruce Kidd recalls seeing prominently displayed when he competed at the 1964 Tokyo Olympics. At the time, "the overarching goal of the Olympics ... to bring people together under sporting culture so they can get to know each other better" was still central to the Olympic project.[23] Elsewhere in this volume, John MacAloon explores – albeit in an early-twentieth-century American Olympic context – the shift in leadership of the domestic Olympic movement at the time of the 1904 St Louis Olympic Games that began the withdrawal of the universalist and humanist aims of the Olympic movement from the foreground of U.S. amateur sport.

These values stand in contrast to the state-funded athlete-support system that ebbed and flowed over the next four decades in Canada until the Canadian Olympic Committee branded its athlete-development strategy in preparation for the 2010 Games as "Own the Podium." The partnership of state, corporate, and sport interests (and investors) had as its goal the leading of the medals table at the 2010 Winter Olympics and finishing in the top twelve at the 2012 London Summer Olympics.[24] The emphasis on medals and performance as the motivation for athlete development and as a theme for hosting the world's athletes troubled some sport leaders. Kidd was especially critical, asking of "Own the Podium," "So why is your slogan, 'Come to Canada so we can own the podium,' i.e., beat the shit out of you? It was contrary to the spirit of what being an Olympic host should be."[25] The emphasis on results was a significant shift in Canadian high-performance sport, which had made a marked turn towards an ethical orientation following the 1988 Seoul Olympics and the Dubin inquiry into the widespread use of steroids and performance-enhancing substances. Rob Beamish's chapter in this volume examines the impact of the Dubin Report twenty years after its release.

"Own the Podium" is one measure of the Canadian government's investment in sport and recreation; the federal government invested $62 million in

2010, funnelled through Sport Canada, in time for the Vancouver Games, while "Own the Podium" boasted an investment in winter sports of over $80 million from government and corporate sources for the Sochi quadrennial.[26] The program's creation when Canada was planning to host the Olympic Games was not a coincidence. It is often the perceived benefits of hosting – including a boost to the local economy, infrastructure development, job creation, and tourism promotion – that generates the desire to bid for international events. (Winnipeg's mayor, Sam Katz, for example, framed the city's hosting of the Canada Summer Games in terms of "contributing an estimated $130 million to our local economy.")[27] While Canada did not lead the medals table at Vancouver in 2010 – it finished third behind Germany and the United States – Canadian athletes won more gold medals (fourteen) than did any other nation and were credited with spurring the outbursts of national pride that greeted the closing of the Games.

This national goodwill, however, came at considerable public and corporate expense. The Games' organizers announced a final budget of $1.7 billion, which included $925 million from the Province of British Columbia – the largest portion ($290 million) of which was spent on Olympic venues – and $554 million from the City of Vancouver. The federal government and corporate sponsors covered the remainder. But even these figures do not reflect the true cost of hosting the Olympic Games. They do not include nearly $1 billion in federal money spent on security; $1.9 billion spent on a local rapid-transit line in Vancouver; $600 million paid to upgrade the Sea-to-Sky Highway that connects Vancouver with Whistler; or $900 million spent by the city on a new convention centre, which was used exclusively by Olympic broadcasters during the Games.[28] These infrastructural developments were a tangible outcome of the 2010 Olympics, and while the public cost of 2010 paled in comparison to the estimated $51 billion spent by Russia on the 2014 Sochi Winter Olympics, critics argued that they could only be realized with the substantial public investment in the Games themselves.

Yet scholars such as David Black have noted that the tangible benefits *directly* associated with hosting international sport events are difficult to quantify or qualify.[29] One pre-Olympic community program in Vancouver, funded by a hardware store chain, trained under-employed persons in woodworking skills to build the medal podiums, and the program continued after the Games, with the podiums being cut into souvenirs. While far from sustainable employment, this program was called by one media outlet the Games' "only social inclusion legacy."[30] As Hart Cantelon and James Riordan note in their chapter in this volume, debates over the funding of the subsequent Winter Olympic Games – 2014 in Sochi – are very different from those that surrounded the 2010 Games in Vancouver.

The allocation of significant resources (public and private) for building elite sport venues and hosting international competitions of short duration is also a public policy issue in the global South. Some concerns garnered increasing attention, beginning in 2010, as the world's biggest sporting events expanded their global brands into the southern hemisphere with the FIFA World Cup taking place in South Africa, and the Commonwealth Games being hosted in Delhi, India. This trend continued with the 2011 International Cricket Council's (ICC's) Cricket World Cup jointly hosted by India, Sri Lanka, and Bangladesh, followed by the 2014 FIFA World Cup in Brazil and the 2016 Summer Olympic Games in Rio de Janeiro. In anticipation of these events, media reports in the West focused on whether organizers in the developing world would have facilities built and operational in time for the Opening Ceremonies.[31] One Canadian journalist at the 2014 World Cup opined, after the first week of competition in Brazil, that "the stadium in São Paulo wasn't ready and, as I understand it, in the EU, no country would have been allowed it to be used and accommodate the crowd for the opening match."[32]

Concerns over the allocation of state funds in societies with considerable poverty, as well as the dislocation resulting from stadium and venue construction, typically receive less attention from the mainstream media. There is evidence, though, that this is beginning to change. When Brazil hosted the 2013 FIFA Confederations Cup, a quadrennial pre–World Cup tournament intended to test a host's readiness for the subsequent event while capturing an additional slice of the world's sports media pie, the event was met by widespread protest in the South American nation. Sparked by the imposition of transit-fare hikes to pay for World Cup venue construction, the protests highlighted, as journalist Dave Zirin notes, "the spending priorities for stadiums, security, and all attendant infrastructure [which] were monstrous, given the health and education needs of the Brazilian people."[33] Protests continued unabated through the opening of the World Cup in June 2014, with Zirin noting that "it is difficult even to keep up with the parade of stories of dissatisfaction, waste, protest, and tumult that appeared almost daily."[34]

Back in South Africa in 2010 the non-governmental organization (NGO) Umthombo, which works with street children in Durban, sought to raise awareness of the efforts made by local security authorities to forcibly remove impoverished children from the streets of Durban to the city's outskirts during the World Cup.[35] Other agencies pointed to the human dislocation – often of a community's most marginalized residents – caused by stadium construction and renovation prior to the World Cup in South Africa.[36] Sadly, these were not novel occurrences. The Geneva-based Centre on Housing Rights and Evictions (COHRE) gathered considerable data on the displacement caused by international sport (as well as by other capital development projects), noting, for example, that "in the lead up to the 2008 Olympic Games in Beijing, over 1.25 million people were displaced due to Olympics-related urban redevelopment."[37] Similar narratives were revisited in Brazil, as the 2014 World Cup got underway. The Homeless Workers Movement called off planned protests after receiving assurances from the government that two thousand homes would be built on land near São Paulo's stadium that was occupied by five thousand homeless people.[38] As Richard Gruneau argues in his chapter in this volume, international sport is doing little to redress global poverty despite the rhetoric of economic benefits and legacies.

Issues such as these are not unique to China, Brazil, or the global South. Indeed, COHRE reported that preparations for the 1996 Atlanta Summer Olympics included the prior displacement of thirty thousand people for "Olympics-related gentrification and development," and during the Games "9,000 arrest citations were issued to homeless persons, mostly racial minorities, as part of an Olympics-inspired campaign to, quote, 'clean the streets.'"[39] Awareness of these issues was highlighted by the Metro Atlanta Task Force for the Homeless, an early example of the social activism that arose in response to the hosting of international sporting events and which subsequently grew to include protest groups such as Bread Not Circuses in Toronto and the Impact of the Olympics on Community Coalition in Vancouver.[40] The latter was one of the many groups that voiced opposition to the hosting of the 2010 Olympic Games in British Columbia's Lower Mainland, protests that focused on poverty, homelessness, environmental issues, and aboriginal land claims; I highlight these narratives in my chapter in this volume.

For all its complexity, and despite the ways in which it is embedded within global capital structures, sport does offer opportunities for the expression of a social conscience. Such accountability often comes from the varied NGOs, watch-dogs, and activists who promote equity within and through sport. Among athletes the most iconic image is that of Tommie Smith and John Carlos raising black-gloved fists on the Olympic podium in Mexico in 1968.[41] A similarly silent and peaceful protest took place at the Harare Sports Club before Zimbabwe's first match of the 2003 Cricket World Cup when Zimbabwean cricketers Andy Flower and Henry Olonga wore black armbands (and released a statement explaining their actions) in opposition to the human rights abuses and the "death of democracy" in Robert Mugabe's regime.[42] While others have protested the administration of sport – Canadian race walker Ann Peel, for example, led the fight to ensure that female athletes did not lose their state funding if they were pregnant[43] – sport has often been a platform from which some activists have waved the banner of human rights. In February 2011 the most significant international news came from across the world as protestors remained in Cairo's Tahrir Square, angry over President Mubarak's refusal to step down and the army's reluctance to speed his departure. Egyptian soccer became central to some of the demonstrations. Although the Cairo club Zamalek, which historically was a Mubarak ally (a Zamalek board member publicly supported the regime), the club's former goal-keeper Nader el-Sayed led protests in Tahrir Square, and Zamalek coach Hossam Hassan and striker Mido were also among the demonstrators.[44]

This book is a reminder, if we needed one, that on almost any given day sport matters to people around the world, not only because of its cultural significance but also because sport – at the grassroots level as well as in its corporatized media guise – is implicated in people's lives in ways that often seemingly have little to do with sport. (It is on this latter point that the social protest attaching itself to sport, in part because of the visibility of sport, is too easily dismissed.) So the Jets returned and Winnipeg celebrated, or at least the fans of professional men's hockey did. And well they should have. Yet, in such an environment, where gaining membership to the oligarchy of commercial sport is seen as a victory of civic agitation, the achievement of deeper social change within sport, and as advocated by association with sport, can be lost or neglected altogether.

This collection pursues multiple avenues of inquiry into the cultural significance of sport: interrogating the deep interconnections of sport, popular culture, economic interests, the media, and the state, and by implication asserting that sport plays a cultural role (substantially) beyond its contribution to individual health; situating the significance of these issues at local, regional, national, and international levels; and, finally, affirming the public responsibility of scholars, whether through acting on contemporary research that documents inequity or by advocating for the important connection between history and activism. The chapters and the four sections into which they have been apportioned reflect many of the themes that have dominated the critical study of sport and physical activity. *Playing for Change* features both historical and sociological scholarship, emphasizing theoretical considerations at times, and empiricism at others; most important, the contributors explore the relationship between advocacy and scholarship.

Part 1 focuses on the Olympic Games and international sport, reflecting upon the values that inform Olympic competition, both those represented by athletes on the field and those that attract bidding cities from around the world. This collection begins with a consideration of sport for development and peace (SDP) and of the debates over sport's utility and worth beyond the stadium. Cities throughout the world confront these issues every time a "mega-event" is contemplated, but it could be argued that they are magnified in the developing world when the institution that is international sport comes calling. In chapter 1, Richard Gruneau offers a powerful essay on the role that international sport plays in perpetuating inequity. We inhabit a world, especially in the global South, faced with rapidly increasing rates of urbanization and population drain from rural areas, populations that increasingly are under-housed or squatting. At the same time, in the pursuit of markets, global sporting events (with the Commonwealth Games and ICC Cricket World Cup having already been held in South Asia, and the FIFA World Cup in South Africa and Brazil, and the 2016 Summer Olympic Games being destined for Rio de Janeiro) are now targeting major centres in the global South, without moderating their expectations of local resource allocation for facilities and infrastructure. In both the South and the North there is, as Gruneau argues, a "conventional wisdom among booster coalitions in bid cities or hosting cities that such investments are justified because of the capacity for large-scale sporting events and projects to become powerful engines of economic development." However, he questions whether the public investments (improved infrastructure and transportation networks) will address issues of poverty and homelessness, to say nothing of the evictions and considerable forced relocations that have accompanied the preparations for large-scale sporting events. It is at the intersection of these two trends – increasing urban slum populations in the very cities that are bidding to host international sporting events – that, Gruneau argues, "the challenge of slums requires greater attention in research and writing on global sport."

These issues gained the attention in the late-twentieth century of NGOs that engaged in a wide variety of development projects in the South, which, Gruneau notes, "reflected a broader trend towards non-state approaches to development." At the same time that the international sports community has turned its gaze southward, the number of sport-focused NGOs practising SDP has increased dramatically, evidence of what Gruneau calls the "recent enthusiasm for sport as an aspect of development policy." He notes that the scholarship in support of SDP initiatives "lacks depth and critical reflexivity." The work that has been undertaken has been "consistently more programmatic than analytical" and has displayed an "inadequate consideration of the systemic underpinnings of global poverty." Advocates of sport for development and peace have yet to adequately demonstrate, argues Gruneau, that their programs are "a meaningful response to the challenge of slums." So while advocates of sport for development and peace are being forced to confront the role that sport can play in the alleviation of global poverty in empirical as well as programmatic ways, the increasing desire to host mega-events in the South forces a perhaps even more challenging question: does the organization of contemporary global sporting events contribute to the exacerbation of global poverty?

Even in the North, bid cities for events such as the Olympic Games often tout ancillary goals, such as economic development and tourism promotion, although not without contestation.[45] A civic plebiscite in February 2003, seven years in advance of the 2010 Olympic Winter Games, asked Vancouver residents to influence whether or not organizers should, with the support of taxpayers, continue with their planned bid; it posed the question, "Do you support or do you oppose the City of Vancouver's participation in hosting the 2010 Olympic Winter Games and Paralympic Winter Games?"[46] A voter turn-out of 46 per cent approved the pursuit of the Games by a 64:36 margin.[47] However, as I outline in chapter 2, groups in Vancouver and Whistler, British Columbia, beyond VANOC (the official Olympic organizing committee) resisted the Province's Olympic project and the distribution and use of state funds in very different ways and over a wide variety of issues.

Anti-poverty activists protested over the use of funds that they felt could have been directed towards addressing poverty and housing shortages in Vancouver's Downtown Eastside, and against real estate speculation that resulted in the eviction of many of the neighbourhood's residents. Environmentalists highlighted – and at times forcibly blocked – construction on the Sea-to-Sky Highway, which connects Vancouver to Whistler, because of the expansion of the transportation corridor to a four-lane highway, which passed through and ultimately destroyed a unique ecosystem on Eagle Ridge Bluff. Finally, indigenous rights protestors, whose concerns had to with both the ownership of tribal land and the socio-economic circumstances of Canada's First Peoples – were prominent in their opposition to the Vancouver Games, succeeding in obstructing the pre-Games torch relay in a number of Canadian cities. I situate the protests over the 2010 Games within a new "culture war" (borrowing a phrase that Kidd used to describe the social and political context of Quebec prior to and during the 1976 Montreal Olympics) as many of the protestors found their inspiration in the emergence of late-twentieth-century globalization protests.[48] I explore not only the goals of the protesters but also their inability to translate their concerns into widespread resistance to the impact of the Olympic Games on Canada's third-largest city.

The planning for the subsequent Winter Olympics, the 2014 Games in Sochi, Russia, took place in a vastly different context, one that largely precluded dissent and debate over the allocation of resources. In chapter 3, Hart Cantelon and James Riordan examine the financing of the Sochi Winter Olympic Games and the considerable involvement of Russia's billionaire sector – the oligarchs – and consider the consequences for competitive high-performance sport. Following the collapse of the Soviet Union, the rapid transformation to a market economy under Boris Yeltsin was enabled by a period of what Naomi Klein has called "robber capitalism," during which the class of entrepreneurs and black-market exploiters who had benefited from cronyism and nepotism in Soviet economic affairs prospered. It was to these men that Yeltsin turned for election financing, and in return they received state resources as collateral. Thus the "oligarchs" were born, and in post-Soviet Russia "criminality remains rife, poverty is extensive, and the citizenry has little opportunity to defend itself against the threats of the rich and powerful." This system continues today, Cantelon and Riordan argue, as "for personal capital donations and political loyalty, the Kremlin and Putin turn a blind eye to the ever-increasing gap between rich and poor in Russia."

This influence extends into all areas of Russian society, so that the dominant position assumed by the oligarchs in the Russian economy has been mirrored by the significant role they have come to play in sport. Commercial sport has become a place for these resource tycoons to both invest wealth and cleanse ill-gotten gains. Most prominently, like Chelsea Football Club owner Roman Abramovich, the oligarchs have invested in the ownership of football (soccer) and ice hockey teams. In the lead-up to the 2014 Winter Olympics in the Black Sea coastal city of Sochi, Cantelon and Riordan observe, the oligarchs became intimately involved in the financing of the Games. It was "the state's insistence," they note, "that the very wealthy would (and did) bankroll major capital projects necessary for the hosting of the Games." As a result, the organizing committee "can guarantee that whatever funding is needed will be forthcoming." The presence of the oligarchs in Sochi did not trouble the International Olympic Committee (IOC), Cantelon and Riordan argue. Not only is their wealth often obtained under dubious circumstances, but there is no mechanism by which to hold the oligarchs accountable.

The increasing commercialization of the Games and the attendant governance challenges – to which the presence of the oligarchs lends a particularly Russian hue – is not the only issue that the Olympics have faced in the late-twentieth and early-twenty-first centuries. The use of steroids and other banned performance-enhancing substances has drawn considerable attention in the wake of the Ben Johnson positive drug test following the 100-metre men's sprint final at the 1988 Seoul Olympic Games. The subsequent Canadian inquiry into those events – the Commission of Inquiry into the Use of Drugs and Banned Practices Intended to Increase Athletic Performance – was headed by the former chief justice of Ontario, Charles Dubin. He noted the structural conditions within the Canadian and international high-performance sport systems that had fostered what Kidd called the "ideology of excellence," one of whose eventual outcomes in the pursuit of sporting success and the maintenance of athletic support and funding was the use of performance-enhancing substances among track-and-field athletes, not only in Canada but around the world.[49] For some, the Dubin Report ushered in a radical restructuring of the Canadian sport system. Two decades after its release, the report is revisited by Rob Beamish in chapter 4. He considers its lasting impact, less for its challenge to the drug culture in sport and more for its being "one of the most systematic and thorough analyses of Olympic sport ever conducted." Moreover, it remains "the best reference point for understanding the dialectic of high-performance sport within the context of modernity."

Beamish argues that the founder of the modern Olympic Games, Baron Pierre de Coubertin, imbued his project with a particularly anti-modern vision, one that sought to overcome the "ills" of an industrializing European society. Although his enterprise failed to resist the forces of modernity, "the promise of Coubertin's imagery has persisted." The Coubertin vision, what Beamish calls "the social value of sport," is a trans-historical, essentialist notion of athletic competition in which the pursuit of individual achievement and perfection results in physical and mental health, strengthened character, and a renewed sense of citizenship. The influence of performance-enhancing substances in sport was not a failure of these values but the result of their ultimate rejection in an ever-increasing lust for medals. The Dubin Report, Beamish argues, accepted the values and placed within the hands of the state the imperative to refocus sport in the direction of "broad participation – not solely elite sport – increased access to all Canadians, the encouragement of women to participate in sport with equal access to sport and athletic facilities, support for the disabled, and an amelioration of the regional disparities in access to facilities and sports programs." Although governments held the ultimate leverage – funding – over the way that sport was to be imagined or re-imagined, the efforts to clean up the system and to return it to Coubertin's trans-historical vision have ultimately failed. There has been a renewed commitment to an instrumental rationality that still favours the pursuit of medals above all, albeit now in a drug-free environment with new ethical institutions in place, including the World Anti-Doping Agency, the Canadian Centre for Ethics in Sport, and a process of alternative dispute resolution made available to Canadian high-performance athletes.

Debates over the nature and organization of sport do not only play themselves out at the international level. Much as Beamish asserts that the post-Dubin era was more a rejection of Coubertin's philosophical values for the Olympics rather than a failure of those values, John MacAloon argues in chapter 5 that the failed Chicago bid for the 2016 Summer Olympic Games was, in many ways, "structurally pre-formed by the 1904 experience of Chicago and St Louis." He contends that the organization of the Olympic movement in the

United States, led primarily by the United States Olympic Committee (USOC), has drifted since 1904 from the values and intentions of the Olympic movement. This is the subject of one of the three historical case studies in part 2 that highlight debates over the meaning and form of commercial and amateur sport in North America in the first half of the twentieth century.

The dominant sport ethos at the outset of this period – amateurism – was embodied in the emergence of the modern Olympic Games in the last decade of the nineteenth century. As a vision of sport that incorporated a dedication to physical culture, selflessness, and education and a commitment to engaged citizenship (among almost exclusively male participants), amateur sport took root in a variety of civic institutions, including universities. "International sport was," observes MacAloon, "embedded with other university projects to the end of increasing intercultural education." The Canadian Olympic community in the first decades of the twentieth century (if such an entity could be distinguished from amateur sports leaders at the time) was rooted, Kidd notes, in the staunch amateurism of the Canadian Amateur Athletic Union and was dominated by men with connections to institutions such as the University of Toronto (Maurice Hutton, Nathaniel Burwash) and McGill University (A.S. Lamb).[50] There were similar configurations evident in the United States at this time, but while men such as these wielded considerable influence over the nature of Canadian sport in the years before and after the First World War, as MacAloon argues, the first hosting of the Olympic Games in the United States – 1904 in St Louis – "represented simultaneously the apogee and ... the swansong of 'university men' in American Olympic affairs."

The 1904 St Louis Olympic Games were originally scheduled to be held in Chicago. MacAloon recounts in part the machinations surrounding the shift of the Games from Chicago to St Louis, but his larger project – based upon the papers of Henry (Harry) J. Furber Jr., co-leader of the Chicago bid and president of the organizing committee for Chicago's unrealized Olympic project – is to examine the impact that this shift had on the nature of American Olympic leadership. In discussing the original organizing group, the Chicago Association for the International Olympian Games (CAIOG), MacAloon notes that its "special relevance for the ensuing structuration of American Olympism lies in the social characteristics and particularities of its composition." The association's membership was populated with industrialists and professionals (bankers, lawyers, architects), but "mainly university professors and higher-education reformers steered the ship," and "elected politicians played little front-stage role in the Chicago Olympic effort." The composition of the organizing group changed after the Olympic project left for St Louis. Although Chicago would have staged in 1904 an Olympic Games, MacAloon argues, "with a cultural and educational atmosphere vastly different from that of Paris [in 1900] and from that eventuated in St Louis," the impact of the ultimately unrealized Chicago Games was that "university professors were increasingly driven to the margins in subsequent U.S. Olympic history."

In chapter 6, Stephen Hardy offers another reconsideration of the impact of amateur sport and takes direct aim at Kidd's assertion that hockey in Canada was damaged by the expansion of the NHL into the United States in the 1920s. Kidd argues that, symbolic of the "accelerating penetration of American industry and culture into Canada," this embedded a Canadian game in the continental entertainment economy of capitalist sport.[51] The attraction of the U.S. market for the owners of the NHL's Canadian franchises was the financial stability and rewards offered by association with entrepreneurs who could deliver more sizeable audiences and facilities and thus greater profits. Hardy, however, reimagines this distinction and rejects the notion that ice hockey was a "Canadian" game being taken over by U.S. capital, with its very essence as a community game altered, as asserted by Kidd and Macfarlane in *The Death of Hockey*.

Hardy instead characterizes North American commercial sport in the early-twentieth century using a "two-way" model, in which hockey as a North American cultural form is not reduced to a Canadian export south of the border, but American influences on the game include practices transmitted northward. Indeed, American hockey promoters sought to shape their own version of the sport. As Hardy argues, "there is abundant evidence to suggest a complex American model, one that promoters and their consumers developed interactively, with both a respect for Canada's dominance and a desire for distinct American brands." This included forging links between grassroots hockey and the professional game that were unseen north of the border, as the NHL "brand" of hockey with its emphasis on profits and markets overwhelmed amateur hockey in Canada.

The emergence of the NHL as the "definitive" version of hockey, in a landscape where other organizing principles for the sport existed, was mirrored south of the border when Major League Baseball, and its many affiliated minor leagues, sought to control access to what was officially "baseball" and to marginalize non-sanctioned leagues as "outlaw" outfits. In chapter 7, Colin Howell examines the ways in which outlaw leagues in both Mexico and Canada challenged Major League Baseball's continental hegemony. Major League Baseball is celebrated for, and indeed celebrates, its own history of racial inclusion in the mid-twentieth century – marked most prominently by Jackie Robinson joining the Brooklyn Dodgers in 1947 and breaking baseball's "colour barrier." Robinson was followed by a steady progression of other African American players, many of them Negro League veterans, and dark-skinned Latinos. Howell, while noting the importance of these achievements, argues that the progressiveness of these initiatives also worked to extend the commercial dominance of "major league" baseball, based as it was entirely in the United States.

Elsewhere in North America, however, both entrepreneurs and professional players were engaged in what Howell calls a "process of resistance and accommodation to the expansionist designs of Major League Baseball beyond the continental boundaries of the United States." He focuses on Jorge Pasquel's Mexican League, the Quebec Provincial League, and winter baseball in Cuba in the post-war period. These organizations were framed by Major League Baseball as "outlaw" leagues, and Howell considers the ideological weight of such a term. While typically framed in racialized terms as a "bandit," stealing players from the major leagues, Pasquel is reframed by Howell as emblematic of a Mexican ruling class interested in asserting its entrepreneurial clout in nationalist terms. Many of the players who jumped to the Mexican League were banned from "Organized Baseball" (the very terrain contested by these renegade leagues) by Commissioner Happy Chandler for five years; he also sought to extend major league influence beyond the boundaries of the United States by aiding supportive winter baseball leagues in Latin America. Quebec-born pitcher Jean-Pierre Roy, "property" of the Brooklyn Dodgers, was one player who flouted such a ban, playing wherever he chose, spurning both the Dodgers and Pasquel's Mexican League before turning to the Quebec Provincial League. As Howell notes, the actions of the independent leagues in Canada were rarely framed in the same racialized terms as those in Latin America. These patterns have influenced the continentalization of baseball. The game remains stronger and more independent in countries south of the United States – and decidedly more nationalist – than it does north of the forty-ninth parallel.

It is not just the organization of commercial sport that is open to contestation. With the contours of class and race still very much evident, the three chapters that comprise part 3 are informed by a desire to examine the accessibility of recreation and physical activity at the local level. In chapter 8, Parissa Safai explores the role of sport and physical activity as a vehicle of inclusion among immigrants in Toronto, specifically by considering the accessibility of recreational opportunities. In a city that touts its multiculturalism and diversity, and which has the highest concentration of visible minorities in Canada (49 per cent in 2011), access to recreation resources is far from equitable. While statistics suggest a diverse community, Toronto is a city of neighbourhoods, which means, Safai argues, that the city differs for different ethnic communities. Not all communities have equal access to sport and physical activity opportunities, and the barriers are typically not religious or ethnocultural proscriptions but a lack of facilities and programming that meet the needs of a culturally diverse population. Safai's objective, however, is not only to enumerate barriers to participation but to consider strategies that minimize barriers and promote social inclusion.

Sport and physical activity can be a place in which social inclusion is fostered – and perhaps community is built and strengthened – but the process of inclusion is a "shared responsibility." As newcomers adapt to Canada, the organizations and services that they access must also adapt to meet the changing needs of an increasingly diverse city. Moreover, Safai argues that the struggle for equitable access to public resources necessitates "the mobilization of public advocates" – what she terms "change agents." Ultimately the aim is to reduce barriers but also to empower marginalized voices to have an active say in shaping their active city. She encourages us "to be radical change agents and to attend … to the ways in which certain social groups come to experience the city, ways that are different from those of others." She concludes, "Let us be change agents and use physical activity and sport spaces to address the tensions between the need to adapt to new conditions of community, the desire to maintain cultural continuity, and the newness of emergent, potential hybrid or third spaces."

A similar spirit of activism informs the case study of recreational land use presented in chapter 9. Although, as Robert Pitter and Glyn Bissix make clear, debates over the direction of civic activism and the nature of any resultant impact on public policy can be hotly contested. They examine a conflict that erupted over the development and use of a public trail in Kings County, Nova Scotia. A citizens' group, the Kieran Pathways Society, sought to develop this trail into an active transportation network that would connect four local communities. Their efforts met resistance from off-highway vehicle (OHV) users, including all-terrain vehicle riders. The trail was subsequently designated by the province as "shared use," meaning it could be used by both OHVs and the walkers, cyclists, and cross-country skiers whose activities comprised active transportation. Conflict over the trail ultimately resulted in debates over the recreational use of public spaces, what was permissible, what was desirable, what was sustainable, and ultimately what constituted recreation.

Pitter and Bissix examine the discourses employed by all three constituencies – active transportation advocates, the OHV lobby, and the provincial government – in advancing their positions. Each stakeholder sought to associate itself with environmental stewardship; however, Pitter and Bissix contend that each group alternately invoked economic, health, or sport discourses to advance its agenda for trail use, each attesting that such an argument was its way of privileging the environment. They also note the inconsistencies between the sustainability aims of provincial environmental legislation and the realities of supporting the OHV-users lobby.

The differing influences of sport and recreation groups, some with and some without access to policymakers, are also central to Victoria Paraschak's analysis of recreation in the Canadian north in the last four decades of the twentieth century. In chapter 10 she undertakes a historical evaluation of the delivery of sport and recreation services in Canada's Northwest Territories (NWT). Paraschak acknowledges the various abilities of the groups and individuals in sport and recreation to act within particular rules and with different resources. This context, she argues, accounts for the differences in sport and recreation delivery in southern and northern Canada and explains the collaborative system, comprising seven groups, that has evolved in the north. Opportunities for sport and recreation in the NWT were provided by government agencies, sport groups tied to national federations, recreation professionals, professional associations, community groups, and the Aboriginal Sport Circle of the Western Arctic. In the NWT, such an arrangement has mirrored the apportioning of resources in other sectors since the early 1990s, when there emerged "an ongoing presence of inter-organizational partnerships in the NWT as an integral way of doing business, especially for the territorial government."

These partnerships, however, have reflected shifting and unequal power relations. Initially, the government of the NWT had the largest resource base and the greatest legitimacy on which to set the agenda for sport and recreation in the territories, but a shifting landscape – the waning relative power of the territorial government – enabled other actors to influence the direction and delivery of community recreation. With the growing professionalization of sport delivery in the area, opportunities increasingly came to resemble those in the south, with little adaptation to the northern context, as "programs were often adopted from other jurisdictions, such as the National Coaching Certification Program or the Active Living Strategy, and federal or national resources were accessed." Nevertheless, Paraschak argues, there evolved "northern forms and values that continued to make activities distinctive from the mainstream ways of 'doing' sport and recreation in southern Canada." These included prioritizing inclusion over achievement in sport, incorporating traditional aboriginal games, and integrating aboriginal and non-aboriginal sport and recreation services, as local actors sought to overcome apparent power differentials to ensure that sport and recreation at the local level reflected local priorities.

Paraschak makes clear that the shaping of northern forms of recreation reflected attempts to moderate the hegemonic influence of southern culture. In the spirit of the engaged public history called for by Nancy Bouchier and Ken Cruikshank, her goal was "to write a history for northerners that would inspire them to continue creating the system for sport and recreation that best meets particular needs." Similarly, Safai, Pitter, and Bissix begin to answer Peter Donnelly and Michael Atkinson's call for a more engaged public sociology. The role of the public intellectual is the subject of the four chapters that comprise part 4, which outline a framework for an engaged and critical socio-cultural study of sport and recreation, one in which scholarship advances progressive positions and encourages activism.

In chapter 11, Bouchier and Cruikshank reflect on their public history initiatives. They recognize the value of public history and indeed assert the importance of historical knowledge to effect and support change, as well as its potential to build community; however, they take this opportunity to consider the impact of historians on such public processes. Bouchier and Cruikshank do so in the context of their ongoing investigation into "the social and environmental transformation of an urban waterfront in a Canadian industrial city," in this case, Hamilton, Ontario. Their research into the recreational and other uses of the land adjacent to Hamilton harbour has resulted in the production of academic papers and presentations as well as the making of an educational film (*The People and the Bay*) and the mounting of a museum exhibit. In addition, Bouchier and Cruikshank's research has been incorporated into artistic discourses as members of the local visual arts community represent the state of Hamilton harbour in their work.

Historians, including sport historians, have a role to play in the public understandings of such places. However, Bouchier and Cruikshank consider the ways in which historians – even those with the most progressive of intentions – impose themselves into attempts to broaden an understanding of the past, and inform, in their particular case, future environmental remediation efforts. In celebrating the vibrant harbour life that once was, they worry that continuing struggles over pollution and public access to the waterfront, among other issues, may fade into the background and that "voices of popular resistance" are at risk of being silenced. While the authors acknowledge that their engagement with the local communities surrounding Hamilton harbour was informed by a desire to "help them to change their world for the better," they contend that this remains "both one of the best rewards and one of the greatest challenges that we as academic historians have faced."

In chapter 12, Donnelly and Atkinson continue the emphasis on scholarly engagement beyond the academy by exploring the resurgence of public sociology, arguing that "sociological knowledge is *practical* knowledge." This practical sociology "combines rigour, ethics, and honesty in the research process with an ongoing responsibility for the widespread dissemination of findings and for the consequences of those findings." They consider the application of recent debates in public sociology – and the assertion or re-assertion of the importance of "speaking truth to power" – to the critical study of sport and physical activity. There has been sport sociological research that has "contributed to or is contributing to larger public debates, or has actually resulted in progressive social changes," including collecting data that act as quantitative representations of inequity, challenging the still-pervasive functionalist view of sport as an unquestionably positive force in the lives of participants, and revealing the ways in which sport acts to reproduce particular forms of gender, race, and class relations. In attempting to re-centre the public obligation of the sociological researcher, Donnelly and Atkinson argue that too often the critical examination of sport "rests on its own intellectual laurels" without engaging in "a concerted and unapologetic ritual of transformative praxis."

Donnelly and Atkinson acknowledge that there are barriers to achieving their vision of a public sociology of sport. Mainstream media outlets and the state and commercial sport organizations upon which they rely may be resistant to the implications of critical sport sociology. However, Donnelly and Atkinson express the greatest concern for the barriers that exist within the academy as social scientists compete for resources in multidisciplinary faculties and departments with health science researchers and human movement scientists. Although they note that it is necessary for scientists of all stripes to "ask where our academic responsibilities end," they lament that too often the public efforts of social scientists are sidetracked by a competition for resources and respect as well as by the instrumental priorities of grant writing and peer-reviewed publishing.

Patricia Vertinsky contemplates the impact of similar barriers – what Donnelly and Atkinson call "the constraining conditions of knowledge production now faced by many in the academy." However, in chapter 13, she offers a different vision for the future of "physical cultural studies." Vertinsky does not doubt that "the influence of the managerial class in setting agendas and defining excellence is indeed critical in today's research university," nor does she question that in kinesiology and other human movement faculties and departments there was an "epistemological hierarchy that continued to privilege positivist over post-positivist, quantitative over qualitative, and predictive over interpretive ways of knowing." Nevertheless, Vertinksy argues that many of the best scientific researchers do not debate the inclusion of a variety of perspectives and the value of interdisciplinary research. Research is being conducted increasingly by collaborative networks – especially as funding agencies prioritize team-oriented research – which include social science and cultural studies components.

To make the case for proactively engaging in team research, Vertinsky considers some of the "shadow disciplines" (for example, area studies, cultural studies, women's studies, gender studies, race studies, science studies, performance studies, and media studies) that emerged in the 1960s and 1970s. She contends that the history of these shadow disciplines is instructive for the future of a critical study of sport and physical activity (she frames her discussion around "physical cultural studies," as articulated most prominently by David Andrews of the University of Maryland). The lessons of some of these earlier studies indicate that adopting a perspective aggressively critical of the epistemology of lab-based science may alienate social science researchers from their colleagues and the rest of the academy. She argues that sport scholars should neither "retreat to our core disciplines" nor "avoid the tough disciplinary work of holding up our own methods of inquiry to constant scrutiny." Instead, physical cultural studies, with scholars working to set research priorities and engaging colleagues from a variety of disciplines, can be a place with "potential as an inter- or trans-disciplinary arrangement, a place for constantly shifting problem-specific collaborations, and/or a space for novelty and shifting post-disciplinary liaisons." Rather than having social science perspectives included in a token way on research teams, such an approach keeps the cultural studies agenda at the forefront while not sacrificing a politically activist agenda.

Refocusing and promoting physical cultural studies within the contemporary institutional landscape in the ways suggested by Vertinsky, as well as by Donnelly and Atkinson, requires strong leadership. Vertinsky praises Bruce Kidd, who as Dean of Physical Education and Health at the University of Toronto "brought critique to his science-oriented faculty, indeed all his faculty and students, while supporting putting the active back into activism." During the period of shifting nomenclature and priorities identified by Vertinsky – as the study of physical education and human movement became kinesiology – Kidd was not only a senior administrator but also a high-profile scholar, one who brought an activist sensibility to his research agenda. His work not only critiqued but occurred within the changing political economy of knowledge production in North America. The nature and products of this explicitly progressive research program are the focus of Douglas Booth's close reading of Kidd's oeuvre in chapter 14. Booth seeks to "examine Kidd's historical scholarship as an element of his activism" and also generally to reconcile the claims of historical scholarship with the aims of progressive researchers such as Kidd.

Booth situates Kidd's scholarship within the social history that emerged in the 1970s. Historians who were committed to this approach explicitly connected their research to a larger emancipatory project and often conceived of their narratives as telling "history from below." Yet, Booth argues, they "remain committed to the empiricism, logic, and reason of modernist-inspired history." He contends that social historians such as Kidd make choices about the content and form of their narratives. "Those decisions," Booth writes, "prefigure the narrative and configure its content and form." This makes tenuous any claims about empiricism. "Historians who configure their narratives to conform to an emancipatory mission," he continues, "cannot claim allegiance to an empirical-analytical epistemology and pretend that their histories arise from an objective mining of ethical data from the past."

Booth's intention is not to malign social history but to call attention to its methodological and epistemological claims and the nature of narrative construction in historical scholarship. Indeed, he praises "Kidd's (refreshingly) explicit positioning of himself and his narratives" and his commitment "to democratize sport and to change the status quo" through his writing and public activities. Kidd's current project in this regard is an advocacy for SDP and a call to sport leaders to imagine the ways in which development goals can be made more central to their athletic priorities.

That Richard Gruneau (to return to our starting point) and Bruce Kidd – long both friends and debaters – might disagree over the impact that sport can have on international development and global poverty does not diminish the importance of having this discussion. The research and positions elaborated in *Playing for Change* continue the debates about the structural organization of and equitable access to opportunities for sport and physical activity. Sport does indeed matter, but what also matters is the critical reflection on its cultural significance, which continues here.

NOTES

1 Fiona Hill and Clifford Gaddy, *The Siberian Curse: How Communist Planners Left Russia Out in the Cold* (Washington, DC: Brookings Institution, 2003). Page 228 (table E-1) shows the top twenty-five coldest cities in North America and Russia with populations over five hundred thousand. All but two (Winnipeg, sixth, and Edmonton, thirteenth) are in Russia. Page 229 (table E-2) lists the world's coldest cities having more than one million people. All are in Russia except for Ottawa-Hull, tenth.

2 Morris Mott and John Allardyce, *Curling Capital: Winnipeg and the Roarin' Game, 1876–1988* (Winnipeg: University of Manitoba Press, 1989); see also http://www.curlingrink.ca.

3 Winnipeg is one of only two cities to have hosted the Pan American Games twice; Mexico City is the other. Until 2015, when the Pan Am Games was hosted in Toronto and southern Ontario, Winnipeg was the only Canadian city to have hosted the event.

4 Greg Dicresce, "The Sweet Summer of the Jets," *Winnipeg Sun*, 30 August 2011, 13.

5 For the best analysis of the opposition to the "Save the Jets" campaign see Jim
   Silver, *Thin Ice: Money, Politics, and the Demise of an NHL Franchise* (Halifax, NS:
   Fernwood Publishing, 1996).
6 Gerald Friesen, "Hockey and Prairie Cultural History," in Gerald Friesen (ed.),
   River Road: Essays on Manitoba and Prairie History (Winnipeg: University of Manitoba Press, 1996), 219.
7 The scholars who have made significant contributions to these fields are too
   numerous to mention, but, in the North American context, a glance at the membership and annual conference programs of the North American Society for Sport
   History (www.nassh.org) and the North American Society for the Sociology of
   Sport (www.nasss.org) is a good starting point.
8 Friesen, *River Road*, 218, 219.
9 Bruce Kidd and John Macfarlane, *The Death of Hockey* (Toronto: New Press, 1972),
   12, 15.
10 Ibid., 16.
11 Much could also be said – about the profit imperative and the commingling of
   sport and militarism – of the new team's decision to replace the cherished logo of a
   commercial jet airliner with a new logo that features an F-18 fighter jet.
12 Philip Moore, "Practical Nostalgia and the Critique of Commodification: On the
   'Death of Hockey' and the National Hockey League," *Australian Journal of Anthropology* 13, no. 3 (2002): 310.
13 Ibid., 316.
14 "Grey Cup Ratings Reveal Game Was Most Watch Sports Program of the Year,"
   Globe and Mail, 25 November 2013, http://www.theglobeandmail.com/sports/foot-
   ball/grey-cup-ratings-reveal-game-was-most-watched-sports-program-of-2013/
   article15596026/; "Despite Blowout Game, Super Bowl Breaks American TV Ratings Record," *Globe and Mail*, 3 February 2014, http://www.theglobeandmail.com/
   arts/television/despite-the-blowout-game-super-bowl-breaks-american-tv-ratings-
   record/article16670936/.
15 Moore, "Practical Nostalgia," 312.
16 "Sochi 2014: Gay Rights Protests Target Russia's Games," BBC News, 5 February
   2014, http://www.bbc.com/news/world-europe-26043872.
17 Alan Tomlinson and Christopher Young, "Culture, Politics, and Spectacle in
   the Global Sports Event: An Introduction," in Alan Tomlinson and Christopher
   Young (eds.), *National Identity and Global Sports Events: Culture, Politics, and
   Spectacle in the Olympics and the Football World Cup* (Albany, NY: SUNY Press,
   2006), 1.
18 See, for example, David Whitson and Donald Macintosh, "Becoming a World-Class
   City: Hallmark Events and Sport Franchises in the Growth Strategies of Western
   Canadian Cities," *Sociology of Sport Journal* 10 (1993): 221–40; John Hannigan,

Fantasy City: Pleasure and Profit in the Postmodern Metropolis (London and New York: Routledge, 1998).

19 "2010 Gold Medal Game Is the Apex of TV Viewing in Canada as Legend of '72 Summit Series Finally Laid to Rest," Newswire.ca, 12 March 2010, http://www. newswire.ca/en/story/575679/2010-gold-medal-game-is-the-apex-of-tv-viewing-in-canada-as-legend-of-72-summit-series-finally-laid-to-rest.

20 Tomlinson and Young, "Culture, Politics, and Spectacle," 1.

21 Stephen Brunt, "He Deserved Better," *Globe and Mail*, 9 February 2011, S4. Brunt also makes an important argument concerning the role of the media in covering the death of Georgian luger Nodar Kumaritashvili in the hours before the Opening Ceremonies, noting the implication of the sports media in the preferred narrative of mega-events and its desire to wrap up the Kumaritashvili story without the necessary due diligence to fully investigate the safety concerns it raised: "there is also the troubling realization that in our desire to get on with the party, to have our big Canadian moment, we wanted this over with as quickly as possible."

22 "Winnipeg to Host 2017 Canada Summer Games," CBC News, 26 April 2013, http://www.cbc.ca/news/canada/manitoba/winnipeg-to-host-2017-canada-summer-games-1.1363620. To be fair, Winnipeg "won" the Games after it was the only remaining bid city during a Canada Games cycle when the event was slated to take place in Manitoba.

23 Cited in Sandro Contenta, "Profile of Bruce Kidd, Former Star Athlete and Fitness Advocate," *Toronto Star*, 21 May, 2010, http://www.thestar.com/news/insight/2010/05/21/profile_of_bruce_kidd_former_star_athlete_and_fitness_advocate.html.

24 Canada's medal position in Vancouver and Whistler is discussed later in the introduction. In London, Canada finished thirteenth in the medals table with eighteen medals (one gold, five silver, twelve bronze). There were also goals for the Paralympic Games: to be in the top three in gold medals at the 2010 Paralympic Winter Games (Canada finished third with ten golds,) and in the top eight in gold medals in the 2012 Paralympic (Summer) Games (Canada finished twentieth with seven golds, winning thirty-one medals overall). http://ownthepodium.org/About-OTP.aspx.

25 Cited in Contenta, "Profile of Bruce Kidd."

26 http://ownthepodium.org/Funding/Winter-Historical-Comparison.aspx.

27 "Winnipeg to Host 2017 Canada Summer Games."

28 "Olympics Cost B.C. $925M," CBC News, 9 July 2010, http://www.cbc.ca/news/canada/british-columbia/olympics-cost-b-c-925m-1.934931.

29 David Black, "Dreaming Big: The Pursuit of Second Order Games a Strategic Response to Globalisation," *Sport and Society* 11, no. 4 (2008): 467–79.

30 "Olympic Legacy Providing Hope of Skilled Jobs," CBC News, 9 February 2011, http://www.cbc.ca/news/canada/british-columbia/olympic-legacy-providing-hope-of-skilled-jobs-1.1090108.

31 See, for example, Steve McMorran, "Could Next Month's Commonwealth Games Be Cancelled?," Associated Press, 21 September 2010, http://www.thestar.com/sports/2010/09/21/could_next_months_commonwealth_games_be_cancelled.

32 John Doyle (with Cathal Kelly), "This Week in Footie," *Globe and Mail*, 21 June 2014, S1.

33 Dave Zirin, *Brazil's Dance with the Devil: The World Cup, the Olympics, and the Fight for Democracy* (Chicago: Haymarket Books, 2014), 206–7.

34 Ibid., 13–14.

35 Kyle G. Brown, "Rounded Up and Run Out of Town," *Toronto Star*, 10 June 2010, http://www.thestar.com/news/world/2010/06/10/rounded_up_and_run_out_of_town.html.

36 See, for example, www.sportforsolidarity.org.

37 COHRE, *Fair Play for Housing Rights: Mega-events, Olympic Games, and Housing Rights; Opportunities for the Olympic Movement and Others* (Geneva: COHRE, 2007). http://www.ruig-gian.org/ressources/Report%20Fair%20Play%20FINAL%20FINAL%20070531.pdf.

38 "A Threat to World Cup Averted: Brazil's Homeless Movement Withdraws Vow to Stage Big Protests," Huffington Post, 10 June 2014, http://www.huffingtonpost.ca/2014/06/10/a-threat-to-world-cup-ave_n_5479028.html.

39 COHRE, *Fair Play for Housing Rights*.

40 Helen Jefferson Lenskyj, *Inside the Olympic Industry: Power, Politics, and Activism* (Albany, NY: SUNY Press, 2000), 133.

41 See Douglas Hartmann, *Race, Culture, and the Revolt of the Black Athlete: The 1968 Olympic Protests and Their Aftermath* (Chicago and London: University of Chicago Press, 2003). A recent analysis reads this event through the lens of peace and conflict studies to suggest that Smith and Carlos were not punching the sky with the "Black power" salute, but offering a less violent display inspired by Martin Luther King and Mahatma Gandhi (see Christopher Hrynkow, "Players or Pawns? Student-Athletes, Human Rights Activism, Nonviolent Protest, and the Cultures of Peace at the 1968 Summer Olympics" unpublished PhD diss., University of Manitoba, 2013).

42 Callie Batts, "'In Good Conscience': Andy Flower, Henry Olonga, and the Death of Democracy in Zimbabwe," *Sport in Society* 13, no. 1 (2010): 43–58.

43 Ann Peel, "The Athlete as Sisyphus: Reflections of an Athlete Advocate," *Sport in Society* 13, no. 1 (2010): 22–3.

44 James Dorsey, "Former Zamalek Goalkeeper Joins Tahrir Square Protests," The Turbulent World of Middle East Soccer, 8 February 2011, http://mideastsoccer.blogspot.ca/2011/02/former-zamalek-goalkeeper-joins-tahrir.html.

45 Black, "Dreaming Big," 470.
46 "Vancouver 2010 Bid Plebiscite Question Announced," GamesBids.com, 12 December, 2002, http://gamesbids.com/eng/other-news/vancouver-2010-bid-plebiscite-question-announced/.
47 "64% Support Olympic Bid in Vancouver Plebiscite," GamesBids.com, 23 February, 2003, http://gamesbids.com/eng/other-news/64-support-olympic-bid-in-vancouver-plebiscite/.
48 Bruce Kidd, "The Culture Wars of the Montreal Olympics," *International Review for the Sociology of Sport* 27, no. 2 (1992): 151–64.
49 Bruce Kidd, "The Philosophy of Excellence: Olympic Performances, Class Power, and the Canadian State," in Pasquale J. Galasso (ed.), *Philosophy of Sport and Physical Activity: Issues and Concepts* (Toronto: Canadian Scholars' Press, 1988), 11–31.
50 Bruce Kidd, *The Struggle for Canadian Sport* (Toronto: University of Toronto Press, 1996), 39.
51 Ibid., 224.

PART ONE

Global Promises: The Contested Terrain of International Sport

1 Sport, Development, and the Challenge of Slums

RICHARD GRUNEAU

In the opening passages of his book *Planet of Slums* Mike Davis notes that there were eighty-six cities in the world in 1950 with a population of more than one million people. By 2015, Davis continues, "there will be at least 550" cities in this category.[1] China, in particular, is urbanizing at a rate that is unprecedented in human history. Between 1978 and 2007 the number of official cities in China jumped from 193 to 640, and more than 160 of these now have a population in excess of a million people.[2] In Africa urban population growth since the 1950s has followed a similar pattern. Dhaka, Kinshasa, and Lagos have evolved into sprawling megacities that are already nearly forty times the size they were in 1950.[3] According to the United Nations Human Settlements Programme, UN-Habitat, of the twenty-five largest cities in the world, twenty-four can be found in the global South – cities such as Mexico City, São Paolo, Mumbai, Cairo, and Lagos.[4]

In Southern nations – the so-called developing world – this extraordinary urban growth has been driven by a complex set of global forces that have either pushed people out of rural areas against their will or drawn them to the city with promises of a better life. Across Africa, South Asia, Latin America, and South America the mechanization of agriculture, the consolidation of small holdings into larger ones, and the competition from international agribusiness have challenged the ability of subsistence farmers to generate enough money for water, clothing, or school books.[5] In many parts of Africa these pressures have been exacerbated by recurring drought and civil war. In China, migration from the countryside has been driven by an erosion of the social guarantees that once protected rural living standards, matched with the promise of steady factory wages in the city and more cosmopolitan lifestyles. Some estimates suggest that by 2020 a staggering 300 million to 500 million people in China will have moved from the countryside to urban areas.[6]

All of this has led to unrelenting economic and social pressures in cities across the global South. People continue to stream into the largest urban areas despite ongoing economic weaknesses in many cities and the cities' inability to provide adequate housing, public services, or sanitation. Accordingly, the most visible feature of urban development since the mid-twentieth century has been the dramatic spread of squatter cities, shanty towns, and tenement districts. These slum districts now absorb the majority of population growth in many of the world's poorest countries. It is estimated that the number of squatters, people living illegally on land they do not own, is now over a billion worldwide, approximately one out of every six human beings on the planet.[7] Similarly, there are projections that by 2015 "Africa will have 332 million slum dwellers, a number that will continue to double every fifteen years."[8] Even in North America and Europe, while the trends are far less dramatic, research has shown a pattern of increasing homelessness and squatting and the displacement of former slum populations into peripheral pockets of suburban poverty.[9]

In this chapter I argue that the challenge of slums requires greater attention in research and writing on global sport. There is some encouraging work that has begun to take up this challenge in areas such as sport and globalization, sport and social movements, and sport and subaltern studies.[10] In addition, in the past decade there has been considerable enthusiasm for the use of sport in social and economic development, and the literature in this area is growing.[11] There has also been a groundswell in the number of international agencies and NGOs who have initiated sport and development programs of various types in barrios, favelas, and shanty towns around the world.[12]

Nonetheless, when it comes to the analysis of sport and urban poverty, there are striking absences in the literature. In particular, much of the work on sport and development lacks depth and critical reflexivity. For example, there continues to be a lack of research on the social factors underlying the growth of interest in sport as a tool for development in recent years, and we do not know enough about the way in which these factors have shaped major policy agendas. There is also insufficient research on the political and economic interests and the ideological assumptions associated with sport and development initiatives of various types, particularly those that claim to include poverty reduction as an objective. With these concerns in mind, the analysis that follows situates the enthusiasm for sport as an aspect of development policy in its historical and political economic context. This leads to an evaluation of the extent to which several key policy documents, and the solutions they suggest, provide a meaningful response to the challenge of slums.

Anyone who writes on the topic of sport and development will be struck by the important role that Bruce Kidd has played in the area, with respect both to scholarly research and to the shaping of recent policy directions. Since the late 1960s Kidd's scholarly work has regularly provided new insights into Canadian sport history, as well as deep and probing analyses of the ways that contemporary social class and corporate interests have shaped Canadian sport. He has also consistently taken principled and progressive positions on a variety of social issues. His many contributions include leading the charge in Canada against South African sporting apartheid in the 1970s; staking out an early pro-feminist position with respect to women's involvement in sport and being a pioneering critic against homophobia in sport; and promoting tirelessly the use of sport to support the goals of peace, international co-operation, and progressive social change. His impact and personal legacy in both the practice and the study of Canadian sport have been immeasurable. For nearly forty years, in addition to being a friend and colleague, I have been one of Bruce Kidd's biggest fans. Still, that does not mean that I always agree with him. While I know that Kidd will see common ground in the analysis that follows, much of the chapter provides a measure of our differences.

A Better World for All? Slums, Civil Society, Sport, and Development

For most people the word *slum* refers to large-scale zones of urban habitation that are economically impoverished, over-crowded, and lacking an adequate health and service infrastructure. Yet, it is an imprecise term that blurs the vast distinctions between the environments inhabited by the world's dispossessed. The word *slum* also often carries with it an implicit sense of judgment.[13] On this point Robert Neuwirth notes that slums are everything that people who do not live in slums tend to fear: dirt, decay, disease, despair, degradation, horror, abuse, crime, uncertainty, and danger. To use the word *slum* risks conjuring an implicit morality. *Slum* means something bad and, indeed for outsiders who often have the best of intentions, something to be "improved" or "developed."[14]

Still, in contrast to this depiction and for all their problems, slums are also neighbourhoods and communities – sometimes in the best sense of these terms. While slum neighbourhoods may be economically depressed, they are also often alive with an anarchic blend of mutualism matched with high levels of individual freedom and creative energy. It is important not to romanticize these communities, where people often lead very desperate lives, but slum communities should be neither demonized nor patronized. Too often, programs to eradicate slums seem merely intent to relocate "the problem" elsewhere or to seek paternalistic solutions from outside the community. Alternatively, many slum development programs tend to be temporary and ameliorative, unable to respond to the structural dynamics that are creating the problem of slums in the first place. Neuwirth suggests that the only practical solution to the problem of slums is not to try to eliminate slum conditions; rather, the solution lies in *not* treating poor urban communities as slums – that is, as "horrific, scary and criminal – and start treating them as neighbourhoods that can be improved."[15]

Nonetheless, the phrase *poor neighbourhoods* lacks the evocative power of the word *slum*, and it is the latter word that has figured centrally in recent programmatic discussions of global urban poverty. In 2003 UN-Habitat released a landmark report, *The Challenge of Slums*, that urged donors and governments to improve the lives of five million to ten million slum dwellers by 2005, and one hundred million by 2020, in line with the broader Millennium Goals (UNMGs) announced in the United Nations' *Millennium Declaration* in 2000.[16] In its declaration the United Nations announced a commitment to work towards the eradication of extreme global poverty and hunger by 2015 (an impossible target that has since been revised).[17] Other UNMGs included the achievement of universal primary education; promotion of gender equality and women's empowerment; reduction of child mortality; improvement in maternal health; the combating of HIV/AIDS, malaria, and other diseases; environmental sustainability; and the pursuit of global partnerships for development. *The Challenge of Slums* embraces a similarly broad set of objectives including "leading a worldwide effort to move from pilot projects to city-wide and nation-wide upgrading, and to generate the required resources to do so; and investing in global knowledge, learning and capacity in slum upgrading, and reducing the growth of new slums."[18] The report suggests that such broad-ranging objectives will only be achieved by increasing investments aimed at providing basic services to the world's urban poor.

In the early post-war era it was widely assumed that national governments would be the most likely source of such investments. However, since the late 1980s the United Nations has paid growing attention to the importance of NGOs in civil society as potential partners in development. In its simplest form the phrase *civil society* refers to social organizations and associations that are independent of the state.[19] Enthusiasm for civil society organizations in international development occurred in conjunction with a loss of faith across much of North America and Europe in the ability of state organizations to resolve major social problems. It also reflected a trend towards non-state approaches to development that was ascendant during the 1980s in large international economic organizations such as the International Monetary Fund and the World Bank.[20] The collapse of state socialism in Eastern Europe and the Soviet Union contributed to a retreat from state-based approaches to social problems, further opening the door to a neo-liberal ideology that extolled free market principles and the ideals of entrepreneurialism and individual initiative.[21]

In an environment permeated by distrust of state agencies' abilities to find solutions to contemporary social problems a turn to civil society organizations, buttressed by donor-partners in the corporate sector, came to be seen as an inevitable, and in some cases a progressive, alternative. For progressively minded individuals and groups the NGO path to development connected strongly to an emphasis on the role of autonomous organizations and groups in civil society as agents of change, against the inequities and constraints of the state and the market. For post-war free marketeers, who tended to be suspicious of the state, the pathway to social progress was seen to lie with the private sector in combination with other "stakeholders" represented through civil society organizations. Each of these political perspectives embraced the importance of civil society organizations in social change and development, albeit for different reasons. Nonetheless, from the 1980s onwards the idea of NGO-led approaches to development was able to draw subtly on both traditions in making a claim to legitimacy, sometimes blurring their lines in new ways.

By the early 1990s the idea of necessary partnerships between large multilateral organizations – such as the United Nations and its agencies, national governments, NGOs, and new national and multinational corporate supporters – was emerging as the cutting edge in international development circles. According to the World Bank, 12 per cent of foreign aid to developing countries was already being channelled through NGOs in 1994, and by 1996 the total amount was $7 billion worldwide. In Africa alone NGOs managed nearly $3.5 billion in external aid in 1998, compared to under $1 billion in 1990.[22] Still, many NGOs were finding it difficult to raise enough money from memberships and private donations to take on the larger role that they were being invited to fill, and there was increasing competition for these traditional sources of funds arising from the proliferation of new NGO competitors. The logical solution to such funding problems was to augment the traditional sources of donor revenue through new partnerships with governments and the private sector. An international framework for such partnerships was initiated in 1999 when the United Nations launched a new Global Compact (UNGC) program with more than three thousand companies willing to partner with NGOs, governments, and other international agencies to work towards meeting United Nations development goals. In this global compact, public-minded corporations and NGOs committed themselves to principles of sustainability, social justice, health, and economic development to build what the UNGC final report called "a better world for all."[23]

It is not surprising that sport would quickly be seen as a useful ground for forging development partnerships through the Global Compact. The idea of individual, social, and cultural development through sport has a long history stretching back to nineteenth-century middle- and working-class movements for rational recreation and muscular Christianity. As Bruce Kidd notes, this tradition was taken up by professional physical educators and amateur sports organizations and found its way into the emerging philosophy of Olympism, with its emphasis on fair play and internationalism. A belief that sport can be a source of social improvement and development can also be found in sources as diverse as the playground movement of the early-twentieth century and the workers' sports movements of the inter-war period.[24]

However, Kidd suggests that the more recent manifestation of sport as a vehicle for development is markedly different even though it draws on some of the ideas and assumptions of earlier traditions. It is different "in the rapid explosion of the agencies and organizations that are involved, the tremendous appeal it has for youth volunteering, the financial support it enjoys from the powerful international sports federations and the extent to which it has been championed by the United Nations, its agencies and significant partners."[25] In addition, Kidd notes that a growing movement, which he calls "sport for development and peace," was able to take root in the 1990s given the collapse of the Cold War and its attendant complications for development programs. Just like the NGO sector more broadly, the triumphant neo-liberalism of that decade enabled a "new focus on entrepreneurship as a strategy for social development, creating new openings for the creation of non-governmental organizations and private foundations."[26] At the same time, the movement also fed on a spirit of "humanitarian intervention" associated with the growing legitimation of international legislative bodies, such as the International Court of Justice, and the accompanying notion of the "right to protect" in the wake of the "genocides in Rwanda and the former Yugoslavia, the tremendous visibility of the worldwide appeals to combat famine and the pandemic of HIV/AIDs in Africa," as well as various campaigns to end global poverty.[27]

In this context, older connections between sports organizations and the United Nations solidified in new ways. United Nations agencies had used major sporting events and star athletes in the past in campaigns to promote immunization against childhood diseases, and other public health measures, and to support human rights, especially the post-war fight against racism and apartheid. The right to play and to participate in sports regardless of race, ethnicity, or gender was solidified in UN policy through such events as the Convention on the Elimination of Discrimination against Women in 1979 and the later ratification of the International Convention on the Rights of the Child in 1990.

Since the early 1990s UN agencies such as UNESCO, UNICEF, and the UN Development Program (UNDP) have worked out co-operative agreements and programs with international sporting associations in the interests of promoting social responsibility and meeting the UNMGs. Major examples include the International Olympic Committee (IOC), which continues to form alliances with a diversity of UN agencies and is a partner in a variety of innovative development projects, and the Fédération Internationale de Football Association (FIFA), which has established working relationships with the World Health Organization and UNICEF for campaigns against polio and for the Rights of the Child.[28]

Kidd argues that these transitions were significantly influenced by a generation of "highly educated and media savvy" athletes and sports leaders who emerged between the 1970s and the 1990s and sought to take "more responsibility for the direction and governance of their sports."[29] Following the accusations of widespread drug taking in international sport in the wake of the Seoul Olympics, and the bribery and doping scandals of 1998, a number of these activist athletes and sports leaders – including Kidd himself – pushed for reforms in international sports organizations, stressing a need for international sport to embrace a broader humanitarian mandate. Kidd's own pioneering involvement in Commonwealth Games Canada's program International Development through Sport, stretching back to the mid-1990s, is one example. There are many others, including former speed skater Johann Olav Koss, founder of the now high-profile international organization Right to Play; and former Canadian race walker, Ann Peel, who led a group of athletes at the 1994 Commonwealth Games to create a program designed to provide sports leadership in disadvantaged communities around the Commonwealth.[30]

By the turn of the twenty-first century it was impossible to ignore the seemingly insatiable desire for sport in countries around the world, the increasing size of global audiences for international sporting events, and the striking growth in the numbers of sports organizations and NGOs interested either in developing sport opportunities in disadvantaged communities and countries or in using sport as a platform for promoting non-sport development programs in areas such as maternal health, gender equity, and HIV/AIDS promotion. In an attempt to promote and co-ordinate these developments better, in 2002 the United Nations created the Inter-Agency Task Force on Sport for Development and Peace. The task force released its report, *Sport for Development and Peace: Towards Achieving the Millennium Development Goals,*[31] in 2003, the same year that UN-Habitat released its report *The Challenge of Slums.*

The two reports are a study in contrasts. *The Challenge of Slums* is a culmination of years of research and analysis developed through a large UN agency, whereas the 2003 *Sport for Development and Peace* report is a preliminary state-ment from a small task force, which was meant to pave the way for subsequent organizational co-ordination, research, and development. In contrast to the 310 pages of research and discussion in *The Challenge of Slums,* the UN inter-agency task force's report is a mere 36 pages, consisting mostly of program-matic statements drawn from other UN documents, a superficial and selective use of academic research, and some examples of existing programs. Although *The Challenge of Slums* is not without its limitations, it nonetheless makes an attempt at detailed social analysis, including discussions of the global ascend-ency of neo-liberalism and the comparative failure of market-oriented glo-balization strategies espoused through organizations such as the International Monetary Fund. At the other end of the spectrum, the UN task force's report on sport for development and peace is filled with platitudes and generalizations and contains little social analysis of any depth or consequence. Significantly, while much is made in *Sport for Development and Peace* about using sport to achieve UNMGs, the vitally important millennium goal of eradicating extreme global poverty and hunger by 2015 is ignored in favour of a few passing obser-vations to suggest how sport can help with economic development.

It is important to acknowledge that the 2003 UN inter-agency task force report on sport and development was meant only as a springboard for sub-sequent development and analysis, and on these terms it was successful. The report led to the creation of a Sport for Development and Peace International Working Group (SDP IWG) at the Athens Olympics in 2004 (affiliated with the prominent NGO Right to Play), in addition to a United Nations Office on Sport for Development and Peace. The report also paved the way for the United Nations to declare 2005 the International Year of Sport and Physical Education, with a strong emphasis on the ideals of social responsibility, development, and sustainability, and it provided a base for a growing body of more developed work. Examples include the literature review prepared by Donnelly, Coakley, Darnell, and Wells in 2007 for the SDP IWG Secretariat in Toronto, as well as a 176-page SDP/IWG Preliminary Report in 2006, and a final report that was presented at the Bejing Olympics in 2008.[32] The 2003 inter-agency task force report also provided a set of working principles upon which multilateral agen-cies, NGOs, and corporations could begin to form more effective partnerships.

Still, these later documents and studies have been consistently more pro-grammatic than analytical. They map existing sport and development initia-tives in various countries and make programmatic assertions but offer little in the way of detailed social analysis or critical reflection. More important, later SDP IWG reports also reproduce the inadequate consideration of global pov-erty that is evident in the initial 2003 inter-agency task force's report. Nowhere in any of these documents can one find a detailed analysis of how sport might be mobilized to meet the key UNMG target of substantially reducing global poverty or how some approaches to meeting this goal might be more or less successful than others. When there is any discussion of the way in which sport might advance the goal of global poverty reduction, the analytical position in SDP IWG reports typically defaults to the broader development goals and objectives of major players in the UN Global Compact, such as the World Bank and the International Monetary Fund.

Consider, in this regard, the brief discussion of how sport might be used to meet the UN anti-poverty targets outlined in the 2006 SDP IWG interim report, *From Practice to Policy*. After asserting that sport can play a role in meeting the UN Millennium Goal of poverty reduction, the report acknowledges that "most countries will not be able to attain the eight goals by 2015."[33] The report then goes on to list the "common reasons for shortfalls in the attainment of the MDGs" in different countries, including "poor governance, poverty traps with local and national economies unable to make investments, unequal distribution of economic development within countries, areas with multiple complex challenges that defy solutions, and the simultaneous occurrence of all or some of these factors."[34] Despite these problems, the report concludes that "urgent action is needed" and that success will depend "on the international community's willingness to make significant economic investments and, in many cases, policy and institutional improvements to allow implementation of practical measures that have already been shown to work."[35]

Once more, a comparison with the UN-Habitat's 2003 report *The Challenge of Slums* is instructive. In contrast to a single sentence in the SDP IWG interim report that lists some possible reasons for the likely shortfall in meeting the UNMGs, the 2003 UN-Habitat report offers a much more sustained analysis, including discussion of histories of colonial underdevelopment and consideration of the failures of more recent market-centred policies such as the structural adjustment policies of the International Monetary Fund.[36] Yet, there is not even the slightest critical reflex in the SDP IWG interim report, let alone any suggestion of the need for a comparable socio-historical analysis of sport or of sport development policies. Instead the report suggests that developing countries currently already have the tools to meet anti-poverty goals through national Poverty Reduction Strategy Papers (PRSPS) prepared "through a participatory process involving civil society and development partners, such as the World Bank and the International Monetary Fund."[37]

The confidence expressed in this assertion about PRSPs is both striking and dubious given competing assertions found in documents from other UN agencies as well as in the substantial literature in the field of international development studies.[38] At one moment the SDP IWG 2006 report makes the claim that sport can play a role in meeting the UN Millennium Goal of poverty reduction, but at another moment it passes up the opportunity to develop the point and suggests that national governments should simply work harder to integrate sport into IMF-supported national poverty reduction strategies that are now widely criticized.[39] To be fair, the SPD IWG interim report does argue for investment in programs for poverty reduction; however, it is vague about what such investments might look like and what priorities should guide them. The 2006 report merely echoes the suggestions introduced in the 2003 SPD IWG report, namely that sport can play a role in economic development and that economic growth has a positive effect on poverty reduction.

Making Poverty History? Sport in the Neo-liberal Discourse of Rights, Stakeholders, and Partnerships

The superficial treatment of the problem of global poverty in SDP IWG reports exists in conjunction with a broad rights-oriented perspective that is pervasive in the mission statements of related UN agencies and NGOs. Despite frequent mention of the need to eradicate global poverty and hunger, most of the programs and policy statements from these groups focus on the expansion of individual rights associated with such things as the right to health, education, social inclusion, and, of course, to play. Not surprisingly, the inadequate consideration of global poverty found in the documents produced by sport and development groups is reproduced in their organizational structures. For example, the SDP IWG has working subgroups listed on the website of the UN Office on Sport for Development and Peace in the areas of sport and health; sport, child, and youth development; sport and gender; sport and persons with disabilities; and sport and peace. But there is no SDP IWG subgroup listed in the area of sport and global poverty.[40]

Admittedly, it is asking a lot of development policies involving sport to contribute substantially to the resolution of such complex problems as global poverty and the expansion of slums. So it is perfectly understandable that supporters of sport and development policies focus instead on expanding the terrain of rights and opportunities for individuals and communities in more modest and immediately achievable ways. Examples include opening up opportunities for sports participation or coaching in disadvantaged communities or, more ambitiously, using sport for the advancement of broader agendas such as the promotion of anti-racism, the rights of the disabled, the empowerment of girls and women, HIV/AIDS prevention, and peace in war-torn societies. If we accept Robert Neuwirth's view of slums as "neighborhoods to be improved," many recent sport and development programs appear to be doing exactly that. For example, one of the most commonly noted success stories in the literature on sport and development is the Mathare Youth Sports Association (MYSA) located in a crowded and desperately poor slum community of Nairobi, Kenya.[41] The MYSA was started in 1987 by a Canadian UN diplomat, Bob Munro, as a self-help project to organize sports while involving local youth in environmental clean-ups. Since then the MYSA has grown to approximately twenty thousand members, with numerous football (soccer) teams, ranging from recreational to semi-professional, and several development initiatives in areas such as AIDS prevention, leadership training, and the empowerment of girls and women.

The apparent success of the MYSA shows the impact that NGO-led sport and development programs can have on an impoverished community. Providing opportunities to participate in sport undoubtedly creates new and positive experiences for young people in these communities. This may include a sense of confidence and personal fulfilment as well as a sense of belonging and citizenship beyond the immediate needs of day-to-day economic survival. By the promotion of health-care messages and the provision of new opportunities for individual empowerment, self-expression, and belonging, it is easy to see how sport can play a small role in the fight against various forms of impoverishment. In other words, despite the seeming intractability of so many of the world's greatest problems, proponents of sport as an agency of development are not being unrealistic when they claim that sport can at least do *something* to help. Indeed, as John Sugden has suggested, for socially conscious individuals, "doing nothing may no longer be an option."[42] More and more people in recent years appear to feel this way. According to Kidd, in 2008 there were 166 organizations devoted to sport and development programs listed on the International Platform on Sport for Development maintained by the Swiss Academy for Development, and this list appears to be far from exhaustive.[43] Using sport to "build a better world" now has unprecedented social, political, and cultural momentum.

Unfortunately when an idea develops such widespread social, political, and cultural momentum, the urge to *act* sometimes pushes critical reflection aside in favour of unreflective evangelism. In the area of sport and development, that evangelism is positive in so far as it provides the energy for NGOs and UN- and government-affiliated organizations to do good work. However, it also lends itself to silences and blind spots, some of which are evident in the priority given to civil society organizations in international development and in the tendency to downplay the systemic causes of poverty in favour of a focus on individual rights. This rights-based discourse has not emerged in the area of sport and development simply as a pragmatic response to the unmanageable nature of the world's greatest problems; it is also a corollary to a policy logic that shifts responsibility for development away from national and regional governments and towards international partnerships of civil society organizations, state agencies, and corporations. A focus on improving human rights in development promises to open up opportunities for marginalized individuals but also risks deflecting attention from less immediately evident social and organizational features that reproduce broader inequalities in condition. When this latter situation occurs, rights-based approaches to development can become disconnected from the structural changes that many community groups argue are necessary to improve the lives of the world's poorest citizens.

Commenting on this point in the case of Africa, the Tanzanian legal scholar Issa Shivji notes that NGO-led development policies originating in the global North since the 1990s have often been justified by arguments about the corruption of African governments, or a fear of African-based social movements struggling for autonomy and greater control of self-destiny. Rather than working with activist groups and governments in ways that respect their autonomy, the challenge of development has typically been passed on to experts in Northern-based multilateral organizations, NGOs, and their public and corporate partners.[44] The aid that comes to Africa is well intentioned, there is often consultation in local communities, and many of the programs provide real opportunities for certain individuals and communities, but the policy logic is almost always developed by educated elites in the North and applied to problems viewed from afar and in a global political economic environment where Northern ambitions and agendas shape international circuits of economic exchange and political power, typically to the detriment of former colonial societies.

The result is a widespread tendency to lose sight of the way that real people live their lives in favour of abstractions such as "the chronically poor," who then become the "subject matter of papers on strategies for poverty reduction authored by consultants and discussed at stakeholders workshops in which the poor are represented by NGOs."[45] Too often, Shivji claims, "the "poor," the diseased, the disabled, the AIDS-infected, the ignorant, the marginalized," are not seen as active agents themselves in the development process; rather, such groups tend to become objectified in a paternalistic equation – the needy recipients of humanitarian aid given by well-meaning "friends" in the North "and dispensed by non-partisan, non-political and presumably non-involved, nongovernmental organizations. In these societies, where stakeholders never tire of policy making on the poor, there isn't its twin opposite, the rich. These societies apparently do not have producers and appropriators of wealth; they only have the poor and the wealth creators."[46]

The last comment points to a half-hidden theory of society implicit in discourses of development centred on the idea of a global compact of partnerships between civil society, NGOs, the state, and corporate stakeholders. This theory posits a world that may be unequal and unjust but is composed of multi-party groups who have a shared will for change matched with broadly shared political, cultural, and economic interests. In this perspective, while various stakeholders may have conflicts or disagreements, there is no perception of a fundamental contradiction between their interests. The result is a chronic inability to analyse the way in which some stakeholders in development partnerships may be more powerful than others and able to pursue their own interests to the detriment of others. It is one thing to say that we should "make poverty history" (to use the phrase adopted by a prominent activist coalition), but this will only happen if we understand the history of poverty.[47] Wealth creation does not necessarily lead to poverty reduction in situations where certain groups in societies are able to appropriate more of the wealth for themselves than for others, especially when these groups are able to make the resulting forms of inequality seem natural, inevitable, or representative of the general public interest.

Even a cursory analysis of the history of poverty over the past two centuries underlines this point in dramatic fashion. While urban poverty and slums are as old as human cities themselves, the nature and character of global poverty in the late-nineteenth and early-twentieth centuries changed in conjunction with the rise of factory-based industrialism, burgeoning monopoly capitalism, the consolidation of the modern global state system, and the formation of new colonial networks. Industrialization featured the first modern migrations of dispossessed rural residents to cities, where they became factory labour forces and slum dwellers in industrialized Northern nations. At the same time, colonization accelerated the international ascendency of Western industrialism and finance capital, with disastrous consequences in many parts of the global South.[48]

New ways of organizing economic production in the early-twentieth century, along with increasing state intervention in economic life and the fall-out from the two world wars, began to shift the disposition of global political and economic forces, accentuating the elevation of the United States to a position of global power, accompanied by a decline in European colonial dominance in many parts of the world. Following the Great Depression of the 1930s and the Second World War, and especially in the United States, a door opened for increased state involvement in capitalist economies. Research shows that inequality in many parts of the world decreased in the post-war period from 1945 to the early 1970s.[49] Wages rose with increased productivity, and full employment was not uncommon. Governments worked hard to keep economies stable, "using new techniques of Keynesian pump priming through the public sector."[50] Under pressure from communist countries, and "with growing social democratic and socialist movements at home, the capitalist regimes, already enfeebled by the Great Depression, conceded to dramatic and far-reaching social reforms" such as "unemployment benefits and pensions, paid vacations, the 40-hour week, guaranteed and free education and health care for all, and trade union protection of workers."[51]

At the same time that these events were unfolding in Northern nations many of the countries in the global South won independence from colonial rule, creating a situation in which "dreams of industrialization and "catching up" could be realistically entertained."[52] Over the period of post-war growth between 1950 and approximately 1972, inequality not only fell within countries but also lessened somewhat between countries. In some parts of the world this trend extended into the late 1970s, although it is important not to overstate the extent of post-colonial "catching up."[53] At the peak of the post-war boom, in 1970, "the top 20 per cent of the world's people in the richest countries had 32 times the income of the poorest 20 per cent."[54] Still, while the reduction of inequality between nations may have been modest in the early post-war period, there was at least a brief time during which the economic chasm between North and South seemed to be eroding. In contrast, from 1973 to the present, inequality has increased dramatically.[55] The gap between the top 20 per cent of world's people in the richest countries grew to forty-five times in 1980, fifty-nine times in 1989, and about seventy-eight times in 2003.[56] The gap between rich and poor within countries also began to grow, against the tide of the comparative gains of the 1945–72 period.[57]

Who Benefits? Sport, Consumption-Based Development, and Poverty in the Age of Neo-liberal Globalization

It is more than coincidental that growing social inequality around the world from the early 1970s to the present day correlates with a dramatic growth in the economic scale and significance of the world's largest international sporting events. There is no direct causal relationship between these two circumstances, but international sporting events have benefited from and contributed to new economic and political policies around the world that have exacerbated global poverty. Three developments in particular have contributed both to the growth of these policies and to the accelerating economic importance of international sporting events between the 1960s and the present day.

First, the global deflation of the mid-1970s demonstrated substantial limitations to the settlement of the international economic and political interests that had emerged at the end of the Second World War. A "stagflationary spiral of high inflation and low growth proved resistant to all conventional measures," opening up a debate about the apparent weaknesses of Keynesian economics.[58] This opened the door to a new coalition of political and economic actors in North America and Europe who were determined to liberalize what they saw as excessive regulation in both national and international economies. The mantra of this new coalition was focused on the need to reduce state regulation of the economy in the interests of promoting greater flexibility in production and easier mobility for capital.[59]

Second, in conjunction with this push for deregulation and flexibility there was an aggressive campaign in many Northern nations to reduce public expenditures, while providing tax incentives to induce private investment and to reorient state policies towards activities that would be economically beneficial. The social-democratic movements of the earlier post-war period were weakened, and the "collapse of communism eliminated the external threat and made global capitalism ... free to pursue unhindered its objectives of profit maximization – without much regard for social consequences."[60] In this context, campaigns for debt reduction by federal and regional state governments, matched with a growing political commitment to reduce taxes in general, meant a widespread offloading of public sector responsibilities onto lower levels of government, such as municipalities and cities. In addition, the mid-twentieth-century evaluation of the worth of public investment to meet broad social needs shifted to accommodate a stronger emphasis on policies that promoted entrepreneurialism, capital accumulation, and economic growth.[61]

Finally, in an emerging digital age, new technologies became the mechanism for accomplishing a late-twentieth-century neo-liberal agenda and extending it to new global networks. Taking advantage of the vistas of managerial control opened by new technologies of communication, computerization, and robotics, firms moved aggressively towards automated decentralization. The drive to more flexible production and accumulation included "just in time" and small-batch production techniques, and new forms of inventory control, as well as the hiving off and contracting out of many functions previously performed in house. Reliance on standardized products did not die out, but the older form of mass production was increasingly augmented or challenged by market segmentation and the need for customization.[62] Meanwhile, the deregulation and privatization of the post-war welfare state opened up new areas of commodification, as capital became more mobile and nomadic, taking advantage of geographical differentials in market opportunity and labour costs on a broader international scale than ever before. Faced with such changes, the old mid-twentieth-century industrial labour force in Northern nations was fractured and remade to include a new breed of knowledge or cultural worker.[63] At the same time, older forms of sweat-shop labour grew steadily in deregulated free trade zones of Southern nations and even began to re-emerge in many cities in the North.

These wide-ranging changes accompanied, and contributed to, a significant growth in the cultural economies of cities and nations around the world. In an age of dramatic economic, political, and social recomposition the "production of events" in cities in the developed Northern nations increasingly came to rival the more traditional making of things.[64] The growing capacity for global media to construct both larger and more focused audiences created new sources for profit – new media markets – and intensified the promotional value of those international events that were seen to have the highest status and the highest levels of global interest. While civic boosters have long sought to attract big events to their cities for reasons of pride and the promotion of place, a "new entrepreneurialism," as David Harvey calls it, became centrally focused on remaking the city to take advantage of the cultural economy.[65] In the late-twentieth century the predominant vision of urban revitalization became linked to the construction of spectacular sites for consumption that were meant to attract international tourists and convention-goers as well as new cultural workers into the downtown area. Not only did this strategy involve upgrading urban infrastructure in transportation and communications, but it was also built on real estate speculation associated with the creation of gentrified housing and shopping spaces.[66] The huge scale of investment required in such projects, in an age of diminished city budgets, required a growing reliance on partnerships with outside groups, which resulted in the diffusion of some of the traditional power of city governments.[67]

In combination with a more sophisticated approach to maximizing revenues on the part of international sports organizations, these trends over the past thirty years have created an immensely lucrative seller's market for the rights to host international sporting events and for the trademark rights associated with them. The result has been escalating profits for international sponsoring associations, such as the IOC or FIFA, as well as for many of their NGO and private sector partners. For example, according to Giannoulakis and Stotler, sponsorship revenue to the IOC rose from $95 million in 1986 to $650 million in 2004.[68] Similarly, FIFA's revenues in 2007–10 were twelve times greater than in 1995–8, up from $257 million to $3.2 billion.[69] These global market dynamics have also worked to give new value to "second-tier" international or regional sporting events, such as the Asian Games and the Commonwealth Games. Over the past half century, and especially in the past twenty years of neo-liberal globalization, the dream of hosting such events has become no less a part of the agenda of upwardly striving elites in cities of the economically ascendant countries of East and South Asia, as well as of other parts of the global South. From Delhi to Guangzhou, Cape Town, and Rio, cities have been lining up to invest in large-scale sporting events and related projects, with marketers around the world cheering them on.

It is now conventional wisdom among booster coalitions in bid cities or hosting cities that such investments are justified because of the capacity for large-scale sporting events and projects to become powerful engines of economic development. To cite just one of many examples, in Delhi the India Olympic Committee, the governing body for the 2010 Commonwealth Games, was emphatic in arguing that the 2010 Games "will be the catalyst for the development of the city of Delhi and its environs."[70] Similar arguments have been put forward by every Olympic organizing committee since the mid-1980s and are also constantly present in contemporary policy documents associated with the promotion of sport and development generally. The 2003 UN Inter-Agency Task Force report, *Sport for Development and Peace*, provides an instructive example because many of its suggestions about sport and economic growth are repeated without much elaboration in later policy documents. The report argues that sport can act as both a catalyst and an engine for economic growth through "the economic weight, resulting from activities such as the manufacture of sporting goods, sports events, sport-related services and the media," and by "providing employment opportunities," stimulating "demand for goods and services," and acting as "an important source of public and private expenditure such as that spent on infrastructure, during major events and on consumption."[71]

No reasonable person can deny that major sporting events such as the Olympics or the World Cup generate substantial economic activity, particularly in the areas of construction, real estate development, tourism, increased foreign investment, and trade. It is also clear that such events can be catalysts for public investment in civic infrastructure in areas such as transportation and communications, the environmental clean-up and revitalization of former industrial districts, and the construction of sporting facilities that leave a highly visible legacy for certain groups within the urban community. Still, there is a deep suspicion among economists, sociologists, and urban geographers about the extent to which major sporting events, and related large-scale facilities construction and infrastructure development projects, generate the kind of growth they promise, and, more important, about whether the development that does occur is inclusive, sustainable, and worth high levels of public investment.[72]

Projections of the economic impact of investment in large sporting events, or accompanying sports facilities, are often speculative and prone to exaggeration by event promoters.[73] In addition, the booster coalitions who support and promote such events tend to downplay their cost. Bookkeeping around these events typically overlooks the full range of public subsidy involved, especially in situations where local or regional governments have been able to use the event to leverage infrastructure investments from higher levels of government. There is also never assurance that the economic returns associated with a major sporting event or facilities project in one city or region will be automatically similar to those in other cities and regions. Indeed, Flyvberg, Swyngedouw and their colleagues note that project-based or event-driven approaches to urban development tend to be so tied to volatile real estate markets that they are filled with levels of risk that would never be accepted in any other form of public investment.[74] Research has shown that the level of economic activity associated with large-scale sporting events can vary dramatically from city to city and is highly contingent on global events beyond the control of local promoters. In addition to issues at the site of the actual event (such as labour shortages or labour unrest), increases in oil prices or interest rates on the global stage can wreak havoc on budgets. If estimates or planning go even slightly wrong in the game of international event roulette, as in the case of the 2004 Athens Summer Olympics, the result can be a legacy of crippling debt and decaying facilities.[75] Yet the various partners involved in organizing and staging these activities do not similarly share the risk. International sports organizations such as the IOC and FIFA are guaranteed profit, while local taxpayers, along with the users of public services, carry a disproportionate part of the risk.

Furthermore, when civic boosters and event promoters make claims about the positive economic benefits of investing in major sporting events, they never compare them to the possible economic benefits that might flow from other types of large-scale public investments. How would the social and economic returns on investment in an international sporting event compare to the returns that would be generated if a city suddenly spent billions of dollars to upgrade sanitation and public health infrastructure, create affordable housing on a large scale, subsidize community arts and job retraining, as well as to build new parks, community centres, affordable technical colleges, and universities, along with smaller and more localized sport and recreational facilities? We do not know enough about such comparisons, because the local and transnational coalitions of economic and political interests who push for investment in large-scale sporting events tend to view such alternative social investments as secondary and dependent upon the greater priorities of entrepreneurialism and wealth creation. Wealth creation, the argument runs, will create employment, put money in people's pockets, and bring tax revenues into government coffers that can be used to strengthen a city's social services, including support for the poor and the homeless. It is for this reason that supporters of so-called world-class sporting events, and related urban development projects, argue that these truly are *public* events and projects with widespread benefits that accrue to the community as a whole.

Yet the suggestion that large international sporting events are part of the public domain or serve democratically accountable public interests is an ironic exaggeration on many levels. First, organizations such as the IOC or FIFA are not accessible to the public, and they are certainly not accountable to elected public bodies anywhere in the world. Similarly, while many of the corporate partners of international sporting associations are publicly traded companies, as private sector organizations they are not subject to the traditions of democratic governance typically found in the public sphere of Northern democracies. None of the more than three thousand companies who signed the 1999 UNGC statement is legally responsible to any international body if the company fails to live up to its UN commitment to operate in a manner that helps build "a better world for all." Likewise, the IOC's 1999 commitment to sustainable development is not enforceable by any higher-level body, and the committee has only ever "invited" national Olympic associations to share in the commitment "to the best of their ability."[76] By the same token, the essentially private organizing committees that form to run large-scale international sporting events, such as the Olympic organizing committees, are also not accountable to public bodies and are prone to operate in ways that are far less transparent than would be tolerated in any public institution in a democratic society.[77]

In an exhaustive study of thirteen large-scale urban development projects (including the Athens Olympics) in twelve European countries Swyngedouw, Moulaert, and Rodriguez conclude that such projects have too often been used to establish exceptional measures in planning that are part of very selective "middle- and upper-middle-class" interests associated with "new forms of governing." These forms of governance have entrenched inequalities in access to decision making that are not reflective of broader democratic public priorities.[78] While local grassroots movements have sometimes won concessions in the planning and staging of large-scale urban events and projects, local democratic mechanisms are not always respected or are used unevenly.

Swyngedouw and his colleagues suggest that the project-based and event-driven forms of development so favoured in recent years reveal a "new choreography of elite power" in major European cities, based partly on the desire of urban elites to elevate the international visibility of the city in the interests of economic growth, with a view to positioning the city better in global trade and financial networks and elevating it as a destination site for international tourists. However, in almost all of the cities studied, large-scale urban development projects were found to have accentuated social polarization in the cities rather than reduced it. This occurred primarily through changes in the priorities of public budgets that were redirected from more traditional social objectives "to investments in the built environment and the restructuring of the labour market.[79] In addition, polarization resulted from both price rises associated with gentrification and the physical displacement of lower-income urban residents in conjunction with project-based or event-driven development.[80]

The conclusions made by Swyngedouw and his colleagues about the social and economic dimensions of large-scale urban development events and projects in Europe are similar to the conclusions reached about similar events and projects in other parts of the world.[81] Similarly, recent literature on the economic impact of international sporting events, and the facility construction and infrastructure projects associated with them, offers no substantial deviation from the social-polarization thesis outlined in the analysis of World's Fairs, festival markets, and other forms of tourist-oriented urban revitalization.[82]

Thus we are faced with a haunting paradox. International sporting organizations such as the IOC endorse the Millennium Goal of poverty reduction by 2015 and claim to be committed to the broader values of sustainability and inclusiveness. They support sport-for-development-and-peace initiatives and often form partnerships with well-intentioned NGOs that are making an effort to do good work in slums around the world. But the major events and projects that bring money into international sporting organizations, and the forms of urban governance and public spending typically associated with these events, are implicated in deepening social polarization in the world's major cities with an accompanying exacerbation of the problems of poverty and slums.

It is useful at this point to return to the conclusion reached in UN-Habitat's 2003 report *The Challenge of Slums*: there can be no solution to the growth in homelessness in many parts of the world, or to the spread of slums, without dramatic investments aimed at providing basic services to the world's urban poor. When they are asked, residents of the world's slums say they want to be empowered to run their own communities.[83] They want shelter on which they can count, clean water, and better sanitation as well as work, personal security, and improved access to health care, transportation, and education. They want these things more than they want renovated airports, up-market shopping malls, gentrified townhouse complexes, gorgeous hotels, and "world-class" sports events and facilities. Yet, while there always seems to be public money available to fund the large-scale events and projects, there rarely seems to be enough to make the dramatic investments needed to meet the interrelated challenges of poverty, homelessness, and slum conditions. While there is considerable rhetoric from international sporting associations, bid committees, and NGOs about making these kinds of investments, the results have been disappointing, to say the least.[84] Similarly, there is little evidence to support the claim that the money spent on such investments will create enough wealth to trickle down to improve the lives of the majority of people in poor urban neighbourhoods.

More troubling is the fact that large-scale international sporting events and the development projects associated with them have been accompanied often by evictions and forced relocations of slum dwellers in an attempt to put a city's best face forward to the world and to create attractive, gentrified spaces in the downtown area. In 2007 the Geneva-based Centre for Housing Rights and Evictions (COHRE) issued a devastating report on the numbers of evictions and forced relocations associated with past Olympic Games. The scale ranges from several hundred to thousands of people in Olympic cities in Northern nations to even larger numbers in recent Olympic cities in the global South. For example, COHRE claims that more than 720,000 slum dwellers, including both squatters and property owners, were displaced through expropriation or forced eviction prior to the Seoul Olympics in order to "beautify" the parts of the city that Olympic organizers thought would receive the greatest media attention."[85] The Asian Coalition for Housing Rights estimates that the number of forced evictions was even higher, exceeding a million people.[86]

The scale of evictions and slum demolition in recent Chinese urban rede-velopment has been equally dramatic, despite the Chinese Communist Par-ty's professed commitment to universal housing. Over the past three decades China has emerged as a global economic powerhouse, based largely on a strat-egy of attracting investments in manufacturing through the creation of special economic zones.[87] A lessening of Communist Party restrictions has also created opportunities for ambitious cities to pursue so-called world-class events and projects to attract international attention, foreign investment, and tourism. In this context several Chinese cities have responded to the challenge of slums simply by obliterating whole communities and removing their residents to sprawling high-rise complexes on the city's periphery.[88] In Shanghai, for exam-ple, rebuilding the downtown area for up-market developments such as the Xintiendi commercial district, and, more recently, for the 2010 World Expo, involved the relocation of more than 500,000 Shanghai residents.[89] Although property owners were moved to new housing and were paid compensation, the rate was often far below market prices, and there was little room to negotiate prices or to resist relocation. Reactions to the levels of compensation that was paid to evicted residents, and to the quality of the new accommodations, have been mixed, but many older residents say that they feel depressed, isolated, and lonely with the loss of their former communities.[90]

In Guangzhou, where it is estimated that the city spent more than $27 billion on the 2010 Asian Games, the Shanghai pattern has been repeated. Many slum dwellers were forced to move out to the city's periphery, through either evictions or an inability to pay newly inflated downtown real estate prices.[91] On an even larger scale, Beijing is said to have spent in excess of $43 billion preparing for the 2008 Summer Olympic Games, with projections ranging in the hundreds of billions if security costs and related infrastructure projects are included.[92] COHRE has estimated that between 1.25 and 1.5 million people were displaced in the run-up to the Games, with many evicted forcibly. Of the total number of persons displaced in Olympics-related development, COHRE claims that each year between 2006 and 2008 "as many as 33,000 people with sustainable livelihoods were pushed into poverty, or deeper poverty, because their homes and neighbourhoods were demolished."[93]

A pattern in which event preparation, facility construction, and urban beautification schemes lead to the destruction of whole neighbourhoods and to the forced relocation of residents appears to have become the norm in many parts of the global South. In Delhi activists and former residents of the Yamuna Pushta slum settlement claim that 140,000 people were removed and 40,000 homes bulldozed to make way for the Commonwealth Games athletes village, Metrorail headquarters, and land slated for up-market accommodation.[94] Yamuna Pushta was one of Delhi's oldest slum communities and contained schools, temples, and mosques, but many residents were squatters and were not offered compensation for lost homes or possessions. According to Samara, "less than a quarter of the residents were offered resettlement aid, while being relocated to a peripheral area with few public services. The rest were left to fend for themselves."[95] Like Beijing's and Guangzhou's, Delhi's approach to urban development through sport has involved a widespread cleansing of the urban underclass. Ironically, the international sporting associations that sponsored the events triggering this underclass cleansing are strong supporters of sport for development and peace.

Conclusion

The challenge of slums invites deeper critical reflection about sport and development: the programs that seem to work better than others; the interests that count most in certain approaches to development, and the interests that count less; the dominant ideologies that shape perceptions of the problems that matter most and the solutions that make the most sense. One key issue is the extent to which international sports organizations and their corporate and NGO partners profess commitments to socially progressive goals of inclusivity but also participate in staging events and projects that are far from economically or politically inclusive. Research shows that these events and projects promote forms of urban governance that are not democratic and, rather than trickling benefits down to the poor, are more likely to promote social and political polarization in communities and exacerbate divisions in wealth and power.

It is important not to tar all sport and development initiatives with the same brush, and there are certainly many NGOs and development organizations that are rooted deeply in the communities they serve. Many of these organizations, companies, and agencies are involved in activist work, either by seeking to improve the daily lives of people who live in poor communities or, in some cases, by taking on a much more politicized and adversarial role in the struggles around economic development and land use. Harvey, Horne, and Safai have made an important first step in mapping and classifying the groups and movements associated with sport that claim to give priority to the "values of democracy, justice, environmental protection and human rights" over "purely economic concerns."[96]

Still, it can be exceptionally difficult to distinguish the stated intentions of seemingly progressive groups and movements in sport from the economic or social consequences of their actions. This is especially true with organizations that have a mainstream global presence. For example, UN-Habitat has recently begun to work with sport and recreation organizations in slum areas "to empower young people and help inform them about the challenges facing them as well as offering alternative life skills geared towards conquering life in informal settlements."[97] However, UN-Habitat has been unwilling to push organizations such as FIFA or the IOC to make the kinds of substantial investments in slums that were called for in 2003 in *The Challenge of Slums*.

Solving problems of homelessness and squatting in many communities will surely require more than informing young people about the "challenges" facing them, or providing "alternative life skills" for life in slum environments. Instead, the solutions to such problems may require decisions about property rights, and the uses of urban space, that are likely to be opposed by powerful economic interests. Similarly, making substantial investments in sanitation infrastructure or in the universal availability of health care in times of economic crisis, high public debt, and deficit may mean taking money away from "wealth creation" projects such as building stadiums, hosting large sporting events, or improving local airports. Development programs always require judgments about priorities, and these inevitably involve questions of power. In the end, UN agencies have little power to make such judgments. Furthermore, UN agencies such as UNDP and UN-Habitat, which have sometimes shown resistance to neoliberalism, have been dragged into its political orbit, leading them to retreat from the more politicized standpoints and towards the more impartial UNGC language of stakeholders and partnerships. For example, Neuwirth notes that UN-Habitat has long claimed to take a progressive position regarding squatters, but whenever a situation has arisen in which the agency has had a chance to defend the rights of squatters in decision making, it has remained silent.[98] Furthermore, there has been a growing tendency for international development agencies and NGOs to adapt their vision of success to criteria adopted from the corporate sector in order to successfully integrate into the new international order typified by the UNGC.[99] By adopting corporate models of governance and evaluation, these agencies and NGOs tend to develop their own vested interests, resulting in a cascading proliferation of agencies all trying to do roughly similar things.

None of this is new to Bruce Kidd, who has recognized that the proliferation of NGOs in the sport and development area in recent years has created a chaotic situation in which objectives are not always shared, the agendas of NGOs can become more driven by their donors than by community needs, and NGOs can become more concerned with their own organizational growth and survival than with their original mandate.[100] In response, Kidd argues for "bringing the state back" into development, and he has championed this perspective in his own work with the Commonwealth Games. Kidd has also long been committed to a political agenda of trying to hold international sports organizations and partnering corporations to their rhetorical pronouncements. In promoting sport for development and peace, he sees the idealistic rhetoric of Olympism as powerful leverage in the push to make the IOC more accountable and more seriously committed to sustainability and inclusiveness. COHRE and many other critics share this latter position, and it makes sense as a front-line reformist political strategy. Inclusivity and sustainability will be enhanced if international sports associations and their corporate partners are held accountable, through various forms of public pressure, to honour their UNGC commitments to build a better world for all.

Still, there is good reason to be sceptical about how successful this public pressure can be on its own terms. Nearly everyone these days seems to profess a commitment to some social cause or another, and it is often difficult to differentiate genuine commitment from marketing rhetoric. There is good business in philanthropy if it provides brand recognition or satisfies consumers' desires to feel good about the products they purchase.[101] Social investments can also build audiences or markets for one's products. For example, over the past decade FIFA's expenditures in developing soccer programs, coaching, and facilities in poor communities around the world have increased at a rate that exceeds the rate of increase in the organization's profits.[102] These programs provide opportunities for many disadvantaged young people, but they also build attachments to global soccer culture and to famous players and teams and create larger markets for the sale of merchandise. Slums may be poor, but their sheer scale and the nature of their informal economies create substantial global markets for light consumer goods such as mobile phones, sun-glasses, energy drinks, DVDs, inexpensive sports apparel, and equipment.

At the same time, in a world where neo-liberalism has emerged as an international form of common sense, contemporary politics have moved in a hyper-individualistic direction. In many of the Northern nations the game of politics is now played out in the media or expressed through acts of "ethical" individual consumption, such as boycotting Nike or drinking fair-trade coffee. The more activist variant of this game involves volunteering through work with well-meaning NGOS for the provision of programs designed to meet local community needs. Yet, what is largely missing in all of this is an emphasis on engaged *collective* forms of democratic action, particularly when it comes to supporting individuals and groups who lack the resources to compete with entrenched economic and political interests, both in their home communities and on the global stage. In the case of sport for development and peace this may well mean engaging with local activist groups who oppose public investments in large-scale sporting events, in favour of the provision of non-sporting public goods and services.

During the World Cup in South Africa in 2010 one of the most interesting examples of such groups was Abahlali baseMjondolo, the Durban Shack Dwellers Movement, which has organized a sixteen-team soccer league in Durban, South Africa, as well as other cultural activities, but was an outspoken critic of World Cup expenditure. The Durban Shack Dwellers see themselves as a political organization with a responsibility to challenge the "uncritical assumption of a right to lead the local struggles of the poor in the name of privileged access to the global (i.e., Northern donors, academics, and NGOs) that remains typical of most of the NGO-based left."[103] They particularly rejected the premise that economic growth and wealth creation were enough to solve the challenge of slums, and they protested in the run-up to the World Cup against the forced removal of Durban's slum dwellers and for greater access to education and the provision of water, electricity, sanitation, and health care.

Self-consciously politicized groups such as the Durban Shack Dwellers understand clearly that they will never sit as equals at the international development table with the IOC, FIFA, and their sponsoring corporations or even with Northern-based aid agencies and NGOs. Instead, such groups typically seek partnerships with other activist movements and advocacy organizations around the world. In this regard, the Shack Dwellers have developed partnerships with the Landless People's Movement and Poor People's Alliance in Africa, and the Landless Worker's movement in Brazil.[104] However, while the diverse groups who belong to such coalitions all work for local community empowerment and generally oppose approaches to development associated with neo-liberal globalization, there can be considerable philosophical and strategic eclecticism among them. For example, the large and widespread protests in Brazil surrounding the lead-up to the 2014 World Cup and the 2016 Olympics involved a broad spectrum of groups with a diverse inventory of grievances, including corruption, poverty, and inadequate access to transportation and education, as well as a concern for favela clearances, "pacification," and forced gentrification.[105]

In some instances these groups focused their criticisms on very local issues, such as increases in transit fares or workplace unrest. In other instances activist groups in Brazil situated their critique of public spending on sporting facilities and events as part of a broader criticism of their socialist government for adopting neo-liberal approaches to economic development, promoting a divisive class and racial politics, and suppressing dissent through police state tactics. Still, beneath their differences, and whether one considers activist groups who protested Brazil's 2014 World Cup and 2016 Olympics or those who opposed South Africa's 2010 World Cup, it is possible to find some important commonalities. In my view, three commonly shared ideas stand out: (1) an emphasis on "autonomy," on the centrality of local consultation and local community authority in development; (2) recognition that coalitions of international, national, and local elites cannot be trusted on their own to do the right thing for slum dwellers; and (3) a belief that development for poverty reduction depends on structural changes that will necessarily involve collective organization and active forms of political resistance. In my view, these three simple ideas contain more wisdom than all of the agency reports on sport for development and peace put together.

NOTES

1 Mike Davis, *Planet of Slums* (London: Verso, 2006), 1.

2 Ibid., 7.

3 Ibid., 2.

4 UN-Habitat, *The Challenge of Slums: Global Report on Human Settlements* (London, 2003), composite data from this report summarized in Davis, *Planet of Slums*, 4–5.

5 Davis, *Planet of Slums*, 16–17.

6 "China Encourages Mass Urban Migration," *People's Daily Online*, 28 November 2003, http://enlist.people.cm.

7 Robert Neuwirth, *Shadow Cities: A Billion Squatters, a New Urban World* (New York and London: Routledge, 2005), 9.

8 John Vidal, "Cities Are Now the Frontline of Poverty," *Guardian*, 2 February 2005, cited in Davis, *Planet of Slums*, 19.

9 For example, see *Homes, Not Handcuffs: The Criminalization of Homelessness in U.S. Cities* (Washington, DC: The National Law Center on Homelessness and Poverty and the National Coalition for the Homeless, July 2009); Laszlo Andor and Martin Summers, *Market Failure: Eastern Europe's "Economic Miracle"* (London: Pluto Press, 1998); Joseph Stiglitz, *Globalization and Its Discontents*, (New York: Norton, 2002).

10 Examples include Toby Miller, Geoffrey Lawrence, Jim McKay, and David Rowe, *Globalization and Sport: Playing the World* (Thousand Oaks, CA: Sage, 2001); Richard Giulianotti and Roland Robertson (eds.), *Sport and Globalization* (London: Blackwell, 2009); J. Harvey and F. Houle, "Sport, World Economy, Global Culture, and New Social Movements," *Sociology of Sport Journal* 11, no. 4 (1994): 337–55; and James Mills (ed.), *Subaltern Sports: Politics and Sport in South Asia* (London: Anthem Press, 2005).

11 For a review see Peter Donnelly and Jay Coakley (with Simon Darnell and Sandy Wells), *Literature Reviews on Sport for Development and Peace*, Sport for Development and Peace International Working Group (STP/IWG) Secretariat, Faculty of Physical Education and Health, University of Toronto, October 2007. Also see Roger Levermore and Aaron Beacom (eds.), *Sport and International Development* (Basingstroke, UK: Palgrave Macmillan, 2009); and Simon Darnell, *Sport for Development and Peace: A Critical Sociology* (New York: Bloomsbury, 2012).

12 There are two distinct types of sport and development programs, although sometimes the lines between them are blurred. The first focuses on development *in* sport through, for example, the provision of new opportunities for coaching and facilities. In this tradition, reference is often made to *capacity building* in disadvantaged countries and communities that lack a well-developed sporting infrastructure. A second type of development program uses sports as a means to accomplish non-sport objectives associated with, for example, maternal health, HIV/AIDS reduction, or conflict resolution. Sometimes these programs are referred to as sport *for* development to indicate the extent to which sporting objectives are ancillary to broader social objectives. In this paper, while recognizing the distinctions above, I have adopted the more generic phrase *sport and development* to encompass both of these variations. For more on these types of distinctions see Bruce Kidd, "A New Social Movement: Sport for Development and Peace," *Sport in Society* 11, no. 4 (2008): 370–80; Fred Coulter, "Sport in Development: Accountability

or Development?" in Levermore and Beacom (eds.) *Sport and International Development*, 57–8.

13 Neuwirth, *Shadow Cities*, 16.

14 Ibid.

15 Ibid., 249.

16 UN-Habitat, *The Challenge of Slums: Global Report on Human Settlements* (London, 2003), 167.

17 See United Nations *Millennium Declaration Resolution*, adopted by the General Assembly, 18 September 2000, http://www.un.org/millennium/declaration/ares552e.pdf.

18 UN-Habitat, *The Challenge of Slums*, 167.

19 This brief definition of *civil society* works for my purposes here; however, in modern political philosophy the concept is far more complex. See the essays in Virginia A. Hodgkinson and Michael Foley (eds.), *The Civil Society Reader* (Lebanon, NH: University Press of New England, 2003).

20 UN-Habitat, *The Challenge of Slums*, 36–8.

21 On the rise of late-twentieth-century neo-liberalism see David Harvey, *A Brief History of Neoliberalism* (Oxford: Oxford University Press, 2005).

22 Sam Chege, "Donor's Shift More Aid to NGOs," *Africa Recovery* 13, no. 1, June 1999.

23 *A Better World for All* (New York and London: United Nations, Organization for Economic Cooperation and Development; World Bank; and International Monetary Fund, 2000). An online summary of "partners" in the Global Compact can be found at http://www.unglobalcompact.org/.

24 Kidd, "A New Social Movement," 371.

25 Ibid., 374.

26 Ibid.

27 Ibid.

28 Recent overviews of ongoing IOC-sponsored projects for sport and development and for sport and peace can be found on the IOC's official website, http://www.olympic.org/olympism-in-action.

29 Kidd, "A New Social Movement," 375.

30 Ibid.

31 *Sport for Development and Peace: Towards Achieving the Millennium Development Goals*, Report from the United Nations Inter-Agency Task Force on Sport for Development and Peace (Geneva: United Nations, 2003).

32 Links to these reports can be found on the United Nations Office, Sport for Development and Peace, website at http://www.un.org/wcm/content/site/sport/home.

33 *Sport for Development and Peace: From Practice to Policy*, Preliminary Report of the Sport for Development and Peace International Working Group, Toronto, Canada, June, 2006.

34 *From Practice to Policy*, 9.

35 Ibid.

36 On the failures of IMF structural adjustment policies see R. Peet, *Unholy Trinity: The IMF, World Bank, and WTO* (London: Zed Press, 2009). By the early-twenty-first century many mainstream social institutions, and even some sectors within the World Bank, were beginning to have concerns about the failures of the IMF emphasis on debt reduction and free market principles in development policy. See *The Policy Roots of Economic Crisis and Poverty: A Multi-country Participatory Assessment of Structural Adjustment* (Washington, DC: Structural Adjustment Participatory Review International Network, 2001), http://www.saprin.org/SAPRIN_Synthesis_11-16-01.pdf.

37 *From Practice to Policy*, 10.

38 In addition to the critical analysis developed in the UN-Habitat report *The Challenge of Slums*, see the more trenchant critiques in R. Peet, "Madness and Civilization: Global Financial Capitalism and the Anti-poverty Discourse," *Human Geography* 1, no. 1 (2008): 82–9, and the more developed analysis in Peet, *Unholy Trinity*. Also see J. Brohman, *Popular Development: Rethinking the Theory and Practice of Development* (Oxford: Blackwell, 1996).

39 The SDP IWG also remarks on a partnership with the UNDP to survey the extent to which sport figures in the poverty-reduction strategies in twenty-six different nations. The 2006 *From Practice to Policy* report summarizes the UNDP results (p. 10) and suggests that to be successful in poverty-reduction strategies sport would have to be "positioned as a cross-cutting tool in national development strategies for achieving the MDGs"; that countries need more information on the way in which sport can be used to advance their development objectives; and that national governments and NGOs need "advocacy and support" from the United Nations. There is nothing new in these pronouncements. However, the UNDP concluded that the effective use of sport poverty-reduction programs would need to ensure "local ownership" as well as an understanding of "local contexts." Unfortunately these latter ideas are not developed significantly.

40 Information taken from the UN Sport for Development and Peace website: http://www.un.org/wcm/content/site/sport/home/unplayers/memberstates/sdpiwg_structure.

41 My description of the MYSA draws from Fred Coulter, "Sport in Development: Accountability or Development," in Levermore and Beacom, *Sport and International Development*, 59–60, and from the MYSA website, http://www.mysakenya.org/.

42 John Sugden, cited in Donnelly, Coakley, Darnell, and Wells, *Literature Reviews on Sport for Development and Peace*, 186.

43 Kidd, "A New Social Movement," 370. The International Platform on Sport for Development can be found at http://www.sportanddev.org/.

44 Issa G. Shivji, "The Silences in the NGO Discourse: The Role and Future of NGOs in Africa." *Pambazuka Special Report 14* (Nairobi: Fahamu, 2006), 10–11.

45 Ibid., 10.

46 Ibid., 11.

47 Ibid., 14. A link to the website of the Make Poverty History coalition can be found at http://www.makepovertyhistory.org/takeaction/.

48 For example, in 1800 China's per capita income was equal to or higher than Britain's per capita income, and Asian countries produced 56 per cent of the world's gross domestic product, compared to Western Europe's 24 per cent. Throughout the nineteenth century there was a significant drop in Asian GDP relative to that of Northern nations. By the end of the century the colonial and industrial North had achieved a position of economic and political dominance over most of Asia. UN-Habitat, *The Challenge of Slums*, 36.

49 See S. Margolin and J.B. Schor (eds.), *The Golden Age of Capitalism: Reinterpreting the Postwar Experience* (Oxford: Oxford University Press, 1999); and Robert Skidelsky, *Keynes: The Return of the Master* (New York: Public Affairs, 2009).

50 UN-Habitat, *The Challenge of Slums*, 36.

51 Ibid.

52 Ibid.

53 Ibid., 36–8. For a much more developed analysis see Giovanni Arrighi, *The Long Twentieth Century: Money, Power, and the Origins of our Times* (London: Verso, 1994).

54 UN-Habitat, *The Challenge of Slums*, 36.

55 Ibid. There was some dispute about this point during the 1990s, with both the World Bank and the UNDP claiming that overall economic growth in the world was contributing to a reduction in world poverty. However, the sheer volume of evidence suggesting the contrary has made such assertions increasingly untenable. By the early-twenty-first century, for example, UN-Habitat has taken a position counter to the earlier UNDP position. See Peet, "Madness and Civilization," 82–9.

56 UN-Habitat, *The Challenge of Slums*, 36.

57 Ibid.

58 Ibid.

59 David Harvey, *The Condition of Postmodernity* (Oxford: Basil Blackwell, 1989), 141–88, and *A Brief History of Neoliberalism* (Oxford: Oxford University Press, 2005).

60 UN-Habitat, *The Challenge of Slums*, 36.

61 See Harvey, *A Brief History of Neoliberalism*, 64–86.

62 Nick Witheford and Richard Gruneau, "Between the Politics of Production and the Politics of the Sign: Post-Marxism, Postmodernism, and 'New Times,'" in Ben Agger (ed.), *Current Perspectives in Social Theory* 13 (1993): 82–4 (Greenwich, CT: JAI Press).

63 More developed discussion of this point can be found in Nick Dyer-Witherford, *Cyber-Marx: Circuits of Struggle in High Technology Capitalism* (Urbana: University of Illinois Press, 1999); and Michael Hardt and Antonio Negri, *Empire* (Cambridge, MA: Harvard University Press, 2001).

64 Harvey, *The Condition of Postmodernity*, 179.

65 On these trends see David Harvey, "From Managerialism to Entrepreneurialism: The Transformation in Urban Governance in Late Capitalism," *Geografiska Annaler* 71B, 1989: 3–18; Sharon Zukin, *Landscapes of Power: From Detroit to Disney World* (Berkeley: University of California Press, 1991); J. Hannigan, *Fantasy City: Pleasure and Profit in the Postmodern Metropolis* (New York: Routledge, 1998); and the essays in Dennis R. Judd and Susan S. Fainstein (eds.), *The Tourist City* (New Haven, CT: Yale University Press, 1999).

66 Neil Smith, "New Globalism, New Urbanism: Gentrification as Global Urban Strategy," *Antipode* 34, no. 3 (2002): 427–50. Brief but excellent summary discussions of many of these points can be found in Timothy A. Gibson, *Securing the Spectacular City: The Politics of Revitalization and Homelessness in Downtown Seattle* (Lanham, MD: Lexington Books, 2004); and Mark Lowes, *Indy Dreams and Urban Nightmares: Speed Merchants, Spectacle and the Struggle Over Space in the World-Class City* (Toronto: University of Toronto Press, 2002).

67 Erik Swyngedouw, Frank Moulaert, and Arantxa Rodriques, "Neoliberal Urbanization in Europe: Large Scale Urban Development Projects and the New Urban Policy," *Antipode* 34, no. 3 (2002): 545–82.

68 C. Giannoulakis and D. Stotlar, "Evolution of Olympic Sponsorship and Its Impact on the Olympic Movement," in Nigel B. Crowther, Robert K. Barney, and Michael K. Heine (eds.), *Cultural Imperialism in Action: Critiques in the Global Olympic Trust* (London, ON: International Centre for Olympic Studies, University of Western Ontario, 2006), 182.

69 Kevin Fylan, "FIFA Reveals Billion Dollar Equity, Big Profits," *Reuters*, 10 June 2010.

70 Cited in Tony Samara, "Paving the Way for Neoliberal Development: Urban Transformation and the Mega-Event," *Global Studies Review* 5, no. 1 (Spring 2009): 1, http://www.globality-gmu.net/archives/14.

71 United Nations Inter-Agency Task Force on Sport for Development and Peace, *Sport for Development and Peace*, 4.

72 Useful overviews can be found in Bent Flyvberg, Nils Bruzelius, and Werner Rothengatter, *Megaprojects and Risk: An Anatomy of Ambition* (Cambridge: Cambridge

University Press, 2003); Maurice Roche, *Mega-Events and Modernity* (London: Routledge, 2000); H. Preuss, *The Economics of Staging the Olympics* (Northampton, MA: Edward Elgar Publishing, 2004).

73 On this point see Andrew Zimbalist, *Circus Maximus: The Economic Gamble behind Hosting the Olympics and the World Cup* (Washington, DC: Brookings Institution Press, 2015). The tendency towards speculative and exaggerated economic impacts also extends to North American major league sports franchises and sports arenas. See J. Siegfried and A. Zimbalist, "The Economics of Sports Facilities and Their Communities," *Journal of Economic Perspectives* 14, no. 3 (2000): 95–114.

74 Flyvberg, Bruzelius, and Rothengatter, *Megaprojects and Risk*, and Swyngedouw, Moulaert, and Rodriquez, "Neoliberal Urbanization in Europe."

75 See S. Giorgiakis and J. Nauright, "Creating the Scarecrow: The 2004 Athens Olympic Games and the Greek Financial Crisis," George Mason University: Centre for the Study of Sport and Leisure in Society Working Papers, https://www.academia.edu/1922581/Creating_The_Scarecrow_The_2004_Athens_Olympic_Games_and_the_Greek_Financial_Crisis.

76 Helen Jefferson Lenskyj, "The Olympic (Affordable) Housing Legacy and Social Responsibility," in Crowther, Barney, and Heine (eds.), *Cultural Imperialism in Action*, 196.

77 Greg Androvich, Matthew J. Burbank, and Charles H. Heying, "Olympic Cities: Lessons Learned from Mega-event Politics," *Journal of Urban Affairs* 23, no. 2 (2001): 123–4.

78 Swyngedouw, Moulaert, and Rodriquez, "Neoliberal Urbanization in Europe," 547.

79 Ibid.

80 Ibid., 547–8.

81 For some North American examples see Kris Olds, "Urban Mega Events and Housing Rights: The Canadian Case," *Current Issues in Tourism* 1, no. 1 (1998,): 2–46; David Whitson, "World Class Leisure and Consumption: Social Polarization and the Politics of Place," in C. Andrew et al. (eds.), *World Class Cities: Can Canada Play?* (Ottawa: University of Ottawa Press, 1999), 303–20; Mark Levine, "Tourism, Urban Redevelopment, and the 'World Class' City? The Cases of Baltimore and Montreal," in Andrew et al., *World Class Cities*, 421–50; P.K. Eisinger, "The Politics of Bread and Circuses: Building the City for the Visitor Class," *Urban Affairs Review* 35, no. 3 (2000): 316–33. Although the social context is very different, the polarization argument is also made in countries outside Europe and North America: He Shenjing, "State-Sponsored Gentrification under Market Transition: The Case of Shanghai," *Urban Affairs Review* 43, no. 2: 171–98; R. Forest, A. La Grange, and N. Yip, "Hong Kong as a Global City? Social Distance and Social Differentiation," *Urban Studies* 41, no. 1 (January 2004); Y.-F. Huang, *Spectacular Post-Colonial*

Cities: Markets, Ideology, and Globalization in the Making of Shanghai and Hong Kong, unpublished PhD diss., School of Communication, Simon Fraser University, 2008.

82 For example, M.J. Burbank, G.D. Andranovich, and C.H. Heying, *Olympic Dreams: The Impact of Mega-events on Local Politics* (Boulder, CO: Lynne Reinner Publishers, 2001); H. Hiller, "Mega-events, Urban Boosterism, and Growth Strategies: An Analysis of the Objectives and Legitimation of the Cape Town 2004 Olympic Bid," *International Journal of Urban and Regional Research* 24, no. 2 (2000): 439–58; C.M. Hall, "Selling Places: Hallmark Events and the Reimagining of Sydney and Toronto," in J. Nauright and K. Schimmell (eds.), *The Political Economy of Sport* (New York: Palgrave Macmillan, 2005); H. Lenskyj, *The Best Olympics Ever? Social Impacts of Sydney 2000* (New York: State University of New York Press, 2002); and B. Surborg, R. VanWynsberghe, and E. Wyly, "Mapping the Olympic Growth Machine," *City* 12, no. 3: 341–55.

83 This is a major theme in Neuwirth, *Shadow Cities*; see his summary in chapter 10.

84 On these failures and on the IOC's historical lack of interest in such investments see *Fair Play for Housing Rights: Mega-events, Olympic Games, and Housing Rights* (Geneva: Centre on Housing Rights and Evictions [COHRE], 2007); and Lenskyj, "The Olympic (Affordable) Housing Legacy," 195–7.

85 *Fair Play for Housing Rights*, 42.

86 Cited in Lenskyj, "The Olympic (Affordable) Housing Legacy," 193.

87 On China's economic ascendency see Giovanni Arrighi. *Adam Smith in Beijing: Lineages of the Twenty-First Century* (London: Verso, 2007).

88 For some examples see Huang, *Spectacular Post-Colonial Cities*.

89 *Global Survey of Forced Evictions: Violations of Human Rights*, 2003–6 (Geneva: Centre on Housing Rights and Evictions, 2006); and Huang, *Spectacular Post-Colonial Cities*, ch. 4.

90 Samara, "Paving the Way for Neoliberal Development," 3. Also see Veronique Dupont, "Infrastructure Project, Beautification, and Forced Evictions in Delhi: The Exemplary Story of a Cluster of Slum Dwellers Rendered Homeless," paper presented at the Conference on Rethinking Development in an Age of Scarcity and Uncertainty, York University, 19–22 September 2011, available online at http://eadi.org/gc2011/dupont-624.pdf; and "The Dream of Delhi as a Global City," *International Journal of Urban and Regional Research* 35, no. 3 (May 2011): 533–54.

91 Wei Liming, Xie Liangbing, and Yang Xingyun, "Chinese Migrant Workers in Transition: Part 1," *Economic Observer News*, 2008, http://www.eeo.com.cn/ens/feature/2008/08/04/109335.html.

92 Steven Towns, "China's Massive Infrastructure Spending for the 08 Olympics and Beyond," *Wall Street Journal*, 16 October 2006.

93 *Fair Play for Housing Rights*, 154.

94 Samara, "Paving the Way for Neoliberal Development," 3.

95 Ibid.

96 Jean Harvey, John Horne, and Parissa Safai, "Alterglobalization: Global Social Movements and the Possibility of Political Transformation through Sport," *Sociology of Sport Journal* 26 (2009): 383.

97 A description of UN-Habitat's use of sport in their programs is found on the website of *Sport for Development and Peace, the UN System in Action*, http://www.un.org/wcm/content/site/sport/unhabitat.

98 Neuwirth, *Shadow Cities*, 249.

99 Shivji, "The Silences in the NGO Discourse," 10.

100 Kidd, "A New Social Movement," 376–7.

101 See Matthew Bishop and Michael Green, *Philanthrocapitalism: How the Rich Can Save the World* (New York: Bloomsbury Press, 2008).

102 Fylan, "FIFA Reveals Billion Dollar Equity."

103 "A Short History of Abahlali baseMjondolo, the Durban Shack Dweller's Movement," http://abahlali.org/a-short-history-of-abahlali-basemjondolo-the-durban-shack-dwellers-movement/.

104 Toussaint Losier, "The Struggle for Land and Housing in Post-Apartheid South Africa," *Indybay International*, http://www.indybay.org/news-items/2009/01/12/18562116.php; and MST, Landless Worker's Movement of Brazil, http://www.mstbrazil.org/.

105 For examples of earlier community organization in Rio's slum districts see Brodwyn Fischer, *A Poverty of Rights: Citizenship and Inequality in Twentieth-Century Rio de Janeiro* (Stanford, CA: Stanford University Press, 2008). Discussion of resistance to the Olympics in Rio's slums is also found in Simon Romero, "Slum Dwellers Are Defying Brazil's Grand Design for Olympics," *New York Times*, 5 March 2012, http://www.nytimes.com/2012/03/05/world/americas/brazil-faces-obstacles-in-preparations-for-rio-olympics.html?pagewanted=2&_r=2&ref=americas.

2 The New "Culture Wars": The Vancouver 2010 Olympics, Public Protest, and the Politics of Resistance

RUSSELL FIELD

In February 2010 Canada hosted the world's largest multi-sport event for the third time, when the twenty-first Winter Olympic Games were held in Vancouver and Whistler, British Columbia.[1] Popular media accounts lamented early technical and organizational glitches, as well as reporting the tragic death of luger Nodar Kumaritashvili in the hours before the opening ceremonies. Two weeks later the focus had shifted, at least domestically, to the successful execution of the Games and to the host nation's ascent up the medals table as the Canadian team sought to realize the Canadian Olympic Committee's stated goal of "owning the podium." The highlights of the 2010 Winter Olympics for many Canadians included Sidney Crosby's gold-medal-winning overtime goal in the men's hockey final, scenes of wild street partiers enjoying the unseasonably mild weather, and the signature, souvenir red Olympic mittens. However, ever since the Games had been awarded in July 2003 to the bid group that became the local Vancouver Olympic organizing committee, VANOC, the event had been a lightning rod for local protest and controversy. Such civic ambivalence, which saw debate and protest occur on a wide variety of issues, was reflected in the varied groups that organized active opposition to the Games. These groups included the Impact of the Olympics on Community Coalition, No Games on Stolen Native Land, No Games 2010, and the Olympic Resistance Network, and they had very different memories of the Olympic Games that had been held in the province's Lower Mainland. As one prominent Olympic opponent, Chris Shaw of 2010 Watch, lamented, "I'm glad people had a wonderful party, they paid for it. That party came at the expense of other things that most people simply are oblivious to or don't care about."[2]

While the concerns raised by the hosting of the Games tapped into local concerns, these were articulated within and informed by the larger narratives of the anti-globalization movement that had emerged in the last decade of the twentieth century. In April 2008, with the at-times contentious Beijing Olympics only months away, Jörgen Johansen wondered whether the Olympic Games would be "the next arena for global protests." It was likely, he asserted, that "the Olympic Games for some decades to come will be a platform for resistance."[3] While Olympic resistance pre-dates the Beijing or Vancouver Games, it appears to have taken on a new flavour in the decade after the widespread anti-globalization protests. Yet, the issues central to many of the protests in Vancouver reflected particular local concerns. This chapter examines the issues on which the anti-Olympic groups in Vancouver focused, as well as their efforts to garner both attention and support for their causes. It is important, as Bruce Kidd argues, to "understand sports as sites of cultural struggle, where different groups with widely varying abilities contend to impose the meanings they prefer."[4] The debates over the state investment in and policing of the 2010 Games revealed the contours of this struggle in an age of increasing protests, while the varied nature and tactics of the protesters, as well as the strength of the dominant narratives they contested, laid bare the power relations inherent in the struggle to impose meaning.

Boosterism and Dissent as the Games Come to Town

Not only was 2010 not the first occasion on which Canada had hosted the Olympics, but it was not the first time that local debates over the priorities and organization of civil society had accompanied the arrival of this global sporting event on Canadian soil. The preparations for the 1976 Summer Olympics in Montreal had taken place during the tensions and debates of the English-French cultural divide in Quebec, a moment in Canadian history when these issues were especially politicized. In 1976 the Olympic Games were embroiled within what Bruce Kidd has called "the culture wars." Thirty-four years later, on Canada's west coast, another culture war played itself out on the Olympic stage, contesting the role of the neo-liberal state in the Olympic enterprise.

Increasingly, mega-events such as the Olympic Games promise their hosts global exposure as world-class cities and nations, with opportunities to secure state and corporate funds for local economic invigoration. As Dave Whitson and Don Macintosh identified nearly twenty years ago (and as scholars such as political scientist David Black continue to examine), there are primarily three perceived benefits of events that are typically claimed by the host cities – precisely, the capital-cultural elites that represent the host cities in this process, or, as Andrew Ross puts it, the "creative industries."[5] They include the legacies, most visibly, of sporting facilities, but there are other types of legacies such as those of volunteerism and community involvement; infrastructure

development, through both direct and indirect investment, the former including sport-specific facilities, and the latter featuring tangential but hardly inci-
dental development in transportation networks and tourism inventory (newly
built hotels, restaurants, and other services); and, serviced by this new infrastructure, increased tourism – both at the time of the mega-event and after the
fact in host communities, who seek to promote their region to both tourists
and the tourist industry. All such claims are informed by a healthy dose of civic
boosterism, and, as Vancouver city councillor Ellen Woodsworth noted following the 2010 Games, it was thanks to the Olympics that Vancouverites "got a
real sense of what we can be on the world stage."[6]

Yet in Vancouver and Whistler, as in Montreal, "the very definition of the
host nation and the purpose of sports – both of which frame the staging and
interpretation of an Olympics – were openly and fiercely debated."[7] In Montreal
in 1976 this contestation had taken place "in the context of growing federalist-
separatist and English-French tensions."[8] In Vancouver and Whistler there was
again a local context. Protest discourses highlighted First Nations' land claims,
environmental stewardship, poverty and homelessness, and the right to freely
express dissent on these and other issues before and during the Games. These
local narratives were further inflected by an international dynamic of public
protest over and resistance to state funding of the expressions of a neo-liberal
order. The unfurling of debates over these issues, and the ways in which the
Games came to occupy a space in which protesters could have their voices
heard (and silenced) on issues both connected to and/or exacerbated by the
host of a mega-event, made the 2010 Winter Olympics the site of a new "culture
war" in sport.

On the first full day of competition in the twenty-first Winter Olympic
Games, the world was treated to images of balaclava-clad protesters in Vancouver marching through the downtown and smashing store windows.[9] Visitors
could be left to wonder if Vancouver really wanted them there. The national
newspaper *The Globe and Mail* offered reassurance that the "silent majority"
were enjoying themselves. In fact, thanks to the Games the city had discovered a sense of civic pride, where "seemingly everyone" had taken a new pride
in their city. While there may have been voices critical of the Winter Olympics in the build-up to the Games, "few [were] saying that now."[10] Yet, resistance and objections had orbited these Games since the bidding stage, and, as
the Opening Ceremonies loomed, one observer noted that Vancouver was "a
city divided." The decisions made by VANOC and officials at all three levels of
government had created an "environment" and a "context" in which "a protest
movement was born."[11] Indeed, as David Eby of the B.C. Civil Liberties Association notes, "there were demonstrations almost every day of the first week of

the Olympics."[12] If not divided, the citizens of the Vancouver that hosted the 2010 Winter Olympics certainly seemed conflicted about the event.

Issues of Protest in Vancouver

As the 2010 Games approached, there were sport-specific protests and debates centring on the case of female ski jumpers who took VANOC to court, charging discrimination under the Canadian Charter of Rights and Freedoms for the International Olympic Committee's refusal to include their discipline within the Olympic program of events. They argued, ultimately unsuccessfully, that their exclusion constituted gender discrimination, banned by the Charter, which took precedence over the IOC rules on Canadian soil because VANOC received public funding.[13] However, the issues around which the resistance to the Vancouver and Whistler Olympics coalesced extended far beyond sport. In the months leading up to the Games a series of what the media portrayed as embarrassing missteps by VANOC engendered charges of overzealous management at best and of infringement on the right to free expression at worst. The contracts that the artists who had been invited to participate in the Olympics' cultural program were asked to sign precluded criticism of the Olympic Games, noting that artists "must refrain from making any negative or derogatory remarks respecting VANOC, the 2010 Olympic and Paralympic Games, the Olympic movement generally, Bell and/or other sponsors associated with VANOC."[14] These conditions led the city's poet laureate, Brad Cran, to refuse an invitation to participate in the Games.[15] The NGO Right to Play was banned from the Olympic Village by VANOC after it was revealed that Right to Play had been sponsored by an automobile manufacturer other than the VANOC automotive partner, and VANOC feared an attempt at ambush marketing.[16] Finally, there was the implication of the censorship of public dissent and freedom of expression that accompanied the detention of an American journalist, Amy Goodman of Democracy Now, at the Canadian border on 25 November 2009 for fear that her public lecture that evening in Vancouver would include comments on the 2010 Games.[17]

Despite these events, such issues were not the central feature of the protests that had been gathering steam since the early part of the decade, when the nascent Vancouver Games remained in the bidding stage. Resistance centred on three discourses of social inequity. The first was a discourse of indigeneity that foregrounded issues of aboriginal rights and featured protests by First Nations activists, including the group No Games on Stolen Native Lands, which argued that the Olympics were taking place on land that had never been legitimately ceded by local First Nations tribes. Despite the presence of four "host

First Nations" – Lil'wat, Musqueam, Squamish, and Tsleil-Waututh – within VANOC's organizational structure, Coast Salish Territories–based activist Harsha Walia notes: "In 2002, members of the St'at'imc and Secwepemc Nations filed a submission with the International Olympic Committee to oppose the bid. Since then Indigenous peoples have been disproportionately impacted by the pillage and theft of their lands, poverty and homelessness in urban areas, and repressive policing and surveillance tactics. In this context, Indigenous resisters on the land and in urban areas have provided powerful opposition to government propaganda about Native consent to the games."[18] Before the end of 2009, protests drawing attention to these issues had successfully obstructed the Olympic torch relay in both Toronto and Guelph, Ontario.[19] Aboriginal concerns also focused on the official VANOC 2010 logo, a stylized inukshuk, which critics argued was appropriated for aesthetic reasons (and the resulting commercial gain) because none of the four host First Nations that were partners in Vancouver and Whistler 2010 was either Inuit or the other Arctic first peoples for whom the inukshuk would have cultural significance.[20]

A second discourse surrounding the Vancouver 2010 protests invoked the rhetoric of environmentalism. Environmental protests highlighted the impact of the 2010 Games preparations, specifically the expansion and development of the Sea-to-Sky Highway from a two-lane highway to a four-lane thoroughfare running between Vancouver and Whistler, and the subsequent destruction of the ecosystem at Eagle Ridge Bluffs. There were also other issues of environmental concern, with those in Whistler being given voice by AWARE (the Association of Whistler Area Residents for the Environment), a local public education and advocacy group. AWARE tracked the environmental impact of the development of the Whistler venues, including the sliding centre and the expansion of the cross-country skiing venue at Callaghan Valley.[21] Discourses of environmentalism highlighted the perceived irony of the IOC's promotion of environmental stewardship as one of the principles of the Olympic movement enshrined in the Olympic charter, with all Olympic bids, including Vancouver's, assessed in part on their environmental impact.

A third discourse of protest was articulated, by activists against poverty and homelessness in Vancouver's Downtown Eastside, over the investment of public funds in Olympic facilities at the perceived expense of public housing and over the resulting real estate speculation that prompted the eviction of low-income residents from shelter that was marginal at best. Anger was fuelled by the growth of Vancouver's homeless population in the years leading up to the Games – to 300,000 – an increase of "three-fold since the city won the Olympic bid, despite city and provincial promises to increase social housing programs in the lead up to the Games."[22] Instead of social housing, real estate development in the Downtown Eastside was bringing expensive condominiums to an area whose residents had long felt underserved by the state and who were now feeling pushed out of their neighbourhood. Condos in the Downtown Eastside, argues Jean Swanson, come with "more high-end stores, security guards, rent increases, displacement and homelessness."[23]

A wide variety of local groups attempted both to raise awareness of these issues and to engage in direct action. These included the Anti-Poverty Committee (APC), its No2010.com website, the Impact of the Olympics on Community Coalition, and Pivot Legal Society. The APC organized a series of squat campaigns in late 2006 and 2007, including one near the city hall, all of which resulted in the arrest of over twenty APC members. Thanks to these efforts, local activist Gord Hill notes, "homelessness became a central issue in the Vancouver civic elections in fall 2008."[24] Another attempt to raise awareness of homelessness during the Games came in the form of the visible red-tent campaign. The tents – labelled with slogans such as "Housing is a right" – appeared at a rally outside of Science World in Vancouver and became part of a take-over of a vacant lot in downtown Vancouver during the Olympics, in which a "tent city" was created.[25]

These discourses inflected concerns over freedom of expression. In October 2009 a local Vancouver artist and Downtown Eastside support worker, Jesse Corcoran, painted a mural to express his feelings about the 2010 Games: "I created this piece, the Olympic rings with four unhappy faces and one happy face, mostly hoping to get people talking about this issue." His misstep was to include the Olympic five-ring symbol. The city ordered the mural to be removed. Frustration over and resistance to such limitation of civil rights and free expression were issues that united the groups opposed to the Vancouver Olympics. Anger over the perceived misdirection of government resources and priorities was another strand around which anti-Olympic sentiment converged. For Corcoran, working with marginalized peoples in the Downtown Eastside for whom state assistance was hard to come by, it was easy to conclude in the light of three levels of government supporting the 2010 Olympics that "the powers that be seem to be OK with the majority suffering for the enjoyment of the minority."[26]

Protest in the Anti-globalization Era

In such a context the Olympic movement has invariably been forced to confront issues of social protest. Although perhaps not well remembered, campaigns that highlighted ecological issues (in contemporary jargon) had successfully derailed earlier Olympic bids by emphasizing the potential impact on the natural environment of what are now called mega-events. In 1965 and early 1966 the

IOC president, Avery Brundage, was shocked by the volume of letters from committed local residents who opposed a Calgary and Banff bid for the 1972 Winter Games. Brundage was "at a loss to understand the attitude of the Banff people," but, as he told James Worrall, president of the Canadian Olympic Association, he had been "deluged with letters of protest against the Banff site from Canadian citizens and organizations."[27] These organizations included the Canadian Society of Wildlife and Fishery Biologists, which passed a resolution at its April 1965 annual meeting to oppose the construction of sports facilities in Banff National Park because these were "incompatible with the primary function of National Parks" and "would cause serious localized changes in the environment."[28] Similarly, the World Wildlife Fund publicly regretted what it perceived to be Canada's repudiation of nearly a century's worth of leadership in parkland preservation. As IOC delegates gathered in Rome in April 1966 for the annual IOC session, on the agenda of which was the awarding of the 1972 Winter Games, they found a telegram waiting for them from a group of "residents[,] parents[,] and Canadian citizens," signalling their commitment to "protest the holding of Olympic Games in National Parks for sake of future of National Parks in Canada and world."[29] The 1972 Winter Olympics were awarded to Sapporo, Japan.

Six years later similar citizens groups, equally dedicated to local ecological preservation in the face of a global sporting event, managed to compel the relocation of a Winter Olympic Games. After Denver had been awarded the 1976 Winter Olympics, local residents began to raise concerns over the increasing costs, to be funded by public dollars, as well as the potential environmental damage that might accompany development of the Games' venues. A local activist group, Citizens for Colorado's Future, succeeded in having a question regarding the investment of Colorado state funds placed on the November 1972 ballot. The Games were rejected by 60 per cent of voters.[30] While the IOC sought an alternate site – eventually settling on a return to the 1964 host, Innsbruck – local lawyer Harry Arkin tried to revive the Denver Games by working to raise the necessary funds privately. This news only ratcheted up the local protest, and Brundage's successor as IOC president, Lord Killanin, was similarly flooded with letters suggesting that it was more than just the use of public funds that had spurred local opposition to a Colorado Winter Games. One citizen from Denver told Killanin that "we do not want the games no matter where the money comes from"; indeed, a gentleman from Boulder wrote, "We are unalterably opposed to any plan, no matter what its financing might be, to having the Olympics assigned to the mountains we cherish." The commitment of the activists who had successfully won the plebiscite would not waver. "We want no Olympics in Colorado on any terms," noted a resident of Littleton, "and will organize to fight their proponents each time they try again."[31]

Resisters did indeed continue to organize, and partly owing to their efforts, calls for accountability and inclusion have become a hallmark of the contemporary mega-event. Well-documented by Helen Jefferson Lenskyj, these efforts have highlighted a wide array of issues associated with public investment in sport facilities and their ancillary infrastructure. They included Rentwatchers in Sydney and the Metro Atlanta Task Force for the Homeless. One of the regrets expressed by the latter was that their efforts had not started prior to Atlanta being awarded the 1996 Games.[32] Consequently, local activists have recently engaged with these issues during the bidding process, as was the case in Vancouver. A prominent example of such a group is Bread Not Circuses, a coalition of "antipoverty activists, trade unionists, women's groups, community agencies and others opposed to the bid" who campaigned against Toronto's 1996 and 2008 bids.[33] Recently NoLondon2012 organized resistance to the British capital's ultimately successful bid.[34]

Nevertheless, the "success" of the protests over Banff, for example, should not be overstated. In 1965–6 the IOC was confronting a host of geopolitical challenges in an attempt to buttress Brundage's belief that sport should be kept separate from politics. These issues included the two Chinas and the two Germanys, the increasingly problematic apartheid regime in South Africa, and the incorporation of the newly decolonizing countries of Africa and Asia into the Olympic movement. It is perhaps not surprising that, in the face of domestic opposition to the Calgary and Banff bid for 1972, Brundage noted that "the International Olympic Committee cannot very well be blamed for not wanting to place itself in the middle of a controversy of this kind."[35] Indeed, at the 1966 IOC session Brundage stated to the assembled members that "the I.O.C. should not, in principle, be the cause of a controversy within a country, with its international implications, and risk hostile demonstrations at the time of the Games."[36] The impact that the Banff and Denver protests were able to exert on the process of the IOC's bidding decisions only highlights the dramatic shift in the political economies of sport and anti-establishment protest that took place in the succeeding four decades. In 1965 a variety of groups came together in Olympic opposition. It was relatively straightforward for the World Wildlife Fund and the Canadian Society of Wildlife and Fishery Biologists, for example, to wage a common cause; moreover, their ecological stance, while not always popular in the mainstream media and with civic boosters and business interests, offered a consistent message on a single issue. In 2010, by contrast, Olympic resistance was framed in the language of "convergence."

The modern anti-globalization movement has its roots in rural Mexico, and a direct line can be drawn from the Zapatista resistance against the impact of global capitalism in rural Chiapas that began in 1994 to the high-profile confrontations between protesters and police at the World Trade Organization (WTO) meetings in Seattle five years later.[37] Collectively they represented what were to become regular, multi-issue protests at meetings of the world's self-proclaimed economic leaders (such as the WTO, G8, G20, World Bank, and World Economic Forum), resistance that travelled from Quebec City to Davos and incorporated activists from both north and south. The movement, loosely organized on principle, has been characterized as anti-globalization, but some advocate for a global moniker such as the "global resistance movement"[38] or "global social movements."[39] As Noam Chomsky notes, the movement "is about ways and means of transferring leadership from centres of power to the general population, and that's a global ambition."[40] While its critics claim that the global resistance movement lacks both a coherent focus and programmatic alternatives, its proponents tout the opportunity for convergence – that is, world economic meetings have provided the basis for activists to converge and protest over their varied concerns, "from the erosion of democracy to over-consumption, from environmental destruction to privatisation, from corporate power to colonialist development models."[41] The issues of concern, however, the disjuncture between the promise and the reality of capitalism, were not new. Indeed, as Jeffrey Juris notes, "although Seattle was an important moment of visibility, grassroots movements had been organizing against corporate globalization for years. Indigenous communities, peasants, and workers in the South were among the first to rise up against neoliberal policies and practices in the 1970s and 1980s, challenging IMF austerity programs, privatization, World Bank–financed infrastructure programs, mining, oil, drilling, and genetically modified foods."[42]

Environmentalism, a central tenet of the global resistance movement, has its own radical history dating to the philosophy of Deep Ecology and the action politics of Earth First!, which "emerged in 1980 and changed the face of environmental struggle with militant civil disobedience and monkeywrenching actions."[43] The activist environmental movement has deep roots in British Columbia, from the founding of Greenpeace in 1971 to anti-logging protests in the 1980s.[44] Such a history hinted at the potential for the issues around which the anti-Olympic forces coalesced to find a receptive audience in Vancouver. But the uneasy history between environmental advocates and organized labour – Salazar and Alper characterize it as a struggle over redistributing versus redefining wealth[45] – also pointed to tensions that influenced actions around the Games.

The 1999 WTO protests in Seattle "demonstrated the power of a convergence of class, environmental, and other new social movement politics," notes John-Henry Harter, "while hinting at the inherent difficulties of such a union."[46] Nevertheless, global resistance actions, especially after Seattle, spawned a new optimism.

"It seemed the world was suddenly swept away by this new 'anti-globalisation movement,'" recalls Paul Kingsnorth, on which "hung the hopes of a generation."[47] It was on the tide of such optimism that early in the twenty-first century activists in Vancouver articulated their anti-Olympic project within the language and politics of convergence. As Shaw explains, "a lot of groups are now linking up the Olympics ... not just as something that comes on the coattails of kind of a globalization phenomenon, but actually part of the problem."[48] For activists such as Harjap Grewal the occasion of the 2010 Games was "a unique moment in history, because a call for a convergence normally happens at the G8, WTO and World Bank summits that happen around the world, and this time organizers have actually called for a demonstration against the Olympics industry. We don't see the Olympics industry as being that much different than these other institutions that are unaccountable to the people of the world. The IOC is like the WTO. The IOC is like the IMF, is like the World Bank. And it encourages the transfer of wealth from public hands to private pockets."[49]

Celebrating Resistance, Debating Tactics

The context for the "culture war" in 2010 was that the Olympics would generate infrastructure development and civic prestige or they would be a wasteful two-week party that perpetuated inequity and privileged economic elites. The struggle to define the meaning(s) of the 2010 Games played out on the ground, especially during the most visible protests that took place during the first two days of the Olympics, the reactions to which were shaped by both the media portrayal of these events and the protesters' own perceptions of the most visible protests, especially as the tactics employed were debated.

A variety of people gravitated to the issues raised by preparations for the 2010 Games. One protester at the rally on the day of the opening ceremonies (Friday, 12 February), Greg Hamilton, recalls, "We had grandmothers, we had kids ... It was just an unbelievable group of protesters, just basically saying we don't like the Olympics."[50] This protest was perhaps the most successfully visible moment of the anti-Olympic movement in Vancouver. The "Take Back Our City" rally took place on the north side of the Vancouver Art Gallery, which Hamilton notes is "a traditional gathering place for protests."[51] The approximately two thousand protesters moved their demonstration towards the site of the Opening Ceremonies "to march to and be visible to the people attending the Opening Ceremonies at BC Place," according to David Eby. For Hamilton, "it was an awesome protest."[52]

For many, the euphoria of mass public demonstration soured on the following day, when another march wended its way through downtown Vancouver.

During the Friday march to BC Place stadium Mark Hasiuk had marvelled at the diversity of the group: young women, First Nations elders, and "stilt walkers dressed like spruce trees" – reminiscent of the ways in which Juris has argued that "mass counter-summit protests provide multiple theatrical spaces."[53] However, Hasiuk was also troubled watching "a suburban brat in a black ski mask launch a sharpened wooded stick at a police officer," representative as he was of "a group of self-described anarchists, composed of skinny young men in black hoodies and balaclavas."[54] On Saturday this "Black Bloc" took centre stage, and the anti-Olympic message was swamped by headlines that read "Anti-Olympics rioters smash Vancouver store windows." The public to whom the protesters were trying to communicate, who were already inundated with Olympic results and "feel-good" stories, read in their local news that "more than 200 masked protesters smashed windows, vandalized cars and newspaper boxes and intimidated pedestrians in downtown Vancouver Saturday morning before being confronted and dispersed by police in riot gear."[55]

The tactics of the Black Bloc, and the media reaction to the images of smashed department store and bank windows – and the presumed impact that this would have on public opinion of *all* resistance efforts – became a subject of considerable debate among protesters. One response was to argue that using a diversity of tactics was central to the moment of convergence offered by anti-Olympic resistance. As the *Georgia Strait* reminded its readers, "this wasn't the traditional placard-carrying protest that many are familiar with. It wasn't a peaceful and pretty event. As organizers have long advertised, it was one where a diversity of tactics were to be employed."[56] Columnist Charlie Smith noted that the Black Bloc protest was but one point on an anti-Games continuum, as "this is just the most extreme manifestation of a growing sense of dissatisfaction with the way the Olympic industry operates in host cities."[57] Moreover, First Nations activist Harsha Walia argued that Black Bloc participants supported other protest actions, as "some of the anonymous, black-clad protesters are the same activists who use other tactics and who are at the front lines of helping the poor and disenfranchised."[58] Most important, Black Bloc tactics "create room" for other protest forms to be more effective "because they seem quite reasonable in comparison."[59]

The opening ceremonies march and the Black Bloc protest were indeed not the only moments of Olympic opposition. Protests on Monday, 15 February, focused on housing and the war in Afghanistan and were part of a week of varied protests throughout Vancouver. Pivot Legal Society organizers unfurled a forty-five-foot-long banner reading "Homes for All" from the Cambie Street Bridge, a visible landmark leading in and out of downtown Vancouver. Directly facing the Athletes' Village, the banner was part of the organization's red-tent campaign to raise awareness of homelessness.[60] Campaigns such as these resulted in thirty-five to forty tent-city residents being placed in BC Housing units in the Lower Mainland before the end of the Games.[61] The successful unfurling of the "Homes for All" banner, which draped over the major thoroughfare for twenty minutes (negotiated in advance with the 2010 Integrated Security Unit), was featured on the front page (accompanied by a photograph) of the *Courier*, a local Vancouver newspaper.

The alternative press (and blogs) such as the *Courier* offered the most sympathetic and varied coverage of anti-Olympic protest. In the *Georgia Strait* Smith wrote that "this year's Winter Games feature something we haven't seen on this scale before: a concerted backlash against the Olympic brand in the host city." Bemoaning the organizers' and the provincial and municipal governments' lack of transparency regarding finances and governance, the reneging on inner-city housing agreements, and the damage to the environment, Smith concluded that "the demonstrations reflect a fair amount of discomfort with the tactics that Olympic supporters ... have employed on the road to the Games."[62]

Ironically, Smith's editorial appeared in an issue of the *Georgia Strait* that featured considerable typically mainstream coverage of the 2010 Olympics. By and large, it was within the mainstream and popular media that anti-Olympic protesters found their efforts characterized with little nuance, which often failed to distinguish between the protesters who had demonstrated at the art gallery on Friday and the balaclava-clad protesters who had smashed windows on Saturday. All fell under the umbrella of "anti-Olympic protesters."[63] Although discourses of resistance had begun to circulate through the mainstream media in the days and weeks leading up to the Opening Ceremonies, Norman Spector claimed in the national *Globe and Mail* that "Vancouverites were almost universally excited about their Olympic Games and about the prospect of having the eyes of the world on their magnificent city for two weeks."[64] However, when resistance occurred, especially in its most visible forms, the *National Post* was especially critical, noting that such "kvetching is exasperating." Its editorial board went on to reassure readers that "Vancouver and Whistler have done an excellent job of it," before imploring "people to lay down their grievances and enjoy the spectacle on offer ... notwithstanding the one-issue activists who will be telling you the podium is a shrine to Canadian wickedness."[65] Elsewhere, the *National Post* dismissed the protests as "petty exercises in vacuous Marxist agitation," the protesters as lacking "a coherent explanation for why they were protesting," and the entire movement as indicative of a "uniquely Canadian obsession with regionalism and identity politics."[66]

Before considering debates within the anti-Olympic movement about varied tactics – and not all protest groups rued their cause being painted with broad brush strokes – it is worth noting that some resistance efforts in Vancouver did indeed elicit sympathetic treatment. Smith claimed that "the media focused on the most radical protesters," while the *National Post* expressed a similar sentiment, although from a very different starting point, asserting that anti-Olympic protest was "over-hyped by a media that seems intent on turning the Games into a microcosm of Canadian class struggle."[67] Spector, however, rejected such claims, noting instead that "the violent protesters in Vancouver were roundly and uniformly denounced by the local media; I cannot think of a single journalist or member of the chattering class who expressed even a modicum of sympathy for the 'cause.'"[68]

At the outset of the Games the *Globe and Mail's* Rick Salutin called the Olympics a "tarnished spectacle." In recognizing the resistance movements that had been gaining local and increasingly national attention, he noted there was indeed "lots to protest at the Games that start tonight … About $1-billion for mostly stupid security, an amount that would be better spent on a city core with crying social needs. The usual baloney about economic gains that won't materialize, aside from a faster ride to the airport and some high-priced condos. A 'muzzle clause' for Olympiad artists that makes them promise not to say anything mean about the Games or the sponsors … So it does make sense to protest against the hypocrisy, hype and rotten priorities."[69] As the Games drew to a close, the *Vancouver Sun* did not shy away, in its summary of what it considered to be a largely good-news local story, from the fact that "there was protest, quite rightly drawing attention to everything from the grizzly bear hunt to homelessness. But it was, for the most part, marked by civility."[70] Civility, perhaps; civic pride, to be sure. As Spector claims, "the residents of Vancouver were not prepared to cut the violent demonstrators any slack, or to assist them in any way. On the contrary: In several instances, ordinary citizens took matters into their own hands in defeating the Black Bloc tactics. As a result, Vancouver ended up looking good in the eyes of the world."[71]

The mainstream media may have crafted a consensual civic response to Black Bloc tactics, but supporters of the anti-Olympic movement were less unanimous in their condemnation. One protester, Alex Hundert, rued these debates: "We need to stop qualifying some tactics as good and others as bad. The media and the cops are going to do that; we should not do it for them."[72] Nevertheless, the media had made this very characterization, and some anti-Olympic activists argued, in a second reaction to Black Bloc tactics (the first being that they created "room" for other actions), that highly visible, violent protest had worked to alienate some members of the movement and to inhibit additional large, peaceful gatherings. As one activist, Tom Sandborn, noted, "the events of the 13th were an enormous gift to the supporters of the Olympics, who dismissed all criticism of the obnoxious commodity sports/advertising orgy as the work of crazy people who break windows."[73] For Shaw, at worst, "going around breaking windows, frankly, I think is a pretty stupid tactic." At best, "anyone [in the general public] who was still listening after the Friday, wasn't listening by Saturday night."[74]

Arguing in favour of diversity of tactics, Juris writes that "sustaining a mass movement is a complex art, requiring a delicate balance between periodic outbursts of embodied agency and their controlled management, improvisation, and staged repetition."[75] Shaw lived this complex balance in Vancouver, recalling that "it's hard to maintain that kind of thing that we had done on the Friday for 17 days. I mean no one's got the time, or the money, or the resources to do that compared to VANOC." With limited resources and energies, "once the Black Bloc had done their thing on the Saturday, the people who liked it had thought they were done, the people who didn't like it thought, oh my god, I don't want to go out there anymore."[76] Hundert insisted that activists "had no business condemning the [Black Bloc] action," but Shaw, among others, was adamant that "the different groups hadn't discussed in enough detail what diversity of tactics means, what's acceptable, what's not, [and] how do you keep the momentum going."[77] The question remains, then, what other tactics, what other actions, could have been undertaken in pursuit of an anti-Olympic convergence that would have highlighted important local issues related to poverty, the environment, and the rights and living conditions of the First Nations?

It became clear in talking to both anti-Olympic activists and Olympic spectators or visitors in Vancouver and Whistler that the former had expended little effort attempting to win over the latter to their cause. Greg Hamilton had been involved in the production of an anti-Olympic documentary film, *Five Ring Circus*, and during the Games the film was screened at a suburban public library, far from the Olympic venues and largely to a sympathetic audience already familiar with the film and the issues it raised.[78] Outreach to the public, especially with a mainstream media privileging feel-good Olympic stories, was always going to be a challenge, but, as Shaw asks, "do you always just want to talk to the same people all the time and have your group grow smaller and smaller or do you actually want to broaden the circumstance and have more people come in?" He offers no shortage of alternate tactics. Protestors could have "sat down on the Lion's Gate Bridge and forced the police to arrest them for civil disobedience without breaking anything – the impact would have been far greater; if they really wanted to do vandalism, I mean all those VANOC SUVs with single passengers driving around town would have been perfect targets for stickers or tagging; a very effective strategy would have been just walking around and talking to people; [and] just walk through the crowds and hand out leaflets."[79]

Nevertheless, Shaw maintains that "I don't particularly have a problem with breaking things if it serves a purpose at large." Violent action has "gotta mean something and it's gotta communicate something and it's gotta be educational and/or it's gotta be defensive in nature. You don't just break shit to break shit. That's stupid. And it's too easy to be characterized therefore as a mindless vandal."[80] But such characterizations did circulate – among security forces, the media, and protesters themselves. These had an impact on the nature of subsequent actions and participants. David Eby of the B.C. Civil Liberties Association explains:

> Demonstrators were painted as the most radical, unsafe, dangerous terrorists, you know, insert whatever inflammatory word you want. And so, as a result, more mainstream people who had objections to the public spending or were concerned about the environmental impact or whatever were reluctant to become involved because it sort of had this stigma that these were the real radicals. And so it was sort of a self-fulfilling prophecy, that the people who ended up participating in large part were people who were not the traditional folks, [who] felt the traditional leaflets, picket signs, picket lines, were not among the more effective means of demonstration, that the more effective means of demonstration are direct action or civil disobedience, and so there weren't a lot of the leafleting kind of groups out, because this sort of narrative had been successfully created by the security forces that people who did this stuff were security threats.[81]

The Struggle for the Space to Resist

In an environment where the dominant Olympic narrative avoided anti-Games stories, the culture war in 2010 became about defining and defending the "spaces" within which dissent and critique of the Olympic enterprise could take place. This occurred most obviously with debates over what was and was not permissible within the physical space that the Olympics occupied in downtown Vancouver.

In the context of the 1999 WTO protests in Seattle, Steve Herbert considers a variety of frames through which to view the role of the state in regulating public protest, including the ways in which "the state has often used territorial restrictions to regulate dissent," in the knowledge of "the importance of spatial tactics to social movements."[82] Attempts to regulate the spatial dimension of anti-Olympic protest were a feature of the lead-up to the 2010 Games. The City of Vancouver passed a by-law that created "zones of exemption" around Olympic venues, which established a perimeter (initially) of about forty downtown blocks within which "you weren't allowed to hold a sign that was not a celebratory sign." Eby continues: "Celebratory was defined in the by-law as a sign that increased the positive feelings around the Olympic Games or increased the festive spirit around the Olympic Games. And all other signs were verboten unless they were official VANOC way-finding signs or signs that had permits from the City of Vancouver." To increase the stakes, the Province included within a Miscellaneous Statutes Amendments Act a provision that allowed the City to increase the penalty for violations, from $2,000 to $10,000. Collectively, according to Eby, state restrictions "functionally meant that the City could, without notice, enter property – beyond knocking – to remove anti-Olympic signs that were visible publicly." Eby and the B.C. Civil Liberties Association sued the City, "and they re-wrote the by-law to remove the celebratory sign prohibitions and to re-draw perimeters tightly against the venues."[83]

In such a situation the focus was on anti-Olympic sentiment rather than on protest that offered a prospect of violence or illegal actions. As Herbert notes of the 1999 WTO protests in Seattle, the state was not opposed to dangerous protest or interested solely in preserving public safety but took the position of a blanket opposition to all protest against the WTO, so that "police did nothing to ascertain whether anyone entering downtown possessed the means to perpetrate violence. Instead, they focused on evidence that pedestrians opposed the WTO."[84] Moreover, although the celebratory signage by-law was an attempt to regulate the content of anti-Olympic sentiment, efforts that focus on spatial restrictions are often undertaken in the name of public safety. For, as Herbert argues, "to regulate the space of protest – rather than the content of speech aired in that space – is presumptively a neutral endeavor. And such regulation can be an indispensable means to create public order."[85] But, as Nanes points out, the "line between regulating speech and regulating where speech occurs is not always clear."[86] Rumours of the creation in Vancouver and Whistler of designated protest zones, similar to those that had been established in Beijing for the 2008 Olympics – rumours that were denied by ISU chief Bud Mercer – could be understood in similar ways.[87] "Indeed, in the end," Don Mitchell asks, "isn't protest zoning really just a way of controlling the content of debate without really acknowledging that that is what is being done?"[88] Ultimately, in the struggle for a physical place and space to express anti-Olympic sentiment, "if protest is marginalized spatially, it is also marginalized politically."[89]

This was not the only way in which some activists felt that their efforts had been marginalized. As noted earlier, many people within Vancouver's Olympic resistance movement were sensitive to the role played by the media in shaping public opinion towards the protesters and the significance of their issues during the Olympic fortnight. The Olympic Resistance Network had outreach and media and communications groups, but the Black Bloc protest on Saturday quickly became the focus of mainstream attention. This was perhaps not surprising; as Juris notes of the high-profile 1999 anti-globalization protests at the WTO meetings, "it was largely the mass media images generated by the confrontations between direct action protestors and police that caught the world's attention in Seattle."[90] While primarily concerned with the "performative and affective dimensions of anti-corporate globalization activism"[91] among participants, he highlights an important paradox for movement activists debating a variety of tactics and at the same time hoping to engage the mainstream media in an effort to win the battle for public opinion: "The most spectacular, confrontational free-form actions, which are particularly potent in emotional terms [for participants], often contribute to media frames that stigmatize or belittle protestors ... Conversely ... peaceful protests are often ignored [by the media but, when covered] ... are more likely to elicit sympathetic treatment."[92]

It is within such a perspective that the media focused on the Saturday Black Bloc protest, highlighting its tactics while obscuring its politics (and its possible links to other, non-violent elements of the anti-Olympic movement). Shaw was critical of the protesters' tactics: "When they broke windows they didn't do a poster drop or a flyer drop, which would have said, 'Okay, we're breaking the windows of Hudson's Bay Company because,' so the media was left to kind of make it up, which they did." But the struggle for media space at the Olympics may have been unlike other moments of convergence. Juris argues that the "anti-corporate globalization activists attempt to hijack the global media stage afforded by multilateral summits, making power visible and challenging dominant symbolic codes."[93] Anti-globalization protesters can take up media space because the WTO, G8, and other economic summit meetings are often closed to the public (or, more to the point, closed to the media) and afford poor television content, so that theatrical protests fill the media's need for stories. But does the feel-good nature of Olympic coverage and the very fact that Olympic content is designed to be television friendly limit the ability of anti-Olympic protesters to have the same impact as their counterparts protesting economic summits? Olympic proceedings are intentionally visible and designed to take up media space, leaving little room for counter-narratives, especially when media outlets have purchased rights to the content they are privileging.

During global events there is a strong perception among activists that the state is on the side of international organizations, setting aside the issues raised by concerned citizens. Denise Cooper, one of the protesters arrested in Seattle during the 1999 WTO protests, remarked, "I really do think that they [officials of the state] were more on the side of the folks attending the meeting than they were on folks who wanted to talk about what the meeting was about."[94] Indeed, Gorringe and Rosie argue that social justice protests are "framed by narratives relating to the (il)legitimacy of the various protestors."[95] They argue, in the case of protests surrounding the 2005 G8 Summit in Scotland, that the organizers of the Make Poverty History campaign looked to distance themselves from the "anarchist" protest that had attracted so much attention in Seattle in 1999, because of the stigma attached to those protesters.[96] Such associations are made by officials of the state as well as by protesters. In Scotland in 2005 the authorities' preconceptions about "anarchists" were transferred to all protesters in spite of the significant differences in both issues and tactics among protest groups. Gorringe and Rosie observe that "groups were treated as a dangerous *collective* partly because there was a preconception of 'anarchists' as troublemakers."[97] At an event such as the Olympic Games, constructed as it is around feel-good stories of athletic accomplishment and host-city achievement, "once the party aspect starts," Shaw observes, "it's very hard to get a negative message out." Nevertheless, even as they were restricted within physical space and media space, activists struggled to establish a discursive space within which protest could occur and counter-narratives could be articulated. To the extent that these efforts were successful, they were realized because of the groundwork that had been laid by the anti-Olympic movement in the years leading up to the Games. According to Eby,

> We really created a narrative where it was impossible for the police to do anything that would be seen to restrict free expression, because the media was so sensitized to the issue. And the police were aware of that reality, and actually come the Games they were more hands-off on demonstrations than they are during a regular time in Vancouver ... When people were marching in the streets, they were allowed to march in the streets ... There was a very visible security presence, and it was very heavy-handed in terms of its presence. But in terms of its operation, for those people who had the guts to show up, there was no prevention of people from protesting or demonstrating.[98]

These very real achievements in creating a discursive space in which narratives of Olympic resistance were possible were mediated by the contested nature of the ideological space of resistance. The varied ideals of global convergence, the priorities of local activists, and debates over the efficacy of different tactics signalled the varied composition and objectives of the groups ostensibly united in their opposition to the 2010 Games' being hosted in Vancouver. There were "places" – often virtual, such as the website of the Olympic Resistance Network – where protesters shared their common cause. Nevertheless, a unity of issues, aims, and tactics was difficult to achieve, although some proponents of convergence would argue that enabling the expression of diverse interests is a strength of the global resistance movement. However, take, for instance, the contentious relationship between environmentalists and organized labour mentioned earlier. Eeva Berglund and David Anderson note, with regard to environmental issues, land use, and ecological preservation, that these debates are often informed by differences in social class and beliefs about leisure, so that calls for access to space can clash with advocacy for preservation.[99] In the Canadian context both Harter, and Salazar and Alper, point out that "the history of the environmental movement has been marked by conflict with labour."[100] In this vein it is worth asking about the affinities, for example, shared by the environmental protesters in affluent West Vancouver and the activists in the Downtown Eastside, besides an opposition to the Games. Moreover, these communities were also faced with their own internal divisions, as Harsha Walia notes: "In Vancouver's Downtown Eastside, for example, there are pro-Olympic residents and/or groups that are complicit in Olympic-related gentrification through funding partnerships. In Indigenous communities, there are members of the Four Host First Nations that are part of the Olympics industry."[101]

The presence of internal divisions within the communities opposed to the 2010 Games did not necessarily undermine their political project, for, as Walia continues, "alliances are based on shared values, principles, and analysis, and not simply on one's identity."[102] From a tactical perspective, however, Eby notes that during the actions of the 2010 Games "organized labour wasn't there." According to Eby, the practical significance of this absence for the communication of the anti-Olympic message was that

> when I think about leaflets and more traditional forms of protest, it's usually organized labour involved to some degree. And they weren't there. And the main reason was the largest union in the Lower Mainland, CUPE [Canadian Union of Public Employees], many of their members were working overtime, were very busy on Olympic projects. The building trades, although they were critical certainly of many aspects of the Olympics, it was difficult for them to be out there protesting the Olympics when essentially they'd be demonstrating around venues that were occupied and worked at by their own members. So a traditional base for demonstration against government excess and spending social money on parties simply wasn't at the table, because their members were actively working. Everybody was working full-time plus over the Olympics.[103]

Postscript

The critiques offered by the anti-Olympic movement (and the form that these critiques took is as important as their content) were more an indictment of the

Olympic enterprise than of the athletic competitions themselves. But as much as some of the financial windfall (in real estate speculation, for example) was unconnected to the Games but took advantage of the Games coming to Vancouver and Whistler, some of the protests unconnected to sport gained needed visibility because of the Games and because in many ways the problems they sought to ameliorate were exacerbated by the arrival of the Olympics. While the global resistance movement has often been criticized for being "high on energy and low on strategy," as Hundert comments, "there were many victories on the streets of Vancouver despite the fact that we did not stop the Olympics or stem the tide of gross nationalism that swept the country during the hockey finals."[104] To the extent that this is accurate, it has much to do with the ways in which the global issues were articulated within local issues. Gorringe and Rosie argue, in the case of the protests surrounding the 2005 G8 Summit in Scotland, that "protests followed a 'national' as much, if not more, than a 'global' logic."[105] In addition, it can be argued that it was this local context that enabled the success achieved by the Olympic resistance movement in Vancouver. Local issues – of indigenity, poverty and homelessness, and the environment – informed and provided energy to the movement.

Gorringe and Rosie further note that "global protests [are] mediated by local social, political and historical contexts."[106] Their final adjective, *historical*, is significant. It was the history of active resistance in British Columbia's Lower Mainland that fomented resistance in 2010 and the years leading up to the Games. Smith draws an important analogy between anti-Olympic protesters and opponents of the BC forest industry in the 1980s, which included "the Earth First types." He reminds us that "the anti-Olympic movement, like the environmental movement of the 1980s, is multisegmented," and, important, that "the protestors who smashed the windows of the Bay and a Toronto-Dominion bank branch in Vancouver were the Earth Firsters of the anti-Olympic movement, going straight at a corporate target with direct action."[107]

Moreover, while the local context of the 2010 Games actions cannot be overlooked, the momentum for this particular culture war at this particular Olympics was provided by the emergence of the global resistance movement. However, the response to the protests also requires contextualization. While Seattle 1999 proved to be a euphoric and galvanizing moment for many activists, "11 September [2001] changed everything," recalls columnist Paul Kingsnorth. "It was clear within minutes that there would be no more appetite for street showdowns, and that states the world over would no longer tolerate even mild dissent."[108] (It is too early to know, but it is at least worth highlighting the potential that the Arab Spring and, in the West, the Occupy Wall Street and the other Occupy actions that it spawned have to revise such an assessment.) In this context the achievements of the anti-Olympic movement were not inconsiderable, beginning with realizing the 2003 plebiscite and continuing with agitation on the post-Games usage of the Athletes' Village.[109] While Shaw laments the "missed opportunity," another activist, Mandy Hiscocks, asserts that "Vancouver was probably the most effectively organized protest against a major event that I have ever been a part of."[110] At the very least, the protests were "probably one of the more dramatic things that's happened in Vancouver."[111]

NOTES

1 The Paralympic Winter Games took place in the same two cities in March 2010.

2 Interview with Chris Shaw, 2010Watch.com, 14 April 2010.

3 Jörgen Johansen, "Olympic Games: The Next Arena for Global Protests?," 20 April 2008, http://resistancestudies.org/?p=301.

4 Bruce Kidd, "The Culture Wars of the Montreal Olympics," *International Review for the Sociology of Sport* 27, no. 2 (1992): 153. Kidd cites John Hargreaves, *Sport, Power, and Culture* (Cambridge: Polity Press, 1996).

5 See David Black, "The Pursuit of 'Second Order' Games as a Strategic Response to Globalization," *Sport in Society* 11 (2008): 467–80; David Whitson and Donald Macintosh, "Becoming a World-Class City: Hallmark Events and Sport Franchises in the Growth Strategies of Western Canadian Cities," *Sociology of Sport Journal* 10 (1993): 221–40; Andrew Ross, *Nice Work If You Can Get It: Life and Labor in Precarious Times* (New York: New York University Press, 2009).

6 Cited in Rod Mickleburgh, "Games Awaken Vancouver's Civic Pride," *Globe and Mail*, 25 February 2010, a portion of which is archived at http://www.sportsbusinessdaily.com/Daily/Issues/2010/02/Issue-114/Olympics/Jacques-Rogge-Lauds-Vancouver-For-Embracing-Winter-Olympics.aspx.

7 Kidd, "The Culture Wars of the Montreal Olympics," 153.

8 Ibid., 157.

9 "Anti-Olympics Rioters Smash Vancouver Store Windows," CBC News, 13 February 2010, http://www.cbc.ca/olympics/story/2010/02/13/bc-vancouver-olympic-protest.html.

10 Mickleburgh, "Games Awaken Vancouver's Civic Pride."

11 Am Johal, "Vancouver 2010: A City Divided," Rabble.ca, 11 February 2010, rabble.ca/blogs/bloggers/amjohal/2010/02/vancouver-2010-city-divided.

12 Interview with David Eby, B.C. Civil Liberties Association, 14 April 2010.

13 "Women's Ski Jumping Lawsuit Wraps Up in Vancouver," CBC News, 13 January 2010, www.cbc.ca/sports/amateur/story/2009/04/24/sp-skijumpers-vanoc.html.

14 Cited in Janaya Fuller-Evans, "Vancouver's Poet Laureate Bows Out of Games in Protest," *Vancouver Courier*, 17 February 2010, 27.

15 His invitation accompanied a list of topics on which to write that included "equality." He felt that his poem on equality and female ski jumpers would violate the spirit of the clause that he was being asked to sign, and so he bowed out. Also within the arts community, the Vancouver Symphony Orchestra refused to pre-record music for the Games' Opening Ceremonies after it was learned that the VSO would not appear in person during the event and would be replaced by stand-in "musicians" and a conductor "miming" the actions of an actual maestro. Ibid. See also Laura Robinson, "A Shameful Track Record," *Literary Review of Canada*, January–February 2010, http://reviewcanada.ca/magazine/2010/01/a-shameful-track-record/; "Vancouver Symphony Says No to Olympic Opening,'" CBC News, 19 December 2009, http://www.cbc.ca/news/arts/vancouver-symphony-says-no-to-olympic-opening-1.799049.

16 "Charity Booted from 2010 Olympic Village over Sponsorship Conflicts," CBC News, 2 October 2008, http://www.cbc.ca/news/canada/british-columbia/charity-booted-from-2010-olympic-village-over-sponsorship-conflicts-1.725855.

17 "U.S. Journalist Grilled at Canada Border Crossing," CBC News, 26 November 2009, http://www.cbc.ca/news/canada/british-columbia/u-s-journalist-grilled-at-canada-border-crossing-1.801755; "Amy Goodman Detained at Border Services," Rabble.ca, 26 November 2009, www.rabble.ca/books/reviews/2009/11/amy-goodman-dissent-what-will-save-us.

18 Cited in Maryann Abbs, Caelie Frampton, and Jessica Peart, "Going for Gold on Stolen Land: A Roundtable on Anti-Olympic Organizing," *Upping the Anti* 9 (2009): 144.

19 "Olympic torch delayed by Toronto protesters," CBC News, 17 December 2009, http://www.cbc.ca/news/canada/toronto/olympic-torch-delayed-by-toronto-protesters-1.804943; "Olympic Torchbearer Knocked Down," CBC News, 28 December 2009, http://www.cbc.ca/news/canada/toronto/olympic-torchbearer-knocked-down-1.810974.

20 "Olympic Inukshuk Irks Inuit Leader," CBC Sports, 27 April 2005, http://www.cbc.ca/sports/olympic-inukshuk-irks-inuit-leader-1.548870.

21 Interview with Sara Jennings, AWARE, 26 February 2010.

22 Mara Kardas-Nelson, "'We Can End Homelessness, and We Can End It Now': Two Vancouver Actions Call For a National Housing Strategy," Rabble.ca, 20 February 2010, http://rabble.ca/blogs/bloggers/marajenn/2010/02/%E2%80%9Cwe-can-end-homelessness-and-we-can-end-it-now%E2%80%9D-two-vancouver-action.

23 Jean Swanson, "My Megaphone: Jean Swanson on the Poverty of the Olympics," *Megaphone* 47 (2010): 11.

24 Cited in Abbs, Frampton, and Peart, "Going for Gold," 144.

25 Mara Kardas-Nelson, "Two Pro-social Housing Successes Mark the End of the 2010 Olympic Games," Rabble.ca, 5 March 2010, www.rabble.ca/blogs/bloggers/marajenn/2010/03/two-pro-social-housing-successes-mark-end-2010-olympic-games; Harsha Walia, "Chronicles of the Olympic Tent Village," Vancouver Media Co-Op, vancouver.mediacoop.ca/story/2908.
26 "Olympic Special," *The Agora* 3 (February 2010): 1.
27 Avery Brundage to John A. Fraser, Garibaldi Olympic Development Association, 16 May 1966; Avery Brundage to James Worrall, 1 April 1966, Candidatures for the Olympic Winter Games in 1972, sous-dossier: Banff, 1964–1966, Olympic Studies Centre (OSC), Lausanne, Switzerland.
28 "Resolution submitted to the Annual Meeting of the Canadian Society of Wildlife and Fishery Biologists, at Calgary, on April 3, 1965," Candidatures for the Olympic Winter Games in 1972, sous-dossier: Banff, 1964–1966, OSC.
29 Cable to International Olympic Committee, Rome, Italy, 25 April 1966, Candidatures for the Olympic Winter Games in 1972, sous-dossier: Banff, 1964–1966, OSC.
30 L.L.K. Olson, "Power, Public Policy, and the Environment: The Defeat of the 1976 Winter Olympics in Colorado" (PhD diss, University of Colorado, 1974), cited in Stephen Essex and Brian Chalkley, "Driving Urban Change: The Impact of the Winter Olympics, 1924–2002" (University of Plymouth, UK, undated), www.etsav.upc.es/personals/iphs2004/pdf/052_p.pdf.
31 Lettres de protestation contre M. Arkin, sous-dossier 1: Lettres de protestation contre M. Arkin, 1972, CIO JO-1976W-DENVE-PROTE, OSC.
32 Helen Jefferson Lenskyj, *Inside the Olympic Industry: Power, Politics, and Activism* (Albany: SUNY Press, 2000), 133.
33 Ibid., 67.
34 Finlo Rohrer, "Saying No to London 2012," BBC News, 17 February 2005, news.bbc.co.uk/2/hi/uk_news/4272113.stm.
35 Avery Brundage to John A. Fraser, Garibaldi Olympic Development Association, 16 May 1966, Candidatures for the Olympic Winter Games in 1972, sous-dossier: Banff, 1964–1966, OSC.
36 Minutes of the 64th Meeting of the International Olympic Committee, Rome, Italy, 24–26 April 1966, OSC, 9.
37 Paul Kingsnorth, *One No, Many Yesses: A Journey to the Heart of the Global Resistance Movement* (London: Free Press, 2003).
38 Ibid. In 2014, the G8 became known as the G7 with the expulsion of Russia.
39 Bettina Köhler and Markus Wissen, "Glocalizing Protest: Urban Conflicts and Global Social Movements," *International Journal of Urban and Regional Research* 27, no. 4 (December 2003): 942–51.
40 Cited in Kingsnorth, *One No, Many Yesses*, 218.
41 Kingsnorth, *One No, Many Yesses*, 208.

42 Jeffrey Juris, "Performing Politics: Image, Embodiment, and Affective Solidarity during Anti-corporate Globalization Protests," *Ethnography* 9, no. 1 (2008): 67.

43 Steven Best and Anthony J. Nocella, II, "A Fire in the Belly of the Beast: The Emergence of Revolutionary Environmentalism," in Steven Best and Anthony J. Nocella, II (eds.), *Igniting a Revolution: Voices in Defense of the Earth* (Oakland, CA: AK Press, 2006), 17.

44 Ramachandra Guha, *Environmentalism: A Global History* (New York: Longman, 2000), 87.

45 Debra J. Salazar and Donald K. Alper, "Reconciling Environmentalism and the Left: Perspectives on Democracy and Social Justice in British Columbia's Environmental Movement," *Canadian Journal of Political Science* 35, no. 3 (2008): 528.

46 John-Henry Harter, "Environmental Justice for Whom? Class, New Social Movements, and the Environment: A Case Study of Greenpeace Canada, 1971–2000," *Labour / Le Travail* 54 (Fall 2004): 83.

47 Paul Kingsnorth, "Protest Still Matters," *New Statesman* 135 (8 May 2006): 28.

48 Interview with Chris Shaw.

49 "Vancouver Activists Greet Winter Olympics Opening Ceremony with People's Summit, Protest," Democracy Now, 12 February 2010, http://www.democracynow.org/2010/2/12/olympics.

50 Interview with Greg Hamilton, *Five Ring Circus*, 19 February 2010.

51 Ibid.

52 Interview with David Eby.

53 Juris, "Performing Politics," 65.

54 Mark Hasiuk, "Police Turn Blind Eye to Spear-Chucking Vandals," *Vancouver Courier*, 17 February 2010, 7.

55 CBC News, "Anti-Olympics Rioters Smash Vancouver Store Windows," 13 February 2010, http://www.cbc.ca/olympics/story/2010/02/13/bc-vancouver-olympic-protest.html.

56 Carlito Pablo, "2010 Heart Attack Disrupts Vancouver on Day Two of Winter Olympics," *Georgia Strait*, 13 February 2010, http://www.straight.com/article-289546/vancouver/2010-heart-attack-disrupts-vancouver-day-two-winter-olympics/.

57 Charlie Smith, "Why the IOC Is Taking Notice of the Protests," *Georgia Strait* 44, no. 2200 (18–25 February 2010): 21.

58 Charlie Smith, "W2 Forum Focuses on Black Bloc Tactics in February 13 Protest against Vancouver Olympics," *Georgia Strait*, 20 February 2010, http://www.straight.com/article-292307/vancouver/w2-forum-focuses-black-bloc-tactics-february-13-protest-against-vancouver-olympics/. Another activist, Tom Sandborn, was quick to note that "at least some of the masked marauders were members of our broader social movement." Tom Sandborn, "Diversity of Tactics: February 13

and the Black Bloc," *Columbia Journal* 15 (July 2010), www.columbiajournal.ca/10-07/08%20Diversity.html.

59 Smith, "W2 Forum Focuses on Black Bloc Tactics."

60 Mike Howell, "Housing Activists Drop Banner, Pitch Tents during Games," *Vancouver Courier* 101 (14), 17 February 2010, 1, 4.

61 Kardas-Nelson, "Two Pro-social Housing Successes"; Walia, "Chronicles of the Olympic Tent Village."

62 Smith, "Why the IOC is Taking Notice of the Protests."

63 CBC News, "Anti-Olympic Rioters Smash Vancouver Store Windows."

64 Norman Spector, "Olympics, G20, and Black Bloc," *Globe and Mail*, 30 June 2010, http://www.theglobeandmail.com/news/opinions/olympics-g20-and-black-bloc/article1623465/.

65 *National Post*, "The Olympics and Their Spoilsports," editorial, 13 February 2010, http://oped.ca/National-Post/national-post-editorial-board-the-olympics-and-their-spoilsports/.

66 *National Post*, "Gold-Medal Nation," editorial, 28 February, 2010; http://www.nationalpost.com.

67 Smith, "Why the IOC Is Taking Notice of the Protests"; *National Post*, "The Olympics and Their Spoilsports."

68 Spector, "Olympics, G20, and Black Bloc."

69 Rick Salutin, "Making Do with Tarnished Spectacles – So Enjoy the Olympics," *Globe and Mail*, 11 February 2010, http://www.theglobeandmail.com/news/opinions/making-do-with-tarnished-spectacles-so-enjoy-the-olympics/article1465048/.

70 Stephen Hume, "Scoffs and Sneers Can't Break Our Cheers: Games Win Gold," *Vancouver Sun*, 28 February 2010, http://www.vancouversun.com/sports/2010wintergames/news/Scoffs+sneers+break+cheers+Games+gold/4231251/story.html.

71 Spector, "Olympics, G20, and Black Bloc."

72 Alex Hundert, "Diversity of Tactics from Vancouver to Toronto," letter, *Upping the Anti* 10 (2010), http://uppingtheanti.org/journal/article/10-diversity-of-tactics-from-vancouver-to-toronto/.

73 Sandborn, "Diversity of Tactics."

74 Interview with Chris Shaw.

75 Juris, "Performing Politics," 90–1.

76 Interview with Chris Shaw.

77 Hundert, "Diversity of Tactics from Vancouver to Toronto"; interview with Chris Shaw.

78 Conrad Schmidt (dir.), *Five Ring Circus*, Ragtag Productions, 2007.

79 Interview with Chris Shaw.

80 Ibid.

81 Interview with David Eby.

82 Steve Herbert, "The 'Battle of Seattle' Revisited: Or, Seven Views of a Protest-Zoning State," *Political Geography* 26 (2007): 602.

83 Interview with David Eby. Continued efforts by the BCCLA during the Games included a legal observer program that provided neutral observers at all public demonstrations.

84 Herbert, "The 'Battle of Seattle' Revisited," 608.

85 Ibid., 607.

86 S. Nanes, "The Constitutional Infringement Zone: Protest Pens and Demonstration Zones at the 2004 National Political Conventions," *Louisiana Law Review* 66 (2005): 210, cited in Herbert, "The 'Battle of Seattle' Revisited," 607.

87 CBC News, "2010 Security Plans Include 'Free Speech Areas,'" 8 July 2009, http://www.cbc.ca/news/canada/british-columbia/story/2009/07/08/bc-olympic-security-plans-free-speech-areas.html; Carlito Pablo, "Olympic Protest Zones Don't Exist, VPD Says," *Georgia Straight*, 21 January 2010, www.straight.com/article-281369/vancouver/olympic-protest-zones-dont-exist-vpd-says.

88 Don Mitchell, "The Liberalization of Free Speech: Or, How Protest in Public Space Is Silenced," *Stanford Agora* 4 (2003): 40, cited in Herbert, "The 'Battle of Seattle' Revisited," 607.

89 Herbert, "The 'Battle of Seattle' Revisited," 616.

90 Juris, "Performing Politics," 67–8.

91 Ibid., 63.

92 Ibid., 89. Kingsnorth makes a similar argument concerning regional "social forums," which were created as an alternative to economic forums: "They rarely garner the media attention that a good tear-gas and cobblestones punch up with police does" (*One No, Many Yesses*, 211).

93 Juris, "Performing Politics," 64–5.

94 Cited in Herbert, "The 'Battle of Seattle' Revisited, 615.

95 Hugo Gorringe and Michael Rosie, "The Polis of 'Global' Protest: Policing Protest at the G8 in Scotland," *Current Sociology* 56, no. 5 (2008): 692.

96 It is worth noting that Gorringe and Rosie argue that "in freezing out radical voices," Make Poverty History "contributed to a delegitimatization of anti-systemic protest" (693).

97 Gorringe and Rosie, "The Polis of 'Global' Protest," 707; emphasis original.

98 Interview with David Eby.

99 Eeva Berglund and David G. Anderson, "Introduction: Towards an Ethnography of Ecological Underprivilege," in Anderson and Berglund (eds.), *Ethnographies of Conservation: Environmentalism and the Distribution of Privilege* (New York and Oxford: Berghahn Books, 2003), 1–15.

100 Salazar and Alper, "Reconciling Environmentalism and the Left," 527.
101 Cited in Abbs, Frampton, and Peart, "Going for Gold," 149.
102 Ibid.
103 Interview with David Eby.
104 Paul Kingsnorth, "So Where Did Global Resistance Go?," *New Statesman* 134 (11 July 2005): 20; Hundert, "Diversity of Tactics from Vancouver to Toronto."
105 Gorringe and Rosie, "The Polis of 'Global' Protest," 706.
106 Ibid.
107 Smith, "Why the IOC Is Taking Notice of the Protests."
108 Kingsnorth, "So Where Did Global Resistance Go?"
109 CBC News, "Protest Shuts Down Olympic Village Condo Sale," 15 May 2010, http://www.cbc.ca/news/canada/british-columbia/protest-shuts-down-olympic-village-condo-sale-1.882067.
110 Mandy Hiscocks, "Anti-Olympics Organizing and the G-20 in Toronto," letter, *Upping the Anti* 10 (2010), http://uppingtheanti.org/journal/article/10-anti-olympics-organizing-and-the-g-20-in-toronto/.
111 Interview with Chris Shaw.

3 Sochi 2014: The Russian Oligarchy and Winter Games Funding

HART CANTELON AND JAMES RIORDAN

The IOC's Olympic Games constitute a major hallmark event that guarantees worldwide interest, and few would argue that every four years the summer or winter festival virtually wipes all other sports off the media's production schedule. Consequently there is a constant stream of academic research questions that can be addressed with the Olympic Games as the primary case study. This chapter focuses on an important consideration concerning the financing of the Sochi 2014 Winter Games, which was problematic given the presence and considerable involvement of Russia's billionaire sector, the oligarchs. As such, the underlying theme of this chapter might best be summarized with a rhetorical question: Given the existence of the Russian billionaire oligarchs, what were the consequences (intended and unintended) for competitive high-performance sport, especially the 2014 Sochi Olympic Games?

The chapter is organized chronologically. First, the social conditions that led to the creation of the Russian oligarchy are summarized. Then follows a discussion of the oligarchy's entrance into an involvement with high-performance competitive sport, especially professional team ownership. The final two sections outline Vladimir Putin's insistence on the oligarchs' compensating the state for their often ill-gained wealth and, specifically, on their giving considerable financial support to the Sochi Olympic Games.

The Social Conditions Leading to Russian Oligarchy

The circumstances that allowed economic oligarchy to be developed in post-Soviet Russia are presented here, albeit briefly and in no order of importance.

Leonid Brezhnev and the Period of Economic Stagnation

Soviet economic stagnation under Brezhnev is best marked by two events, which indicated that neither serious discussion nor reforms (even within the limited Soviet circumstances) would be allowed. These were the Sinyavsky-Daniel trial (1965–6) and the Prague Spring (1968), both of which spelled out that serious debate and/or criticism of Marxist-Leninist ideology, Soviet-style state socialism, its leaders, or Soviet public policy were to be branded as anti-Soviet propaganda.[1]

Coupled with this social and political censorship was the blatant proliferation of cronyism (*blat*), corruption, and economic stagnation. In their 1995 *Theory and Society* article, Hanley, Yershova, and Anderson note that the bureaucratic nepotism, characteristic of much of Soviet history, was particularly stifling under the later days of the Brezhnev regime. Mikhail Gorbachev, speaking after the fact, in January 1987, would complain that "sometimes necessary personnel changes and a flow of new people would not occur for decades." Brezhnev's solution to such inertia, the authors argue, "had the genius of simplicity": he invited one and all in the state and party bureaucracy to "augment their salaries with corruption."[2]

To fully understand the level of corruption, consider the example provided by these scholars.

> We cannot, of course, assess the scale of corruption with any exactitude. Nevertheless the anecdotal evidence makes it seem ubiquitous. Brezhnev made his son-in-law national chief of police, and the son-in-law became bagman for a bribery and extortion racket on a national scale. The police collected tribute from directors of factories, who would rent their facilities to private entrepreneurs. The entrepreneurs employed the factory labor force to use state-supplied materials in production of commercial goods that the entrepreneur would then distribute through unofficial retail networks. Under threat of arrest (with the death penalty in force for "economic crimes"), the police extracted tribute from all parties. When economic officials refrained from unofficial transactions, the police sometimes forced them to sign false confessions implicating themselves and others in the second economy. Needing to pay tribute to the police, innocent officials found themselves forced to turn to corrupt practices.[3]

Meritocratic Structure and Quality of Soviet Education

Certainly since at least 1957 and the Soviet sputnik space program there has been considerable, if reluctant, admiration (at least in the West) of the education system in the USSR, and later Russia, especially in engineering and the sciences.[4] De Witt notes, "If the aim of education is to develop a creative intellect critical of society and its values, then Soviet higher education is an obvious failure. If its aim is to develop applied professional skills enabling the individual to perform specialized, functional tasks, then Soviet higher education is unquestionably a success."[5]

Some oligarchs have earned doctoral degrees in their chosen area of specialization. Further, there is evidence of substantial generational social mobility of the oligarchs in comparison to that of their parents. Indeed, some of the Russian super-rich can legitimately claim authentic peasant status, which under Stalin was a trump card for advancement to state or party positions. The stagnation, acute under Brezhnev, left many of these highly educated, but frustrated, "red circled" young specialists eager for revolutionary change that would allow them to put into practice the theories, scientific practices, and skills that they had learned in the classroom and workplace.

The Soviet *nomenklatura* will be discussed later, but here it is expedient to make one observation. It has been commonplace to suggest that the Russian oligarchs (the economic billionaires) as a group realized their fortunes solely because of the loans-for-shares program, that is, robber capitalism. While this is true for such as Roman Abramovich, Mikhail Khodorkovsky, Boris Berezovsky, Vagit Alekperov, and Mikhail Fridman, it is also true that some like Alexander Abramov and Viktor Rashnikov realized their wealth because of their labour connections, professional experience, and leadership expertise realized through earned degrees in specialized sciences and engineering. In recognizing the latter cohort, we in no way wish to ignore the blatant corruption associated with Russian billionaire status.

Political Advancement of Mikhail Gorbachev

The cliché "being in the right place at the right time" fits the political advancement of Mikhail Gorbachev. Simply put, Gorbachev benefited politically from the aging Communist leadership. Brezhnev had died in 1982, and those who had not died had retired, to be replaced by younger men (with the emphasis on *men*). By 1985 Gorbachev had become the General Secretary of the Communist Party of the Soviet Union (CPSU), a position he held until 1991. In addition, he was president of the Soviet Union from 1990 to 1991.

Mikhail Gorbachev is associated most closely with two Russian terms: *perestroika* (restructuring) and *glasnost* (openness). In the interest of brevity we simply note that from his position of authority in the state and party administration Gorbachev, in a CNN 2006 interview, stated that he and his cadre "were coming to the conclusion that the system needed drastic changes."[6] The latter were widely interpreted by the bourgeoning middle-class Soviet citizen as increased grassroots democratization and the taking into account of far more meritocratic principles for employment and promotion. Gorbachev also anticipated the level of resistance and hostility directed at him and his proposed changes, from the "old guard" *nomenklatura,* that is those state and party personnel who had benefited from the practice of cronyism, especially under Brezhnev. What Gorbachev did not anticipate, we would argue, was the pace with which the state and party structure collapsed, leading to the election of Boris Yeltsin.[7] With unprecedented speed, Yeltsin dismantled the edifices of the planned economy begun in 1928. We would further suggest that Gorbachev vastly under-estimated the economic ingenuity and organized sophistication of the underground (grey and black) economy.

Yeltsin and Robber Capitalism

Boris Yeltsin, in his rise to power, was elected president of Russia in June 1991 in the first direct presidential election in Russian history. One of his campaign promises was the rapid transformation towards a market-oriented economy, similar to that which had taken place in Poland, that is shock economic reform. As Naomi Klein notes in *The Shock Doctrine: The Rise of Disaster Capitalism,* such economic thinking originated with Milton Friedman and his Chicago school disciples.[8]

Yeltsin placed his deputy prime minister, Yegor Gaidar, in charge of the shock economic reform. When Gaidar died in December 2009 at the age of fifty-four, obituary comments were mixed.[9] According to Klein, Gaidar was one of a group of Soviet economists who, while never having studied at the University of Chicago, "had formed a kind of free-market book club, reading the basic texts of the Chicago School thinkers and discussing how the theories could be applied to Russia."[10] One of the earliest shock economic treatments came on 2 January 1992 when Yeltsin ordered the liberalization of foreign trade, prices, and currency, which resulted in the removal of all planned economic principles – price controls and subsidies to state farms and industries – and the dismantling of legal barriers to private trade and manufacture. The latter was particularly poignant for the black marketers, for now they could operate as legitimate business entrepreneurs. Moreover, as was the case in Lenin's emergency New Economic Policy period, foreign investment and imports were welcomed. The immediate Yeltsin strategy was the unbridled destruction of the state monopoly's power.

Arguably more than any other policy strategy, the decrees led to the subsequent characterization of this period as that of "robber capitalism." Marketplace liberalization created winners and losers, and there were far more of the latter than the former. Those who won most were the self-same entrepreneurs and black-market exploiters who had expanded their presence under Brezhnev and Gorbachev. This group seamlessly aligned with select party *apparachiks*, who, like rats fleeing a sinking ship, sought any and every means to maintain the social privilege afforded by their former Communist Party status.[11] Those who lost were the elderly, those on fixed incomes, and generally all citizens who, whether they agreed fully with the CPSU policies or not, had toiled in the planned economy throughout their working lives.

It is important to recognize that for most former Soviet citizens life remains extremely difficult. It has led social philosopher John McMurtry to write that the shock-therapy-market movement "has been by every measure far more destructive of people's daily and long-term security and well-being than any Communist Party policy since the Second World War."[12] Riordan echoes McMurtry's concerns:

> The uncertainty and destruction of people's living standards that accompanied the break-up of the Soviet Union have resulted in two disastrous consequences. The first concerns health and education. The World Health Organisation today (2008) ranks Russia at 127th out of its 192 member nations, and at 75th according to the amount the government spends on health care. Not surprisingly, life expectancy has drastically fallen, especially for men – down to 58, six years less than it was under Brezhnev in 1965.
>
> The second consequence is that from a Soviet population of 286m people, the population of Russia is now 149m; but with the swiftly falling birth rate, the population could be half as much, 75m, by 2050. This has resulted in the government having to encourage large-scale immigration for the first time in history – initially from China, India and Vietnam.[13]

Professional hockey coach Dave King and his wife, Linda, experienced first-hand what McMurtry and Riordan have stated, when King coached the Russian Super League Metallurg Magnitogorsk in 2005–6. Regularly the Kings would purchase sunflower seeds from a local citizen, who they affectionately dubbed "the Sunflower Seed Man." The man, except on extremely cold days, would be found from dawn to nightfall selling seeds from a parking lot kiosk. Sales were made to supplement his meagre pension, and when the Kings paid a hundred rubles for a ten-ruble cup, the man could not believe his good fortune. Imagine how pleased he was when the Kings gave him five hundred rubles for the ten-ruble cup as a going-away present on their last day in Magnitogorsk. As King explains, it "works out to about seventeen dollars and to him represents about a month of selling because he doesn't sell a lot."[14]

Evidence from Russian social-attitude surveys suggests that many citizens consistently yearn for the stability provided under the former Soviet regime.[15] This same sense of yearning may well have fuelled the discontent with the radical changes in neighbouring Ukraine and the rise in popularity of Vladimir Putin with the take-over of Crimea.

Such nostalgia is not surprising when one realizes what Yeltsin's shock reforms did to the social fabric of the society. The McMurtry and Riordan observations parallel those of other analysts. For example, in 1998 the number of Russians living in poverty stood at 63 per cent, and Russia rivals Brazil as a world leader in unequal distribution of income. In 2004 it was estimated that more than one million lives ended earlier in Russia than would have happened in the former Soviet Union.[16]

As Klein documents, the consequence of Friedman principles imposed on the former Soviet Union was, quite literally, armed revolt when street riots rocked Moscow on 2–3 October 1993.[17] While Yeltsin ultimately surfaced victorious, there were 187 deaths and 437 wounded citizens in the insurrection. The resistance and fervent opposition to Yeltsin was not eradicated but simply went underground. It was clear to the president that he was unlikely to gain re-election in a fair and open political campaign. It was from this insight that the infamous loans-for-shares scheme was born: in exchange for loans to finance his re-election bid, Yeltsin offered valuable state resources as collateral. This scheme in turn led to the further rise of the oligarchs.

Scholars such as Lane and Lewin cite examples of so-called Communists who gain party membership with about the same level of commitment as those who choose to seek affiliation in service clubs like Rotary or Kiwanis.[18] Some of this ilk also came to positions of privilege and authority in the Soviet *nomenklatura*.[19] If one thinks of the English language nomenclature (that is, systematic naming), one will have a close approximation of the Russian word. It is, as Harasymiw notes, "a list of positions arranged in order of seniority, including a description of the duties of each office."[20]

The legacy of the *nomenklatura* extends at least from the reign of Tsar Peter the Great (1689–1725) and his Scheme of Service, *the chin*, to Lenin's uneasiness with tsarist bureaucrats employed by the Bolsheviks,[21] to Stalin and the expansion of the shock worker vanguard program, which eventually led to the administrative entrenchment of the *nomenklatura*. In other words, there have always been those who have accessed positions of privilege through proximity to the seat of power and through party status, the approved birthright (peasant or worker background), and, later, higher educational achievement.[22] For some this translated into the undeniable right to "feather their own nest." Conversely, there were those who, for exactly opposite reasons, were denied access to positions of privilege and authority. For some in this latter category a career in the "second economy" seemed a viable and personally profitable option. Ironically, both the party or state *apparatchik* and the black-market entrepreneur mutually benefited from the political and policy decisions put in place by Gorbachev and Yeltsin.

The highly centralized administrative structure of the former Soviet Union did not simply disappear with the dismantling of the USSR. *Nomenklatura* insiders, while intent on directives to dismantle the planned economy, had access to state assets and could clandestinely transfer funds to Swiss accounts, British real estate, or American banks.[23] Others, as the planned economic structure was dismembered, created banks or businesses or purchased particular segments of the massive state enterprises in minerals, oil, gas, and agriculture.[24] Still others, like Roman Abramovich and Boris Berezovsky, merged CPSU-insider privilege with black-market acumen.

This insider knowledge was critical and placed the *nomenklatura* figures on the ground floor, either independently or with black-market entrepreneurs, to successfully tender and "win exclusive government contracts and licenses and to acquire financial credits and supplies at artificially low, state-subsidized prices in order to transact business at high market-value prices. Great fortunes were made almost overnight."[25] Consider the case of Roman Abramovich, current owner of the Chelsea football club, who along with Kremlin insider Boris Berezovsky in 1995 doled out US$100,000 each to buy the planned economy's oil conglomerate Sibneft. Ten years later Putin's state-run Gazprom bought Abramovich's shares in Sibneft for US$13 billion. Berezovsky meanwhile, according to online *Pravda* reports, was persona non grata, facing serious criminal charges in both Russia and Brazil if he entered either country.[26] (Berezovsky died in London on 23 March 2013, thus ending the Russian demand for his extradition to face the legal accusations levelled against him.)

The loans-for-shares program only flamed an already smouldering process of corruption and deceit. The well-placed were joined by other potential oligarchs, some who were without powerful political patrons but had higher-education degrees, valuable professional experience in state industries (mostly in far eastern Siberia), and, important, an entrepreneurial spirit that would have been applauded by the early captains of industry.[27]

The Yeltsin strategy was a crass example, we would argue, of the allusion of democracy. The government declared that the transformation to a market economy should have an impact upon as many citizens as possible and indirectly lead to greater political support for Yeltsin and the shock-therapy policies. Alongside the loans-for-shares program a system of free vouchers was implemented to give mass privatization a jump-start and to allow the ordinary citizen the opportunity to purchase shares in the dismantling of the planned economy. All well and good, except that the industrial workers and the state and collective farm workers, seeing their standard of living drastically reduced, were in dire need of rubles to purchase the basic necessities of life. The almost-hourly increases in inflation did not make the funds go far at any rate. Enter those intermediaries with suitcases full of rubles, quite willing to buy the vouchers for cash, particularly those associated with the desirable enterprises in energy, telecommunications, and metallurgy. The consequence was inevitable. The voucher give-away of valuable state assets quickly polarized under the control of a few powerful, well-connected individuals. In fact, BBC news reporter Rupert Wingfield-Hayes estimated in 2007 that fully 25 per cent of the Russian economy was then owned by thirty-six men and one woman.[28]

It is important to emphasize that there is much about the culture and psyche of the former Soviet citizen that affects the decisions made and the life views held. Just as there was a stubborn reluctance to participate in the collectivization of agriculture, fierce resistance to the Bolshevik appropriation of grain, and lukewarm support for the transfer of state farms to co-operatives, so too was there a great deal of angst surrounding the privatization of the economy. It is no surprise that the oligarchs had come from either the black-market economy or the *nomenklatura*. Nor is it surprising that few ordinary Russians understood or took advantage of Yeltsin's voucher scheme. Since most needed immediate cash for basic sustenance, they were easy pickings for those who had the cash to buy vouchers.

As the Abramovich example demonstrates, all oligarchs are very rich. *Forbes Magazine,* which annually lists the world's billionaires, estimated in its 2005 list that, based on standard economic indicators, the twenty-seven richest Russians accounted for 17 per cent of the total gross national product of Russia.[29] It should also be noted that billionaire nouveau riche status can be a fleeting thing. The *Forbes* list of 2008 identified eighty-seven Russian billionaires; one year later there were fifty-eight fewer members of this selective club. Finally, while one may gain or lose a position in the *Forbes'* club, these remain very wealthy individuals. For example, Riordan estimates that presently there are hundreds of U.S. dollar millionaires and at least 100,000 euro millionaires in Russia.[30]

Many follow the Soviet tradition of the likes of Laventii Beria and Vasilii Stalin in their patronage of sport.[31] We can now turn to a summary analysis of this patronage.

Russian Oligarchy and Sport

In the wake of the crumbling Communist edifice a deadly struggle commenced for control of sport. The ostentatiously rich robber barons, the so-called New Russians (succeeded by the "Very Newest Russians"), went about acquiring symbols of wealth. For some like Viktor Vekselberg this meant the acquisition of the largest collection of Fabergé eggs in the world (fifteen) and the repatriation of the Lowell House Bells from Harvard University to the Danilov Monastery.[32] For many oligarchs, however, sport became a convenient place to invest their extensive and suspected ill-gotten wealth.

By the turn of this century the new Russian elite had accumulated so much wealth that they had to seek ways of both investing it and hiding it from the tax authorities. Sport, especially top-flight football, basketball, and ice hockey, seemed to be a convenient shroud to cover their less sporting activities; an enjoyable plaything that brought with it popular acclaim and prestige; and a legitimate means to launder illicit money.[33] As a result we want to explore this phenomenon in the context of investments in football and ice hockey respectively, as well as the recent oligarch involvement in the financing of the Sochi 2014 Winter Olympics.

Like the primitive capitalism that led to oligarch wealth acquisition, the methods used to intervene in sport were equally primitive in the extreme. They included the fixing of results, the bribing and intimidation of referees, and even the "hit" killings of those who stood in their way or tried to expose their nefarious operations. Assassinations are common and rarely lead to convictions. Hockey's Valentin Sich, instrumental in the organization of the 1972 National Hockey League Soviet and 1974 World Hockey Association Soviet hockey series, was gunned down in 1997.[34] In the same year Larissa Nechayeva, the general manager of Spartak, Moscow's most popular football team, was shot dead at her dacha outside Moscow in what was rumoured to be a dispute over television rights. Five years previously, the Chernomorets (Black Sea) Novorossiysk chairman, Vladimir Boot, was assassinated, and his footballing son had to seek shelter from the Russian mafia in Germany, where he played for Borussia Dortmund. In February 2005 the son of the chairman of the Central Sports Club of the Army (TsSKA), Vadim Giner, survived a murder attempt when his car was shot at in Moscow.[35] As recently as November 2009, Shabtai Kalmanovich, the owner of the Spartak women's basketball team, was gunned down in a drive-by shooting.[36] No one has been convicted of any of these crimes.

Initially oligarchs treated sport clubs like any other turf that had to be won and retained. They took control, by fair means or foul, of the major Russian and often foreign (especially British) football clubs and tried to "buy" success in domestic and international tournaments. This included outrageous gestures, such as Leonid Fedun's promise of a gift of Mercedes automobiles to outstanding Croatian players for defeating England in a November 2007 competition. The 3–2 Croatia victory ensured that Russia and not England would advance in the 2008 European Football Championship.[37] Fedun delivered four vehicles to the delighted Croatian goal scorers and goalkeeper.

In case one might think such practices were part of the teething of the corrupt Yeltsin regime, as late as 2007 *Moscow Times* complained that "there has been one fixed football match in every week of the second half of the season."[38] Similarly, Dave King has suspicions that select Kontinental Hockey League (KHL) games might be fixed. In fact, coach King was told by one of his veteran players, who had experience in both Russian hockey and the NHL, that no KHL team coached by a foreigner would ever win the domestic title. King's Metallurg club finished third while challenging for the title up until the last weeks of the 2005–6 season.[39] (By the 2012–13 season this prediction was history; Canadian-born Mike Keenan led Mettallurg to the KHL title.)

The oligarch intervention in sport has had negative effects on Olympic sport. For those with athletic ability and the motivation to aspire to "Olympic Gold" there was much to recommend the Soviet sports organization. "Own the Podium" might have been a Roger Jackson–inspired slogan for Canadian athletes at Vancouver 2010, but at least by the 1930s the Soviet Union's planned economy had fully funded sport and physical culture with impressive athletic performances by Soviet athletes in any number of Olympic sports.[40] However, the shock economic reform included a weakened Russian interest in the Olympic movement and led to the erasure of the state amateur status of Russian high-performance athletes. Financial sinecures in the military and in postsecondary education were removed. The trade union sports societies, as well as the KGB-sponsored *Dinamo* and the sports club of the armed forces (TsSKA), mostly disappeared in favour of private sports, health, and recreation clubs.

The erosion of the "Giant Red Machine" (as the Soviet national teams were dubbed in the Western press) is no more clearly demonstrated than in the respective performance of the Russians at the 2010 Vancouver Winter Olympic and Paralympic Games and the 2012 London Summer Olympics. Prior to the Vancouver Winter Olympic Opening Ceremonies, *Moscow Times* reporter Alex Anishyuk noted that sports officials interviewed by the *Isvestia* newspaper expected Russian athletes to capture thirty medals in Vancouver, with at least seven being gold.[41] The outcome was dramatically different. In fact, Russia experienced its worst Olympic performance ever. The result was the insistence that senior sports ministers resign,[42] and President Dmitry Medvedev complained that the leadership had "capitalized on the Soviet potential for too long" and that in future "athletes must be the focus of attention, and not the federations, which now look like fat cats."[43] (At London 2012, Russia was in fourth place for medal count and finished in third place in Paralympic competition.)

Medvedev went on to warn that the Soviet sports system should not be idealized but that it was fair to note that the radical shift in sport policy obscured many of the positive features of Communist sport in the former Soviet Union. The old system was generally open to those with talent, regardless of the discipline, and, unlike much of sport in Western nation states, could be pursued at minimal cost to the individual.

Such was not the case at the 2010 Vancouver Winter Olympic Games. Valery Silakov, president of the Russian Luge Federation, complained that his athletes had had to build their own sleds because of a lack of government funding, and (until the 2014 Sochi Games construction) they only had access to a practice facility in 2008. The international standard luge track, built during the Soviet Union era, is located in post-Soviet Latvia and in 2008 was not regularly accessible to Russian lugers. Paralympic athletes had similar complaints, having to travel to Finland for training purposes.[44]

The performance of the Paralympic athletes in Vancouver, unlike that of their able-bodied comrades, was impressive (the Russians won more medals than did any other team, thirty-eight, but placed second in the number of golds, one short of Germany's thirteen). If the able-bodied sporting situation is a far cry from that of the Soviet era, the domestic situation for the Paralympic competitors is even more desperate. They receive little money for training and are a highly marginalized group, given the lack of accessibility to public sports facilities. Even adequate housing is lacking, and most public transportation and retail shops remain wheelchair inaccessible.[45]

When twenty-year-old Maria Iovleva, who is deaf and a paraplegic, won a gold medal in cross-country skiing and a silver medal in sitting biathalon at the Vancouver Games, her life changed. She had only obtained a competitive performance wheelchair in 2007 after a fundraising campaign by the local newspaper in her home city of Syktyvkar in the Komi republic. Her coach had assembled her previous wheelchair by himself and also covered most of the cost of the US$4,000 German-made rifle used by Iovleva in winning the biathalon silver medal. Her medal performances parlayed into €100,000 for gold and €60,000 for silver, monetary incentives provided by the Russian government. With her €160,000 Iovleva would be able to purchase a modest apartment and leave the single room she occupies in a collective home for disabled young women. Ironically, Maria Iovleva still faced considerable challenges when she trained for Sochi. There is modest sponsorship funding from the sports oligarchs, who favour highly visible professional male sports, and government funding was earmarked for capital construction at Sochi.[46] In fact, reporter Thomas Grove calculates that by February 2013 the Sochi Games were on track to be the most expensive of any of the IOC festivals, summer or winter. He goes on to cite data from RIA Novosti that estimates that, of the US$50 billion spent, a full one-half comes from private investment.[47]

In short, the way of life for post-Soviet athletes is much different than that provided under the Soviet planned economy.[48] For the elite performer it has reverted to a profitable occupation.[49] Like Iovleva, all Olympic medal winners are rewarded handsomely. London 2012 medal winners earned 4 million rubles, 2.5 million rubles, and 1.7 million rubles for first-, second-, and third-place finishes, respectively. In addition each medal winner received an automobile for his or her London success: Audi A8 (gold), Audi A7 (silver), and Audi A6 (bronze). Not coincidentally, all rewards come from the Russian Olympians Foundation, financed by oligarch funding.[50]

It is not only lack of stable organizational funding that differentiates present-day Russian sport from the Soviet-era sport. When the USSR sought membership in the International Olympic Committee after the devastation of the Second World War, it did so with considerable reverence for Olympism, Coubertin, and Olympic ritual and decorum. One practical embodiment of this reverence was a contribution to the Olympic solidarity with Third World nations by offering training and coaching opportunities to their athletes and coaches. Much of this aid was free. None of it was disinterested, but it also went to the oppressed, as was the case with the Soviet-led campaign against apartheid in sport and the success in having racist South Africa banished from world sport forums and arenas. Having allowed the nation to bare its soul, the leaders in the post-Gorbachev era radically changed their scale of priorities. They no longer saw the need to demonstrate the advantages of socialism, in so far as they were trying to distance themselves from the command economy that had failed so badly and from the totalitarian political system that had accompanied the imposition of state socialism from above.

Putin, Oligarch Alliances, and Loyalty

Such a radical shift in policy was bound to have its repercussions, in particular in the figure of Vladimir Putin. When the global recession of 1998 only exacerbated the shock-therapy strategies, Boris Yeltsin was in political free fall. After a series of political dismissals, new appointments, and questions about Yeltsin's health and his increasingly erratic behaviour in public, Vladimir Putin was named by the president to head the government. The State Duma approved the appointment by a narrow margin.

The KGB-trained Putin dramatically increased his popularity by taking an uncompromising stance against Chechnya in the vicious Second Chechen War, to be repeated with the annexation of Crimea in 2014 following the Ukrainian unrest and eventual ousting of President Victor Yanukovich. This legacy may come back to haunt the former secret-police operative. When Yeltsin resigned from the presidency at the end of 1999, Putin became acting president, and then went on to win the position of president outright in the 26 March 2000 election. Since his presidential victory Putin has moved to the post of prime minister, with his selected favourite, Dmitry Medvedev, assuming the presidency. In the 2012 election Putin and Medvedev merely switched government portfolios.

Putin's political policies are worth noting, given that they have ramifications for the potential return to Soviet-style sport policy. He has admitted that the fall of Soviet rule has been detrimental to the lifestyle of ordinary Russians.[51] The Russian Axis organization, in its analysis of the 2004 re-election of Putin, has noted the impact that the oligarch control of the economy has had on the life of ordinary Russians. It suggested, with a good deal of accuracy, the strategies that Putin would take to address the problems faced by the population.[52]

Putin's approach to Chechnyan aspirations for independence was a precursor to his approach to governance generally.[53] He has introduced violence as a method of political struggle, and significant power was concentrated first in the Russian presidency, then in the prime minister's office, and currently back to the presidency. In short, wherever Putin resides, so too does the power base.

Previously elected state positions (both regional governorships and the judiciary) reverted to appointment from Moscow.[54] Putin may publicly bemoan the plight of ordinary Russians, but criminality remains rife, and poverty extensive, and the citizenry has little opportunity to defend itself against the threats or initiatives of the rich and powerful. The international outrage voiced at the draconian sentences handed down to the punk-rocker women (Pussy Riot) is evidence of the inequity that characterizes contemporary Russia. Any example of gross inequity, like Putin's Chechnyan policy, had serious implications for the Winter Olympics in Sochi.

As a former KGB operative, Putin has the paramilitary discipline and mindset that comes with recruitment and graduation from security force training. This background is relevant for sport, given the frequency of assassinations of sport officials, almost all of which go unsolved. In his book *Putin's Labyrinth* Steve LeVine, former Moscow-based foreign correspondent for *Business Weekly*, raises an unsettling observation in this regard: "A high-profile murder can go unsolved anywhere. A hostage situation can go awry even when police are highly skilled. But after the third, fourth, or fifth such outrage, it becomes clear that something fundamental is amiss."[55]

LeVine implicitly raises what is repeatedly suggested as the modus operandi of the Russian or Soviet security service, namely that the leadership may not directly sign a death contract, but any unsolved murder does leave questions about complicity of inaction. A mantle of suspicion is always close by. For rhetorically based examples consider: What role did the Kremlin play in the murder of Moscow-based *Forbes* reporter Paul Klebnikov for his identification of oligarchs who wished to remain invisible? Was *Novaya gazeta* correspondent Anna Politkovskaya assassinated because of her highly critical image of Putin and his policies with regard to Chechnya? Did Putin sign Alexander Litvineko's death warrant? Did the Kremlin have any involvement in the tragic Polish air disaster, given that the passengers were en route to visit Katyn, the memorial site of Polish military officers brutally murdered by Stalin, and said passengers were the self-same persons who were seeking closer alliance with NATO and the United States, rather than with Russia? Did the Kremlin–Russian Orthodox Church coalition unduly influence the verdict in the Pussy Riot trial? The Russian government and Putin personally may have nothing whatsoever to do with any of these situations. However, as LeVine observes, the frequency with which they occur, the lack of progress leading to conviction of the perpetrators associated with some events, and the draconian sentences imposed in others translate into suggested state complicity. It does not help that Putin insists on non-intervention when foreigners are the target of harassment, as, for example, the expulsion from Russia of *Guardian* correspondent Luke Harding.[56]

What is factual is Putin's allegiance to high-performance sport, particularly judo; his personal enthusiasm for bringing the Olympic Games to Sochi; and his iron-fisted approach to leadership. Putin has attained black-belt standard as a judoka and has won several high-level competitions in his native St Petersburg. He regularly appeared in Sochi 2014 media photo opportunities, participating in sport, skiing in the Caucasus, or judo training; arguably his commitment to high-performance sport is best illustrated by the press story covering Putin's first trip to the United Kingdom. When given the option of meeting any number of government officials or celebrities, Putin only expressed a keen interest in meeting Kate Howey. She expressed puzzlement at such a request but later discovered that it came from her double Olympic medal success in the sport of judo.[57] As for his commitment to Sochi, numerous media reports suggest that while the city was the preferred IOC choice over Pyeongchang (Korea) and Salzburg (Austria), Putin's personal intervention and emotional address to the committee sealed the deal for Russia.[58]

It is obvious that Putin has brought his KGB discipline to his political leadership. He will and does crush those who offend him. Most notable in this regard is the case of Mikhail Khodorkovsky, who was stripped of his considerable wealth and sent to a hard-labour camp in 2003.[59] Later the state brought further charges against Khodorkovsky, extending his incarceration. Khodorkovsky remains unrepentant, claiming that the accusations are politically motivated because he financed the campaigns of candidates running against Putin and his United Russia party in the December 2003 parliamentary elections. What is telling about the Khodorkovsky case is the fact that while he is guilty of irregularities and conniving in gaining wealth, Khodorkovsky is no better or worse than other oligarchs. Thus the fundamental question is not what is he guilty of, but why him and not others. Both the Russian Axis analysis and Steve LeVine share a poignant observation: "There is no leniency for perceived political transgressors; Putin is hypersensitive in this regard."[60]

We support these observations. When Vladimir Putin took over as Russian president, some of the illegal Mafiosi reconstituted themselves as "legal" oligarchs operating within bounds set by the regime. The oligarchs were those tolerated and supported by the Russian president, who operates not exactly as a godfather – although Roman Abramovich consistently addresses the president with the formal patronymic, and Putin is reputed to have insisted that Abramovich legally divorce his wife before appearing in public any more with Dariya Zhukova, his mistress (now wife number three). It is not Godfather Vlad, but Putin is a neo-authoritarian dictator, who has made it perfectly clear that as long as the oligarchs do not threaten his power, they may coexist with the regime. If, however, they overstep the mark (as did Boris Berezovsky, based in Britain prior to his death, or Badri Patarkatsishvili, based in Georgia), they have to seek political asylum abroad. If they remain in Russia and challenge Putin's power base (United Russia), as did Khodorkovsky in his position as head of the Yukos Petroleum Company office, they can find themselves stripped of their wealth and incarcerated on legitimate grounds of financial fraud and tax evasion. (Khodorkovsky was granted a pardon by Putin just prior to the Sochi Olympic Games and now resides in Switzerland.)

Putin's underlying objective is *state capitalism,* whereby "Kremlin Inc.," as it is known, becomes the major shareholder in the newly privatized society. Besides being fabulously wealthy owners of state firms, the Russian oligarchs must also serve the bidding of the Kremlin and toe the political line. Suffice it to say, we contend that Vladimir Putin is and has been instrumental in deciding who can and who cannot maintain oligarchic status. He is also, as noted earlier, not overly pleased with the massive transformation of Soviet Russia resulting from the intended reforms envisioned by Mikhail Gorbachev. Arguably the best example of his position in this regard is Putin's approach to nationalized property versus privately owned property. In his detailed study of the rise of economic nationalism in Russia, Kari Liuhto, Director of the Pan-European

Institute, Turku School of Economics, quotes a Putin address to the State Duma in April 2005. Putin stated, "It is time we clearly determined the economic sectors where the interests of bolstering Russia's independence and security call for predominant control by national, including state, capital."[61]

Professor Liuhto goes on to carefully document the economic and natural resource sectors that are considered "security vulnerable" and those that are not. Not fortuitous, the former seems to be generally those owned or formerly controlled by oligarchs who are not in favour at the Kremlin. Even more telling, Professor Liuhto observes that "even without direct ownership, the Kremlin uses its indirect control via persons loyal to the state's strategic goals."[62] The trusted oligarchs are those who, while maintaining a lavish billionaire lifestyle, willingly see (or, as in the case of Mikhail Gutseriev, owner of the oil and gas company Russneft, are forced to see) their individual capital as national capital as well.[63] In other words, often with not-so-subtle nudges from Putin, the favoured oligarchs, even those not living in Russia, are expected to turn over considerable sums to the Kremlin for infrastructure projects.

Alexander Wolff has documented just how open Vladimir Putin and the Kremlin have been in their expectation of considerable contribution of funds from the oligarchs for Russian sport. Wolff also notes Putin's dismissive attitude towards the oligarchs: "Putin told the *New York Times*, 'The state appointed them as billionaires. It simply gave out a huge amount of property, practically for free. Then they got the impression that everything is permitted to them.'"[64]

Wolff maintains that in July 2000 Putin summoned the most prominent oligarchs to the Kremlin. He goes on to suggest that the message presented was clear. Personal wealth could be retained. They could operate their corporations freely, but the Kremlin would dictate the taxes owing. For some this was the entire tax roll of identified poverty-stricken rural regions. Putin also asserted his displeasure at those who would meddle in politics and in the expectation that personal wealth would be tithed in the interests of the state.

To reiterate this last, very important, point, it is the expectation of Vladimir Putin that the oligarchs will accept willingly (or be coerced into accepting) their social obligations towards the Russian collective. These social obligations cover a wide rubric of public policy initiatives including government or state service, full or substantial support of social welfare initiatives (housing, schools, hospitals, sports and recreation facilities), ownership or sponsorship of major sports clubs in Russia, and, specific to this chapter, funding for the Sochi Olympic Games in 2014. In return for personal capital donations and political loyalty, the Kremlin and Putin turn a blind eye to the ever-increasing gap between rich and poor in Russia.

Sochi 2014 and Oligarch Contributions

Much can be stated concerning the oligarchs and funding of the 2014 Games in Sochi. In the interest of brevity we will limit our observations to the Games bid and the infrastructure facility construction. The uniqueness of the Sochi funding lay in the state's insistence that the very wealthy would (and did) bankroll major capital projects necessary for the hosting of the Games. As already noted, athlete compensation for the medals won was also the responsibility of the oligarchs.

Contrast this to what has been dubbed the first IOC Commercial Games, that is, Los Angeles 1984.[65] Organizing committee president Peter Ueberroth insisted that he would not spend tax dollars but would organize the Games with private capital. To do so, Ueberroth relied heavily on American nationalism to gain major commercial sponsorship. Success sometimes was hard to come by, as in the case of Ueberroth's attempts to acquire motor vehicles for the Games: "Datsun and Toyota essentially offered us blank checks; Mercedes indicated interest, too; but Detroit wanted nothing to do with us. We were rejected more than once by Ford, General Motors, and Chrysler."[66]

Ueberroth's Sochi counterpart, Dmitry Chernyshenko, would have been bemused by such experiences; he guaranteed that whatever funding was needed would be forthcoming – and considerable funding was necessary. Indeed, in March 2010 Chernyshenko declared that domestic sponsorship funding had exceeded US$1 billion, three times greater than the amount first budgeted by the organizing committee.[67] Table 1 summarizes, up to the opening of the Olympic Games, the explicit oligarch funding for Sochi 2014. It is assumed that others, such as Viktor Rashnikov, owner of Metallurg Magnitogorsk hockey team, also contributed to the national ice hockey team. The table does not identify those who, while not enjoying billionaire status, were still very wealthy and would have been expected to contribute to the Games. The table itself has been developed through extensive search of each of the oligarchs, including the source of their individual wealth, their business partners, and, where relevant, their involvement in high-performance sport. As a starting point, each billionaire was identified from the *Forbes* list of most wealthy persons in the global economy.

At first glance, such commitment would appear to be nothing but positive. Indeed recent Canadian sports-policy statements have noted that the private sector must be more involved in the support of high-performance Canadian sport.[68] However, as we have argued in this chapter, there are consequences, both positive and negative, of the oligarchic intervention in sport. Further, it is still open for debate as to whether or not this involvement is voluntary or is proscribed by the Kremlin. Certainly there must be some sense of social

Table 1. Oligarch Funding for Sochi 2014

Oligarch	Sochi Contribution
Roman Abramovich	Sochi infrastructure construction; athlete funding (Russian football)
Vahid Alakbarov, Leonid Fedun, and Vagit Alekperov	Through ownership and executive status of Lukoil, heavily involved in the Russian Olympic Committee (official sponsor), the national alpine ski teams (primary sponsor), and elite athletes (direct sponsorship through Russian Olympian Support Fund); support of the Application Committee Sochi 2014
Elena Baturina	Her company Inteco built guest hotels for the Games
Oleg Boyko	Funding for Paralympic Games through his membership in the Russian Committee for the Development of the Paralympics Movement
Oleg Deripaska	Contributed to funding the construction of Athletes' Village, Press Centre, new airport terminal; funding to Russian Olympian Support Fund (which funds medal winners)
Vladimir Potanin	Reputed to have personally funded much of the Sochi 2014 Games bid; his Rosa Khutor resort was upgraded for alpine skiing and snowboarding; funding to Russian Olympian Support Fund
Alisher Usmanov and Viktor Vekselberg	Funding to Russian Olympian Support Fund

responsibility in the oligarchs' behaviour. The oligarchs are products of the Soviet propaganda mill of creating new socialist men and women. Like their Soviet athletic counterparts, therefore, there are expectations and obligations demanded of them. Just as the state-supported Soviet amateur was expected to contribute to USSR physical culture and sport specifically, as well as Soviet society generally, so too is the oligarch.

What remains problematic about the oligarch presence at Sochi 2014 is threefold. First, one could argue that there is a real possibility that oligarch money was ill gotten. Sponsorship in Sochi 2014, given the high-profile status of the Olympic Games and the potential for oligarch expropriation and control of facilities after the event, may have been little more than a safe haven for money laundering. Further, since much of the oligarch presence in Sochi 2014 was visible, there is the distinct possibility that oligarch sponsorship was socially constructed as good corporate citizenship rather than as criminality. (For example, Sochi's Bolshoi Palace Arena is now home to Hockey Club Sochi, with former NHL player Vyacheslav Butsayev as the team coach).[69]

The second problematic reflects the autocratic ideology emanating from the Kremlin. Resistance or debate concerning facility construction in Sochi was simply not tolerated. The Sochi Organizing Committee did not negotiate with the local population; it demanded. (It is important to remember also that Sochi lies in a geographical region that experiences sparse winter climatic conditions.) These autocratic manoeuvres were merely the latest in the tsarist legacy of the Russification of the Caucasus regions, much to the resentment of the indigenous populations.

The third problematic, and arguably the most serious one, is the actual history of the relationship between the indigenous peoples of the Caucasus and the Russian overlords (tsarist and Soviet alike). To enter into any detailed account of Caucasus-Russian history would go far beyond the scope of this chapter. Suffice it to say that most individuals are well aware of the continued tensions between Moscow and Chechnya, with the Moscow subway and St Petersburg airport bombings being examples of the level of animosity that exists between the two. Putin's rise to power and popularity through a heavy-handed second war in Chechnya does not help either. While the western Caucasus, in which Sochi is situated, remained relatively calm, there was ample room for concern in the hosting of such a highly visible hallmark event as the Olympic Games. In his extensive memoirs, former Soviet president and CPSU general secretary Mikhail Gorbachev suggested as much: "The tsars fought wars for decades in North Caucasus, creating a system of fortresses, Cossack settlements, punishing, threatening, destroying, and all for naught, for nothing good came from all this."[70]

Gorbachev is a source to heed, given his birth and childhood in the Caucasus region. Others expressed similar concern. Alina Inayeh, Director of the Black Sea Trust for Regional Cooperation for the German Marshall Fund (GMF), had serious reservations about Sochi 2014. It is apropos to conclude with Inayeh's rhetorical observation at the time: "Four years from now, the Winter Olympic Games will be held in Sochi, Russia. Unlike Vancouver, Sochi, and the eastern Black Sea region where it sits, is synonymous with poverty, corruption and violence. The question to ask between now and the closing ceremony of the Sochi Games is: Will the bright glow of the Olympics influence Sochi and its neighborhood positively, or will the unstable character of the region tarnish the Olympic spirit?"[71] Hindsight allows us to answer Inayeh's question. The Games were a success, much to the satisfaction of Vladimir Putin.

NOTES

1 Mikhail Gorbachev, *Memoirs* (New York: Bantam Books, 1996); Academy of Sciences of the USSR, *Leonid I. Brezhnev: Pages from His Life* (New York: Simon & Schuster, 1978).

2 Eric Hanley, Natasha Yershova, and Richard Anderson, "Russia: Old Wine in a New Bottle? The Circulation and Reproduction of Russian Elites, 1983–1993," *Theory and Society* 24 (1995): 645.

3 Ibid., 646.

4 See Margaret A. Coulson and Carol Riddell, *Approaching Sociology: Fully Revised Edition* (London: Routledge & Kegan Paul, 1980); Nicholas De Witt, *Education and Professional Employment in the U.S.S.R.* (Washington, DC: United States Government Printing Office, 1961); Urie Brofenbrenner, *Two Worlds of Childhood: U.S. and U.S.S.R.* (New York: Simon & Schuster, 1970); Landon Pearson, *Children of Glasnost: Growing Up Soviet* (Toronto: Lester & Orpen Dennys, 1990).

5 De Witt, *Education and Professional Employment in the U.S.S.R.*, 548.

6 CNN Interactive, "The Cold War: Episode 23, The Wall Comes Down – Mikhail Gorbachev, Soviet Leader," 6 July 2006, www.cnn.com/SPECIALS/cold.war/episodes/23/interviews/gorbachev/.

7 See Gorbachev, *Memoirs*.

8 Naomi Klein, *The Shock Doctrine: The Rise of Disaster Capitalism* (Toronto: Alfred A. Knopf Canada, 2007).

9 "More Than 8,000 People Pay Last Tributes to Late Reformer Yegor Gaidar," ITAR TASS, 19 December 2009, www.tass.ru; Yulia Latynina, "Gaidar's Dislike for Power Did Him In," *Moscow Times*, 23 December 2009, www.themoscowtimes.com/opinion/article/gaidars-dislike-for-power-did-him-in/396673.html; Konstantin Sonin, "The Death of Russia's Premier Shock Therapist," *Moscow Times*, 18 December 2009, www.themoscowtimes.com/opinion/article/the-death-of-russias-premier-shock-therapist/396363.html; "Average Russian 8 Times Poorer Than Average European," *Pravda-ru,* 3 December 2009, english.pravda.ru/business/finance/03-12-2009/110908-russian_european-0/; Anders Aaslund, "Life Is Not Fair," *St Petersburg Times*, no. 1539, 28 December 2009, www.sptimesrussia.com/index.php?action_id=2&story_id=30606; Joseph F. Dresen, "*The Piratization of Russia: Russian Reform Goes Awry,*" book review, Kennan Institute, www.wilsoncenter.org/publication/the-piratization-russia-russian-reform-goes-awry.

10 Klein, *The Shock Doctrine*, 267.

11 Gorbachev, *Memoirs*.

12 John McMurtry, *Unequal Freedoms: The Global Market as an Ethical System* (Toronto: Garamond Press, 1998), 208.

13 James Riordan, "Athletic Development in Post-Soviet Russia," paper presented at the Centre for Olympic Studies and Research Seminar, Loughborough University, 25 April 2008, 2–3.

14 Dave King, *King of Russia: A Year in the Russian Super League* (Toronto: McClelland & Stewart, 2007), 242.

15 Lisa Karpova, "Sixty Percent of Russians Nostalgic for Soviet Union," *Pravda-ru*, 22 December 2009, http://english.pravda.ru/society/22-12-2009/111328-sovietnostalgia-0/.

16 See Graeme Smith, " Five-Part Series on Russia: Part 1, Russia Shrinks; Part 2, Russians Dying of AIDS, Drugs, Despair; Part 3, Tensions in Lenin's Hometown; Part 4, From Russia with Hate; Part 5, Old Cossacks Gain New Respect in Protecting Russian Outposts," *Globe and Mail*, 22 and 24–27 April 2006, www.theglobeandmail.com; Aleksander Buzgalin, "Signs of Change: The Economic Situation in Russia in 2000–2001, *IV Online Magazine*, no. 340 (May 2002), www.internationalviewpoint.org/spip.php?id_article=454&page=print_article; Riordan, "Athletic Development in Post-Soviet Russia"; James Riordan, "Sport after the Cold War: Implications for Russia and Eastern Europe," unpublished paper, 2007; James Riordan, "Sport, Civilisation, and Violence: Russian Football Is Murder," unpublished paper, 2006.

17 Klein, *The Shock Doctrine*.

18 David Lane, "Transition under Yeltsin: The Nomenklatura and Political Elite Circulation," *Political Studies Journal* 45, no. 5 (1997): 855–74; Moshe Lewin, *The Soviet Century* (London: Verso, 2005).

19 Michael Voslensky, *Nomenklatura: The Soviet Ruling Class* (Garden City, NY: Doubleday, 1984).

20 Bohdan Harasymiw, "Nomenklatura: The Soviet Communist Party's Recruitment Program," *Canadian Journal of Political Science* 2, no. 4 (1969): 494.

21 V.I. Lenin and Leon Trotsky, *Lenin's Fight against* Stalinism, edited with an introduction by Russell Block (New York: Pathfinder Press, 1975).

22 Simon Sebag Montefiore, *Stalin: The Court of the Red Tsar* (London: Phoenix, 2003).

23 Michael Freedman, "Welcome to Londongrad," *Forbes.com*, 23 May 2005, www.forbes.com/forbes/2005/0523/158.html; Rupert Wingfield-Hayes, "Moscow's Suburb for Billionaires," *BBC News*, 21 April 2007, news.bbc.co.uk/2/hi/programmes/from_our_own_correspondent/6577129.stm; James Brookfield, "Bank of New York Probe Exposes Ties between Western Financiers and Russian Mafia," World Socialist website, 27 August 1999, www.wsws.org/articles/1999/aug1999/russ-a27.shtml.

24 Pyotr Johannevich van de Waal-Palms, "The 200 Largest Russian Companies Available for Acquisition: Directory of Industries Interesting for Investment," no date, IV 340, www.peterpalms.com/russia/texts/pd70.html

25 Gorbachev's description of the Gaider shock-therapy solution. Gorbachev, *Memoirs*, 485.

26 "Berezovsky, Brazil, and a Chronology of a Crime," *Pravda.ru*, 6 January 2010, http://english.pravda.ru/hotspots/crimes/06-01-2010/111564-berezovskybrazil-0/;

"Boris Berezovsky to Be Questioned in London about Corruption in Brazilian Football," *Pravda.ru*, 19 March 2010, http://english.pravda.ru/russia/politics/19-03-2010/112650-berezovsky_questioned_in_london-0/.

27 Max Weber, *The Protestant Ethic and the Spirit of Capitalism* (New York: Charles Scribner, 1958).

28 Wingfield-Hayes, "Moscow's Suburb for Billionaires."

29 "New Billionaires on Forbes List Replace Yukos' Lost Fortunes," *Moscow Times*, 14 March 2005, www.themoscowtimes.com/business/article/new-billionaires-on-forbes-list-replace-yukos-lost-fortunes/224618.html.

30 Riordan, "Athletic Development in Post-Soviet Russia."

31 Robert Edelman, *Spartak Moscow: A History of the People's Team in the Workers' State* (Ithaca, NY: Cornell University Press, 2009); Ian Thomsen, "Russian Revolution," *Sports Illustrated*, 28 April 2008, sportsillustrated.cnn.com/vault/article/magazine/MAG1130720/index.htm; Alexander Wolff, "To Russia with Love," *Sports Illustrated*, 15 December 2008, sportsillustrated.cnn.com/vault/article/magazine/MAG1149632/index.htm; Tom Bower, "The Big Sell Out," *Observer*, 29 July 2007, www.theguardian.com/football/2007/jul/29/newsstory.sport; "Is Leonid Fedun Russia's True Football Hero?," *Dalje.com*, 22 November 2007, dalje.com/en-sports/is-leonid-fedun-russias-true-football-hero/100577; Sam Knight, "Dein Sells Arsenal Stake to Russian Oligarch for £75m," *Times*, 30 August 2007, www.timesonline.co.uk/tol/sport/football/premier_league/arsenal/article2357110.ece; Ben James, "Oligarchs Warned Over Multiple Ownership," 3 September 2006, *Deutsche Presse-Agentur*, www.rawstory.com/news/2006/Oligarchs_warned_over_multiple_owne_09032006.html; James Riordan, *Sport in Soviet Society: Development of Sport and Physical Education in Russia and the USSR* (Cambridge: Cambridge University Press, 1977); Henry W. Morton, *Soviet Sport: Mirror of Society* (London: Collier-Macmillan, 1963).

32 Wolff, "To Russia with Love."

33 "Prokhorov Steps Toward NBA," Associated Press, 18 December 2009, www.themoscowtimes.com/business/article/prokhorov-steps-toward-nba/396372.html.

34 Dave King, telephone interview, 8 February 2010.

35 Riordan, "Sport, Civilisation, and Violence: Russian Football Is Murder."

36 Alexander Bratersky, "Spy with 'Twisted Biography' Is Laid to Rest," *Moscow Times*, 6 November 2009, www.themoscowtimes.com/news/article/spy-with-twisted-biography-is-laid-to-rest/388977.html.

37 "Is Leonid Fedun Russia's True Football Hero?"

38 Nick Walsh-Paton, "Putin's Russia," *Guardian*, 6 July 2005, G2, 4.

39 Dave King, telephone interview, 8 February 2010.

40 See Riordan, *Sport in Soviet Society*; Hart Cantelon, "The Social Reproduction of Sport: A Weberian Analysis of the Rational Development of Ice Hockey under

Scientific Socialism in the Soviet Union," unpublished PhD thesis, University of Birmingham, 1981.

41 Alex Anishyuk, "State's Expectations High for Vancouver Team," *Moscow Times*, 12 February 2010, www.themoscowtimes.com/olympic_coverage/article/states-expectations-high-for-vancouver-team/399602.html.

42 Alexander Arkhangelsky, "Olympic Victory in Defeat," *Moscow News*, 1 March 2010, themoscownews.com/proetcontra/20100301/55416751.html; "Russian President Blasts Sports Officials," Associated Press, 1 March 2010, www.cbc.ca/olympics/story/2010/03/01/spo-olympics-russia-medvedev.html; Alexander Bratersky, " Russia Plays Its Worst Ever Olympics," *St Petersburg Times*, 2 March 2010, http://www.sptimesrussia.com/index.php?story_id=30889&action_id=2; Evgeniya Chaykovskaya, "Heads Roll after Russia's Fiasco in Vancouver," *Moscow News*, 4 March 2010, themoscownews.com/sports/20100304/55417569.html; Alexandra Odynova, "Heads to Roll Over Poor Olympic Results," *Moscow Times*, 2 March 2010, www.themoscowtimes.com/olympic_coverage/article/heads-to-roll-over-poor-olympic-results/400730.html; Andy Potts, "Olympic Blame Games Begin," *Moscow News*, 4 March 2010, themoscownews.com/news/20100304/55417953.html; "Head of Russia's Olympic Committee Resigns Beautifully," *Pravda-ru*, 5 March 2010, english.pravda.ru/sports/games/05-03-2010/112491-russia_olympics-0/; Winter Olympics 2010 to Become Worst Ever for Team Russia," *Pravda-ru*, 19 February 2010, english.pravda.ru/sports/games/19-02-2010/112302-olympics_russia-0/; Scott Rose, "Lawmakers Say Heads Will Roll for Dismal Olympic Performance," *Moscow Times*, 19 February 2010, www.themoscowtimes.com/news/article/lawmakers-say-heads-will-roll-for-dismal-olympic-performance/400098.html; Nikolaus von Twickel, "Sports Minister Ready to Quit Over Olympics," *Moscow Times*, www.themoscowtimes.com/news/article/sports-minister-ready-to-quit-over-olympics/400820.html.

43 "Medvedev Dmitry: Russia Needs Cardinal Reform of Athletes" Training," Tatar-inform, 2 March 2010, http://eng.tatar-inform.ru/news/2010/03/02/28574/.

44 Alexander Bratersky, "Disabled Athletes Show Up Olympics Team," *Moscow News*, 18 March 2010, www.themoscowtimes.com/news/article/disabled-athletes-show-up-olympics-team/402021.html.

45 Vladimir Kozlov, "Russia's Paralympic Triumph Hides Cash Woes," *Moscow News*, 22 March 2010, themoscownews.com/news/20100322/55424022.html.

46 Bratersky, "Disabled Athletes Show Up Olympics Team."

47 Thomas Grove, *Special Report: Russia's $50 billion Olympic Gamble*, 21 February 2013, www.reutersreprints.com.

48 Bratersky, "Russia Plays Its Worst Ever Olympics"; Natalya Krainova, "Russian Paralympians at Top with 38 Medals," *Moscow Times*, 23 March 2010, www.themoscowtimes.com/news/article/russian-paralympians-at-top-with-38-medals/402316.html.

49 John Nelson Washburn, *Censored Statutes Used to Develop the USSR Sports Complex for International Competition after World War II*, Hearings before the Committee on Commerce, Science, and Transportation, United States Senate, Ninety-fifth Congress (Washington: U.S. Government Printing Office, Serial No. 95–53, 1978).

50 Jonathan Earle, "Olympic Medalists Get Luxury Cars," *Moscow Times*, 16 August 2012, www.themoscowtimes.com/news/article/olympic-medalists-get-luxury-cars/466643.html.

51 Henry E. Hale, "Russia's Presidential Election and the Fate of Democracy: Taking the Cake," *AAASS Newsletter* (May 2004): 1–6.

52 Russian Axis, "Vladmir Putin's Second Presidential Term and the Coming Campaign of De-oligarchisation: Possible Scenarios; Preliminary Research," 2004, www.russianaxis.org.

53 See Steve LeVine, *Putin's Labyrinth: Spies, Murder, and the Dark Heart of the New Russia* (New York: Random House, 2008); Anna Politkovskaya, *Putin's Russia* (London: Harvill Press, 2004).

54 Nikolay Petrov and Michael McFaul, "How Much Has Federal Power Increased under President Putin?," Carnegie Endowment for International Peace, 8 September 2004, http://carnegieendowment.org/2004/09/08/how-much-has-federal-power-increased-under-president-putin/27j5; Jodi Koehn, "Putin's Reforms and Russia's Governors: The Impact of Putin's Reforms on Russia's Governors," Woodrow Wilson International Center for Scholars, 2001, www.wilsoncenter.org/publication/putins-reforms-and-russias-governors.

55 LeVine, *Putin's Labyrinth*, xx.

56 Luke Harding, *Expelled: A Journalist's Descent into the Russian Mafia State* (New York: Palgrave Macmillan, 2012).

57 Owen Slot, "Oligarchs Made to Foot the Bill for Rebuilding Russia Machine," *Times*, 29 September 2008, timesonline.co.uk/tol/sport/olympics/article4843061.ece.

58 Mark Grossekathöfer, "Putin's Winter Fairy Tale: Russia's Big Plans for Sochi 2014." *Spiegel Online International*, 26 February 2009, www.spiegel.de/international/world/putin-s-winter-fairy-tale-russia-s-big-plans-for-sochi-2014-a-610096.html; Alexander Katner, "Will Sochi Host 2014 Olympics?" *Sport Express Daily*, 12 April 2007, english.sport-express.ru; "Victory will Change Russian Lives for Ever (Reuters)," Sochi.ru 2014, official website of the Organizing Committee of the XXII Olympic Winter Games and XI Paralympic Winter Games of 2014 in Sochi, 4 July 2007, www.sochi2014.com/en/media/press/publications/7253/.

59 Frontline, "Special Report on Mikhail Khodorkovsky," 28 October 2003, PBS, www.pbs.org/frontlineworld/stories/moscow/khodorkovsky.html.

60 LeVine, *Putin's Labyrinth*, xxi; See also Russian Axis, "Vladmir Putin's Second Presidential Term."

61 Kari Liuhto, "Genesis of Economic Nationalism in Russia," Electronic Publications of Pan-European Institute 3/2008, Turku School of Economics, www.balticseaweb. com/files/files/publications/pan/2008/Liuhto_32008.pdf, 3.

62 Ibid, 19.

63 Andrew E. Kramer, "Mikhail Gutseriev, the Owner of Russneft, Accuses Putin of Forcing a Sale," *New York Times*, 30 July 2007, www.nytimes.com/2007/07/30/ business/worldbusiness/30iht-ruble.4.6903032.html.

64 Wolff, "To Russia with Love."

65 See Peter Ueberroth, *Made in America: His Own Story – Peter Ueberroth* (New York: Wm. Morrow, 1985); Richard Gruneau and Hart Cantelon, "Capitalism, Commercialism, and the Olympics," in Jeffrey Seagrave and Donald Chu (eds.), *The Olympic Games in Transition* (Champaign-Urbana, IL: Human Kinetics Press, 1987).

66 Ueberroth, *Made In America*, 71.

67 Reuters, "Sochi Sponsorships Top $1Bln," 1 March 2010, www.themoscowtimes. com/olympic_coverage/article/sochi-sponsorships-top-1bln/400631.html.

68 Canadian Sport Policy, 2002, Government of Canada; Dennis Mills, "Sport in Canada: Leadership, Partnership, and Accountability – Everybody's Business," Standing Committee on Canadian Heritage, Sub-Committee on the Study of Sport in Canada, 1998, House of Commons Canada.

69 www.en.khl.ru.

70 Gorbachev, *Memoirs*, 438.

71 Alina Inayeh, "Will Olympic Flame Dim in Sochi?" *Spiegel Online International*, 26 February 2010, www.spiegel.de/international/world/opinion-will-olympic-flame-dim-in-sochi-a-680560.html.

4 The Dialectic of Modern, High-Performance Sport: Returning to the Dubin Inquiry to Move Forward

ROB BEAMISH

In conducting their work, sociologists face three distinct, monumental challenges. The first involves identifying the "structure" of the society they are examining. The second concerns locating that society within history. The final challenge is determining the men and women who are prevailing or coming to prevail.[1] Within each of the three there are deeper, subtler, and profounder issues because the ultimate objective of good sociology is to create change, seeking what many have now cast aside as the naive, grand narratives of the Enlightenment's promise of social progress and human emancipation.

One of the difficulties with structure is the term itself; while the noun *structure* conveys the relatively enduring nature of social relationships, it easily lends itself to reification and a misleading sense of permanence and objectiveness or to biological analogies of organic structures serving specific functions for the larger, systemic whole. But structure is simply an abstraction that reminds us that human action takes place within a relatively enduring context, that all social action involves the interpenetration of micro and macro. Sociologists as diverse as Jeffrey Alexander, Pierre Bourdieu, Anthony Giddens, Jürgen Habermas, Richard Münch, and George Ritzer have all attempted to explicitly and consciously forge conceptions of the way in which the micro level of everyday action and human agency is entwined with the macro context within which action takes place.[2] Each of their particular formulations recognizes the constraining and enabling aspects posed by the macro social context, while also remaining true to the productive agency and resistance found in the struggle for greater freedom and human control by knowledgeable, individual, and collective agents acting within that larger social context. The true dialectic – there is, unfortunately, no better term despite its numerous trivializations – of immediate and mediated, material and abstract, and micro and macro and within the concept of structure itself is paramount to understanding how, despite the fact that people seek to change and improve the social world within which they live, their actions are always determined by the enabling and constraining, productive or reproductive dialectic of social structure.

The question of structure also entails an identification of the structure or structures. While sociologists rarely attempt to enumerate all aspects of the structure of the society on which they are focused, they must identify those features that are relevant to the issues under investigation.

The complexity of structure does not end there. After the linguistic turn in social theory, sociologists have drawn upon the work of Claude Lévi-Strauss and Roland Barthes to use language and linguistic structures as heuristics for understanding the social-structural parameters of social life.[3] Still others have followed Michel Foucault and his notion of discourse in which one is not interested in spoken language but focuses instead on the regularities of bodies of knowledge (that is, a discourse) that operate in the absence of speaking subjects and hence establish a structured organization to thought and action.[4]

Next, consider history. "History," Fernand Braudel reminds us, "operates in tenses, on scales and in units which frequently vary: day by day, year by year, decade by decade, or in whole centuries." In each instance, "the unit of measurement modifies the view." Most important, "it is the contrasts between the realities observed on different time-scales that make possible history's dialectic."[5]

Finally, while identifying the men and women who prevail at a particular point in time is never easy and without caveats and questions, determining those who are coming to prevail is even more complex and undetermined, particularly when several competing bodies are struggling to control the social institutions, groups, or relationships under consideration. In each instance sociologists must wade into questions of power, social inertia, and the mobilization of resources, all of which are complex concepts and processes. Yet the fact remains that men and women make their history, so one must identify the conditions under which those in positions of power are shaping the world and who is rising to challenge their domination, seeking to restructure specific aspects – or the totality – of social life.

Hegel maintained that ultimately no philosophy can transcend its age; sociologists face a similar dilemma. While detailed sociological analysis can determine who has prevailed and indicate who may be coming to prevail, an accurate prediction is dependent upon so many factors that the best one can offer is possible scenarios. Yet these scenarios are the most critical aspects of sociological work undertaken in the interest of change and progress. Thus, just as Hegel engaged with the most critical issues in philosophical thought in the opening decades of the nineteenth century, sociologists cannot retreat from public issues of social structure that are in need of change irrespective of what might ultimately transpire.

The significance of each of the three major challenges that sociologists face, and their inner complexities, will become evident in the remainder of this chapter as I focus on the standing of the Olympic project in the wake of the 2010 Winter Games in Vancouver, British Columbia. To do that, however, involves two detours, one brief and the other constituting the bulk of the chapter. The first concerns Baron Pierre de Coubertin's original objectives in mounting the modern Olympic Games based upon his philosophy of Olympism, and the second entails a detailed discussion of one of the most systematic and thorough analyses of Olympic sport ever conducted, *The Commission of Inquiry into the Use of Drugs and Banned Practices Intended to Increase Athletic Performance*, conducted between November 1988 and June 1990 by the Honourable Charles Dubin.[6]

Olympism: The Olympic Project

"The athlete enjoys his effort," Coubertin wrote. "He likes the constraint that he imposes on his muscles and nerves, through which he comes close to victory even if he does not manage to achieve it." The dynamic struggle and euphoria are internal. However, Coubertin continued, "imagine if it were to expand outward, becoming intertwined with the joy of nature and the flights of art. Picture it radiant with sunlight, exalted by music, framed in the architecture of porticoes. It was thus that the glittering dream of ancient Olympism was born on the banks of the Alphaeus, the vision of which dominated ancient society for so many centuries."[7] Coubertin's imagery is simple, yet powerfully inspiring. In the 1890s Coubertin wanted to mobilize the Promethean symbolic power of Classical Greece, Olympia, and human athletic performance to resist, challenge, and hopefully undermine modernity's spread and growing influence in fin-de-siècle Europe.

The modern Olympic Games, Coubertin maintained, would constitute a temple, high above "the great free-for-all" of modern, urban life.[8] Within the Games, the youth of Europe would discover "a delicate balance of mind and body, the joy of a fresher and more intense life, the harmony of the faculties, [and] a calm and happy strength."[9] The youth of Europe, focused on the sacred, spiritual experience of the Games rather than on the profane reality of the industrialized life world, would form a new "*aristocracy*, an *elite*," which would "also be a *knighthood*" – "brave energetic men united by a bond that is stronger than that of mere camaraderie, which is powerful enough in itself." The Olympics would build chivalrous brothers in arms, where "the idea of competition, of effort opposing effort for the love of effort itself, of courteous yet violent struggle, is superimposed on the notion of mutual assistance."[10]

Coubertin's motto, "*Athletae proprium est se ipsum noscere, ducere et vincere* [it is the duty and the essence of the athlete to know, to lead and to conquer himself]," encapsulates the "whole lesson in manly athletic education" – the "transposition from the muscular to the moral sphere, the basis of athletic education."[11] It is also the sense within which the Games' branded motto, "Citius, Altius, Fortius," must be understood rather than the modernist reading it now receives.

Coubertin was not alone in his reluctance to embrace modernity. On the one hand, he shared many of the same deep concerns as those of cultural conservatives like Samuel Coleridge, Thomas Carlyle, J.H. Newman, and Matthew Arnold about the impact that capitalist industrialization and the forces of modernity were having on traditional European culture and values.[12] With the cultural conservatives, Coubertin feared that the growing market-based orientation of Europe and the spread of its commercial ethos would slowly debase the great cultural achievements of Western civilization, push high culture from centre stage, and replace it with a shallow, ersatz commodified culture cheaply sold to mass publics in department stores. Coubertin believed that even if the Games could not change the entire course of European cultural history, they would at least ensure the proper enculturation of Europe's future elite, thereby guaranteeing the preservation of Europe's most treasured, long-standing values.[13]

As a traditionalist, Coubertin shared the pivotal values and beliefs found in the social and political commentaries that began with Edmund Burke's *Reflections on the French Revolution* and extended through the works of Joseph de Maistre, Louis de Bonald, and Hugues Felicité de Lamennais to François René de Chateaubriand and others.[14] More than anything, Coubertin shared the conservatives' fear of the spectre of social disorganization and disintegration.

For members of the conservative tradition the French Revolution was not the epoch-making event that it was for the members of the third estate. For conservatives the events of 1789 and the ensuing social instability and chaos were simply the inevitable outcomes of the social decline and fragmentation that the Renaissance, the Reformation, and the Age of Reason had ushered in through the promotion of individualism, science, the mechanistic world view, expanding markets, and industrialization.

Coubertin shared with Bonald, for example, the conviction that authority and social hierarchy must take precedence over individual liberty. Both celebrated the stability of medieval Europe, its time-honoured institutions, organic functional integration, hierarchical structure, and emphasis upon duty and membership over freedom and individualism. Bonald's *Theory of Power* focused on three key elements – political power, religious power, and social education – which resonated with Coubertin's image of a stable social order and the role of educational experiences in shaping elites and leaders. Like Bonald, Coubertin feared that even though industry and commerce brought people together in an increasingly urbanized world, it did not join them in any meaningful, cohesive solidarity. Social order stemmed from the integrating forces found in the long-established values of medieval Europe, values that gave people a powerful sense of historical connection and common, national purpose.

To emphasize the extent to which the rise of modernity, and the social upheaval it represented, concerned social and political thinkers and activists in nineteenth-century Europe, it is important to note that the radical left also focused on the same aspects of modernity that concerned Coubertin and others in the conservative tradition, even though their proposed solutions were vastly different. In fact, the problems of modernity were best captured in Marx's evocative phrasing in the *Communist Manifesto*. In the era of modernity, Marx noted, the bourgeoisie had become the dominant class and, "wherever it has got the upper hand, has put an end to all feudal, patriarchal, idyllic relations."

> [The bourgeoisie has] pitilessly torn asunder the motley feudal ties that bound man to his "natural superiors," and has left no other nexus between people than naked self-interest, than callous "cash payment" ... It has resolved personal worth into exchange value, and in place of the numberless indefeasible chartered freedoms, has set up that single, unconscionable freedom – Free Trade. In one word, for exploitation, veiled by religious and political illusions, it has substituted naked, shameless, direct, brutal exploitation.
>
> The bourgeoisie has stripped of its halo every occupation hitherto honoured and looked up to with reverent awe. It has converted the physician, the lawyer, the priest, the poet, the man of science, into its paid wage-labourers.[15]

The modern era was unlike any before it; tradition, the mystification of magic or religion, and "natural rights" would no longer structure social relationships. The cash nexus and the ethos of progress through continuous development and perpetual change dominated production, interpersonal relations, the social structure as a whole, and its dominant discursive formation.[16]

While replacing a veiled form of exploitation with a naked, direct form that left factory workers toiling long hours for meagre wages, the bourgeoisie demonstrated the power of industrial, market-based production. The accomplishments of modernity were breathtaking, producing "wonders far surpassing Egyptian pyramids, Roman aqueducts, and Gothic cathedrals."[17] Most important, the impetus for change and progress permeated all aspects of social life. "Conservation of the old modes of production in unaltered form," Marx wrote, was "the first condition of existence for all earlier industrial classes." But under modernity's unlimited drive for progress there was the "constant revolutionizing of production, uninterrupted disturbance of all social conditions, everlasting uncertainty and agitation ... All fixed, fast frozen relations, with their train of ancient and venerable prejudices and opinions, are swept away, all new-formed ones become antiquated before they can ossify. All that is solid melts into air, all that is holy is profaned, and man is at last compelled to face with sober senses his real condition of life and his relations with his kind."[18] Although Marx and Coubertin differed vastly on the solutions they proposed to the modern world that they saw before them, they both felt deep concerns over the impact that modernity was having upon individuals as well as the social fabric as a whole.

While Marx viewed the evils of modernity in the mid-nineteenth century within the context of class struggle and exploitation, Max Weber, writing from the vantage point of the opening decades of the twentieth century, argued that the most powerful, insidious, driving force in the modern world was the increasing domination of instrumental, goal-rational action, a theme that members of the Frankfurt School would develop much further from the 1930s onwards.[19]

In "The Protestant Ethic and the 'Spirit' of Capitalism" Weber maintained that "a constituent part of modern culture" was the rational conduct of one's life. More important, Weber emphasized that the "essential elements of the attitude which is there [in Benjamin Franklin's works] termed the 'spirit of capitalism' are precisely those which we found to be the content of Puritan asceticism of the calling, only *without* the religious foundation, which had already ceased to exist at the time of Franklin."[20] Weber continued:

> The Puritans *wanted* to be men of the calling – we, on the other hand, *must be*. For when asceticism moved out of the monastic cells and into working life, and began to dominate innerworldly morality, it helped to build that mighty cosmos of the modern economic order (which is bound to the technical and economic conditions of mechanical and machine production). Today this mighty cosmos determines, with overwhelming coercion, the style of life *not only* of those directly involved in business but of every individual who is born into this mechanism, and may well continue to do so until the day that the last ton of fossil fuel has been consumed.[21]

Weber concluded the thought with one of his most famous images: for the ascetic Puritans, worldly possessions should sit lightly on their shoulders "like a thin cloak which can be thrown off at any time," but, Weber continued, fate has decreed that "the cloak [of ascetic rationality] shall become a shell as hard as steel [*stahlhartes Gehäuse*]."[22]

Although Talcott Parsons' early rendering of *stahlhartes Gehäuse* as "iron cage" is more widely known, and Peter Baehr and Gordon Wells's "shell as hard as steel" is less pithy, it is more precise and conveys key elements in Weber's text that were missing in Parsons' translation.[23] The cloak of ascetic rationality that dominates the modern world is not something one can easily cast aside; it is a solid, heavy, virtually indestructible shell. Steel is a modern alloy, engineered for its strength and ability to resist, far better than any natural element such as iron, the elements, and time; the goal-rational asceticism of modernity, Weber suggested, promises us an enclosed, enduring, hollow existence from which there may be no escape. The image and concern were completely consistent with Coubertin's view of the modern, industrial, capitalist world.

Herbert Marcuse and Jürgen Habermas elaborated upon the connection between goal-rational action and the ultimate domination of instrumental reason that Weber suggested but did not fully develop.[24] The connection is important because the rise of instrumental reason as the dominant, institutionalized way of approaching the world is central to the thrust of modernity, and it is an immanent process arising from within the precepts of goal-rational action. Habermas indicated that Weber used the concept of rationality "to define the form of capitalist economic activity, bourgeois private law, and bureaucratic authority."[25] As social labour was progressively industrialized, instrumental action penetrated into other areas of social life, leading to the progressive rationalization of society. Through this process, more and more aspects of social action conformed to goal-rational – means-ends efficiency – decision-making processes. "The progressive 'rationalization' of society," Habermas noted, "is linked to the institutionalization of scientific and technical development." The immanent development of instrumental reason undermines and replaces the former taken-for-granted notions of conducting routine social action:

> To the extent that technology and science permeate social institutions and thus transform them, old legitimations are destroyed. The secularization and "disenchantment" of action-orienting world views, of cultural traditions as a whole, is the obverse of the growing "rationality" of social action. Herbert Marcuse has taken these analyses as a point of departure in order to demonstrate that the formal concept of rationality – which Weber derived from the purposive-rational action of the capitalist entrepreneur, the industrial wage labourer, the abstract legal person, and the modern administrative official and based on the criteria of science as well as technology – has specific substantive implications. Marcuse is convinced

that what Weber called "rationalization" realizes not rationality as such but rather, in the name of rationality, a specific form of unacknowledged political domination. Because this sort of rationality extends to the correct choice among strategies, the appropriate application of technologies, and the efficient establishment of systems (with *presupposed* aims in *given* situations), it removes the total social framework of interests in which strategies are chosen, technologies applied, and systems established, from the scope of reflection and rational reconstruction ... By virtue of its structure, purposive-rational action is the exercise of control. That is why, in accordance with this rationality, the "rationalization" of the conditions of life is synonymous with the institutionalization of a form of domination whose political character becomes unrecognizable: the technical reason of a social system of purposive-rational action does not lose its political content.[26]

The prospects of modernity, according to Weber, Marcuse, and Habermas, are even less appealing than Coubertin and the conservatives had anticipated as industrial capitalism gathered steam heading into the twentieth century.

Despite Coubertin's lofty goals and principles, scholars as diverse as Jean-Marie Brohm, Peter Donnelly, Richard Gruneau, Allen Guttmann, John Hoberman, Alan Ingham, Bruce Kidd, Ian Ritchie, Debra Shogan, Steven Ungerleider, and Ivan Waddington, to name just a few, have documented in various and detailed ways the extent to which Coubertin and his successors were unable to overturn the forces of modernity, on the whole, and the growing domination of instrumental rationality as outlined by Habermas.[27] Yet, while it is the failure of the Olympic Games, as an institutionalized practice, to contain and limit the domination of goal-rational action in sport that has caused the greatest problems for the Olympic movement, the promise of Coubertin's imagery has persisted. In fact, the dialectical tension between the material practices of the Games and their ideological inspiration keeps intensifying their appeal, particularly as performances continue to push back the outer limits of human athletic performance within a spectacle that is the most heavily resourced, symbolically rich, media production viewed around the world.

Making Olympic History

On 24 September 1988, taking forty-eight strides in under 9.8 seconds, Ben Johnson not only annihilated his arch rival, Carl Lewis, at the Seoul Summer Games but also opened a critically new chapter in Olympic history. Within seventy-two hours of his spectacular victory, following a positive test for the banned steroid stanozolol, Johnson became the first gold-medal winner in one of the Games' premier events to be disqualified for using a banned substance.

From the 5 October 1988 Order in Council PC 1988–2361, through an inquiry that began on 15 November 1988 and extended to 3 October 1989, involving 119 witnesses and 295 exhibits, a staggering 86 volumes with 14,817 pages of transcripts and 26 additional briefs submitted by the public, to the release of his final report on 26 June 1990, the Honourable Charles Dubin sought to make, or roll back, Olympic history in his own way as the domination of instrumental rationality had become clearly visible and turned into a crisis of Olympic proportions.

Although the Commission of Inquiry into the Use of Drugs and Banned Practices was not the only major investigation into drug use in sport undertaken in the wake of the Seoul Games, in terms of the resources expended, the status of those providing testimony under oath, and the scope of the material presented, the Dubin Inquiry stood as, and remains, the most thorough investigation into the nature of contemporary, world-class, high-performance sport ever undertaken by an independent investigator.[28] For this reason it stands as the best reference point for understanding the dialectic of high-performance sport within the context of modernity. Although twenty-five years have passed since the report's release, the only changes of significance in the nature of high-performance sport are the intensification of instrumental reason, the increased resources directed at creating gold-medal-winning athletes, and the ever greater performance demands required to reach the podium.

The inquiry and its representation in the 1990 report are fascinating social constructions of what members of the International Olympic Committee, sport administrators, politicians, and the media have portrayed as the most pressing problem in world-class, high-performance sport. The inquiry's mandate contributed to that particular construction. The Order in Council stated:

WHEREAS there is a clear public concern with respect to the use of drugs and banned practices intended to increase athletic performance;

AND WHEREAS recent events warrant the establishment of an inquiry with the capacity to examine the issues and determine the facts with respect to the use of drugs and banned practices;

Therefore, the Committee of the Privy Council, on the recommendation of its Prime Minister, advises that a Commission do issue under Part I of the Inquiries Act and under the Great Seal of Canada, appointing the Honourable Charles Leonard Dubin, the Associate Chief Justice of Ontario, to be a Commissioner to inquire into and report on the facts and circumstances surrounding the use of such drugs and banned practices by Canadian athletes, including the recent cases involving athletes who were to, or did, compete in the Olympic Games in Seoul, South Korea, and to inquire into and to make recommendations regarding the issues related to the use of such drugs and banned practices in sport.[29]

The remaining paragraphs in the order covered issues related to the way in which the commissioner would conduct the inquiry.[30]

The order established five points of particular significance. First, the inquiry was initiated on the basis of the claim that there was "a clear public concern with respect to the use of drugs and banned practices intended to increase athletic performance." Second, the inquiry was to look into "the facts and circumstances surrounding the use of such drugs and banned practices by Canadian athletes" in general. Third, that investigation would include "the recent cases involving athletes who were to, or did, compete in the Olympic Games in Seoul, South Korea." Fourth, the inquiry was to "make recommendations regarding the issues related to the use of such drugs and banned practices in sport." Finally, it was up to the commissioner to determine the appropriate methods and procedures for the inquiry, establish advisory panels comprising "sports, medical or legal experts" as he felt necessary, and he was authorized to consult with "groups, bodies or individuals having responsibility for, or authority or expertise in dealing with, on a national or international basis, the use of such drugs and practices," which he felt would assist the inquiry.[31]

Before I examine the report in detail, there are three specific points to be established. First, the discoveries made by Dubin regarding Canada's high-performance-sport system did not demonstrate that it was unique among the sport systems existing in other Western, liberal democracies. Whether one looked then, or looks now, at Australia, Austria, Canada, the Federal Republic of Germany, Great Britain, Sweden, or the United States, for example, it is clear that after the Soviets had entered the Olympic Games in 1952, Western governments became increasingly involved in providing financial support and other resources for the development of more and more sophisticated, heavily resourced, scientifically based systems of athlete development.[32]

Second, not only did Dubin's investigation accurately capture the extent of such involvement and the complex, performance-oriented systems that Canada and other Western nations had developed, but he also identified many of the most important internal contradictions that existed between the high-performance sport systems, as they developed, and the practices that were pursued with them, on the one hand, and the pronouncements that were often used to justify their existence, on the other. This was particularly true in the Canadian case where government policies and statements emphasized themes of national fitness and health promotion through broader participation in sport, the increasing democratization of opportunity, and greater inclusion through the removal of barriers related to racialization, ethnicity, gender, regional disparity, or disability, while funnelling a growing proportion of federal funds into the elite levels of high-performance sport and introducing funding-allocation schemes that were increasingly based on medal counts and other measures of athlete performance.

Finally, despite all of the resources at his behest, and his formal recognition of how professionalized high-performance sport had become, Dubin did not really address the three key questions that I noted at the outset of this chapter. As a result, despite what Dubin discovered and his acting in good faith, his recommendations suggested that the forces of modernity, despite their deeply engrained presence in contemporary high-performance sport, could be overcome through acts of will on the part of athletes, international sport leaders, and national governments. The way in which Dubin came to that conclusion and the manner in which it shaped his recommendations become apparent through a detailed examination of his final report.

The Report of the Commission of Inquiry

On the surface the Commission of Inquiry and, more important, the report issued from it appeared to fully and precisely follow through on the commissioner's mandate. Thus, for example, the report is 638 pages in length, including appendices and notes; it is 581 pages in length from "Part One: Overview of Government Involvement in Sport" to the end of the recommendations. In the latter case, the mid-way point of the report (pages 290–1) falls in a section ominously entitled "The Positive Test." This section discusses the events immediately leading up to Johnson's positive test in Seoul. If one considers the entire report, then the midpoint (page 319) is at the end of the discussion of the athletes disqualified from competition for positive tests. In other words, the heart of the report is focused on the highest-profile Canadian athletes who had tested positive for banned substances. In addition, that discussion is preceded by an overview of some key issues involved in the history and use of performance-enhancing substances, and followed by a discussion of their control.

The report is broken into six parts: "Part One: Overview of Government Involvement in Sport"; "Part Two: Overview of Doping"; "Part Three: The Sports and Events Examined"; "Part Four: Use and Control of Banned Substances"; "Part Five: Rights and Ethical Considerations"; and "Part Six: Conclusions and Recommendations."[33] Once again, if one sets aside the recommendations section and focuses on the material upon which the recommendations are based, then the middle section of the report concerns the sports and events examined by the inquiry, and the parts immediately preceding and following that discussion focus on banned substances. However, the report is constructed in a subtler manner than it first appears.

The apparent substance of the report is supported by two bookends: the overview of government involvement in sport and a discussion of ethics and morality. While most were interested in the material found between these two bookends and Dubin's specific recommendations, it is the bookends themselves that actually shape the report, contour its recommendations, and represent the most salient aspects of Dubin's analysis of high-performance sport.

With respect to the first bookend, although Dubin began the inquiry with testimony from Lyle Makosky, the assistant deputy minister for fitness and amateur sport at the time, and Abby Hoffman, then director general of Sport Canada, which outlined the structure of Canada's sport system in general, and the high-performance-sport system in particular, and it was not until 12 September 1989, the fifth-to-last day of public hearings, that Canadian sport-policy analyst Donald Macintosh testified before the inquiry, Dubin opened the report with a selection of statements and arguments that cast government investment in sport within the broader mandate to govern and meet the needs of the country as a whole. Thus, for example, one of Dubin's key premises came directly out of Donald Macintosh, Tom Bedecki, and Ned Franks's *Sport and Politics in Canada: Government Involvement since 1961*: "Government has a legitimate and essential role to play in sport. Promoting sport and physical activity for all Canadians is one such role. Providing equality of opportunity to high-performance sport is another. Sport also has an important role to play in any government efforts to promote unity and a unique Canadian identity. Government support of sport for these purposes is justified to the same extent as these functions are widely accepted in other areas of cultural practice."[34] Dubin mirrored the quotation with a series of bullet points that were direct citations or paraphrases from then Minister of State for Fitness and Amateur Sport Jean Charest's lengthy introduction and contextualization to the 1988 task force report *Toward 2000: Building Canada's Sport Systems*:

- Sport genuinely reflects the nature of this country – diverse, proud, and competitive. The physical activities we choose to undertake – and the meaning we draw from them – say a lot about Canadians and who we are.
- Sport has always played a prominent role in Canadian life. It is a component of our culture, an element of our economy, and a way of presenting ourselves proudly to the world.
- The federal government "invests" in the sport system for several important reasons. First, we support sport simply for what it is – a part of human nature; a social movement made accessible and equitable through the national sport system. We also invest in the system because sport forms a major part of our national identity and is an expression of our culture and

who we are. As well, sport supports individual Canadians as they pursue excellence to the highest levels and provides opportunities for Canadians in general to observe and share in their pursuit and their celebration and to draw important meanings from their performances.

• I believe the financing of sport is a worthy and important social responsibility of government.[35]

During the inquiry Dubin had heard similar sentiments expressed by several high-profile members of the Canadian sporting community – people with impeccable sport, civic, and professional credentials. Thus, for example, when asked how he would eliminate the use of banned performance-enhancing substances in sport, Bruce Kidd noted that prohibition, increased testing, and better surveillance were not the answer. "Arming the police," he began figuratively, "is simply not a way of dealing with it." One needs to recreate "sport as an important international cultural practice where people are valued, regardless of their position, for outstanding performances." "I think," Kidd continued, "we need to recreate the moral basis of sport. You know it is almost as if the exchange-value of sport is the only value." He also indicated that he did not feel that most Canadians shared the attitude that "if you win you are a hero and make millions, if you lose you are a bum."[36]

In the first chapter Dubin documented that although these sentiments had existed at the outset of government involvement in sport, they had been pushed aside as the system grew. To indicate the philosophy that had shaped early government involvement Dubin cited from the pivotal 1969 *Task Force Report on Sports for Canadians*. Despite the report's overall sport- and performance-oriented emphasis, its authors recognized that Canadians felt that the federal government was there "not just to govern us, but first to create our country, and then constantly to recreate it in terms of the challenges thrown up to each generation."[37]

From the 1970 government White Paper *A Proposed Sports Policy for Canadians*, which established Sport Canada and Recreation Canada, moving sport and recreation planning from the kitchen table tops of Canada to government board rooms, Dubin underlined the main philosophy that informed government involvement in sport.[38] During a period of time in which, as Martin Jay once noted, alienation had "become the chief cant phrase of our time," the 1970 *Proposed Sports Policy for Canadians* emphasized that sport helped "restore a human soul and sense of human fraternity to what otherwise might remain just another agent of depersonalization." Government involvement would help revitalize people by providing greater opportunity and more facilities so that Canadians could easily engage in constructive leisure pursuits.[39]

Despite the claims for inclusion and building a broad base of participation, Dubin recognized that there was an overall emphasis on sport and elite-level performance in the 1970 White Paper. "Notwithstanding the paper's fine sentiments," Dubin wrote, "it is a fact that the specific program proposals it contained were geared to establishing the agencies and programs recommended by the 1969 task force report. These agencies and programs focused upon – and continue to have their focus [upon] – high-level competitive sport."[40]

As he proceeded through ensuing White Papers and policy documents – the 1979 *Partners in Pursuit of Excellence*, the 1981 *A Challenge to the Nation: Fitness and Amateur Sport in the '80s*, and the 1988 task force report *Toward 2000: Building Canada's Sport Systems* – Dubin did more than simply use the material that Lyle Makosky had presented to describe the overall structure of Canada's high-performance-sport system. Dubin indicated the extent to which the federal government had essentially removed itself from maintaining the original principles upon which the system had been initiated. "In principle," Dubin wrote, "Mr. Makosky is correct in stating that the role of the federal government is restricted to financial contribution. In practice, however, federal funding props up the entire sport system, and so its role appears to be much more significant. It is appropriate that, because the Government of Canada makes such a substantial financial contribution to the sport organizations, it be concerned with the manner in which these funds are expended and have the authority to withdraw funding if those organizations are not carrying out the objectives for which they receive such moneys. In that sense, the government does exercise regulatory authority. Indeed, one of Sport Canada's major roles is to coordinate, promote, and develop high-performance sport."[41] In fact, citing extensively from *Toward 2000*, Dubin documented the extent to which Sport Canada and the federal government fully supported a performance-oriented system in the 1980s.[42] "*The thrust of the report of the 1988 task force*," Dubin emphasized, "*stresses government funding for the winning of medals primarily in major and international competition and uses that focus as one of the principal criteria for the determination of the level of future government funding.*"[43]

The discussion contained in the section "Sport as a Policy Instrument" returns to the nation-building and welfare-state themes of the 1970 *Proposed Sports Policy*. Dubin considers sport as a means of improving Canadians' health and fitness, promoting and facilitating gender equality, increasing opportunities for those with disabilities and backgrounds of low socio-economic status, and forging a national identity.[44] "In sum," concluded Dubin in his discussion of sport as a policy instrument, "the federal government, in its role as guide, motivator, mentor, and source of funds for sport, is perhaps the only entity capable of exercising sufficient moral and economic suasion to ensure equality of access by all Canadians – regardless of gender, physical disability, socio-economic or cultural background, or language – to sport, to sport facilities, and to programs it supports."[45]

In his summary to part 1, Dubin noted that since 1969, when the federal government became increasingly involved in funding sport, as "the degree of involvement in and funding of sport [had] increased," there had been "a shift in the nature and focus of that involvement." In spite of lip-service to the benefits of broad-based participation, government support for sport, "particularly since the mid-1970s, had increasingly been channelled towards the narrow objectives of winning medals in international competition." "Notwithstanding protestations to the contrary," Dubin stated categorically, "the primary objective has become the gold medal. This changed emphasis from broad-based support of sport for the general community of ordinary Canadians to high-level competitive sport demands a re-examination of the role and mandate of government sport agencies. In light of the evidence and disclosures made before this Commission, I think the time has come for the Government of Canada to consider whether those premises upon which government involvement in and funding of sport have been founded are still valid and whether, if they are indeed still valid, the legitimate objectives of such involvement are being pursued and achieved."[46]

Sport, Ethics, and Morality

With an overview of government involvement in sport established as one bookend, Dubin constructed the other in part 5 within his discussion of "Athletes and Coaches against Drugs" and "Ethics and Morality in Sport."[47] In the first section of part 5 he began with testimony from three of Canada's long-standing, prominent, highly regarded former athletes and pillars of Canadian civic life: Bill Crothers, one of the world's premier middle-distance runners when he was competing; his University of Toronto and East York Track Club teammate, Bruce Kidd; and former athlete turned track-and-field specialist and educator at the University of Toronto, Andy Higgins.

Based upon information presented at the inquiry and Crothers' testimony, Dubin noted that during Crothers' highly successful international career, track was always "an avocation that took second place to his schooling." "Mr Crothers," Dubin wrote, "considers money to be the root of the current problems in athletics," and supported the point with a lengthy excerpt from Crothers' testimony:

As long as there is sufficient money in the sport to produce the kind of rewards that the athletes can receive for their performances, and, more importantly, that there is enough money to support all the support personnel, the trainers, the physicians, the agents, the promoters, that is far more important. As long as there is sufficient money in sport to make it possible for them to benefit by the performances of individual athletes, there will always be the problem. Because ... they achieve their benefits, not by virtue of the enjoyment they get out of the sport, but they achieve their benefits by virtue of the success that the individual athlete receives.

And as long as they can receive material, significant material benefits from that, there will always be ... some people who are looking for an edge and an angle.[48]

While indicating the significance of money, Crothers was really indicating the extent to which an elaborate system, with specific interests and goals, now existed in high-performance sport and dictated its entire ethos. As long as there were the resources to support that system, the use of banned substances and practices would continue.

From Kidd's testimony at the inquiry, Dubin focused on one particular incident: a shift in Kidd's training plan. Kidd had testified that in 1963 he had introduced a morning run into his training program. At the Highland Games in Edinburgh that year Kidd mentioned it to a fellow competitor. Martin Hyman, "easily among the top 10 in the world" in his event and an older competitor whom Kidd deeply respected, responded with vehemence: "And I still remember that," Kidd testified, "because I was trying to defend the new approach, training twice a day, and I was surprised I was under attack. 'You know,'" Kidd recounted Hyman saying, "'you represent the thin edge of the wedge. If it gets to the point where people are training twice a day, then they will move on to three times a day because probably there is a marginal efficiency to be gained with a lot more training. And it will become a full time occupation and the life we lead will be impossible. And it will mean that people such as us will be forced to choose from being a full time athlete, focusing on nothing but sport, or a recreational athlete with little opportunity to travel and compete at a high level.'"[49] Kidd continued in his testimony, and Dubin included in the report, that he now realized "how prophetic that was because subsequent Canadian athletes have experienced great difficulty trying to make that choice. And nowadays there is no question ... Athletes today identify themselves as full time athletes."[50]

Citing from the testimony of Andy Higgins before the inquiry, Dubin focused on Higgins' discussion about why anyone should care how far a person can project sixteen pounds of metal (that is, in the shot put). "I mean, we have machinery today that can make it go much further, so just projecting metal through the air some distance is an absolutely useless activity." So what is the point of putting a shot or running around a track? "I think that's a discussion that has to be generated from the very beginning," Higgins had testified. "It is a discussion," he continued, "that we should have in Canada, and it must begin at the top."

> We should understand why we are doing sport, and the only value, it seems to me, is what happens to the individual in the process of trying to make that piece of metal go as far as he is capable of making it go. Because once one commits to that kind of endeavour, then all kinds of possibilities begin to arise. We are going to meet all the challenges that many of these athletes [who have testified before the inquiry] spoke about, and they will come in minor ways and in major ways, and at every challenge we are faced with options.
>
> It seems to me the value of sport to the individual and to the country is to help young people to make the choice that will make them stronger when you meet the challenge, and not go the easy route, not to take what I refer to as the "fear choice."[51]

Dubin continued the section by citing material and ideas from current athletes: distance runner and 1984 Olympic Games silver medalist Lynn Williams; decathlete and 1988 Games bronze medalist Dave Steen; Canadian sprinter Angela Bailey, who, as Dubin pointed out in the report, remained in the shadow of Angella Issajenko throughout much of her career; race walker Ann Peel; and the Canadian record holder in the high jump, Milt Ottey. On the basis of the material drawn from their testimony and presented in the report, Dubin concluded that each of those athletes "realizes that there is something more to sport than the mere winning of medals, and, if sport is to survive, heed must be given to those moral and ethical values which form such an important part of its definition."[52]

Before presenting conclusions and making his recommendations, Dubin completed the second bookend to the report with a chapter entitled "Ethics and Morality in Sport," in which he expressed the same concerns found within the conservative tradition that had influenced and inspired Coubertin. Dubin emphasized that people look to sport "to build character, teach the virtues of dedication, perseverance, endurance, and self-discipline." One may learn from defeat as much as from victory. Most important, "we look to sport to impart something of moral and social values and, in integrating us as individuals, to bring about a healthy, integrated society."[53]

Dubin noted that Canada's international athletes are ambassadors for the nation, representing the principles that Canadians value. Cheating, he emphasized, "is not one of those principles."[54]

Dubin used this final section to bring together the two key issues he wanted to feature in each of the bookends and use to hold the entire report together – the principles behind government involvement in sport, and ethical conduct. If winning a gold medal at all costs – including risking one's health and cheating – is the only goal of high-performance sport, then, he unequivocally affirmed, "there can be no justification for continued public financial assistance."[55]

To put high-performance sport in its full social context, Dubin drew from an unusual source, Jean-Marie Brohm's *Sport: A Prison of Measured Time*.[56] The use of Brohm indicates a theme that I noted in the discussion of Coubertin's original Olympic project: the extent to which conservatives' and traditionalists' concerns about sport under modernity overlap with critics from the social democratic, socialist, or communist left even though their proposed solutions differ dramatically. "It is impossible to deny," René Maheu wrote in text cited by Brohm, "that the development of spectator sport has turned attention away from the moral value of sport for the individual towards its entertainment potential. For the mass of people, sport has become a form of entertainment of which they are mere spectators; radio and television spare them even the trouble of getting to the sportsground. The success of spectator sport and the importance it has come to assume in everyday life are unfortunately too often exploited for purposes alien or even opposed to sport – commercialism, chauvinism and politics – which corrupt and deform it. *If we want to save sports' soul, the time has come to react and react quickly.*"[57]

To frame his understanding of the social value of sport Dubin returned to Coubertin directly. In 1892, addressing the members of the Union des sports athlétiques assembled at the Sorbonne, Coubertin had noted: "Before all things it is necessary that we should preserve in sport those characteristics of nobility and chivalry which have distinguished it in the past, so that it may continue to play the same part in the education of the peoples of today as it played so admirably in the days of ancient Greece."[58]

Dubin proceeded to address a number of key issues, bringing each one back to the question of moral integrity. Lowering the performance standard for federal funding, without a change in moral integrity among athletes, would accomplish nothing; the athlete who is struggling to meet that lower standard will find reasons to use banned performance-enhancing substances for the same reasons that certain athletes make that decision if they are struggling to meet the higher standards or attain the podium.

Coaching is critical. As Higgins had noted, coaches are extremely influential educators; they have a unique, intense relationship with their athletes, and the commitment from both towards their common goal is enormous. Dubin cited, with added emphasis, a similar view towards coaching offered by Dr Andrew Pipe: "*The care, training and athletic education of an athlete should be in accord with the highest standards of ethical behavior and scientific knowledge.*"[59]

Dubin maintained that "it is only when winning is the sole purpose of sport that ethics and morality are cast aside." Fortunately, he claimed, that is not the case with the majority of Canadian athletes. Failing to meet an appropriate moral standard, Dubin argued, had serious implications for the athletes themselves because "personal integrity cannot be compartmentalized … We live in a competitive society, and an athlete who cheats in athletic events may carry this attitude over to the everyday world in which he or she must now compete."

Dubin drew his discussion to a close with the following final remarks: "As Bruce Kidd said in his testimony, Canadians must re-create the moral basis of sport. We must examine to what extent our expectations of our athletes have contributed to the current unacceptable situation in sports in Canada. We must examine, too, whether the programs supported by the federal government have contributed to the problem, and indeed whether the funds provided by the government are being utilized in a manner consistent with the fostering of those values and ethics which are so important to us as Canadians."[60]

Despite the fact that the inquiry centred on banned substances and practices, the material and evidence presented to Dubin ranged from the structure of Canada's high-performance-sport system to the resources invested in it to government policy documents to some history of the Games, and to the use of banned substances and practices, as well as including detailed testimony by athletes, coaches, and sport administrators. In the end, however, Dubin's report and recommendations rested on key questions of philosophy and ethics. Adopting a trans-historical, essentialist notion of sport, Dubin noted in the report's preface, "The use of banned performance-enhancing drugs is cheating, which is the antithesis of sport. The widespread use of such drugs has threatened the essential integrity of sport and is destructive of its very objectives. It also erodes the ethical and moral values of athletes who use them, endangering their mental and physical welfare while demoralizing the entire sport community. I have endeavoured to define the true values of sport and restore its integrity so that it can continue to be an important part of our culture, unifying and giving pleasure to Canadians while promoting their health and vitality."[61] The "true values of sport," "its integrity," and sport's place in Canadian culture as a unifying, pleasurable activity, despite all of the territory that Dubin covered throughout his inquiry, became the central issues in his report and his most far-reaching recommendations.

The Commission of Inquiry's Conclusions and Main Recommendation

Dubin drew his report to a close by bringing the inquiry full circle. In the first public session of the inquiry, Dubin noted, he had asked: "Have we, as Canadians, lost track of what athletic competition is all about? Is there too much emphasis by the public and by the media on the winning of a gold medal in Olympic competition as the only achievement worthy of recognition?"[62] "In my opinion," Dubin now commented, "the answers will in large measure determine the future of sport in Canada."[63]

Before moving into his seventy recommendations, Dubin framed them within the "fundamental principles of the Olympic movement" as they are stated in the Olympic Charter:

1. The aims of the Olympic Movement are:
   - to promote the development of those physical and moral qualities which are the basis of sport,
   - to educate young people through sport in a spirit of better understanding between each other and of friendship, thereby helping to build a better and more peaceful world,
   - to spread the Olympic principles throughout the world, thereby creating international goodwill,
   - to bring together the athletes of the world in the great four-yearly sport festival, the Olympic Games.[64]

Dubin then noted that the Charter also states: "3. The Olympic Games take place every four years. *They unite Olympic competitors of all countries in fair and equal competition.*[65] 'Unfortunately,'" Dubin candidly continued, "the noble sentiments and lofty ideals proclaimed in the Olympic Charter are a far cry from the reality of international competition. This reality has not until recently been widely known, but the conspiracy of silence has now been broken and the truth revealed. Truth is not always pleasant."

Dubin's preamble to his first recommendation sketched some of that difficult truth, documented in detail throughout the report.[66] He emphasized, in several ways, the manner and extent to which he believed that the use of banned performance-enhancing substances undermined the integrity of sport; Dubin noted how widespread the use of banned substances had become along with the various social pressures that encouraged or supported their use; he was extremely critical of athletes, officials, sports governing bodies, and Olympic officials for not doing more to eradicate their use in sport; Dubin also expressed concern for athletes' health and, more important, the "carryover effect of a breach of ethical standards in one field, sport, to other areas of an individual's life, and about the consequent erosion of the entire value system." He continued:

> We cannot allow sport, which we expect to build character, to become a means of destroying it, encouraging hypocrisy and cynicism in athletes and other young people.

There will be those who say that this view of sport [expressed in the overview] and its purpose is idealistic and out of date, that I have taken too high a moral tone, that the modern world of sport has progressed beyond the point where the original amateur ideals of fair play, honest striving to do one's best, camaraderie, and wholesome competition have any meaning or validity. If that is indeed the view of Canadians (and I do not accept that it is), then there is no justification for government support and funding of sport.[67]

With his framework in place Dubin proceeded to his recommendations, focusing first on government funding.[68] Since this was, potentially at least, Dubin's most significant and far-reaching recommendation, its immediate context merits full citation.

It is the essence of athletic competition that it should be conducted fairly, with an equal opportunity for all who compete based on their natural ability, and in accordance with the underlying principles of ethics and morality. That is what sport is all about. International competition is intended to promote the development of those physical and moral qualities that are the basis of sport. In addition, it is intended to bring athletes from different countries and cultures together in a spirit of friendship and better understanding.

Based on such premises, there are valid and legitimate reasons to justify government involvement in and funding of sport. To that end and to further these worthy social and national objectives, the Government of Canada, by the expenditure of public funds, has made a very substantial commitment to and investment in sport and, over the last thirty years, has become more and more involved in the development and funding of sport.

However, as the degree of involvement in and funding of sport has increased, there has been a shift of emphasis in the nature and focus of that involvement. While task force reports and government white papers acknowledge the broad objectives set forth above and the benefits of widely based participation in sport, in fact government support of sport, particularly since the mid-1970s, has more and more been channelled towards the narrow objective of winning medals in international competition. Notwithstanding protestations to the contrary, the primary objective has become the gold medal.[69]

As a result, Dubin's first and most far-reaching recommendation was that the mandate for the government funding of sport must "reflect a commitment to those principles on which government funding was originally based" – broad participation, not solely elite sport, increased access to all Canadians; the encouragement of women to participate in sport, ensuring equal access to sport and athletic facilities; support for the disabled; and an amelioration of the regional disparities in access to facilities and sport programs.[70]

Instrumental Reason, and the Dialectic of High-Performance Sport

In the two decades since the release of the Commission of Inquiry's report, what has changed? In short, little to nothing, and everything.

The fundamental nature and inspirational promise of Coubertin's project remains. His quest to wrap the ethos of modernity within a code of chivalry, as brothers in arms are forged in the cauldron of competitive struggle among international comrades, where character development is valued far above victory, still inspires many around the globe. In pursuit of that elusive goal, advocates for Olympism continue to champion Coubertin's vision and his festival.

In the aftermath of the Commission of Inquiry the Canadian government continues to fund high-performance sport. Canadian athletes still compete and excel on the international stage. And athletes around the world have not stopped using banned performance-enhancing substances and practices, although the actual extent of their use continues to remain a matter of educated speculation.

At the same time, everything has changed internationally and within Canada itself. In the post–Commission of Inquiry world, the pursuit of the podium has intensified as governments, national sports organizations, and national Olympic committees fund and amass larger and more sophisticated teams of applied sport scientists (for example, exercise physiologists, biomechanicians, and sport psychologists) and applied technologists (for example, materials engineers, product designers, inventors), and a growing army of sport medicine professionals (for example, trainers, physiotherapists, masseurs, sport physicians), so that their athletes have the resources needed to win at the world-class level. Athletes are increasingly committed to driving themselves towards achieving performances that are at the very outer limits of human athletic potential. Athletes and coaches dedicate the best years of their lives to the full-time pursuit of gaining mere millimetres of distance or reducing increasingly minute slivers of time – one one-thousandth of a second in many sports – to win gold.

Within Canada, despite the Commission of Inquiry's report and recommendations, Sport Canada, the Canadian Olympic Committee, the federal government, and, in the wake of the 2010 Games, the Canadian media and public at large have firmly embraced "Own the Podium 2010," which ties funding directly to success measured in medal counts.[71] Moreover, "Own the Podium" has raised the bar on technological advancement and the systematic and focused use of sport science, pure science, and applied science to make athletes faster, push them higher, and build them even stronger. Even though Dubin was particularly critical of the performance-oriented thrust of *Towards 2000*, "Own the Podium" has taken performance objectives, medal targets, and the twinning of funding with medal-winning athletes to new heights within the history of Canada's high-performance-sport system.

None of this is surprising – not to a good sociologist, at least. The bookends to the inquiry's final report suggested that an overzealous commitment to winning gold medals was due to a failure of will and ethical integrity. The problem was easily resolved if athletes and coaches wanted to return to Coubertin's original vision for the modern Games. And there was leverage – in Canada it resided in the government's control of resources. The one who was paying the piper should call the tune. Dubin's primary recommendation seemed like tough medicine, but his staging of the recommendation suggested it would be effective, especially in the aftermath of the crisis in Seoul.

In spite of Dubin's good intentions his inquiry fell well shy of what was really required to fully grasp the nature of high-performance sport in the modern era, let alone tackle the enduring contradictions that exist between Coubertin's imagery and the humanistic promise of sport, on the one hand, and the reality of sport within the forces of modernity, on the other. As a result, even though the Commission of Inquiry gathered a good deal of critical information related to high-performance sport, it was not enough for a genuine, in-depth, sociological analysis of contemporary, world-class sport. One could detail where the inquiry failed to gather sufficient information and was thus unable to fully address each of sociology's three key questions, but the real Achilles heel of the investigation was the extent to which it, like Coubertin, underestimated or failed to recognize the hard-as-steel grip in which instrumental rationality holds the modern world.

Whether one draws upon Foucault and his notions of discursive formations and power/knowledge, Alfred Schütz and Thomas Luckmann and their concept of life world, the critical theory of Horkheimer and Adorno or Habermas, or Giddens' theory of structuration – to name just four possible frameworks – Weber's insight and fears about instrumental reason have to be addressed openly, systematically, and honestly.[72] The *stahlhartes Gehäuse* of instrumental rationality is not a cloak that is easily cast aside. It shapes and contours all thoroughly institutionalized forms of social action including – perhaps one should say, *especially* – sport. With the disenchantment of the medieval world, a new ethos – a new form of domination – arose, and until it is determinately negated and transcended, the promise of ludic freedom and cultural expression in international, high-performance sport will remain entrapped in the enduring hollow shell of modernity.

All of the above leads to two very different conclusions. First, following "Own the Podium" and the 2010 Vancouver Games, it is clear that Canada's high-performance-sport system is fully committed to the money-for-medals mentality that Dubin had tried to eradicate. Rather than writing a new chapter in Olympic history and re-establishing Coubertin's original vision for the modern Games, modernity – not Dubin – has prevailed. The ongoing quest to push back the outer limits of human athletic performance continues; indeed, it does so with even more resources and legitimacy than ever before. "Own the Podium" has not only kicked the Commission of Inquiry report into the proverbial dustbin of history, but it has made the objectives of Canada's high-performance-sport system crystal clear.

While many support this direction, they must now be willing, to paraphrase Marx, to confront with sober senses the real conditions of high-performance sport and the relations within which athletes labour; they must be ready to confront the dialectical reality of high-performance sport under modernity. What does this mean, especially with respect to instrumental rationality?

Although often trivialized, and sometimes made so convoluted that it is incomprehensible, the dialectic for Hegel is actually quite simple. It involves taking something seriously, absolutely seriously. In his lectures on the history of philosophy Hegel took seriously every philosophical system he discussed. He followed the logic of each one to its ultimate consequences, and it was then that each system's internal contradictions became apparent and the way to positively transcend them was clear. The same is now true of high-performance sport.

As instrumental rationality pushes human athletic performance to greater and greater heights through a growing army of performance-enhancing support personnel and continual technological advance, two outcomes will emerge. First, it will become impossible to keep new technologies at bay and more and more difficult to determine which technologies – which performance-enhancing substances and practices – should be banned as others are adopted and needed to push the value of the Olympic spectacle even higher. Second, if the history of prohibition and sanction has proven to be an absolute failure between 1973 and the present, as technologies become more highly developed, the future success of prohibition is even less sanguine than in the past. Indeed, as the ethos of modernity and technological development extend into the future, the overall safety of more and more athletes will quickly become the overriding concern at the Games. As the system proceeds towards the full expression of the logic of modernity, the focus will have to turn from policing athletes to ensuring their safety. Policies of prohibition will have to give way to those of harm reduction.

At the very moment when contemporary high-performance sport seems to have condemned the report of the Commission of Inquiry to the trash, one might want to retrieve it and finally implement Dubin's first and most significant recommendation: government funding of sport should only continue if it reflects the commitment upon which it was originally based – building a broad base of active participation, expanding access to facilities and opportunities, and building a sense of what it means to be Canadian within a genuinely multicultural society. This is the second major conclusion to emerge from the discussion. In the midst of the country's greatest crisis of inactivity, it is time to recognize that high-performance sport is a market-oriented, market-driven media spectacle in which private interests profit from the sale of a heavily promoted commodity or spectacle. It is time to let the market bear the full costs of the enterprise. World-class, high-performance sport can be sustained by the forces of the great colossus of the modern economy – caveat emptor.

In an era where government resources are scarce and are most needed to stimulate Canadians to become physically active, the dialectic of high-performance sport within modernity represents a powerful argument for returning to Dubin's first recommendation in order to move forward from the present reality of high-performance sport in Canada.

NOTES

1 See C. Wright Mills, *The Sociological Imagination* (New York: Oxford University Press, 1959), 6–7.
2 See Jeffrey Alexander, *Theoretical Logic in Sociology*, 4 vols. (Berkeley CA: University of California Press, 1982–3); Pierre Bourdieu, *The Logic of Practice*, trans. R. Nice (Stanford CA: Stanford University Press, 1990); Anthony Giddens, *The Constitution of Society* (Berkeley: University of California Press, 1984); Jürgen Habermas, *The Theory of Communicative Action*, 2 vols., trans. T. McCarthy (Boston: Beacon Press, 1984, 1987); Richard Münch, *Theorie des Handelns: Zur Rekonstruktion der Beiträge von Talcott Parsons, Emile Durkheim, und Max Weber* [Theory of Action: Towards a Reconstruction of the Contributions by Talcott Parsons, Emile Durkheim, and Max Weber], (Frankfurt: Suhrkamp Verlag, 1982); George Ritzer, *Metatheorizing in Sociology* (Lexington MA: Lexington Books, 1991).
3 See Claude Lévi-Strauss, *The Savage Mind* (Chicago: University of Chicago Press, 1968); Roland Barthes, *Mythologies*, trans. A. Lavers (New York: Hill & Wang, 1972).
4 See Michel Foucault, *The Order of Things: An Archaeology of the Human Sciences*, trans. A. Sheridan (New York: Pantheon Books, 1971); *The Archaeology of Knowledge*,

trans. A. Sheridan (London: Tavistock, 1972); *Discipline and Punish: The Birth of the Prison*, trans. A. Sheridan (New York: Vintage Books, 1977).

5 Fernand Braudel, *A History of Civilizations*, trans. R. Mayne (New York: Penguin Books, 1993), 34.

6 Charles Dubin, *The Commission of Inquiry into the Use of Drugs and Banned Practices Intended to Increase Athletic Performance* (Ottawa: Canadian Government Publishing Centre, 1990), xviii–xxii, 585–6.

7 Pierre de Coubertin, *Olympism: Selected Writings*, selected by Norbert Muller (Lausanne: International Olympic Committee, 2000), 552.

8 Ibid., 559.

9 Ibid., 536.

10 Ibid., 581.

11 Ibid., 593.

12 Samuel Coleridge, *Confessions of an Inquiring Spirit and Some Miscellaneous Pieces* (London: Wm. Pickering, 1849); Thomas Carlyle, *Works of Thomas Carlyle*, vol. 2 (London: Chapman & Hall, 1896); J.H. Newman, *On the Scope and Nature of University Education* (New York: E.P. Dutton, 1915); Matthew Arnold, *Culture and Anarchy: An Essay in Political and Social Criticism* (Cambridge: Cambridge University Press, 1932 [1875]); see also Raymond Williams, *Culture and Society: 1780–1950* (New York: Pelican Books, 1961).

13 See Coubertin, *Olympism*, 559.

14 See Edmund Burke, *Reflections on the Revolution in France and on the Proceedings in Certain Societies in London Relative to that Event*, 5th ed. (London: J. Dodsley, 1790); Louis de Bonald, *La théorie du pouvoir, politique, et religieux dans la société civile* [The Theory of Power, Politics, and Religion in Civil Society], 4th ed. (Brussels: Société nationale, 1845 [1796]); Robert Nisbet, "Conservatism," in Tom Bottomore and Robert Nisbet (eds.), *A History of Sociological Analysis* (London: Heinemann, 1978), 80–117.

15 Karl Marx and Friedrich Engels, *The Manifesto of the Communist Party* (London: Martin Lawrence Ltd., 1934 [1848]), 12.

16 See Foucault, *The Order of Things*, 250–302.

17 Marx and Engels, *The Manifesto of the Communist Party*, 12.

18 Ibid., 12–13.

19 See Jürgen Habermas, "Technology and Science as Ideology," in *Toward a Rational Society*, trans. J. Shapiro (Boston: Beacon Press, 1971), 81–122; Max Horkheimer, *Critique of Instrumental Reason*, trans. M. O'Connell (New York: Seabury Press, 1974); Horkheimer and Theodor Adorno, *Dialectic of Enlightenment: Philosophical Fragments*, trans. E. Jephcott (Stanford, CA: Stanford University Press, 2002); Herbert Marcuse, "Industrialization and Capitalism," in Otto Stammer (ed.), *Max Weber and Sociology Today* (New York: Harper Torchbooks, 1971), 133–86.

20 Max Weber, *The Protestant Ethic and the "Spirit" of Capitalism and Other Writings*, trans. P. Baehr and G. Wells (New York: Penguin Books, 2002), 120.

21 Ibid., 120–1.

22 Ibid., 121.

23 See Max Weber, *The Protestant Ethic and the Spirit of Capitalism*, trans. Talcott Parsons (New York: Charles Scribner's Sons, 1958), 181.

24 Habermas, "Technology and Science as Ideology," and Marcuse, "Industrialization and Capitalism."

25 Habermas, "Technology and Science as Ideology," 81.

26 Ibid., 81–2; see also Richard Münch, *Die Kultur der Moderne* [The Culture of Modernity] (Frankfurt: Suhrkamp, Verlag, 1986).

27 Rob Beamish and Ian Ritchie, *Fastest, Highest, Strongest: A Critique of High-Performance Sport* (New York: Routledge, 2006); Jean-Marie Brohm, *Sport: A Prison of Measured Time*, trans. I. Fraser (London: Ink Link, 1978); Peter Donnelly and L. Petherick, "Workers' Playtime? Child Labour at the Extremes of the Sporting Spectrum," in D. McArdle and R. Giulianotti (eds.), *Sport, Civil Liberties, and Human Rights* (London: Routledge, 2006), 9–29; Richard Gruneau, *Class, Sports, and Social Development* (Amherst: University of Massachusetts Press, 1983); Allen Guttmann, *From Ritual to Record: The Nature of Modern Sports* (New York: Columbia University Press, 1978); *The Olympics: A History of the Modern Games* (Chicago: University of Illinois Press, 2002); John Hoberman, *Mortal Engines: The Science of Performance and the Dehumanization of Sport* (Toronto: Maxwell Macmillan Canada, 1992); Alan Ingham, "Occupational Subcultures in the Work World of Sport," in Don Ball and John Loy (eds.), *Sport and the Social Order* (Reading, MA: Addison-Wesley, 1975), 395–455; Bruce Kidd, *The Struggle for Canadian Sport* (Toronto: University of Toronto Press, 1996); Debra Shogan, *The Making of High-Performance Athletes* (Toronto: University of Toronto Press, 1999); Steven Ungerleider, *Faust's Gold: Inside the East German Doping Machine* (New York: St Martin's Press, 2001); Ivan Waddington and Andy Smith, *An Introduction to Drugs in Sport* (London: Routledge, 2008).

28 See Rob Beamish, "Torn between Founding Principles and the Realities of Modernity: Canada's Anti-doping Policies," in Lucie Thibault and Jean Harvey (eds.), *Sport Policy in Canada* (Ottawa: University of Ottawa Press, 2013), 217–42; House of Representatives, *The Anabolic Steroid Restriction Act of 1989: Hearings before the Subcommittee on Crime of the Committee of the Judiciary of the House of Representatives*, 101st Congress, 1st Session, 1989; House of Representatives, *The Anabolic Steroid Restriction Act of 1990: Hearings before the Subcommittee on Crime of the Committee of the Judiciary of the House of Representatives*, 101st Congress, 2nd Session, 1990.

29 Dubin, *The Commission of Inquiry*, 585.

30 Ibid., 585–6.
31 Ibid.; Canada, *Hearings: Commission of Inquiry into the Use of Drugs and Banned Practices Intended to Increase Athletic Performance*, 86 vols. (Ottawa: Government of Canada), 3–11.
32 See Beamish and Ritchie, *Fastest, Highest, Strongest.*
33 See Dubin, *The Commission of Inquiry*, 1–65, 67–136, 137–332, 333–470, 471–512, 513–81.
34 See Donald Macintosh, Tom Bedecki, and C.E.S. Franks, *Sport and Politics in Canada: Government Involvement since 1961* (Montreal: McGill-Queen's Press, 1987), 186; cited in Dubin, *The Commission of Inquiry*, 4.
35 Dubin, *The Commission of Inquiry*, 4; see also National Sports Policy Task Force, *Toward 2000: Building Canada's Sport Systems* (Otttawa: Government of Canada, Fitness and Amateur Sport), 16–17.
36 Canada, *Hearings: Commission of Inquiry*, 10710.
37 Dubin, *The Commission of Inquiry*, 12.
38 Ibid., 14.
39 Martin Jay, *The Dialectical Imagination* (London: Heinemann, 1973), 1.
40 Dubin, *The Commission of Inquiry*, 16.
41 Ibid., 27.
42 Ibid., 48–9.
43 Ibid., 52.
44 Ibid., 53–4, 54–7, 57–8, 58–60, 60–2.
45 Ibid., 61–2.
46 Ibid., 64.
47 Ibid., 473–89, 499–512.
48 Ibid., 474.
49 See Canada, *Hearings: Commission of Inquiry*, 10688–9; cited in Dubin, *The Commission of Inquiry*, 475.
50 Cited in Dubin, *The Commission of Inquiry*, 476; see Canada, *Hearings: Commission of Inquiry*, 10689.
51 Cited in Dubin, *The Commission of Inquiry*, 476.
52 Dubin, *The Commission of Inquiry*, 488.
53 Ibid., 499.
54 Ibid., 500.
55 Ibid., 501.
56 Ibid.
57 Brohm, *Sport: A Prison of Measured Time*, 8; emphasis in Brohm and Dubin.
58 Cited in Dubin, *The Commission of Inquiry*, 502.
59 Cited in Dubin, *The Commission of Inquiry*, 509.
60 Dubin, *The Commission of Inquiry*, 511.

61 Ibid., xxii.
62 Ibid., 515; see Canada, *Hearings: Commission of Inquiry*, 17.
63 Dubin, *The Commission of Inquiry*, 515.
64 Ibid., 516.
65 Ibid., Dubin's emphasis.
66 Ibid., 517–24.
67 Ibid., 523.
68 Ibid., 524–81.
69 Ibid., 525.
70 Ibid., 527.
71 See Own the Podium, *Pillars of Excellence*, http://www.ownthepodium2010.com/ About/objectives.aspx (accessed 17 May 2010); Government of Canada, *Own the Podium 2010*, http://www.canada2010.gc.ca/invsts/podium/030701-eng.cfm (accessed 17 January 2010); Cathy Priestner Allinger and Todd Allinger, *Own the Podium – 2010: Final Report with Recommendations of the Independent Task Force for Winter NSOs and Funding Partners*, http://www.sportmatters.ca/Groups/ SMG%20Resources/Sport%20and%20PA%20Policy/otp_report_-_final_-_e.pdf (accessed 17 January 2010).
72 See Foucault, *Discipline and Punish*; *Power/Knowledge: Selected Interviews & Other Writings, 1972–1977*, ed. C. Gordon (New York: Pantheon Books, 1980); Alfred Schütz and Thomas Luckmann, *The Structures of the Life-World*, 2 vols. (Evanston, IL: Northwestern University Press, 1973, 1989); Horkheimer and Adorno, *Dialectic of Enlightenment*; Habermas, *The Theory of Communicative Action*; Giddens, *The Constitution of Society*.

PART TWO

Continental Divides: Revisiting the Shaping of Sport in North America

5 The 1904 Chicago–St Louis Transition and the Social Structuration of the American Olympic Movement

JOHN J. MACALOON

Historiography of the second modern Olympiad – the four-year period from the 1900 Paris to the 1904 Chicago–St Louis Olympic Games – has been largely stagnant for over a decade.[1] Absence of new source material has chiefly been responsible, but so has the limited agenda of straight historical narrative in the Olympic studies mode that has organized previous work on the topic.[2] This chapter makes the first scholarly use of the papers of Henry (Harry) J. Furber Jr, co-leader of the Chicago bid and president of the organizing committee for the 1904 Olympic Games before they were transferred from Chicago to St Louis.[3] Clarifications and emendations of the standard Olympic studies account suggested by the Furber papers will be offered en passant here, but full revisions to the established narrative must await another occasion. The main purpose of this chapter is not chronicle but interpretation. I endeavour to show that in the total matrix of events and conditions comprising the award to Chicago of the rights to the 1904 Olympic Games, Chicago's preparations, the transfer of the Games to St Louis, and their eventual conduct in that city lies much of the "structuration" (in Anthony Giddens' awkward but indispensable term)[4] of subsequent American Olympic history. I conclude by pointing out how thoroughly Chicago's second Olympic bid, for 2016, was structurally pre-formed by the 1904 Chicago–St Louis experience.

The Chicago Association for the International Olympian Games of 1904

If the chief significance for Olympic studies of the Chicago Association for the International Olympian Games (CAIOG)[5] is as the first Olympic bid committee (to use contemporary terms), producing the first Olympic bid book (booklet, actually),[6] its special relevance for the ensuing structuration of

American Olympism lies in the social characteristics and particularities of its composition.

As the first organized body of any kind in American Olympic history, CAIOG had no precedent or model on the Olympic sports side.[7] Charter efforts towards what would eventually become a permanent national Olympic committee were not made until the end of the 1910s.[8] As for Olympic Games delegation management, William Milligan Sloane, distinguished Princeton (and later Columbia) professor of history and inaugural president of the American Historical Association, had been a one-man committee in shepherding a team of U.S. collegians and club members to Athens in 1896.[9] Sloane was an inaugural member of the International Olympic Committee (IOC) and Coubertin's closest international friend and confidant; though he followed and supported Chicago's effort, Sloane played no direct role in the formation or functioning of CAIOG. For the 1900 Games, Albert Spalding had extracted from his friend Ferdinand Peck, the U.S. general commissioner for the Paris Exposition, supervision of the athletic mission, an assignment he endlessly aggrandized in his company's publications. In fact, Spalding had little authority over what was less an organized delegation than a congeries of participating club and college coaches, officials, and athletes, as well as unattached entrants. In Paris, Spalding concerned himself as much with the commercial displays of his sporting goods company as with team affairs.[10] He appointed his publishing company employee James E. Sullivan, also Amateur Athletic Union (AAU) chief, as his Paris deputy, and Sullivan famously took the opportunity to consolidate an intense animosity towards Coubertin and the Europe-based IOC and to begin plotting to overthrow them.[11]

The Furber papers confirm that neither Spalding nor Sullivan had any part in the initial formation of CAIOG, despite the former being the most sports-prominent Chicagoan.[12] As is well known, in the beginning Sullivan was antagonistic to the whole Chicago project, given his grandiose plans for his own "Olympic Games" under AAU control at the Buffalo Pan American Exposition of 1901 and his presumptuous and delusional claims to have replaced Coubertin and the IOC with a new organization.[13] These initiatives coming to naught, Sullivan pronounced himself in favour of Chicago[14] and later insinuated himself, as we shall see, into the umbra of the Chicago committee, where he existed for a time as a double agent for the St Louis exposition, over whose Olympic Games he would himself eventually and fatefully preside. The Furber archive also makes clear what has not previously been appreciated: A.G. Spalding was a chief backstage agent of the transition from Chicago to St Louis.[15]

The actual template for the Chicago Olympic committee was a local one, the 1893 World's Fair organization, not surprisingly since much of the domestic impetus for a Chicago Olympics was to get the city moving again a decade thereafter. "It is the intention of our citizens to render the [Olympic] event as important in a way as was the World's Columbian Exposition."[16] In both organizations, "city fathers" and "civic leaders," that is to say, leading industrialists and professionals (bankers, lawyers, architects) provided the core membership. CAIOG included as active members many of the biggest names in Chicago industry, retailing, and finance. In two other respects, however, CAIOG differed significantly from its 1893 model. First of all, elected politicians played little front-stage role in the Chicago Olympic effort. Of course, the mayor and eventually the governors of Illinois and surrounding states were solicited for expressions of support, but they played no leadership role in either the bid or the organizing committee phases.[17] Instead – and this is the historical feature of CAIOG that must absolutely be marked – university professors and higher-education reformers mainly steered the ship. CAIOG represented simultaneously the apogee and (as we shall see) the swansong of "university men" in American Olympic affairs.

As Coubertin's memoirs note and I have documented, during his 1893 visit to the Chicago world's fair, the would-be founder of the modern Olympic Games visited with William Rainey Harper, the founding president of the new University of Chicago, helping to set the stage for the eventual award of the rights to the 1904 Olympics to a Chicago committee under Harper's active presidency.[18] At the Paris Games in 1900, Amos Alonzo Stagg led a delegation of University of Chicago athletes and discussed a university-based 1904 Chicago Olympics with "European representatives."[19] Harper himself is reported to have been in direct communication with Coubertin on the matter.[20] It is well known in the standard account that it was Henry Furber who pushed Harper in the autumn of 1900 to get on with the candidature process.[21] What has remained opaque until now is whence Furber was coming and why he so interested himself in an Olympic project. In default of any real information, the standard account has implied that Furber was simply an ambitious young hot-shot seizing on any random opportunity to distinguish himself in Chicago public affairs.[22]

In fact, Furber's acquaintance with the Olympics was academic in origin and context and could not have been any closer to a mainspring of Coubertin's Olympic revival. International sport was embedded with other university projects to the end of increasing intercultural education. Furber had pursued graduate studies and was awarded a doctorate in history in Germany, and, as a charter member of the Franco-American Committee in the mid-1890s, he devoted himself to the task of making French universities as accessible to American students as were German ones.[23] This project was completely congruent with the work of Coubertin in comparing and linking American and

French universities and seeking student exchanges among them, as well as with the career of Professor Sloane, Coubertin's closest American interlocutor.[24] President Harper was directly associated as well; indeed, he would become president of the Franco-American Committee (later the Alliance Française) in 1903.[25] Harper's papers contain an 1897 letter from a newspaper editor continuing their discussion of "a movement relating to the influence on a nation of having considerable numbers of its students receive a part of their education in some other land." Enclosed with the letter was a recent clipping from the *New York Evening Post*:

> Baron Pierre de Coubertin, best known as the reviver of the Olympic games, is the prime mover in the effort to extend among the seats of learning in the United States a "juster knowledge of French civilization." In the course of an extended tour in America in connection with the idea of the revival of the Olympic games, he was struck by what he describes as the characteristic prejudice against France arising out of the general ignorance of the best things which Frenchmen have done and said in the world, and the corresponding sympathy for Germany and German scholarship, which results in the departure, year after year, for German universities of hundreds of graduates of American universities and colleges. Unwilling that France should mean to the Anglo-Saxon foreigner only Paris, and Paris only the boulevards or the Moulin Rouge, he associated with him a number of Frenchmen, lay and professional, such men as M. Paul Bourget, the Duc de Noailles, Dr. Pozzi, Prof. Bréal, and the Comte de Rochambeau, in the formation of a society known as the Union Française des Universités d'Amérique, and the other night the first meeting was held [in Paris] in the rooms of the Geographical Society. In the presence of the members and a large assembly of American professors and students, as well as members of the American colony, Baron de Coubertin spoke on the national ideal of the United States, illustrating his lecture by magic-lantern pictures of the leading American universities. Prof. Sloane of Columbia was one of the speakers.[26]

There is evidence that Furber had met Coubertin prior to the Chicago Olympic project, doubtless in connection with their overlapping networks in these international education initiatives.[27] Among the extraordinary roster of Instituteurs and members of the Académie française joining Furber in the "French branch" of the Franco-American Committee were Jules Simon, Coubertin's most important patron, and Michel Bréal, the world-renowned philologist, father of the field of semantics, and a wide-ranging educational reformer. Michel Bréal could not have been closer to the new modern Olympic project. He attended and indeed addressed Coubertin's 1894 Sorbonne Congress that declared the

Olympic revival, and it was Bréal, an Alsatian Jewish professor at the Collège de France, who invented the marathon race, offering Coubertin and the Greeks a silver cup for the winner if in 1896 they would make a modern formal contest of the legendary ancient soldier's run from Marathon to Athens. (As I have elsewhere argued, the charisma of that contest in Athens did more than anything to keep the nascent Olympics alive through the organizational disasters that followed.) Bréal was also a leading member of the inaugural French National Olympic Committee established by Coubertin.[28]

Henri (usually signing himself "Henry") Bréal, Michel's younger kinsman and protégé, was secretary general of the Franco-American Committee and a close friend of Furber. If Furber needed any additional encouragement to pursue an Olympics in Chicago, Henry Bréal provided it, pushing Furber to get Harper going on the project, and serving in 1900–1 as Chicago's chief lobbyist with Coubertin and the French establishment in Paris, working in close concert with Henri Merou, the French consul in Chicago.[29] After the Games were awarded to Chicago, Henry Bréal spent much of the following summer in the city, meeting with Harper, Furber, and CAIOG, reviewing the plans, and reporting enthusiastically back to Coubertin.[30]

Harper's commitment to the Chicago Olympic project was intellectual, moral, and pedagogical, as well as civic institutional in nature. The spatial and temporal congruence of the 1893 World's Fair and the foundation of the university left Harper and his colleagues and donors with a strongly performative sense of institution and city building. The University of Chicago was a private institution, founded with John D. Rockefeller's money, and higher education as a philanthropy of businessmen is marked in the present context by today's University of Chicago buildings and amenities – Noyes, Hutchinson, Vincent, Bartlett, Ryerson – named after industrialists and faculty members who served together on CAIOG committees. But there should be no underestimating Harper's muscular Christianity and his personal and pedagogical commitment to Christian manliness and the strenuous life. It was he who made the archetypical American muscular Christian educator Amos Alonso Stagg one of the first regularly tenured professors of physical culture in the world. Although their joint enterprise in the expansion of college football is much better known, Harper had sent Stagg and his university athletes to the Paris 1900 Olympics, where, as we noted, Stagg promoted the possibility of Chicago Olympics. Moreover, as a professor of classical languages and Biblical studies, Harper was fully in concert with a university version of the philhellenism that in part motivated Coubertin and provided him with a language to dignify the educational and moral mission of modern sport. Although utterly different from the jingoistic and ethnically overdetermined nationalism of persons like Sullivan and Spalding, Harper himself promoted a cosmopolitan version of American patriotism and national strength fully of a piece with his muscular Christianity. While Furber was the man in the trenches, Harper's leadership of CAIOG was anything but academic. He offered the university's grounds and facilities gratis for the Games,[31] and his speeches and appearances helped make the University of Chicago student body the most enthusiastic booster group in the city. Whenever CAIOG seemed to falter, Harper threw more Chicago professors and officers onto its committees. Harper himself was cultivated by the Louisiana Purchase Exposition – being appointed on 18 December 1902 to the advisory board of the fair's International Congress of Arts and Sciences, after having been offered a paying position the previous year as director of exposition congresses – but he was one of the leading Chicago diehards, vowing to Coubertin to fight on for a Chicago Olympics regardless of the odds.[32] Most of his university community followed him in bitterly resisting the transfer to St Louis even as it was being "negotiated" by Furber and Spalding.[33]

CAIOG's initial planning for the para-sport aspects of the festival will be discussed later, but the intense involvement of the university officers and faculty and their ideological commitments to what would come to be known as Olympism would have surely led to a Games with a cultural and educational atmosphere vastly different from that of Paris and from what eventuated in St Louis. There, for reasons we shall see, scholars and university professors were much involved with the wider fair but hardly at all with the Olympic Games themselves. In Chicago, by contrast, the Olympic project was situated from the outset in a university context, and the civic and commercial forces engaged found no occasion to doubt or complain of this. Far from it. In Chicago's elite culture of the period, "downtown" the university was itself perceived as a civic and economic force, just as Harper counted on Chicago's civic ambition and commercial philanthropy to help build the finest research university in the country.[34]

Such a thoroughgoing academic and commercial philanthropic collaboration, with the university men in the ideological and managerial driver's seat, has never been repeated in American Olympic history. Denied fruition in a successful Chicago Olympics, and thereby the possibility of becoming a structuring model for the future, university professors were increasingly driven to the margins in subsequent U.S. Olympic history. Harper was the first and the last university president, and Furber the first and the last international higher-education reformer, to lead an American Olympic bid or Olympic Games organizing committee. After Sloane, no university professor has ever served as an IOC member in the United States. No president or secretary general of the national Olympic committee – today's United States Olympic Committee (USOC) – has ever issued from the arts and sciences faculty of a regular university.

Of course, a number of university men and women over the years have served on specialized committees or on the ceremonial roster of notables transiently connected to constituted Olympic bodies, but the structural point is that, since 1904, such persons and roles have always been marginal to the central fields of power, with their very different social correlates in American Olympic affairs.

After 1904, university leaders were additionally driven from the international sport field by the need to defend their own intercollegiate turf. The history of struggle between the AAU and the National Collegiate Athletic Association (NCAA) has probably been the principal theme in the historiography of U.S. amateur sport, and, until the Amateur Sports Act of 1978, governance issues in the national Olympic committee were deeply inflected by it, giving it another incentive to be wary of academics in Olympic leadership positions. However, specific agents have also played a key role in actively working to keep out the professors and intellectuals, beginning, as we shall see, with the "winners" after the transfer of the 1904 games to St Louis. Consequential contemporary facts, such as the USOC's international reputation across the past thirty years for caring only about money and medals and paying mere lip service to Olympism, cannot be adequately explained, in my opinion, without discovery of the relevant structurations acting over the *longue durée*. My experience at the centre of the Chicago 2016 Olympic bid – the only professor to be found there, incidentally – convinced me that many of the USOC characteristics that soured us with the IOC voters had their constitutive precedents and sources in the 1904 Chicago–St Louis experience.

State Responsibility, Funding, and the Military

The single most structuring condition of U.S. Olympic history has been the refusal of the federal state to engage directly in Olympic affairs by either administering U.S. sports bodies or funding Olympic celebrations. If one seeks a historical point source of this critical development, it too can be found to lie in the Chicago–St Louis transition. In the construction of the standard narrative much ink has been spilled in debating whether Coubertin prevaricated in his memoirs (he did) by claiming that Theodore Roosevelt had made the final decision to move the 1904 Games to St Louis (he did not).[35] Of immensely greater historical importance is the letter that Roosevelt sent on 28 May 1902 addressed to Harper, Crane, Payne, Noyes, and Furber in response to CAIOG's year-long solicitation of federal government support.

> Gentlemen:- I earnestly wish you success in your undertaking. While I regret that the United States can not officially take charge or be responsible for the games,

I shall do all in my power to contribute to their success, and it will give me pleasure to open them and to send to them bodies of United States troops and United States sailors to take part in the contests, in which representatives of the armies and navies of all nations are expected to enter. I hope these exercises will include feats of horsemanship and marksmanship as well as tests of endurance and strength under service conditions.[36]

Here one (long) sentence announces the practices that for the following century would actually determine U.S. government engagement with the Olympic Games hosted by U.S. cities: active moral, rhetorical, and political support and collaboration from the president and government agencies, but no federal management or direct funding ("responsibility"); the U.S. president to open the Games; and federal security personnel on loan for the event. Over the course of ensuing American Olympic projects, U.S. presidential support, lobbying, and even (for Chicago in 2009) delegation leading would be added to the U.S. candidature process, together with Congressional resolutions and international lobbying by government agencies and personnel. Every U.S. Games would indeed be declared open by the sitting president or vice-president. Continuous (and growing) commitment of federal military and paramilitary personnel for security and public safety would come to be joined with extensive diplomatic, customs, commercial, communications, and legal services, eventually amounting to hundreds of millions of dollars in value. However, since these federal services and personnel would always be provided on a value-in-kind basis, the fiction could be (and has been) maintained in the rhetoric of U.S. politicians and lawmakers, the public discourse of American Olympic authorities, and U.S. popular culture that there is no state funding of U.S. Olympics and that American federal taxpayer dollars are never used to pay for them.[37]

Here is a stunning example of the phenomenon of an important policy formulation both seeming to appear from out of the blue and turning out to be definitive in national life. Of course, Roosevelt did not dictate his letter completely offhandedly. His personal passions for sport in its connection with both the individual character building and the martial-national virtues of the strenuous life are too well known to require any further documentation here. Roosevelt was the international icon of the militant colonialist wing of muscular Christianity, deferred to by all in this respect, including Pierre de Coubertin, who dedicated two books to him.[38] Although Roosevelt had no precedent to go on, this being the first Olympic project on American soil, he had been pressed by CAIOG representatives ever since he had assumed the presidency in September 1901, most especially in a face-to-face White House meeting in early May 1902 with Furber and Benjamin Rosenthal.[39] In November 1901

Coubertin had written to Roosevelt – as he had earlier to President McKinley, without response – asking that he accept honorary presidency of the Chicago Olympics. Roosevelt declined by letter of 8 December 1901 on the grounds that he did not wish to "give the unavoidable impression of governmental connection with the Games." He further specified that he took the decision "after consultation with members of the cabinet."[40] In the absence of any further record of Roosevelt's personal deliberations and consultations, this hugely significant historical event, the single most fateful from a structuring point of view in U.S. Olympic history, must itself be understood as notable evidence of the value of the social scientific concept of structuration, that processual combination of individual agency and political projects with particular social and cultural contexts that, in and through the event, becomes reproducible and thereafter governs socio-cultural reproduction.

Awareness of the subsequent history of American Olympic bodies having to search, obsessively and as the very condition of their continued existence, for private funding in the absence of government cash grants has helped to encourage an emphasis on the financial factor in the literature preoccupied with Chicago's 1903 "capitulation" to St Louis.[41] There can be no question of CAIOG's own keen awareness of the multimillion-dollar federal subsidy to the St Louis Exposition, justified chiefly for its trade promotion functions. These financial subsidies were regularly mentioned in CAIOG's communications with Coubertin. David Francis and his colleagues were free to parcel out monies to their fair's Physical Culture Department and its Olympic Games as they saw fit. After his May meetings in Washington, Furber had convinced himself, as he told Coubertin, that "in addition to the appropriations made for the military and naval displays ... the Government of the United States will make us an appropriation of at least $500,000." No such appropriation was forthcoming, yet until the very end CAIOG officials fantasized about a backstage or last-minute federal subsidy for Chicago that would somewhat level the playing field.[42]

At the same time it is a very serious mistake to discount the role of national patriotism, or rather the threat of being accused of a parochial lack of it, in the weakening of Chicago's resolve to fight the Exposition authorities who were bound and determined to eliminate a competing festival in Chicago. Furber became one of the most fearful ones on this score and also joined others in taking seriously the threat of Sullivan to diminish Chicago's Olympian sports contests, through his AAU power and St Louis's pocketbook, sufficiently to have an impact on participation, press interest, and gate revenues.[43] Chicago, more than anywhere, understood the power of a world's fair. To suggest that her city fathers should have known that a free-standing American Olympics could successfully compete would be presentist indeed, there never having been one to contemplate and no Chicagoan having been present in Athens to see an autonomous, if foreign, Olympic Games. One may also posit a certain world's fair solidarity, given the importance of 1893 to Chicago history. In his final letter to Coubertin, vowing to host a Chicago Olympics if the transfer was rejected by the IOC, Harper wrote: "Our only desire was to show a spirit of accommodation to our friends in St. Louis. We did not wish to do anything which would interfere with their work."[44]

This all being said, financing remained a critical issue, and the main point is that it was Chicago that first demonstrated the challenge of funding an Olympic festival independent of a world's fair in the United States, once federal Olympic policy had been articulated by Roosevelt. When that policy became ideologized and proved permanent, becoming what Pierre Bourdieu terms a "structuring structure,"[45] so did the fiscal challenge facing all subsequent American initiatives up to and including Chicago 2016. Whether Chicago 1904 would eventually have pulled off its Games, probably on a reduced scale, cannot ever be known. The record suggests two particular points of fiscal challenge and ambiguity that also would reproduce themselves through subsequent American Olympic history.

Individual and corporate philanthropic donations – the distinction being harder to discern in the different legal environment of the time – were expected to comprise the bulk of Chicago's capitalization. In a 2 May 1901 letter to Casper Whitney, Harper gave a more detailed and intimate portrait of the situation just before Chicago won the rights to the Games.

A large interest has been excited in the minds of Chicago's leading citizens. Actual subscriptions have been pledged, by representatives of different interests, conditional on the entire amount being secured. In order, however, that there should be no doubt about the matter, twenty of the strongest men of the city have signed a paper in which they practically guarantee the money needed for the games. This guaranty, I may say is not in a form which would involve their heirs if they were to die, but I need hardly say that the pledge of men like Mr. Harry Selfridge, of the firm of Marshall Field & Company, Mr. H.H. Kohlsaat, of "The Record-Herald," Mr. E.A. Potter, of The American Trust and Savings Bank, Mr. Volney W. Foster, President of The Union League Club, is sufficiently strong. I am, therefore, from my personal knowledge of the situation, able to give you the strongest assurances that Chicago will do even more than is necessary to make the games a great success. I ought to say that in all of our calculations we have supposed the sum of two hundred thousand dollars necessary to cover the expenses and have been proceeding on that basis.[46]

The funding strategy had an additional aspect, organizing the Chicago Olympics as in part a joint stock company. Charles Crane recruited actual investors from outside the city. At a September meeting in Chicago's Rookery Building, J.R Anthony, Arthur A. Burnham, F.E. Weaver, and P.A. Kirby became the shareholders of record, each holding 5,000 shares with a pledged value of $50,000, for the total capitalization of $200,000 promised in the bid booklet.[47] The Furber papers suggest that a return of 10 per cent had been agreed to on each stockholder's investment. Nothing in the archive indicates that the investors ever went back on their commitment. Indeed, in November 1902, Furber got Coubertin to change the payout formula to the IOC in order to "greatly facilitate the disposition of our stock."[48] At the same time, the absence of bank books or deposit certificates in the archive makes it thus far impossible to know how much (if any) cash was actually handed over (and when) to CAIOG. The same condition obtains with respect to the individual and corporate pledges. CAIOG clearly had enough cash on hand to pursue its planning over two years and to hire a paid executive secretary, but it finished the process with a debt of $10,160.52. As part of the deal to make Chicago succumb, the St Louis Exposition paid most of these debts; CAIOG directors covered $3,000. The final accounting by Rosenthal made no mention of any payments to the stockholders.[49] Either they forsook their claim on a profit, the Games having never taken place, and received back their principal alone or their $200,000 had never actually changed hands in the first place.[50] We simply do not know as yet. In either case, the addition of private, profit-seeking, stockholder-investors to Olympic Games funding strategy has never, to my recollection, been tried again in the United States.

Announcement of the plans and release of the architectural drawings for a new Chicago stadium for the Games caused a bigger sensation in the newspapers than did anything else connected with the 1904 project. The Furber papers make it possible to definitively attribute this huge neoclassical edifice, featuring such radical innovations as a retractable roof, to the architectural firm of Holabird and Roche.[51] What remains opaque in the record is the precise plan for funding this project, which according to an after-the-fact newspaper source required $300,000.[52] If funding was not achieved and this stadium remained unbuilt – there were controversies over the proposed site as well – it is apparent that events would take place instead on a refurbished Marshall Field on the University of Chicago campus.[53] As it turned out, Chicago did not get a lakefront stadium until twenty years later,[54] and main stadium funding remained a defining problematic through the entire subsequent history of American summer Olympic Games projects.[55]

The second half of Roosevelt's 28 May declaration has received only cursory notice in the literature. The importance to CAIOG of leveraging the president's interest in military games and exercises is borne out by the volume of minutes and plans of the CAIOG Military Affairs Committee preserved in the Furber archive.[56] Its 10 June 1902 "Circular No. 1 on the General Outline of the Military Division" foresaw:

> Two branches: the first of contests; the second of conventions. The branch of contests will again be divided into: (1) Contests in general athletics for military contestants; (2) contests or competitive exhibitions in military proficiency of every sort; (3) contests in marksmanship; (4) contests in swordsmanship ... [In the conventions branch] there will ... be not only an interchange of opinions and reports of facts upon the various purely technical topics of military science, but also and particularly upon the physical aspects of military service, as will be especially in keeping with the scope of the Games in general ... There is every ground to expect that many, at least, among foreign powers will send representative organizations to compete, as well as delegates to observe and report upon the exhibitions made in the different competitions.[57]

While it is impossible to predict their eventual shape, particularly the degree of their multinationality, it is clear that, had Chicago gone forward, military contests would have been prominently featured as both medal and demonstration events (as we say today). Whatever Coubertin's IOC might have thought of this, it would have been powerless to intervene. We know that Coubertin himself could not have been entirely unfavourably disposed, going on, as he did, to invent – surely in part under Rooseveltian inspiration – the modern pentathlon that he inserted into the Olympic program for 1912.

I cannot enter here into speculative analysis of the way in which the subsequent course of international Olympic history might have been changed had separate events for serving military personnel (as opposed to their inclusion as national representatives in the regular contests) become established in Chicago, as Roosevelt had insisted and for which CAIOG had actively planned. Suffice it to say, the ideological as well as political impacts would have been highly unpredictable and considerable.[58] Instead, I wish to emphasize here the structuring impact on ensuing American Olympic history of this presidential invitation to circumvent strictures on direct state involvement with the Olympics through a strategy of engagement with the U.S. military. For some reason – ethnographic ignorance, state restriction of information, political discomfort, outright taboo – American Olympic scholarship has not yet come to grips with the systemic characteristics and effects of U.S. military, paramilitary, and state security service engagements with U.S. Olympic institutions across the twentieth century, particularly in the Cold War years.[59] From Olympic athlete provision and preparation to the national Olympic committee's contemporary existence – USOC headquarters and its main training centre today rest on land provided by the U.S. military – the structuring effect of Chicago has in yet another way been pronounced.

The Social Composition of American Olympic Authority

In January 1902 Coubertin sent word to Furber through Bréal of his "distress" that in the Chicago committee "men from sport don't have a sufficiently important place." More than the number of spectators and everything on the "exposition" side, it would be the "excellent organization of the competitions, the number of contestants, and the quality of the contests" that would determine whether Chicago would be an "organizational success," particularly in attracting "European spirits to the idea of Chicago." "It's the sporting world that we have to attract; this is the world for whom the Games were revived; it's this world that includes partisans from all social situations, and above all from among the cultivated [*milieux distingués*] seeing that it's a question of the amateurism that made such a great success at the Athens Games … You could have tens of thousands of spectators for Games among Americans [but] your Olympiad will be a failure in sport history and public opinion if all the nations aren't represented."[60] Perhaps it would have served just as well for Chicago, had her Olympics taken place, but strangely enough Bréal and Coubertin here wrote in advance the epitaph of the St Louis Olympic Games, for most of the European (and South American) sporting world never showed up there, leaving it indeed largely a contest among Americans, and remembered unfavourably for that in sports history.

CAIOG did send promotional delegations to Europe in the summer and fall of 1902, but they mainly aimed their attentions at social and political elites and not at sports bodies. Meanwhile, back in Chicago, efforts were being made to more thoroughly engage leading men of sport in the 1904 Olympic project, and the unintended result would be to help deliver the games into the hands of St Louis. The key figures were Spalding and Sullivan, the two most powerful persons in American sport, both based in New York and neither of them, in the slightest, university men.

Once he had taken over the CAIOG Final Athletics Committee, Spalding moved methodically to reconstitute it with his own sports colleagues from across the country, including a significant AAU presence.[61] Although it is not clear that Sullivan was ever formally made a committee member, his employer kept him closely informed, in the end on Furber's behalf. In April 1902 Sullivan had AAU president Edward Babb write a letter of "hearty good will and cooperation" to Spalding's committee.[62] As long as Sullivan's public statements remained pro-Chicago, the CAIOG leadership treated him as part of their wider team, even when executive secretary A.A. Burnham spread word through the committee in August 1902 that "St. Louis was making love to the AAU," offering financial incentives, and preparing to lay siege to the next AAU meeting in November in New York. Burnham expected Sullivan, as well as the AAU officials who had joined Spalding's committee, to be an ally at that meeting.[63] Spalding's partiality to Sullivan and the AAU is highlighted by an extraordinary letter asking Furber to take up anew, with the IOC, Sullivan's old complaint of having been denied his rightful place as a member of that body because of "friction" with Coubertin. Furber honoured the request but wisely shifted from Sullivan to Babb as the AAU official whom Coubertin ought to appoint to the IOC. Furber also assured Spalding that Coubertin had agreed months earlier that AAU representatives would be invited to the Olympic congress scheduled for Brussels and that any competition rules set there would be purely advisory, American rules obtaining for the sports contests in Chicago.[64]

Anxiety over St Louis grew during the summer among the most active CAIOG members, so much so that they discussed sending a group of directors to have it out directly with Exposition officials in St Louis. Spalding's influence was waxing within the committee in this same period,[65] and his was the leading voice of sanguinity about St Louis. On 2 October John Barton Payne informed Furber in Europe:

> At the insistence of Spalding a meeting was held at the Athletic Club last evening ... A very full and general talk was had covering the whole subject and especially of the St. Louis and A.A.U. features. As might be supposed Spalding was not nearly so much alarmed about St. Louis as was [Final Athletics Committee vice-chairman] Churchill. The meeting was quite satisfactory. Spalding displayed the greatest interest and seemed to have a very comprehensive notion, but wanted to be particularly informed about all our plans, our finances, date when the [sports] meeting would be held, and generally every detail. His idea was that it was idle to attempt to stop St. Louis from having an athletic meet; that perhaps it would be best not to stop it; that if the A.A.U. wanted to have their United States meeting at St. Louis it would relieve us from many embarrassments; that the Championships contested there would be local, while those contested for here would be world. His impression was that we had nothing to fear from the A.A.U. and that by a little diplomacy the matter could be arranged so that one might even help the other. Of course there was much talk but when it was all over it was left like this: Spalding wants to advice himself fully, see just what could be accomplished, and you were to meet him in New York when you landed and then decide definitely what to do ...

The plan which Rosenthal, Noyes and I have discussed of having a committee go to St. Louis will be abandoned for the time, and that will be left in the hands of Spalding as indicated.[66]

Later in October Gordon Strong noted that Spalding, in contrast to other CAIOG members, showed "very little interest" in defending against St Louis by getting the national sports unions in foreign countries like Canada to certify that the International Olympian Games would be the only world championships in 1904.[67] On 18 October Burnham commented to Furber that "Spalding is waiting to confer with you. The St. Louis people are anxious to get him into their athletic features, but he will stay with the [Chicago] games, I am sure."[68]

Spalding wasted no time getting his "diplomacy" going (if it had not already been underway for some time). St Louis sources both before and after the Exposition are clear and consistent in crediting Spalding for playing the chief role in prying the Olympics away from Chicago. Based on a 9 October letter from Spalding to Skiff in the Exposition's executive committee minutes, Dyreson goes so far as to state that "negotiations by two 'Chicago men' – A.G. Spalding and the director of exhibits at the St. Louis world's fair, Frederick J.V. Skiff (who was also a member of the AAU's national organizing committee) – pushed Chicago to yield to St. Louis."[69] As we have just seen from materials in the Furber archive, Spalding certainly did not do this openly. Instead he worked in the fall of 1902 to dampen CAIOG alarm about St Louis, to soften its approach to the AAU, and to block more aggressive anti–St Louis initiatives proposed by his CAIOG colleagues, like negotiating directly with foreign sports unions and sending the Rosenthal-Payne delegation to confront the Exposition leadership.

A confidential letter from Furber to Spalding on 14 November is the nearest direct evidence we have suggesting a conspiracy among these two, Sullivan, and Governor Francis. Furber advises Spalding of his upcoming secret trip to St Louis – "the fact of Mr. Furber's visit was carefully guarded by exposition officials, and it was not generally known until his departure"[70] – the purpose of which was to prepare and issue with Francis a joint communication to the AAU. Spalding was instructed to tell no one but Sullivan, to stay by his New York office phone at the appointed time on 17 November, and to expect that Francis and Furber would "address copies of our joint telegram both to you and Mr. Sullivan." The immediate issue concerned an upcoming AAU vote on the location of its 1904 championships. "In view of the negotiations now pending between St. Louis and Chicago which are not yet sufficiently ripe for publication, neither Governor Francis nor I desire the A.A.U. to take any action in its upcoming meeting, from which inferences may be drawn."[71]

On 26 November Furber sent his famous double letter to Coubertin, one version public, one private, "acquainting [the IOC president] with certain very serious embarrassments arising from a conflict in dates"; requesting that if the Olympian Games were to stay in Chicago, they be postponed until 1905; and half-heartedly suggesting that Chicago would persevere if so ordered by the IOC, while reiterating the undesirability of doing so.[72] Furber followed with a 3 December telegram to Coubertin asking rather presumptuously that, if the IOC granted the postponement to 1905, Coubertin keep the decision secret "until we advise you," so that CAIOG "may secure the best terms from St. Louis." Coubertin was clearly taken aback and on 6 December sent a letter of deepest concern to Harper. The CAIOG chairman answered with a cable, followed up by a letter on 27 December, stating and restating that he was "very sorry that there has been a misunderstanding. The Chicago Committee has been ready and is still ready to go forward with the plans."[73]

Was Furber entirely on his own initiative "negotiating" with the Exposition authorities and the IOC? His papers contain no indication whatsoever of any formal mandate from the CAIOG directors to be doing what he was, and Furber's understanding of the situation obviously differed significantly from Harper's. Harper remonstrated with Furber, forcing him to write to Coubertin on 31 December, apologizing for the "confusion" generated in Paris by Furber's telegram. "My object was to devise a plan for making St. Louis, in case of postponement, as active in supporting us [in 1905] as possible."[74]

Was Furber merely naive and inexperienced in confronting a difficult situation or had he already gone in over his head in his backstage dealings with the Exposition and the AAU? On 11 December, while all of this was occurring, Furber was back in St Louis, and on this trip the Exposition publicly offered to make him the head of its athletics department, inviting him to bring others from Chicago, most particularly Spalding. "Under the direction of President Furber and A.G. Spalding, the latter the chairman of the final athletics committee, much work has been done in a preliminary way [in Chicago] toward preparing for the games and it was with the idea that a transfer at the present time would cause a loss of time, that the position of athletic director was tendered Mr. Furber."[75] Far from feeling embarrassed or compromised by the offer of an Exposition job while the Chicago–St Louis question was not finally settled, Furber talked extensively about the opportunity with the St Louis newspapers.[76]

Other evidence suggests that it was more Spalding than Furber about whom the canny Exposition authorities seriously cared and with whom they engaged. Edward Hoch, an official of the Exposition's division of exhibits, writing in the official *World's Fair Bulletin* in March 1903, just after the transfer had been completed, states unequivocally that the St Louis victory was "largely through the aid of Mr. A.G. Spalding," though A.L. Shapleigh rather than Frederick J.V. Skiff is singled out as Spalding's chief St Louis collaborator.[77] In his St Louis Olympic Games official report, published, naturally, in *Spalding's Official Athletic Almanac*, Sullivan also asserted that the conflict with Chicago had been "averted ... mainly through the instrumentality of Mr. A.G. Spalding and Mr. Frederick J.V. Skiff."[78] Sullivan could have been just flattering his employer, but the backstage facts were clearly known to him, and others had been speaking to the same effect for over a year.

So Spalding clearly played both sides of the street, but was he a fifth column figure within CAIOG, wanting to know all its plans, finances, dates, and "generally every detail" in order to report them to the St Louis Exposition authorities? Perhaps, but absent any documentary smoking gun, I prefer another interpretation. Spalding was a businessman with goods to sell; indeed at that time he was the largest purveyor of sporting goods in the world. He cared about markets above all, wherever they were to be found. On the subject of the social ideology of sport, his biographer has this to say of him:

> [Spalding] could declaim alphabetically that baseball was "the exponent of American Courage, Confidence, Combativeness; American Dash, Discipline, Determination; American Energy, Eagerness, Enthusiasm; American Pluck, Persistence, Performance; American Spirit, Sagacity, Success; American Vim, Vigor, Virility." A.G., however was not a professional reformer, social critic, or moralist. Although he shared many of the sentiments and goals of such people, he was above all a flamboyant entrepreneur, out to enhance his personal fortune, a man who recognized that it was good business to promote sport in terms of its social promise.[79]

Thus, any ideological resemblance between Spalding and figures like Harper, Sloane, Stagg, Roosevelt, or Coubertin was entirely superficial. For them, transnational educational values in the "republic of sport" were rather more than a merchandizing tool.[80] For Spalding, there was a national and increasingly international business to develop; that is what he cared about above all else. To suggest that Chicago and St Louis, or CAIOG and the AAU, might help one another, as Spalding did, should be read, I believe, as a simple acknowledgment that there was money to be made for the Spalding & Brothers Company in each of these locales. Wherever the Olympics took place and whatever form they took, Spalding would be the supplier of the equipment and outfitter of the sports facilities. Most of the expertise and publicity would also issue from within his empire, and he certainly knew how to leverage it all to further build, as we would say today, the Spalding brand.

Indeed, Spalding was the first serious "official supplier" in Olympic history. We cannot quite call him an Olympic sponsor, in the contemporary sense of the term, because his company took; it did not give, except perhaps a few discounts and a little value in kind. Spalding's business interests in the Chicago Olympics took a very different practical form than did those of the CAIOG directors, whose pledges as individuals or companies presented them as firmly within the ambit of civic philanthropy. Not that these industrial tycoons and bankers did not expect a return, but it was in social and political capital, and in economic capital only indirectly through that. (The CAIOG "stockholders" were a different matter.) If the Games went to St Louis, Spalding would be on the more familiar ground of a world's fair. As in Paris, Spalding & Brothers would exhibit their wares and win all the prizes in category, only this time the company would also have a monopoly on outfitting the Olympic installations and a special entrée to athletes and teams as well. Indeed, if one merely wanted to read the official results, one would have to consume dozens of pages of Spalding advertisements to do so. However, if the Olympics were to stay in Chicago, Spalding already had the key athletics committee well in hand, and he was manoeuvring to dominate his status-betters in the general CAIOG organization as well. The planned sporting goods exhibit in Chicago would be smaller and less well attended than a World Fair's, but his Chicago monopoly would be complete. Maybe a free-standing Olympics was a different marketing challenge, but either way Spalding was prepared to win.

Not so for Sullivan. While Spalding liked to play the self-made man when it suited him – the modestly educated sports hero turned entrepreneur – he understood that his success had depended on his mother's capital.[81] James E. Sullivan, however, was the real thing. The son of an immigrant Irish railroad worker, he had grown up hard in New York City, left school at sixteen, was a modest success as an athlete, found a nascent identity as a sports organizer, then got his big break when Spalding hired him to run the American Sports Publishing Company. A lifelong employee, Sullivan depended on his Spalding paycheque to be able to help organize, put himself forward in, and eventually to dominate amateur sports bodies and fixtures.[82] His boss saw business value in Sullivan's administrative work, and the suite of Spalding publications offered Sullivan an unmitigated opportunity for self-promotion in service of his passion to dominate American amateur sport as American sport dominated the world. The Spalding-Sullivan partnership had already laid the foundations for much of the American sports landscape, and now they wanted to add the newish Olympic sport to the hegemony they already possessed over professional and amateur club sport.[83] They had had a practice session in Paris 1900, which they had subsequently aggrandized to their own benefits at the expense especially of university sports leaders like Sloane and Stagg. Now they had the opportunity to take real control over an entire Olympic Games. The duo hedged their bets with Chicago, Spalding by joining CAIOG and Sullivan by professing publicly his support. But Spalding saw a world's fair as his clearer business opportunity, and Sullivan saw his chance to run an Olympic Games however he pleased and to his own public credit.

Sullivan was not formally announced as director of the Exposition's Physical Culture Department and its Olympic Games until July of 1903, receiving the big treatment in the *World's Fair Bulletin* in August.[84] Whether the offer of the same position to Furber the previous December was serious or a feint to further entice this ineffectual man's allegiance, once the transfer was complete and Furber was out of the picture, Sullivan had the St Louis field to himself. Most likely, he had been setting the stage all along with Francis, who had every reason to be grateful for the AAU role in cornering Chicago. Moreover, we have noted testimonies to the influence that Spalding would have had over the decision as to who would run a St Louis Olympics. In fact, Sullivan cleverly managed to leverage Coubertin in getting control for himself in St Louis. With no university men in sight there, perhaps worn down by lobbying such as Furber's, and finally willing to seek a rapprochement with the AAU, Coubertin deputized that organization in the spring of 1903 to take authority over the St Louis Olympics.[85] The AAU would act as the IOC's sub-contractor. The AAU leadership used this to insist that Francis had to appoint an AAU man as director, and Sullivan made repeated trips to St Louis to curry personal favour while keeping the institutional pressure on the Louisiana Purchase Exposition (LPE). Other AAU leaders were volunteers with day jobs. Although they complained of temporizing by the LPE, Sullivan had his way in the end and wasted no time in letting everyone know just how in charge he was.[86]

The higher-educational foundations of the Chicago Games and the presence of Harper and Stagg meant that the colleges would always counterbalance the AAU there, limiting what Sullivan could ever claim for himself. Chicago was further associated with Coubertin and the disrespect and humiliation that Sullivan felt he had received at these European hands. In St Louis he could keep the universities at bay and run things as he saw fit. Coubertin and the Europeans would have no choice but to defer to him.[87] After St Louis, Sullivan would necessarily be the chief man in arranging what would finally become the duly constituted American Olympic Committee (AOC). Sent to the sidelines by the transfer of the Games from Chicago to St Louis, the professors and educators would thereafter find themselves dismissed from American Olympic affairs. We may pause to recall here that a main purpose of Giddens' theory of structuration – and of Bourdieu's closely related understandings of habitus and structuring structures – is to create theoretical space for such individual subjects and their projects, a space missing from classical structural functionalist and Marxist approaches.

John Lucas established our picture of Sullivan's personality and interpersonal style: tough minded, coarse, pugnacious, blunt, no-nonsense, a pragmatist without a shred of cosmopolitanism, given to furious tirades.[88] Sullivan was also deeply class conscious and resentful of anything he took to be status privilege, including especially university education and foreign-language facility. Sullivan's personality and social attitudes sorted out and justified themselves in a fiercely formal and meritocratic rationality. His AAU work was distinguished by a fanatically self-righteous enforcement of the amateur code, his estimation of others by a narrow and uncompromising definition of sports expertise, and his public persona by an "America First" style of braggadocio nationalism. As Steven Hardy perfectly puts it, "Sullivan respected his social superiors only if they deferred to his expertise in sport. The industry could be open to the masses and favored by gentlemen and college presidents, but it should be controlled by middle class expert bureaucrats like James E. Sullivan. Such an attitude blended well with Sullivan's quest for national victory."[89]

Indeed, when aroused, Sullivan did not shrink from identifying the country with his own person. He resented Coubertin because, as he told him, "you have not recognized me in the slightest way in your organization, or, in your good work you have never asked me for my cooperation; you have gone along with the idea that you could get along *without America*." With regard to university educators like Sloane, Sullivan dripped sarcasm and disgust: "Professor Sloane is a lovely gentleman; I have met him once. He knows absolutely nothing about athletics, although he is *an educational man and stands very high*. I doubt if he ever attended an important athletic meeting in America. Certainly he is unknown in the athletic legislative halls of this country, in either college, scholastic or athletic club circles."[90] Of course, those whom he antagonized gave back as good as they got. Sloane wrote that "Sullivan is a ghetto-poor Irish-American, a man whose great faults are those of his birth and breeding, but he is unfortunately *a representative man* and holds the organized athletes of the clubs in the hollow of his hand."[91] That Sullivan's outlandish American nationalism was overdetermined by the second-generation immigrant's fears and self-doubt was further evidenced when he could not resist crowing after the 1906 Athens Games that it was "the pick of Ireland's greatest jumpers who were competing and having their points recorded for Great Britain."[92] The novel American lower-middle-class occupational path of sports administrator was deeply conditioned by urban ethnicity and status mobility. The Irish ascendancy in the politics of Tammany Hall New York and in Chicago – where 80 per cent of aldermanic seats were held by Irish-Americans at the time of CAIOG – was simultaneously an engine of mobility and the object of upper-class Protestant contempt and backlash.[93] As was made apparent in his obituaries, James Sullivan's lifelong contributions to New York's public school sports and Police Athletic League were probably his most sustained and important achievements, but he himself much preferred to tout his AAU and Olympic work.

It is hardly inappropriate, then, that the James E. Sullivan Award has been the top U.S. Olympic honour for nearly eighty years. By taking power in the nascent American Olympic movement in 1902–4, Spalding and Sullivan established a class-located and culturally particular hegemony of leadership that grew permanent as the American Olympic Committee evolved into today's USOC across the next century. To be sure, one can find in this history the occasional representative of old money, the intelligentsia, or progressive internationalism engaged in or near American Olympic leadership, but the domination of politically conservative, upper-middle-class, commercial men in alliance with equally conservative, upwardly mobile sports bureaucrats would prove so thoroughgoing that it has been seriously challenged only now and again by American military men.

Consider only the most dominant successor figure for purposes of illustration. Except for his university degree and modest foreign-language skills, Avery Brundage was a pure combination of Spalding and Sullivan: a former athlete, an amateurism fanatic, a bare-knuckles bureaucratic infighter, an America-firster like Sullivan, but like Spalding a Chicagoan who had made his own independent fortune in business. As for organizational priorities, the AOC, and then USOC, consistently followed the Sullivan path in valuing national Olympic medal counts above all else, while preoccupying itself with raising the money to achieve them and to fund the organization in the absence of direct state investment.[94] Correspondingly, the higher-educational, intercultural, and international peace movement characteristics and aspirations of the Olympic movement have been of only marginal and chiefly rhetorical interest to the USOC over the years and are still today.[95]

The Logic of the Spectacle

Besides the failure to attract international competitors, the St Louis Games are best known today for their denaturing and diffusion of the term *Olympic* to the point almost of comedy. Sullivan's Physical Culture Department scheduled scores of competitions of every sort throughout the fair and insisted on labelling each of them *Olympic*, with the result that a university (my own), a club (the New York Athletic Club), and several other domestic organizations still claim to have "won the 1904 Olympics" (in events that had no foreign competitors).[96] Such was the situation that sorting out the "real" Olympic competitions has required a lot of work and a good deal of anachronism on the part of sport chroniclers.[97] All this betrays what I have elsewhere analysed as the logic and ethos of the spectacle, conceived as a specific genre of cultural performance.[98] In St. Louis the "more is better" ethos of the spectacle triumphed as the encompassing frame of the sports contests for the same reason as in Paris 1900. From each of its departments a world's fair demands as many "attractions" as possible to draw paying customers across the entire duration of the event. Indeed, the international expositions were themselves the prototypical nineteenth-century consolidation of the genre of modern spectacle, gigantic extravaganzas for the visual consumption of multitudes of spectators, aiming to induce in them, above all, the emotions of wonder and awe. Personal political projects intensified this structuration effect in St Louis, namely Sullivan's imperial desire to put his imprimatur on every kind of sport contest – the amateur code being strictly observed, of course – that he could attract to the fair and that his AAU had an interest in later governing. The multiplication of "Olympic" events in turn multiplied the number of visual and potentially commercial consumers of Spalding products, spectacle being the performance genre most congruent with mass consumption capitalism.

Ritual is the cultural performance genre most contrastive with the spectacle,[99] and it is not accidental that the development of Olympic ritual ceased between the two Athens games of 1896 and 1906. Neither Paris nor Sullivan's Olympics had any rituals of note. In St Louis the Opening Ceremonies, if they can even be called that, were multiple, perfunctory, ill attended, and lacking most of the athletic participants. Victory ceremonies were highly variable and ill organized, and there was no highly formalized closing ceremony. How could there be, when the "Olympics" went on and on? It is reasonable to imagine that with Harper committed above all to dignity, with the habitus of academic ritual present to infuse the proceedings, and with a more focused and delimited spatio-temporal format, a Chicago Olympics would have been much more highly developed on the ritual front.[100]

At the same time, the CAIOG planners, and particularly Furber, were hardly free of the intrusive logic of the spectacle.[101] Chicago had not forgotten its world's fair. In order to maintain interest over the course of a month-long Olympic festival and to generate additional tourism and gate receipts, a long roster of ancillary events and exhibitions was imagined for Chicago too.[102] The unifying theme was an exploration of global physical culture and education. Indeed, Sullivan borrowed some of these plans for St Louis, albeit in a typically cruder form.[103] Caspar Whitney publicly implored Furber and CAIOG to avoid surrendering to the logic of the spectacle, to "not forget their classical reading, and seek to make an Athletic Midway out of these traditional games. There is significance in the retention of the original simple programme, significance and sentiment … *The Olympics need no side shows*."[104] When word came of the transfer to St Louis despite his opposition, Whitney knew that the "deplorable" business aspect was chiefly to blame, and he tore into CAIOG for being seduced by it.

> The conduct of the Chicago committee that originally pleaded for the Olympian Games, and subsequently had arrangements in hand for their holding, is strikingly illuminative of the commercialism which attaches to any venture in the field of sport *by certain types of Americans*. It was not enough for these Chicago committeemen that they had been granted these historic games; it was not enough to hold the simple games on the traditional lines redrawn eight years ago on the first revival at Athens, and repeated (rather poorly) at Paris four years later; not at all; the Chicago gentlemen seized upon it as an opportunity to advertise themselves and their city; they scented a chance to boom business, to attract the country merchant to town, perhaps to make money. They would make the Olympian Games the side show to a huge vaudeville, to a congress of performers gathered from the corners of the earth to attract the country merchant. But this was exactly what St. Louis was very properly planning to do for its Fair; and as St. Louis was not to be denied, Chicago surrendered as a fitting close to utter and needless failure on top of an ignorant conception of the Olympian Games. Had the Chicago committee been content to abide by the traditional lines it was the wish of the International Committee to perpetuate, the Games could have been held in Chicago with success.[105]

Whitney's critique – as penetrating today of American Olympic affairs as when he uttered it – most certainly captured the drift of many in CAIOG's larger circle into the logic of the spectacle, as against the logics of ritual and game. But Whitney underestimated the push-back that would eventually come from Harper, Stagg, and other university and civic arts leaders. In St Louis there was no one at all to push back. From a cultural performance point of view Chicago would surely have differed in a more integrated direction. The mere presence of real ritual upon which the educators would have insisted would have made its performance system both more complex and more nested, as I have elsewhere defined these terms.[106]

Sullivan himself had guilty intimations of the problem of spectacular diffusion. In his official report on the St Louis Games he wrote: "Early in the season, the Department of Physical Culture was notified that it was the desire of the

International Olympic Committee that all sports that were to be given under the auspice of the LPE must bear the name 'Olympic,' and as a result Olympic championships in different sports were announced." This is an outright and self-defensive prevarication. There is no evidence of any such instruction coming from Coubertin, and the notion of him issuing such an instruction – in effect, to repeat Paris in the extreme – is absurd. At best, Sullivan was asserting that the American IOC members never objected. Sullivan further defended the multiplicity of "Olympic" competitions on the grounds of American egalitarianism: "Owing to the conditions in America, particularly the athletic conditions, and the advanced stage we are now in, the Olympic games were held for many classes."[107] That such competitions and exhibitions were held during the fair is unobjectionable; that Sullivan labelled all of them "Olympic" was the spectacular affront.

After he had seen the 1906 Athens Games first-hand, Sullivan got the point and repented in an important statement that is far too little known among Olympic historians. "The Olympic Games at St. Louis had been a pronounced success athletically and we had a large audience, but now that I have been in Athens I can see how poorly we managed the Olympic games of St. Louis in 1904 and at Paris in 1900. They were not Olympic Games at all; merely International athletic meetings. I am convinced that we learned a lot at Athens in 1906."[108] What he learned, in my interpretation, is the necessity of limited spatio-temporal focus on one social type of international competition and the necessity of encasing the athletic contests within evocative ritual performances that reproduce the universal paradigm of rites of passage. Sullivan came to understand the destructive effects of an unfettered logic and ethos of the spectacle. The struggle continues today.

Chicago 1904 and Chicago 2016

Between 2006 and 2009 hundreds of Chicagoans and extramural experts and allies sought to bring the Olympic Games of 2016 to Chicago. Chicago–St Louis 1904 was seldom mentioned during this process, and certainly never in front of the IOC members. Hill & Knowlton, the public relations firm that dictated a great deal of Chicago's strategy,[109] had convinced the leadership that "since Chicago had given up the Games in 1904," it was wise never to mention that part of the city's Olympic history to the IOC voters. When the only professor on the committee – and the only Chicagoan whom the IOC knew when the city's new bid process commenced – protested that many IOC members knew and understood the history better than the committee and most Chicagoans did (except those few who had visited the 2004 Hellenic Museum exhibition), he was overruled. Instead of mentioning how much better off the Olympic movement might have been had the Games stayed in Chicago in 1904 and been independent of a world's fair for the first time since Athens, the bid books and other promotional materials were intentionally silent on Chicago's real Olympic history. When the IOC Evaluation Commission was given its formal tour of Chicago as a potential Olympic city, the sites associated with Coubertin's visit, CAIOG, and the planned Olympics were never even pointed out, even as the motorcade passed by or through them. Owing to the controversies surrounding his tenure as IOC president, Avery Brundage also received the silent treatment; visiting IOC members were never shown the hotel headquarters from which Brundage ran the global Olympic movement for decades.[110]

The irony is that Chicago–St Louis 1904 could not have been more present for Chicago 2016. The 1904 Games may have been tabooed in discourse, but the core "structuring structures" of American Olympic affairs that I have traced in this paper governed much, if not most, of what Chicago 2016 confronted. There were differences and variations, of course. Structures organize the contextual possibilities; they do not mechanically determine outcomes. Unlike CAIOG and the LPE Physical Culture Department, and like New York 2012, the Chicago bid was called into being and managed backstage by an elected politician, Mayor Richard Daley. Selected by the mayor to run the bid committee on a volunteer basis was a self-made insurance tycoon, Pat Ryan, a billionaire with a strong record of civic philanthropy supporting flagship arts institutions and private universities. He was also a sport man, with an ownership interest in a Chicago professional team, and his name on the football stadium at Northwestern University, though he had had nothing to do previously with Olympic sport and would be in for repeated shocks in dealing with the USOC. The paid staff consisted for the most part of migratory Olympic technical experts (nonexistent in 1904) and a few local professionals. Much of the work was actually accomplished on a pro bono basis by Chicago corporations, who also seconded their executives to the bid committee, where they were joined by scores of volunteers.

Why such a complexity (and often confusion) in staffing? Because of an underlying structural fact with which we have become familiar: no government funding or staffing by regular government officials. Chicago's rivals, by contrast – Tokyo, Madrid, and Rio – had most of their bids paid for by federal, state, and city governments, and much of their bid work was done within government ministries. That is the global norm; the United States is the global exception. Chicago 2016 raised $72.8 million over a forty-two month period, nearly all of which came from individual and corporate donations. An additional $16.2 million came in as corporate value-in-kind contributions. The

Chicago mayor had promised that no local public funds would go into the bid, though the city did purchase the land that would have been the site for the Olympic village, and some city services for bid-related events went unreimbursed. While this private fundraising capacity was admired by some IOC members, many others remained sceptical about scaling it up to fund an Olympic Games. Few IOC members today are anti-commercial and anti-corporate per se, but many remember Atlanta unfavourably as the Games where the constant pressure of corporate fundraising and budgetary shortfalls was widely believed to have led the Atlanta OCOG to cut back on important games services for the "Olympic Family." No one wanted a repeat of that experience, and the IOC's technical evaluation commission judged Chicago 2016's commercial fundraising targets as "ambitious" – diplomatic speak for "don't count on it." Meanwhile the national governments of rival cities were basically offering blank cheque guarantees.

The Chicago 2016 bid committee, of course, knew that the U.S. government contribution would actually be in the hundreds of millions of dollars for security and public safety and that Chicago had every likelihood, particularly with an Obama White House, of receiving over a billion dollars in additional federal grants for transportation improvements, as happened most recently for Salt Lake. But the IOC only allows funds in hand or legally committed to figure in bid committee financial proposals, and in the United States the actual federal financial outlays for the Olympics are not too loudly bruited about, lest politicians get cold feet about seeming too eager to violate our culturally enshrined "national tradition." After Los Angeles 1984, Atlanta 1996, and Salt Lake 2002, IOC members are perfectly aware of these American traditions, but that does not mean that they understand or approve of them. Many who issue from state-centred sports systems argue quite openly that if America really cared about Olympic sport and the Olympic Movement, then the government would directly and openly invest in them. To counter such sentiments, President Obama announced the opening of a White House Office of Olympic and Youth Sport led by Valerie Jarrett, his close adviser and a former Chicago 2016 officer.[111] In a first for a U.S. president, Mr. Obama also travelled with the first lady to Copenhagen, where both spoke during Chicago's final presentation.

Then there was the vexing matter of the USOC. Since the passage of the Amateur Sports Act in 1978, the professionalization of Olympic sport, the take-off of Olympic television rights revenues, and the IOC initiation of worldwide commercial sponsorships, the USOC has been in a struggle with the IOC over the division of Olympic revenues. To make a long story short, the USOC has been living for some time from its cut of IOC television and sponsorship contracts through a series of sweetheart deals stretching back to the 1980s.[112] Against a background of general international Olympic discontent with a USOC seemingly interested only in American money and medals, often led by monolingual chauvinists, and uninvolved with the institutions of a wider Olympism, leading IOC factions rebelled, demanding that the USOC's cut of Olympic revenues – "more than all the other NOCs combined" – be radically reduced. As Chicago was bidding for the Olympics, the USOC was refusing even to negotiate, and under the presidency of Peter Ueberroth indeed seemed to be delighting in its defiance of growing Olympic Family opinion. As the leadership of the anti-USOC faction in the IOC liked to put it, "if your government won't fund you, that's your problem, not the IOC's." To the gratification of Chicago, Ueberroth was eventually eased out, but an agreement to postpone the revenue-sharing discussions until after the decision on the 2016 host city had been made in Copenhagen in October 2009, satisfied next to no one outside the USOC.

Meanwhile the president and the executive director of the USOC who were appointed in the heat of final battle were persons with no international Olympic experience, no standing in the Olympic sports community, and only corporate success to their supposed credit, which reinforced every stereotype of American Olympic leadership going back to its roots in the period I have been analysing in this chapter. A new and very effective USOC international relations department staffed by persons who were in every way different was insufficient to overcome many IOC members' distaste at the thought of gratifying the USOC leadership by voting for another American Olympic Games. As a key IOC member put it to me after Chicago had garnered only eighteen votes and was eliminated in the first round, "this was not a defeat for Chicago, you had the best technical bid. This was a defeat for the United States Olympic Committee." It was a defeat whose deepest roots extend back to the same town in the first years of the twentieth century.

NOTES

1 A text of John Findling will be discussed below. More typical of the period was a quasi-academic volume by amateur historian George Matthews (*America's First Olympics: The St. Louis Games of 1904* [Columbia: University of Missouri Press, 2005]), occasioned by the centennial of the St Louis Olympics. With respect to matters of direct concern in this essay, no new archival sources made their appearance in this text. Matthews's summary narrative of the events of the transition – reasonably reliable until it declines into boosterism masquerading as revisionism in the claim that the St Louis Games were actually a rousing success – is based entirely on stitching together earlier academic sources (with inadequate citation). These

included bits of my own work *This Great Symbol: Pierre de Coubertin and the Origins of the Modern Olympic Games*, 2nd edition (London: Routledge, 2007), and, more notably, work by the physical educationists: Robert Barney, "Born from Dilemma: America Awakens to the Modern Olympic Movement, 1901–1903," *Olimpika* 1 (1992): 92–135; John Lucas, "Early Olympic Antagonists: Pierre de Coubertin versus James E. Sullivan," *Stadion* 3, no. 2 (1979): 258–72; and Bill Mallon, *The 1904 Olympic Games* (Jefferson, NC: McFarland, 1999).

2 What I am calling the Olympic studies agenda consists in taking the series of Olympic Games as the orienting events and generating a historical narrative that carries from one to and through the next, a narrative centred on Coubertin and the International Olympic Committee (IOC). Local actors and contexts appear, of course, but their concerns and projects are rarely of as much intrinsic interest as are the development and consolidation of the central international bodies and practices we know today. John Lucas's work has certainly been concerned with the evolution of American Olympic institutions, but it really does not depart from this paradigm, and it is proudly innocent of social scientific conceptualizations. Mark Dyreson's writing might be taken as an exception, but for this reader his concept of nationalism is so generic as to be of little help in differentiating specific class fractions and social projects in the structuration of American Olympic institutions. See Dyreson, "The Playing Fields of Progress: American Athletic Nationalism and the St. Louis Olympics of 1904," *Gateway Heritage* 14 (Fall 1993): 4–23, and "'America's Athletic Missionaries': Political Performance, Olympic Spectacle, and the Quest for a National Culture, 1896–1912," *International Journal of the History of Sport* 25, no. 2 (2008): 185–203. The official IOC centennial history – *The International Olympic Committee: One Hundred Years*, 3 vols. (Lausanne: Imprimeries Réunies, 1994) – turns scholarly and professional in its later volumes, edited by Otto Schantz, Fernand Landry, and Magdaleine Yerlès, but Yves-Pierre Boulongne's treatment of our period in the first volume is riddled with errors.

3 The Henry J. Furber Jr papers (hereafter HFP) are held in the special collections of the Neville Public Museum of Brown County in Green Bay, Wisconsin, the Furber family seat. They consist of four boxes, under the accession numbers 33–57–4/2146, 3576/2355, 3355–2/2146. (Folders 1–3 in box 3 are not relevant here, as they concern Furber's later involvement with the invention of the phonotelemeter, a device for detecting submarine batteries.) I wish to thank the Neville curator of collections, Louise Pfotenhauer, and archivist Jacqueline D. Frank for facilitating my study of the HFP in the spring of 2004. According to Neville Museum records at the time, I was the first Olympic scholar to research this archive.

In preparation for an exhibit on the 1904 Chicago Olympic project that ran from 23 May to 14 November 2004 at the Chicago Hellenic Museum and Cultural Center, mounted to honour the Athens Olympic Games, I set our advisory group the task of locating the Furber archives. Although often referred to by Olympics writers as lost, non-existent ("Furber left none of his private papers to posterity": Barney, "Born from Dilemma," 96), or even "destroyed" (Gary Allison, personal communication, 1988), the collection has long been listed in specialized standard librarian's references (Wayne Wilson, personal communication, 2004. See for example, Ed Talent, *Library Journal/Archives USA* [New York: Chadwyck-Healey, 1999]). Our contact with the archive, however, came about in another way. Noting that the Furber family was from Green Bay, Hellenic Museum curator Alison Heller chanced a call to her Neville Museum colleague Louise Pfotenhauer. Heller and Professor Rose Economou of Columbia College visited Green Bay in late winter of 2004 to cull documentary artifacts from the collection for exhibit in Chicago, including the first Olympic "bid book(let)," the original ceremonial stock certificate, and key letters of Pierre de Coubertin and Henry Furber. (In 2008, for reasons never provided, Neville refused requests from the Chicago 2016 Olympic bid committee for loan of these same materials.) Economou and Heller left professional historical analysis of the archive to me, a francophone, Coubertin biographer, and Olympic history specialist.

Alerted to the location of the Furber papers by our Hellenic Museum exhibition, John E. Findling, a now-retired professor of history at Indiana University Southeast, published in October 2004 "Chicago Loses the 1904 Olympics" in the *Journal of Olympic History* 12, no.3: 24–9. A casual reader might come away with the impression that Findling had actually visited the archive to prepare his article. A careful reader, however, would have noted that he twice misidentifies the collection's site as the "Nevill Green Museum" and cites materials from it only as "Henry J. Furber Papers" without any professional citation data. Moreover, his assertion to the contrary notwithstanding (p. 25), his narrative relies more on newspapers than on materials from the archive. Professor Findling has kindly clarified that he had not visited Green Bay before publishing his text and that the archival materials he cites came from what he saw at the Hellenic Museum exhibit. He did spend some time in the archive at the end of April 2005 and two days later gave a modestly revised version of his paper at the meetings of the North American Society for Sport History in Green Bay. The differences between his texts, he reports, were not so great as to merit a new publication (John E. Findling, e-mail personal communications, 8–9 August 2010.) The agenda of Findling's article was a purely Olympic studies one. Relying on one outdated journalistic source (Lord Killanin and John Rodda, *The Olympic Games* [London: Barrie & Jenkins, 1975]) as "the standard Olympic history," and an encyclopedia entry (C. Robert Barnett, "The Games of the Third Olympics," *Encyclopedia of the Modern Olympic Movement*, ed. J.E. Findling and Kimberley Pelle [Westport, CT: Greenwood Publishing, 2004]) that does mention some of the specialized scholarship, Findling sought to rectify, where he could, the "traditional narrative" of the Chicago–St Louis transfer. Although his conclusions are generally left in the form of rhetorical questions, one of them – that Chicago had certainly not been inactive since the award of the games, a feature of the standard account – is most certainly borne out by a full study of the HFP.

4 There being no space here for a theoretical discussion, I deploy the concept in its orthodox usage, emphasizing in my presentation the duality of structure, that is, the mutual constitution of the projects of individual agents and social and cultural rules and resources. See Giddens, *The Constitution of Society: Outline of a Theory of Structuration* (Cambridge: Polity Press, 1984).

5 This is the proper, letterhead name that the Chicago project gave to itself upon formal establishment. The members variously referred to themselves as the "committee for" or "association for" this project. CAIOG is my own shorthand. Coubertin actually wrote to Furber on 13 November 1901 to "call your attention to the inconvenience of the title chosen: 'International Olympian Games Association' brings forth the idea of a permanent association such as is our committee, not of an association specially formed to hold the Games of 1904." HFP, box 3, folder 4. Hence the subsequent inclusion of 1904 in the title. St Louis later changed *Olympian* to *Olympic* in proper preference for Hellenic over Latinate usage.

6 No formal candidature process existed for the 1896 Games, much less any organized bid committees. After backstage conversations, the incipient IOC simply awarded the first modern Games to Athens. See MacAloon, *This Great Symbol*, 167–79; Konstantinos Georgiadis, *Olympic Revival* (Athens: Ekdotike Athenon, 2003), 73–7. No formal candidatures appeared for what became Paris 1900, and Coubertin's self-constructed proto-organizing committee was quickly put out of business by the French and Paris City governments acting through their world's fair commissions. The 1896 Athens Games certainly relied on private philanthropy, but they were in the end, like 1900 Paris, a state project. Chicago, by contrast was almost entirely a private sector and civil society project, a necessary and fateful development, as we shall see.

    Two copies of the formal Chicago prospectus or bid booklet are known by me to exist, one in the Furber archive (HFP box 1, folder 2), and the other in the IOC archives in Lausanne (folder: 1904 Olympic Games, Chicago/St. Louis). The document was officially prepared by the Chicago committee, forwarded to Paris with copies to Coubertin and chief Chicago lobbyist Henry Bréal on 1 May 1901, and formally presented by American IOC member Theodore Stanton to the IOC session in Paris on 21 May 1901. The session unanimously voted the Games to Chicago.

    The cover letter accompanying the prospectus (HFP box 1, folder 2) was signed by Harry G. Selfridge (department store magnate), E. Fletcher Ingalls (professor of medicine and comptroller of Rush Medical Center), Frank O. Louden (lawyer and later Illinois governor), James H. Eckles (lawyer, bank president, and former U.S. comptroller of the currency), William A. Giles (manufacturer), John Barton Payne (lawyer, former Superior Court judge, and later U.S. secretary of the interior), Volney W. Foster (president of the Union League Club), William R. Harper (president of the University of Chicago), Benjamin J. Rosenthal (merchant, real estate tycoon, and philanthropist), H.J. Furber Jr, Chas. L. Hutchinson (treasurer of the University of Chicago and director of the Art Institute of Chicago), H.H. Kohlsaat (newspaper magnate), and E.A. Potter [*sic*, Porter] (bank president).

This letter is remarkable for Olympic historians in that it offers the first direct financial incentives to the IOC itself. "We further agree that all gate receipts and other revenues derived from holding of said games, over and above moneys thereon and in connection therewith actually expended plus % 10 [*sic*] per annum for the term of the investment, shall, in the manner set forth in the said prospectus, become the property of the International Olympian [*sic*] Committee." Chicago concluded by offering to cover all IOC members' expenses for travel to and attendance at the Games in Chicago, another first. Coubertin later agreed to reduce the financial commitment to the IOC to a lump sum payment of $25,000 "to be paid out of our gate-receipts after discharging all other obligations," in response to a request from Furber, stipulating that the IOC did not wish to be seen as trafficking in gate-receipts and would "gladly surrender ... all claim to pecuniary benefit if the coming games require it." Furber to Coubertin, 1 October, 6 October 1902; Furber, Report on 1902 European trip, HFP, box 3, folder 5.

7 Newspapers in this early period might casually refer to an American Olympic Committee, as the *New York Times* did on 28 July 1900 (Barney, "Born from Dilemma," 122), but the fact that the paper included Sloane, Whitney, and Sullivan as "members" demonstrates that there was no such organization. These three did meet in New York with Coubertin on his American trip, and on that basis, Sullivan, source for many later quotes, tendentiously hypostasized the grouping into "the American Olympic Committee of the International Olympic Committee" in order to buttress his claim to have been appointed an IOC member. Some recent U.S. Olympic Committee official histories have backdated the organization's foundation to include this fictitious entity, and, alas, some historians have naively followed along.

By *formally organized*, I mean incorporated and legally registered, with an established board of directors, officers, and (at least pledged) stockholders. Coubertin himself was so impressed that he published in French these details and even part of the organizational chart from the Chicago prospectus. Coubertin, "Courrier de Chicago," *Revue Olympique* 4 (1901): 55–7.

8 20 January 1906 is one date reasonably identified for the real foundation of the American Olympic Committee, though, by my definition of formal organization, the process stretched into the next decade. See John Lucas, "Casper Whitney," *Journal of Olympic History* (May 2000): 30–8.

9 MacAloon, *This Great Symbol*.

10 Peter Levine, *A.G. Spalding and the Rise of Baseball: The Promise of American Sport* (Oxford: Oxford University Press, 1985), 88.

11 Casper Whitney complained in advance of the "bungling" represented by the appointment of the Spalding-Sullivan team for Paris, ensuring that "whatever athletic representation America will have in Paris will be sent by individual colleges." *Outing* 36 (April–September, 1900): 98–9. Without calling out Sullivan by name, Whitney later mocked his pretensions at claiming to replace the IOC (of which Whitney had become a member), as well as the general standing of the AAU in comparison with the intercollegiate world in the production of high-level amateur sport. *Outing 37* (October 1900–March 1901): 473–5.

12 Furber did, however, propose Frank W. Gerould of the A.G. Spalding Company and George K. Herman, secretary of the AAU's western section as members of the Committee on Preliminary and Local Athletics two months after the award of the Games to Chicago. Furber to Harper, 9 August 1901, University of Chicago Library Special Collections, University Presidents' Papers, 1889–1925, box 50, folder 13 (hereafter, WHP). By December 1901, however, Spalding had managed to insert himself into CAIOG. Levine, *A.G. Spalding*, 98, citing a newspaper notice.

13 John A. Lucas, *John Apostal Lucas: Collected Essays* (Lemont, PA: Eifrig Publishing, 2009), 42–3.

14 Barney, "Born from Dilemma," 99.

15 Findling ("Chicago Loses," 24, 29) notices this.

16 Furber to Dr William T. Harris, 5 March 1902, HFP box 3, folder 4.

17 Mayor Carter Harrison Jr was at this period of his career widely associated with the tolerance of urban vice. The Chicago civic luminaries may well have preferred to avoid direct association with him. The young William Hale Thompson, newly elected alderman, served on the Preliminary Athletics Committee and did lead the political effort to have the proposed stadium approved. Thompson later became Chicago's most corrupt mayor, a pawn of Al Capone and organized crime. Other city officials were appointed to relevant committees, such as the chief and assistant chief of police and the fire marshal to the Public Order Committee.

18 MacAloon, *This Great Symbol*, 164–5. Pierre de Coubertin, *Mémoires Olympiques* (Lausanne: Bureau international de pédagogie sportive, 1931), 15, 61, 63. Coubertin's claim forty years later that during their 1893 visit Harper compared his new university's efficiency to that of the Pullman Railroad Company has always seemed suspect to me, an imaginative conflation of Coubertin's visit on the same day to the Pullman industrial community. John Boyer, leading Harper scholar and present dean of the University of Chicago College, agrees that the purported remark seems most un-Harper-like (personal communication, 2008).

The Harper and Stagg papers at the University of Chicago Library Special Collections Department were first reviewed for Olympic materials in the 1980s by my

student Byron Trott, now an accomplished Chicago financier and leading supporter of the Chicago 2016 Olympic candidacy, and again, in 1992, by Jill Dupont,
then a graduate student, now professor of history at the College of St Scholastica.
I provided this file of archival materials to Robert Barney, who used them extensively for his articles on the second Olympiad. While Professor Barney was kind
enough to thank us privately, he neglected to mention in print the role especially
of Jill Dupont's archival research in providing him with his primary sources from
these archives.

19 "Greek Games for the City in Year 1904: President Harper Hopes to Secure
Next Series of Olympian Contests for the University of Chicago," *Times-Herald*,
11 November 1900.

20 Ibid. "It has only been known to a few of Dr. Harper's friends that he has been in
communication with Baron Coubertin, but those who have been made acquainted
with the plans proposed assert that President Harper is in earnest in his endeavor
to make Chicago the mecca of the world's greatest athletes." *Times-Herald*,
11 November 1900. No further record of this communication has yet emerged, to
my knowledge, from either the Harper or the Coubertin archives.

21 On 19 October 1900, Furber received a letter from Henry Bréal renewing his earlier
calls for serious action from Chicago, this time in light of efforts by representatives
of the University of Pennsylvania to secure the 1904 Games. In his own letter to
Harper on 30 October, Furber noted the disinformation coming from Sullivan concerning Buffalo, quoted Bréal's information about the University of Pennsylvania,
and relayed Bréal's outline of what a bid prospectus from Chicago should look like.
This important letter makes plain the proximate origin of the project – "Consul
Merou of Chicago, at present in Paris, and Mr. Bréal, as well as myself, have
undertaken to create a movement in favor of Chicago" – and pressed Harper that
"a committee such as we already have considered, be appointed at once; in order
that we may formulate some definite plan of action and be able to follow up our
somewhat general declaration of intentions by a definite proposition." In response,
on 1 November, Harper appointed members of his faculty – George E. Vincent,
A.A. Stagg, Frank F. Abbott, Shailer Matthews, and O.J. Thatcher to join Furber,
Merou, and Bréal on the nascent bid committee. The original committee therefore
consisted, to echo my main interpretive point, of six university professors, two
higher-education reformers, and one intercultural diplomat; the commercial and
professional elites were added subsequently. Furber to Harper, 30 October 1900;
Harper to Furber, 1 November 1900, WHP, box 50, folder 13.

22 Matthews, following Barney, can do no better than speculate that the Chicago bid
derived from city elites, including Furber, excitedly reading newspaper accounts
of University of Chicago athletes' doings in Paris 1900. Matthews, *America's
First Olympics*, 9; Barney, "Born from Dilemma," 97. Barney notes Henry Bréal's

position on the Franco-American Committee but is unaware of the committee's mission, Furber's membership and devotion to its agenda, and its intersection with Pierre de Coubertin.

23 The American branch of the Franco-American Committee included eight university presidents, the U.S. commissioners of education and labour and other federal officials, and scientific society presidents. Henry Bréal to Furber, June 1900, HFP, box 3, folder 4.

24 Pierre de Coubertin, *Universités transatlantiques* (Paris: Hachette, 1890).

25 WHP, box 3, folders 17–18.

26 W.L. Eaton to William Rainey Harper, 2 April 1897, WHP, box 50, folder 13. Coubertin was a prolific founder of organizations and committees. To my recollection, the Union Française des Universités d'Amérique has not previously been noted in the literature. It does not seem to have endured for long. Aside from an overlapping agenda and membership, further information on the precise relationship between this body and the Franco-American Committee is lacking.

27 In a letter to Coubertin on 2 March 1903 Furber states that "one of the most gratifying results of my connection with [the Chicago Olympic project] has been the pleasure of *renewing our acquaintance*." Furber to Coubertin, HFB, box 4, folder 1, emphasis added.

28 For the legend and the inaugural marathon see MacAloon, *This Great Symbol*, 225–41. For Coubertin and Bréal, see Coubertin, *Une Campagne de vingt-et-un ans, 1887–1908* (Paris: Librairie de l'éducation physique, 1909): 89–98, 121–2.

29 An important feature of the HFP is its collection of letters from Merou to Coubertin reporting and commenting on the progress of CAIOG through most of its existence. While a complete analysis will be postponed to another occasion, this correspondence, together with Coubertin's previously unknown letters to Furber and Merou offering a stream of advice, put paid to the impression in the standard narrative that Coubertin was uninformed of and uninvolved in Chicago's preparations. How much he understood and how helpful he actually was are, of course, different questions.

30 Coubertin, *Revue Olympique* 4 (1901): 57. Coubertin to Furber, 13 November 1901, HFP, box 3, folder 4.

31 Harper to the Olympian Games Committee of Chicago, 1 May 1901, WHP, box 50, folder 13.

32 See John J. MacAloon, ed. *Muscular Christianity in Colonial and Postcolonial Worlds* (London: Routledge, 2008), and *This Great Symbol*; John W. Boyer, *"Broad and Christian in the Fullest Sense": William Rainey Harper and the University of Chicago* (Chicago: University of Chicago Press, 2006); Robin Lester, *Stagg's University* (Champaign: University of Illinois Press, 1999). For Harper's St Louis appointments, WHP, box 6, folder 21. Harper was a leading intellectual and

university figure of the time, but coming at the height of the Chicago–St Louis struggle and juxtaposed with the offer of a paying job in the exposition administration to Furber, it might appear that the timing was not altogether fortuitous. In fact, however, David Francis had tried throughout 1901 to recruit Harper to the exposition as director of its Department of International Congresses, making him a formal offer of the position on 23 November, at a salary of $8,000 and allowing him to apportion his time between Chicago and St Louis as he saw fit. In a letter to his brother on 3 December Harper refers to a $10,000 salary and choosing university colleague Albion Small as vice-director, while also noting that "Mr. Rockefeller does not seem quite willing." WHP, box 6, folder 20; box 32, folder 22.

33 For example, after impassioned speeches by Professor Maxime Ingres and alumni association officials loudly decrying the possibility of losing the Games, a mass meeting of students in early December passed a unanimous formal resolution demanding of the IOC that the athletic festival remain in Chicago. *The Daily Maroon*, 5 December 1902.

Several newspapers had been editorializing to the same end. For example, the *Chicago Daily News* (14 November 1902) wrote prophetically: "Should Chicago now announce that it had decided to pass the Olympian games along to another city, the Europeans who are interested in the enterprise would be likely to resent or at least to misinterpret the action. If by any mischance the games in St. Louis should fall short of success the blame of necessity would fall on Chicago. Can Chicago afford to run the risk of bringing a great international enterprise to possible disaster through its failure to discharge the responsibility placed upon it?" The *Chicago Record-Herald* (23 November 1902) acknowledged that the CAIOG officials had "shown that they too feel the appeal which St. Louis made on the grounds of patriotism." Then the article proceeded, with great perspicacity as it turned out, to illuminate all the reasons St. Louis would be a poor host.

The indefatigable Henri Merou gave a long interview to the *Chicago Record-Herald* (1 December 1902), reviewing his entire engagement in the Chicago Olympic project and insisting yet again on why Chicago was preferable to St Louis for the Games. Newspaper sentiment was not entirely unanimous, however. The *Inter Ocean* (14 November 1902) editorialized that Chicago "can afford to be generous" because she is now "the intellectual and financial capital of an empire and her interests are those of the great middle West which is tributary to her."

34 Nowhere in the FHP can I detect any town-and-gown tensions within CAIOG. Even with respect to the composition of the Final Athletics Committee, the general CAIOG milieu and the presence of Stagg meant that the tendentious Spalding-Sullivan dichotomy between "real sports experts" and well-meaning "academic dilettantes" gained little traction in Chicago, whereas, as we shall see, it was given free and constitutive rein in St Louis. Non-American readers should be reminded that

U.S. private universities like the University of Chicago are non-profit entities legally "owned" by and having as final authority boards of trustees made up largely of local business elites who are expected to be major donors. Harper's success as a university president depended in no small part on his close collaboration with (some would say manipulation of) leading industrialists (Boyer, *Broad and Christian*), and the purchased perception of these business elites as "university men" through their trusteeships and philanthropies could be critical in their own status contests. All were aligned shoulder to shoulder in Chicago's city-on-the-make culture of the time.

35 Robert Barney, "A Myth Arrested: Theodore Roosevelt and the 1904 Olympic Games," in *Umbruch und Kontinuitat im Sport*, ed. Andreas Luh and Edgar Beckers (Bochum, Germany: Universitat Verlag, 1991), 218–29. John Lucas, "Theodore Roosevelt and Baron Pierre de Coubertin: Entangling Olympic Games Involvement, 1901–1918," *Stadion* 8, no. 9: 137–50.

36 Theodore Roosevelt to Harper et al., 28 May 1902, WHP, box 57, folder 3.

37 The U.S. Government General Accounting Office ("Olympic Games: Costs to Plan and Stage the Games in the United States," November 2001) has documented federal government expenditures on recent American Olympic Games. Counting only direct costs and setting aside nearly all personnel costs and many security and transportation improvements treated as "normal" expenditures, the GAO's baseline figures are Lake Placid 1980, $179 million; Los Angeles 1984, $77 million; Atlanta 1996, $193 million; Salt Lake City 2002, $342 million.

Los Angeles 1984 chief, Peter Ueberroth, a conservative Reagan Republican and an ideologue of capitalist entrepreneurship, managed to establish a rhetorical picture of his Games as "the first entirely privately financed," despite the actual facts. Ueberroth and the Los Angeles Olympic Organizing Committee (LAOOC) also treated as unmentionable and unreimbursable the additional millions of dollars in local and state services provided at taxpayers' expense. The Atlanta organizing committee (ACOG) and its conservative Republican leader, Billy Payne, did reimburse much of the state and local government investment but not any of the federal dollars spent. Internal ACOG discourse often more accurately referred to a "public-private partnership," but strategic recourse to the rhetoric of "privately funded Games" was the norm in its public statements. Future Republican presidential candidate Mitt Romney, the chief of the Salt Lake Olympics, actually forced the General Accounting Office to append to its 2001 report a letter from him pointing out that federal funds as a percentage of the OCOG budget had actually fallen from 52 to 18 per cent between Lake Placid and Salt Lake. Within the Chicago 2016 bid committee it was a continual (and often losing) battle to keep Patrick Ryan, the billionaire businessman and moderate Republican who led the bid, and Democrat Mayor Daley from referring to a "privately financed" Games, rather than to a public-private partnership.

At every level, these facts provide the clearest contrast with the social and cultural organization of Olympic sport in other countries, including Canada despite its proximity and apparent familiarity. See MacAloon, "Popular Cultures of Sport in Canada and the U.S." in *The Beaver Bites Back*, ed. F. Manning and D. Flaherty (Montreal: McGill-Queens University Press, 1994), 126–51. I remain exceptionally grateful to Bruce Kidd of the University of Toronto for the opportunities that he has provided to me over thirty years for comparative ethnography of the Canadian Olympic system.

38 In contrast to the Christian socialist wing of the movement's originators, Hughes, Kingsley, and Maurice. See MacAloon, *Muscular Christianity*.

39 Furber to Roosevelt, 24 May 1902, HFP, box 1, folder 7. Low-level suggestions of government funding of American Olympic delegations had been made in 1896 and 1900, but Washington never took any formal notice of them.

40 Barney, "Born from Dilemma," 104–5.

41 For example, Barney, "Born from Dilemma," 100, 192, 192n67. The fact that fundraising was a challenge to be approached cautiously has too quickly been turned into suggestions that it immediately proved overwhelming for CAIOG. Barney's speculations rely far too much, in my opinion, on a single early letter from Merou to Coubertin, containing unconfirmed assertions about Harper. (Harper's own 2 May letter to Casper Whitney, quoted below, gives a quite different impression.) The HFP contain several of Merou's reports and musings to Coubertin, which could be quite self-serving and ill informed. A full analysis cannot be offered here, but suffice it to say that they record CAIOG ups as well as downs across a period of months. The presence of copies in his archive suggests that Furber was fully informed of this correspondence. In any case, these documents further discredit suggestions that CAIOG was dormant over long periods or that Coubertin was uninformed or insufficiently interested in the development of the Chicago Games.

42 Furber to Coubertin, 6 May 1902, HFP, box 1, folder 10. In November 1902 Furber understood the federal U.S. financial appropriation for the St Louis Exposition to be "nearly, $6,500,000." Three times he mentions Chicago's continuing "efforts to secure governmental recognition and financial aid." Furber to Coubertin, 26 November 1902, HFP, box 4, folder 2.

43 Furber's report to Coubertin and analysis of the situation after meeting in New York with St Louis officials, the document that announced his own ill-starred proposal for a postponement of the Olympics to 1905, strikes each of these chords. The Exposition "has the official recognition of our government," while the Chicago Olympics did not, and this could confuse international collaborators. Furber worried that "St. Louis might place Chicago in the light of mischievously competing with an enterprise in whose success the honor of our nation is in a sense

involved, and might thereby estrange from us the popular support which has been our greatest presage of success." Furber highlighted "the importance of placing ourselves in the attitude of dealing with the obstacles in front of us in a broad, generous, and patriotic manner." Then there were the explicit counter-threats. "[St. Louis] Exposition officials … informed me politely but clearly, that the Olympian Games in 1904 threatened the success of their World's Fair; and that if we insisted in carrying out our program, they would develop their athletic department so as to eclipse our Games. While doubting their ability to excel our efforts, I recognized that they could injure us seriously." This was because Furber knew that St Louis was ingratiating itself with Sullivan and the AAU. Furber to Coubertin, 26 November 1902, HFP, box 4, folder 2.

44 Harper to Coubertin, 27 December 1902, IOC Archives, folder: Chicago/St.Louis.

45 Pierre Bourdieu, *Language and Symbolic Power* (Cambridge, MA: Harvard University Press, 1991), 165.

46 Harper to Caspar Whitney, 2 May 1901, WHP, box 50, folder 13. In service of his speculative scepticism about Chicago's finances, Barney highlights the "conditionality" in the first part of this quote and ignores entirely the personal guarantees in the second part. Barney, "Born of Dilemma," 126n49.

47 According to a November 1900 newspaper report, the original plan was to create a joint stock company, "The Olympian Games Company," to sell 20,000 shares at $10 each, giving the target capital of $200,000, against an expected expense budget of $175,000. "Greek Games in This City in the Year 1904," *Times-Herald*, 11 November 1900, HFP, box 1, folder 3. At the September 1901 meeting Anthony was elected chair of the board, and Furber its secretary In addition to Harper, Furber, Selfridge, Rosenthal, Hutchinson, and Ingals who had signed the prospectus, added directors included Hiram A. [Hiram R.] McCullough, Stanley McCormick, Chas. R. Crane, Walter H. Wilson, LaVerne W. Noyes, James Deering, and Edwin Potter, among the most prominent railroad men, financiers, and industrialists in Chicago at the time (including one later known as "the Mad Millionaire"). "Minutes of the Stockholders Meeting, International Olympian Games Association, September 11, 1901," HFP, box 1, folder 2. A beautifully rendered charter and stockholder's certificate is in the Furber archive and was exhibited at the Chicago Hellenic Museum in 2004. The legal status of the document is dubious; it appears entirely ceremonial.

48 Furber, "Report on 1902 European Trip," HFP, box 3, folder 5. In a letter to Coubertin on 1 October 1902 Furber had specified that "the promised payment of a considerable contingent sum to an institution largely foreign would be embarrassing; and might lead either to the refusal of State and national aid or to a provision that the sums appropriated be repaid out of receipts accruing from the games. In this case probably no surplus would remain to the use of the Comité International Olympique." Hence CAIOG's suggestion of a lump sum "in the nature of a donation

to the expenses of a collaborating organization" to be paid to the IOC "*before the declaration of any dividend on stock.*" FHP, box 3, folder 5, emphasis added.

49 Benjamin J. Rosenthal, "Statement of Receipts and Disbursements on Account of Preparation for the Olympian Games of 1904, at Chicago, U.S.A., February 13, 1903." The Louisiana Purchase Exposition Company paid Chicago $6,954.47 to settle its debt of $10,160.52, which included a loan with interest for $3,857.10 from E.A. Potter's American Trust Savings Bank. HFP, box 4, folder 1.

50 All this makes ludicrous the assertion by the normally reliable Mark Dyreson that Furber and Chicago "had raised a $1 million war chest to make European trips boosting Chicago's image at IOC meetings." Dyreson, *Making the American Team: Sport, Culture, and the Olympic Experience* (Champaign-Urbana: University of Illinois Press, 1998), 74. Rosenthal's final accounting says that just over $3,000 had been spent to this purpose.

51 At the time, the source of the stadium drawings was not revealed to the public, a curious matter highlighted in contemporary newspapers and in our 2004 exhibition at the Hellenic Museum. The Furber archive contains a memo documenting the physical return of the architectural drawings to the offices of Holabird and Roche, William Holabird having served as chairman of the CAIOG construction committee, of which Louis Sullivan was also a member. My own guess as to the secrecy is that the plans were originally drawn up by Holabird for another client. Newspaper accounts also noted that the cost, source of potential funding for the stadium, and precise location were left opaque in the CAIOG press conference presenting the project.

52 Barney, "Born from Dilemma," 126n48.

53 This was the original plan, already stated in the newspapers in November 1900. "Plans have already been set on foot at the university to have Marshall field rushed to completion. It is intended to include the two blocks now inclosed [*sic*] into one field with a high ornamental fence surrounding all. A running track will circle the entire field, and on the inside will be separate fields for football, baseball, and tennis. The gymnasium will be built on the corner of Lexington avenue and Fifty-seventh street. Should it be decided to hold the games in Chicago it is part of the plans to dedicate the field and perhaps the gymnasium with the international contests. Every energy will be bent toward the consummation of the plan." "Greek Games for This City in Year 1904: President Harper Hopes to Secure Next Series of Olympian Contests for the University of Chicago," *Times-Herald*, 11 November 1900.

54 See Liam Ford, *Soldier Field: A Stadium and Its History* (Chicago: University of Chicago Press, 2009).

55 The St Louis stadium was an entirely modest affair on the Washington University campus, upgraded with Exposition funds, and later named after David Francis. The pre-existing Los Angeles Memorial Coliseum had only to be expanded by

25,000 seats for the 1932 Games and refurbished for 1984. The Atlanta stadium was designed and funded to be repurposed for the city's professional baseball team. The New York 2012 bid was ravaged when a Manhattan stadium deal involving a professional football team fell through at the last minute. Chicago 2016 was led to an innovative plan for an entirely temporary, and therefore relatively inexpensive, main stadium, a project that would solve the "white elephant" problem.

56 HFP, box 4, folder 1. CAIOG had at least twenty-five standing committees: Executive, By-Laws, Nominations, Finance, Auditing, Publicity, Preliminary and Local Athletics, Final Athletics, Yachting and Aquatics, Site, Construction, Prizes, Concessions, Receptions, Invitations, Ceremonials, Banquet, Music, Decorations, Illuminations, Spectacular Displays, Program, Badges and Carriages, Transportation, Public Order, as well as Military Affairs (HFP boxes 1 and 3, various folders). Unfortunately, the minutes books of these other committees have not been discovered, but if their work was even a fraction as extensive as that of Military Affairs, CAIOG as a whole was, in contrast to the predominant impression in the literature, a veritable hive of planning activity. HFP, box 2, folder 1.

57 International Olympian Games Committee on Military Affairs, circular no.1, 10 June 1902, HFP, box 3, folder 7, and box 2.

58 The St Louis Exposition included a plethora of military performances, but they were diffused throughout the fair and did not become associated with the 1904 Olympic Games. Had such international military contests actually taken place in Chicago, it is not impossible to imagine their production of a scandal of invidious comparison analogous to Sullivan's infamous Anthropology Days in St Louis. Susan Brownell (ed.), *The 1904 Anthropology Days and Olympic Games* (Lincoln: University of Nebraska Press, 2008).

59 MacAloon, "You Don't Say: Why There Were No Spies in American Sport" (unpublished manuscript, 1993).

60 Henry Bréal to Harry Furber, 10 January 1902, HFP, box 2, folder 3, my translation. The customary familiarity of the address and signature are juxtaposed with the formality of the salutation ("Cher Monsieur Furber"), signalling the intended importance of the message.

61 Spalding to Furber, 10 June 1902, HFP, box 3, folder 10. Including three members from St Louis. "Fair Officers Sure of Olympic Games," *The Republic*, 12 December 1902. Furber, Churchill, and others pleaded for a "residential sub-committee" on athletics in Chicago that the "absentee landlord" Spalding in New York was slower to organize.

62 Edward E. Babb to Durand Churchill, 16 April 1902, HFP, box 3, folder 9.

63 Burnham to Furber, 4 August 1902, HFP, box 3, folder 10.

64 Spalding to Furber, 3 June 1902, Furber to Spalding, 7 June 1902, Furber to Coubertin, 9 June 1902, HFP, box 3, folder 10. Although Spalding explicitly denies it,

his letter seems dictated by Sullivan. For the original Sullivan-Coubertin imbroglio see Lucas, "Early Olympic Antagonists." Nothing so embittered Sullivan in his professional life as the thought that he had been robbed of a seat on the IOC by Coubertin's personal fiat. Sullivan refused to acknowledge that he never had such a seat in the first place, and to the end rationalized away the fact that it was he who first insulted and tried to finish off Coubertin. Sullivan reviewed the whole relationship from his point of view in an extraordinary letter written after the 1906 Athens Games, a letter in which he states that after Athens he realized that his St Louis Games "were not Olympic Games at all." Sullivan to Coubertin, 26 June 1906, Avery Brundage Collection, University of Illinois-Champaign Library Special Collections, box 103.

65 Furber was himself in Europe. Given my interpretation, it should be noted that, from the perspective of visibility in the Furber archive during this period, Harper and Spalding were on inverse trajectories.

66 John Barton Payne to Furber, 2 October 1902, HFP, box 3, folder 10. Spalding's claim about "one local games and one world games" either missed or more likely dissembled on the point that St Louis was insisting that it would hold its games simultaneously with any in Chicago, forcing the AAU to choose one over the other. If St Louis won over the AAU, and Sullivan sanctioned AAU club athletes to compete only in St Louis, then America would be represented in Chicago solely by college athletes who might not be the country's best in their disciplines. Hence, Chicago could no longer really claim to be hosting "world championships," as Sullivan could be counted on to make plain to the newspapers and to anyone else who might listen.

67 Gordon Strong to Furber, 20 October 1902, HFP, box 3, folder 10.

68 A.A. Burnham to Furber, 18 October 1902, HFP, box 3, folder 10. A story about the recruitment of Spalding to the Exposition team even appeared in a St Louis newspaper in July. Dyreson, *Making the American Team*, 76.

69 Dyreson, *Making the American Team*, 76, 222n11.

70 "World's Fair Athletics," *The Republic*, 19 November 1902.

71 Furber to Spalding, 14 November 1902, HFP, box 3, folder 10.

72 Furber understood that the quadrennial principle was sacred to Coubertin and that he was unlikely to yield on the point. Nevertheless, Furber was clearly sincere in his arguments for a postponement to 1905. History doctorate that he had, he even wrote to University of Chicago classicist William B. Owen asking if there were any ancient precedents for an Olympic postponement. Furber to Owen, HFP, box 3, folder 10.

73 Harper to Coubertin, 27 December 1902, IOC Archives, folder: Chicago/St.Louis.

74 Furber to Coubertin, 31 December 1902, IOC Archives, folder: Chicago/St. Louis.

75 That Furber and Spalding came to be so closely associated with one another in the minds of Exposition leaders during this period is a most interesting fact, as they had actually had relatively little direct contact back in Chicago, Furber having been

in Europe during the height of Spalding's CAIOG activity. Spalding showed no special regard for Furber, particularly in the matter of sports organization. The clear implication is that both were seen by the Exposition as St Louis's leading friends in CAIOG. Further evidence is, however, lacking.

76 "I want to say that we feel highly the compliment paid in offering to allow the committee to stand as it is," declared Furber. "As to whether I can accept the offer is another matter. I am deeply interested in athletics and will do all that I can to help the games along, but there are several conditions that I will have to consider before accepting. It would mean that I would have to give up my legal business temporarily, or, at least, not be able to give it the time it should have. Then I have no practical knowledge of the workings of such a large event, and would hesitate before undertaking the task on this account." "Fair Officers Sure of Olympian Games," *The Republic*, 12 December 1902. Whatever Furber's CAIOG colleagues might have had to say to him concerning these developments is not to be found in the Furber papers, but reading such statements makes it unsurprising that Harper had soured on Furber and may have intended to have him replaced. George Vincent to Harper, 5 November 1902, WHP, box 50, folder 13.

77 Edmund S. Hoch, "The Olympian Games to Be Held in St. Louis as a Part of the World's Fair," *World's Fair Bulletin*, March 1903. Partisans of the financial risk theory of Chicago's demise will note that Edwin Potter and Charles Crane, two of CAIOG's three chief money men, are singled out by name in this article as representing "the utmost friendship and cordiality toward St. Louis" of "the Chicago Committee." (Rosenthal, as we have noted, was a die-hard.)

78 J.E. Sullivan, "Special Olympic Number Containing the Official Report of the Olympic Games 1904," *Spalding's Official Athletic Almanac for 1905* (New York: American Publishing Co.), 157.

79 Levine, *A.G. Spalding*, 99.

80 The term *republic of sport* is now especially Mark Dyreson's. In their laudable and otherwise successful efforts to discern a general ideological and social formation, texts like "America's Athletic Missionaries" and *Making the American Team* too often ignore extremely serious differences among key figures, factions, and class fractions, even where these are in frank political opposition to one another. Neither nationalism nor republicanism is any one simple thing, save, as Roland Barthes would put it, in "mythic speech."

81 Levine, *A.G. Spalding*, 73.

82 Details of Sullivan's compensation, if any, during his long tenure as secretary and secretary-treasurer of the AAU have not yet come to light. It would be very interesting to know whether during his brief tenure as president of the organization Sullivan relinquished any such compensation, thus confirming his status anxieties and ambitions.

83 Only college sport eluded the full Spalding-Sullivan hegemony. This fact under-girds what has come to be referred to in the sports history literature as the NCAA-AAU wars.

84 "Physical Culture at the World's Fair," *World's Fair Bulletin*, August 1903.

85 Jean Drury (ed.), *Coubertin autographe, 1889–1915* (Bière, Switzerland: CABED-ITA, 2003), 55.

86 F.J.V. Skiff to Walter Liginger, 1 April 1903; Liginger to Coubertin, 28 April 1903. Sullivan to Coubertin, 2 May 1902: "I am very glad for the good of sport that the Olympian Games have been transferred to St. Louis. I have been out there and have had several conferences with the directors in connection with the Olympian Games and other matters athletic. I think they will handle things in a way that will please you and your Committee." Sullivan to Coubertin, 22 July 1903: "As you will see, I have been appointed Chief of the Department of Physical Culture at the World's Fair ... The Fair is to be a big thing, and no doubt the Olympian Games will be a big thing." HFP, box 4, folders 1–4; IOC Archives, folder: Chicago/St. Louis.

87 The neutering of Sloane, who had only an international sports presence by this point, helped considerably here.

88 Lucas, "Early Olympic Antagonists."

89 Steven Hardy, "Entrepreneurs, Structures, and the Sportgeist: Old Tensions in a Modern Industry," in *Essays on Sport History and Sport Mythology*, ed. Donald Kyle and Gary Stark (Arlington: Texas A&M University Press, 1990), 68.

90 Sullivan to Coubertin, 26 June 1906, emphasis added. This important letter swings schizophrenically between righteous anger and plaintive abjection. It makes painful reading (at least to this great-grandson of an immigrant Irish railroad worker). Many of Sullivan's criticisms of Coubertin's management style (or lack of it) were completely accurate and appropriate, and while he always acknowledged Couber-tin's larger achievement, Sullivan had no intellectual context in which to actually appreciate it. Not only Sullivan's habitus but his very self-respect depended on the bureaucrat's commitment to formal rationality, whereas the claims of Coubertin, who had never been an employee of any kind, much less a bureaucrat, belonged to the domain of substantive rationality.

91 Carl Posey, *The Olympic Century: III Olympiad, St. Louis 1904 and Athens 1906* (Los Angeles: World Sport Research and Publications, 1998), 10, emphasis added.

92 James E. Sullivan, "America's Athletes in Ancient Athens," *American Monthly Review of Reviews* 34 (July 1906): 48.

93 Edward M. Levine, *The Irish and Irish Politicians* (South Bend, IN: Notre Dame University Press, 1966).

94 "Bulletin #1, Objects of American Olympic Committee," the original mission state-ment of the organization, begins: "Objects of the American Olympic Committee are the stimulation of public interest and participation in the Olympic movement

and the selection, organization, and financing of the strongest possible team to represent the United States in the Olympic Games." Only down the page does the document mention international goodwill, inspiring in youth "the love of competition … the mainspring of the American system," health, crime prevention, clean living, and meritocratic values. Document contained in the Amos Alonzo Stagg papers, University of Chicago Library Special Collections, box 82, folder 4.

95   I stress that I am talking about these structurations as related to the USOC – from their points of consolidation in particular events and agentic political projects at the turn of the twentieth century to their continuing importance at the opening of the twenty-first century – and not of American Olympic bid and Olympic organizing committees (OCOGs). While there must by IOC statute and national practice be considerable formal and legal relationship between the relevant National Olympic Committee (NOC) and a bid committee or OCOG, particularly after the IOC 2000 Commission reforms, the latter organizations have a considerably wider range of stakeholders, officials, and functions, only some of which readily conform to the culture and established practices of the NOCs. In the American case, the IOC reforms were in fact occasioned by that organization's perception of unfortunate organizational relations between the USOC and the second Salt Lake City bid committee. See John MacAloon, "Scandal and Governance: Inside and Outside the IOC 2000 Commission," in *The International Olympic Committee Reforms*, ed. Bruce Kidd and Peter Donnelly, Special Issue, *Journal of Sport in Society* 14, no. 3 (2011): 292–308. Moreover, the dominant attitude of the leaderships of the Atlanta, New York, and Chicago bid committees towards the USOC has been highly sceptical and often antagonistic, because of the perennial hold of the structuration that I am analysing over the culture and practices of the American NOC. This claim is based on extensive ethnographic fieldwork within the Atlanta, New York, and Chicago committees.

96   "We had in St. Louis under the Olympic banner handicap athletic meets, interscholastic meets, Turner mass exercises, base ball, international gymnastics championships, swimming championships, basketball championships, one of the best regattas ever seen, bicycle championships, roque tournaments, a fencing tournament, a special week for the Olympic YMCA championships, a tennis tournament, a golf tournament, an archery tournament, boxing and gymnastics tournaments, as well as the Olympic games that decided the world's championships of track and field sports." This list was hardly the half of it, allowing Sullivan to claim 4,000 athletes "for the games decided in the Olympic series," and 9,000 including the participants in "mass exercises." Sullivan, *Official Report*, 159. The problem was not the multi-sport nature of the program but that few of these events were Olympic in exclusively involving adults representing their nations in manifestly international competition.

In a 1903 letter to Coubertin, Sullivan betrayed how thoroughly weak were his understandings of and commitments to the international architecture of Olympic sport. About St Louis he wrote, "I do hope there will be representatives from the foreign countries, this is what is going to add interest to the meeting" (Sullivan to Coubertin, 18 August 1903, IOC Archives, folder: Chicago/St. Louis). As if there could be anything Olympic without representatives of the foreign countries! In Sullivan's mindset of the time, if the world's best were there, what would it matter if they were all Americans? The logic of the spectacle ("create mass interest") is here combined with modernist technical universalism. As previously noted, after seeing Athens 1906 first-hand, Sullivan would recant and admit that St Louis had not been particularly Olympic at all.

97 Mallon, *The 1904 Olympic Games.*

98 MacAloon, "Olympic Games and the Theory of Spectacle in Modern Societies," in *Rite, Drama, Festival, Spectacle: Rehearsals Toward a Theory of Cultural Performance*, ed. John MacAloon (Philadelphia: Human Issues Press, 1984), 241–80; "The Theory of Spectacle: Reviewing Olympic Ethnography," in *National Identity and Global Sports Events*, ed. A. Tomlinson and C. Young (Albany, NY: SUNY Press, 2006), 15–40.

99 MacAloon, "Olympic Games and the Theory of Spectacle" and "The Theory of Spectacle."

100 Harper to Caspar Whitney, 2 May 1901, WHP, box 50, folder 13.

101 Clan solidarity (despite cultural performance theorist discomfort) leads me to note that a Chicago journalist and press agent, Charles R. Macloon, conceived of celebrating a "Chicago Centennial Jubilee" in 1904. He wrote to Benjamin Rosenthal and then met with the CAIOG finance committee and the State Street Business Council in the effort to combine this celebration with the International Olympian Games. "Mr. Macloon's ... proposition ... was enthusiastically received by the men of trade, who are willing to meet the promoters halfway. State Street will contribute generously toward placing the project on a sound footing." Macloon dated his centennial from Kinzie's first (white) settler house in 1804 and foresaw its celebration in purely spectacular terms. "This anniversary also gives admirable material and opportunity for historical pageants, illuminations, historical pyrotechnic spectacles, centennial mass meetings and possibly a centennial exposition of trades and industries, lasting about a month." ("Olympian Games as Celebration of Chicago's Centennial Year," unsourced newspaper clipping, HFP, box 1, folder 4.) When the Olympic project fell through, Macloon held his centennial celebration from 26 September to 1 October 1903, opportunistically backdating the centennial to the foundation of Fort Dearborn. Newton Bateman and Paul Selby, "Chicago Centennial Jubilee," *Encyclopedia of Illinois*, 758–65. Macloon's career as a press agent for Chicago spectacles also included

the inauguration of the Chicago Coliseum in 1900 and the Chicago Electrical
Exposition in 1906.

102 Coubertin had urged CAIOG to limit its festival to two weeks, concentrating
on the sports contests, but he was politely ignored by a leadership needing gate
receipts, uncertain that sport alone could draw sufficient attention and financial
benefits to the city, and still dominated by the spectacle logic of the world's fair.
So, besides the "world's championship contests … in the standard sports," there
would be "exhibitions … of the sports peculiar to various countries of the world"
[folk games and sports], "historical displays of a spectacular nature" [costume
pageants], "military sports and exercises and a naval display," a "comprehensive
exhibition of sporting apparatus and equipment," an "Olympic Congress" [one of
the first uses of that phrase in Olympic history], and continuous "illuminations,
musical contests, and art exhibitions." "Le Programme de 1904," reprinted in
Revue Olympique, no. 7 (1902): 36–43.

   Additional evidence for the articulation of the spectacle frame is the presence
of what I call "the Durante effect," after the comedian who famously complained
that "everybody wants to get into the act." One of the more interesting letters in
the Furber archive is the three-page proposal by a Mr O.E. Skiff of the Pain Fire-
works Manufacturing Co. of St Louis for a spectacular presentation in Olympic
Chicago after a prior show at the LPE. "Our historical reenactment of 'The Last
Days of Pompeii' is known so well that businessmen, Commercial Clubs, Boards
of Trade, Chambers of Commerce, etc., from the various cities have made such
demands on us for this work that we have been compelled to build three immense
[displays] for public exhibit." Skiff to Furber, 20 May 1902, HFP, box 1, folder 3.
(One presumes that this Mr Skiff was related to the LPE director of exhibits who
was manoeuvring at the time to have the Olympics removed to St Louis.) What
does Pompeii have to do with the Olympic Games? In the logic of the spectacle,
no need to ask if both are "really big shows."

103 Chicago had planned its Olympic Congress as a major international academic conference on global physical culture, with sections on history and literature, physiology,
psychology, ethics, and ethnology. Sullivan co-operated with the LPE Department
of Congresses to produce one on physical culture that was not international, only
quasi-academic, and way off to the side of the Olympic Games. The Chicago Olympic Congress in its ethnology section was scheduled to take up discursive "comparison of the sports of different races." Sullivan produced the notorious "Anthropology
Days." See Brownell, *The 1904 Anthropology Days and Olympic Games*.

104 Caspar Whitney, "Olympian Games Not an Athletic Midway," *Outing* 41, no.1
(October 1902): 120, emphasis added.

105 Caspar Whitney, "Chicago Olympian Games Committee Sails across the Ocean –
and Back Again," *Outing* 42, no. 1 (April 1903): 119.

106 MacAloon, "Olympic Games and the Theory of Spectacle."

107 Sullivan, *Official Report*, 157–9.

108 Sullivan to Coubertin, 26 June 1906.

109 For the influence of global professional consultants on the Olympic sports industry today, see MacAloon, "'Legacy' as Managerial/Magical Discourse in Contemporary Olympic Affairs," *International Journal of the History of Sport* 25, no. 14
(2008): 2060–71, and "Scandal and Governance."

110 The one exception was a terrible faux pas, in which his public relations consultants had Chicago 2016 chairman Patrick Ryan present IOC president Jacques
Rogge with a "rare volume" of his predecessor Avery Brundage's speeches, in total
ignorance of the fact that Brundage had so stuffed Lausanne with copies of this
book that the Olympic Museum had been giving them away for years.

111 There was a good deal of IOC confusion over this Obama initiative. Working
from within their own national frames of reference, many IOC members initially
thought that Ms Jarrett was being appointed a cabinet-level secretary of sport
and that the USOC would now report to this new government ministry. They
were most disappointed to learn that this was not at all the case, that American
exceptionalism was holding fast, and that the USOC, its Congressional charter
notwithstanding, remained free to go about its business unchecked by the state.

112 For a primer up until 2000, see Robert Barney, Stephen Wenn, and Scott Martyn,
"Family Feud: Olympic Revenue and IOC/USOC Relations," *Olympika* 9 (2000):
49–90.

6 Two-Way Hockey: Selling Canada's Game in North America, 1875–1935

STEPHEN HARDY

Hockey's American Bogeyman

Wayne Gretzky's August 1988 trade from Edmonton to Los Angeles tweaked Canada's ulnar nerve, prompting some writers to shriek with critical prose, lamenting and analysing a deepening crisis for hockey and for Canadian identity. The maple leaf was dripping dry, its sweet hockey sap diverted south. To some Canadian minds, American colleges, minor leagues, and National Hockey League (NHL) franchises had leveraged their stronger currency to lure hockey talent. Gretzky's loss was symbolic of a larger threat, the "Americanization" of Canada. His father, Walter, offered *Newsweek* a summary of the nation's indignation: "You Americans think you can buy anything we have. That's not the way I feel, that's reality." Two decades later the story was retold in several new books, including Stephen Brunt's *Gretzky's Tears: Hockey, Canada, and the Day Everything Changed.*[1]

Since Gretzky's trade, the story seemed to get worse. In 1993 the NHL anointed yet another non-Canadian as its commissioner, and this American Gary Bettman was not even a hockey guy. He had cut and grown his sports teeth in the National Basketball Association. His orders were to grow the game of hockey and fashion a continental (perhaps intercontinental) presence like the NBA's. This did not sit well with hard-core fans on either side of the border. To them, expansion meant degradation. The 1994–5 lockout exacerbated the situation. America's *Sports Illustrated* ran a story entitled "Giant Sucking Sound: That's the Noise Distraught Canadian Hockey Fans Hear as Their Game Heads South." Writer Michael Farber quoted a sympathetic Brian Burke (an American then working as NHL director of operations): "I view the migration of teams and star players south of the border like a mother putting her baby up for adoption. Canadians don't want to hand that baby over to any but a Canadian." Americans were now stealing babies.[2]

Other hockey writers joined this chorus. As the jacket blurb on one critical book, *The Death of Hockey* (1998), put it, a game of "speed, grace, and power" had evaporated: "Somehow, since the 1980s, but particularly in the last five years, that game has disappeared. It has migrated from the lands of ice and snow where it belongs to regions more suitable for beach volleyball. Along the way, it has been transformed into a cartoon-like spectacle that alternates between mayhem and a snorefest." America was stealing, and then euthanizing the baby.[3]

So what has been America's role in hockey's development? Have American markets and capitalists simply served as a siphon of talent or, worse yet, some evil workshop that fashioned a dumbed-down spectacle more worthy of professional wrestling? For that matter, has America's hockey history been fundamentally different from Canada's?

There is a long history of this concern about America's greedy capitalists and hungry markets sucking the life blood from Canada's national sport. The angst has been naturally heightened during periods of instability or failure among Canada's top-level teams and leagues. For instance, in 1972 Bruce Kidd and John Macfarlane published a very important book entitled *The Death of Hockey*. A tumultuous year, 1972 included the birth of a rival professional league (the World Hockey Association) with more American franchises, and a Summit Series that suggested (to many) that Canada's top professionals were not superior to the Soviet Union's state-supported "amateurs."[4]

Kidd and Macfarlane dedicated their book to "the rightful owners of hockey, the Canadian people." In their words, the game was the nation's great metaphor, representing winter, wilderness, and struggle: "In a land so inescapably and inhospitably cold, hockey is the dance of life, an affirmation that despite the deathly chill of winter we are alive." But hockey also represented Canada's uncertain identity. Was she a sovereign nation or a colony, "first of the British Empire and now of the American"? For them, the answer was clear. "We live in a country we no longer own. We merely lease it from the Americans." Like the timber, oil, gas, and minerals that Americans had taken over, hockey players who had grown up with dreams of Maple Leafs or Canadiens would more than likely play in the U.S. markets. In their most telling metaphor they concluded that hockey "may be our national religion, but the services are held in the United States."[5]

Kidd and Macfarlane did not focus solely on the American "problem," however, and this is one reason that their book deserves more sustained attention. Most of their narrative outlined the historical alternatives *within* Canadian hockey, between what they called the "commercial" and the "community" traditions. In their words, "a community team, amateur or professional, existed to provide hockey for the enjoyment of the community. A commercial team existed to make money." Before the Second World War, they claimed, "for every professional team in Canada there were 10 to 15 amateur teams representing private athletic clubs, universities, regiments and businesses. Many of them were far more popular than the professional clubs." The years since 1939 had not been kind to community hockey, they argued. Every gain in NHL popularity was a loss for the local community teams. Every advance in the NHL's control of player development was another nail in the coffin. The big league's expansions into the United States were logical: "As commercial hockey prospered, it was only natural that the men who owned it would try to sell it in the United States." After all, the rest of Canada's industrial magnates were doing the same thing with the nation's other resources like iron, natural gas, and hydroelectric power.[6]

Bruce Kidd pursued some of these themes in his award-winning book *The Struggle for Canadian Sport* (1996), one of the more important sport-history monographs of the last forty years. In this work he returned to the central drama of choice and transformation. He brilliantly placed the rise of the NHL between two world wars, in a broader national context that included alternative and popular visions or systems of participation, for females and males across a range of sports. Embroiled in this competitive environment, the NHL had struggled for domination. Its success as an exemplar of commercial or capitalist sport, however, could not be taken for granted. Bruce Kidd skilfully outlined the strategies that the NHL's magnates employed to position their brand as *the* brand of hockey and sport in Canada. In so doing, they kept one eye south of the border, where Major League Baseball had already developed a coveted model of hegemony.[7]

NHL magnates like Frank Calder, Tom Gorman, and George Kendall (aka Kennedy) were Kidd's focus of discussion, as they were in *The Death of Hockey*: "The promoters of the new league were unabashed sports capitalists. They sought to forge identities that could be turned into consumer loyalties. If in order to profit, they needed to alter the rules, transform the labour relations of the game, or move their operations to other communities, even another country, they were prepared to do it." More interestingly, *The Struggle for Canadian Sport* seemed to hasten the NHL's victory over community hockey by a decade or so. While noting that in 1917 (the NHL's birth year) the amateurs still got top billing, Kidd concluded that "in just two decades, the NHL became the best-known sports organization in Canada, with its players household names and the term 'professional' synonymous with 'excellence.'"[8]

Then there was America. In Kidd's words, "in the United States, where the game was 'foreign' to most regions and cities, hockey had to be carefully explained and popularized." However, as he also noted, in both the United States *and Canada*, the NHL took advantage of newspapers, magazines, and radio to promote "a number of strategies to increase the attractiveness of their 'product.'" Among these were rules to speed up the game, exclusive control of the Stanley Cup, a divisional play-off system that gave the new U.S. franchises more opportunity to make the post-season, and promotion of a select group of stars. Kidd concluded that the NHL strategies worked to create an NHL brand that dominated the imaginations of Canadians.[9]

One of the problems in hockey literature, both popular and scholarly, has been a fixation on the NHL. Historians must start somewhere, however, and it is certainly easier to find memoirs, newspaper and magazine articles, or archival materials on the big leagues of any sport. Several historians have recently argued that this tendency "toward Whiggishness" has been true of business history in general. A focus on the winners, though, often risks "jumping to the conclusion that the enterprises they have been researching are superior in some robust way." Consequently, to date there has been far less research into the history of what Kidd called community-based hockey.[10]

The focus on alternatives is perhaps Kidd's fundamental legacy to the historiography of hockey. In hindsight, his 1972 manifesto is especially important, because 1972 may be logically marked as a turning point, particularly when the game is viewed internationally. It was only after 1972, the Summit Series, and the WHA that the broader hockey markets in America and Europe began to converge towards the NHL's version of the game. Yet, as Richard Gruneau and David Whitson argued in their now-classic *Hockey Night in Canada*, perhaps there have always been more than just two versions of the game – community and capitalist: "It is difficult to determine the foundation for the argument that there is any one single legitimate 'intended use' for hockey [such as Kidd's notion of 'community' hockey]. Hockey has always had a range of different meanings and intended uses for various groups in Canada. The game has variously been a form of backyard play, a type of 'civilizing' amateur sport, an opportunity to drink and gamble, a source of profit, and a community symbol. Moreover, these different uses of hockey have often blended together in complex ways." The challenge for historians is to recover those alternatives. In other words, we must return to a more fundamental question, well parsed by Andrew Ross in his elegant dissertation on the NHL's first fifty years: "How did the hockey business grow, and why did it take the particular form it did?" Beyond this, we may ask if American entrepreneurs and markets were fundamentally different from their Canadian counterparts.[11]

Conceptualizing Two-Way Hockey

From its foundation in the decades after the well-documented 1875 Victoria Rink premier, the Montreal game has resonated and connected with American entrepreneurs and markets. However, that relationship and hockey's growth must be understood as a dynamic interaction on several levels. On the one hand is the cultural level – between the Canadian and the American. Andy Holman made this clear in his study of hockey in the borderlands. In parts of the western states and provinces the Montreal game flowed north and south as early as it flowed from east to west. From the beginning it was a shared experience. In Holman's words, "among the logging, smelting, and mining towns of the Northwest Interior at the turn of the twentieth century … ice hockey was an important part of trans-boundary regional culture, something that bound Canadian and American borderland dwellers, even as the border was supposed to keep them apart." Andrew Ross has furthered this viewpoint in his study of the NHL's first fifty years. As he noted, it is myopic to think only of how American tastes have somehow infected Canadian purity: "We are often left with a unidirectional model of cultural transmission where the mutual interchange and sharing of culture – asymmetrical as it may be – is ignored. Canadian-American comparative cultural studies show this deficiency insofar as they tend toward the study of US influence on Canada, and not that of Canada on the US."[12]

At the same time, historians must consider how entrepreneurs interacted with their audiences and markets at various levels and not just at the top. Successful sales are seldom a one-way proposition. Yet hockey history, like much sport history, has been written from a one-way perspective. Russell Field recently questioned our glib assumptions and "popular representations" about the experiences of fans. Beyond this, how influential were hockey spectators in the game's evolution on the ice? As Morris Mott suggested twenty-five years ago, every contest, every season, and every era should be considered "not primarily as productions put on *for* spectators, but as ceremonies accomplished *with* them." Marketers have understood this for some time. So have the wiliest magnates, like the Patrick brothers, Tex Rickard, and Conn Smythe. As difficult as it is to tease out what is now called the "consumer experience" and its influence on the game, we must not abandon the effort. In both regards – Canada vis-à-vis America and entrepreneurs vis-à-vis their markets – there is a need for more focus on interaction, what we might call "two-way" hockey.[13]

Games on ice – with skates, sticks, and balls – have a long history. There is nothing distinctly Canadian about them. The English of the Fens District had their bandy. The boys of St Paul's School in Concord, New Hampshire, played "hockey" on ice from the school's inception in 1860; by 1875 they had published rules to govern play. In fact, the *Montreal Herald's* account of the "first" game in Victoria Rink included the following note: "the game of hockey, though much in vogue on the ice in New England and other parts of the United

States, is not much known here." As historian Bill Fitsell has outlined in his exhaustive research, hockey's builders were grabbing rules and names from a variety of old folk games. They scanned many national and cultural borders, borrowing and discarding as they tinkered.[14]

In November 1883, for instance, the St Paul's boys published a complete set of new "hockey" rules in their school newspaper. Their athletic association president prefaced the document with a note indicating an awareness of "Montreal" rules. Later school accounts suggest that a master had attended the famous Montreal carnival earlier that year. Perhaps he had returned with a document. In any event, the Concordians expressed themselves "at a loss to understand the terms employed in the rules of the Montreal club." Concluding that "they would be of little value" in New Hampshire, the boys went their own way. Within a year, however, the school's hockey writers were recommending "the use of the Canadian blocks [i.e., pucks], which are so made that they cannot rise from the ice, thereby freeing the players from the danger of being hit in the face or head." Two-way hockey came early to America.[15]

Innovation in rules and equipment flowed across the borders. More important, so did players and teams. The mid-1890s were the take-off years for Montreal hockey in the United States. The primary factor was a technological breakthrough in artificial ice-making, which spawned indoor rinks in Baltimore, New York, Washington (DC), Pittsburgh, and other cities. Local athletes and Canadian transplants took to the ice with their sticks and pucks. They faced competition, however, from ice polo (a game with a ball and short sticks). America's conversion was due in large part to a series of tours by teams from Kingston, Montreal, and Ottawa, but the first tour actually went from *south to north* in December 1894 when a group of northeast American collegians played a series of challenge matches in Montreal, Toronto, Kingston, and Ottawa. The real twist was that half the games were the American ice polo. The press in Boston, New York, and Canada covered the action. Toronto's *Globe* noted that the tour was "arousing great excitement and interest in society and sporting circles." The *New York Times* added that "Canadians anticipate the result of the American visit will probably be the adoption of the Canadian game."[16]

The *Times* was correct. American rink managers quickly salivated at the prospect of exhibitions by crack players from Canada's top hockey teams, especially winners of the new Stanley Cup competition. The visits came early and with some regularity in the years that followed. With indoor artificial ice, a game could now be scheduled in advance and heavily promoted, with virtual certainty that the event would actually occur. This meant that investments would pay off. This new calculus had major implications for hockey in both countries. Canadian promoters understood this.

Two-Way Hockey, from the Start

While Canadians were slower to build artificial-ice plants, they still needed indoor rinks to ensure competition. Such capital investments, however, also required revenue streams to pay bonds or loans or to satisfy investors. This is where Kidd's dichotomous model of community versus commercial or capitalist hockey requires some adjustment. Rinks brought a new form of two-way hockey. They made the game entrepreneurial, both in the sense of risk and in the Schumpeterian sense of innovation. Rinks required an eye on the marketplace, the source of revenue, even for those who might have the purist of community motives. This happened in Canada as early as it did in America. As Alan Metcalfe has argued, a roof might tame winter or possibly a January thaw, but a roof could not slow the escalating taxes assessed on valuable property. And a roof could not protect investors from the public's fickleness or boredom. Very quickly, then, even the most private of operations was forced to look for new ways to bring a paying public through its doors. Montreal's elites learned this quickly after they had invested $20,000 to build the Victoria Skating Rink in 1862–3. The brick and truss-frame structure had a large (200 by 85 feet) ice surface surrounded by a raised, yard-wide promenade. A gallery big enough for seven hundred spectators wrapped around one end of the rink. Large windows offered daylight; six huge gas chandeliers guaranteed a bright skating surface at night. Those nights were filled with gala masquerade balls and skating festivals. By 1873, however, operating profits were under $1,000. Was the public getting bored with skating?[17]

Perhaps this explains an interesting twist to the "birth" of hockey in this same arena. On 3 March 1875 the following notice appeared in the *Montreal Gazette*:

> Victoria Rink – A game of Hockey will be played at the Victoria Rink this evening between two nines chosen from among the members. Good fun may be expected, as some of the players are reputed to be exceedingly expert at the game. Some fears have been expressed on the part of intending spectators that accidents were likely to occur through the ball flying about in a too lively manner, to the imminent danger of on lookers, but we understand that the game will be played with a flat, circular piece of wood, thus preventing all danger of its leaving the surface of the ice.

This story was more likely a notice prepared by the players and sent to the *Gazette* (and perhaps other papers) in hopes of attracting spectators. More crucial to their marketing plans, the fundamental innovation – replacing the ball with a flat block – was described *not* as a means to a more appealing game but as a *protection for spectators*. We may reasonably guess that earlier indoor hockey-like games had been hindered by errant balls and that spectator danger was well understood by the normal patrons of the Victoria Rink. These player-promoters, supposedly the modern game's fathers, recognized the need to sell a spectacle, not just a sport.[18]

"Organized" hockey meant organized competition, between clubs and between markets. Canadian teams and their communities, much like their American counterparts in baseball, found it difficult to square amateur purity with the desire to win. Success for a team like northwest Ontario's Rat Portage (Kenora) Thistles meant investments in larger indoor arenas and in players. In their quests for the Stanley Cup the Thistles evolved from assemblages of home-grown amateurs to collections of the best players that money could buy, from wherever necessary. For instance, after they had lost the cup to Montreal in 1907, Kenora's *Miner and Semi-Weekly News* justified the use of three imported professionals: "Imported players have been a factor in hockey for a number of years and the eastern clubs have been the most familiar with it. This is the first season that the Thistles have ever been abroad for assistance or offered inducements. The team had been the product of the town itself, and no change would have been made in this program, had it not been rendered necessary in self defence by the actions of eastern teams." One can find similar apologies in the history of baseball, basketball, and football (in its abundant variety of codes). There is nothing distinctly American in this evolution. Entrepreneurs on both sides of the border pressed the boundaries of pure community or amateur hockey as they built competitive teams that attracted audiences. Often this meant paying players under the table or securing them sinecure jobs.[19]

The transition from community hockey to openly professional hockey moved quickly in one borderlands town – Houghton, Michigan. Canadian émigrés, including Dr John L. Gibson, showed the locals how the game could be played in the nearby Hancock Palace Ice Rink. The hunt for competition, and more talent, was on. Within two years (1902) Houghton had a new rink that could seat 2,500 spectators, care of a dedicated stock company headed by a local hotel magnate. In order to challenge for mythical American championships against teams from Pittsburgh, Houghton's Portage Lake Club recruited the best players and paid them well. Soon two other Michigan communities joined Houghton, Pittsburgh, and the Canadian "Soo" (Sault Ste Marie) to organize hockey's first avowedly professional league – the International Hockey League. As historian Daniel Mason has concluded, however, "the seeds" of such commercialization "were sown prior to the migration of hockey to the United States." Entrepreneurs in both countries had learned to fill their rinks by sating "spectator demand for high-caliber competition."[20]

The game's top players – especially the top Canadians – took what they could from the changing landscape. Fred Taylor of Listowel, Ontario, needed no American model to fashion a career as hockey's most successful vagabond. If anything, American baseball players would have envied his craftiness and his daring. He jumped to whatever team offered the most money. He recalled years later: "Relatively speaking, the money for playing pro hockey wasn't bad in 1908. A good pro could make between $1,200 and $1,500." Taylor would not be hampered by averages. He understood the advantages of two-way hockey and leveraged media exposure in New York City for higher pay back home. For instance, in 1908 and 1909 his Ottawa Senators played exhibition games in New York's St Nicholas Rink. Gotham's media played up both his skill and his remarkable resemblance to the recently retired heavyweight boxer Jim Jeffries, who was then being pressured to return to action as the "Great White Hope" against Jack Johnson. All of this was good news for Taylor, who later explained, "Right after my first visit to New York, my salary went up to $5,260." When he returned in 1910, the *New York Evening Telegraph* reported that, on a per-game basis, Taylor's salary "shames what is paid to our star baseball players." Taylor was neither the first nor the last Canadian athlete to enjoy the reach of New York's media attention.[21]

There was much to learn in the Big Apple. Taylor's tour mates, Frank and Lester Patrick, were among the most astute students. Taylor recalled that the Patrick brothers skipped the Broadway nightlife in favour of a broader Manhattan tour. In his words, "they always gave the impression that they were filing information away for future reference. Frank couldn't get over the size of the big arena on Madison Avenue [the old Madison Square Garden, which had no ice]. Frank made sketches of the Garden." Lester Patrick later told writer Eric Whitehead that the New York City visit had planted a seed in his head, which sprouted the next year when he and Frank visited their father, Joe, in British Columbia. They talked of moving west and bringing a grand vision. "It was at the first of these discussions," he recalled, "that the idea was firmly planted to ... start a new hockey league and pioneer Canada's first artificial-ice rinks. They would be of the type we had seen in New York." They were soon in operation.[22]

The Patrick brothers may have seen a vision in New York City, but a few days were hardly the stuff of business savvy. That was all homegrown in Canada. As historian John Wong has argued, "turn-of-the-century Canada provided a haven for entrepreneurs such as Lester and Frank Patrick, who had been helping their father run the family lumber business in British Columbia. In this favorable business climate, the Patricks decided to apply their expertise as businessmen and hockey experts when they formed the PCHA." Much like American promoters in New York, Boston, and Pittsburgh, the Patricks "had to cultivate consumer demand" for a new product. And the Pacific northwest *was* a new market. When the Pacific Coast Hockey Association (PCHA) opened in January 1912, the *Vancouver Province* ran a long, instructive article outlining hockey's fine points and acknowledging that "only a small percentage of the city's population" had actually seen a game. Teaching was one thing; playing was another. So the Patricks raided eastern Canadian teams for western *Canadian* markets. Beyond this, they tinkered with the rules, adopting forward passing, which purists argued would drastically change the game, all of which was done for Canadian consumers. The PCHA would not open a Portland, Oregon, franchise for another year.[23]

The PCHA was surely a cauldron for innovation in the game. As Wong suggested, however, the prompt was not change for its own sake. The Patricks faced stiff odds in a new market. Their greatest innovation was not with the rules; it lay in their control of every league arena and franchise. Today this arrangement is called a "single entity league," and it is used in the Women's National Basketball Association, Major League Soccer, and other leagues, largely to control labour costs. In 1912, however, it was called a "syndicate" approach, and it was not viewed kindly by the press. The problem had its roots in American baseball, where league wars and economic depression in the 1890s had led many owners to bankruptcy. More successful rivals took advantage of fire-sale prices to gobble up majority positions and even sole ownership in more than one club within the same league. Bizarre trades and transfers between these clubs – sometimes announced in mid-season – prompted bitter backlash from fans and their press patrons. In 1901 the New York Giants' owner, Andrew Freedman, floated a plan that would have turned the *entire* National League into a single joint stock company, wherein the company could make trades at will to even up competition on the field. It made great business sense, but "Freedmanism" became a cause célèbre in the sporting press. There was something about having an owner who was dedicated to just one market, not two or three.

Canadian writers, especially in the eastern cities that the Patricks had raided, wrote relentlessly about the PCHA and its "syndicate" hockey. Could the fans in one city really expect their players to fight for *just them* if they all worked for the Patrick brothers? Cynicism increased when the three PCHA franchises ended the first season with records of 9–6, 7–8, and 7–9. The competitive parity was just a little too neat. Some wondered if the players, with a nudge from the Patricks, were making sure that the league race stayed close. Frank Patrick later recalled: "Little did we dream when we took over this very difficult and costly venture at the sacrifice of much of our family's timber profits, that this sort of prejudice would arise to taunt and accuse us." They posted a notice in the league's rinks offering a reward for proof of any game fixing.[24]

Lester remembered: "We had much to learn as executives … Our ideas of improving the game were never at fault … but we were too young to appreciate the fact that the population in the West – and therefore the drawing possibilities – was very limited. I'm convinced that had we gone eastward and developed our ideas in the larger centers of population hockey history might have been different, and for us certainly more profitable." The Patricks may indeed have been ahead of the market.[25]

From the turn of the century, others had looked to American cities, especially in the northeast. There had been speculation about professional hockey franchises in Boston and New York as early as the days of the International Hockey League, with its one eastern team in Pittsburgh. The speculation increased in 1910, when an arena opened in Boston, but nothing happened on the professional level until 1924. As Bruce Kidd, John Wong, and Andrew Ross have clarified in their detailed research, the impresario behind the NHL's move to American markets in the 1920s was a *Canadian*, Tom Duggan, who had first tried to buy franchises in Montreal and Quebec. Failing in those efforts – because franchise values were already too high – he bought options to franchises in Boston and New York. Elmer Ferguson later wrote that it was Duggan, "lovable, financially careless but clever and imaginative … who was responsible for the great international edifice that is today the National Hockey League – Tom, and no one else."[26]

Duggan found American investors with deep pockets, but it was a governing body with a Canadian majority that accepted franchises in Boston, Pittsburgh, and New York and then changed the league's constitution in May 1926 to allow new franchise applications to be approved by a two-thirds vote rather than unanimous consent. This opened the gates for franchises in Detroit and Chicago. Charles Adams of Boston may have pushed, but he needed Canadian votes. Those votes were lubricated, then as later, by lucrative expansion franchise fees. In the end, Canadian owners were no different from their American counterparts. John Wong called them "capitalists whose main interest was the profitability of their franchises." Kidd and Macfarlane put it another way: "It was just that the opportunity for a quick, easy profit was too great. A buck is a buck."[27]

The NHL's arrival was certainly big news in America. Professional hockey attracted an up-scale audience in new giant arenas that were part of the whole strategy in New York, Chicago, Detroit, and Boston. Tex Rickard had built the new Madison Square Garden in 1925, which housed the new "Americans" franchise. He arrived in Chicago in April 1926 to announce plans for another "MSG" in Chicago that would support his bid to have the NHL franchise in the Windy City. "In New York," he crowed, "society comes to the games, in evening wear. We turn people away, for the sport takes hold of the women as well as the men. I never knew what a wonderful game it was until I tried it. It is better than baseball for interest in the scientific end." Big-time hockey was a big-time deal in America's largest cities.[28]

Andrew Ross has concluded that, while the NHL was "not the only brand," it eventually became the "dominant industrial mode of hockey in the United States," effectively controlling and moulding rival leagues "in its own image." Ross is surely correct if he were painting a picture of American hockey in 2010, or even in 1990, but his comprehensive NHL history ends in 1967, when distinct alternatives to an NHL model were quite alive and well in America. While we await more detailed histories of community hockey in any country, there is abundant evidence to suggest a complex American model, one that promoters and their consumers developed interactively, with both a respect for Canada's dominance and a desire for distinct American brands. Some of them were aggressively independent of professional influence.[29]

This attitude rose early in New York City, where the game's initial patrons hoped to nurture home-grown amateurs. They knew from experience in other sports that national competition fuelled impurity. As one hockey analyst wrote in the February 1903 issue of *Outing* (a mouthpiece of amateurism), championships had "engendered a degree of competition which created a demand for Canadian players," who were imported with little concern for amateur status. Pittsburgh's crack team, he claimed, was filled with players "who have been suspended by the Ontario Hockey Association for professionalism." The New York league, he added, had "leading players" who were imported and "inducted into more or less lucrative commercial positions in order that they might play upon local teams." There was nothing new here except the country of export. Creeping professionalism had happened in baseball, track and field, football, and basketball. Besides the moral issue, however, the hockey analyst recognized a more strategic problem. A continued pursuit of imports "hinders the development of the only possible adequate base of supply, for the permanence of the game below the international boundary line depends upon the maintenance of a home-bred school of recruits, constantly at practice, and with the possibility of making one of the expert teams as an incentive." How to build and sustain the grassroots? That was a fundamental problem that had additional twists in warmer climates.[30]

American "hockeyists" – as promoters and zealots were called at the time – approached selling and building the game in several ways. The first was an almost unfettered optimism in rink technology. The second was a frequently expressed desire to nurture "our own" game at a local, regional, and national level. The third, and the most successful, was a recognition of potential synergies between professional and grassroots hockey.

The Promise of Rink Technology

When the Montreal game was first played beyond the borderlands in the eastern United States, early in 1895 and 1896, it landed in Baltimore, Pittsburgh, Washington (DC), and New York City, places hardly renowned for outdoor winter sports. The reason was simple. These cities had new artificial-ice rinks, which completely changed the dynamics of winter. To be sure, earlier American skating booms, such as the 1860s, had prompted investment in indoor, natural ice rinks around the country, including Chicago, Boston, New York, Brooklyn, Detroit, St Louis, Pittsburgh, Cleveland, Springfield (Illinois), Indianapolis, Rochester (New York), and Columbus (Ohio). New York's Empire City Rink had opened in 1868 with a huge ice bed, 200 by 130 feet. A number of these buildings were built and operated by the Hervey brothers, who were native Canadians. Paul DeLoca's exhaustive research indicates that the Hervey brothers built and managed dozens of rinks "from Quebec to Chicago to New York to Philadelphia," using their patented design, which was engineered to pull in cold, outside air along the ice surface, while retaining some warmer air above. It was crude science that often resulted in slushy ice. Most of these rinks offered amenities beyond the ice. The Boston Skating Rink (1868–9) on Tremont Street boasted of its ability to "accommodate 5,000 persons, including skaters and spectators," and of its "warm and comfortable rooms ... where polite attendants will always be found to assist in putting on skates." The restaurant was a proto-skybox, with "a front entirely of glass" that offered a "fine view of the ice surface, and of the entire audience." It was a place to skate, to see, and be seen.[31]

These rinks, however, could sustain neither hard ice nor participation. Engineers and investors in North America and Europe looked for a better system of refrigeration, one that could produce ice for sale as well as ice for skating. Condenser efficiency, coolant effectiveness, refrigerant leakage – these problems plagued designers who attempted to freeze large ice surfaces. Newspapers and magazines covered announcements of technological breakthroughs. In 1889, for instance, the *Washington Post* ran a story from the west coast that captured the vision of technology: "Despite the fact that the weather is not cold enough in San Francisco to snow more than once in a dozen years, the city is to have an ice rink, and while flowers are blooming in front of the place there will soon be a building here where skaters may turn in on the glistening surface and try their skill at winter sport." San Franciscans would have to wait a few years. It was not until the mid-1890s that the answers came together and prompted a boom in artificial-ice rinks, which in turn boosted hockey's prospects in the warmer climates of America and Europe. The promise of big rinks, year-round skating, and hockey would pepper western and southern American cities repeatedly in the years to come.[32]

On 30 December 1900 the *Brooklyn Eagle* published a Nostradamus-like article, projecting the future of sport in twentieth-century America. The prognosticators expected baseball to decline while football, hockey, and yachting would gain participants and audiences. In American hockey's case, the future would "depend upon the artificial congealing of the skating surface – a process complicated and expensive." The *Eagle* also recognized a crucial reality for many of the newly codified sports being introduced to markets across the world, including football (in its various forms), hockey, and basketball. Long-term success depended on a synergy between playing and watching. A truly popular sport would have many more spectators than players. In this regard, it appeared that hockey was on solid ground in the New York area. The core of avid, skilled players was attracting crowds of "several thousand" to the "bigger matches to see a game that has probably never been played by one out of every fifty of the spectators." The game's future in America, concluded the *Eagle*, rested on more artificial-ice rinks, where more college teams could develop (college athletics being the gold standard for most team sports beyond baseball). These teams, in turn, would attract more spectators, who would help to promote the game to more players, and thereby build the crucial synergy between the sport and the spectacle. It seemed to be a given: "When the manufacture of ice becomes cheaper and the artificial rinks are fixtures of every college town, then we shall have a game that will rival football." This mantra was just beginning.[33]

In the four decades that followed, some of the new arenas were built for large-scale spectacle – Madison Square Garden, Chicago Stadium, Detroit's Olympia, Boston Garden. These have naturally captured the attention of historians because they garnered most of the contemporary media descriptions. Analysts knew that indoor artificial ice was essential for hockey's expansion. The technology went beyond the ice, however. The real genius lay in balancing a cold ice surface with warm seats. As Edward L. Bigelow, who had played and coached at Harvard, argued in 1928, fans no longer had to be "hardy Spartans" facing bitter winds: "Today an enthusiast can take a taxi after dinner to one of these arenas where from a raised seat in a comfortably heated building every detail of play can be seen clearly." Other experts and hockey writers predicted a similar, "can't-miss" future for hockey in America.[34]

Most of the indoor rinks, though, were on a smaller scale, built to expand participation in skating and hockey. Paid admission for spectators was an important revenue stream, but it was supplemental. Many of these rinks sprouted in established hockey country, such as Boston (Massachusetts) or Eveleth (Minnesota). They rose on solid foundations, relentlessly piled down to frozen cultural bedrock by the faithful and frigid sweat of countless players and managers whose teams had succeeded for a generation or two on natural ice. A new artificial-ice arena simply cemented existing winter tradition. But others were in warm, sometimes desert climates. Obscure guidebooks and magazines, not digitized major daily newspapers, contain many of these stories. What strikes the historian who digs them out are both the grand openings in places like San Antonio (Texas) and the *assurance* that indoor artificial ice would *guarantee* a fast-growing market. With historical hindsight, this optimism sometimes rings as a monotonous chorus of the doomed, filled with the irony of Graeco-tragic hubris.

Examples abound. For instance, Spalding's *Official Ice Hockey Guide* for 1909 included a four-page story on "Hockey in Cleveland." Correspondent W.H. McAvoy credited some Canadian transplants with founding the Cleveland Hockey Club in 1901. With no indoor rink, members took to local ponds. It was rough skating. As McAvoy insisted, "playing hockey is no pink tea affair, even when the best of facilities are provided." Creditable showings against sevens from Pittsburgh and St Louis would not be enough to keep the flame alive. Cleveland needed a rink. It came in 1907 with the Elysium, built and run by the "greatest amusement promoters in Ohio," the Humphrey Company. This spurred a renaissance that included the formation of the Northern Ohio Hockey Association, a four-team league, with a twelve-game schedule that filled the Elysium with "lusty-lunged supporters, who cheered themselves hoarse as their steel-shod favorites pursued the elusive rubber." Female fans, "not to be outdone, shrieked their approval through megaphones." Visiting teams from Duluth, Princeton, Pittsburgh, and Montreal swelled the gate, all of which, McAvoy concluded, "substantiates the fact that hockey, fast, furious, and brilliant, the offspring of Our Lady of the Snows, will thrive and flourish in Ohio."[35]

"Thrive and flourish" might be a stretch, although Cleveland supported minor league hockey franchises from the mid-1920s on. What counted most was optimism. It came to the west coast in 1915. Correspondent W.A. Kearns insisted in the Spalding guide that regardless if "few Oregonians" had ever "seen a hockey stick, much less a hockey match," Portland's huge new hippodrome (built for the PCHA franchise Rosebuds) would guarantee success. Despite the reality that all the professional and amateur players were Canadian or eastern American transplants, "a year or two will undoubtedly find some native players as good as the transplanted variety."[36] Before America's entry into the First World War, San Franciscans were turning out to watch senior amateur, collegiate, and women's teams compete on artificial ice. Los Angeles had its Ice Palace, which opened in early 1917 to the awe of one local writer who concluded that "compared to ice hockey, the old-time sport of feeding people into a lion's den looks like a drab and uninteresting commonplace." It was a game unlike all others, he claimed, for its combination of speed, skill, and physical collisions.[37]

By the late 1920s the bug had reached Texas, where investors built arenas in Houston and San Antonio. Despite their small size the rinks supported the development of local talent at both the high school and the senior amateur level. As a Houston correspondent wrote, dependable ice gave "young skaters an opportunity to develop into very capable, if not expert hockey players." On the Mexican borderlands there was optimism and even gloating that "weather conditions, noted so frequently in reports from hockey centers in the Northern states, have no standing in Texas, for the presence of artificial rinks in several of the cities has set the matter of weather at naught." The formula appeared simple: build the rinks and they will come.[38]

Reports from some of these rinks, however, faded away in the years to come. It was not easy to sustain the booms. By the late 1920s, for instance, the University of Southern California (USC), the University of California–Los Angeles (UCLA), Loyola University, and University of California–Berkeley (CAL) had organized teams. Local promoters crowed that hockey had fully arrived. Nonetheless, the powerhouse Trojans represented the limits of such visions. Led by the great pioneer Dr Charles Hartley – who had brought the Montreal game to Germany in his medical school days – USC's thirty-five-game winning streak from 1930 through 1933 rested on the backs of players imported from the likes of Brandon (Manitoba), Ely (Michigan), St Paul (Minnesota), and Boston. Not a single Californian was on the squad. CAL dropped hockey in 1936–7. A correspondent wrote in the *NCAA Guide* the following year that attempts to resurrect the program enjoyed "only slight progress," largely "due to the presence of a professional team in San Francisco and inadequate rink facilities." For the next four decades these two factors – the professionals and inadequate ice – would be the focus of attention for those who hoped to build *American* hockey.[39]

The Search for an American Brand

Controlling mother nature was a daunting task; so too was taming the game's inherent tension – a yin and yang that delicately fused science, skill, and speed with savagery and mayhem. Canadians have long suspected that Americans were incapable of mastering and governing this balance. These doubts were famously articulated in the early 1970s when bench-clearing brawls at the youth levels triggered an investigation by Ontario's Ministry of Community and Social Services. The McMurtry Report (1974) spread the blame to be sure, but it focused attention on a "trickle-down effect" from the NHL, and a certain cause was the league's expansion to new markets in the United States, where the wide audience "understand a hockey brawl far more easily than the intricacies and finesse of the game." This conclusion may have been soothing to some, but was it accurate?[40]

Historical sources suggest Americans approached and embraced the game in much the same ways as did their Canadian counterparts. Hockey had something for just about any fan of action, but managing the perfect mix was no easy task, as Canadians knew well. In fact, Montreal hockey's 1875 "birth" had ended in a brawl, as Bill Fitsell discovered when he dug into newspaper accounts. While the *Montreal Gazette* had the spectators leaving "well satisfied with the evening's entertainment," the *Montreal Witness* and Kingston's *Daily British Whig* had another take. The *Whig* described a "disgraceful sight," with "shins and heads … battered, benches smashed" and the "lady spectators" fleeing "in confusion." Apparently, wrote the *Witness*, some boys had skated out on the ice during play, where one was "struck across the head," leading to a larger altercation, a "regular fight," the broken benches, and the fleeing ladies. A boxing promoter could not have wished for more.[41]

Alan Metcalfe and many others have described how this new game on ice developed in a cultural swirl of tensions – many openly debated – about what it meant to be a man (especially a bourgeois man) in a society of burgeoning cities, factories, national railroads, huge inflows of immigrants, and labour and ethnic strife. A sport that somehow fused science with savagery seemed to promise an education for succeeding in life's struggle. So the Montreal game – with its frequent scenes of blood and butchery –was quickly rationalized and ritualized. It was never quite tamed, as Cornwall's Owen McCourt learned tragically in 1907 when Ottawa's Charles Masson chopped him lethally over the head. Masson was tried for manslaughter and acquitted. Since a teammate had whacked McCourt for good measure, it was impossible to know who had delivered the kill shot.[42]

American bourgeoisie approached its version of football along the same lines during the very same years. It was a delicate dance to justify primitive and atavistic forms of violence, particularly those produced by gentlemen from the nation's most prestigious universities. It was done repeatedly, however, in the name of science and manliness. This general discourse had been well established when the sensational new ice sport arrived in the mid-1890s. Some markets, including New York, Boston, and the Twin Cities, had supported "polo" for over a decade. Those audiences were familiar with speed, goal scoring, and stick control, as well as slashes and gashes. Hockey's promoters pushed the "scientific" improvements brought by a puck, a longer and broad-bladed stick, and a rule that forced players to stay "onside" of the disc.[43]

Canadian players were recognized for both their skill and their toughness. In March 1896, for instance, New York's new Ice Palace hosted its first big exhibition – a stop on the Shamrocks-Montreals tour. While the New York Hockey Club was stocked with Canadian transplants, the visitors promised something better. One local writer suggested that the difference would be toughness. The club had recently played a rough match against a Baltimore seven. The *Times* writer scoffed that it would seem like a "pillow fight as compared to a prize fight with the game the two teams of Canucks will put up." Such players "don't stop to pay any attention to a few barked shins and cracked heads when they get thoroughly warmed up at the sport." A post-game story claimed that the crowd had sat "as if spellbound" when skaters rushed "like an arrow, nursing, passing, lifting, or pucking the little rubber disc." Although one player was struck in the eye with a stick, the play was judged to be "uniformly gentlemanly." As to fears of barbaric roughness and altercations, the *Times* concluded that the deference to the referee and the general "absence of disputes" was a striking contrast to the "squabbling and disputations" and the "exhibitions of temper" that were common at football games. Later tours with the likes of Cyclone Taylor continued to awe American crowds.[44]

Some well-positioned writers and critics worried about the violence. Caspar Whitney, one of amateurism's most strident apologists, wrote a February 1903 *Outing* article on "Hoodlumism in Hockey." Seldom was there a game in New York, he claimed "which does not disclose the foulest kind of foul play, yet on the majority of occasions the offender escapes free of penalty, or the penalty is so absurdly inadequate as to bestir the indignation of spectators." Whitney blamed the young New York Hockey League and its officials for not controlling play. "The ruffianism of the players and indifference of the League," he warned, "is hurting hockey around New York beyond repair."[45]

One Canadian transplant, who may well have been an object of Whitney's ire, wondered if American audiences were *too* vigilant *against* roughness. Thomas A. Howard had captained the Winnipeg Vics before coming to New York to lead the NYAC, then the New York Wanderers. By 1905 he was writing for the Spalding guide. That year he claimed that American spectators were "less charitable" towards players because they "criticized harshly" those sent off for penalties that "across the border would not call forth even passing comment." He continued that Americans could not adequately "discriminate" between the player who was "intentionally unfair" from the player who might "accidentally offend." Howard did not clarify the penalties involved, but it is possible that American audiences in some arenas were rejecting "ruffiansim," "hoodlumism," and the most vicious type of stick-swinging violence that was also nagging at the game's integrity north of the border.[46]

The public's desire for violence was fluid and gendered. As Andrew Holman has uncovered, northeast women's teams in the years around the Great War were stocked with players who had skill and toughness; many had learned their skill from older brothers. One was Boston's Ruth Denesha, who played for the Girl's Hockey Club of Boston. In March 1917 the *Boston Herald's* hockey-beat writer, John Hallihan, covered a highly touted "first-time" match at the Arena between the Bostons and a club from New York's St Nicholas Rink. His post-game analysis concluded that "while hockey is altogether too strenuous a game at times for men, it did not prove too hard for women to tackle last night." He added, in passing, that "of course, there were several bumps, tosses, and falls, but no serious damage was reported, only that Miss Ruth Denesha had a couple of teeth loosened." Holman found that, after the war, rink managers in Boston, New York, and Philadelphia had organized women's hockey on a commercial basis that paralleled senior men's amateur leagues. In the end, he concluded, this hurt the women's game. While Denesha and her peers displayed speed and skill, they could never match the *paying* public's expectation for collisions.[47]

Over the next three decades, as hockey expanded south and west, American audiences embraced the same mix of elements that attracted Canadians. Sophistication was not a matter of national breeding; it was a matter of education. As one 1925 spectator's guidebook to winter sports cautioned, a first-time fan might be confused by the seemingly "wild scramble on skates, to the tune of swinging clubs and skimming puck." With a little experience, however, "there is no more scientific or intelligent game." At the same time, as the *New York World's* Gertrude Lynahan wrote of the NHL, "hockey offers more chance for men to lame, maim, bruise, batter, smash and slash each other than any other game." While historians have not uncovered evidence from anyone's marketing plan, it appears that professional hockey was sold aggressively to the same audiences that supported football and boxing. By the 1920s football had cleaned off its bloodiest veneer. Boxing still danced in and out of scandal's shadow. Benny Leonard, a recent lightweight champion boxer, invested in the Pittsburgh NHL team. In 1929 he told the *New York World* that "hockey will, or already has, cut into boxing considerably." He was "agreeably surprised" at a home opener when he "spotted hundreds of fans that I recognized as 'front-rowers' at all the important fights." A Philadelphia writer supported Leonard's marketing sense. The hockey fan, he wrote, "is seldom disappointed and, in addition, sees for his money many fights and near-riots that are not advertised as 'special added attractions' but are fought, nevertheless, with the same vigor that Tunney fought Dempsey or Princeton fights Yale." It was the same science and savagery, at higher speeds.[48]

At least one American governing body attempted, with real success, to craft a brand that was an alternative to the NHL. Although American colleges had established hockey leagues as early as the 1890s, they had typically adopted the rules of other amateur governing bodies, such as the Amateur Hockey Association of Canada, the Ontario Hockey Association, or the Canadian Amateur Hockey Association. This changed in 1926 when the National Collegiate Athletic Association (NCAA) – as part of a wider branding effort – established its first ice hockey committee. The NCAA committee was chaired by Albert Prettyman, coach and athletic director at Hamilton College. Rufus Trimble, a faculty member at Columbia University, served in the powerful role as secretary-editor. Two years later the Spalding's *Official Ice Hockey Guide* moved under the aegis of the NCAA, becoming part of the association's "plan to issue rules on all sports participated in by college teams." For the next six decades the NCAA Ice Hockey Rules Committee consciously worked to distinguish its game from other forms of hockey, especially the professional forms. The committee carefully articulated distinctions from others in its minutes and published rules. Among its central goals, the NCAA committee wanted to promote "greater appreciation" of skill "in contrast to the 'approval,' and even encouragement, of reprehensible rough play now sometimes unfortunately manifested by spectators." In a jab at the NHL, it concluded that "the extension of professional hockey in the United States should not interfere with the improvement of intercollegiate play in this respect." [49]

Believing that the onside game was more scientific, the NCAA committee stubbornly maintained the old rules well after the professionals had allowed forward passing in the neutral and attacking zones. While the collegians eventually changed their offsides rule to parallel most of the professional version, checking and fighting were another matter. From 1931 to 1972 the American college game (like the international game) included restrictions on body checking (at first, allowed only in the defensive zone; then only in the defensive half; then only up to the offensive blue line). Even when the final checking barrier came down, however, the NCAA brand's most distinguishing attribute held up – the automatic disqualification for fighting.

The original rules of Montreal hockey (1877, lifted verbatim from published rules for field hockey) included one lump section on egregious fouls: "charging from behind, tripping, collaring, kicking, or shinning shall not be allowed." In the decades that followed, the list grew longer, but the referee had full range to penalize offensive behaviour "for any time in his discretion." By the early 1920s most governing bodies were spelling out penalty types and times in more detail. "Fighting" or "slugging" were among the clearly articulated infractions. In 1921, for instance, the NHL rules listed "fighting" as a "match" foul, although the fine print explained that a match foul could mean anything from a ten-minute penalty to a game disqualification –"such length of time as in the opinion of the referee shall constitute an adequate penalty."[50]

Within a decade the American collegians separated fundamentally on the matter of fighting. The very first set of NCAA rules were unequivocal: "slugging incurs a five-minute penalty and disqualification of the offending player for the remainder of the game." As if this were not clear enough, two years later the phrase was expanded to "slugging, fighting, fisticuffs, *or attempting to hit or slug*." Meanwhile the NHL was moving to redefine fighting from a discretionary "match" penalty to a "major" penalty of five-minutes duration. At their 1933 meeting the NCAA Ice Hockey Rules Committee seemed clearly aware of this divergence in rules. "Although it is possible," the secretary-editor wrote, "in some cases fighting and 'dirty' play may add interest and increase attendance, nevertheless the type of rough play that develops into slugging, kicking, and near riots on the ice is not in harmony with the principles of sportsmanship which are advocated by schools and colleges and hence should be strictly ruled out of the game." To this day, this remains a "fire-wall" philosophy.[51]

Most American high schools adopted NCAA rules. For some forty years, then, the vast majority of American hockey players and a large portion of American hockey fans focused their attention on a style of play that had far less hitting and fighting than did the Canadian-dominated NHL and its related minor leagues. In some respects, the fire wall seriously reduced the chances that an American would play in the NHL. By the 1940s almost none did. Few of the players cared. American school and college hockey was their alternative universe.[52]

At the same time, American promoters, players, and their fans happily drew comparisons and made connections with the professionals. Americans enjoyed the game of two-way hockey. Success *depended* on making connections – between nations, between markets, between roles as spectators and players, and between commercial, corporate, and community elements. This became particularly important when the economy crashed in 1929. In 1931, for instance, Minneapolis's assistant director of recreation reported a municipal hockey program that included 275 registered teams, 2,750 players, and 50 officials engaged in over four hundred scheduled games on "twenty-six brilliantly lighted rinks systematically placed throughout the park system, with a view of developing the hockey spirit and play in every neighborhood." Team registration fees between five and ten dollars were coupled with sponsor dollars from "settlement houses, athletic clubs, social center bodies, men's church clubs of every denomination, Y.M.C.A., Knights of Columbus, Masonic organizations." All made the program self-sustaining. Sectional round robins, leading to city-wide play-offs, nurtured "a deeper sense" of local community. One of the program's linchpins, however, was the Minneapolis Arena, site of senior amateur and professional hockey. In this model, commercial spectacle provided inspiration for grassroots players. "The skillful play in evidence at the Arena, the tremendous attendance and enthusiasm accompanying these paid programs," he stressed, "naturally interest the young boys of the city and they want to go out on the park ice and do likewise." Synergy beckoned in a land of two-way hockey.[53]

No group understood this better than sporting goods dealers. In January 1931 the industry's national trade magazine, *Sporting Goods Dealer*, ran a feature story entitled "A Big Skate Season Is Afoot." Correspondent J.T. Meek reported on the skating boom in Chicago, a result of collaboration between grassroots recreation groups, sporting goods dealers, and big-time hockey. The Chicago board of education flooded 118 areas for supervised skating. The South Park board offered eighteen "small parks with rinks." Some three thousand skaters enjoyed the Midway area on the first afternoon of public skating. Speed skaters had formed the Illinois-Western Skating Association as a regional affiliate with the Amateur Skating Union of America to govern some twenty new clubs. And "hundreds" of new hockey teams vied for their share of ice time. Outdoor rinks alone were not the total trigger for such demand. "You'll find," Meek noted, "an intention [among local sporting goods dealers] to tie up closely with the community skating rinks, with the associations, and with the two professional skating groups – the Blackhawks and Americans – that thrill thousands with their skill at hockey throughout the winter."[54]

The strategy seemed to work, even in the Depression's trough. In December of 1933 the *Sporting Goods Dealer* ran a triumphant story about amateur hockey "booming in Chicago." The correspondent claimed that the old Coliseum was packed with an average of six thousand fans on Tuesday, Thursday, and Saturday afternoons to cheer on the senior "amateur" Butterfingers, Blue Ribbons, Baby Ruths, or Nestor Johnsons. The magazine credited Emil Iverson (a Canadian who had coached the Blackhawks the prior season) as the league's architect. Iverson had a vision that today's sport psychologists would call *modelling*. A set of top amateur teams "would arouse the interest of the boys in their neighborhoods, [which would] result in the formation of minor amateur teams." In turn, the minors would be "constantly feeding the rosters" of the top teams. In this ideal hockey world, passion would "permeate down into the neighborhood structure until every youngster was going for ice hockey." Charles Johnson, owner of the Nestor Johnson skate line, agreed in full with this wonderful fantasy. What worked for baseball, he wrote in a letter to local dealers, would work for hockey. "Hockey is new," said Johnson. "It packs a wallop. And it has a big future." With a good pyramid of competition in place and "with the right leadership" in the game's "promotion," the future was better than bright – "1,000 teams are entirely possible." Better yet, "lots of skates and equipment can be sold."[55]

A year later J.T. Meek outlined the synergy between Chicago's professional, commercial, and grassroots hockey elements. At the top perched the Blackhawks in their mammoth Chicago Stadium, which seated 18,078 for hockey and which saw the overall number of paid admissions increase from 138,546 in 1932–3 to 208,458 in 1933–4. Meek quoted Blackhawks general manager William Tobin as adding the next step in the formula: "The more people who attend the hockey game, the more people who want to skate." In Meek's theory of hockey consumer behaviour, "pro hockey tends to make people conversant with the game and with ice skating." Tobin went even further. Within five years, he claimed, artificial-ice rinks would be found in most of the modern playgrounds of the country. It was almost inevitable, he predicted, especially since "the old $100,000 artificial-ice skating plant has been trimmed down to a $7,500 figure by some manufacturers, and might get lower." This was ballyhoo from hockey heaven. The Blackhawks, concluded Meek, "go out of their way to increase interest and to build up a love for the fascinating sport."[56]

Skate manufacturers did not sit on the sidelines. In one promotion the Nestor Johnson Mfg. Co. paid for the distribution of fifty thousand copies of the Blackhawks' NHL champion team photograph. Requests, Meek claimed, were pouring in "from New Zealand, Australia, various countries of Europe – almost everywhere on the good old globe." Right in the Windy City, fans at Chicago Stadium could see "200–300 youngsters trooping around the players," trying to get their autographs on the picture. In conclusion, Meek recognized that Chicago's story of successful synergy, which resulted in ever-increasing levels of attendance, skate sales, participation, and "columns and columns of newspaper stories," could be replicated almost anywhere. "Is it too much," he asked, "to expect that such news cannot permeate into your city?"[57]

Similar visions appeared with regularity in American newspapers, magazines, and guidebooks. NHL expansion – whether in the 1920s, 1960s, or 1990s – prompted a spike in such stories. An NHL franchise presented the prospect of a complete top-to-bottom pyramid of participation and spectacle. It is a mistake, however, to think that American entrepreneurs were dependent on the NHL. Rink owners, coaches, administrators, dealers, and their media allies looked to "grow the game" for a range of interests that often had little to do with the league. Some, like the NCAA Rules Committee, wrote stridently about building their brand in strong opposition to professional hockey's "commercial" model, even as their member schools operated on a highly commercial level. In the end, though, we must ask if such a muddled marketplace was really much different from Canada's.

Conclusion

In 1928 Joseph Schumpeter published "The Instability of Capitalism" in the *Economic Journal*, the premier quarterly journal in the field of economics. Schumpeter was midway in an academic career that would mark him as one of capitalism's top twentieth-century theoreticians. In 1913 he had first visited America (which became his home in 1932). During the course of five months he travelled cross-country by rail. As his most recent biographer notes, he was impressed with "how the unfettered release of entrepreneurial energy, much of it financed with borrowed money," had made the United States both rich and vibrant. If Karl Marx, Charles Dickens, and others had stunningly articulated the dark and rapacious side of industry and business, Schumpeter would explore and explain its underlying mechanisms of growth and change. He was a child of the Austro-Hungarian Empire. He had both prospered from its traditions and suffered with its dissolution after the First World War. He had made and lost fortunes in banking and trading. For Schumpeter, the key to capitalism was "creative destruction." He returned to this theme repeatedly. As he wrote in "The Instability of Capitalism," change was endemic to this economic system, and it was driven internally by entrepreneurs who worked to "destroy any equilibrium" by constantly introducing new products, new technologies, new markets, and new business organizations.[58]

Schumpeter informs us about the history of two-way hockey. It has a long and complicated past, too often simplified by Canadians who have lamented a loss to the greedy southern capitalists, and too often misunderstood by American pundits and entrepreneurs on the make. The Patrick brothers, Thomas Howard, Tex Rickard, Rufus Trimble, William Tobin, and others represented the realities of capitalism in North America – a vibrant economy of "creative destruction" that spawned a range of hockeys. The concepts of community and commercial, or amateur and professional, help us appreciate alternatives. They are important intellectual tools. Schumpeter tips us off, however, to a more important reality. Their historical existence was neither concrete nor stable. They hovered in a system of change and disequilibrium, in a complex industry that flowed across segments, across countries, and between entrepreneurs and their audiences. Some visions succeeded, and some failed. The same will be true of the latest expansion into America's Sun Belt. As the sport industry's top trade magazine concluded in the middle of the 2009 Phoenix Coyotes bankruptcy case, "just how bright hockey's future will be in the Sun Belt remains unknown. To date, it has been successful in some markets but unsuccessful in others, and beneficial to the NHL in some ways but damaging to it in others."[59] Amen to that.

NOTES

My thanks to Andy Holman, Andrew Ross, John Wong, and Roger Godin for their help and suggestions on this essay, and to Bruce Kidd for many years of friendship and inspiration.

1 Walter Gretzky, quoted in Bill Barol, "Gretzky Puts Edmonton on Ice," *Newsweek*, 22 August 1988, 60. For a very thoughtful analysis of the immediate "crisis," see Steven J. Jackson, "Gretzky Nation: Canada, Crisis, and Nationalism," in *The Cultural Politics of Sporting Celebrity*, ed. David Andrews and Steven J. Jackson (London: Routledge, 2001), 164–86. Stephen Brunt's *Gretzky's Tears: Hockey, Canada, and the Day Everything Changed* (Knopf, 2009); Terry McConnell and J'lyn Nye with Peter Pocklington, and foreword by Wayne Gretzky, *I'd Trade Him Again: On Gretzky, Politics, and the Pursuit of the Perfect Deal* (Key Porter Books, 2009).
2 John Ziegler was the first American to serve as the NHL's chief executive officer (1977–92). Although he had been a hockey guy (via the Red Wings), his reign was highly controversial. Prior to Bettman, the CEO's title had been president. Michael Farber, "Giant Sucking Sound: That's the Noise Distraught Canadian Hockey Fans Hear as Their Game Heads South," *Sports Illustrated*, 20 March 1995, 107. Daniel S. Mason, "'Get the Puck Outta Here!' Media Transnationalism and Canadian Identity," *Journal of Sport and Social Issues* 26, no. 2 (May 2002): 140–67. The seminal book on hockey and Canadian identity is Richard Gruneau and David Whitson's *Hockey Night in Canada: Sport, Identities, and Cultural Politics* (Toronto: Garamond, 1993). The first full treatment of Bettmann is Jonathon Gatehouse, *The Instigator: How Gary Bettmann Remade the NHL and Changed the Game Forever* (Chicago: Triumph Books, 2012).
3 Jeff Z. Klein and Karl-Eric Reif, *The Death of Hockey* (Toronto: Macmillan Canada, 1998), cover, 8.
4 Bruce Kidd and John Macfarlane, *The Death of Hockey* (Toronto: New Press, 1972). For a critique of this book as "practical nostalgia," see Philip Moore, "Practical Nostalgia and the Critique of Commodification: On the 'Death of Hockey' and the National Hockey League," *Australian Journal of Anthropology* 13, no. 2 (202): 309–22.
5 Bruce Kidd and John Macfarlane, *The Death of Hockey*, 4, 16–17.
6 Ibid., 104, 105, 109.
7 Bruce Kidd, *The Struggle for Canadian Sport* (Toronto: University of Toronto Press, 1996), 186, 190. Kidd had switched terms from *community* to *capitalist*.
8 Ibid., 184–5.
9 Ibid., 209.
10 Naomi R. Lamoreaux, Daniel M.G. Raff, and Peter Temin, "Economic Theory and Business History," in *Oxford Handbook of Business History*, ed. Geoffrey Jones and Jonathan Zeitlin (New York: Oxford University Press, 2008), 38.

11 Richard Gruneau and David Whitson, *Hockey Night in Canada: Sport, Identities, and Cultural Politics* (Toronto: Garamond, 1993), 27. James Andrew Ross, "Hockey Capital: Commerce, Culture, and the National Hockey League, 1917–1967" (PhD diss., University of Western Ontario, 2008), 7. For an attempt at periodizing hockey history, see Stephen Hardy and Andrew Holman, "Periodizing Hockey History: One Approach," in *Now Is the Winter: Thinking about Hockey*, ed. Richard Harrison and Jamie Dopp (Hamilton, ON: Wolsak & Wynn, 2009), 19–36. For a valuable answer to the question of American exceptionalism, see Craig Hyatt and Julie Stevens, "Are Americans Really Hockey's Villains? A New Perspective on the American Influence on Canada's National Game," in *Canada's Game: Hockey and Identity*, ed. Andrew C. Holman (Montreal: McGill-Queens University Press, 2009), 26–43.

12 Andrew C. Holman, "Playing in the Neutral Zone: Meanings and Uses of Ice Hockey in the Canada-U.S. Borderlands, 1895–1915," *American Review of Canadian Studies* 34, no. 1 (Spring 2004): 34–5; Ross, "Hockey Capital," 14. Battles over the "birthplace" of hockey are ongoing, but scholars agree that the game as we know it came out of Montreal in the decade or so after 1875. See online materials at Library and Archives Canada, http://www.collectionscanada.gc.ca/hockey/index-e.html?PHPSESSID=7jtqj0cbm1k6ge2uru1rfp2rs3, and the Society for International Hockey Research, http://www.sihrhockey.org/main.cfm.

13 Russell Field, "'There's More People Here Tonight Than at a First Night of the Metropolitan": Professional Hockey Spectatorship in the 1920s and 1930s in New York and Toronto," in *Canada's Game: Hockey and Identity*, ed. Andrew C. Holman (Montreal: McGill-Queens University Press, 2009), 131; Morris Mott, "Flawed Games, Splendid Ceremonies: The Hockey Matches of the Winnipeg Vics, 1890–1903," *Prairie Forum* 10, no. 1 (1985): 178.

14 "Hockey," *Montreal Gazette*, 4 March 1875, available at http://www.collectionscanada.gc.ca/hockey/024002-119.01-e.php?hockey_id_nbr=3&PHPSESSID=7jtqj0cbm1k6ge2uru1rfp2rs3; J.W. (Bill) Fitsell, *Hockey's Captains, Colonels, and Kings* (Erin, ON: Boston Mills Press, 1987); Bill Fitsell, *How Hockey Happened: A Pictorial History of Canada's National Winter Game* (Kingston, ON: Quarry Press, 2006). For European roots see Carl Giden, Patrick Houda, and Jean-Patrice Martel, *On the Origin of Hockey* (Stockholm and Chambly: Hockey Origin Publishing, 2014).

15 *Horae Scholasticae*, 17 (29 November 1883); 18 (17 December 1884), school newspaper in Saint Paul's School Archives, Concord, New Hampshire. For more on St Paul's hockey, see Stephen Hardy, "Performance, Memory, and History: The Making of American Ice Hockey at St. Paul's School, 1860–1915," *International Journal of History of Sport* 14, no. 1 (April 1997): 97–115. On the Montreal carnival, see Don Morrow, "Frozen Festivals: Ceremony and the *Carnaval* in the Montreal Winter Carnivals, 1883–1889," *Sport History Review* 27 (1996): 173–90.

16 *Globe* [Toronto], 24 December 1894, 6; *New York Times*, 28 December 1894, 7. Stephen Hardy, "'Polo at the Rinks': Shaping Markets for Ice Hockey, 1880–1900," *Journal of Sport History* 33, no. 2 (Spring 2006), 156–74; Bill Fitsell has a short account of the tour in *Hockey's Captains, Colonels, and Kings*, 99–101.

17 Alan Metcalfe, *Canada Learns to Play: The Emergence of Organized Sport, 1807–1914* (Toronto: McLelland & Stewart, 1987), 135–6; Don Morrow, Mary Keyes, Wayne Simpson, Frank Cosentino, and Ron Lappage, *The Concise History of Sport in Canada* (Toronto: Oxford University Press, 1989), 11–12.

18 Fitsell, *Hockey's Captains, Colonels, and Kings*, 31–6.

19 *Kenora Miner and News*, 20 March 1907, quoted in R.S. Lappage, "The Kenora Thistles Stanley Cup Trail," *Canadian Journal of History of Sport* 19, no. 2 (December 1988): 92. For an excellent study of the Thistles' evolution as a club, see John Wong, "From Rat Portage to Kenora: The Death of a (Big-Time) Hockey Dream," *Journal of Sport History* 33 (Summer 2006): 175–91. See also Rob Kossuth, "Chinook Country Hockey: The Emergence of Hockey in Pre-second World War Southern Alberta," in *Coast to Coast: Hockey in Canada to the Second World War*, ed. John Wong (Toronto: University of Toronto Press, 2009), 203–22.

20 Daniel S. Mason, "The International Hockey League and the Professionalization of Ice Hockey, 1904–1907," *Journal of Sport History* 25, no. 1 (Spring 1998): 10. In this quote Mason was responding directly to Kidd and Macfarlane's suggestion that the United States was somehow to blame. See also Daniel S. Mason, "Hockey's First Professional Team: The Portage Lakes Hockey Club of Houghton, Michigan," *Sport History Review* 27 (1996): 49–71. For the rise of professionalism in Ontario see Stephen J. Harper, *A Great Game: The Forgotten Leafs and the Rise of Professional Hockey* (Toronto: Simon & Schuster Canada, 2013).

21 Quotes in Stan Fischler, *Metro Ice: A Century of Hockey in Greater New York* (New York: H&M Publications, 1999), 17, 19. The best biographical treatment of Taylor is Eric Whitehead, *Cyclone Taylor: A Hockey Legend* (New York: Doubleday, 1977).

22 Taylor quoted in Fischler, *Metro Ice*, 19. Patrick quoted in Eric Whitehead, *The Patricks: Hockey's Royal Family* (Toronto: Doubleday, 1980), 93. Craig Bowlsby offers a full chronicle of early hockey in the Pacific Northwest in his self-published books *The Knights of Winter: The History of British Columbia Hockey from 1895 to 1911* (2006) and *Empire of Ice: The Rise and Fall of the Pacific Coast Hockey Association* (2012). In both books he raises questions about some of the Patrick brothers' later recollections.

23 Quotes in John Chi-Kit Wong, "Boomtown Hockey: The Vancouver Millionaires," in *Coast to Coast*, 240. John Chi-Kit Wong, *Lords of the Rinks: The Emergence of the National Hockey League, 1875–1936* (Toronto: University of Toronto Press, 2005), 65; see also Charles L. Coleman, *The Trail of the Stanley Cup, Volume 1: 1893–1926* (NHL, 1966), 257–8, 275, 286.

24 Whitehead, *The Patricks*, 111.

25 Ibid., 94.

26 Elmer Ferguson, "Arena Dramas," [part 2] *Maclean's Magazine*, 1 July 1938, 26; quoted in Ross, "Hockey Capital,"187. See also Kidd, *The Struggle for Canadian Sport*, 203; and Wong, *Lords of the Rinks*, 84–5.

27 Wong, *Lords of the Rinks*, 91. Kidd and Macfarlane, *Death of Hockey*, 111.

28 *Chicago Daily News*, 17 April 1926, 23. For the NHL's arrival in the established Boston market, see Stephen Hardy, "Long before Orr: Placing Hockey in Boston, 1897–1929," in *The Rock, the Curse, and the Hub: Random Histories of Boston Sports*. ed. Randy Roberts (Cambridge, MA: Harvard University Press, 2005), 245–89.

29 Ross, "Hockey Capital," 138–9.

30 Charles Patterson, "Hockey: A National Winter Game," *Outing* 41 (February 1903): 627. As Andy Holman has noted, the border worked in two-ways: "For some, the international border helped keep amateur hockey players in Canada safe from the enticements of professional pay with hockey clubs in the U.S." For others, the border insulated American gentlemen "from the plebeian thuggery of the Canadian brand." Holman, "Playing in the Neutral Zone," 37.

31 James Bird, *The Diagram: Containing Plans of Theatres and Other Places of Amusement in Boston* (Boston: Harper, 1869), 37. My thanks to Paul DeLoca for sharing this source and his manuscript on skating, "The Ice and the Eagle: Skating's Shift from Saint to Show and from Chaos to Science, 1380–1915." On the 1860s skating boom see Luna Lambert, "The American Skating Mania," *Journal of American Culture* 1, no. 4 (1978): 685–6.

32 For the new process of condensing ammonia and chilling brine, see "Skating on Artificial Ice," *Scientific American* 7 (January 1893): 11; *Washington Post*, 8 September 1889, 1.

33 "Automobile Promises to Be the Fad of the New Era," *Brooklyn Eagle*, 30 December 1900, 34.

34 Bigelow quoted in "Thrills That Rock the Hockey Fan Benches," *Literary Digest* 96 (25 February 1928): 54. For an assured prediction that hockey would soon rival football and baseball, see Walter Trumbull, "Hockey Fans Are Demanding More Scoring in Contests," *Boston Evening Globe*, 1 February 1929, 21.

35 W.H. McAvoy, "Hockey in Cleveland," in *Official Ice Hockey Guide, 1909*, ed. Frederick Toombs (New York: American Sports Publishing, 1908), 53, 55, 57. For two excellent books on early hockey in Minnesota, see Roger Godin, *Before the Stars: Early Major League Hockey and the St. Paul Athletic Club* (St Paul: Minnesota Historical Society, 2005), and Roger Godin, *Red, White, and Blue on Ice: Minnesota's Elite Teams and Players of the 1920s, '30s, and '40s* (Haworth, NJ: St Johann Press, 2010).

36 W.A Kearns, "Amateur Hockey in Oregon," in *Official Ice Hockey Guide, 1916* (New York: American Sports Publishing, 1915), 51.

37 "Ice Hockey in San Francisco," in *Official Ice Hockey Guide, 1918*, ed. Thomas A. Howard (New York: American Sports Publishing, 1917), 49–51; "Ice Hockey in Los Angeles," ibid., 52. See also Seamus O. Coughlin, *Squaw Valley Gold: American Hockey's Olympic Odyssey* (Lincoln, NE: Writer's Showcase, 2001).

38 "Ice Hockey in Houston Texas," in *NCAA Ice Hockey Rules and Official Ice Hockey Guide, 1938–39*, ed. Louis Keller (New York: American Sports Publishing, 1938), 69–70; "Texas Military Institute, San Antonio," in *Official Ice Hockey Rules of the NCAA, 1928–29*, ed. Rufus James Trimble (New York: American Sports Publishing, 1928), 75.

39 "University of Southern California," in *NCAA Ice Hockey Rules and Official Ice Hockey Guide, 1933–34*, ed. Louis Keller (New York: American Sports Publishing, 1933), 53. "University of California," in *NCAA Ice Hockey Rules and Official Ice Hockey Guide*, 1937–38, ed. Louis Keller (New York: American Sports Publishing, 1938), 51.

40 William R. McMurtry, *Investigation and Inquiry into Violence in Amateur Hockey* (Ontario Ministry of Community and Social Services, 1974), 21.

41 Account in Fitsell, *Captains, Colonels, and Kings*, 36.

42 For a useful review of some of this literature, see Stacy L. Lorenz and Geraint B. Osborne, "Brutal Butchery, Strenuous Spectacle: Hockey Violence, Manhood, and the 1907 Season," in *Coast to Coast: Hockey in Canada to the Second World War*, ed. John Chi-Kit Wong (Toronto: University of Toronto Press, 2009), 160–202; John Matthew Barlow, "Scientific Aggression: Manliness, Class, and Commercialization in the Shamrock Hockey Club of Montreal, 1894–1901," in Wong (ed.), *Coast to Coast*, 35–85.

43 For the debate over football, see Ronald A. Smith, *Sports and Freedom: The Rise of Big-Time College Athletics* (New York: Oxford University Press, 1988), 83–98. For the sport of "polo," which was played on either roller or ice skates, see Hardy, "Polo at the Rinks," and Fitsell, *How Hockey Happened*.

44 "Club Chat about Sports," *New York Times*, 8 March 1896, 6; 11 March 1896, 6.

45 Caspar Whitney, "Hoodlumism in Hockey," *Outing, an Illustrated Monthly Magazine of Recreation* 41 (February 1903): 635.

46 Thomas A. Howard, "Hockey in the United States," in *Ice Hockey and Ice Polo Guide, 1905*, comp. Arthur Farrell (New York: American Sports Publishing, 1905), 89. Arthur Farrell was a Canadian hockey player who wrote his country's first guidebook to the game, in 1899, two years after the Spalding firm had published the first hockey guide in America. Within a few years he was writing and editing for the Spalding guides.

47 *Boston Herald*, 23 March 1917, 9. Andrew Holman, "Stops and Starts: Ideology, Commercialism, and the Fall of American Women's Hockey in the 1920s," *Journal*

of Sport History 32, no. 3 (Fall 2005): 328–50. For early women's hockey, see Joanna Avery and Julie Stevens, *Too Many Men on the Ice: Women's Hockey in North America* (Victoria, BC: Polestar, 1997); Gai Berlage, "The Development of Intercollegiate Women's Ice Hockey in the United States," *Colby Quarterly*, 32 (March 1996): 58–71; Carly Adams, "'Queens of the Ice Lanes': The Preston Rivulettes and Women's Hockey in Canada, 1931–40," *Sport History Review* 39, no. 1, (2008): 1–29.

48 W. Dustin White, *Book of Winter Sports* (Boston: Houghton Mifflin, 1925), 96. Lynahan quoted in in "Why Stitches Decorate the Hockey Player's Dome," *Literary Digest* 92 (12 February 1927): 75. Benny Leonard and Philadelphia writer in "Thrills and Spills in the Hockey Rink," *Literary Digest*, 12 January 1929: 56. For contemporary thoughts on the science of hockey, see "Thrills That Rock the Hockey Fan Benches," *Literary Digest* 96 (25 February 1928): 52–6.

49 "Foreword," "Rules Changes for 1928–1929," "Uniformity of Amateur Rules Desirable," and "Unnecessary Rough Play," in *NCAA Ice Hockey Rules and Official Ice Hockey Guide, 1928–29*, ed. Rufus James Trimble (New York: American Sports Publishing, 1928), 29. NCAA Ice Hockey Committee Minutes in Charles E. Holt Archives of American Hockey, Dimond Library, University of New Hampshire; http://www.library.unh.edu/find/special/subject/holt-hockey-archives.

50 "Hockey on Ice," *Montreal Gazette*, 27 February 1877, 4. Compare to "CAHA Rules," in *Official Ice Hockey Guide and Winter Sports Almanac, 1921*, ed. Tom Howard (New York: American Sports Publishing, 1921), 68; "Playing Rules of the United States Amateur Hockey Association," *in Official Ice Hockey Guide, 1924*, ed. Tom Howard (New York: American Sports Publishing, 1924), 92; NHL from "Laws of Hockey as Compiled by the National Professional Hockey League," in *Official Ice Hockey Guide and Winter Sports Almanac, 1921*, 63. For an overview of Canadian rules, see Ronald C. Watson and Gegory D. Rickwood, "Stewards of Ice Hockey: A Historical Review of Safety Rules in Canadian Ice Hockey," *Sport History Review* 30 (1999): 27–38.

51 NCAA Ice Hockey Rules Committee Minutes, June 1933, p. 2, NCAA collection, mc 206, box 1, folder 1; Charles Holt Archives of American Hockey, Dimond Library, University of New Hampshire. *Official Rules for Ice Hockey, 1926–27* (NCAA, 1926), 18; *Official Ice Hockey Rules of the NCAA, 1928–29*, ed. Rufus Trimble (New York: American Sports Publishing, 1928). NHL 1930–31, Rule 34 stated: "A major penalty [five minutes] shall be imposed on any player who starts fisticuffs. A minor penalty shall be given the adversary if he has responded with a blow, or attempted blow, but he shall be permitted to hold his opponent without penalty." Note that a player who received a second major for any reason (for example, throwing stick, causing injury with stick) would have a ten-minute major. The third would be disqualification. See "National Hockey League Laws of Hockey

(Professional)," in *Official Rules for Ice Hockey, Speed Skating, Figure Skating, and Curling* (New York: American Sports Publishing, 1930), 11.

52 At least until the 1950s and 1960s, when a surge of Canadian recruits seemed to threaten short-lived traditions. As Andrew Holman concluded in his research on this topic, observers in both countries considered this influx an "acute problem that threatened the integrity and identity of the game." See Andrew Holman, "The Canadian Hockey Player Problem: Cultural Reckoning and National Identities in American Collegiate Sport, 1947–80," *Canadian Historical Review*, 88 (September 2007): 439–68, quote at 448.

53 W.H. Fox, "Municipal Hockey in Minneapolis," in *NCAA Ice Hockey Rules and Official Ice Hockey Guide, 1931–32*, ed. Trimble (New York: American Sports Publishing, 1931), 63. For links between community and commercial sport in Canada during this time, see Daniel Macdonald, "Class, Community, and Commercialism: Hockey in Industrial Cape Breton, 1917–1937," in Wong, ed. *Coast to Coast*, 3–34.

54 J.T. Meek, "A Big Skate Season Is Afoot," *Sporting Goods Dealer*, January 1931: 117–18. My thanks to Larry Fielding for his generous assistance in tracking down hockey-focused stories in the *Dealer*.

55 "Amateur Hockey Booming in Chicago," *Sporting Goods Dealer*, December 1933, 107.

56 J.T. Meek, "Hockey's Coming Along in a Hurry," *Sporting Goods Dealer*, December 1934, 34, 74.

57 Meek, "Hockey's Coming Along in a Hurry," 34, 74. Tobin's boss, Blackhawks owner Frederick McLaughlin, would soon hatch a plan to "Americanize" his franchise.

58 Thomas McCraw, *Prophet of Innovation: Joseph Schumpeter and Creative Destruction* (Cambridge, MA: Harvard University Press, 2007), 82, 164. Joseph Schumpeter, "The Instability of Capitalism," *Economic Journal* 38 (September 1928): 361–86; Joseph A. Schumpeter, "The Creative Response in Economic History," *Journal of Economic History* 7 (November 1947): 149–59; reprinted in Joseph A. Schumpeter, *Essays on Entrepreneurs, Innovations, Business Cycles, and the Evolution of Capitalism*, ed. Richard V. Clemence (Addison-Wesley, 1951; reprinted New Brunswick, NJ: Transaction Publishers, 2008), 221–31.

59 Tripp Mickle, "Sun Belt Hot and Cold for NHL," *Street and Smith's Sports Business Journal*, 5–11 October 2009, 1, 17–22; quote on page 22.

7 Continentalization and America's Contested Baseball Hegemony: The Post-War Challenge to Major League Baseball in Mexico, Quebec, and the Caribbean, 1945–55

COLIN HOWELL

The years immediately following the Second World War are most often understood in relation to baseball's "great experiment," the gradual breaking down of barriers to participation for African Americans and other peoples of colour in American professional baseball. This process of inclusion, which grew out of the new demographics and commercial possibilities of the post-war era and in response to pressure from civil liberties advocates, the black press, and the Communist Party, has become a centrepiece of baseball's broader narrative of increasing democratization in the post-war years. The liberal interpretation of baseball's important place in the incipient civil rights movement implies the socially redemptive character of America's "national pastime" and highlights its democratic sensibilities. The inclusion of visible minorities – beginning with the signing of five players by the Brooklyn Dodgers in 1946 and the eventual involvement of Latino players in considerable numbers in the 1950s – is seen as one of the most pivotal developments in the history of Major League Baseball. Of course, the democratization of the game was and is a gradual process. As Jules Tygiel, Patrick Harrigan, Sam Regalado, Adrian Burgos, and others have demonstrated, black and Latino players faced continuing discrimination during these years and continue to do so today.[1]

One would be hard pressed to ignore the significance of the eradication of baseball's "apartheid" policies, or the often-heroic struggle of black and Latino players to secure their place in the game, but the persuasiveness of this story often masks another contested and arguably related process. As Adrian Burgos has pointed out, the end of segregation in baseball meant that major league owners and league officials no longer had to "balance their commercial goals of expanding markets and dominating labor with the goal of maintaining a racially restrictive system."[2] This facilitated in turn an extension of America's post-war baseball hegemony both northward into Canada and southward into Latin America. Yet "playing America's game" was not uncontested. This chapter focuses on the process of resistance and accommodation to the expansionist designs of Major League Baseball beyond the continental boundaries of the United States. It addresses in turn Don Jorge Pasquel's Mexican League experiment, the subsequent experience of blacklisted players such as Jean-Pierre Roy, Roland Gladu, and Stan Breard in the Quebec Provincial League, and of Napoleon Reyes, Silvio Garcia, Tomas de la Cruz, and others in the Cuban National Association in the immediate post-war period. It is not my intention here to recount in detail the story of Pasquel's challenge, for that has already been done elsewhere. Instead I focus on discourses, the ideological weight attached to terms such as *outlaw leagues, banditry, player slavery,* and *peonage* and what one might call the "naturalization of American power" reflected in the self-appropriation of the term *Organized Baseball.* As Rob Elias points out in his recent study of baseball's connection to American imperial expansion, it makes a difference whether hegemonic internationalism "is experienced from the bottom up by peoples and nations or imposed from the top down by the dominant powers."[3] Rather than seeing these years as ones in which people of colour fought to establish their place in the major leagues, this chapter looks at those who resisted and accommodated themselves to America's growing hegemony.

Jorge Pasquel: The Nationalist Owner as Outlaw

In Mexican history outlaws and bandits have been variously interpreted. Yet if the meaning of *banditry* – like contemporary terms such as *terrorism* or *insurgency* – is broadly contested, the stereotypical physical image of Mexican outlaws is relatively uniform. On the front page of its 25 February 1946 edition *The Sporting News* presented a commonplace image (see figure 7.1). The Willard Mullin cartoon depicted there parodied the challenge to Organized Baseball mounted by Pasquel and his four brothers. Beneath the headline "Game's Officials Act to Meet Outlaw Threat" the cartoon depicts an audacious and menacing Mexican bandit replete with sombrero, serape over the shoulder, and six-shooter in hand, holding up Organized Baseball in its respectable business suit and tie. Clutched in the outlaw's raised right fist are a number of the players snatched from their Major League clubs: Tomas de la Cruz, Adrian Zabala, Nap Reyes, Bobby Estalella, Danny Gardella, and Luis Olmo.

The Pasquels represented a rather unusual kind of outlawry. Members of a wealthy Mexican family with close ties to the Mexican government, they had amassed substantial fortunes in banking, ranching, transportation, and the import-export trade. Connected by marriage to former Mexican president

7.1 References to Mexico's baseball "outlaws" were commonplace in the 1940s, as indicated in this Willard Mullin illustration. Image courtesy of Shirley Mullin Rhodes.

Elias Callas, and by friendship and business partnership with Miguel Aleman who became president of Mexico in 1946, the Pasquels had both political and financial capital at their disposal.[4] Armed with over $30 million to make the Mexican League "as good as, or better than, baseball in the United States,"[5] the Pasquels convinced more than two-dozen players to jump their existing major- and minor-league contracts in the spring of 1946. Some of these players, such as Sal Maglie and Max Lanier, had signed contracts for the 1946 season; others like Danny Gardella were bound to their clubs by the reserve clause in existing contracts. All except those who returned to their major league clubs before the opening of the 1946 season were handed five-year suspensions from Organized Baseball by Commissioner A.B. "Happy" Chandler.

Like elsewhere in North America, the end of the war had released pent-up demand for leisure and recreation activities in Mexico, and Pasquel envisaged the revamping of the country's professional sport infrastructure to meet the expanding market for spectator sport. The post-war years witnessed rapid economic growth, infrastructure improvements, and the coming of consumer culture to Mexico.[6] In addition to attracting major league stars, Pasquel announced plans to construct a $2.2 million baseball stadium in Mexico City that would accommodate 52,000 fans in soft cushioned theatre seats and rival the city's new 46,000-seat bullring and 70,000-seat soccer stadium. Noting that the present outdated ballpark would only hold 22,000 fans and that crowds of 100,000 would not be out of the question if the facilities were available, Pasquel spoke of plans for "ultra-modern" parks in all Mexican League cities.[7] Obviously, this fascination with modernity is hardly the stuff of the traditional outlaw. The *bandido* of Mexican folklore was at odds with the process of modernity as presided over by the state. By contrast, the plutocratic Pasquels were clearly committed to the modernizing project of the post-war era. Determined to present an image of the nation as stable, progressive, and forward looking, they chafed at their characterization as "outlaws." "Why do they refer to our Mexican League as an outlaw organization?" Pasquel asked. "I resent that and may take Organized ball into the courts to make them prove that we are not operating fully within the laws of ... Mexico."[8]

In his classic study of banditry in peasant societies Eric Hobsbawm advanced the idea of social banditry, arguing that embedded beneath the social violence in which outlaws engaged, there often were deeper social purposes. Rough around the edges, disorderly and violent, and threatening the established rule of law, some outlaws were "primitive rebels" and avengers of wrongs. In refusing to acquiesce to established authority or to live the life of the subject peasant, moreover, *bandidos* often became champions of the plebeian community from which they originated.[9] Historians have hotly debated the merits of the "social bandit" concept and continue to do so today. Chris Frazer points out that popular narratives of the *bandido* in Mexico arose amidst a broader cultural struggle involving issues of class, gender, and national identity, and that discourses about banditry were fiercely contested. Positive constructions of the *bandido* often appeared in popular ballads, which presented commonplace notions of appropriate masculinity and vented the Mexican underclass's hostility to its social oppressors.[10] For members of the Mexican elite, like Pasquel, outlaws were atavistic figures who represented cultural backwardness rather than social progress.[11] From the late-nineteenth century Porfiriato well into the twentieth century, tensions between modernity and traditionalism enlivened debates about both banditry and the making of sporting culture.[12]

Rather than conforming to Hobsbawm's notion of the social bandit, Pasquel is better understood as reflecting the nationalist presumptions of the Mexican post-war ruling class. In his study of baseball along the Mexican-American border Alan Klein spoke of three different presentations of nationalism: auto-nationalism, binationationalism, and transnationalism. According to Klein, binationalism and transnationalism imply a shared experience, a pragmatic working out of cross-border problems, and even a borderland culture in which residents share cultural identities. Autonationalism involves a collective identification with a society articulated by its borders, excluding those beyond and often identifying the "other" as an enemy. At times, autonationalism involves the "puffery, bluster and sabre-rattling that accompanies testicular politics," and the machismo of the outlaw. In trying to apply these categories to the Mexico–United States baseball dispute, Klein asks whether Pasquel's nationalism was "a constructive, collective sense of self, or … a collective demonizing of an enemy?" He concludes that Pasquel was "only erratically autonationalist."[13]

However they are labelled, the Pasquels considered themselves social reformers and modernizing nationalists, defending Mexican interests, dispelling stereotypical assumptions about cultural decadence and backwardness, and providing a bulwark against the destructive cultural imperialism that the expansion of Organized Baseball represented.[14] In their defence of Mexican baseball – indeed of Mexico itself – the Pasquels fashioned an adroit critique of baseball in the United States that turned traditional images of American freedom and prosperity and Mexican corruption and poverty on their head. Organized Baseball, they argued, was like a "slave market," its players held in virtual peonage as a result of the reserve clause.[15] In a Rafael Freyre cartoon from the Mexico City newspaper *Excelsior*, reprinted in the *Sporting News*, for example, Organized Baseball was likened to a meat grinder, with Ford Frick and Lee McPhail turning players into processed meat. At the border an agent of the Mexican League waved a cheque book, beckoning players to choose wealth and freedom over contract slavery and exploitation.

The Mexican usurpation of post-war images of American liberty in a world of tyranny, and the use of racially charged references to player slavery at the very time that Organized Baseball was priding itself on lifting the colour bar, invited a quick rejoinder from the American baseball establishment. In the *Sporting News* of 21 March 1946, J.G. Taylor Spink complained about Latin American newspapers' attacks on the reserve clause: "Ballplayers in this country do not challenge the reserve clause. The player knows that he is receiving every dime to which he is entitled by the box office. If the money comes in, the club owner is only too glad to pass the benefits on to his players." Of course, many players would have taken exception to this rosy picture, even if they were reluctant to challenge the authority of the owners.[16] Spink also derided Mexican charges of player "peonage" in professional baseball. "For certain people in Latin America to use the word peonage is highly inadvisable," he said, arguing that "while no peonage exists in the United States, it prevailed in Latin America."[17] As the historian Mark Reisler has pointed out, the stereotype of ordinary Mexicans as "Indian peons" had congealed in the United States during the inter-war years and endured into the post-war era.[18]

Although rhetoric framed the debate, the contract question was the nub of the issue. For the most part, Americans believed in the idea of sanctity of the contract, which was a foundation of the legal system and the cornerstone of the collective bargaining process. As far as Mexican baseball officials were concerned, however, Organized Baseball defended its own contract rights vociferously but had little interest in the rights of others. Pasquel pointed out that for years the major and minor leagues had raided the Mexican League for Latin stars of light complexion, and hinted that, with the dropping of the colour bar, Negro League contracts were likely to be ignored as well. There was a widespread belief in Mexico that Americans used contracts when it suited them, violated contracts when it did not, and used their might to achieve their own interests when all else failed. It is worth remembering that Pasquel's challenge to existing contracts took place in a broader context of contested relations relating to contract labour. Under the Bracero program established in 1942 to meet war-time labour shortages in the United States, Mexican contract labourers in the country routinely found themselves working for employers who violated contract guarantees.[19]

From the Mexican point of view, American presumptions about the sanctity of contract obscured the contradictions inherent in the processes of underdevelopment and dependence. Not surprisingly, notions of honour, respect, and gentlemanly behaviour resonated more powerfully among the Mexican ruling class than did allusions to sanctity of contract. A situation involving Don Aurelio Ferrara, Mexican League vice-president and chief executive of the Monterrey club, and Joseph "Papa Joe" Cambria of the Washington Senators illustrates the point. Ferrara accused Cambria of abusing Mexican hospitality and stealing two of his players, Lamalla Torreon and Hec Leal, while Cambria was a guest in his home. Cambria vigorously denied the report, saying that he had never been in Ferrara's home, had paid for his own ticket to watch Monterrey play, and was "chased out [of town] at the point of a gun." What is more, he had signed them in Cuba when their Mexican contracts had expired.[20] Cambria believed that he was simply facilitating the entrance of Latino players into the major leagues and that the Mexican challenge stood in the way of a more integrated and ethnically diverse system of professional baseball in the United States. Hired in the 1930s by the parsimonious owner of the Washington Senators, Clark Griffith, to bring low-salaried Cuban players to the United States, Cambria lured a score of Cubans to the United States during the 1940s and brought hundreds more to the country in the 1950s.[21] He became so popular in Cuba that a cigar was named in his honour.[22]

Whomever one believes in the dispute between Ferrara and Cambria, what is interesting is the way in which contract inviolability, personal honour, and the exercise of power – at the point of a gun – were woven into the story. By arguing that the major leagues had once been able to violate Mexican contracts with impunity because of their extensive capital resources, Pasquel essentially reframed the discussion, focusing less on contract and more on the questions of power, access to capital, and honour and respect. "I took my losses for years when Organized Ball moved in and took my players because I was unable to compete with their salary offers," said Pasquel. "Today, it's a different story. I am ready to compete with Organized Ball, dollar for dollar and peso for peso, for the best talent available."[23]

The ability to compete as equals implied, moreover, that any attempt to resolve the dispute required a negotiation framework that reflected that reality. With Dodgers general manager Branch Rickey calling for a tough stance against "deserters," and with Pasquel signing more and more players, the *Sporting News* called for negotiations between Pasquel and Commissioner Happy Chandler. Although Pasquel was willing to deal – and may even have considered affiliating his Mexican League with Organized Baseball if certain conditions were met – he did not want to present the image of being at Chandler's beck and call and suggested that negotiations take place in a border city or in Havana. The *Sporting News* was amazed at this affrontery. "Pasquel's 'ultimatum,'" wrote Spink, "smacks of the days when Pancho Villa was raiding Columbus, N.M., and relations between the United States and outlaw Mexican elements were close to actual war."[24]

Although there was some understanding in the United States that Pasquel was responding to what many Mexicans considered "shabby treatment" by Organized Baseball,[25] it is also interesting to note the tendency of journalists to reinforce traditional stereotypes about Mexican emotionalism, hot-headedness, and political instability. "Americans, probably, cannot fully appreciate the situation," one commentator wrote, "for although Mexico is a hotbed of howling rabid fans, there is a powerful factor of Mexican politics, filled with implacable hatreds and rivalries, and the enmity of the Pasquels who are throwing millions of dollars into a fight to get vengeance."[26] Mexican baseball itself seemed undisciplined and rowdy. An article in the 11 April 1946 *Sporting News* described the Mexican League as the equivalent of class A minor league ball, with long, dragged-out games, exploding firecrackers, and people stretching after each inning. "Betting is illegal, plentiful, but unorganized," it reported. "Gamblers shout their odds on a pitch or inning."[27] All of this suggested a league unwilling to play by the rules, and helped to portray Pasquel and his associates as outlaws. But the tendency to think of Pasquel as Pancho Villa in business attire, or as a vengeful autonationalist motivated by an irrational anti-Americanism, ignores a number of important realities and accepts as natural the attempt of Organized Baseball to control baseball in Latin America.

In the end, Pasquel's challenge to Major League Baseball collapsed. As losses increased and as many of the Cuban and Negro League players outperformed high-priced major league stars,[28] Pasquel began to lose interest in his Mexican operation. The bubble finally burst in September 1948 when the league ended its pennant race five weeks early. Pasquel summoned team managers to a meeting on 19 September to inform them that "the season is over. Tell your players I am not paying a single cent more."[29] Over three seasons the league had suffered losses estimated at $362,000.[30] Although Pasquel's dream of a rival major league in Mexico was never realized, it led in the long run to a stronger Mexican baseball system under Mexican control. Even when the Mexican League rejoined Organized Baseball in 1955 and was designated as a Double-A and later a Triple-A circuit, it retained a relatively independent position, and does so even today.

Outlaws at Home: Nap Reyes, Tomas de la Cruz, Silvio García, and Winter Baseball in Cuba, 1946–8

During and immediately after the war Commissioner Happy Chandler took steps to extend the reach of Organized Baseball outside of the continental boundaries of the United States. He was urged on in this endeavour by a number of owners, especially Clark Griffith of the Washington Senators who supported intervention in Cuba and Mexico and had visions of Organized Baseball building up leagues in Central and South America.[31] Unlike many of his counterparts who dismissed Latinos as "good field, no hit" players, Griffith respected the skill of Cuban ballplayers and encouraged "Papa Joe" Cambria to scour the island for baseball talent.[32] Like Cambria, Alex Pompez, the long-time Negro League owner of the Cuban Stars and later a New York Giants scout, had for years imported talent from Cuba, the Dominican Republic, Puerto Rico, and Panama and was an influential figure in the post-war importation of Latino players into Major League Baseball.[33] J. Alvin Gardner, president of the Texas League, was another exuberant advocate of baseball's expansionist project.

Noting the popularity of baseball in Mexico among children aged ten to sixteen, and of pick-up games on every vacant lot, Gardner believed that it was time for baseball to become an important element of American foreign policy in Latin America. According to Gardner, "the Latins close to our borders have long been ready to receive American baseball with open arms."[34] He may have exaggerated their interest. In fact, the strategy of Organized Baseball to establish teams and leagues under its control in Mexico and Cuba was met with considerable suspicion.

In its attempt to undercut the legitimacy of Pasquel's Mexican League, Organized Baseball became closely associated with the Mexican National League (MNL). Established in 1943 with franchises in El Paso, Juarez, Chihuahua City, Torreon, Saltillo, and Mexico City, the MNL was a bitter rival of Pasquel's circuit. Between 1943 and 1945 it operated as an unaffiliated league, but in 1946 it was absorbed into the minor league system within Organized Baseball. Griffith argued that Major League Baseball "should help in every way to develop this league, and also help the fans of Mexico to the realization that baseball and gambling cannot mix, and that the American way is the only way." Pasquel, however, saw Organized Baseball's association with the MNL as provocative, a threat to the integrity and control by Mexicans of the Mexican baseball system. The Mexican League had operated since 1920. Pasquel bridled at the assumption of major league officials that the Mexican League was an outlaw league and that the upstart MNL represented order and respectability. During these years the Pasquels fought a tenacious battle against the MNL, sewing up the only good stadium in Mexico City and making sure that there was no press coverage of the MNL Aztecs in Mexico City. Squeezed on all sides by the Pasquels, the MNL's franchises in Mexico City and Torreon collapsed. On the American side of the border the situation was reversed. In El Paso, the Spanish language newspaper *El Continental* carried regular reports on Major League Baseball and MNL competition but ignored Pasquel's Mexican League completely. The MNL played to small crowds, however, and finally collapsed in the summer of 1946.[35]

At the same time that Organized Baseball cultivated the MNL as its surrogate in the battle against the Pasquels, the Florida International League (FIL), which had not operated during the war, opened play in 1946 with a team in Havana. The Havana club was eventually controlled by co-owners Clark Griffith and Joe Cambria and became a farm team for the Washington Senators.[36] Over that summer the Havana club was the class of the league, winning the pennant by seven games even though it had been stripped of seventeen victories by the league's president for using too many over-age players.[37] In 1947 the club captured its second straight FIL pennant, with 105 victories in 150 games. Havana was equally successful at the gate: its attendance of 264,813 fans was double that of the Miami club, its closest competitor.[38] Despite the success of the franchise, Cuban baseball officials were wary of the FIL and considered it an American camel sticking its nose under the Cuban tent. They deeply resented in turn the suggestion by Happy Chandler that "Cuba must either conform to America's system of Organized Baseball or fall into the category of the so-called Mexican outlaw league."[39] According to columnist Shirley Povich, there were fifteen newspapers in Havana representing various shades of opinion but united on one thing: "They don't want Americans telling Cubans how they should run their baseball leagues."[40]

Like Mexico, Cuba had welcomed visits by American major league teams over the years.[41] Yet, while many of its players barnstormed in the United States and while Cubans were proud of Adolfo Luque, Bobby Estalella, Nap Reyes, and Alex Carrasquel for their major league achievements, an independent spirit prevailed among Mexican and Cuban baseball officials alike.[42] This was evident during the 1946–7 winter league season when Organized Baseball supported a new league restricted to players in good standing with Major League Baseball. A dispute quickly arose between the newly established National Baseball Federation, which was made up of sanctioned Cuban and American players, and the older Cuban Winter League, which included a number of ineligible players from the Mexican League.[43] In an attempt to work out a compromise arrangement with Organized Baseball, Cuban Winter League president Julio Sanguilly initially offered to respect the ban against twelve ineligible players from the Mexican League if Chandler would forgive Cuban players who had gone to Mexico. Among the players who would have been barred were Stan Breard, J.-P. Roy, Roland Gladu, Bucky Tanner, Freddy Martin, and Max Lanier. Sanguilly pointed out the irony of not allowing Cuban stars like Tomas de la Cruz, Alex Carrasquel, Nap Reyes, and Mike Gonzalez to play at home.[44] Sanguilly's offer was rejected, however, and the Cuban Winter League proceeded to play with players blacklisted by Major League Baseball. In response to the hard line taken by Chandler, the Cuban Winter League announced that it would bar for three years any player leaving it to play with the National Baseball Federation.[45]

It soon became clear where the allegiance of the Cuban fans lay. The press lambasted Chandler on a regular basis. Lilio Jiminez, sports editor of *Informacion,* echoed the feelings of most baseball fans in Cuba when he claimed that Chandler wanted "to make us have Class D baseball when we want major league ball."[46] Although the sanctioned league had some high-quality Cuban players such as shortstop Silvio Garcia,[47] and a number of Negro League stars like Don Newcombe and Ray Dandridge, it could not match the quality of the traditional winter league. The teams in this league dated back to before the turn of the century, and according to Roberto Gonzalez Echevarria, "their rivalry moved thousands of fans to passion. It defined and divided families, endangered friendships and was the financial mainstay of Cuban baseball."[48] Attendance in the National Baseball Federation was spotty, while the four-team winter league was a smashing success. During more than sixty games at the brand new Gran Stadium el Cerro, the Havana Lions drew over 750,000 fans, including a crowd of more than 35,000 who witnessed a pitching matchup between Max Lanier of the Alamanderes Scorpions and Freddy Martin of Havana. On 1 January 1947 the National Baseball Federation collapsed. Later that spring the Brooklyn Dodgers arrived in Cuba for spring training, hoping to provide a more congenial setting for Jackie Robinson than Florida, but Cuban fans seemed more interested in their own leagues than in the major league brand, and crowds were disappointing for the major league exhibition games.[49]

Still smarting from the failure of the National Baseball Federation, and the fact that fifty-four players had played in the unsanctioned Cuban Winter League without permission from Organized Baseball,[50] Happy Chandler threatened to suspend any player who played alongside blacklisted players in Cuba during the forthcoming 1947 winter season. He was forced to compromise with Cuban officials, however, and on 11 July 1947 a newly organized Cuban League received the blessing of Organized Baseball. Many Cuban players had their earlier suspensions lifted, and the teams were limited to eight American players who had no more than four years' experience in the minor leagues. The newly sanctioned league included the teams from the older winter league in Havana, Alamanderes, Cienfuegos, and Marianao. For those under continuing suspension, a rival four-team Players Federation was established, sporting a number of star players including Bobby Avila, Danny Gardella, Adrian Zabala, Myron Hayworth, Sal Maglie, Fred Martin, and Canadians Roland Gladu, Stan Breard, Paul Calvert, and Jean-Pierre Roy. The only player who would not play in the major leagues during his career was Breard, but not because of a lack of talent. In 1948 the *Sporting News* noted that Breard was "fifth among hitters in *Liga Nacional* … looks good in every department … Moving fast and fielding steadily."[51] The involvement of these Canadian players, and of Roy and Gladu in particular, was important in the final act of the story, the subsequent development of the Quebec Provincial League as a "haven" for blacklisted stars following the collapse of the Mexican League experiment.

Jean-Pierre Roy: The Player as Outlaw

As the opening of the 1946 major league season loomed, the resentment against the Pasquels' high-handed raiding tactics reached the boiling point.

On 25 March the Brooklyn Dodgers' spring-training camp was in a state of high alert, occasioned by the visit of Mexican League player's agent Robert Janis to the training site of the Brooklyn affiliate Montreal Royals. Janis reportedly offered Jackie Robinson $6,000 to jump across the Rio Grande. Later that same day Dodgers general manager Branch Rickey and manager Leo Durocher confronted the interloper. Along with an angry demeanour Durocher carried a baseball bat, while Rickey took off his coat and challenged Janis to a fight. According to one reporter, Rickey accompanied his "warlike gesture with a string of naughty words that would have made Larry McPhail stop his ears."[52] Janis, a six-foot-four bodybuilder from New York who had been hired by Pasquel to contact major league players from the Dodgers, Giants, and Yankees, was so shaken by the incident that he quickly left the site, checked out of his hotel, and registered elsewhere under an assumed name.[53]

On the following day the Dodgers' camp at Daytona Beach was abuzz again when a figure in a wide-brimmed sombrero and a Mexican blanket strode out onto the field. Walking confidently to the mound, the intruder turned, bowed, and, in a dramatic flourish, threw back the blanket. Immediately the tension in the air turned to laughter. The mystery man was none other than Jean-Pierre Roy.[54] Always irreverent and often in trouble with the clubs for whom he played, Roy had been one of the first Dodgers whom Pasquel had contacted to play in Mexico. Rickey was less than amused with Roy's antics. Some even suspected him to be Pasquel's clubhouse agent, a charge he later denied. Whatever the case, Roy flitted back and forth between Mexico and the Dodgers in 1946, escaping suspension by starting the season on the Dodger roster.

A graduate of the University of Montreal with a burning ambition to pitch for the Montreal Royals, Roy turned professional in 1940 with Trois-Rivières of the Quebec Provincial League, winning ten games that year and fourteen the following season. Purchased by the Cardinals in 1942, he played two seasons for Rochester of the International League until a row with manager Eddie Dyer resulted in his sale to the Royals. Roy had a playboy reputation; he was described by one scribe as "a patron of the nocturnal gaities, a late supper devotee."[55] However, he had a live arm, a fastball with movement, and a good curveball to go with it. He quickly became the workhorse of the Royals' pitching staff. Montreal sportswriter Lloyd McGowan penned the following fictitious note from Royals manager Bruno Betzel to Leo Durocher following the 1945 season: "This will introduce Jean-Pierre Roy, 25, right-hander with a fast ball, explosive temper, fine curve; rugged, of average stature, good pitch, good hit, good field ... but handle with care" since he "is an unusual young Frenchman, edging to the border-line of eccentricity."[56] In 1945 Roy completed twenty-nine games, winning twenty-five during the regular season and three more in the play-offs. He tied Hank Oana of Buffalo for the league lead in strikeouts with a hundred and thirty-five, and racked up almost three hundred innings pitched. Roy's teammates included fellow Canadians Roland Gladu, who led the club in batting with a .338 average, and infielder Stan Breard who hit .275 but, for the second year in succession, led the league's shortstops in fielding. All three would eventually end up playing in Mexico, as would another Royals teammate, William "Bucky" Tanner. Two other Dodgers, Canadian Goody Rosen and the flamboyant Franco-American Stan "Frenchy" Bordagaray, felt secure enough with the big-league club to ignore opportunities to play in Mexico. Ironically, the Dodgers cut Bordagaray at the end of spring training in 1946 and sent him north as manager of the Canadian-American League club in Trois-Rivières.

In early February 1946 reports circulated that Roy and Gladu had signed to play in Mexico and that Luis Olmo was poised to do the same. Although Roy and Gladu had turned in eye-popping minor league performances the year before, both felt that the return of war veterans would deny them a shot at making the Dodgers. While in Cuba over the winter, Gladu and Roy seriously considered offers from Pasquel to play in Mexico. Since the Dodgers offered him less than he had received the year before in Montreal, Gladu had his mind firmly made up to play in Mexico. But Roy vacillated. In late February, on his way home to Canada from Cuba, he took a detour to the Dodgers' camp in Daytona Beach. Although sporting a gold bracelet inscribed with the letters J.P. – signifying the alliance of Jorge Pasquel and Jean-Pierre – he met with Rickey, who assured him that the Dodgers wanted him. Fifteen minutes later Roy signed his Dodgers contract.[57]

After a good spring training in which he secured a spot on the Dodgers' roster, Roy found himself in the bullpen with few opportunities to pitch. Through mid-May he made but one start and two relief appearances with the Dodgers, pitching well in his first two outings but having control problems in the third. In the meantime he was again in contact with Pasquel. Offered a $3,300 signing bonus and a $15,000 per year contract, Roy went AWOL for a couple of weeks to investigate the Mexican option. Although he was known to talk of Mexico as "the land of golden dreams," Roy was disappointed with what he found. "Players were lucky to get a shower bath," he observed, "and hotel rooms were lighted by a single candle."[58] Without playing a single game there, he set what the *Sporting News* called the "new jumping bean record of all time" by bouncing back to Brooklyn.[59] Chastened and contrite – at least for the moment – Roy was reinstated by Branch Rickey and sent to Montreal.[60]

Roy spent the rest of the 1946 season with the Royals alongside Stan Breard, who had spurned an offer to play in Mexico and still dreamed of making the Dodgers' roster despite the return of Pee Wee Reese from war-time service.

Roy's other former teammates Bucky Tanner and Roland Gladu were now in Mexico under five-year suspensions. Like Roy, Tanner was a free spirit. A hard-throwing, six-foot-eight, and two hundred-pound righthander from Rattlesnake, Florida, Tanner had signed with the Dodgers in 1944 as a seventeen-year-old and been sent to Newport News, where he threw two no-hitters that year. In one, he walked the first eight batters, but manager Jake Pitler told him not to quit since Brooklyn scouts wanted to see how long he could smoke the ball. Tanner finished the no-hit game with thirteen walks and lost 6–0. After pitching for Montreal in 1945, Tanner was offered $12,000 to come to Mexico. Already married with four kids, the twenty-year-old agreed and was assigned first to Pasquel's Veracruz Club and later to Torreon. Although he pitched well, at one point besting Max Lanier in a pitcher's duel that broke Lanier's six-game unbeaten streak, Tanner did not return to Mexico after the 1946 season. He later kicked around Quebec and Nova Scotia until his reinstatement in 1949. Tanner gained some notoriety when he pitched an eleven-inning no-hitter for Fort Lauderdale of the FIL against Miami in 1950. The third no-hitter of his career, this was the first no-hit game in baseball history to be televised.[61]

After the 1946 season Roy and Breard defied Happy Chandler's edict against playing in the Cuban Winter League and, along with another Quebecker, pitcher Paul Calvert, were suspended for two years. Breard immediately signed a Veracruz Blues contract, and Calvert joined Gladu in San Luis Potosi. Roy found himself with few options, however. Since he had already burned his bridges with both Pasquel and Rickey and could not expect another pardon to play with the Royals, he agreed to pitch and manage St Jean of the independent Quebec Provincial League (QPL).[62] This decision was an important one for the league but also for the majority of the players who were presently under suspension.[63] Over the next two-and-a-half years, as Pasquel's experiment began to unravel, Quebec (and, to a lesser extent, Nova Scotia) became sanctuaries for a number of players from Cuba, the Negro Leagues in the United States, and Mexico. Roland Gladu, who finished third in batting behind Bobby Avila and Ray Dandridge in Mexico in 1947, returned to Quebec late in the year. When Pasquel announced salary cuts of as much as 50 per cent for the 1948 season, Gladu stayed home, as did Stan Breard. Between them, Roy, Gladu, and Breard convinced a number of their former teammates in Mexico and Cuba to come north for the summer.

The place of Canada in the continentalization of baseball at this time was far less contentious than that of Mexico or of Cuba. In Canada, independent leagues and those affiliated with Organized Baseball had coexisted since before the First World War and demonstrated little animosity towards each other.[64] This helps explain why there was little resentment or antagonism when blacklisted players ended up in the independent QPL as the Mexican experiment began to founder. Rather than being seen as a threat to Organized Baseball, or characterized by a *bandido* spirit, the QPL was more often pictured as a sanctuary for those sinners who had broken their contract with the gods of Organized Baseball.[65] In a story about Max Lanier, who received an "astonishing" $10,000 to play for Drummondville, the headline noted as well: "Other Former Major Leaguers Find Haven in Canadian Loop."[66] This imagery, of course, conformed to the prevailing stereotypes of Quebec in the years before its "Quiet Revolution," as a priest-ridden community dominated by the Catholic Church and respectful of established authority.

A number of players from the Mexican and Negro Leagues ended up in the QPL. Over the years most of these had played with Roy, Gladu, Breard, and Paul Calvert in Mexico and were aware that the QPL, like the Man-Dak League with franchises on both sides of the North Dakota–Manitoba border,[67] provided both a competitive salary structure and a hospitable environment for players of darker skin. Of more than three dozen players from the Mexican League, eighteen signed with QPL clubs in 1948 and fifteen in 1949. When suspended players were reinstated in June 1949, Calvert, Carrasquel, Estalella, Klein, Lanier, and Zabala signed with their former major league clubs. Roy and Tanner returned to Organized Baseball in the International League and the Florida International League, respectively. There were others, including Sal Maglie, who chose not to jump back immediately, finishing out the year with their QPL clubs.

In the meantime, negotiations had begun to bring the Quebec Provincial League back into the Organized Baseball fold. About a month after the blacklist had ended, Albert Molini, QPL president, met with Walter Mulbry, assistant to Commissioner Chandler, to discuss the future of the league. The meeting, brokered by Buzzy Bavasi, general manager of the Montreal Royals, led to two points of agreement. Molini pointed out that the QPL had no quarrel with Organized Baseball. The QPL teams were not "raiders" and did not permit tampering with players under contract to teams in the major or minor leagues. In turn, Mulbry assured Molini that the QPL was not considered an outlaw circuit. Second, the QPL made a firm guarantee that it would not approach players signed with Organized Baseball in the future.[68] In 1950 the league returned to the Organized Baseball fold as a class C operation. Many of those who had played in the league when it had operated independently continued to play under the new arrangements, and the stars of the 1950 season were familiar names. Silvio Garcia won the league batting title with a .365 average and twenty-one home runs. Others included Gladu (a .355 average and five home runs) and Vic Power (a .334 average and fourteen home runs); homebrews Norm Dussault (.329), Nick Malfara (.311), Stan Breard (.307), and Roger Breard (.301); old Negro

Leaguers Wee Willie Pope (.300) and Quincy Barbee (.284); and Cuban veteran Lauro Pascual (.234).

By the time that the QPL had returned to Organized Baseball, Pasquel had resigned as president of the Mexican League and had handed the reins over to Eduardo Quijano Pitman. Pitman had to deal with the whiff of failure that now was associated with the league. According to Pitman, the Pasquel raids set Mexican baseball back a decade. Not only did the league neglect to develop its own younger players, but many sound baseball men, like Castor Montoto of the Puebla club, and Dr Alfredo Cantu of the Tampico team, simply dropped out of baseball completely. To be sure, the Pasquel brothers continued to run the Veracruz Blues and had interest in Mexico City teams for a while, but at the end of the 1951 season they wound up their baseball operations. For a few years afterwards Pitman and other Mexican club owners were determined to maintain their independence and continued to complain that American clubs (particularly those close to the border) were violating Mexican contracts. Finally, in January 1955 a deal was struck that would admit the Mexican League to Organized Baseball as a class AA league and protect Mexican teams from raiding by other teams in Organized Baseball. Although some saw this as capitulation, it should be remembered that the Mexican baseball system is still largely under Mexican control.[69]

The post-war history of Cuban baseball took a somewhat different course. As we have seen, the period immediately after the war witnessed a time of Cuban resistance to and eventual accommodation with Organized Baseball's attempt to extend its hegemony over baseball on the island. According to Peter Bjarkman, the post-war "Americanization of Cuban winter baseball was in one sense only part and parcel of the lust for all things American that came with the prosperity following the end of the world war."[70] During the 1950s the integration of Cuban baseball into the American baseball system proceeded with the involvement of the Havana Cubans in the Florida International League and of the subsequent Havana Sugar Kings in the AAA International League. All of this came to an end with Fidel Castro's overthrowing of the government of Fulgencio Bastista, and the subsequent decision by Organized Baseball to revoke the Sugar Kings franchise and move it to Jersey City. For Major League Baseball this meant greater involvement in areas of Latin America other than Mexico and Cuba where the original attempts to extend its authority after the Second World War had been undertaken.

While the Mexicans and Cubans both reflected an independent state of mind, baseball in Canada remained intimately connected to the United States. Since the beginning of the nineteenth century Canadian baseball had been characterized by both independent and affiliated leagues and clubs and by a relatively unproblematic relationship with Organized Baseball. In 1953 there were sixteen minor league teams in Canada, thirteen more than in all of New England, and the league offices of the International League and the Western International League were located in Montreal and Vancouver, respectively.[71] While images of outlaws bedevilled the relationship between U.S. and Mexican baseball officials and spoke to deeper concerns related to the place of the United States in Latin America, the post-war Quebec Provincial League and other independent circuits in Canada were more often thought of as havens or sanctuaries for those on the margins of the professional baseball world. In this sense, Jorge Pasquel, Nap Reyes, and Jean-Pierre Roy and their compatriots represent some of the subtle dynamics of the relationship of Mexico, Canada, and Cuba to their powerful neighbour across their northern and southern borders.

In the longer term the patterns of development that accompanied the post-war continentalization of baseball have continued to influence the contemporary baseball scene. While Major League Baseball has extended its influence throughout the Caribbean and increasingly draws upon the pool of players in Puerto Rico, the Dominican Republic, Panama, and Venezuela, its influence in Cuba and Mexico is tenuous. Canada, however, has a relatively weak national baseball system and serves in increasing numbers to supply its best players to Organized Baseball in the United States. Indeed, for many years there was no national senior baseball championship in Canada. This was true as well for many other sports, hockey being the great exception. Ironically, the connection of Canadian baseball to the United States has contributed to the growing influence of Canadian baseball on the international scene. Canada now is often in contention for medal status at the World Baseball Championships and has performed well in its recent involvement in the World Baseball Classic, even defeating the United States in the inaugural event in Phoenix in 2006. It is one of the ironies associated with Major League Baseball's continental expansion in the post-war years that it has contributed to the strength of baseball at the national level throughout the entire region. For how long will it be that the major league's "World Series" can resist the future development of a World Cup of baseball?

NOTES

1 Jules Tygiel, *Baseball's Great Experiment: Jackie Robinson and His Legacy* (New York: Vintage Books, 1983); Samuel O. Regalado, *Viva Baseball! Latin Major Leagues and Their Special Hunger* (Urbana and Chicago: University of Illinois Press, 1998); Patrick Harrigan, *The Detroit Tigers: Club and Community, 1945–1995* (Toronto: University of Toronto Press, 1997); Adrian Burgos Jr, *Playing America's Game: Baseball, Latinos, and the Color Line* (Berkeley and Los Angeles: University of California Press, 2007).

2 Burgos, *Playing America's Game*, 2.
3 Robert Elias, *The Empire Strikes Out: How Baseball Sold U.S. Foreign Policy and Promoted the American Way Abroad* (New York and London: New Press, 2010), 286.
4 Gerald F. Vaughan, "Jorge Pasquel and the Evolution of the Mexican League," *The National Pastime: A Review of Baseball History* 12 (1992): 9–13.
5 "Mexican League Earmarks $30,000,000 for Battle: 'O.B. Getting Dose of Own Medicine – Pasquel,'" *Sporting News*, 28 February 1946.
6 David E. Lorey, *The U.S.-Mexican Border in the Twentieth Century* (Wilmington, DE: Scholarly Resources, 1999), ch. 4.
7 *Sporting News*, 28 February 1946.
8 Ibid.
9 E.J. Hobsbawm, *Primitive Rebels: Banditry, Mafia, Millenarians, Anarchists, Sicilian Fasci, the City Mob, Labour Sects, Ritual, Sermons, and Oaths* (Manchester, UK: Manchester University Press, 1959).
10 Chris Frazer, *Bandit Nation: A History of Outlaws and Cultural Struggle in Mexico, 1810–1920* (Lincoln: University of Nebraska Press, 2006).
11 Richard Slatta, *Bandidos: The Varieties of Latin American Banditry* (Westport, CT: Greenwood Press, 1987).
12 William H. Beezley, *Judas at the Jockey Club and Other Episodes of Porfirian Mexico* (Lincoln: University of Nebraska Press, 1989).
13 Alan M. Klein, *Baseball on the Border: A Tale of Two Laredos* (Princeton: Princeton University Press, 1997), 9–16, 151.
14 Vaughan, "Jorge Pasquel," describes the Mexican League experiment as "a mere exercise in nationalism," 13.
15 *Sporting News*, 7 March 1946.
16 Charles P. Korr, *The End of Baseball as We Knew It: The Players Union, 1960–81* (Urbana and Chicago: University of Illinois Press, 2002), 5.
17 *Sporting News*, 21 March 1946.
18 Mark Reisler, "Always the Laborer, Never the Citizen: Anglo Perceptions of the Mexican Immigrant during the 1920s," in David Gutierrez (ed.), *Between Two Worlds: Mexican Immigrants in the United States* (Wilmington, DE: Scholarly Resources, 1996), 28–36.
19 Manuel Garcia y Griego, "The Importation of Mexican Contract Laborers to the United States, 1942–64," in Gutierrez, *Between Two Worlds*, 55–67.
20 *Sporting News*, 14 March 1946.
21 Peter Bjarkman, *A History of Cuban Baseball, 1864–2006* (Jefferson, NC: McFarland, 2007), 64–5.
22 Regalado, *Viva Baseball!*, 26.
23 *Sporting News*, 28 February 1946.

24 *Sporting News*, 21 March 1946.

25 According to Sam Breadon of the St Louis Cardinals, the Pasquels "think they are doing the honorable thing in building up baseball for Mexico. They believe they are merely retaliating in a big way for what American baseball scouts in the past have done to Mexico in a small way." The *Bisbee Daily Review* agreed, noting that the United States had enough players to furnish U.S. cities and cities in Mexico as well. "It is in the best interest of international harmony and the future of baseball that we work with our fellow athletes south of the border," *Bisbee Daily Review*, 3 July 1946.

26 *Sporting News*, 11 April 1946.

27 Ibid.

28 Major league players were often overshadowed by players from the Cuban or American Negro leagues who had been playing in Mexico for some time. John Virtue, *South of the Color Barrier: How Jorge Pasquel and the Mexican League Pushed Baseball toward Racial Integration* (Jefferson, NC: McFarland, 2008), 166–7. Pitchers were particularly disappointing, many of them finding that in the thin air their curve balls broke after they crossed the plate. Among the more disappointing players were pitchers Alex Carrasquel and former New York Giants Harry Feldman and "Ace" Adams. *Douglas Daily Dispatch*, 23 May 1946. See also *Sporting News*, 14 August 1946.

29 *Sporting News*, 29 September 1948.

30 Vaughan, "Jorge Pasquel," 13.

31 G. Richard McKelvey, *Mexican Raiders in the Major Leagues: The Pasquel Brothers against Organized Baseball, 1946* (Jefferson, NC: McFarland, 2006).

32 Regalado, *Viva Baseball!*, 25–30.

33 Adrian Burgos, *Cuban Star: How One Negro League Owner Changed the Face of Baseball* (New York: Hill & Wang, 2011). Among the Latin American players that Pompez signed were future stars Minnie Minoso, Juan Marichal, and Orlando Cepeda.

34 Virtue, *South of the Color Barrier*, 144.

35 Information on the Mexican National League is drawn from the *Sporting News* archives subject files, "Amateur and Semipro Baseball, Baseball in Mexico." Thanks go to archivists Steven Gietscher and Jim Meier for their assistance. See in particular *Sporting News*, 2 May 1946.

36 Jose E. Figueredo, *Cuban Baseball: A Statistical History, 1878–1961* (Jefferson, NC: McFarland, 2003), 269.

37 *Baseball Guide and Record Book, 1947* (St Louis, MO: Charles C. Spink & Son, 1947), 385.

38 *Baseball Guide and Record Book, 1948* (St Louis, MO: Charles C. Spink & Son, 1948), 389.

39 *Sporting News*, 21 March 1946.

40 Ibid.

41 See the article in the *Sporting News*, 4 February 1937, outlining the positive influ-
    ence of visiting U.S. teams on the development of baseball in Mexico.
42 Peter J. Bjarkman, *Diamonds around the Globe: The Encyclopedia of International
    Baseball* (Westport, CT: Greenwood Press, 2005).
43 *Sporting News*, 6 November 1946.
44 *Sporting News*, 22 January 1947.
45 *Sporting News*, 13 November 1946.
46 *Sporting News*, 26 November 1946.
47 *Sporting News*, 7 March 1946. According to Durocher, Garcia "was the best I ever
    saw. He can do everything Marty Marion can do and he can do it better." Before
    settling on Jackie Robinson to break the colour bar, Branch Rickey may have briefly
    considered the dark-skinned African Cuban as a good candidate for the task.
    Bjarkman, *History of Cuban Baseball*, 148–9.
48 Roberto Echevaria, "The '47 Dodgers on Havana: Baseball at a Crossroads," *Spring
    Training History*, 1996, 20–1.
49 Ibid., 21. See also Roberto Gonzalez Echevarria, *The Pride of Havana: A History of
    Cuban Baseball* (New York: Oxford University Press, 1999).
50 *Sporting News*, 14 March 1946.
51 *Sporting News*, 4 February 1948. Breard finished the season with a .288 batting
    average. Roland Gladu won the batting crown with a .330 average. Bjarkman,
    History of Cuban Baseball, 124; Figueroa, *Cuban Baseball*, 313.
52 *Sporting News*, 28 March 1946. *Sporting News* referred to Janis incorrectly as
    Roberto Jaimez.   .
53 Virtue, *South of the Color Barrier*, 128.
54 *Sporting News*, 28 March 1946.
55 *Sporting News*, 21 June 1945.
56 Draft letter by Lloyd McGowan, undated. Jean-Pierre Roy file, *The Sporting News*
    Archives, St Louis, Missouri.
57 "Roy in Detour to Mexico, Signs Brooklyn Contract," *Sporting News*, 28 February
    1946.
58 "Mexico Brings Disillusion, Roy Back in Royal Family," *Sporting News*, 26 June
    1946.
59 *Sporting News*, 12 March 1947.
60 Rory Costello, "Jean Pierre Roy," *The SABR Baseball Biography Project*, provides an
    interesting online biographical profile of Roy. See also "Mexico Brings Disillusion,
    Roy Back in Royal Family," *Sporting News*, 26 June 1946.
61 *Sporting News*, 24 May 1950.
62 "Jean Roy, Barred by O.B., to Hurl in Canadian Loop," *Sporting News*, 12 March
    1947. Although Roy was reinstated later in the year and assigned to Mobile of the
    Southern Association, he announced that he would not report. Instead he played

in the unsanctioned Cuban League during the winter and rejoined St Jean in the Quebec Provincial league in 1948. *Sporting News*, 5 November 1947.

63 Merritt Clifton, *Disorganized Baseball: The Provincial League from Laroque to the Expos* (Brigham, QC: Merritt Clifton, 1982).

64 Colin D. Howell, *Northern Sandlots: A Social History of Maritime Baseball* (Toronto: University of Toronto Press, 1995); William Humber, *Diamonds of the North* (Toronto: Oxford University Press, 1995); Colin Howell, "Baseball in Canada," in George Gmelch (ed.), *Baseball without Borders: The International Pastime* (Lincoln: University of Nebraska Press, 2006).

65 "Quebec Haven for Ineligibles," *Sporting News*, 23 June 1948.

66 "Lanier to Get $10,000 This Year at Drummondville, City of 30,000. Other Former Major Leaguers Find Haven in Canadian Loop," *Sporting News*, 1 June 1949.

67 Barry Swanton, *The Mandak League: Haven for Former Negro League Ballplayers, 1950–1957* (Jefferson, NC: McFarland, 2006).

68 *Sporting News*, 1 June 1949.

69 Tomas Morales Fernandez, *Los Diablos Rojos* (Mexico City: D.F. Publishers, 1972), 193.

70 Bjarkman, *History of Cuban Baseball*, 98.

71 This contrasts starkly with the number of baseball franchises in Canada at the present time. See Robert Bellamy and David Whitson, "Going South: Professional Baseball's Contraction in Canada, *NINE, a Journal of Baseball History* 18, no. 1 (Fall 2009): 86–106.

PART THREE

Local Contours: Debating Access to Physical Activity in Canadian Communities

8 Change Rooms and Change Agents: The Struggle against Barriers to Opportunities for Physical Activity and Sport in Ethnocultural Communities in Toronto

PARISSA SAFAI

Critically engaged scholars have been prominent voices in articulating the belief that physical activity is a vital part of the human spirit, that it must be considered a human right worthy of protection, and that it must be made accessible to all.[1] Chief among these has been Bruce Kidd, whose incorporation of the personal, professional, and political into his daily practices as scholar, athlete, and activist has become the model to which many of his colleagues aspire. It should come as no surprise then that the focus of this chapter – an exploration of the various ways in which certain social groups come to experience physical activity and sport in the city of Toronto – is as much personal as it is professional. The purpose of this chapter is to explore the barriers to and the opportunities for the inclusive partici-pation and representation of ethnocultural and racial communities in sport and physical activity in Toronto, as well as the strategies to minimize and overcome such barriers in order to reach inclusiveness and representation. In focusing on the sport and physical activity experiences of ethnocultural and racial communi-ties in Toronto, one of Canada's most ethnically diverse metropolitan areas, we can see examples of not only the establishment and enhancement of equitable and accessible sport for all but also the mobilization of public advocates (change agents) in the fight for equal access to all sport and physical activity services, facilities, and programs regardless of race and national or ethnic origin.

The Colouring of Toronto

> Vital cities have marvelous innate abilities for understanding, communicating, contriving and inventing what is required to combat their difficulties.[2]

In 2006 the Canadian Institute for Health Information (CIHI) released a Canadian Population Health Initiative report entitled *Improving the Health of*

Canadians: An Introduction to Health in Urban Places.[3] Drawing on data from the 2001 census, the report examined the health of Canadians living in five urban centres (Vancouver, Calgary, Toronto, Montreal, and Halifax) in efforts to explore the reasons that people in some urban communities are healthier than in others.[4] For CIHI researchers, cities are not just hubs for large masses of people but rather complex systems where individuals live in households nested within neighbourhoods that are, in turn, nested within cities.[5] The health of individuals is affected by determinants that operate within and cut across these locations. Using red, orange, light green, and dark green to represent the health of individuals in the community, the researchers painted the neighbourhoods of each city to create a patchwork quilt of health status as framed by space (the physical or geographic characteristics of a location) and place (the social meaning of a location). Simply put, health varied depending on where people lived and who lived there. Those who lived in dark-green neighbourhoods reported better health and were more likely to be post-secondary graduates and to earn higher-than-average income. Those who lived in red neighbourhoods reported the poorest health; these neighbourhoods were the cities' more socio-economically disadvantaged with lower-than-average income earners, fewer post-secondary graduates, more single-parent families, and greater proportions of recent immigrants. It should come as no surprise then that the individuals who reported better health had greater leisure time and higher rates of participation in physical activity during leisure time compared to those individuals with poorer health, who were less likely to report being physically active or to report injury to a medical clinician.

In Toronto's case there was no shortage of green (both dark and light), orange, and red neighbourhoods, yet the colours fell into a particular pattern that has since been replicated in other studies of the health and well-being of Toronto's population: the healthiest (dark-green) neighbourhoods occupy a central position immediately north of the city's downtown area and dominate the suburbs, while the least healthy (red) neighbourhoods fan out of the downtown, scattered predominantly to the east and west of the city.[6] In fact, we could superimpose a map of the City of Toronto's thirteen "priority areas" (now referred to as neighbourhood improvement areas) – identified by city councillors and key community representatives, including the United Way of Greater Toronto following the release of its landmark *Poverty by Postal Code Report*, as being at risk and requiring concerted public intervention and investment to boost community services and facilities – onto the CIHI's 2006 snapshot of the city and find little to no difference in the V-shaped mapping of disparity and disadvantage.[7]

There is tremendous irony in this "colouring" of Toronto's neighbourhoods and mapping of its pockets of ill health given the city's reputation for and pride in its diverse neighbourhoods. Every day, neighbourhoods are performed all across the city for residents and visitors alike; in fact, Toronto is known as the city of neighbourhoods. I was born and raised in Toronto, have lived there most of my life, and yet only moved recently into the city proper from the suburbs in the north. I now live on a very pretty and quiet residential street – tree-lined and filled with the voices of children going to and from the local YMCA. The quiet nature of the street sometimes surprises me because I need only to walk a block and I find myself on Bloor Street West with its frenetic energy and the hustle and bustle of cars and pedestrians. My favourite restaurant is close to my new home, the food there is delicious, and, perhaps more important, the beer is cold and cheap. At times there are long waits for a table, which is a true test of perseverance when platters of delicious *tibs*, *kitfo*, and *injera* bread keep coming out of the kitchen. I share these details because I am fascinated by the energy and character of this neighbourhood of mine. My neighbourhood has a name, Bloorcourt Village, and it lies next to other named neighbourhoods: Dufferin Grove, Bickford Park, Palmerston, Trinity-Bellwoods, and South Annex. But Bloorcourt Village does not capture the other names and identities mapped onto its visible, invisible, and imagined spatial borders. I live a touch west of Koreatown, east of Little Poland, a bit north of Chinatown, around Little Italy and Little Portugal.

As I travel north to see my parents, who live in the suburbs, I travel through Tehranto, a twisting of the name *Toronto* in acknowledgment of the large Iranian community that eats, shops, and lives on Yonge Street between Finch Avenue and Steeles Avenue. It is fitting that I travel through Tehranto to go to my parents' home as they themselves chose to leave their home in Tehran and immigrate to Canada in the early 1970s. Although the rumblings of political unrest were in the air, they migrated before the Iranian Revolution in 1979, and they chose Toronto out of a sense of hope, promise, and adventure. They never returned to Iran, recognizing that their children, particularly their only daughter, would never experience the same opportunities there as they would here. I am Toronto born, but I live, breathe, eat, and sleep with my parents' migration and displacement – through their experiences, memories, and nostalgia of an Iran that under the current regime really no longer exists and of a Canada that they selected as their new home. I continually negotiate my hyphenated identity. When people ask me where I come from, often Toronto is not what they want to hear. I am certain that my story and my parents' story of immigration resonate with many of the people who live in the city. Toronto's city of neighbourhoods is a city of immigrants. Data from the 2011 census/National Household Survey (NHS) showed that the City of Toronto and Greater Toronto Area was home to nearly 18.1 per cent of Canada's total population and to approximately one-third (32.8 per cent) of newcomers who arrived between 2001 and 2011 (as compared to 40.4 per cent in 2006). About half (49 per cent) of those living in the City of Toronto identified as immigrants – a significantly higher rate than the rest of the Greater Toronto Area (38 per cent) and nationally (21 per cent). Furthermore, 49 per cent of those living in the City of Toronto identified as a visible minority as compared to 19 per cent nationally.[8]

More so than ever, this city of neighbourhoods is a city of newcomers, and city life is understood as structured around the actual and not-just-imagined "being together of strangers."[9] Cities are sites where diversity ebbs and flows, such that they are the "place of our meeting with the other,"[10] and city dwellers are always "people in the presence of otherness."[11] These neighbourhoods – Little Italy, Little Poland, Koreatown, Tehranto – are constructed in part to facilitate a sense of belonging in the face of displacement and otherness; they are daily attempts to construct or reconstruct familiarity and tradition on the sidewalks of a new country.[12] Yet these little countries – the conflation of the national or international with the local – mapped onto Toronto's streets are not carbon copies of homelands and cultures of origin; they are in fact complicated mixtures of nostalgia, memory, and new constructions of hyphenated or hybrid identities that change and transform within and across generations of immigrants and their families. For scholars such as Stuart Hall, the displacement and construction or reconstruction of home experienced by diasporic communities "is defined, not by essence or purity, but by the recognition of a necessary heterogeneity and diversity; by a conception of 'identity' which lives with and through, not despite, difference; by hybridity. Diaspora identities are those which are constantly producing and reproducing themselves anew, through transformation and difference."[13] Hall highlights the productive, resistant, self-representational activities and subjectivities of diasporic people in efforts to demonstrate that hybrid identities are not fixed straightforwardly in processes of acculturation, assimilation, or pluralism.[14] Much like Hall and Gilroy, Bhabha views hybridity as process – not "two original moments from which a third emerges" but a third space of cultural production and reproduction that does not conform to either original space.[15]

Diversity and hybridity are sustained features of the city, and socially determined power relations contribute to and operate through complex entanglements of identity and place such that marginalized groups can, through politics of identity and of place, be oppressed or can resist and subvert.[16] We must be cognizant of the ways in which located politics of difference shape urban lives and are, in turn, shaped by the contingent circumstances of specific people in specific settings.[17] Furthermore, we must also be cognizant of the ways in which our practices of identification and analysis continually pull hybridity – that which can be transgressive, subversive, or ambivalent – back into fixity as an object of knowledge, that which can be known.[18] In fact, conceptualizing Toronto as a city of many ethnocultural neighbourhoods both attends to the social distinctions that occur there and represents "one more articulation in the ongoing discursive constitution of those categories of distinction."[19] Attempts to map difference assume stable categories even though identity is multiply and variably positioned along multiple axes of privilege and oppression.[20] At any one time we occupy more than one system of difference – race, class, sex, ability, to name a few; thus, how we present ourselves to others is then always provisional and contextual as we, at any one time, may be fixed into or may strategically mobilize different aspects of ourselves.[21] This chapter focuses on one axis of power – racial or ethnocultural identity – with regard to physical activity and sport; however, I am mindful of the complex intersections of multiple determinants of identity that influence and are influenced by physical activity and sport.

Many applaud the diversity and hybridity of Toronto, pointing towards it as the true example of multiculturalism, particularly when it is politically useful (for example, as part of the promotion of Toronto as host for the Pan American or Parapan American Games or during World Cup celebrations).[22] However, multiculturalism – the state-legislated preservation of cultural heritage – in and of itself is a tricky concept. Multicultural policy, introduced by the Trudeau government in 1971 and given royal assent in the late eighties through the Multicultural Act of 1988, is well intentioned in its focus on the social integration of all people into all aspects of Canadian society regardless of race or national or ethnic origin. As Fleras and Kunz note, multiculturalism assumes that ethnocultural identity is compatible with national unity and that multiculturalism, as a policy, can be employed to organize and regulate various practices and institutions through the celebration of difference, equity, or civic multiculturalism.[23]

However, we must be cognizant of how people in Canada take up multiculturalism on a daily basis and how it (and the policies, programs, and services that are borne of it) may actually deflect attention from the barriers experienced by members of ethnocultural communities.[24] Usually understood at the level of statistics (that is, the number of different cultures, religions, languages, etc., in a community), multiculturalism allows some individuals and groups to further some interests by promoting multicultural issues (for example, hiring diverse employees) or by using multiculturalism as "leverage to prod, embarrass, and provoke central policy structures by holding them accountable."[25] Yet, critiques of multiculturalism suggest that the room for genuine social and civic participation and contestation provided within the discourse of multiculturalism is limited in its depoliticized focus on racial and cultural accommodation and tolerance.[26] Smyth notes: "If the discourse of Canadian multiculturalism relies upon an understanding of 'difference' that sees racial and ethnic identities as fixed, historical, and discrete categories, then the multicultural model cannot imagine the shifting of identifications back and forth across these categories, or of identifications refracted through other categories that are just as pertinent to the exercise of cultural citizenship."[27] In the educational context, James and Woods add that school-based multicultural activities (for example, bake sales, multicultural days) attempt to raise cultural awareness and resist racism and xenophobia among students, staff, and teachers, but that "this kind of 'tourist' approach posits culture as a set of static, uncomplicated information and observable items and practices that can be identified, displayed, communicated and easily represented, rather than as something dynamic that people make together. Moreover, it marks certain groups as 'immigrants-for-life,' thereby cementing their outside status."[28] Thus, diversity is to be celebrated or consumed but only in ways that are comfortable within and "bound by the rules of established institutions (i.e., legal, economic, political, etc.) that tend to represent the views of the dominant cultural group."[29]

Reflecting on the neighbourhoods described above – Little Italy, Chinatown, Tehranto – on the one hand, and as noted above, we can argue that the ethnic neighbourhoods of Toronto are pockets of belonging and communal identity for diasporic communities. Yet, on the other hand, we must question whether "the existence of so-called 'ethnic communities' [is] in fact, a reflection of a differentiated and stratified society, belying the claim of harmonious and comfortable living that city politicians and others boast about."[30] If we envision social integration as the full participation of all individuals – including "the migrants, the minorities, the diasporic"[31] – in the social, political, educational, and cultural activities and institutions of Canadian society, why the need for such "enclosures of difference" that mark some communities as different from the norm?[32] What are the lived barriers experienced by racial, ethnic, religious, and linguistic minorities and migrants in the city broadly, and around physical activity and health specifically?

Living Health and Physical Activity in Colour

In a project entitled "Revisiting Personal Is Political: Immigrant Women's Health Promotion," Denise Gastaldo and colleagues explored the settlement experiences of immigrant women who arrived in Canada and settled in Toronto.[33] With the employment of participatory action research methods that saw the active involvement of study participants in the generation and representation of knowledge (including poetry writing), the main goal of the study was to analyse the social determinants of women's health in the context of recent immigration. Participants revealed that multiple and competing factors and narratives shaped their experiences as immigrant women in Canada, such that they were living in a state of limbo; for the women in the study, "Toronto is a place full of worries for immigrants."[34] They experienced challenges around language, social welfare, access to immediate health care, affordable housing, and child care, and the high cost of higher education that, for some, became an unexpected requirement in order for them to convert their already high credentials as professionals into the Canadian context.[35] These experiences were combined with a very limited social network to support them in their initial months; as a result, for most women, very quickly Canada no longer was the country that selected them according to professional qualification, where they would find jobs and contribute to society. In fact, after living in Toronto for a few years, no participant in the study had found a job equivalent to her existing professional credentials.[36]

Gastaldo et al.'s participants kept busy through volunteer and community work, school activities, minor jobs, or caregiving; yet, after living in Toronto for a few years, the majority of participants described their everyday lives simply as "busy and tired."[37] While participants had some knowledge of street names, public places, and public transportation, most had a very limited use of the city; "there were a few malls, squares, food stores, second-hand stores and particular [average-to-poor] neighbourhoods that framed these immigrants' everyday living."[38] The women had good knowledge of free services such as libraries, swimming pools, community centres, religious centres, and museums, but most had neither visited "the city's attractions nor entered in a home of someone who was not an immigrant."[39] Despite the hardships of the participants, the researchers found that they continued to reproduce and promote a discourse of hopefulness and perseverance:

> Being a good immigrant required a constant manifestation of gratitude for being accepted into the country, hard work, being self-conscious for having limited or broken English, full or partial acceptance that education from other countries is not sufficient preparation to work in Canada, that volunteer work is a central element in becoming Canadian, that previous professional and experiential knowledge are very limited because "Canada is different" and finally, despite all these elements for hopelessness, a belief that immigrants should persevere through hardships in their lives because "eventually they will succeed."[40]

For Gastaldo et al., such discourse served to only act in a disciplinary manner and deflected attention from the systemic barriers faced by the participants.

The poetry from these women is illuminating. In a poem entitled "Walking Partners" one participant, Nataliya, writes of how she and her husband supported each other through the immigration process:

> We walk every evening
> We go out and walk
> Maybe for one hour
> We don't worry about winter
> We know winter
> We walk every evening
> We had a dog, but he was 14 and he died
> We continue without dog
> We talk and speak a lot
> We speak of everything, family, plans
> We exercise and I hold his arm while we walk
> People see me and my husband and say: hello lovebirds![41]

In Nataliya's case, the simple act of walking represents not just exercise but a moment for connection with her husband at a time when they are living in a state of limbo. What makes this poem remarkable is that it is the only one in the collection of thirty that touches on physical activity. What about physical activity then in this city of neighbourhoods? How do physical activity and sport figure as sites of community building, rebuilding, or marginalization within and across the city of Toronto?

The benefits of participation in physical activity and sport have been clearly identified. The intent of this chapter is not to dispute the consistent evidence that supports the value of physical activity and sport participation (at certain intensities and levels of organization) in such areas as lifelong health, learning, leadership, and citizenship.[42] Rather, the focus here is to recognize that the benefits of participation in physical activity and sport are neither automatic nor equally experienced by all.[43] Traditionally there has been a tendency for sport and recreation providers to assume that cultural differences and beliefs, most often religious ones, inhibit participation. Yet, we know that minority populations would like to participate in sport and recreation but often cannot do so because of the limited number of existing facilities, programs, and services that meet their cultural, social, and religious needs.[44] Furthermore, the predominant approach to sport and physical activity programming is the provision of Western games, dances, and other activities; many individuals from racial and ethnocultural communities do participate in these programs, but they are disproportionately under-represented because of structural or procedural barriers, including the fact that these activities are not always culturally meaningful.

Contemporary state sport policies do not explicitly discriminate against visible minorities, but they constitute a form of "institutionalized racism" by the lack of attention to the experiences and needs of those from racial and ethnocultural minority groups. Donnelly and Nakamura state explicitly:

> The most striking finding of [our] study is the absence, at the high performance and provincial levels of Canadian sport, of any consideration of multiculturalism, or any sense of responsibility for social inclusion beyond general statements about diversity and "open door" policies. Sport Canada holds NSOs [national sport organizations] responsible for implementing policies regarding gender equity, official languages, the provision of disability sport opportunities, and the establishment of procedures to combat sexual harassment and abuse. However, other than some parenthood statements about "overcoming barriers to participation," there are no policies to deal specifically with ethnic and racial diversity, social inclusion, or multiculturalism, and no statements or policies dealing with anti-racism.[45]

Paraschak and Tirone note that Canadian sport has largely been defined by and structured on the values of people from white, European backgrounds.[46] The authors use the term *whitestream sport* to indicate this racially based dominance of mainstream sport that they suggest has marginalized and discriminated against Canadians who are not of Euro-Canadian heritage.[47]

Immigrants to Canada face particular challenges in sport and physical activity. Doherty and Taylor interviewed eighty-five youths who had recently moved to Canada, and found that they faced a number of barriers to full participation in sport.[48] These included language and cultural differences, social exclusion, school and/or part-time work, family commitments, financial cost, and culturally specific issues such as the appropriateness of required clothing. Many of these barriers are affected by gender, with women generally regarding them as more significant constraints than do men.[49] Yet, sport and physical activity can be sites where social inclusion does occur – where individuals can learn about Canadian social and civic life through participation in Canadian activities, or where (opportunity for) intercultural exchange occurs through newcomers' use of community facilities to engage in their own physical practices.[50] This process of social inclusion requires shared responsibility in that, as newcomers adapt to Canada, Canadian institutions, organizations, and services need to adjust their policies, programs, and practices in order to remove barriers to participation and thus enhance equality of access or outcome.[51] It is believed that, when newcomers' needs are responded to and addressed in services and organizations, this can facilitate the realization of immigrants' participation in their community. For example, a community centre may take steps to offer activities in a manner that accommodates the needs of a particular immigrant group that may wish to use the facilities in efforts to increase interest and participation in the specific program or activity. Newcomers, in return, may contribute to Canadian social and community life by introducing new, or by preserving, sporting or physical cultural practices.[52]

In its *Parks, Forestry, and Recreation Strategic Plan* the City of Toronto recognizes the capacity of sport for social inclusion, stating that sport and physical activity can "guide a newcomer's way into the heart of a new community," and adding that the City is involved in facilitating this guidance: "to follow a path, one has to know it's there, and that it can be used by everyone."[53] In other words, to facilitate the participation of recent immigrants in the recreational opportunities of the city and subsequently welcome them into Toronto, steps must be taken to ensure that these individuals are aware of and can access such opportunities. For example, in response to the needs of a religious community, the Parks, Forestry, and Recreation (PFR) department began offering female-only swim hours and lessons, with female lifeguards and instructors on deck, and the windows of gyms were also covered to further ensure women's privacy.[54] Such provisions have been found to encourage Muslim women, among others, to participate in swimming and use physical activity facilities in their community.[55] We should not wish to diminish the steps that the City of Toronto has taken to integrate and accommodate immigrants through its PFR services (although it is important to point out that, at present, women-only leisure swimming and lessons are available at only nine of the over two hundred City of Toronto public swimming pools), but the policy oversimplifies social inclusion and integration.[56] When the document posits that, "if doing winter sports is Canadian, learning winter sports can turn everybody into a Canadian," the process of "becoming Canadian" is presented as uncomplicated and without negotiation and, sometimes, resistance.[57]

Sport and physical activity is a site where social inclusion and mutual obligation can occur in the city, yet relatively little is known about the potential effects of sport and physical activity on genuine and long-lasting community inclusion and about the conditions needed for the effective and long-term utilization of sport and physical activity for community inclusion and engagement – in spite of the consistent evidence that newcomers in Toronto experience heightened levels of unemployment and workplace discrimination, higher rates of poverty, higher rates of food insecurity, increased incidence of illness (for example, diabetes), and greater social marginalization.[58] With regard to sport and physical activity, a 2010 report from Get Active Toronto (a collaborative effort between the City and several public-private entities) identified a number of disturbing trends around the participation of ethnocultural groups in physical activity: half (50 per cent) of visible minority students in kindergarten through grade six participate in extracurricular sports, compared to 70 per cent of their non-visible minority counterparts; and immigrant youth aged twelve to nineteen are more likely to be inactive (43 per cent) than are their Canadian-born counterparts (39 per cent).[59] More important, the report identified the lack of sufficient data around the physical activity participation of visible minorities and newcomers in Toronto.

This report is consistent with other analyses acknowledging that while there is some research on the patterns of sport, physical activity, and recreation participation by specific and self-identified racial or ethnocultural minority groups within Canada and within specific large cities, much of the scholarly research on the barriers to physical activity for ethnocultural groups has come from elsewhere.[60] Methodologically, research in this area is challenging, and we must resist explanations that pathologize minority communities.[61] One challenge in trying to conduct research with groups that have been historically marginalized is gaining access to these communities and doing outreach work that does not pathologize or patronize. Another challenge rests in designing research that actively integrates community members from the beginning of the research process and which provides them with participatory mechanisms throughout.[62] In a project attempting to identify the barriers faced by ethnocultural and racial minority groups when they try to access the programs and facilities at the University of Toronto's Athletic Centre, Lorena Gajardo and I faced numerous challenges in collecting data from the university community because of a lack of positive response to various recruitment strategies including extensive contact work with different campus groups through telephone calls, emails, in-person meetings, and poster campaigns.[63] In a last ditch effort to elicit participation, we chose to hold a town hall meeting that was widely advertised throughout campus, and even that event failed to draw many participants. Those who did come to the town hall meeting, however, provided us with a wealth of information about the ethnocultural and racial minority communities' experiences and barriers at the Athletic Centre. Methodologically, what became clear following this process was that our assumption that traditional methods of data collection (interviews, focus groups, and town hall meetings) would yield satisfactory results was misguided: "In fact, one of our respondents pointed out that minority groups may have grown tired of a methodological approach which does not include the voices and knowledge of minority groups at all levels of the research project. *That is, ethnocultural and racial minority groups do not want to be asked through a previously designed methodology to answer questions about their particular conditions and experiences. Rather, they would prefer collaborative approaches that include them at all levels of the process.*[64] Such an approach acknowledges not just that there are systemic barriers to access and representation for some ethnocultural communities and individuals but also that ethnocultural individuals and groups themselves possess valuable skills and knowledge that must be incorporated into any scholarly endeavour that seeks to understand their experiences.[65]

Change Agents and Change Rooms

In the days leading up to my public presentation of an earlier version of this chapter, *Toronto Sun* columnist Steve Buffery wrote: "In the second session, Dr. Parissa Safai from York University will talk about: 'Change Rooms and Change Agents: The Struggle against Barriers to Opportunities for Ethnocultural Communities in Toronto.' Again, I have no idea what any of that means. But I have a sneaking suspicion that, when it's over, I'll feel guilt and shame."[66] Neither guilt nor shame is the intent of that presentation or this chapter. To dwell on guilt and shame is to focus on what we have not done, and we need to focus on what we can do. To do that compels us to hope and strive for change that is positive, powerful, and empowering. And there are examples of change; case in point, the Toronto Sport Leadership Program.

As highlighted in the *2010 Get Active Toronto Report*, following the "summer of the gun" in 2005, the Toronto Community Foundation called on a wide range of community members and leaders to explore the challenges facing Toronto's youth (for example, high rates of youth violence, youth unemployment, school drop-outs, and drop-offs in youth recreation) and to converge and collaborate together around one goal: increase access to opportunities for youth in training, employment, and community leadership.[67] The Toronto Sport Leadership Program was born out of a partnership with the Toronto Community Foundation; the United Way of Greater Toronto; the City's Parks, Forestry, and Recreation department; the Toronto District School Board (TDSB); the Toronto Catholic District School Board (TCDSB); and the YMCA of Greater Toronto. The program provides training and certification for youth sport coaches (identified in TDSB schools) from high-risk (financially and socially vulnerable) Toronto neighbourhoods, and graduates of the program are employed by the City of Toronto and the YMCA in an effort to help traditionally disenfranchised young people to find the confidence, skills, and experience to obtain employment and lead their communities. Many of these students come from the racially and culturally diverse communities in the city that are mapped red in the CIHI study or are identified as "priority areas" in need of investment by the City.[68]

The Toronto Sport Leadership Program is the first of its kind in Canada, and in its first seven years more than eight hundred young Torontonians graduated from the program, gaining transferable, marketable skills, and forming a roster of diverse, qualified sports staff for public and private employers.[69]

Despite some successes, challenges still remain. In a multidisciplinary pilot project at York University (located in Toronto) I was part of a research team interested in exploring the barriers to and opportunities for physical activity participation among immigrant women of low socio-economic status, as a function of the built environment in the Jane-Finch community that neighbours York University. It was a multifaceted, mixed-methods pilot project that explored such things as the walkability of the area, its aesthetic appeal, ecological features of the community, and the role and impact of policing in the community, as well as municipal policy on neighbourhood services. I conducted a number of focus groups and particularly noticed the impact of seemingly subtle municipal-level policy changes on participation. As one woman from Sri Lanka asked me, when the City decides to no longer shovel the sidewalk around her building because of diminished public budgets, how can she and her elderly mother go for a daily walk given that that is the only activity they can afford?[70] What such a question brings to light is the precariousness of life and isolation felt by those marginalized in the community, particularly members of ethnocultural and racial minority groups including immigrants and new Canadians.

As noted in the introduction to this chapter, a key focus is the mobilization of public physical activity advocates – the change agents in our communities who, via such spaces as the change room, the ice rink, the soccer pitch, the cricket field, the running track, the classroom, the municipal council room, and even the board room, push for equitable physical activity and sport access for all. In doing so, these advocates use physical activity and sport as a way in which to fight the social isolation experienced by many in our communities: the precariousness of life felt by the Sri Lankan woman and her mother noted above; the sense of vulnerability lived by marginalized people who are neglected, in the neatly colour-coded maps of the city; the isolation that Nataliya and her husband evade on their walks together; and the anxiety of separation that Toronto's ethnic neighbourhoods both resist and contribute to in their construction or reconstruction of familiarity and tradition.

A word of caution, however. The battle against social isolation is not won by simply providing sports equipment or access to physical activity facilities. Authentic and sustained action against social isolation – or, in other words, authentic and sustained action for equitable social and civic inclusion – occurs through outreach, alliance building, and a commitment to both participational and representational access.[71] This means looking not just to who is participating but to who is at the decision-making table; as Jane Jacobs writes in *The Death and Life of Great American Cities*, "cities have the capability of providing something for everybody, only because, and only when, they are created by everybody."[72] This means looking at the variety of systemic barriers – infrastructural, superstructural, and procedural – that may work to prevent access to physical activity and sport.[73] It means recognizing that systemic barriers may result from limitations in material and tangible wealth, such as cost, transportation, or physical access, but more frequently arise in a more subtle form in which, according to Donnelly and Harvey, barriers tend to be based on the assumption that all individuals have a similar background. Faced with such barriers, many individuals will assume that they do not belong in such surroundings or that they have no chance of success in a system where they are treated in the same way as those from more privileged backgrounds. As Donnelly and Harvey emphasize, it is important to empower: "Potential participants in active living initiatives must be empowered to determine their own form of activity, as well as to have some control over the provision of services. This may be achieved only through the development of community action at the local level."[74]

In a testament to physical activity advocacy in the city, there has been no shortage of community action at the local level in Toronto. In addition to the Toronto Sport Leadership Program, the *2010 Get Active Toronto Report* highlighted the activities and actions of people involved with the Aquatic Working Group (AWG).[75] With almost forty pools slated for closure in 2008 and 2009 owing to lack of funding for either continued operations or much-needed facility repair, the AWG was created to find a long-term sustainable solution for the continued operation of school-based pools that were accessed by community members on evenings and weekends. The working group pulled together all those who had an interest in and care for aquatics in Toronto: the City, the TDSB, advocacy groups, and swim clubs, as well as interested and engaged Torontonians. The AWG was able to come forward with strategies to keep these community assets in the public domain. Pools across the city were audited, an inventory of viable and not-viable pools was created, local champions for pools in different Toronto neighbourhoods (pool captains) were identified, and permit fees were equalized across the schools to encourage the rental of aquatic facilities and to generate permit revenue. In a pivotal breakthrough, the AWG was able to persuade the Province of Ontario to invest in the repair and rebuilding of some pools to the point that communities, led by local champions, could come in and take care of the facilities from that point onwards.

What is most notable about the work of the AWG – and what connects it to the foci of this chapter – is that, for nine pools where the AWG could not find a local pool champion, pool captains from other neighbourhoods stepped in to help organize and mobilize advocacy campaigns. Those nine pools were located in the city's more low-income and ethnoculturally diverse neighbourhoods, areas where people could not afford to lose a community asset like a swimming pool. Rather than parachuting into these ("red") neighbourhoods and dictating a particular political course of action, those who had already "saved their pools" – individuals with capital and capacity (that is, time, money, privilege) to mobilize – continued to advocate for publicly accessible community swimming by identifying local partners in these at-risk neighbourhoods and by collectively developing local neighbourhood-specific solutions. In other words, there was a recognition that different neighbourhoods – as a function of the people who live in those communities – are not served well by one-size-fits-all solutions that often favour those with cultural, social, and economic power and that often produce or reproduce the (obvious and subtle) barriers to full and equitable participation by ethnocultural and racial minority groups. There was also recognition that long-term, sustained change must develop from the ground up and must involve the very people who are so often not involved in the decision-making that will impact their lives.

Let me conclude this chapter by calling on us to be radical change agents and to attend – with sensitivity, diplomacy, and a sense of social justice – to the ways in which certain social groups come to experience the city, ways that are different from those of others. I draw on Jane Jacobs in unpacking the word *radical*; to be radical means to go to the root and to examine the roots of life at ground level.[76] Let us be change agents and use physical activity and sport spaces to address the tensions between the need to adapt to new conditions of community, the desire to maintain cultural continuity, and the newness of emergent, potential hybrid or third spaces. As Kofman writes, "the right to the city [is] not merely a visiting card – it [is] about the right to appropriate space and participate in decision making … a situation in which exchange values [do] not usurp use values, and where the city [can] be added to other abstract rights of the citizen. Thus the right to and respect for difference and diversity in the city is an integral aspect of social citizenship."[77]

Let us as scholars, athletes, and advocates contribute to broader discussions on the need to provide equitable sport and physical opportunities for diasporic communities – those communities that live outside of their natal territories, forced or otherwise, and that recognize that their traditional homelands are reflected deeply in the languages they speak and the cultures they produce. If, as researchers, we are committed to the concept of social justice through physical activity – of making "another world possible" through physical activity – then we must empower those individuals or peoples in our local community and beyond who are living with change as occasioned by displacement and migration and who are creating and re-creating, within the existing framework of Canada, identity, citizenship, sense of belonging, and homeland along national, racial, gendered, political, spatial, and socio-economic lines.[78] As Bhabha notes, "it is from those who have suffered the sentence of history – subjugation, domination, diaspora, displacement – that we learn our most enduring lessons."[79]

NOTES

1 B. Kidd and P. Donnelly, "Human Rights in Sport," *International Review for the Sociology of Sport* 35, no. 2 (2000): 131–48.

2 J. Jacobs, *The Death and Life of Great American Cities* (London: Jonathan Cape, 1962), 447.

3 Canadian Institute for Health Information (CIHI), *Improving the Health of Canadians: An Introduction to Health in Urban Places* (Ottawa: CIHI, 2006).

4 See R.G. Evans and G.L. Stoddart, "Producing Health, Consuming Health Care," in *Why Are Some People Healthy and Others Not? The Determinants of Health of Populations*, ed. R.G. Evans, M.L. Barer, and T.R. Marmor (Hawthorne, NY: Aldine de Gruyter, 1994), 27–66.

5 T. Bryant, "Housing and Health," in *Social Determinants of Health: Canadian Perspectives*, ed. D. Raphael (Toronto: Canadian Scholars' Press, 2004), 217–32.

6 For example, R.H. Glazier and G.L. Booth, with P. Gozdyra, M.I. Creatore, and A. Tynan, *Neighbourhood Environments and Resources for Health Living: A Focus on Diabetes in Toronto; ICES Atlas* (Toronto: Institute for Clinical Evaluative Sciences, 2007); J.D. Hulchanski, "The Three Cities within Toronto: Income Polarization among Toronto's Neighbourhoods, 1970–2000," *Centre for Urban and Community Studies, Research Bulletin 41*, (December 2007), www.urbancentre.utoronto.ca/pdfs/researchbulletins/CUCSRB41_Hulchanski_Three_Cities_Toronto.pdf.

7 United Way of Greater Toronto, *Poverty by Postal Code: The Geography of Neighbourhood Poverty, 1981–2001* (Toronto: United Way of Greater Toronto, 2004); see also City of Toronto, *Strong Neighbourhoods: A Call to Action* (Toronto: City of Toronto, 2005), www.unitedwaytoronto.com/document.doc?id=59.

8 www1.toronto.ca/city_of_toronto/social_development_finance__administration/files/pdf/nhs_backgrounder.pdf.

9 I.M. Young, *Justice and the Politics of Difference* (Princeton: Princeton University Press, 1990), 237; see also D. Brand, *Thirsty* (Toronto: McClelland, 2002); D. Brand, *What We All Long For* (Toronto: Knopf, 2005); H. Smyth, "'The Being Together of Strangers': Dionne Brand's Politics of Difference and the Limits of Multicultural Discourse," *Studies in Canadian Literature* 33, no. 1 (2008): 272–90.

10 R. Barthes, "Semiology and the Urban," in *The City and the Sign: An Introduction to Urban Semiotics*, ed. M. Gottdiener and A.P. Lagopoulos (New York: Columbia University Press, 1981), 96.

11 R. Sennett, *The Conscience of the Eye: The Design and Social Life of Cities* (New York: Knopf, 1990), 23.

12 J. Clifford, "Diasporas," *Cultural Anthropology* 9, no. 3 (1994): 302–38.

13 S. Hall, "Cultural Identity and Diaspora," in *Identity, Community, Culture, Difference*, ed. J. Rutherford (London: Lawrence & Wishart, 1990), 235.

14 See also P. Gilroy, "'It Ain't Where You're From, It's Where You're At …': The Dialectics of Diasporic Identification," *Third Text* 13 (1991): 3–16.

15 H.K. Bhabha, "The Third Space: Interview with Homi Bhabha," in *Identity, Community, Culture, Difference*, ed. J. Rutherford (London: Lawrence & Wishart, 1990), 211.

16 J. Jacobs and R. Fincher, introduction to *Cities of Difference*, ed. R. Fincher and J. Jacobs (New York: Guilford Press, 1998), 1–25.

17 Young suggests that a politics of difference "aims for an understanding of group difference as indeed ambiguous, relational, shifting, without clear borders … Difference now comes to mean not otherness, exclusive opposition, but specifically variation, heterogeneity" (*Justice and the Politics of Difference*, 171).

18 H.K. Bhabha, "Of Mimicry and Man: The Ambivalence of Colonial Discourse," in *The Location of Culture* (London: Routledge, 1994), 85–92.

19 Jacobs and Fincher, introduction to *Cities of Difference*, 6.

20 Cf. H. Bannerji, *The Dark Side of the Nation* (Toronto: Canadian Scholars' Press, 2000); P.H. Collins, "Toward a New Vision: Race, Class, and Gender as Categories of Analysis and Connection," *Race, Sex & Class* 1, no. 1 (1993): 25–46.

21 G. Pratt, "Grids of Difference: Place and Identity Formation," in *Cities of Difference*, ed. R. Fincher and J. Jacobs (New York: Guilford Press, 1998), 26–48.

22 Brand, *What We All Long For*; C.E. James, ed., *Possibilities and Limitations: Multicultural Policies and Programs in Canada* (Halifax: Fernwood Publishing, 2005).

23 According to Fleras and Kunz, the preservation of different cultures is prioritized within the "celebration of difference" model, whereas "equity multiculturalism" prioritizes overcoming barriers to opportunities for new immigrants. "Civic multiculturalism" attempts to include ethnocultural minorities into civic culture. A. Fleras and J.L. Kunz, *Media and Minorities: Representing Diversity in a Multicultural Canada* (Toronto: Thompson Educational Publishing, 2001).

24 Bannerji, *The Dark Side of the Nation*; C.E. James, *Seeing Ourselves: Exploring Race, Ethnicity, and Culture* (Toronto: Thompson Educational Publishing, 2001); C.J. Jansen, "Canadian Multiculturalism," in *Possibilities and Limitations: Multicultural Policies and Programs in Canada*, ed. C.E. James (Halifax: Fernwood Publishing, 2005), 21–33.

25 Fleras and Kunz, *Media and Minorities*, 19.
26 Bannerji, *The Dark Side of the Nation*; Fleras and Kunz, *Media and Minorities*.
27 Smyth, "The Being Together of Strangers," 276.
28 C.E. James and M. Wood, "Multicultural Education in Canada: Opportunities, Limitations, and Contradictions," in *Possibilities and Limitations*, ed. C.E. James, 102. See also G. Sefa Dei, "The Challenge of Promoting Inclusion Education in Ontario Schools: What Does Educational Research Tell Us?," in *From Enforcement and Prevention to Civic Engagement: Research on Community Safety*, ed. B. Kidd and J. Phillips (Toronto: University of Toronto Centre of Criminology, 2004), 184–202.
29 P. Donnelly and Y. Nakamura, *Sport and Multiculturalism: A Dialogue. Report for Canadian Heritage* (Toronto: University of Toronto Centre for Sport and Policy Studies, 2006), 5; see also James, *Seeing Ourselves*.
30 James, *Possibilities and Limitations*, 13.
31 Bhabha, *The Location of Culture*, 169.
32 Brand, *What We All Long For*.
33 D. Gastaldo, N. Khanlou, N. Massaquoi, D. Curling, and A. Gooden, *Revisiting Personal Is Political: Immigrant Women's Health Promotion; Executive Summary* (Toronto: University of Toronto, 2005), www.migrationhealth.ca/sites/default/files/files/3-Page-Executive-Summary.pdf.
34 Gastaldo, Khanlou, et al., *Revisiting Personal Is Political*, 2.
35 See also P. Elabor-Idemuida, "Immigrant Integration in Canada: Policies, Programs and Challenges," in *Possibilities and Limitations*, ed. James, 52–75.
36 D. Gastaldo, G.J. Andrews, and N. Khanlou, "Therapeutic Landscapes of the Mind: Theorizing Some Intersections between Health Geography, Health Promotion, and Immigration Studies," *Critical Public Health* 14, no. 2 (2004): 157–76.
37 Gastaldo, Khanlou, et al., *Revisiting Personal Is Political*, 2.
38 Ibid.
39 Ibid.
40 Ibid., 3.
41 D. Gastaldo, ed. *I'm Not the Woman I Used to Be: 30 Poems by Recent Immigrant Women* (Toronto: Women's Health in Women's Hands Community Health Centre, 2004), 25.
42 P. Donnelly and J. Harvey, *Overcoming Systemic Barriers to Access in Active Living* (Ottawa: Fitness Branch, Health Canada and Active Living Canada, 1996); P. Donnelly, C. McCloy, L. Petherick, and P. Safai, *The Crisis in School Sport: Issues and Resolutions; Centre for Sport Policy Studies Colloquium Report* (Toronto: University of Toronto, Faculty of Physical Education and Health, 2000); P. Safai, "Sport and Health," in *Sport and Society: A Student Introduction*, ed. B. Houlihan (London: Sage, 2007), 155–73; J. Taylor and W. Frisby, "Addressing Inadequate Leisure Access

Policies through Citizen Engagement," in *Decentring Work: Critical Perspectives on Leisure, Social Policy, and Human Development*, ed. H. Mair, S.M. Arai, and D.G. Reid (Calgary: University of Calgary Press, 2010), 30–45.

43 P. Donnelly and J. Coakley, *The Role of Recreation in Promoting Social Inclusion: Perspectives on Social Inclusion Working Paper Series* (Toronto: Laidlaw Foundation, 2002); Donnelly and Nakamura, *Sport and Multiculturalism*.

44 Y. Nakamura, "Beyond the Hijab: Female Muslims and Physical Activity," *Women in Sport and Physical Activity Journal* 11, no. 2 (2002): 21–48.

45 Donnelly and Nakamura, *Sport and Multiculturalism*, 3.

46 V. Paraschak and S. Tirone, "Race and Ethnicity in Canadian Sport," in *Canadian Sport Sociology*, ed. J. Crossman (Toronto: Thomson Nelson, 2003), 119–38.

47 Ibid., 125.

48 A. Doherty and T. Taylor, "Sport and Physical Recreation in the Settlement of Immigrant Youth," *Leisure/Loisir* 31, no. 1 (2007): 27–55.

49 See also Nakamura, "Beyond the Hijab."

50 Donnelly and Nakamura explore the concept of social inclusion, identifying it as a term among many that is "now used either synonymously with multiculturalism, or that overlaps significantly in meaning." They add that "it is not simply the removal of social exclusion. Social inclusion can be multi-faceted (e.g., economic, political, spatial, etc.). It can also be defined in divergent, sometimes oppositional ways. For example, assimilation involves the absorption of minority groups into the majority group, a process that involves deculturation. Social inclusion through integration involves adaptation by the minority groups to the majority group in order to receive equal treatment. Multiculturalism takes a different approach to social inclusion by promoting individual freedoms and promoting cultural diversity. The diverse approaches to social inclusion are related to alternate understandings of national identity and citizenship, and can result in different policies." Donnelly and Nakamura, *Sport and Multiculturalism*, 8.

51 Y. Nakamura, "Swimming Upstream? Exploring Culturally Sensitive Physical Activity Spaces and Programming in the Creation of Welcoming Communities," paper prepared for CERIS – The Metropolis Project, 2010, 2.

52 J. Joseph, "A Perfect Match: Brazilian Martial Arts and the Canadian Multiculturalism Act," unpublished paper, 2005, https://secure.sirc.ca/documents/JJoseph2005.pdf.

53 City of Toronto, *Parks, Forestry, and Recreation Strategic Plan: Our Common Grounds* (Toronto: City of Toronto, 2004), www1.toronto.ca/City%20Of%20Toronto/Parks%20Forestry%20&%20Recreation/05Community%20Involvement/Files/pdf/O/OCG.pdf, 60.

54 Nakamura, "Swimming Upstream?," 2.

55 Nakamura, "Beyond the Hijab."

56 Nakamura, "Swimming Upstream?," 3.

57 City of Toronto, *Parks, Forestry and Recreation Strategic Plan*, 60.

58 Toronto Community Foundation, *Toronto Vital Signs 2009: Full Report* (Toronto: TCF, 2009), https://torontofoundation.ca/sites/default/files/TVS09FullReport.pdf; Toronto Community Foundation. *Toronto Vital Signs 2010: Full Report* (Toronto: TCF, 2010), https://torontofoundation.ca/sites/default/files/TVS10FullReport.pdf.

59 YMCA of Greater Toronto, *Get Active Toronto Report on Physical Activity* (Toronto: YMCA, 2010).

60 L. Gajardo and P. Safai, *Ethnocultural Academic Initiatives Project Report* (Toronto: University of Toronto, Faculty of Physical Education and Health, 1999); Donnelly and Nakamura, *Sport and Multiculturalism*.

61 Gajardo and Safai, *Ethnocultural Academic Initiatives Project Report*.

62 James, *Seeing Ourselves*; Nakamura, "Beyond the Hijab."

63 Gajardo and Safai, *Ethnocultural Academic Initiatives Project Report*.

64 Ibid., 8, emphasis in original.

65 L.T. Smith, *Decolonizing Methodologies: Research and Indigenous Peoples* (London: Zed Books, 1999).

66 S. Buffery, "Just Kidding Around: A Renaissance Man's Retirement Party Will Test What's Left of Beezer's Brain," *Toronto Sun*, 23 April 2010, http://www.torontosun.com/sports/columnists/steve_buffery/2010/04/23/13688976.html.

67 YMCA of Greater Toronto, *Get Active Toronto*.

68 City of Toronto, *Strong Neighbourhoods*, 2005.

69 Donnelly and Nakamura also identify a program developed by the City of Toronto's Parks, Forestry, and Recreation department that implemented coach and leadership training programs targeting particular ethnic groups, including Portuguese and Muslim women. In the city of Vancouver, Wong highlights various diversity initiatives including the hiring of multicultural planners and the publication of a *Newcomers' Guide to the City of Vancouver* that is available in five languages. Donnelly and Nakamura, *Sport and Multiculturalism*; B. Wong, "Diversity and Access: Addressing Newcomers' Needs in the City of Vancouver," in *Our Diverse Cities*, ed. C. Andrew (Ottawa: Metropolis, 2004), 158–9.

70 Such a question also brings to light the complex entanglement of identity, as Jacobs and Fincher note, "with material conditions such that struggles around a politics of identity cohere through processes as much economic as cultural." The 2009 *Toronto Vital Signs* report identified that recent immigrants were three times more likely to have lost jobs (owing to the economic downturn) than were their Canadian-born colleagues and that, for those who still had jobs, the earnings gap widened significantly. Furthermore, immigrant women earned eighty-five cents for each dollar earned by Canadian-born women, twenty-five years ago; as of the 2009 report, they earned just fifty-six cents, even though their levels of education had grown at a rate

that was faster than that of Canadian-born women. When participation in sport and physical activity presupposes disposable income and time, such earning trends highlight additional inequity between immigrant and Canadian-born women and men. Jacobs and Fincher, introduction, 8; Toronto Community Foundation, *Toronto Vital Signs*.

71 Donnelly and Harvey, *Overcoming Systemic Barriers*.
72 Jacobs, *The Death and Life of Great American Cities*, 238.
73 Donnelly and Harvey, *Overcoming Systemic Barriers*.
74 Ibid., 41.
75 YMCA of Greater Toronto, *Get Active Toronto*.
76 Jacobs, *Death and Life of Great American Cities*.
77 E. Kofman, "Whose City? Gender, Class, and Immigrants in Globalizing European Cities," in *Cities of Difference*, ed. R. Fincher and J. Jacobs (New York: Guilford Press, 1998), 291.
78 Cf. J. Harvey, J. Horne, and P. Safai, "Alter-Globalization, Global Social Movements, and the Possibility of Political Transformation through Sport," *Sociology of Sport Journal* 26, no. 3 (2009): 383–403.
79 Bhabha, *Location of Culture*, 246.

9 Political Ecology, Discourse, and Shared-Use Trail Development in Nova Scotia: Braking for or Breaking the Environment?

ROBERT PITTER AND GLYN BISSIX

Environmental issues continue to draw attention in media, popular, and political discourses. Some of this attention has been directed at the environmental impact of large-scale events such as the Olympics and of other high-profile sporting activities such as skiing and golf that appropriate large tracks of land. Generally speaking, however, the accumulative environmental impact of dispersed physical and sporting activities has been neglected. In recent years recreational off-highway vehicles (OHVs) – primarily all-terrain vehicles (ATVs), snowmobiles, and off-road motorcycles (ORMs) – have become increasingly controversial throughout North America because of health, safety, environmental, and community-disturbance concerns. In 2006 a conflict over trail development and land use began to simmer in the rural community of Kings County in Nova Scotia, Canada. The conflict began soon after a group of citizens had organized themselves to form the Kieran Pathways Society in order to develop an active-transportation network connecting four semi-urban communities in a predominantly rural area, a goal that met significant resistance.[1]

Robert Pitter concluded that the Nova Scotia government's policies concerning trail development embodied the character of Giddens's "Third Way" by emphasizing local initiatives where government and civil society work in partnership. However, in this case incompatible positions emerged because Nova Scotia's shared-use trails policy allowed OHVs on the same trails as those of walkers, cyclists, and skiers. This policy raised questions about the compatibility of the activities and their impact on the promotion of healthy, active lifestyles, particularly concerning the displacement of non-motorized activities among the proponents of active transportation.[2]

Positions emerged with "me-first" agendas, and so far neither local nor provincial governments have been able to resolve them. In fact, the provincial government has implemented policies with obviously negative environmental consequences that are contradictory and at odds with its legislated environmental policy objectives. These events have drawn some attention to the ecological issues (including air pollution and fossil-fuel depletion) raised by a sporting practice that has been supported by both governmental and commercial sectors. Pitter argued that at the very least this is a consequence of the provincial government's close alliance with a single-issue group within the civil society sector, namely the organized off-highway recreational vehicle community.[3] This alliance, itself a product of governmental initiative, was first challenged by a competing single-issue group, the Kieran Pathways Society, which is championing health and environmental protection. During the years that have followed, the Kieran Pathways Society has joined with several allies to pressure the Nova Scotia government to change its trail-development policy. Hence, the Nova Scotia government must manage if not deal with the resulting sub-politics.

Writing about the environmental ethics of political conflict, Caroline Merchant argues that egocentric, homocentric, and ecocentric ethics underlie the political positions of various interest groups that are engaged in struggles over land and natural resources. "An egocentric ethic (grounded in the self) ... [has been] associated with the rise of the *laissez-faire* capitalism"; "a homocentric ethic (grounded in the social good) underlies those ecological movements whose primary goal is social justice for all people" (for example, social ecologism); and "an ecocentric ethic (grounded in the cosmos, or whole ecosystem) guides the thinking of most deep ecologists" as well as others.[4] This categorization is helpful because it alludes to normative implications attached to space, whereas we conclude that each faction emphasizes differing valuations of the environment and the appropriateness of allocating recreational space for particular uses. Does each faction promote a discourse dominated by ideas that reflect a particular environmental ethic? How do the discourses evident in these valuations compare to broader environmental discourses and ecological democracy?

Methods

For this study we conducted a discourse analysis and a review of the literature. The discourse analysis is based on information collected in a variety of documents from different sources (including provincial government officials and websites, Canadian news media via online news databases such as Proquest and Factiva, volunteer associations, and individuals who shared written communications). Over fifty documents were analysed, documents ranging in length from a few short paragraphs contained in news media accounts to more than a hundred pages in provincial government strategic plans. The government documents that were collected and analysed related mostly to legislation, policy, and strategy. The largest document group was that of media documents. These documents can be sub-classified into those that speak about the OHV industry in general, those that discuss government policy and legislation affecting OHV users, and those reporting incidents or issues involving the vehicles.

The first author, Robert Pitter, conducted both informal and formal interviews with government and community group representatives. The numerous informal interviews were recorded in field notes. Four formal, semi-structured interviews involved two representatives of the Kieran Pathways Society and one each from the Nova Scotia Departments of Natural Resources and Health Promotion and Protection. These interviews were recorded and transcribed verbatim. During the study the first author also attended three public meetings, totalling twelve hours, at which representatives of various interests spoke. The first and third meetings were approximately two hours long: one was recorded and transcribed verbatim, the other documented as field notes. The second meeting, lasting eight hours, generated field notes consisting of more than four thousand words. Data analysis –including both documents and transcripts – employed latent content analysis with the assistance of ATLAS.ti, a qualitative analysis computer software application.

The literature review focused on the health literature, particularly the epidemiological literature related to active transportation and the use of ATVs. This literature was primarily searched by accessing the medical index PubMed, using keywords such as *all terrain vehicles*, *off highway vehicles*, *snowmobiles*, *cycling*, and *bicycling* in conjunction with *costs*, *benefits*, *economic burden*, and *environmental impact*. The environmental literature was surveyed to assess the impacts of ATV use and active transportation. Here the academic, governmental, and non-governmental-organization sources were helpful. Economics literature was reviewed primarily to consider the costs and benefits of ATV use. The academic literature examining the ATV phenomenon was sparse; there was, however, sizeable industry- and user-group-sponsored literature, and one opposing, polemic, coffee-table-sized publication, that was reviewed. Several scientific indexes were consulted to examine the economic literature, such as EconLit. This was supplemented by Internet searches, particularly with the use of Google and Google Scholar search engines. Much of the industry literature was sourced via Google. Finally a review was made of the social impacts of ATV use and active transportation. The sociological literature was explored through a number of indexes such as Sociological Abstracts and Sport Discus.

Scope of the Issues

Controversy over the Nova Scotia government's shared-use trail policy has escalated since 2006 because the policy mandates shared motorized and non-motorized trail use wherever possible. The debate surrounding the credibility of this policy touches on the broad policy areas of economy, health, and environment. The most vocal critics of the policy – a growing "active transportation" lobby buoyed by concerns about health and the environment – have questioned it in all three areas, to which their "adversaries" (the provincial government and the off-highway-vehicle lobby) have responded with reassurances that the policy is both reasonable and consistent with environmental and related health concerns. All three groups maintain that they value the environment. It appears that they want to be good environmental citizens, but are they? Important questions arise from this dispute. Which of the three environmental ethics framed by Merchant do their actions reflect? How do their ethics intersect with dominant environmental discourses, especially those concerning solutions to environmental problems? What strategies might be best suited to resolving these conflicts?

Our data suggest three primary orientations that seem to be central to the discourses championed by each faction. Each orientation appears, however, to value the environment by association with other interests, namely the economy, health, and sport. We argue that each of the orientations – our environment, our economy; our environment, our health; our environment, our sport – is partially consistent with one of Merchant's environmental ethic categories, but none strongly reflects ecocentrism. Furthermore, the factions' approaches to solving environmental problems fluctuate between the administrative rationalism and the democratic pragmatism described by John Dryzek in *The Politics of the Earth: Environmental Discourses*.[5]

Nova Scotia Government: Our Environment, Our Economy

We begin our discussion by focusing on the Nova Scotia government because it has immediate jurisdiction over abandoned rail-line corridors. Many of them are being converted into a province-wide, integrated trail system; however, the provincial government is increasingly entangled in a public struggle of interests between active-transportation advocates on the one hand and OHV users on the other. Over the past ten years the provincial government has expended considerable time and effort in revising and developing new policy and procedures in the areas of health, economy, and the environment. In fact, in November 2006 a newly created Nova Scotia Department of Health Promotion and

Protection[6] released "Nova Scotia Pathways for People: Framework for Action." The document outlines a vision for active transportation in Nova Scotia and identifies active transportation as an important strategy for reducing environmental concerns such as climate change. It begins with a quotation from Rodney MacDonald (Nova Scotia's premier, 2006–9) made in 2004 when he was minister of the office of health promotion: "Making active choices can help us make strides in addressing many issues associated with chronic disease, obesity, climate change, air quality, and traffic congestion. Our government is committed to improving the health of Nova Scotians from many angles, including Active Transportation."[7] The introduction goes on to note that "MacDonald sums it up well. Our love affair with the automobile has made a majority of us overweight and prone to disease, has negatively affected our relationship with the natural world, and has made our cities congested and unsafe."[8]

Nova Scotia's "extensive and diverse trails system"[9] is cited as one example of the many active-transportation initiatives that the government is supporting along with the "Rails to Trails" policy that is said to link Nova Scotia communities. Several provincial non-governmental organizations are listed as having mandates that support active transportation. Despite their obvious commitment to *motorized* transportation, the Snowmobilers Association and the All Terrain Vehicle Association are on this list. Furthermore, while the government upholds Nova Scotia's shared-use trails as part of an active transportation network, there is little evidence that these trails are used for commuting rather than just recreation.

Less than a year following the release of the policy document "Nova Scotia Pathways for People: Framework for Action," the provincial government passed Bill no. 146, the Environmental Goals and Sustainable Prosperity Act. The 2,584-word act is based on several key principles:

(a) the health of the economy, the health of the environment and the health of the people of the Province are interconnected; (b) environmentally sustainable economic development that recognizes the economic value of the Province's environmental assets is essential to the long-term prosperity of the Province; (c) the environment and the economy of the Province are a shared responsibility of all levels of government, the private sector and all people of the Province; (d) the environment and economy must be managed for the benefit of present and future generations; (e) innovative solutions are necessary to mutually reinforce the environment and the economy; (f) a long-term approach to planning and decision-making is necessary to harmonize the Province's goals of economic prosperity and environmental sustainability; (g) the management of goals for sustainable prosperity, such as emission reduction, energy efficiency programs and increasing the

amount of legally protected land will preserve and improve the Province's environment and economy for future generations.[10]

Every principle listed emphasizes a relationship between the environment of
Nova Scotia and the economy of the province. The long-term objectives of the
act address protecting 12 per cent of the province's total land mass; reducing
emissions of sulphur dioxide, greenhouse gases, and mercury emissions by
20, 50, and 70 per cent, respectively; and other goals related to waste disposal
rates, sustainable procurement, and energy efficiency in homes and business
buildings.

Testing on off-highway vehicles conducted by the U.S. Environmental Protection Agency suggests that a multi-use trail policy that includes motorized
vehicles is at odds with the statements contained in the "Pathways for People" framework and the objectives of the Environmental Goals and Sustainable Prosperity Act. According to their testing,[11] ATVs produce from fifteen to
thirty-three times the amount of air pollution in each hour of operation compared to that of the average family car. In addition, about a fifth of the gasoline
expended during ATV use is emitted into the atmosphere as non-combusted
aerosol. The equivalent-emissions rate for two-stroke snowmobiles is much
worse: ninety-eight times that of the average family car.[12] Efforts by the EPA to
enforce enhanced OHV performance were initially postponed to at least 2012
as a result of opposition from the OHV industrial lobby; however, new engine-
testing regulations were finally adopted by the EPA in February 2015.[13] This
delay of over a decade raises concerns about not only the industry's commitment to cleaner air but also its disregard for users' welfare as ATV users and
snowmobilers regularly travel in convoys. In convoys, riders are exposed to
exhaust plumes from preceding vehicles, and nowhere is this exposure more
intense than in ATV rallies involving large numbers of machines travelling in
close formation.[14]

Nova Scotia government's emphasis on the economy when it comes to environmental issues was also evident in interviews with government officials
employed by the Nova Scotia Departments of Health Promotion and Protection and Natural Resources. They regard the proposed multi-use trail system as
an environmental asset yielding important economic benefits through tourism,
with growth potential. One government official noted that a pub owner publicly
reported a $25,000 loss in revenue when the trail in the town of Paradise was
closed to motorized traffic. Similarly, during public consultations concerning
the re-opening of the Paradise trail, many people spoke about the impact of the
trail system on the local businesses that hope to benefit from the tourism generated. In addition to these anecdotal accounts of the economic impact, another

government official referred to a few commissioned economic-impact studies conducted by Gardner Pinfold and the Atlantic Canada Opportunities Agency.

Economic-impact studies sponsored by the government, the ATV industry, and various user groups document considerable economic activity. However, critics note that few if any of these types of studies incorporate the broad costs of ATV use to society, and consequently overestimate its net value. Inflated estimates are not confined to the ATV industry – several special interest studies in tourism show similar overestimates[15] – and a review of the ATV sector highlights a pattern of methodological shortcomings.[16] The website of Peaceful Roads and Trails Vermont highlights some of these. They draw attention to the failure of several ATV studies to account for the considerable capital leakages that drain from the local purchasing area. Such leakages constitute an "opportunity cost" where alternative expenditures could generate greater local economic welfare. The Vermont website notes, for snowmobiling: "In fact, a lot of the money spent on snowmobiling in Vermont should be seen as money leaving the state, rather than coming in. When a Vermonter buys a new $8,000 snowmobile or a $20,000 truck to tow it, the bulk of that money, everything but the dealer's mark-up and the sales tax, is immediately headed for Detroit, Canada, Japan, or wherever the vehicle was manufactured."[17]

Notwithstanding these criticisms, the Nova Scotia government's position on the environment, and its commitment to multi-use trails, reflects an egocentric ethic that, as Merchant notes, underlies laissez-faire capitalism.[18] She argues that laissez-faire capitalism is limited, and, "because egocentric ethics are based on the assumption that individual good is the highest good, the collective behaviour of human groups or business corporations is not a legitimate subject of investigation." Related to this, writing about ecologism as an ideology, Dobson notes that reduced consumption is essential to ecologism's vision of a sustainable society.[19] Also essential is the idea that sacrifices and standard-of-living changes will be compensated by gains elsewhere. Quality of the economy must supersede quantity.

Active Transportation Advocates: Our Environment, Our Health

After the Kieran Pathways Society had begun to challenge provincial multi-use trail policy in 2006, it formed an alliance with eleven other organizations dispersed throughout the province, becoming known as Nova Scotians Promoting Active-Transportation on Community Trails (NSPACTS).[20] The members of this alliance, however, are not the only groups that have publicly declared their opposition to shared-use trails in Nova Scotia; an anonymous and somewhat extremist group, Save Our Trails, has also advocated for a complete ban on recreational motorized trail development in the province. There are important similarities and differences in each group's goal, agenda, and strategies.

The membership of Save Our Trails communicates solely through its website, SaveOurTrails.ca. The goals of this group are considered rather extremist as its members seek to ban OHVs from recreational trails "that run through or close to residential communities in Nova Scotia." The group chooses to remain anonymous "for the simple reason that we fear for our personal safety, and for the safety of our families." SaveOurTrails.ca made several references to the violent behaviour of OHV users within and outside Nova Scotia, and for a very short time period the site contained a link to another site with information on how to sabotage OHVs. Even so, the website states that is it not "anti-ATV … Although there are many organizations which would like to eradicate them completely, we are not one of them, *for now*."[21]

The objections of Save Our Trails to OHV use near people's homes begins with the right to the "quiet enjoyment of our homes and properties." The group argues that this right has been denied in Nova Scotia owing to the provincial government's lack of law enforcement and support of municipal by-laws, and this lack of enforcement has meant negative consequences for people's health and the environment, as the website expresses:

> We're not talking about occasional petty annoyances caused by ATVs and snow-mobiles. We're talking about people who are developing serious health problems because of them, who find themselves threatened, their livelihoods put at risk, and their properties intentionally damaged, destroyed, and devalued – all the while government looks the other way.
>
> Save Our Trails wants Nova Scotians to know where their taxes go: into ATVANS [All-Terrain Vehicle Association of Nova Scotia], into the destruction of the planet – its air, water, forests, wetlands, and greenways – and into a province-wide assault on citizens, their homes and their health, and the natural assets of their neighborhoods.[22]

While Save Our Trails's anonymity, distaste for and fear of OHVs, and emphasis on rights distinguishes it from other groups, its concerns about OHVs' impact on the environment and related health issues overlaps with that of the more moderate approach of NSPACTS. Like Save Our Trails, NSPACTS is concerned about the impact that trail use policy can have on health; however, the NSPACTS' vision of health is articulated in a broader form: their vision is to "create active, healthy and sustainable community trails and pathways for all Nova Scotians."[23]

NSPACTS has been more visible and vocal in more media than has Save Our Trails. These Nova Scotians have a broader agenda and have been very vocal in promoting their alternate vision for rails-to-trails development in the province. They have worked deliberately and diligently to promote this agenda through press conferences, press releases, and public forums, as well as their website, which states:

> The abandonment of the rail lines throughout Nova Scotia, their subsequent gift to the Trans Canada Trail Foundation and their eventual deed or license back to the province, offers an exceptional opportunity, and we believe an inherent obligation upon the province of Nova Scotia, to create a legacy in keeping with the generosity and vision of the gift. We believe creating an environmentally friendly, sustainable, Active Transportation corridor, a Nova Scotia Greenway, would fulfill that legacy.
>
> NSPACTS believes it is essential that the rail corridor be protected as a designated Active Transportation trail and recognized as a *primary health resource* for the public good. The recommendation to formally designate the rail corridor as Nova Scotia's Greenway recognizes the unique opportunity the rail corridor represents.[24]

This vision is linked to an eleven-item charter, the first point of which implies a concern for the environment. It reads: "Promote and create *sustainable trails and pathways* that accommodate all forms of human powered transportation including reasonable mobility aids."[25] NSPACTS has also been endorsed or received support from environmental organizations including the Atlantic chapter of the Sierra Club and the TRAX project of Ecology Action Centre.

The group's rationale for promoting active transportation integrates environmental issues with health issues in several ways that draw attention to expert research rather than to merely anecdotal evidence. The environment-related health concerns discussed by NSPACTS focus on air and noise quality. The concerns question the consistency between the provincial government's shared-use trail policy (which includes OHVs), the new Environmental Goals and Sustainable Prosperity Act, and the evidence-based strategy for policy development espoused by the Department of Health Promotion and Protection.

The NSPACTS position paper, *Creating Greenway Nova Scotia: A NSPACTS Initiative*, emphasizes ties between environmental health, population health, and economic health. It discusses the contribution of OHVs to air and noise pollution and their association with health risks. It points out: "The noise and emissions generated from off road vehicles discourages hikers, walkers and cyclists attempting to enjoy a pleasant outdoor experience. A comprehensive EPA (US Environmental Protection Agency) [study] compared emissions of various non-road recreational vehicle emissions with ordinary cars. Their study demonstrated one hour of snowmobile operation is equivalent to nearly 100 hours of automobile use while a two-stroke ATV is equivalent to over thirty hours of car driving."[26] Beyond the local and perhaps temporary impacts of OHV use, their nationwide impact in the United States is said to make significant contributions to "mobile-source air pollution." In 2000 these machines represented 13 per cent of the United States' mobile-source hydrocarbon, 6 per cent of carbon monoxide, 3 per cent of oxides of nitrogen, and 1 per cent of particulate matter emissions, despite their relatively fewer numbers and substantially less operational time compared to highway traffic.[27] Given previous annual sales growth, in Minnesota alone the growth was expected to rise by 251 per cent by 2014.[28] Thus, there is good reason for concern as emissions levels could reach as high as 33 per cent of the United States' mobile-source emissions of hydrocarbon and as high as 9 per cent of carbon monoxide emissions, 9 per cent of oxides of nitrogen, and 2 per cent of particulate matter by 2020 if this level of growth in ATV use continues.[29] Despite the problems linked to hydrocarbon emissions, opponents to shared trail use rarely talk about hydrocarbons in public forums as much as they do about the dust raised by ATVs.

The concerns raised by individuals in our interviews, at town meetings, and at press conferences often drew attention to the issues of air quality and noise. Those who spoke against OHV use on trails sometimes equated the impact of OHV use on air quality and health with the impact of smoking:

> I mean philosophically I put ATVs, snowmobile use in the same category as smoking. I mean there was a time when we didn't feel it was fair to post non-smoking signs ... We are not doing ourselves any good and I think there are a lot of parallels because it's not just personal health; it is community health that we are talking about. Because there is a spillover effect just like secondhand smoke. You have noise, and this perceived safety risk is just like secondhand smoke. I think, you can't just sort of say it's a personal choice. You know, "I like riding my ATV; therefore I should be allowed to." "I have human rights," and all this stuff. Well, it's not that simple if you are talking about being a social creature.[30]

Noise was also a recurring concern of the most vocal opponents to OHV use of community trails. At a public meeting in the community of Coldbrook, a member of an NSPACTS affiliated organization reported, "In February 2006 we had a preliminary survey of Cambridge Woods subdivision. It showed 91% of respondents as having concerns with current motorized use, and safety and noise issues were the primary concerns among others."[31]

Save Our Trails and NSPACTS both note that in 2004 the homeowners living along a snowmobile trail in Quebec won damages of between $5 million and $10 million from their provincial government to compensate for health injuries caused by sleeplessness, noise, and fumes.[32] Information reported on the Peaceful Roads and Trails Vermont website states that ATVs can create up to a two-mile "auditory footprint," which means that an ATV can be heard as much as a mile away as it approaches and a mile as it moves away.[33] The website argues that such noise levels create stress among local residents.

Our review literature discovered a dearth of studies on the health impacts of OHV noise within host communities. Some studies on ATV use do identify noise as a problem, but none to date objectively measures its health effects. Nonetheless, some groups have extrapolated health impacts from other noise-related health studies. For example, a 2001 World Health Organization fact sheet noted that ambient noise is considered a significant health concern. This publication points out that, while many countries have regulations on noise associated with rail, road construction, and industrial plants, few have regulations to control ambient noise in communities. The absence of enforceable regulation is "probably owing to the difficulties with its definition, measurement and control." Difficulties identifying the effects of noise on people's well-being also "handicap attempts to prevent and control the problem."[34]

Research shows that recreational use of OHVs can have substantial environmental impacts, some of which have direct implications for population health. These implications impede simple solutions. While improved engine performance will reduce the emissions of new OHVs, for example, it will take many years to replace the OHVs already in use or awaiting sale, which in the short term will do little to improve air quality in and around trails. Also simply addressing noise volume will be insufficient because quieter machines may prove to be more dangerous to other trail users, and the noise quality and intermittence rather than the intensity alone may be a more problematic health issue.

The "our environment, our health" discourse championed by those opposed to shared-use trails extends beyond population health to include economic knock-on effects; their arguments draw attention to the financial costs versus benefits of shared-use trails compared to those of non-motorized trails. Much of the cost-benefit analysis focuses on savings related to health-care costs.

Go for Green, a now-disbanded national group that advocated environmentally responsive, active living, estimated in 2004 that the financial benefits to the Canadian economy of active travel were $3.5 billion annually. This not only considers the health-care savings from a healthier population but also includes the benefits derived from reductions in greenhouse gases, traffic congestion, ground-level air pollution, and noise pollution; increased public safety; and a more engaged and independent community, particularly of the disabled, youth, and the aged.[35] Furthermore, Ron Colman indicated that the annual health-care costs of inactivity in Nova Scotia are around $66.5 million, and, when the burden of premature death and disability is included, this adds a further $247 million in costs. The average cost of each inactive Nova Scotian to the province is estimated at $629 per year. Colman calculates that each year there are 2,224 potential years of life lost as a result of inactivity.[36]

Quoting the Heart and Stroke Foundation of Nova Scotia, NSPACTS points out: "The strength of the evidence makes it impossible to ignore. Our population at all age levels is increasingly inactive, and efforts to change that need to happen now. Governments, communities and individuals cannot continue to bear the high costs associated with the growing levels of inactivity; it costs us in many ways … poor health; caregiver burden; decreasing productivity in schools and workplaces; increasing pollution; growing costs of drugs, physician, hospital and long-term care; and in early death and disability. It is time to take action to reduce these debilitating losses to our health and to the economy."[37]

Motorized trails, NSPACTS argues, put people at risk of injury and/or discourage them from engaging in active transportation, and consequently preclude the economic health benefits that could be associated with active transportation. One interview respondent described this position:

INTERVIEWER: So where do you see the key economic benefits from these trails coming? What areas? Where is the savings or where is the economic gain?
RESPONDENT: I think once we can get more people active and going to work on their bicycles or walking more often. Any time you get them more active, we know from our research that is going to have health benefits. Those health benefits are going to translate over time into the reduction of chronic disease. And we have major chronic disease epidemics in this country as we do in just about every Western country. That includes diabetes, obesity and even forms of cancer, and so on.[38]

Active-transportation advocates argue that displacing potentially active people from a trail has financial implications when no substitute for being active is readily available. They believe that, if one extrapolated Go for Green's estimates, a policy of providing active-transportation infrastructure would pay for itself in health-care savings and in carbon-emission reductions in a very short period, while providing additional value for recreation, tourism, and community cohesion.[39]

Beyond the costs of inactivity, active-transportation advocates are also concerned about the costs associated with traffic injury when individuals use public highways for active transportation. To be fair, they note that such injury costs must be weighed against any health-care dividends. In fact, the Canadian

Safety Council maintains that there are more injuries from bicycling than from both snowmobiling and ATV use, and, according to Brown et al., bicycle and ATV injuries are prevalent among children. The rate of injury per participant for cycling is, however, substantially lower than that for ATV use and snowmobiling.[40] Some support for the need to separate motorized and non-motorized traffic on trails comes from a World Health Organization traffic study that cites a pandemic in injuries and deaths resulting from cyclist and pedestrian collisions with motor vehicles and recommends, wherever feasible, separating active-transportation modalities from motor vehicles.[41]

A few American studies show that the health-care costs attributable to ATV use are considerable.[42] In the United States the costs of ATV-use injuries and deaths rose from $493 million in 1999 to $723 million in 2003 among children (under sixteen years of age), and from $1,706 million to $2,517 million among adults (sixteen years of age and over). In deconstructing these costs, 63.8 per cent represent quality-of-life losses, 36.0 per cent are work losses, and 0.2 per cent are direct medical costs. Of particular note is that males account for 77.5 per cent of the costs attributed to youth, and for 89.0 per cent of those attributed to adults.[43] While there are currently no known equivalent Canadian calculations, active-transportation advocates argue that there is no reason to believe that the comparative costs, pro-rated to the size of participation, would be substantially less. In fact, because most health-care costs are supported by a social health-care system in Canada, taxpayers would be expected to bear a greater burden.

Active-transportation advocates spoke least frequently about concerns related to natural environmental damage. The pictorial compilation of essays entitled *Thrillcraft: The Environmental Consequences of Motorized Recreation* is a comprehensive overview of OHV damage to landscape and wildlife in North America.[44] Very little of the data collected for our study raised this issue, and consequently, given its almost exclusive emphasis on the promotion and protection of human health, the NSPACTS discourse seems to be infused with, and is dominated by, a homocentric ethic inasmuch as NSPACTS promotes environmental protection as a social good important to everyone. There is nonetheless the potential to evolve closer to an ecocentric ethic if NSPACTS embraced the preservation of the environment for its own sake.

OHV Users: Our Environment, Our Sport

Off-highway-vehicle enthusiasts actively promote their sport and defend it against criticisms related to the environment, health, and the economy. Collectively, three groups representing snowmobilers, ATV riders, and off-road motorcyclists have developed an effective lobby that pre-dates NSPACTS and its allies. They have also very aggressively and successfully countered criticisms of their activities by NSPACTS and others.[45] In 2009 the OHV lobby convinced the Nova Scotia government to reopen the trail through Paradise to recreational off-highway vehicles;[46] it had been closed at the request of landowners living adjacent to the trail.[47]

In conjunction with the Nova Scotia civil servants responsible for promoting recreation and sport within the Department of Health Promotion and Protection and various OHV industry partners, OHV users maintain that their sport is a healthy way for people from all walks of life to enjoy the outdoors despite the evidence cited above. A public servant and sometime OHV operator interviewed for this study discussed the health benefits cautiously:

> RESPONDENT: Healthwise, I'm certainly not going to speak to that, because I'm not going to say that driving an OHV is a healthy activity, but I am going to say that operating an OHV – if that is what you choose to do – it can contribute to wellness.
>
> INTERVIEWER: In what ways?
>
> RESPONDENT: I know personally and professionally that there is a tremendous link between mental health and physical health. And if a person is relaxed and enjoying themselves and having fun, there is a tremendous amount of an improved mental state. I truly believe that connects to an improved physical state. I am not saying that driving an ATV or a snowmobile or a motorcycle contributes to physical health in the sense of using your muscles and the kinetics of it. You know I have my own opinions on that. My opinion being that operating them in the past, I know that it is physical. But I'm not prepared, nor do I have the facts that can state besides beyond my own personal opinion that it contributes to physical health.[48]

In a similar anecdotal but less cautious manner, a 2009 press release issued by International Snowmobile Association claims that "snowmobiling provides physical and mental health benefits. Winter recreation fights seasonal affective disorder."[49] Also, a brochure published by the Department of Health Promotion and Protection, Nova Scotia All-Terrain Vehicle Association, and the Nova Scotia Anglers and Hunting Federation states that "ATVing is part of a healthy outdoor lifestyle" (see figure 9.1).[50]

The Nova Scotia Department of Health Promotion and Protection's supporting evidence for that statement in their joint brochure was that "a study is in progress."[51] Contrary to the claims of the department and the ATV community, there are few, if any, validated health benefits from riding an ATV reported in the academic literature. Commissioned by the All-Terrain Quad Council

9.1 Brochure promoting the health benefits of ATV use

of Canada (AQCC) and the Canadian Off-Highways Vehicles Distributors Council, and co-funded by Nova Scotia's Department of Health Promotion and Protection, the aforementioned study is in progress at York University in Toronto.[52] According to a conference abstract, however, this study is finding that the benefits of promoting physical health are weak at best with off-road-motorcycle (dirt-bike) riders and poor among ATV riders.[53] Aerobic levels put ATV riders at the thirty-third percentile, which places them unfavourably among a generally unfit Canadian population.

In a companion study recently published in full by Burr, Jamnik, Shaw, and Gledhill concerning the physiological demands of ATV use and off-highway motorcycling, the authors determined that the aerobic demand of "riding an ATV was approximately 4.6 ml/kg-1/min-1 which is less demanding than moderately paced walking."[54] They wondered, because the participants in their ATV study accumulated on average 420 MET (metabolic equivalents of energy expended) per week, whether this could approximate the recommended dosage of exercise for a physiological benefit. They emphasized, nevertheless, that "it has yet to be determined if infrequent longer bouts summing to the same absolute weekly energy expenditure lead to the same health benefits as shorter duration, frequent exercise."

As reported in the *Halifax Chronicle Herald* and in our observations, members of the organized off-highway-vehicle groups often presented themselves as "stewards of the environment," in direct contrast to the image of them painted by the active-transportation lobby and other groups.[55] James Anderson, former public relations manager for the All-Terrain Vehicle Association of Nova Scotia, claimed that ATV users are "becoming environmental activists … Many would like to be seen as guardians of the environment and woodlands."[56] They have promoted this image in various ways by arguing that OHVs are not an environmental problem in themselves; a few unorganized and irresponsible riders are the problem. Organized riders (meaning riders who are members of the numerous clubs affiliated with one of the three OHV provincial associations) are responsible riders and do not cause problems related to dust, noise, or damage to landscapes and habitats. As one ATV user stated, "it is a problem for us just as much as it is for you, the cowboys that we have in the sport. The police have chosen to do very little about it. We are just as disappointed at the way those people treat our environment and our public property."[57]

OHV groups actively promote environmentally responsible riding, through public relations campaigns, brochures (see figure 9.2), the Internet, and trail-development workshops. At a 2008 province-wide meeting of OHV users, the trail-development co-ordinator for an OHV association discussed sustainable trail development by pointing out that *sustainable* means that resource protection, as well as efficient trail operation and maintenance, is provided. Nova Scotia's OHV associations also promote the national ATV NatureWatch program by distributing promotional materials developed by the Canadian All-Terrain Vehicles Association and the Canadian Ecology Centre. The environment and sensitive habitats are listed first and second among the program's five key areas of concern.[58]

Regarding air and noise pollution issues, we found no arguments challenging or qualifying concerns about air pollution in terms of harmful engine

9.2 Examples of OHV-responsibility promotion

emissions; however, ATV users recognized dust clouds as an important issue. Their solution is to use a material made from crushed shingles for surfacing trails and to mandate that all ATV clubs control dust. Concerns about noise were discussed by the International Snowmobile Association, which maintains that snowmobiles are quieter than ever: "Sound levels for snowmobiles have been reduced 94% since inception. Pre-1969 snowmobiles were noisy. At full throttle, these machines emitted sound levels as high as 102 dB(A) from a distance of 50 feet ... Problems with excessive noise levels do occur when irresponsible snowmobilers modify the snowmobile exhaust system or substitute the factory system with an after-market racing exhaust. In most states and provinces this practice is illegal and grossly misrepresents the sport."[59] ATV users have made similar claims about noise problems being a consequence of irresponsible drivers and modifications to ATVs, as expressed by an ATV user during a public meeting in which noise and dust were raised as community concerns: "Most of the problem is the motor-cross bikes and stuff and people racing. Not everybody drives badly on roads. Whenever I go on trails, I always slow down for people and stuff. The main reason I do that is because it leaves a pile of dust behind me. So I always slow down and once I pass fairly far, I'll start to go fast again and stuff. I try to keep the noise down."[60] They often also point to other activities that they feel are as noisy or noisier. During the same public meeting various ATV users commented:

CITIZEN A: What about noisy trucks?
CITIZEN B: My ATV makes less noise than the average lawnmower.
CITIZEN C: Where I live ... the Brown Trucking operation is against the rail bed on Cambridge road. You can hear that four kilometres away from where I live. That is how noisy it is. If you're worried about noise, why don't you get rid of that noise?

OHV associations also argue they help protect the environment by assisting with the enforcement of trail regulations and with public education. This is accomplished through their contributions to the Nova Scotia Trail Patrol, which began in 2002 and currently has two hundred trail wardens. Many of these wardens are members of the Snowmobilers Association of Nova Scotia and the All-Terrain Vehicle Association of Nova Scotia. A key stated objective of this patrol is the protection of the environment through communication with law enforcement officers and through education.[61]

Supported by these and other activities (for example, the development of low-dust-emitting surfaces), the OHV community argues that they are indeed effective stewards of the environment. They contend that they are protecting and managing the trail environment for the enjoyment of both motorized and non-motorized users. This approach is an essential element for preserving their sport and building a positive image to offset what they consider to be the irresponsible behaviour of a few non-members whose thoughtless actions give the sport a bad name.

This is an approach that has much in common with the egocentric ethics described by Merchant. Organized off-highway-vehicle users frequently point out that every individual has a right to enjoy nature and that there is a reasonable solution to most conflicts or issues involving the environment. However, as Merchant points out, the egocentric approach evident in the OHV position is incompatible with the demands of deep ecology.[62] The *ecocentric* ethic of deep ecology supports the intrinsic right of nature to be undisturbed and hence, as Dobson notes, requires humans to challenge the notion of consumption for the sake of consumption and to justify interfering in the world rather than having to justify not interfering in the world.[63]

Summary and Conclusions

These events in Nova Scotia, especially the Environmental Goals and Sustainable Prosperity Act of 2007, support the observation of political ecologist Andrew Dobson that "one of the most striking political transformations of the past two decades has been the way in which environmental concern has moved from the margins to the mainstream of political life." He adds: "No serious candidate for political office can afford to buck this trend ... This transformation has required of politicians that they assimilate 'the environment' into their respective political positions – and the result has been a series of severe cases of ideological indigestion. These attempts at the appropriation of environmental concern have made it more important than ever to stake clearly the territory of political ideology that has formed around environmental issues."[64]

The most obvious example of ideological indigestion in this case concerns the irritation caused by a growing active-transportation lobby that is drawing attention to apparent contradictions between the government's Environmental Goals and Sustainable Prosperity Act and its promotion of a multi-use trail system that essentially encourages increased and unsustainable environmental damage. However, from a radical political ecology point of view, the environmental ethics of all three groups examined in this chapter are very different from the ecocentric ethics at the heart of ecologism, and even the active-transportation lobby, argued by the ATV lobby to be a small, self-interested, and elitist group, seems to be dealing with its own case of ideological indigestion.

One prescription for this indigestion can be found in Dryzek's *Politics of the Earth* and his discussion of environmental discourses.[65] Dryzek analyses the discourses evident in more than forty years of debate over environmental issues. He maintains that fights over meaning in the arena of environmental issues are everywhere, and that the meanings attached to the ideas we have about the environment change. A significant feature of the conflict over trail development in Nova Scotia is the debate about the evidence that should count, and the rights that people have to enjoy and/or to protect a particular kind of environment. The case we have presented here has a lot in common with the conflicts discussed by Dryzek. For example, it illustrates that activists are often resistant to the evidence produced by government agencies and industry. This case raises such questions as: Why is there no consensus on the evidence that counts, and what evidence constitutes proof? How should risks be approached in the absence of public confidence in scientific standards?[66] Our case also resembles the conflict over logging described by Dryzek, in which the simultaneous pursuit of environmental values and economic values seemed at odds with each other. Which set of rights should be privileged? Is it the rights of property owners who dislike OHVs, the rights of constituents to earn a living in a diverse economy that includes recreational OHVs, the rights of constituents to live in a healthy environment, or the right of the environment to be protected from harm?

In the context of solving environmental problems, Dryzek discusses three discourses that reveal three primary methods for solving ecological problems: administrative rationalism, democratic pragmatism, and economic rationalism.[67] In our study two of these approaches –administrative rationalism and democratic pragmatism – are evident. Dryzek defines *administrative rationalism* "as the problem-solving discourse which emphasizes the role of the expert rather than the citizen or producer/consumer in social problem solving."[68] This discourse comes out very strongly in the arguments put forward by active-transportation advocates who are at least partially responding to the evidence-based approach to health care that is espoused by the Nova Scotia Department of Health Promotion and Protection. Administrative rationalism can be found in the practice of rationalistic policy analysis techniques such as the cost-benefit analyses championed by NSPACTS. NSPACTS's arguments drawn from the often cited paper by Bissix and Medicraft and from other sources are textbook examples of this approach.[69] The policy options of shared-use trails and single-use trails are compared by listing both the desirable and the undesirable effects (benefits and costs). Shadow pricing is used to attach monetary values to both types of effects; a balance sheet summing up the net benefits of each alternative is created; and the option with the greatest net benefit (single-use trails, in this case) is chosen or advocated.

Dryzek describes *democratic pragmatism* as "interactive problem solving within the basic institutional structure of liberal capitalism"[70] and as a style of problem solving that relies on public consultation, alternative dispute resolution, policy dialogue, lay citizen deliberation, public inquires, and right-to-know legislation. This discourse is evident in the approach taken by Nova Scotia's Department of Natural Resources and by OHV enthusiasts. While OHV enthusiasts have responded to the administrative rationalism of NSPACTS with alternative cost-benefit research, they have also pointed out that the public consultation, alternative dispute resolution, and lay citizen deliberation mandated by Nova Scotia's rails-to-trails policy has led to what they feel is a reasonable compromise addressing the environment and the needs of various trail users.

Dryzek argues that an intelligent approach to environmental issues requires a structural analysis of the trajectory of liberal capitalist political economy that identifies what might be done to ensure that this path has ecologically benign consequences. An intelligent approach to environmental issues also requires an ability to "facilitate and engage in social learning in an ecological context."[71] The administrative rationalism that is characteristic of NSPACTS and the Department of Health Promotion and Protection has limited the resources for creating institutions and discourses that are capable of learning about their own deficiencies. Dryzek argues that resources for this type of learning are provided by democratic pragmatism (characteristic of the Department of Natural Resources trail policy supported by OHV users).

For Dryzek, democratic pragmatism promotes dispute resolution through co-operative problem solving by the means noted above. These means work best when there are "authentic democratic discussions, open to all interests, under which political power and strategizing do not determine outcomes."[72] Such open discussions have not necessarily been characteristic of the public consultations concerning shared-use trail development, because those opposed to the policies have good reason to believe that their voices have been muted or drowned out by political and corporate interests. Dryzek seems to suggest that the value of democratic pragmatism can be enhanced when the best parts of three other discourses – sustainable development, ecological modernism, and green radicalism – are added to the mix to create an ecological democracy. None of these discourses was apparent in our study. Dryzek argues that sustainable-development discourse allows for a range of experimentation that promotes learning; ecological modernism can promote discussion of radical institutional change through reflexive development; and green radicalism can promote the sense of urgency that is needed to radicalize democratic pragmatism and the other two discourses. This, he says, could lead to an ecological democracy without boundaries, with institutions that are very different from those of our current industrialized society – institutions that do not distort communication. In resolving the environmental politics disrupting trail development in Nova Scotia, who, if anyone, will use the discourses that will lead to ecological democracy and a shared sense of environmental citizenship?

NOTES

1 Robert Pitter, "Finding the Kieran Way: A Study of Sport, Recreation, and Lifestyle Politics in Rural Nova Scotia," *Journal of Sport and Social Issues* 33, no. 1 (2009): 331–51.
2 Ibid.

3 Ibid.
4 Caroline Merchant, *Radical Ecology: The Search for a Livable World* (New York, 1997), 62.
5 John S. Dryzek, *The Politics of the Earth: Environmental Discourses,* 2nd ed. (Oxford, 2005).
6 The Department of Health Promotion and Protection is now known as the Department of Health and Wellness.
7 Renée Hartleib, "Nova Scotia Pathways for People: Framework for Action" (Halifax, November 2006), 3.
8 Ibid.
9 Ibid., 8.
10 Nova Scotia, "Environmental Goals and Sustainable Prosperity Act," 2007.
11 U.S. Environmental Protection Agency (EPA), Office of Transportation and Air Quality, "Frequently Asked Questions: Environmental Impact of Recreational Vehicles and Other Non-road Engines," EPA420-F-01-030 September 2001, http://www.epa.gov/otaq/regs/nonroad/proposal/f01030.pdf.
12 Ibid.
13 "Regulatory Announcement: Extension of Temporary Exhaust Emission Test Procedure Option for All Terrain Vehicles (ATVs)." Federal Register, vol. 80, no. 33, 19 February 2015, Rules and Regulations, www.epa.gov/otaq/regs/nonroad/recveh/420f07022.pdf; 40 CFR Parts 59, 80, 85, et al. Amendments Related to Tier 3 Motor Vehicle Emission and Fuel Standards, Nonroad Engine and Equipment Programs, and MARPOL, Annex VI Implementation; Direct Final Rule.
14 See A. Switalski and M. Wright, "The Influence of Snowmobile Emissions on Air Quality and Human Health," *Autumn Equinox* 12, no. 3 (2007); Scott Emerson, MD, "New Perspectives Concerning Public Health and Economic Aspects of Snowmobiling for the State of Michigan," position paper presented to the Michigan Natural Resources Commission, July 2003; L.M.S. Fussell, "Carbon Monoxide Exposure by Snowmobile Riders," *Park Science* 17, no. 1 (1997): 7-10.
15 John L. Crompton, "Economic Impact Studies: Instruments for Political Shenanigans?" *Journal of Travel Research* 45, no. 1 (2006): 67-82.
16 Thomas Michael Power, "Inflating the Benefits: The Misuse of Economics to Promote Unfettered Motorized Recreation," in *Thrillcraft: The Environmental Consequences of Motorized Recreation*, ed. George Wuerthner (Sausalito, CA, 2007), 83-90.
17 Peaceful Roads & Rails Vermont, "Economic Impact of Snowmobiling," http://www.prtvt.org/economic-impact-of-snow.mobiling.html.
18 Merchant, *Radical Ecology,* 70
19 Andrew Dobson, *Green Political Thought*, 4th ed. (London, 2007).
20 After the completion of this study, NSPACTS incorporated under the name Greenways Nova Scotia.

21 Save Our Trails, "About Us," www.saveourtrails.ca/about_us.htm, emphasis added. The site is no longer active.

22 Save Our Trails, "Welcome," www.saveourtrails.ca/welcome.htm.

23 Nova Scotians Promoting Active Transportation on Community Trails (NSPACTS), "NSPACTS Vision," http://nspact.ca/vision.html; the vision was a work in progress as this research was conducted; an early version specified trails "devoted to human-powered forms of travel."

24 NSPACTS, "Creating Greenway Nova Scotia: A NSPACTS Initiative," position paper, November 2009, 6, emphasis added.

25 NSPACTS, "NSPACTS Vision," emphasis original.

26 NSPACTS, "Creating Greenway Nova Scotia," 17.

27 EPA, "Frequently Asked Questions," 2.

28 I.E. Schneider and T. Schoenecker, "All-Terrain Vehicles in Minnesota: Economic Impact and Consumer Profile" (St Paul, 2006).

29 EPA, "Frequently Asked Questions," 2.

30 Author's interview with active-transportation advocate, 15 September 2007.

31 Author's transcript of Cornwallis River Pathways Society public meeting, 13 December 2007.

32 www.saveourtrails.ca.

33 Peaceful Roads & Rails Vermont, "Keep ATVs Off Vermont's Roads," http://www.prtvt.org/atv-free-roads.html.

34 World Health Organization, "Occupational and Community Noise: Fact Sheet no. 258," 2001, 2.

35 Go for Green, "Active Transportation: The Business Case for Active Transportation," 2004, http://thirdwavecycling.com/pdfs/at_business_case.pdf.

36 Ron Colman, "The Costs of Chronic Disease in Nova Scotia," GPI Atlantic Online, http://www.gpiatlantic.org/releases/pr_chronicdisease.htm.

37 NSPACTS, "Creating Greenway Nova Scotia," 11.

38 Author's interview with active-transportation advocate, 15 September 2007.

39 Kieran Pathways Society, "The Kieran Pathways Society: The Next Step," brochure, 2006.

40 R.L. Brown, M.E. Koepplinger, C.T. Mehlman, M. Gittelman, and V.F. Garcia, "All-Terrain Vehicle and Bicycle Crashes in Children: Epidemiology and Comparison of Injury Severity," *Journal of Pediatric Surgery* 37, vol. 3 (2002): 375–80.

41 M. Peden, R. Scurfield, D. Sleet, D. Mohan, A. Hydner, E. Jarawan, and C. Mathers, eds., *The World Report on Road Traffic Injury Prevention* (Geneva, 2004).

42 M.A. Finn and J.D. MacDonald, "A Population-Based Study of All-Terrain Vehicle-Related Head and Spine Injuries," *Neurosurgery* 67 (2010): 993–7.

43 Jim Helmkamp and Bruce A. Lawrence, "The Economic Burden of All-Terrain Vehicle–Related Pediatric Deaths in the United States," *Pediatrics* 119 (2007): 223–5.

44 George Wuerthner, ed., *Thrillcraft: The Environmental Consequences of Motorized Recreation* (Sausalito, CA, 2007).

45 Pitter, "Finding the Kieran Way."

46 HFX No. 308491, Supreme Court of Nova Scotia, Between Paradise Active Healthy Living Society Applicant and the Attorney General of Nova Scotia representing Her Majesty the Queen in Right of the Province of Nova Scotia Respondent, item 141, 2009.

47 Melanie Patten, "ATVs Source of Tension, Anger, Even Violence, in Some Rural N.S. Communities," *Canadian Press*, 17 October 2009.

48 Author's interview with public servant, 5 March 2008.

49 International Snowmobile Manufacturers Association, "Snowmobiling Provides Physical and Mental Health Benefits: Winter Recreation Fights Seasonal Affective Disorder," press release, 1 December 2009, www.snowmobile.org/pr_10_2010_health.asp.

50 Nova Scotia Federation of Anglers and Hunters, "Atlantic Canadian Traditions," brochure, 2008.

51 Personal communication, May 2008.

52 "COHV: York University to Conduct First Ever National Study on the Health Benefits of Recreational Off-Road Vehicle Riding," www.marketwired.com/press-release/COHV-York-University-Conduct-First-Ever-National-Study-on-Health-Benefits-Recreational-752539.htm.

53 J.F. Burr, V.K. Jamnik, and N. Gledhill, "Fitness, Health, and Quality of Life of Canadian Off-Road Vehicle Riders," abstract in *Applied Physiology, Nutrition, and Metabolism* 34, suppl. 1 (2009): S12.

54 J.F. Burr, V.K. Jamnik, J.A. Shaw, and N. Gledhill, "The Physiological Demands of Off-Road Vehicle Riding," *Medicine & Science in Sport & Exercise*, published ahead of print ed. (2009).

55 For examples of this see Jeffrey Simpson, "ATV Demonstration Backfires on Riders," *Halifax Chronicle Herald*, 26 November 2009; Gordon Delaney, "Acadia Prof: ATVs Have Little or No Health Benefits," *Halifax Chronicle Herald*, 31 October 2008; and Mary Ellen MacIntyre, "'We're Not All a Bunch of Yahoos': ATV Riders Take Reporter Out to Experience the Fun of Nature," *Halifax Chronicle Herald*, 8 November 2009.

56 Delaney, "Acadia Prof."

57 This statement was made by a Berwick, Nova Scotia, resident and ATV owner during a public meeting, 13 December 2007.

58 *Make a Difference, Environmentally!* www.atvnw.ca.

59 International Snowmobile Manufacturers Association, "Snowmobiling Fact Book: Sound," http://www.snowmobile.org/facts_sound.asp.

60 Author's transcript of a Cornwallis River Pathways Society public meeting, 13 December 2007.

61 S. Patterson, "Trail Patrol Training Slides," 2007, All-Terrain Vehicle Association of Nova Scotia, http://www.atvans.org/component/option,com_docman/task,doc_details/gid,8/Itemid,30/.

62 Merchant, *Radical Ecology.*

63 Dobson, *Green Political Thought.*

64 Ibid., 2.

65 Dryzek, *Politics of the Earth: Environmental Discourses.*

66 Ibid., 6.

67 Ibid., 73–142.

68 Ibid., 75.

69 Glyn Bissix and Justin Medicraft, "Deconstructing a Myth: Identifying ATVing's Health, Environmental, Economic, and Social Impacts," unpublished paper, 2008.

70 Dryzek, *The Politics of the Earth*, 99.

71 Ibid., 232.

72 Ibid., 233.

10 Intertwining Histories, Enhancing Strengths: Sport and Recreation Services in the Northwest Territories, 1962–2000

VICTORIA PARASCHAK

Why do people write histories? I remember, a very long time ago, being assigned that question by Alan Metcalfe when I was his student. I read different accounts of historical methodology and came back with two answers: history can be written for its own sake, or it can be written as information that helps us to understand better our situation today. With the wisdom that comes from living life and carrying out research with individuals who are too often under-served[1] in the larger society, I eventually added a third possibility: histories can be written to inspire others, through historical insights and examples, to actively shape the world they live in today and create for tomorrow. That third possibility has become the type of historical account I prefer to write.

In February 1999 I was contracted by several sport and recreation groups in the Northwest Territories (NWT) to create a comprehensive strategic plan for sport and recreation following a common vision, principles, priorities, end objectives, and evaluation measures. As part of this process, which culminated in the Legacy and New Directions Conference in May 2000,[2] I began to write a history of sport and recreation in the NWT. I opted to begin this history at the year 1962, when the territorial government (located in Ottawa) first hired someone to survey recreation practices in communities across the NWT and Yukon. The history continues to 2000 and thus complements the strategic planning process. The decision was made to write this history in keeping with a particular theoretical approach that has been useful in my research – Anthony Giddens' duality-of-structure framework,[3] which explores how agents (individuals and/or groups) act within the broader conditions (rules and resources) that shape them, and are shaped by them over time. I also decided to bring a strengths perspective to this history,[4] identifying the strengths existent in the sport and recreation system over time, and the ways in which particular agents had drawn upon and/or created rules and resources in their environment that would further those strengths. This approach was adopted to fit with my intent to write a history for northerners that would inspire them to continue creating the system for sport and recreation that best met particular needs.

In the end, the history became secondary to a more pressing need to work with seven sport and recreation groups that varied greatly in their histories, mandates, resources, and activities, if we hoped to develop a common framework and a new approach in a year's time. Members of these groups identified the strengths and challenges of the existing system from their viewpoint, which I recorded while seeking to do the same myself using historical records and interviews with various participants. I continued work on an expanded history over the next decade, identifying the underlying assumptions that tied this history to southern Canadian approaches to sport and recreation, those constructions that challenged an "assimilationist" label, and the ways in which this history fit within the current national strategy for sport – the 2002 Canadian Sport Policy and its four goals of enhanced participation, excellence, capacity, and interaction. The resulting historical account, this chapter, highlights the relative ability of different groups in sport and recreation to shape the contexts surrounding them, in light of the available rules (both written and assumed) and resources (human, financial, and material) that were also created and reproduced by select individuals and groups on an ongoing basis. The outcome – formation of a partnership approach to sport and recreation services – makes more sense once this history has been outlined, because no one organization has been successful in dominating the rules and resources that guide sport and recreation in the NWT. Seven organizations were involved in this partnership: the Sport and Recreation Section of the Government of the Northwest Territories (GNWT),[5] the Sport North Federation, the Recreation Leaders Program, the NWT Recreation and Parks Association, two regional associations (the Mackenzie Recreation Association and the Beaufort Delta Sahtu Recreation Association), and the Aboriginal Sport Circle of the Western Arctic. Outlined first is a brief background on each of the partners within their historical context. For ease of understanding, the following table identifies each organization, its acronym, and the year it began.

Organization	Acronym	Year it began
GNWT Recreation Division; Sport and Recreation Division/Section (government unit)	GNWT Sport and Recreation	1967
Sport North Federation (sport federation)	Sport North	1976
Recreation Leaders Program (college program)	RLP	1986
NWT Recreation and Parks Association (professional organization)	NWTRPA	1988
Aboriginal Sport Circle of the Western Arctic (aboriginal sport organization)	ASCWA	1999
Beaufort Delta Sahtu Recreation Association (regional association)	BDSRA	2001

The Partner Organizations

The (Sport and) Recreation Division: Recreation as a Municipal Responsibility

From their inception in 1962, government recreation services were linked to community development generally. Federal fitness and amateur sport dollars were matched by the NWT government to provide per capita grants and to fund other recreational needs identified by the communities.[6] When the GNWT moved north to Yellowknife in 1967, the Recreation Division was created as part of the Department of Local Government,[7] thus further formalizing recreation's link to broader community development. The government provided financial resources to the division, and bureaucrats were then able to offer programs and funding according to prescribed guidelines, to facilitate recreation development in their desired direction. Much of the funding went to communities for facilities development, leadership training (in sports and in playgroups), aquatics (in waterfronts and above-ground pools), and recreation programming (in sports but also in arts, crafts, fitness, and music).[8]

The Recreation Division remained the dominant organization shaping recreation services in the north. For example, initial facilities grants were relatively small and required matched contributions from the community. This approach shifted, however, in 1983 when the division began a massive facilities construction phase to ensure that basic recreation facilities existed in every community in the NWT (for populations of one hundred or eighteen thousand) within five years, without cost to the community. This was a time of government plenty, when resources were available for construction in the north, with funding as high as $25 million per year for facility construction and the hiring of additional staff needed to oversee this fast-tracking period in recreation development.

Funding and staff were accessed at this time to also enhance leadership development. The Sport and Recreation Division designed a two-year college degree program, which began in 1986, to train local community members as recreation professionals in order to optimize the facilities being developed and the programs that could be offered within these facilities. The division complemented these developments with ongoing efforts to foster a system of community recreation committees accountable to the municipal council – an approach taken by the Department of Local Government generally at that time – and the division refused to fund other groups in the community who might express an interest in recreation. Thus, through its control of financial resources, its concerted development of material resources in the shape of recreation facilities, and its defining of "legitimate" recreation as activities vetted through municipal councils, the division created and reinforced a specific context for the development of recreation.

Access to ongoing government resources continued to provide the Sport and Recreation Division with a dominant place in recreation development. However, government downsizing in the mid-1990s had a serious impact on the relative importance of the then Sport and Recreation Section of the NWT government. Financial resources were greatly curtailed, and available human resources decreased as well, with only two full-time staff members left in government.[9] With the completion of basic facilities in all communities, and the 1990s' decrease in capital projects within the government generally, the section's ability to provide material resources for recreation diminished. A policy shift to devolution by the GNWT meant that the section began to provide block grants in 1995, which went directly to the community for its discretionary use without guidelines. Thus, the Sport and Recreation Section's ability to define the rules that shaped the context for recreation in the north was seriously diminished, along with its ability to provide material, human, or financial resources. These bureaucrats continued to have an important role in the recreation system, but they had to turn to other organizations to provide the services previously offered by government employees, organizations such as the Sport North Federation.

Sport North: A Federation of Sport Associations

A second player in the development of recreation in the NWT has been the Sport North Federation. The government, through the Recreation Division, provided occasional funding to community sport associations beginning in the 1960s.[10] Involvement of NWT athletes in the Canada Games, starting in 1967, as well as in the Arctic Winter Games (AWG), beginning in 1970, increased the profile of sport and of multi-sport games generally in the north. In 1972 the government created a program to fund sport associations because it recognized that these associations aided NWT success in multi-sport games. Unlike the "municipal service, community-based" approach fostered by the Recreation Division, the emergence of sport associations mirrored similar developments in other parts of Canada: local volunteer sport groups affiliated with territorial associations that affiliated with national sport bodies. In 1976 the Sport North Federation became the last sport federation formed in Canada (until Sport Nunavut was created in 1999). The federation saw itself as an organization committed to supporting and funding its member territorial sport associations. Sport North thus maintained accountability to its member organizations, and the volunteers that served within them, rather than to the communities in the NWT. Multi-sport games grew in number and prominence, leading to additional funding for

Sport North from the territorial government, and increased staff. The stability of its funding base increased in 1979 when Sport North signed an agreement with the territorial government to manage the Western Canada Lottery in the NWT and to receive its profits for sporting programs. The federation thus had a base of funding unlike that of other sport and recreation associations in the north, as well as enhanced human (staff) and material (office space) resources that set it apart from all other organizations except for the government's Sport and Recreation Division or Section.

Sport North remained the second most powerful organization (in terms of human and financial resources) for sport and recreation in the NWT but was never able to solidify its legitimacy in the eyes of smaller, largely aboriginal communities. Since its formation the federation has received consistent government funding, but the government has largely defined the guidelines by which that funding can be used. With the creation of the Lottery Agreement, funding increased and became stabler for Sport North, but the signing of this formal agreement with the GNWT (as often as every year, and by 2000 every four years) further laid out for the federation the ways in which the lottery profits could be used. In the 1999 lottery agreement the government stopped funding Sport North apart from the lottery profits and also directed Sport North to broaden its services to include recreation and to provide funding to two other organizations, the NWT Recreation and Parks Association and the Aboriginal Sport Circle of the Western Arctic. While Sport North thus theoretically could have taken a more proactive approach towards defining its programs, the federation in practice largely took its direction from the agreement and thus left much of their leadership potential, by default, in the hands of the government.

The legitimacy of Sport North in the NWT was undercut by its lack of an effective connection to the community level in sport development. Its structure as a federation of sport associations, while logical from a national perspective, inhibited Sport North from proactively developing links to the community in other than an ad hoc, sport-specific manner. Thus, the federation was at times portrayed in the political arena and elsewhere as insensitive to the needs of the smaller, largely aboriginal communities.[11] As those communities grew in importance politically, the concerns took on a legitimacy that undermined – primarily along racial (that is, aboriginal–non-aboriginal) lines – the claim by Sport North that its services were accessible to all individuals across the north.

Recreation Leaders Program: Home-Grown Recreation Professionals

The formation of the Recreation Leaders Program (RLP), a two-year diploma offered in the NWT by Aurora College beginning in 1986,[12] marked the creation of a third group of agents in the sport and recreation system. Prior to this time there had been few recreation professionals in the NWT, all of whom had been trained in southern colleges and universities, and they were almost exclusively from southern Canada. As part of the government's attempt, in the 1980s, to strengthen the municipal system for recreation, the Sport and Recreation Division devised a program that would train local members of NWT communities to be recreation professionals. By the year 2000 there were seventy-four graduates from almost all the communities across the north. The program had secured ongoing funding and been staffed with instructors on a consistent basis, unlike many other programs within the college. The government created an interim-recreation-directors program at the same time, to fund communities that wished to hire a southern-trained recreation professional while they had a local person enrolled in the college program. A number of these interim recreation directors stayed in the north and took employment in other recreation positions, most often with the government or Sport North. The government also contributed towards the salary of trained recreation professionals once they had finished their college program, thereby facilitating through their guidelines and funding the hiring of local recreation professionals in many communities across the north. Thus, the government's decision to fund the creation of this program as well as the interim recreation directors and graduates from the program, greatly increased the numbers of local recreation professionals in NWT communities, further shaping the context of sport and recreation in the north.

NWTRPA, MRA, and BDSRA: Professional Recreation Associations

As the numbers of recreation professionals increased, so did the relevance of professionals. The NWT Recreation and Parks Association (NWTRPA), for example, modelled after the national Canadian Parks and Recreation Association, was formed in 1988 largely through the efforts of recreation professionals who had been trained in southern Canada. At the same time, regional meetings (five regions prior to Division in 1999, two regions post-Division) for community recreation staff were being held on a regular basis, helped out by government funding and regional government sport and recreation staff (that is, recreation development officers).

One of these regional organizations, the Mackenzie Recreation Association (MRA), held its first regional meeting in 1992 and became an active voice on recreation concerns for the nineteen communities it represented.[13] Its call for changes to the sport and recreation system became increasingly organized and legitimized. This legitimacy stemmed from members' primary link back to the communities, and the strong presence of aboriginal northerners, a voice sought by politicians at that time. The MRA thus was seen by politicians as providing the community connection – and community voice – that was being facilitated by the Sport and Recreation Section but was perceived to be lacking in Sport North. An emerging organization, the Beaufort Delta Sahtu Recreation Association (BDSRA), formed the regional recreation association for the thirteen northern communities in the NWT. Its administrative formation was slower; it was not officially incorporated until after 2000.

The strength of these regional recreation organizations lay in an ability to provide direct services to the communities in their region – opportunities such as leadership training, community and inter-community opportunities and competitions, and facility building and maintenance assistance. However, with the shift to block funding of recreation dollars to communities in 1995,[14] there was often a decrease in funding provided by those community councils for local recreation. Regional associations recognized that they had a very important task: to convince councils of the importance of recreation and to garner their commitment to providing the resources (financial, material, and human) to carry out this essential service. The calls by these regional recreation organizations to improve sport and recreation services were joined by those of one final organization, the Aboriginal Sport Circle of the Western Arctic.

The Aboriginal Sport Circle of the Western Arctic: The Segregation of Sport

The Aboriginal Sport Circle of the Western Arctic (ASCWA) became the newest member in the sport and recreation system, incorporating in 1999. Its origin stemmed from the first North American Indigenous Games (NAIG), held in Edmonton in 1990. A group of athletes from the NWT had attended with minimal financial support from the government. As NWT delegates to these games grew over the decade, so did the demands for government assistance through financial and human resources. The issue of funding for the games was raised in the legislative assembly.[15] The ad hoc approach taken towards these games was subsequently formalized through government policy after the 1997 games. In keeping with the direction promoted nationally through the Aboriginal Sport Circle, a separate organization was created in the NWT to cater solely to the sporting needs of aboriginal participants in the north. This organization potentially addressed the longstanding critique of Sport North that services officially available to all residents of the NWT had, in fact, failed to adequately provide for aboriginal northerners from smaller communities. Members of the Aboriginal Sport Circle were also, however, struggling to find their place among the myriad of organizations that already existed to serve the sport and recreation needs of a NWT population of about forty-two thousand people (52 per cent of whom were aboriginal), and a context that had always promoted integration, not segregation, among aboriginal and non-aboriginal NWT residents.[16]

These snapshots depict the collection of sport and recreation organizations that agreed in May 2000 to a joint framework to increase their effectiveness as a totality. Their histories, written from this particular perspective, highlight the agency of these groups: their relative ability to shape their sport and recreation services within boundaries (rules and resources) created by others as well as by themselves. This partnership, however, had been developing for a number of years.

The Partnership

Context for Strategic Partnership Efforts (pre-1999)

Partnerships emerged as a fundamental strategy for creating effective, efficient sport- and recreation-delivery systems in the early 1990s in Canada.[17] Policy documents, such as the GNWT's "Partners in Action: Sport and Recreation Directions for the Nineties" in 1992,[18] and the federal "Sport in Canada: Leadership, Partnership, and Accountability – Everybody's Business" in 1999,[19] helped to naturalize partnerships as the way to do sport and recreation.

Partnerships, however, were not a new concept in the NWT sport and recreation system. There had been an ongoing presence of inter-organizational partnerships in the NWT as an integral way of doing business, especially for the territorial government. For example, GNWT-community partnerships had operated since a territorial recreation director had been hired to support community recreation in 1962. The GNWT–Sport North Federation partnership began in 1976, and a formalized relationship was instituted in 1979, through a series of multi-year lottery agreements enabling Sport North to oversee lottery revenues on behalf of the GNWT. In 1985, GNWT Departments of Recreation and Education jointly created a two-year college training program for recreation leaders. The graduates helped to form the NWTRPA in 1988, another GNWT partnership.

Individuals from these various organizations also had ongoing involvement in the creation of longer-term directions for the sport and recreation system, beginning in 1983 with the "Directions for the '80s" conference. The 1991 "Directions for the '90s" conference produced a proceedings report, titled *Partners in Action*. This first overt reference in policy to the theme of partnerships included an introductory comment by the minister that "a strong network of partnerships is required for the NWT Sport and Recreation System to be successful, particularly during these difficult economic times."[20] Despite the rhetoric, the GNWT to this point had been the sole organizer of the Directions conferences, and the government – not the other organizations – was responsible for addressing the recommendations. By 1991, therefore, there was a history within the NWT sport and recreation system of partnership activities, but these actions tended to occur between governments (for example, federal-territorial, inter-departmental, territorial-local), and between the territorial government and select organizations related to specific projects or areas of joint interest. Partnerships were most often initiated and financially resourced by the government, with volunteer organizations providing human resources as their contribution. A series of events in the mid- and late-1990s, however, helped to push these organizations further towards a more comprehensive and formalized partnership structure.

In terms of political interventions, the division of the NWT and the eventual creation of Nunavut prompted two "Vision for Division" recreation and sport conferences in late 1995 and April 1996 so that delegates from the two eventual territories could reflect separately on their preferred sport and recreation structure. Most of the energy was then focused on preparing the Nunavut structures prior to 1 April 1999; recommendations for the NWT, such as "Creat[ing] opportunities for new partnerships within communities,"[21] were put aside. After the division occurred in 1999, the NWT was left to reassess its new requirements in all areas of life, including sport and recreation.

During this period in NWT history, numerous land claims agreements were also being negotiated. The agreements continued to change the political landscape, as aboriginal organizations were able to restructure political boundaries. This required a rethinking of all services offered by the GNWT, including sport and recreation. For example, band councils and friendship centres, along with community councils, became eligible to receive sport and recreation funding. In addition, the GNWT was going through an organizational restructuring, downsizing its departments including sport and recreation. Departments were told to get out of providing services and instead to have that work done by other organizations. Partnerships became a clear way to do this, especially as government staff numbers in the Sport and Recreation Division or Section had decreased significantly (from about fifteen staff members in 1990 to two in 1997).

Competing organizational versus partnership needs was a second factor affecting partnerships. Major reviews of Sport North[22] and of games involvement broadly[23] were carried out, beginning in 1995, following complaints in the legislative assembly that these programs were not benefiting aboriginal northerners. The Aboriginal Sport Circle emerged as a possible new organization to service specifically aboriginal athletes in the NWT, a departure from the previous integrationist approach taken towards recreation services. Sport North had a history of being criticized for minimal involvement with small aboriginal communities and aboriginal athletes. The newly forming Sport Circle argued that it could take over Sport North funds and do the job properly. This pitted two very different sport organizations – one established and well resourced, the other new, inexperienced, and politically relevant – against each other within the same sport system.

Unequal power relations further shaped the approach taken towards partnerships. The GNWT remained the organization with the largest resource base and greatest legitimacy for leading the sport and recreation system. However, its diminished staff numbers and the imposed shift to unconditional grants for communities in 1995 meant that its relative power was diminished. Sport North was well resourced, even though government funding was removed in 1999, because it had sole access, through the lottery agreement, to the lottery profits. In contrast to the federation, the NWTRPA was floundering, and the emerging regional recreation committees were given no power within the Sport North structure. Associations had negative impressions of each other, and the recreation organizations were clearly underdeveloped and underfunded when compared to the well-established Sport North Federation.

Finally, the distribution or redistribution of resources had an impact on eventual partnership considerations. An economic downturn in the NWT in the 1990s led to a reduction in GNWT staff numbers, budgets, and the ability to have government staff provide direct delivery. The government's approach shifted towards having other organizations provide services, with the government facilitating their efforts.[24] Bi-annual departmental meetings became unnecessary with fewer staff; instead, territorial staff invited three partner organizations to their meetings – Sport North, the NWTRPA, and the RLP. Each organization shared information on its particular activities, and joint projects were created, such as the Recreation and Sport Directory, the Partners' Newsletter, and a joint recruitment approach for the RLP.

The lottery agreement of 1999 became a key development prompting the comprehensive strategic plan process. When Nunavut was created, which greatly reduced the size of the NWT, the staff size of Sport North was not cut back. However, the GNWT expected the federation to meet the majority of its costs with profits from the lottery. The eventual agreement was created around six points that aligned with national themes for sport in Canada: (1) a participant-centred system; (2) leadership; (3) a safe, accessible, equitable, and ethical environment; (4) self-reliance and accountability; (5) sport and recreation development; and (6) benefits of sport, recreation, and physical activity.[25]

In addition, for the first time the GNWT included schedules directing the federation to provide funding from their lottery profits to two other organizations, the NWTRPA and ASCWA. Sport North, looking at the nationally linked points, saw itself as responsible for meeting recreation as well as sport requirements and thus looked to these organizations for help in fulfilling those mandates; if they would not help, Sport North threatened to direct the money elsewhere. The ASCWA and the NWTRPA had no interest in taking direction from a different organization, thus setting up a situation of competing values over access to the lottery funds. Within this context came the impetus for the creation of a comprehensive strategic partnership plan.

Strategic Planning Process (March 1999–May 2000)

GNWT staff initially intended to complete a forty-year history of the sport and recreation system, followed by a Directions conference for the new millenium that would help to clarify the NWT's direction now that Nunavut had been created. Sport North staff, however, expressed their unwillingness to participate in a Directions conference unless a process of consultation preceded the meeting. Since the federation was the largest organization in the system, their request was granted, and the six principles embedded in Sport North's lottery agreement became the starting point for developing principles to underlie a partnership strategic plan.[26] Seven primary organizations became central to this process: the partners already attending the partnership meetings, two regional recreation associations, and the newly formed ASCWA. Other GNWT departments were also invited and participated in the process as resource partners, specifically staff members from the Departments of Health Promotion and Culture who might have resources of value to these organizations.

Trust and the sharing of information were clearly two challenges to be overcome if the organizations were to work together. At the first meeting of representatives from these organizations, in June 1999, delegates were asked to publicly express to the group the specific reason for their interest in being involved in sport and recreation, and these reasons formed the basis of the first draft of the vision statement for the sport and recreation system. They were next asked to identify the elements needed to create a successful framework for working as partners, and these points became the first draft of a partners' code of conduct. Finally, the group documented the items on which they could agree. The items were few but important: the group would use consensus decision making, build on existing strengths, and act only after information had been collected. They agreed on a goal: "To create an agreed-upon vision for the NWT recreation and sport system (including principles and priorities) and to use this vision as a basis for action, for the partner organizations, in keeping with their individual mandates, using simple, relevant evaluation measures."[27] At this point, there were still competing values and a history of poor relations between organizations, but their choice to continue forward with the process was a positive sign.

Individual meetings were then held with each organization separately. They identified the vision that the organization would like to see for sport and recreation, the current strengths and challenges of the system, the appropriate principles and priorities, and the organizational activities focused on these priorities. In November 1999 the second partners' meeting was held. Feedback from all organizations was reviewed, principles redrafted, and end objectives generated for each priority. The resulting draft framework – vision, principles, priorities, and end objectives – was put into a template, and all partners generated three-year plans within this format prior to the Directions conference of May 2000. These plans were shared with new delegates, who were invited to attend the Directions conference and fine-tune the draft partnership framework. Recommended actions were then generated for each priority, with regard to the strengths to build on and the challenges to be addressed. Several GNWT politicians attended, connecting this process to their own "Towards a Better Tomorrow" framework[28] and its complementary vision, priorities, goals, and actions.

Conference participants expressed some concern over the make-up of the delegates, noting the lack of teachers, sport volunteers, and non-physical-recreation organizations (such as Girl Guides and Boy Scouts) in attendance. Despite these concerns, the efforts of the past several months – including the two meetings of all the partners, and the joint generation of a draft framework that was then used by every organization to create a three-year plan – helped to legitimize the partnership approach that was being finalized through the conference. While individual organization delegates did not reach consensus on all the details of the framework, they did agree to work together to offer sport and recreation services in the NWT. This became the first Directions conference in which the process was generated by, and recommendations were linked back to, all seven partners, not just the GNWT. While the GNWT had spearheaded the process, it was a joint effort among the partners. Each organization went back to sort out its direction with its members after the conference and worked interdependently with the partners at follow-up bi-annual meetings.

The reticence of Sport North to fully engage in the partnership process is understandable; while the other partners grew in human and financial resources through the process, Sport North paid the price. Its gain was an increased legitimacy in the eyes of the public, as it could finally be seen by its critics as addressing aboriginal needs through partnership activities. Aboriginal political organizations were increasing in their relative power in the NWT; from their perspective, no organization would be considered effective unless it adequately addressed the needs of aboriginal citizens in the NWT.

The unequal power relations among the various organizations at the start of this process, in terms of financial, human, and material resources, were restructured. Four of the least powerful organizations were substantially strengthened through additional human and financial resources. However, their gains were largely drawn from Sport North's resources, rather than received through the infusion of new dollars to the sport and recreation system. Not surprisingly, internal struggles occurred most in Sport North, as its members questioned the benefits of the partnership for their organization.

However, benefits were generated as well. The combined legitimacy of the sport and recreation system was strengthened, as seen by the subsequent designation of lottery dollars solely for sport and recreation organizations.[29] In addition, GNWT staff continued to facilitate this process and retain legitimacy as the lead organization in NWT sport and recreation, with increases in the numbers of staff members in the regions to help in these efforts. The process of partnerships remained the legacy more so than did the actual strategic framework. Trust remained tenuous among the partners, but their shared actions continued to naturalize partnerships as the way to do business, even though that business was conducted in an environment of political intervention, competing individual and partnership needs, shifting unequal power relations, and constantly reshaping human and financial resources.

"Stubborn Chunks": Persistence in Form and Values

Cultural Products, Assimilation, and Power Relations

The ongoing creation, reproduction, and reshaping of cultural products such as sport and recreation in a context of unequal power relations occurs within all societies. However, the labels commonly used to describe these processes and their resultant products differ, in keeping with unequal power relations *between* different cultural groups. Disadvantaged groups within mainstream cultures are often labelled as having "assimilated" into mainstream culture when, for a variety of reasons, they take on the practices of the mainstream. Meanwhile, mainstream groups that are adopting the practices of a disadvantaged group (which happens far less frequently) remain unexamined and/or unlabelled in that process or are viewed as being "flexible" in order to welcome "disadvantaged" groups into the mainstream system. Yet each group, in the end, shapes or reshapes rules, and provides and/or accesses resources in order to produce or reproduce the social practices that they believe best address the needs of their constituents. A term such as *assimilation*, or the "melting pot" description accorded immigrant groups particularly in the United States, distorts our understanding of cultural production processes in a way that privileges mainstream practices; it simplifies them into a dichotomous process in which marginalized groups either stick to their "traditions" or assimilate into the mainstream. Homi Bhabha provides a different way of imagining this situation. He notes that the "notion of the melting pot has been replaced by a model … of the *menudo chowder*. According to this model most of the ingredients do melt, but some stubborn chunks are condemned merely to float."[30] I have been searching for a more effective way to explore and explain the "chunks" of cultural life that complicate notions of assimilation. In the end, I connected Bhabha's stubborn-chunks model to the past forty years of sport and recreation development in the NWT, to explore its usefulness in explaining historical chunks or practices that refuse to meld into mainstream (that is, southern Canadian) understandings of sport and recreation development.

The ongoing professionalization and institutionalization of NWT recreation and sport services enabled sport and recreation in the NWT to operate in a manner similar to that of other provinces across Canada. As a result, programs were often adopted from other jurisdictions, such as the National Coaching Certification Program or the Active Living Strategy, and federal or national resources were accessed. Locally, recreation directors were trained through a two-year college program in Inuvik and remained members of regional and territorial recreation organizations during that time. The Sport North Federation included territorial sport organizations made up of volunteers who delivered sport services across the NWT and connected to their national counterparts not only for competitions but also for contemporary guiding principles such as gender equity, accountability, and transparency. Territorial teams for sporting competitions such as the Arctic Winter Games (AWG), the Canada Games, and the North American Indigenous Games (NAIG) were selected on merit. These developments within the sport and recreation history easily supported the notion that people in the north had "assimilated" into southern Canadian cultural practices, adopting the rules and accessing, where possible, the resources attached to such processes. By doing so, they provided legitimacy to professionals in the north who were looking to maximize the provision of meaningful recreation to all citizens of the NWT.

However, I decided to look for activities that sat uncomfortably – distinctively apart from southern Canadian cultural practices – issues that pushed for the "indigenizing"[31] or "northernizing" of NWT sport and recreation. These chunks – Raymond Williams might call them residual or oppositional practices[32] – continued to be present despite an available, easily accessible set of rules and resources that aligned with the mainstream Canadian system, and such practices eventually were able to change the allocation of resources and/ or the creation of rules. The changes occurred because individuals in a position of power legitimated this alternative perspective and sought creative ways to address the problem. Politicians, sport and recreation personnel, and territorial delegates at Directions conferences were all key actors in the process. Three stubborn chunks, or northern forms and values that continued to make activities distinct from the mainstream ways of "doing" sport and recreation in southern Canada, included (1) the prioritization of inclusion over achievement in the selection of sport participants; (2) the legitimation of traditional Inuit and Dene games and their underlying values as an integral part of the sport system; and (3) the provision of integrated rather than segregated aboriginal and non-aboriginal sport and recreation services.

"Stubborn Chunks"

The "prolympic"[33] values that underlie the Canadian sport system ensure a focus on achievement as the primary criterion for sport participation – what Susan Birrell has called a meritocracy based on skill.[34] In keeping with this approach, the "best" athletes, determined through regional and/or territorial competitions, earn the right to represent the NWT at multi-sport festivals such as the AWG or the Canada Games, and to access accompanying resources such as funding, travel, and status. The NWT sport system largely reinforced this assumption, but complaints about the system continued to point out that the benefits accruing from sport should be shared among people across the north rather than solely the best athletes, who tended to come from the large centres, especially Yellowknife. This was occasionally put in racial terms: "there are not enough aboriginal participants going to major games." However, most often it was framed in terms of needing more athletic participants from the smaller communities. These communities were predominantly aboriginal; thus, increasing the involvement of smaller communities would increase aboriginal involvement at the same time.

The legislative assembly remained the most public venue for these complaints. An Inuit politician from the Central Arctic, for example, challenged the inclusiveness of the first AWG in 1970. He read a telegram to the largely non-aboriginal assembly, stating that if Central Arctic athletes were not acceptable for the games, then the name of the games should be changed to the Western Arctic Winter Games.[35] No changes followed from his comments, but a new festival, the Northern Games, had its debut that year with active involvement from aboriginal communities across the NWT, including the Central Arctic. This event, governed by aboriginal organizers, focused on the traditional activities of the Inuit peoples as well as on a few Dene games. It provided an alternative vision for legitimate activities in the sport and recreation system and fuelled a movement to document and celebrate the traditional games of the NWT's aboriginal peoples. It also demonstrated that aboriginal people could be involved in large numbers in sport festivals – through the inclusion of traditional activities and through the preferred, more flexible organizational approach to the festival[36] – an achievement that had remained elusive in sport competitions across the north. It also developed a cadre of aboriginal athletes skilled at the traditional games. These individuals attended festivals in southern Canada, such as the 1975 Canada Games, the 1976 Olympics, and the 1978 Commonwealth Games. The attempts by organizers to get traditional arctic sports into the AWG as an event came to fruition in 1974, and it immediately became a spectator favourite. However, overtures to have traditional arctic sports in the Canada Games were consistently rejected.[37]

The Northern Games, and later the Dene Games, while focusing on traditional activities, always remained open to all participants regardless of their heritage. This remained the operational approach taken by sport and recreation professionals in the north. For example, a federal program operated for aboriginal sport and recreation from 1972 to 1981.[38] Funds were awarded to aboriginal political organizations in the provinces, but to the government for those in the NWT. This unique funding approach for the NWT was allowed because the government successfully argued that the integrated territorial sport system in place addressed *all* citizens; thus, to fund the system was to fund aboriginal sport.

Despite claims of an integrated system, patterns developed around those who actually accessed specific services. For example, at Northern and Dene Games festivals the participants were almost always aboriginal, and small communities were well represented. Meanwhile, non-aboriginal northerners from the larger communities in the NWT were over-represented on NWT contingents to the AWG. Evaluation reports in 1976 and 1982 documented that a maximum of 33 per cent of any NWT team to the AWG was aboriginal, even though there was a majority of aboriginal citizens in the north. As well, participants from larger communities dominated the team. In any year only seven to twenty of the sixty NWT communities were represented at these Games.[39]

In 1979 a majority of aboriginal politicians made up the legislative assembly for the first time, and control by aboriginal ministers over the bureaucracy increased. The aboriginal politicians fostered a new approach to government services, emphasizing that aboriginal people, and smaller communities, had a right to the benefits previously accruing primarily to Euro-Canadians in the larger communities of the north. A 1983 statement in the legislative assembly exemplified this intent. Sport executives were criticized over the racial composition of the Canada Games contingent. They were directed to send athletes from all ethnic backgrounds and all parts of the north rather than to send an exclusive Yellowknife contingent composed of only white people.[40] This comment, similar in intent to the 1970 comment, led to action this time. Both rules and resources were altered to benefit smaller communities. For the first time, regional competition costs were covered, not just the costs at the territorial level. An extra region was created so that small communities around Yellowknife could compete against each other before having to face the better-resourced Yellowknife teams at the territorial trials. A Directions conference was held that year,[41] drawing together about fifty people from across the north to generate recommendations for improving the recreation system. Small-community and aboriginal delegates voiced their desire for inter-community competitions with travel funds, and for sport skills clinics. New programs were created to address these needs, and funding increased to smaller communities as a result.

Delegates also echoed concerns raised by the politicians, noting that "selection of athletes and events for competitions presently reflect little input from or consideration for small communities. Thus communities are left reacting to directions rather than setting them."[42] In other words, they wanted to have more involvement in making the rules that governed sport and recreation. They did not accept as "natural" that the system present in southern Canada – sport services offered by territorial sport organizations – adequately addressed their community needs. They asked, instead, if there was some way that communities could have greater access to territorial sport organizations and Sport North.[43] In response to this concern, two new programs were started in 1986 – the Sports Skills Program and the Inter-community Competition Program. These were specifically developed by the GNWT to ensure that smaller communities had the opportunity to participate in sporting opportunities on an annual basis, with hopes that their skills would also improve so that they could qualify for eventual AWG teams and Canada Games teams.

By 1990, many of the recommendations of the 1983 Directions conference had been addressed, and a new Directions process, again involving delegates from across the NWT, outlined their concerns. A desire to use northern insights to address unique northern conditions was noted in a recommendation to "support the development of a circumpolar recreation network instead of only looking at southern models and ideas."[44] This theme carried through in requests that the standardized National Coaching Certification Program be modified, and an introduction to the first level be developed to address community needs.

A concern arose again, in 1993, about the funding provided to send aboriginal participants to the NAIG. A politician raised the issue in the legislative assembly because some of his constituents hoped to attend the 1995 Games but had been turned down for government financial assistance. The Cabinet directed its policy and planning directorate to complete a study of the GNWT's involvement in major multi-sport games. Work began in January 1995, and the final report was reviewed with the minister in February 1997. Earlier concerns on small-community involvement in the AWG had been addressed by this point. The report noted that the AWG were now seen as a broad-based event and that they involved participants from 85 per cent of NWT communities.[45]

Perceptions about the NAIG, however, were quite different. Owing to the restricted participation base of these games – only aboriginal participants were allowed to compete – they raised a different question in the minds of territorial residents. The report noted: "Understanding of the NAIG and its purposes is not widespread. Many [of those surveyed] felt that promoting broad-based integrated sport was more important [than] separate events."[46] Nevertheless, the government and Sport North were directed by the minister to work with interested aboriginal groups to create an organizing committee for these games. Following this recommendation was a telling comment: "A key factor is the establishment of complementary programming for aboriginal athletes without the establishment of a parallel sport system."[47] This commitment to an integrated rather than a segregated system for sport was reiterated in notes on the Traditional Games Program, which included both the Northern and the Dene Games. The notes pointed out that the Games are "open to all residents of the NWT."[48]

Questioning the legitimacy of the NWT sport and recreation system for select constituencies in the NWT was a common theme underlying all three of these "stubborn chunks." Margaret Horn uses the term *indigenizing* to label the reshaping of mainstream practices in a way that uniquely suits aboriginal needs.[49] However, each of the stubborn chunks was also threatened at times in this forty-year history, both within the sport and recreation system and by larger national expectations attached to developments such as the Canada Games, the National Coaching Certification Program, and the Aboriginal Sport Circle. Yet these forms and/or values persisted, undercutting the naturalization of mainstream sport and recreation practices prevalent in southern Canada, despite the resources available through them.

A history of the past forty years suggests that these issues will not go away. Each time a review has occurred, there have been requests for the system to be more responsive to the needs of smaller communities that wish to have a more integral role in the shaping of the sport system. This type of system does not exist elsewhere in Canada, because in no other jurisdiction – except for Nunavut – does the combination of small communities with adequate political representation, aboriginal citizens in great numbers, and living traditional cultural activities exist. Thanks to these conditions, select politicians and delegates from the smaller communities at future Directions conferences will no doubt continue to push for a northern or indigenized sport and recreation system that addresses the local needs, which, like the stubborn chunks in the menudo chowder, will not disappear.

Bhabha notes that in this analytic approach "the future becomes (once again) an *open question*, instead of being specified by the fixity of the past."[50] In documenting the history of these elements of northern life, I am suggesting that sport and recreation in the Northwest Territories has remained, in some important ways, distinct from practices in southern Canada, while they are similar in many other ways. Developments in sport and recreation in the NWT are significant to our understanding of sport in Canada because they demonstrate that the "assimilation" label frequently used for "disadvantaged" groups may be limiting our analysis of cultural practices. "Stubborn chunks" can provide us with insights into the cultural production of disadvantaged groups, but also point us towards the insights that those groups can bring to dominant practices that might otherwise remain unexamined. One example of this follows: an examination of the suitability of the current national sport policy in Canada from the NWT perspective.

The Canadian Sport Policy: A Good Framework for NWT Sport and Recreation?

Policies are socially constructed using dominant ideas. Michael Sam, in his analysis of a national government task-force process on sport, fitness, and leisure in New Zealand, notes that "ideas matter in public policy because they form the basis for framing political judgements and because their meanings are continually translated into future plans and actions."[51] In the Canadian Sport Policy, four goals are identified: enhanced participation, enhanced excellence, enhanced capacity, and enhanced interaction.[52] These broad areas thus become the socially constructed framework within which further rules are constructed and additional resources are assigned. For example, Sport Canada's Policy on Aboriginal Peoples' Participation in Sport, released in May 2005, outlines its commitment to and beliefs about Sport Canada's relationship with aboriginal peoples in terms of the four "dominant ideas" or goals of the Canadian Sport

Policy.[53] The 2002 Canadian Sport Policy has also legitimated increased federal dollars for sport, based on these four goals. Funding is being provided on a cost-shared basis with either national sport organizations or provinces and territories, through bilateral agreements.[54]

Fourteen different governments have committed to this policy; each one is a stakeholder that has helped to shape, and is currently being shaped by, the four goals of the Canadian Sport Policy. One of those stakeholders is the GNWT. Sam clarifies that ideas are "constructions that serve to support some interests and institutions over others."[55] Accordingly, it becomes relevant to ask if the Canadian Sport Policy is a "good" framework for sport and recreation in the NWT?

To assess this question, I looked at the concerns raised about sport and recreation historically through NWT Directions conferences. These policy-forming events, held in 1983, 1991, and 2000, brought together a broad range of individuals from across the north. Drawing from their experiences, the delegates identified strengths and challenges of NWT sport and recreation services and provided recommendations for improving the system.[56] A final policy-forming gathering occurred in July 2000, when twenty delegates from the NWT joined with others from the Yukon and Nunavut to provide a northern perspective on sport – one of six regional conferences held as part of the formation process of the Canadian Sport Policy.[57] I systematically examined the conference reports to see if, and how, the four goals – participation, excellence, capacity, and interaction – were being raised as concerns by delegates, who were all sport and recreation participants within the NWT.

Enhanced Participation

The Canadian Sport Policy seeks, through the first goal, enhanced participation, to generate participation in sport from a greater proportion of Canadians from all segments of society, providing them with high-quality sports activities at all levels, and in all forms of participation.[58] This has been a consistent concern of delegates at the three Directions conferences, who framed their ideas in relation to addressing inequities, reshaping sport practices to suit varying needs, increasing and reshaping the distribution of resources, and developing traditional games as an integral part of the sport system.

In 1983 the delegates voiced concern that the inequities be addressed, such as the differing costs faced by participants in more remote regions or communities. This point was also connected to the difference in competition ability between the large communities, such as Yellowknife, and the much smaller communities that had to face Yellowknife teams in regional trials. Those small-community participants were rarely able to advance to the territorial trials as a result. The delegates built on this concern, encouraging the GNWT to address differences created by population segments, regional interests, community size, and cultural diversity. They recommended the creation of more varied activities, including non-sport forms.[59]

The concern over diversity arose again in 1991, tied to specific suggestions such as developing outdoor facilities, developing multi-use and multi-seasonal facilities, and developing research on traditional games, a suggestion also made in 1983.[60] At the Directions conference in 2000 the language had shifted, but the concerns remained. The seven sport and recreation partner organizations agreed to a vision, along with seven priorities. One of these priorities aligned with the goal of enhanced participation. The first priority, a participant-centred system, had as its end objective "an awareness of (1) who does and who does not participate in sport and recreation, (2) the quality of their experience, and (3) their involvement in decision-making within the sport and recreation system.[61] A few months later, at the Sport Canada–sponsored conference, a more selective message was highlighted by the organizers. While a number of both national and regional recommendations were recorded in the report, six key messages were identified in the conclusion. Three of these were relevant to this goal of enhanced participation, that there be recognition in the Canadian Sport Policy for (1) northern Canada's unique geography, special needs, and rightful place at the national table; (2) aboriginal culture and the challenges faced by its people in contemporary Western society; and (3) support for all levels of sport from grassroots to elite.[62]

These key messages focused on the inequities that northerners face within the national sport system; aboriginal peoples' unique needs and challenges, such as racism and different cultural activities; and the need for support to grassroots as well as elite sport development, since there are very limited opportunities for northern athletes to reach the performance levels expected by the goal of "enhanced excellence."

Enhanced Excellence

The second goal of the Canadian Sport Policy focuses on enhanced excellence, in other words, on increasing consistent world-class results at the highest levels of international competition in sport by increasing the number of talented athletes within a sport system that maintains fair and ethical means.[63] However, few athletes from the NWT make it onto national teams; fewer still excel in international competitions. Perhaps understandably, then, very little was said about this goal in the three NWT Directions conferences. While many delegates were sport participants, few were elite athletes. Their concerns thus consistently focused on the grassroots end of athlete development.[64]

Delegates asked for increased financial and human resources to address this issue. In 1983 they recommended that more travel dollars be provided for inter-community competitions. They also wanted to hold coaching and officials clinics that would be sensitive to the needs of small communities.[65] This desire for increased skilled human resources was repeated in 1991, through a recommendation that the skill level and training of athletes and the certification of coaches and officials be increased.[66]

At the 1983 conference the request for more funding of inter-community competition acknowledged the importance of competition as an aspect of overall sport development. In 1991, "sport" became one of the six broad areas wherein recommendations were made. However, these suggestions focused on broadening opportunities for all ages and communities in a variety of sports, and on increasing training and skill levels of athletes, as well as on training and certification of coaches and officials.[67] The recommendations aligned with those made at the conference in 2000, in particular the fifth priority, sport and recreation development, with the end goal that there be "availability of meaningful sport and recreation opportunities from the grassroots to the elite level."[68] Delegates did identify as a strength the fact that multi-sport games at the inter-community and territorial levels, such as the AWG, promoted community pride and spirit,[69] which is a benefit that happens, Canada-wide, when elite athletes succeed. The delegates also identified as a challenge the point that "[multi-sport] Games need a formal process to work towards equitable representation and fair selection, and a fair funding allocation."[70] This concern aligned with the expectation of the Canadian Sport Policy that the promotion of excellence be done in a fair and ethical manner.

At the Northern Perspective on Sport Conference held later that year, in July 2000, one key message that was noted in the conclusion applied to the goal of enhanced excellence. It called for recognition within a Canadian sport policy for "the importance of the AWG and the NAIG."[71] This was an important reminder to the other government stakeholders that, for the NWT, excellence was achieved most often through these "regional" multi-sport international events, rather than through the world championships and international multi-sport games, such as the Olympics, which are commonly associated with the goal of enhanced excellence.

Enhanced Capacity

Enhanced capacity, the third goal of the Canadian Sport Policy, refers to an increase in human, financial, and material resources in a manner that is ethically based, especially in terms of inclusion and equity.[72] These ideas have been central to all three Directions conferences because they focus on the infrastructure needed to provide effective sport and recreation services. The recommendations focused on four key areas: material resources, financial resources, human resources, and underlying values.

In the 1983 conference, the need for facilities and equipment was identified.[73] A major facilities initiative followed, and by 1991 attention had narrowed to the need for outdoor facilities and multi-use or multi-seasonal facilities.[74] Requests for material resources disappeared at subsequent conferences, but the need for financial and human resources linked to facilities remained. At the 1983 conference, increased funding to pay for the operations and maintenance of facilities was mentioned, along with increased funding for sports competition travel, research on traditional games, and training.[75] These concerns were repeated in 1991, along with a request for more program funding.[76] In 2000, the fourth priority, self-reliance and accountability, had as its end objective "a sport and recreation delivery system that is sustainable and accountable to people in the NWT."[77] This represented a shift in emphasis, away from requesting that the government provide needed resources, to encouraging sport and recreation organizations to take responsibility for generating adequate resources and to be accountable for them.

Human resources have likewise remained a consistent concern in the Directions conferences. The need for trained volunteers, paid staff, facility maintainers, administrators, coaches, officials, and teachers was mentioned in 1983.[78] That request was reiterated in 1991, along with a request for support to the Recreation Leaders Program at Aurora College, which had been created in 1986 to train community recreation leaders. There was also recognition of the need to train individuals specifically for effective financial management, to foster certification for coaches and officials, and to establish a territorial-wide organization responsible for traditional arctic sports.[79] In 2000 this human resources focus aligned with the second priority, leadership, and its end goal of "an effective system for the development and support of leaders through attraction, training, recognition and retention."[80] A key message from the Northern Territorial Conference also addressed human resources; delegates stressed that the Canadian Sport Policy should ensure the "promotion, recognition and support of volunteerism."[81]

The search for increased resources was always couched, however, within a values-based context that aligned with the Canadian Sport Policy's emphasis on inclusion and equity. The stated goal of the 1983 Directions conference was to meet the needs of communities better, leading to recommendations such as leadership clinics being sensitive to the needs of small communities.[82]

Values-based comments stressing inclusion and equity increased in 1991: a holistic approach to sport was recommended; resources should be distributed fairly; communities should be involved in all aspects of facility development; and facility design standards should be reviewed in light of community needs.[83] An awareness of differing sport and recreation needs across the NWT was never far from the minds of the delegates. This became evident at the 2000 conference, not only through the first priority, a participant-centred system, but also through the third priority, a positive environment, which had as its end objective "a fun, safe, accessible, equitable, and ethical environment for sport and recreation in the NWT."[84] Concern about a values-based sport and recreation system in the NWT has thus been consistent for over twenty years.

Enhanced Interaction

The final goal of the Canadian Sport Policy, enhanced interaction, stresses increased collaboration, co-operation, and communication within and among the various stakeholders.[85] These three processes were all discussed to some degree in the Directions conferences. Communication was a big issue in 1983; delegates stressed that people needed to know more about the various programs available, the information needed to be easier to understand, at times the information had to be translated, and the benefits of recreation and sport needed to be promoted.[86] The need to gather and share more information was repeated in 1991.[87] In 2000, the sixth priority, promoting the benefits, had as its end objective the "recognition and understanding by all residents of the NWT of the benefits of sport and recreation to individual and community wellness."[88]

Co-operation and collaboration, two other aspects of this goal, are complementary actions. In 1983 an interest in clarifying the overlaps in the sport and recreation delivery system required co-operation from different organizations. However, collaboration was also stressed, in particular as it related to facility use among schools, communities, and private or commercial organizations.[89] By 1991, collaboration had become broadly considered, with delegates encouraging the development and promotion of new partnerships and the pooling of resources to maximize what was available.[90] This focus on collaboration became foundational in the approach taken at the 2000 Directions conference. Seven sport and recreation organizations agreed to develop a comprehensive strategic "partnership" plan with a jointly constructed vision, set of underlying principles, code of conduct, and seven shared priorities. Their priorities took into account the national themes agreed to in the 1994 Planning Framework for Sport in Canada,[91] but those themes were reshaped to fit the needs present in the NWT. For example, the partners acknowledged that a strong partnership must include strong individual organizations. This was stressed through the seventh priority, organizational well-being, with its end objective of "participants, volunteers and leaders in sport and recreation obtaining support from vibrant and sustainable organizations."[92] The northern regional conference held later that year provided two key messages related to this goal: that the Canadian Sport Policy encourage "improved partnerships among governments and sport organizations at all levels," and that northern Canada's "rightful place at the national [sport] table be recognized.[93]

Sam notes that dominant ideas provide credibility to some ideas over others.[94] Certainly, the four goals identified in the Canadian Sport Policy have naturalized the idea that broad participation, striving after excellence at the international level, compiling necessary material, financial, and human resources, and partnering to maximize those resources – all within an ethically based context – are what the Canadian sport system is all about. In keeping with what Sam contends,[95] these naturalized ideas have been institutionalized in subsequent policy documents, such as the *Federal–Provincial/Territorial Priorities for Collaborative Action, 2002–2005*, and *2006–2009*,[96] and the 2005 Sport Canada Policy on Aboriginal Peoples' Participation in Sport.[97]

A historical exploration from the perspective of one of the stakeholders, the NWT, confirms and challenges some of these naturalized ideas. First, I would argue that the four goals work better as an interlocking set of threads underlying sport and recreation rather than as a set of distinct items. As I read through and categorized the various recommendations, overlaps became apparent. For example, resources are central to the functioning of all four goals, not just capacity building. Inequalities in participation, linked to the first goal, exist because limited resources demand that only select needs can be met. The second goal, enhanced excellence, demands extensive resources of all types for its achievement. The third goal, enhanced capacity, is made possible through the provision of resources, while the importance of the fourth goal, enhanced interaction, arises owing to limited resources and a desire to maximize what is available. Overlaps were similarly evident in terms of a values-based sport system that is athlete centred. These concepts are relevant to each goal because they set the boundaries for how that goal should be achieved. It will thus be important to explore the relationships between these goals, not just each one separately.

Also evident through this analysis was the degree of relevance that each goal has had to the NWT sport and recreation system. Clearly, the goal of enhanced excellence was minimally discussed in Directions conferences, and, when it was discussed, the standard for excellence that was possible in the NWT, as outlined in the Canadian Sport Policy, was beyond the reach of most participants.

However, since the first Directions conference in 1983, the NWT has been actively generating meaningful partnerships, increasing participation, and maximizing resources while trying to address the variability that exists between communities, interests, and needs of participants across the territories. The NWT has thus been working to address several of the Canadian Sport Policy goals for the past twenty-two years.

The historical interplay of the dominant ideas embedded in national policies and in the NWT's specific policies and programs thus deserves further analysis in order to understand better the social construction of national policies in Canada in light of various government stakeholders and underlying power relations. As well, ongoing monitoring of the distribution of federal resources linked to the Canadian Sport Policy is needed in order to assess the distribution of the federal resources linked to these four goals. Will resources be distributed in a manner that respects the orientation of each of the stakeholders to the various goals? Will each of the four "Canadian" goals be resourced equally? Or will one goal, such as enhanced excellence, be awarded the majority of the resources, as was seen in the 2010 Vancouver Olympics, at the expense of other priorities that are more relevant to stakeholders such as the NWT? This monitoring, along with further explorations on the historical construction of national policy, will help to assess how "good" this policy really is for the NWT.

Conclusion

In this historical account I have documented a variety of ways in which northern participants and professionals have actively constructed their sport and recreation services in the NWT between 1962 and 2000. With one eye attentive to national developments and another eye fixed on local conditions, they have at times preceded national trends, while also on occasion choosing to ignore or challenge the national approaches that did not serve their best interests. There have been sustained efforts to set a direction that meets the needs of northerners from small as well as large communities and to create a structure that is more equitable for *all* participants. Through this history I ask questions about the suitability of national policies and programs from the perspective of the recipients – in this case, the citizens of the NWT – based on my assumption that *all* individuals have the right to carve out the life that they most prefer within the broader conditions that they face.

Nelson Mandela has been quoted (incorrectly) as saying, "Our deepest fear is not that we are inadequate. Our deepest fear is that we are powerful beyond measure."[98] Writing histories that show the ability of individuals to effect change, and that inspire people to do so while helping them to understand the broader conditions within which they must operate, provides a road map, laying out one method by which individuals and groups can work actively towards the life – and the society – that they most hope to have.

NOTES

1 The term *underserved* rather than *marginalized* is chosen thanks to Sheldon Baikie, who returned from his work in Labrador saying that he would no longer use the latter term, because the people in the community with whom he had worked did not identify with that word. Their recreational situation was a concern because they cared about it, not because they were a marginalized group in need of assistance.

2 NWT Sport and Recreation Partners, *Legacy and New Directions Conference: The NWT Sport and Recreation System, Hay River, NWT, May 10–11, 2000 Proceedings* (Yellowknife: GNWT Sport and Recreation Section, 2000).

3 Duality of Structure is described in Anthony Giddens, *The Constitution of Society: Outline of the Theory of Structuration* (Berkeley: University of California Press, 1984). For a discussion on duality of structure specific to aboriginal sport, see Victoria Paraschak, "Knowing Ourselves Through the 'Other': Indigenous Peoples in Sport in Canada," in Robyn Jones and Kathleen Armour (Eds.), *Sociology of Sport: Theory and Practice* (Harlow, UK: Longman Press, 2000), 153–66.

4 For an extended discussion on the strengths perspective linked to aboriginal sport, see Sheldon Baikie, "The 'Bright Side of the Road': The Strengths Perspective in Nain, Labrador," in Vicky Paraschak and Janice Forsyth (eds.), *North American Indigenous Games Research Symposium Proceedings* (Winnipeg: University of Manitoba, 2003), 70–6.

5 The Recreation Division became the Sport and Recreation Division in 1984, then the Sport and Recreation Section in the mid-1990s.

6 Federal-Provincial or Territorial matching grants were made available beginning in 1961 through the federal Fitness and Amateur Sport Act. Canada, Laws, Statutes, etc. *An Act to Encourage Fitness and Amateur Sport, 1961*, 9–10 Eliz 2, ch. 59.

7 The Recreation Division, initially located in the Department of Local Government, was briefly shifted to the Department of Natural and Cultural Affairs in 1975, and then was relocated in Local Government in 1979, which became Municipal and Community Affairs in 1986.

8 The history of the Recreation Division in its early years draws from interviews with Jacques Van Pelt in January 2000, and from Municipal and Community Affairs, Sport and Recreation Division, *New Employee Orientation Manual*, January 1991, 7–19.

9 Background on this period was provided by Chris Szabo, who was one of the two full-time staff working in the Sport and Recreation Section of the GNWT at that time.

10 For an extended discussion on the initial years of sport funding in the NWT, see Victoria Paraschak, "Discrepancies between Government Programs and Community Practices: The Case of Recreation in the Northwest Territories," unpublished PhD diss., University of Alberta, 1983, 80–8.

11 For example, in a 1995 *Evaluation of Sport North* completed by Avery, Cooper Consulting, they noted that "a significant portion of the people who do not work directly with Sport North view the organization as remote, fat-cat, and too Yellowknife oriented ... These perceptions tend to be stronger as the communities get smaller, further from Yellowknife and towards the East" (79).

12 A description of NWT leadership programs that includes the Recreation Leaders Program and the Recreation Salary Subsidy Program is found in the Municipal and Community Affairs, Sport and Recreation Division, *New Employee Orientation Manual*, January 1991, 30–3.

13 For an extensive discussion on the Mackenzie Recreation Association, see Shane Thompson, "Regional Approaches to Development and Delivery of Recreation and Sport Programs in the NWT," in Vicky Paraschak and Janice Forsyth (Eds.), *North American Indigenous Games Research Symposium Proceedings* (Winnipeg: University of Manitoba, 2003), 77–84.

14 Block funding of recreation grants meant that the government's recreation funding, which had previously been provided to the community for specific recreation initiatives, was now rolled into one larger block grant from Municipal and Community Affairs for use by the community as it saw fit. This meant that the money could, but would not necessarily, be used for community recreation services.

15 For example, the issue of funding for the 1995 NAIG team from the NWT, and a discussion paper being developed on that issue, was raised by several politicians in the House on 17 October 1994, question 153–12(6).

16 A briefing note for the Minister of MACA on the NAIG, on 14 October 1994, stated, "Our involvement in the NAIG must be carefully planned for the impacts it may have on the relatively successful model we have of integration of indigenous and non-indigenous peoples in sport."

17 This section on partnerships draws from a 2002 North American Society for the Sociology of Sport presentation co-authored with Chris Szabo, who at that time was the GNWT manager, Sport and Recreation Programs. We organized our discussion of partnerships in terms of the economic, political, and social realities leading to pressures for partnerships and the eventual impetus for the strategic planning process (three areas taken from L. Thibault, W. Frisby, and L.M. Kikulis, "Interorganisational Linkages in the Delivery of Local Leisure Services in Canada:

Responding to Economic, Political, and Social Pressures," *Managing Leisure: An International Journal* 4, no. 3 (1999): 125–41).

18 Sport and Recreation Division, *Partners in Action: Sport and Recreation Directions for the Nineties* (Yellowknife: GNWT Municipal and Community Affairs, 1992).

19 Dennis Mills, "Sport in Canada: Leadership, Partnership, and Accountability – Everybody's Business," Sixth Report of the Standing Committee on Canadian Heritage, 1999.

20 *Partners in Action: Directions for the '90s Conference*, 1992, 1.

21 Ministry of Municipal and Community Affairs, Proceedings Document, "Vision for Division," Western Territory Conference, 26–28 April 1996 (Yellowknife, January 1997), 5, point 4.1.7.

22 Avery, Cooper Consulting, *Evaluation of Sport North* (Yellowknife, December 1995).

23 GNWT, *Multi-sports Games Review* (Yellowknife, June 1996).

24 History provided by Chris Szabo, who was a staff member of the Sport and Recreation Section during this time.

25 These six points are not identical to, but clearly align with, *A Planning Framework for Sport in Canada*, a joint document of the Sport Community and Federal/Provincial/Territorial Sport Committee, October 1994.

26 As I was contracted to do this project, this section draws from my personal involvement in overseeing the process. For an overview of the process and outcomes, see NWT Sport and Recreation Partners, *Legacy and New Directions* (Yellowknife, June 2000).

27 NWT Sport and Recreation Partners, *Legacy and New Directions*, 2.

28 Ibid.

29 There had been various groups lobbying for the lottery funds to be extended beyond sport and recreation to other non-profit groups in the NWT, such as cultural and arts organizations.

30 Homi K. Bhabha, *The Location of Culture* (London: Routledge, 1994), 219.

31 Margaret Horn, "Bringing Traditional Practices to Today's Reality," *Action* (Ottawa: CAAWS), 22 November 1998, 26.

32 Raymond Williams, *Marxism and Literature* (Oxford: Oxford University Press, 1977).

33 Peter Donnelly, "Prolympism: Sport Monoculture as Crisis and Opportunity," *Quest* 48, no. 1 (1996): 25–42.

34 Susan Birrell, "Racial Relations Theories and Sport: Suggestions for a More Critical Analysis," *Sociology of Sport Journal* 6 (1989): 212–27.

35 Debates (1970), 41st Session, 6th Council, 272, 19 January.

36 The traditional approach towards organizing aboriginal activities, for example with the Northern Games, is outlined in more detail in Victoria Paraschak, "Variations

in Race Relations: Native Peoples in Sport in Canada," *Sociology of Sport Journal* 14, no. 1 (1997): 1–27.

37 They were included as a demonstration event in the 2007 Canada Winter Games but only for the three territorial teams that competed in the games.

38 The Native Sport and Recreation Program; for more details see Victoria Paraschak, "The Native Sport and Recreation Program, 1972–1981: Patterns of Resistance, Patterns of Reproduction," *Canadian Journal of History of Sport*, 1995: 1–18.

39 See Paraschak, "Discrepancies between Government Programs and Community Practices," 45–54.

40 Debates (1983), 10th Session, 9th Assembly, 829, 7 March.

41 Sport and Recreation Division, *Sport and Recreation Direction Conference Proceedings* (Yellowknife: GNWT Department of Local Government, 1983).

42 Ibid., 3.

43 Ibid., 5.

44 Sport and Recreation Division, *Partners in Action: Sport and Recreation Directions for the Nineties* (Yellowknife: GNWT Municipal and Community Affairs, 1992), 5.

45 Executive Summary, GNWT Multi-sport Games Review, 11 February 1997, 2.

46 Ibid., 4.

47 Ibid., 8.

48 Ibid., 31.

49 Horn, "Bringing Traditional Practices to Today's Reality," 26.

50 Bhahba, *Location of Culture*, 219; italics original.

51 Michael P. Sam, "What's the Big Idea? Reading the Rhetoric of a National Sport Policy Process," *Sociology of Sport Journal* 20, no. 3 (2003): 189.

52 Federal–Provincial/Territorial Sport Ministers, *The Canadian Sport Policy* (Ottawa: Canadian Heritage, 2002).

53 Canadian Heritage, *Sport Canada's Policy on Aboriginal Peoples' Participation in Sport* (Ottawa: Minister of Public Works and Government Services Canada, 2005).

54 Federal–Provincial/Territorial Sport Ministers, *The Canadian Sport Policy: Federal–Provincial/Territorial Priorities for Collaborative Action, 2002–2005* (Ottawa: Canadian Heritage, 2002).

55 Sam, "What's the Big Idea?," 194.

56 The number of delegates at these conferences ranged from forty-five in 1983, to fifty-four in 1991, to eighty in 2000, with ages spanning young adults to elders.

57 Canadian Heritage, *A Northern Perspective on Sport: Report on the Territorial Regional Conference, Yellowknife, NWT, July 12–14, 2000* (Ottawa: Canadian Heritage, 2000).

58 Federal–Provincial/Territorial Sport Ministers, *Canadian Sport Policy*, 2002.

59 Sport and Recreation Division, *Directions Conference, 1983*.

60 Sport and Recreation Division, *Directions Conference, 1992*.

61 NWT Sport and Recreation Partners, *Directions Conference*, 2000, p. 8.
62 Canadian Heritage, *Northern Perspective on Sport*, 2000, 28.
63 Federal–Provincial/Territorial Sport Ministers, *Canadian Sport Policy*, 2002. Those familiar with the 2003 federal Physical Activity and Sport Act will know that a large portion of that act deals with the creation of an alternative sport dispute centre, to ensure that "fair and ethical means" are available to elite athletes in Canada.
64 This would differ from annual general meetings held by the Sport North Federation, where most territorial sport organization delegates are attentive to elite levels of sport development as part of their mandate.
65 Sport and Recreation Division, *Directions Conference*, 1983.
66 Sport and Recreation Division, *Directions Conference*, 1992.
67 Ibid.
68 NWT Sport and Recreation Partners, *Directions Conference*, 2000, p. 8.
69 Ibid., p. 33.
70 Ibid.
71 Canadian Heritage, *Northern Perspective on Sport*, 2000, 28.
72 Federal–Provincial/Territorial Sport Ministers, *Canadian Sport Policy*, 2002.
73 Sport and Recreation Division, *Directions Conference*, 1983.
74 Sport and Recreation Division, *Directions Conference*, 1992.
75 Sport and Recreation Division, *Directions Conference*, 1983.
76 Sport and Recreation Division, *Directions Conference*, 1992.
77 NWT Sport and Recreation Partners, *Directions Conference*, 2000, p. 8
78 Sport and Recreation Division, *Directions Conference*, 1983.
79 Sport and Recreation Division, *Directions Conference*, 1992.
80 NWT Sport and Recreation Partners, *Directions Conference*, 2000, p. 8.
81 Canadian Heritage, *Northern Perspective on Sport*, 2000, 28.
82 Sport and Recreation Division, *Directions Conference*, 1983.
83 Sport and Recreation Division, *Directions Conference*, 1992.
84 NWT Sport and Recreation Partners, *Directions Conference*, 2000, p. 8.
85 Federal–Provincial/Territorial Sport Ministers, *Canadian Sport Policy*, 2002.
86 Sport and Recreation Division, *Directions Conference*, 1983.
87 Sport and Recreation Division, *Directions Conference*, 1992.
88 NWT Sport and Recreation Partners, *Directions Conference*, 2000, p. 8.
89 Sport and Recreation Division, *Directions Conference*, 1983.
90 Sport and Recreation Division, *Directions Conference*, 1992.
91 Sport Community and Federal/Provincial/Territorial Sport Committee, *A Planning Framework for Sport in Canada*, October 1994.
92 NWT Sport and Recreation Partners, *Directions Conference*, 2000, p. 8.
93 Canadian Heritage, *Northern Perspective on Sport*, 2000, 28.

94 Sam, "What's the Big Idea? Reading the Rhetoric of a National Sport Policy Process," 204.
95 Ibid., 206.
96 *Provincial/Territorial Priorities for Collaborative Action, 2002–2005*; *Provincial/Territorial Priorities for Collaborative Action, 2006–2009*.
97 Canadian Heritage, *Sport Canada's Policy on Aboriginal Peoples' Participation in Sport*.
98 Marianne Williamson, *A Return to Love* (New York: HarperCollins, 1992), 165.

PART FOUR

Shifting Ground: Reconsidering the Role of the Public Intellectual in Sport

11 "Can You Do This for My Neighbourhood?": Public Sport History, the Environment, and Community in an Industrial City

NANCY B. BOUCHIER AND KEN CRUIKSHANK

In his *Taking History to Heart: The Power of the Past in Building Social Movements,* American activist and historian James Green observes that contemporary struggles for social justice "call up the past for instruction and inspiration."[1] This idea is well conveyed by the title of a 2008 conference on human rights and sport, "To Remember Is to Resist," hosted by Bruce Kidd at the University of Toronto.[2] Throughout a lifetime of important works as a scholar and social activist Bruce has called up the past for instruction and inspiration to help us change our world in good ways.[3] In the *Globe and Mail's* "Intellectual Muscle" series podcast associated with the 2010 Vancouver Olympic Games, Bruce used the lens of sustainability to turn a critical gaze, connecting the past, present, and the future of our sport system.[4]

Sustainability is a key issue for our times, something with which scholars of sport are quite familiar.[5] They know well that generations of physical-activity and health advocates have held that exercise, sport, good health, and nature are inexorably linked. Indeed, many consider nature to be a key ingredient for regenerating our frazzled bodies and minds.[6] Nowadays, however, the needs of future generations are at risk as we all wrestle with the changes to our planet that we have seen occur during our own lifetimes and with the effect that these "inconvenient truths" have upon our sport and physical activity.[7] Bad air, dirty water, harmful sunrays, and pesticides on our fields – to name just a few problems – make playing outside in nature troublesome. Not long ago *Sports Illustrated* shocked many with its cover image of a professional baseball player standing in a centre field, thigh deep in water, with its foreboding subtitle, "Sports and Global Warming: As the Planet Changes so Do the Games We Play – Time to Pay Attention."[8] Critics point out that when it comes to environmental damage, sport is both culprit and victim.[9]

It is hard not to notice that people are indeed becoming aware of what is happening around us and paying more attention to the environment, and that they are doing something about it. The term *green* has invaded the worlds of policy and marketing and our vocabularies.[10] Concern for the health of our planet is now part of our mainstream consciousness as we separate our garbage, turn off lights, and worry about our ecological footprint. Even recent revisions to the International Olympic Committee (IOC) Charter now articulate the green mission, "to encourage and support a responsible concern for environmental issues, to promote sustainable development in sport, and to require that the Olympic Games are held accordingly."[11] The IOC, along with the United Nations Environment Program (UNEP), and international sports federations have taken up the cause of Agenda 21 (a declaration of the 1992 United Nations Conference on Environment and Development in Rio de Janeiro),[12] regularly holding world conferences on sport and the environment.[13] The IOC gives awards for good environmental practices, and in Canada even athletes participated with their Vancouver 2010 Project Blue Sky, which was aimed at promoting carbon-reducing activities.[14] Into this mix, a new breed of consulting companies has created a particular niche in the sport management world for their work on green, sustainable games.[15] Approaches to working from within, rather than replacing, existing sport systems may not be palatable to some types of environmental activists, but the question remains, how can change ever be effected without large institutions and the corporate capitalist world getting on board? As Eric Falt, former UNEP communications director, observed in his 2006 guest editorial for the *Environmental Health Perspectives* special issue on sport, "confrontation and the blame game just don't work."[16]

For several years our research and writing have dealt with issues of sustainability by reviewing roughly two centuries of the past in our documentation and examination of the social and environmental transformation of an urban waterfront in a Canadian industrial city. Although Hamilton's waterfront has been very polluted for over a century, it is nevertheless well known as a site for elite sport and, perhaps more commonly, as a place for the local population of some half a million people to simply live, work, and play.[17] Our work examines past efforts to sustain, manage, and reshape the social and natural environment of the waterfront and analyses how people have viewed, reacted to, and lived with these efforts.[18] We seek to create understandings now about what happened, in order to inform citizens, governments, and the scientists with whom they work in their environmental remediation efforts to restore Hamilton's gravely polluted watershed.[19]

In this chapter we share some of our thoughts on and experiences in communicating our research in the public domain – for example, through our museum exhibit and documentary film – and on the way in which our local artistic community has incorporated our sport history work into their dialogues about the environment and the city, and vice versa. We begin by examining the recent calls for the historical profession to bridge the academic-public divide, and then turn to Robert Archibald's idea of public history as a tool to build community. Finally, we identify the ways in which our own work on the history of Hamilton Harbour has resonated with a value-centred approach to public history and has helped to inform some contemporary discourses about the environment and community in an industrial city in ways that we could not have anticipated.

"Can you do this for my neighbourhood?" many people have asked us at public screenings of *The People and the Bay*, our historical documentary film, hoping that, by bringing public attention to the environmental issues touching their lives, we can help them to change their world for the better. Our film, which chronicles over a century of the search for, and the conflicts over, waterfront sport and recreational green space around a heavily polluted harbour, has struck a chord apparently.[20] We have found such queries and public calls for historical engagement with difficult environmental issues to be one of the best rewards and one of the greatest challenges that we as academic historians have faced.[21] This work has required us to rethink what we do as academic historians and to see ways in which history and sport historians can play a role in community development and activism.

It is hardly surprising that contemporary environmental struggles have resulted in community calls for public history to document the past in order to help people understand where we have been, and to help inform the future.[22] As James Green points out, "historical narratives can do more than redeem the memory of past struggles; they can help people think of themselves as historical figures with crucial moral and political choices to make, like those who came before them."[23] Judging by the recent survey and interview research of the Canadians and Their Pasts Project, there is an audience primed for such messages. It shows that ordinary Canadians are generally historically engaged people.[24] Their connections to history are manifested in myriad ways, and they typically consume the history that they see, hear, and read critically. This makes the multidisciplinary, inclusive, and outward-looking work of public history challenging.[25] It is a challenge that Canadian historian Margaret Conrad, past president of the Canadian Historical Association, argues can be met through bridge building and opening dialogues between academic historians, public historians, and the public at large.[26] Accomplishing this remains a formidable task. Among academic (including sport) historians there is a growing momentum for public engagement, and they have shown considerable reflexivity about their experiences in translating their work for public audiences. For example, *The Public Historian* recently devoted a special issue to public history in Canada, and the *Journal of Sport History* published a special issue devoted to "our voices in public history."[27]

Public history comes in many shapes, sizes, and forms: from community outreach projects, to exhibits in museums and halls of fame, to film and other media forms such as websites, to name a few. But what makes good and effective public history? We have found that the American local historian Robert Archibald provides a compelling answer to this question, especially given our own experiences with our *People and the Bay* project. Good public history, he argues, both makes and sustains a community. We agree. In his highly personal and thought-provoking book, *A Place to Remember: Using History to Build Community*, Archibald entreats us both to action and to an understanding that history is neither disembodied nor lacking in a point.[28] History, he argues, "is a process of facilitating conversations with which we consider what we have done well, what we have done poorly, and how we can do better, conversations that are a prelude to action."[29] It has an important role in contemporary civic life: "Places, memories, and stories are inextricably connected," he writes, "and we cannot create a real community without these elements."[30] We would argue that it is in such a community that we can realize Bruce Kidd's notion of a "constituency for change."[31] There is another way in which Archibald's and Kidd's work resonates: in their analysis of and advocacy for values-based approaches.[32] Archibald details four core values as sound organizing principles for community-focused public history: acknowledging issues of sustainability to meet the needs of future generations; attending to mutual obligation when engaging in civic enterprise; valuing memory as important to community building; and transcending ordinary life to create stories that speak to human spirit and emotions for inspiration and creativity.[33]

In the case of our research we have found such an approach to be tough but not out of reach. As the issue of environmental pollution is, in the words of one astute observer, "a bit of a downer," it is tempting to tune out the message and feel powerless.[34] We have two strategies: we try to situate issues where people care and connect in the context of their everyday lives; and we tell stories that demonstrate that people can make a difference. We want people to understand that environmental challenges are not new and that previous generations have struggled to balance different uses of the harbour and to create sustainable communities, even if they did not use the term.

In telling our stories, we are conscious that some of our audiences are attuned to, and will be thinking about, contemporary issues. Take for example one commentary coming out of the war-time intensification of Hamilton's industrial activity. In 1946 one observer in the *Hamilton Spectator* labelled Hamilton Harbour "our deceptive bay." Why was it deceptive? The answer came quite simply: "From a distance our bay looks attractive and inviting. Nearby it is seen to be dirty and flecked with foulness, the pollution of its waters being the price we pay for modern urban life. The price may easily be too high."[35] Over half a century later the bay can look attractive even up close, but what is under some of its surface is disturbing and toxic. Local policymakers and activists struggle with what to do with Hamilton's Randle Reef, one of the most highly contaminated sediment sites in North America.[36] It is a huge blob of goo sitting on the harbour floor – apparently big enough to fill our local NHL-ready hockey stadium three times – full of coal tar (or polynuclear aromatic hydrocarbons, PAHs), a by-product of steel making.[37] Scientists have shown that PAHs are recirculating from their underwater site, moving up into the food chain.[38]

It's quite frightening. Scientific research has shown that the Air Pollution Index rates in some areas of the city are generally high and that local people are concerned, for good reason, about the health effects of air quality, black fallout from smokestacks, fugitive dust from trucks, and bad odours. Social science research reveals the uneven distribution of these effects throughout the population.[39] In 1992, just as Mediterranean countries were creating an action plan for their sea, Hamilton was devising its own remedial action plan (RAP) for its heavily polluted harbour.[40] Its RAP aimed to have the harbour de-listed from the International Joint Commission's "Areas of Concern" list by 2015, which has not been achieved.[41] The work of community groups such as the Bay Area Restoration Council (BARC), a grassroots volunteer organization,[42] and the stakeholders of the Bay Area Implementation Team (BAIT)[43] complement the RAP work carried out by scientists. When we talk about history with BARC members, as we have done on several occasions, we know that our audience filters what we say through their own concerns for the contemporary harbour.

Hamilton's RAP reflects a much broader trend in the way that industrial harbours are being used, controlled, thought about, and remembered in many developed nations throughout the world. History appears to matter in this larger discourse, and we believe that sport historians working in the arena of public history have an important role to play.[44] Current debates over redevelopment of industrial ports often treat history simply as a rhetorical device – the source for a particular image that developers, planners, and environmental activists can then promise to "restore" and "preserve" – or as a commodity – the source for a particular "authentic" image that can be packaged by developers and planners to make an area attractive to tourists and other consumers. We are anxious to avoid these traps. Through our work we have shown that a historical perspective, especially one that is sensitive to issues of power and social inequality, can help inform debates over waterfront development today. In our research we ask the question, "Whose harbour?," alluding to its multiple uses and multiple meanings to multiple users. Many groups have expressed differing visions of the harbour during its history through the different ways they have used it: for example, as a commercial and industrial port facility; as a playground in nature for anglers, swimmers, and sailors; as a subsistence and business source of fish, game, ice, and water; as an attractive site for beaches, cottages, and amusement parks; and as a convenient dump for residential and industrial wastes. We document and analyse past uses of the harbour as a way of understanding how different groups of Hamiltonians thought about and used the bay and developed and applied particular understandings of what this common space was and should be.[45] Oftentimes, and particularly in response to environmental change, different groups of Hamiltonians championed their particular conception of the harbour over competing visions.

A contemporary example illustrates the contested nature of Hamilton's waterfront and the tremendous implications that exist for sport and recreation. In 2010, city councillors, Pan American Games promoters, and citizen activists battled over Hamilton's part in Toronto's hosting of the 2015 Pan Am Games. Hamilton was to supply a stadium for the event, but the question was, *where*?[46] Among the sites initially considered, games organizers eyed a location at Confederation Park, along the beach strip between the bay and Lake Ontario in the industrial eastern end of the city.[47] Our research reveals that this area has a long and embattled history.[48] Near the steel mills, it originally had been a working-class neighbourhood of makeshift homes fashioned from cottages. In the late 1950s, city planners used a newly developed city plan – one that did nothing to counter existing and emerging environmental inequalities – to designate the area "appalling," "blighted," and in need of transformation.[49] Those in power identified the residential neighbourhood an "unhealthy" area for human inhabitation to justify its expropriation by the city for a waterfront public amusement park. Yet the park that opened in 1964 fell far short of the grandiose plans of local political leaders and entrepreneurs. By 1980 the city had handed the area over to the local conservation authority, an agency responsible for the area's watershed, which works to defend and sustain natural spaces in the region.[50]

In January 2009, when Pan Am Games promoters were eyeing this green space for their stadium, David Braley, the local architect of the Games bid, along with others dismissed environmental concerns over conservation and

the area's protected status. They argued that a stadium would have little negative effect upon the publicly owned nature area because it would make "a mere
eight-hectare dent in an 83-hectare site."[51] Their opponents, however, were not
so sanguine about the incursion, especially in the wake of a sometimes nasty
and unsuccessful fifty-year battle to stop the building of the Red Hill Expressway through forest and parklands in that area of the city.[52] As one concerned
citizen pointed out in a letter to the editor of the *Spectator*, the preservation
of green space against the incursions of development loomed large: "There is
only a finite amount of green space left in Hamilton ... If we take 'only eight
[hectares]' from Confederation Park today, how do we stop another 'only X
[hectares] tomorrow'?"[53]

The city councillor responsible for the ward, along with conservationists and
other concerned citizens, argued powerfully and successfully that the council
must preserve the park.[54] They voted to nip the Confederation Park stadium
in the bud.[55] The decision to remove the site from the list of potential stadium
sites reconfirmed that, whatever the original intentions for the area in the late
1950s, and however unjust its creation was to those whose homes the city had
destroyed, the park's security as open waterfront green space seems to be in
good form, at least *at the moment*. But who can tell what the future may hold if
people are not vigilant?[56]

To be ever vigilant, one must keep a memory alive, something that local historian Robert Archibald argues is important to community building. We turn
now to some of the ways in which our work has called upon people's memories, and the ways in which it has helped to create stories that work towards a
public dialogue about the environment and a community's health and recreational space. Such stories transcend everyday life and are necessary for community building, according to Archibald, because they are "the wellsprings of
inspiration and creativity that are responsible for many of our most laudable
achievements."[57]

Our project on Hamilton Harbour has been public history from the outset.
In 1994, members of the Ecowise project invited us to undertake historical
research as part of their large interdisciplinary research project on the restoration of the harbour. We began our research and shared our early and
tentative findings both with other researchers and at public events. We soon
found that focused stories and visual presentations proved very effective
in communicating our work.[58] Soon afterwards, historical colleagues who
served on the board of Hamilton's newly opened Ontario Workers Arts and
Heritage Centre invited us to create an exhibit for the new centre.[59] As we
had planned to include oral-history evidence in our project, we used the
exhibit to help generate interest in our work and to draw potential interview

subjects from the population at large. We used something that was fun and familiar – the lens of popular culture and recreation – to identify and address something that was not at all fun, the troubling issue of environmental change in the harbour. Our *People and the Bay* exhibit attracted record numbers to the centre and was extended for several weeks by popular demand. It drew on people's local familiarity with the harbour because the centre itself is located in the North End neighbourhood that served as the original port and industrial district, where Hamilton's working-class families have lived for generations.[60] The exhibit also showed features that were quite unfamiliar because of the way in which the harbour had changed so greatly through time. For example, historical photographs showed different shorelines full of ragged inlets that most people had never seen, shorelines that had not yet been hardened by concrete or steel, as can be seen in the map of figure 11.1. They saw an image of a larger body of water which, since that time, has been made much smaller (by about a third of its size) through infilling and land reclamation. Many of the bay's uses had changed substantially or had been long lost; for example, the ice harvest had long ago died, and swimming beaches were no longer clean or safe. While the exhibit's photographs evoked and inspired memories, they also provoked nostalgic responses of "the good old days." This might have undercut the critical edge of our presentation, had we not balanced our photographic and physical layout with carefully chosen captions and text. Why was our exhibit so popular? we asked ourselves in a piece that reflected upon and analysed our experiences.[61] We believe that it was because we had touched an important nerve in the civic life of the community. Indeed, our exhibit has drawn us deeper into the community, sometimes to comment on or add perspective to harbour-development issues, and sometimes with requests to extend our engagement to other aspects of the city's history.

Using the stories conveyed to us by the elderly people whose memories the museum exhibit had triggered, in addition to other types of documentary sources including land records, directories, old telephone books, and aerial photographs of the area, our research began stitching together memories and records of a place long forgotten in Hamilton history. We used this material in a piece written for the journal *Labour / Le Travail* entitled "The War on the Squatters."[62] The article explored the ways in which Hamilton's middle-class urban planners, conservationists, and moral reformers had sought to reshape the human and natural environment of the bay, often at the expense of other segments of the local population, such as working-class families. The story of the "war" goes like this: Hamilton's city planners in the 1920s and 1930s envisioned the West Harbour and Cootes Paradise wetlands as a place

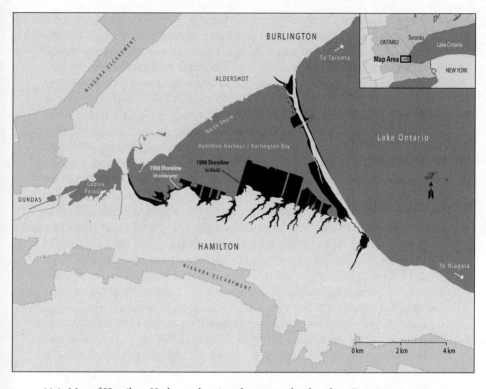

11.1 Map of Hamilton Harbour, showing changes to the shoreline. Data source: © OpenStreetMap contributors, GeoBase®, GeoGratis (© Department of Natural Resources Canada), CanVec (© Department of Natural Resources Canada), and StatCan (Geography Division, Statistics Canada). Credit: Rajiv Rawat

for parklands and gardens. They sought to create a western entrance for the city that would highlight civic beauty, health, and achievement.[63] In doing so, however, they systematically destroyed a community of boathouse dwellers, largely working-class families, who lived there and enjoyed the swimming, boating, and outdoor pursuits of this recreational paradise. These people used the abundant fish and game of the area to put good food on their tables, but its designation as a nature preserve ended that.[64] They resisted their removal as best they could, but over time city authorities, who had many more resources at their disposal, wore their opponents down through expensive litigation and other strategies.

Looking today at the shoreline of the Royal Botanical Gardens along the West Harbour and Cootes Paradise wetlands, one would have had little idea about that rich past, unless one read our article; or saw the historic plaque recently erected alongside the city's new waterfront trail that commemorates the existence of this community, but not its social composition or its struggle to remain alive; or if, in the summer of 2008, one had a chance to catch sight of the art installation *The Urban Moorings Project*, which floated around in Cootes Paradise for a couple of months.[65] Sponsored by Hamilton Artists Inc., the City, and the Royal Botanical Gardens (RBG), the project brought together five artists to create floating sculptures on Cootes relating to the boathouse community and the creation of the RBG, about which we had written.[66] Hamilton's award-winning poet and writer, John Terpstra, praised the manner in which the project "enters the story and transcribes it into eco-innovation in art that recalls and reclaims our past communities and this paradisiacal landscape, in all its complicated and often compromised facets."[67] The aquatic ecologist Tÿs Theÿsmeÿer, head of Conservation and Natural Lands at the RBG (and an active BARC member), noted that the exhibit had a unique way of conveying the environmental message: "to tell stories of the history of the collapse and ongoing rebirth of Cootes Paradise wetland."[68] Curator Nora Hutchinson describes the project as an ever-changing travelling canvas. She extols: "Morning fog, dusk, and the terrible beauty of Hamilton's factory plumes of smoke and fire play a part in this ineffable landscape. Culled into the visual frame of floating homes, there is the call of birds, the hush of wings and the sound of water lapping."[69]

The artists fashioned their works out of "pre-purposed" (aka "used") materials to symbolize aspects of the environmental remediation, such as cleaning the water and creating islands, projects that have engaged water scientists working on the RAP. The sculptures responded in various ways to the story of the boathouse community and Hamilton's waterfront and commented upon the community's environmental past, present, and future. They showed the capacity of RAP projects to inspire human aesthetic dimensions that transcend everyday life. Susan Detwiler's *Green Cleaning House*, shown in figure 11.2, aims to "raise questions about the industrial transformation of nature into toxic waste."[70] She built a green house of familiar cleaning tools – brooms, sweepers, and mops – that sheltered the edible plants growing inside. For artist Steve Mazza, his *Industrial Is a Dirty Word* piece considered "what it means to live in an industrial city, in an industrial province, in a country that doesn't seem to want to be industrial anymore."[71] As seen in figure 11.3, he placed under glass a factory that belched toxins into the air, as if it were a specimen from the past on display in a museum. The artist and musician Tor Lukasik-Foss's

11.2 Cleaning up the bay symbolically. The Urban Moorings Project, Susan Detwiler's *Green Cleaning House*. Photograph by Nancy Bouchier, 2008.

11.3 Waterfront industry as something to be put in a museum, under glass, in the post-modern age. The Urban Moorings Project, Steve Mazza's *Industrial Is a Dirty Word*. Photograph by Nancy Bouchier, 2008.

Viking Soliloquy Chair, a great wooden structure fashioned as a sinking Viking burial ship, became a floating stage for performances by his musical alter ego, Tiny Bill Cody.[72] Like a soapbox at speaker's corner, the chair floated around all summer, a venue beckoning to anyone who cared to climb aboard and express his or her views.

Moorings, the curator of this exhibit explains, "contain hidden anchors and weathered chains." "Likewise," she writes, "our past and public memories are historically concealed, yet live on as vessels decreeing either emptiness or event."[73] We could not have anticipated the way in which our historical research work might become entangled with such creative community engagement. Nor could we be more delighted, because this intervention from the world of art captured people's imaginations and stimulated meaningful discussions about subjective, engaged views of Hamilton's environmental problem, based on people's lived experience.

We were much more intentional about stimulating and creating memory when we created our documentary *The People and the Bay: The Story of Hamilton Harbour* (see figure 11.4).[74] We designed the DVD as part of an outreach program for the new L.R. Wilson Centre (now Institute) for Canadian History at McMaster University, which aims to rethink Canadian history and communicate it to broad audiences.[75] Through the institute our work with area history teachers taught us about some of the constraints that they face daily in the classroom. High costs and the threat of legal liability make class excursions to any historic site, let alone one on the water, difficult, if not impossible. So, we wondered, why not bring the harbour to the classroom? It would be without all of the hassle, and free.[76]

Our upbeat, forty-seven-minute historical and environmental tour around the bay on the *Hamilton Harbour Queen* ship presents popular history with a critical edge. It was designed to appeal to teenage sensibilities by being fast paced, visually eye-catching, and at times – yikes! – kind of goofy, while gently touching on important issues about power, conflict, development, and social and environmental inequality. Its director, Zach Melnick, uses historical re-enactments, archival footage from films and photographs, and the magic of animation to bring life to the bay's past and present. Its storyline foregrounds the search for and the conflicts over the preservation of green space for waterfront sport and recreation in the face of environmental degradation. We highlight the work of citizen activists in "the battle to unchain Hamilton Bay" from its post-war trajectory of industrial and commercial development.[77] The film ends with a message that both acknowledges and (we hope) inspires community involvement. We state: "Nowadays in the West Harbour, fish, people, and seabirds are all making a comeback. It did not *just happen*; people *made*

11.4 *The People and the Bay: A History of Hamilton Harbour.* Zach Melnick, director, and Yvonne Drebert, producer (Pixel Dust Studios, York, ON: L.R. Wilson Centre for Canadian History, McMaster University, 2007) (47 min.). Cover design by Yvonne Drebert.

it happen. For generations, enough people have insisted that the harbour belongs to everyone."[78]

Despite demands for copies of the film, and despite the praise received, on reflection we worry about its role in the shaping of historical memory, a point that we recently raised in a photo essay published in a special environmental issue of *Left History*.[79] The essay's story ends at the West Harbourfront, with the new nature park created out of a toxic dump site formerly known as the Lax lands.[80] These lands had been created in the late 1950s through the early 1970s by a scrap-dealing firm, the Lax Brothers. They filled in water lots initially to create land for industry but later planned it for condominium use. The fight between environmentalists and residents in the city's north end versus the harbour commission and developers over these Lax lands in the early 1970s marked a key turning point in the history of Hamilton's environmental movement. It was the battle over "whose harbour?" it really was. The City eventually

11.5 Bayfront Park and the West Harbour, 1995. How easy it is to forget the once-toxic Lax infill site, which has been replaced by the lush green waterfront park peninsula at the centre of the photograph. Courtesy of Hamilton Port Authority. Photographer unknown.

purchased the contested site in the early 1980s, leaving it vacant until the early 1990s, when the City redeveloped it as a waterfront nature park (the peninsula in the centre of figure 11.5). This happened around the same time that the RAP project began working towards revitalizing the waterfront.

In retrospect, we worry that this storyline and the images used in the film leave viewers with a picture that is *too* upbeat, that the crisp clean visuals of a green waterfront park tend to downplay the harsher messages about pollution and lack of public access to the waterfront – similar to our struggle with the museum exhibit. Despite the waterfront park's lush and ordered loveliness, environmental concerns remain; for example, the ongoing Randle Reef problem still has not been resolved.[81] Will people become complacent? What if we had included an image of the neatly printed row of four signs that stand at Bayfront Park, seen in figure 11.6. They warn people to stay out the water for their health because pollution, poisonous blue-green algae, and the lack of supervision make it unsafe. The signs speak volumes about gaps in achievements. Areas of Hamilton's waterfront are beautiful, green, and lush, but people along the shoreline must still stay out of the water. Swimming in Hamilton's polluted harbour is not advisable for any living thing.

We also worry that the voices of popular resistance that we try to carry forward in our scholarly and public historical work still do not always make their

11.6 Signs warning people to stay out of the water at Bayfront Park. Photograph by Nancy Bouchier, 2009.

way into other, more official versions of historical memory. Consider the images found on historical plaques like the one in figure 11.7, which line the city's new Waterfront Trail.[82] They highlight various aspects of the harbour's history, such as the city's Vision 2020, which aims at environmental sustainability; the work of the RAP and BARC; and the volunteers who planted native trees and plants along the bay's shore. However, the plaques do not memorialize the struggles of local citizen activists like the members of Clear Hamilton of Pollution (CHOP) and Save Our Bay (SOB) in "the battle to unchain Hamilton Bay."[83] Nor do they memorialize the interventions of Hamilton's thriving artistic community on behalf of the environment, like the Robert Yates 1991 exhibit, which visually

11.7 Hamilton's Vision 2020 waterfront plaque, one of the waterfront plaques that do not memorialize the work of citizen activists in "the battle to unchain Hamilton Bay." Photograph by Nancy Bouchier, 2009.

likened the underwater world of the bay to hell.[84] Or Cees van Gemerden's 1989 photo exhibit *No Trespassing*, a damning critique from the left consisting of seventy-eight photograph-and-text panels that documented people's lack of access to their waterfront.[85] He traced the line of fencing that kept people from the bay's southern shore. In 1996 at Aquafest, a festival created for the city's new park, he resurrected the show to remind people of the work still to be done.

The consciousness-raising work done by activist artists like Van Gemerden helped to stimulate and fuel the public outcry about the troubled state of Hamilton's waterfront and bring people on board with remediation efforts.[86] Van Gemerden's 1992 photographic exhibit *Trespassing – More Power Anyone?*, which reveals a hidden world at the Lax lands before their transformation, happened just as Hamilton was beginning its RAP.[87] His shots provide one of the few records of the area during a time of neglect by official authorities, before remediation, and in spite of the toxicity of the land.[88] They show abundant life (despite newspaper reports to the contrary) including a diverse array of trees, plants, and shrubs springing up from the heavily polluted ground, unassisted by human hands.[89] There is no official historical record of this world, beyond

11.8 "The Maple Tree versus Battery Cases." Courtesy of Cees van Gemerden, photographer.

van Gemerden's photographs, of the toxic place that remedial-action planners slated to be refashioned into something more desirable.

Anxious not to let people forget the history of this place, years ago van Gemerden suggested that it would be excellent if the small tree captured in figure 11.8, "The Maple Tree versus Battery Cases," could be preserved in the new Bayfront Park as a historical monument. Somehow the tree had grown up through a pile of discarded battery cases that had been dumped there. As a living monument amidst the toxic waste, the tree would call up the past to instruct and inspire the future. It would forever remind people playing in the otherwise lush green park along the water's edge where we have been and where we do not want to return. As anthropologist and historical archaeologist Donald Hardesty puts it, "the power of toxic waste as a real artifact in its original setting should not be overlooked as a way of conveying to visitors the impact of industrial technologies upon workplaces, communities, and landscapes."[90] It would help to remind people that, in the midst of the large-scale environmental transformations that have been seen in our very own lifetimes, nature and the creation of a sustainable future are important to everyone and everything on this planet.

The tree was not preserved, but van Gemerden's photograph captures it for posterity. It would work well on a historical plaque to record artistic activism and to keep memories alive. Of course, we (perhaps foolishly) mentioned this at a recent community meeting and are now being encouraged to develop a proposal for just such a plaque. "Can you do this for our neighbourhood as well?" we are asked. Clearly, there is much public history work to be done in Hamilton, and by other historical scholars, including sports historians, working across the country. How can we say no, living as we do, and others do, in the inspiring shadow of Bruce Kidd's good works?

NOTES

Nancy Bouchier presented an earlier version of this chapter as the 2009 Seward Staley honour address of the North American Society for Sport History. The Social Sciences and Humanities Research Council of Canada and the Arts Research Board of McMaster University have funded this research.

1 James Green, *Taking History to Heart: The Power of the Past in Building Social Movements* (Amherst: University of Massachusetts Press, 2000), 1.
2 For a commentary by Bruce on the importance of the past for contemporary struggles, see the essays from the conference "'To Remember Is to Resist': 40 Years of Sport and Social Change, 1968–2008," at University of Toronto (2008), published in the January 2010 *Sport in Society* special issue. See particularly, Bruce Kidd, "Epilogue: The Struggles Must Continue," *Sport in Society* 13, no. 1 (January 2010): 157–65.
3 Kidd, "Epilogue." Over a long and productive career Bruce Kidd has linked engaged scholarship and activism, helping Canadians and people throughout the world in their struggles to experience physically active and healthy lives and to understand values and visions for sport and physical activity that have existed and still exist. Reflecting on forty years of human-rights struggles and the role of sport as a site for positive social change, Bruce identifies the importance of the past to contemporary struggles, stating, "It is also clear that a shared, critical understanding of the history of such struggles can contribute significantly to effective activism. Such knowledge has not always been available for those on the front lines" (157).

4 Bruce Kidd, "Sport, Legacy and Sustainability: Is It Worth It?," University of British Columbia Chan Centre (18 March 2010). http://www.chancentre.com/whats-on/ sport-society-sport-legacy-sustainability-bruce-kidd-and-guests.

5 For a good overview and critique, see Brian Wilson, "Reflections on Sport, Carbon Neutrality, and Ecological Modernization," in D. Andrews and M. Silk (Eds.), *Sport and Neo-liberalism* (Philadelphia: Temple University Press, 2012). See also Robert R. Archibald, *A Place to Remember: Using History to Build Community.* (Walnut Creek, CA: Alta Mira Press, 1999). Archibald conceives of sustainability as consisting of multiple components in balance to produce human happiness. He sees it as "not just a principle of environmentally sound economic development but also a vision of the future in which people and communities are nurtured, supported, and safeguarded" (130).

6 See, for example, Johann Guts Muths, *Gymnastics for Youth*, trans. C.G. Salzman (London: J. Johnston, 1800); Sir John Sinclair, *The Code of Health and Longevity* (London: McMillan, 1818); Seward C. Staley, *The Curriculum in Sports* (Philadelphia: W.B. Saunders, 1935), 12–13.

7 To borrow a phrase from Vice-President Al Gore's film of the same name. The list of negative effects goes on and on: polluted air affecting the lungs of athletes and spectators; competitive seasons changed by too much or too little rain; ozone depletion and damaging sunrays; insects invading woods and grasses used for sport; toxic run-offs from chemicals used in greens maintenance; artificial turfs to be relegated, somewhere and at some time, to a garbage dump alongside all of the tons of sports shoes and other sports paraphernalia that will not decompose easily or without toxic effect; and the hormones and other substances to enhance athletic performance, travelling through bodies to find their way into our water and fish.

8 *Sports Illustrated*, 12 March 2007. The U.S. Natural Resources Defense Council responded to this SI issue with a press release hailing it "groundbreaking." NDRC Press Release, "Global Warming Hits *Sports Illustrated* Cover: Groundbreaking Feature Shows Impacts, Solutions, Action," 8 March 2007, http://www.nrdc.org/ media/2007/070308a.asp.[stet]

9 This was revealed, for example, in two special issues published by the *Journal of Sport and Social Issues*, as the journal's guest editors posed the question, "What happens when sport meets nature?" See Diana Mincyte, Monica J. Casper, and C.L. Cole, "Sports, Environmentalism, Land Use, and Urban Development," *Journal of Sport and Social Issues* 33, no. 2 (May 2009): 104; and Mincyte, Casper, and Cole, "Bodies of Nature: Politics of Wilderness, Recreation, and Technology," *Journal of Sport and Social Issues* 33, no. 3 (August 2009). For a fascinating take on the contradictions of sport and environmentalism see Spencer Schaffner, "Environmental Sporting: Birding at Superfund Sites, Landfills, and Sewage Ponds," *Journal of Sport and Social Issues* 33, no. 3 (August 2009): 206–28.

10 Regarding sport, for example see J. Maguire, G. Jarvie, L. Mansfield, and J. Bradley, "Sport, the Environment, and 'Green' Issues," in *Sport Worlds: A Sociological Perspective* (Champaign, IL: Human Kinetics, 2001), 83–97; Grant Jarvie, "Sport and the Environment," in Maguire, Jarvie, Mansfield, and Bradley, *Sport, Culture, and Society: An Introduction* (Routledge, 2006), 237–252.

11 International Olympic Committee, *Olympic Charter* (7 July 2007) (Lausanne, 2007), 15; see also Hart Cantelon and Michael Letters, "The Making of the IOC Environmental Policy as the Third Dimension of the Olympic Movement," *International Review for the Sociology of Sport* 35, no. 3 (2000): 294–308.

12 Some 178 governments adopted Agenda 21, the Rio Declaration on Environment and Development, and the Statement of Principles for the Sustainable Management of Forests at the United Nations Conference on Environment and Development (UNCED) held in Rio de Janeiro, Brazil, 3–14 June 1992, http://www.un.org/esa/sustdev/documents/agenda21/index.htm.

13 United Nations Environment Programme, "Sport and Environment," http://www.olympic.org/Documents/Olympism_in_action/Sport_and_Environment/Awards/Rules-and-Regulations-Extended-IOC-Award-For-Sport-and-the-Environment-2013-eng-V2.pdf; See also International Olympic Committee Sport and Environment Commission, http://www.olympic.org/sport-environment-commission.

14 Project Blue Sky, http://www.offsetters.ca/about-us/current-news/2009/11/16/partners-of-2010-winter-games-sign-on-and-collaborate-with-project-blue-sky-to-help-increase-physical-activity-and-reduce-the-carbon-footprint-in-their-communities; http://olympic.ca/2009/07/08/project-blue-sky/

15 For example, Green & Gold, Inc., "Winning Strategies ... Naturally," http://www.youthxchange.net/main/chernushenko.asp; see also David Chernushenko, with Anna van der Kamp and David Stubbs, *Sustainable Sport Management* (Nairobi: United Nations Environment Programme, 2001); David Chernushenko, *Greening Our Games* (Ottawa: Centurion Publishing & Marketing, 1994).

16 Eric Falt, "Sport and the Environment," *Environmental Health Perspectives* 114, no. 5 (May 2006), guest editorial, http://www.ehponline.org/docs/2006/114-5/editorial.html.

17 In 1930, Hamilton became the birthplace of the British Empire (now Commonwealth) Games. Marathon runners have converged in the city annually since 1894 to run a thirty-kilometre road race, Around the Bay, in an event that is older than the famed Boston Marathon. See Nancy B. Bouchier and Ken Cruikshank, "'The Race Circles This Large Bay ... You Could Sure Smell It': Around the Bay – The Promise and Problems of Sport and the Environment in an Industrial City, Hamilton ON, 1894–2008," paper presented to the 11th International Congress of the International Society for the History of Physical Education and Sport, University of Stirling, Scotland, July 2009. On recreation and environmental inequality

generally, see Matthew Klingle, "Fair Play: Outdoor Recreation and Environmental Inequality in Twentieth-Century Seattle," in Andrew C. Isenberg, *The Nature of Cities* (Rochester, NY: University of Rochester Press, 2001), 122–56.

18 On Hamilton and its waterfront see Ken Cruikshank and Nancy B. Bouchier, "Blighted Areas and Obnoxious Industries: Constructing Environmental Inequality on an Industrial Waterfront, Hamilton, Ontario, 1890–1960," *Environmental History* 9 (July 2004): 464–96. For an examination of cities and water pollution see Joel A. Tarr, *The Search for the Ultimate Sink: Urban Pollution in Historical Perspective* (Akron, OH: University of Akron Press, 1996); and Jamie Benidickson, *The Culture of Flushing: A Social and Legal History of Sewage* (Vancouver: UBC Press, 2007).

19 Our research program is not action-research or the by-product of direct engagement and collaboration with an activist community. On the ways in which historians might work to help inform public choices in environmental decision making, and the importance of locality in the process, see Hugh Gorman, "Urban Areas, Environmental Decision Making, and Uses of History to Inform Public Choices," in Martin V. Melosi and Philip V. Scarpino (Eds.), *Public History and the Environment* (Malabar, FL: Krieger Publishing, 2004), 207–24.

20 *The People and the Bay: A History of Hamilton Harbour* (Zach Melnick, director; Yvonne Drebert, producer; Nancy B. Bouchier and Ken Cruikshank, script), Pixel Dust Studios, York, ON: L.R. Wilson Institute for Canadian History, McMaster University, 2007 (47 min.). For a review of the film see Wade Hemsworth, "Harbour Heritage Documented for Posterity: How We Used It and Abused It," *Spectator*, 19 October 2007.

21 On public history generally, see Roy Rosenzweig and David Thelen, *The Presence of the Past: Popular Uses of History in American Life* (New York: Columbia University Press, 1998); L.J. Jordanova, *History in Practice* (London: Hodder Arnold, 2006); Susan Porter Benson, Steven Brier, and Roy Rosenzweig (Eds.), *Presenting the Past: Essays on History and the Public* (Philadelphia: Temple University Press, 1986); and Phyllis K. Leffler and Joseph Brent, *Public and Academic History: A Philosophy and Paradigm* (Malabar, FL: Robert E. Krieger Publishing, 1990).

22 About the ways in which advocacy is deeply embedded in the academic field of environmental history see Martin V. Melosi. "National Council on Public History, President's Annual Address: Public History and the Environment," *Public Historian* 15, no. 4 (Fall 1993): 11–20; and Carolyn Merchant, *Radical Ecology: The Search for a Liveable World*, 2nd ed. (New York: Routledge, 2005). On public history and advocacy see Martin V. Melosi and Philip V. Scarpino (Eds.), *Public History and the Environment* (Malabar, FL: Krieger Publishing, 2004); a compelling argument and analysis is made regarding labour history and advocacy in Craig Heron, "The Labour Historian and Public History," *Labour / Le Travailleur* 45 (Spring 2000): 171–97.

23 Green, *Taking History to Heart*, 11.
24 This work uses surveys and focus groups and is informed by European, American, and Australian studies. See Margaret Conrad, Jocelyn Létourneau, David Northrup, "Canadians and Their Pasts: An Exploration in Historical Consciousness," *Public Historian* 31, no. 1 (February 2009): 32–3; and Gerald Friesen, Del Muise, and David Northrup, "Variations on the Theme of Remembering: A National Survey of How Canadians Use the Past," *Journal of the Canadian Historical Association* 20, no. 1 (2009): 221–47.
25 According to the 2009 Constitution of the Canadian Committee on Public History, an affiliate of the Canadian Historical Association, among other things public history practitioners "make professional use of evidence about the past to address present-day concerns and foster discussions between creators, consumers and users of history. They serve their clients and audiences in diverse ways - by curating museum exhibits, by conserving and interpreting physical legacies of the past (including buildings and archives), by providing policy analysis and research information, for legal and other purposes, by creating films and other media products and other roles and functions," http://www.chashcacommittees-comitesa.ca/public_history/papers.html.
26 Margaret Conrad, "2007 Presidential Address of the CHA: Public History and Its Discontents or History in the Age of Wikipedia," *Journal of the Canadian Historical Association* 18, no. 1 (2007): 26. See also Margaret Conrad, "Towards a Participatory Historical Culture," paper presented to the CHA, Vancouver 2008, http://www.chashcacommittees-comitesa.ca/public_history/papers.html.
27 "Public History in Canada," *The Public Historian* 31, no. 1 (February 2009); regarding the field of sport history, in the spring of 1989 the *Journal of Sport History* announced a commitment to public history with its new section devoted to film, media, and museum reviews. See, for example, Bruce Kidd, "The Making of a Hockey Artifact: A Review of the Hockey Hall of Fame," *Journal of Sport History* 23, no. 3 (Fall 1996): 328–34. We took the opportunity to critically reflect upon our Ontario Workers Arts and Heritage Centre (OWAHC, now WAHC) museum exhibit in "Reflections on Creating Critical Sport History for a Popular Audience: The People and the Bay," *Journal of Sport History* 25, no. 2 (Summer 1998): 312–19, and "The Pictures are Great But the Text Is a Bit of a Downer: Creating Ways of Seeing and the Challenge of Exhibiting Critical History," *Canadian Historical Review* 80, no. 1 (March 1999): 96–113. For other such sport-history reflections see for example "Our Voices in Public History Forum," *Journal of Sport History* 35, no. 3 (Fall 2008): 371–3; Douglas Booth, "Self Reflections on the Centennial History of Surf Lifesaving Australia," 373–92; Murray G. Phillips, "Public History and Sport History: Evaluating Commissioned Histories and Documentaries," 393–410; Mike Cronin, "It's All About Me: Sports History and Television," 411–420; and Doug Brown, "Commentary," 421–8.

28 Archibald, *A Place to Remember.*
29 Ibid., 24–5.
30 Ibid.
31 Kidd, "Epilogue." He writes: "People should work politically where they happen to be located, where they have experience and are respected for what they contribute to a particular community, field, or institution. With such experience and respect, they can gradually build a constituency for change" (160).
32 On Bruce's analysis of the legacy of value-centred sport see his "Muscular Christianity and Value-Centred Sport: The Legacy of Tom Brown in Canada," *International Journal of History of Sport* 23, no. 5 (August 2006): 701–13; and *The Struggle for Canadian Sport* (Toronto: University of Toronto Press, 1996). Echoes of Bruce's call for re-creating the moral basis for sport are evident in the report by Charles Dubin, *The Commission of Inquiry into the Use of Drugs and Banned Practices Intended to Increase Athletic Performance* (Ottawa: Canadian Government Publishing Centre, 1990); and Rob Beamish's "The Dialectic of Modern, High-Performance Sport: Returning to the Dubin Inquiry to Move Forward," found in this volume.
33 Archibald, "Values at the Core," in *A Place to Remember*, 109–34.
34 Cruikshank and Bouchier, "The Pictures Are Great But the Text Is a Bit of a Downer"; see also Nancy B. Bouchier and Ken Cruikshank, *The People and the Bay: A Social and Environmental History of Hamilton Harbour* (forthcoming, University of British Columbia Press).
35 "Our Deceptive Bay," *Spectator*, 17 August 1946.
36 See, for example, Mel Hawkrigg and Bruce Wood, "Fixing Randle Reef: Hamilton Port Authority 'Willing, Consistent.'" *Spectator*, 19 March 2010; Howard Elliott [editor], "Randle Reef Quagmire," *Spectator*, 18 February 2010; "Randle Reef 101," *Spectator*, 10 November 2007.
37 Howard Elliott, managing editor of the *Hamilton Spectator*, gave this startling description of the size of the mass as related to Copps Coliseum during his address to the Bay Area Restoration Council's annual general meeting (10 June 2010) at the Parks Canada Discovery Centre, Hamilton.
38 Tanya Labencki, *An Assessment of Polychlorinated Biphenyls (PCBs) in the Hamilton Harbour Area of Concern (AOC) in Support of the Beneficial Use Impairment (BUI): Restrictions on Fish and Wildlife Consumption*, Hamilton Harbour Remedial Action Plan Office, 2008. On ongoing efforts to deal with this toxic site see Bay Area Restoration Council (BARC), "Contaminated Sediment: Randle Reef," http://www.hamiltonharbour.ca/index.php?page=index&p=current_and_emerging_challenges; "Harper Government Announces Funding to Clean Up Randle Reef in Hamilton Harbour," Environment Canada news release, 18 December 2012, http://ec.gc.ca/default.asp?lang=En&n=976258C6-1&news=9D3DDA9A-EBD2-45BC-BB5A-EF00E61BEEE5.

39 These effects are most evident in certain of the city's neighborhoods, as brought out in the week-long *Hamilton Spectator* series entitled "Code Red," which ran in the week of 10 April 2010, based on research carried out jointly by the *Spectator* and McMaster University researchers. See Howard Elliott [editor], "Code Red: Call to Action," *Spectator*, 10 April 2010; Steve Buist, "*Spec* Report Finds Health, Wealth Worlds Apart in Hamilton," *Spectator*, 10 April 2010; "About the Series," *Spectator*, 8 April 2010; See also www.cleanair.hamilton.ca.

40 The harbour is one of many areas under remediation in the Great Lakes area. See Environment Canada, "Great Lakes Areas of Concern," http://www.ec.gc.ca/raps-pas/; on Hamilton's RAP, see Environment Canada, "Hamilton Harbour Area of Concern," http://www.ec.gc.ca/raps-pas/default.asp?lang=En&n=3F4F0551-1.

41 John D. Hall, Kristin O'Connor, and Joanna Ranieri, "Progress toward Delisting A Great Lakes Area of Concern: The Role of Integrated Research and Monitoring in the Hamilton Harbour Remedial Action Plan," *Environmental Monitoring and Assessment* 113 (2006): 227–43. In 2012 the RAP co-ordinator announced that the delisting of the harbour had been pushed back five years from the scheduled 2015 date. See Richard Leitner, "Hamilton Harbour to Miss Cleanup Goal," *Spectator*, 19 April 2012.

42 BARC is a community not-for-profit group involved in keeping harbour restoration in the public eye and in assessing and promoting projects aimed at cleaning up the harbour. See http://www.hamiltonharbour.ca/.

43 Consisting of eighteen key stakeholder groups including municipal governments, federal and provincial ministries and agencies, area industry, the port authority, conservation groups, the Waterfront Trust, and the Royal Botanical Gardens, http://hamiltonharbour.ca/index.php?page=index&p=bait_stakeholders.

44 On historians and remediation generally, see Craig E. Colten, "Hazardous Wastes and Environmental Remediation," in Martin V. Melosi and Philip V. Scarpino (Eds.), *Public History and the Environment* (Malabar, FL: Krieger Publishing, 2004), 106–24.

45 On the issue of commons, see Garrett Hardin, "The Tragedy of the Commons," *Science* 162, no. 3859 (13 December 1968): 1243–8.

46 One potential site aimed at brownfield reclamation and remediation along the West Harbour. Howard Elliott [editor], "West Harbour Makes Sense," *Spectator*, 17 February 2010, and "West Harbour Stadium Scores with Our Bloggers," *Spectator*, 16 February 2010; Arne Kurpe, "Why Are Taxpayers Being Stuck for Cleanup Cost of Stadium Site?," letter to editor, *Spectator*, 24 March 2010; "Stadium Talks Progress: Facilitator Says City, Ticats Accept Terms of Reference," *Spectator*, 12 June 2010; "Mayor 'Outraged' at Pan Am Spat: Rules for Talks Ok'd after Fiery Meeting," *Spectator*, 8 June 2010; and "Stadium Site Facilitator to Begin Talks," *Spectator*, 25 May 2010.

47 John Kernaghan, "New Ivor Wynne 2015 Finalist: Where Do You Think the New Stadium Should Go?" *Spectator*, 17 January 2009. Of the Confederation site, against which council voted, the article noted: "Though it has been voted off, it might return due to advantages of public land, highway access, waterfront aesthetics, ongoing revenue prospects, symbolic and image value. Disadvantages are odours and dust from industrial areas and the expense of extending water and sewer service."

48 Ken Cruikshank and Nancy B. Bouchier, "'It Doesn't Bother Me ...': Local Neighborhoods, Planners and the Meaning of Spatial Justice in an Industrial City, 1955–2000," in David Blanchon, Jean Gardin, and Sophie Moreau (Eds.), *Justice et Injustices Environmentales* (Paris: Presses Universitaires de Paris Ouest, 2011), 81–97.

49 Ken Cruikshank and Nancy B. Bouchier, "Blighted Areas and Obnoxious Industries: Constructing Environmental Inequality on an Industrial Waterfront, Hamilton, Ontario, 1890–1960," *Environmental History* 9, no. 3 (July 2004): 464–96.

50 "Farm-in-the-Park Already a Hit," *Spectator*, 16 June 1966. "Campsite Opening Caps an Impressive Decade," *Spectator*, 15 June 1970; "Growing Pains at Confederation Park," *Spectator*, 29 May 1980; "Developers Say Region Unfair in Confederation Park Hotel Deal," *Spectator*, 16 March 1984; Suzanne Bourret, "School's in for Summer," *Spectator*, 15 June 1989. On Hamilton Conservation Authority see http://www.conservationhamilton.ca/.

51 As reported in Rob Faulkner and John Kernaghan, "City Council Shortsighted to Reject Park Site: Braley; Council Unlikely to Revisit Park Site: Noise, Odours Limit 'Legacy' Impact," *Spectator*, 15 January 2009.

52 The city had its expressway (now called the Red Hill Parkway) in November 2007. Many of its opponents are still raw from this lost battle, certain aspects of which lingered in the courts for years, including a case by the City against the federal government. Ironically, the opening of the highway – which so many opposed for environmental and health reasons – was marked by the running of the "Road to Hope" race over its freshly paved asphalt. See Terry Cooke, "Red Hill Valley Parkway Saga Over," *Spectator*, 3 November 2007; "Red Hill Valley Parkway Debuts," *Spectator*, 4 November 2007. Walter G. Peace, "Farm, Forest and Freeway: Red Hill Creek Valley, 1950–1998," in *From Mountain to Lake: The Red Hill Creek Valley* (Hamilton, ON: W.L. Griffin Printing, 1998), 214–46; Friends of the Red Hill Valley Archives, http://rhvna.org/forhv/Start_Page.html.

53 Steve House, "City Took All of Red Hill Valley – Why Not Some of Confederation Park?," letter to editor, *Spectator*, 20 January 2009.

54 Faulkner and Kernaghan, "City Council Shortsighted." Nicole MacIntyre, "Council Puts City Back in Games: Spending $60m on Stadium, Velodrome 'a step in the right direction': mayor," *Spectator*, 24 February 2009.

55 Rob Faulker, "Green Space Argument Snowballed," *Spectator*, 14 January 2009; Robert Howard [editor], "Parochialism Wins – Again," *Spectator*, 16 January 2009; Jason Leach, "Perfect Time to Put Our New Stadium Downtown," letter to the editor, *Spectator*, 20 January 2009; Janina Vanderpost, "No Stadium at Confederation Park," letter to the editor, *Spectator*, 22 January 2009; Linda Jacobs, "Leave Confederation as Is, Put Stadium Elsewhere," letter to the editor, *Spectator*, 24 January 2009. The contentious Pan Am stadium debate dragged on for two more years, with the Confederation Park decision often alluded to but never formally reopened. Many observers point to the debate's role in the defeat of the incumbent mayor during the election of 2010. By February 2011, city council had finally voted to refurbish the existing Ivor Wynne Stadium – constructed for the 1930 British Empire Games, and the home of the Hamilton Tiger Cats – rather than construct an entirely new facility. See Emma Reilly, "Ivor Wynne OK: TO2015; Pan Am Stadium Saga Ends as Games Site Approved," *Spectator*, 26 February 2011, A3; Emma Reilly, "DONE DEAL; A Unanimous Council Decides on Ivor Wynne Just in the Nick of Time," *Spectator*, 1 February 2011, A1.

56 Memories of earlier beach-strip expropriations were stirred when the city expropriated and demolished West Harbour homes to make way for a stadium that was never to be. See Hamilton, "Expropriations Act: Notice of Application for Approval to Expropriate Land," advertisement, *Spectator*, 16 June 2010; John Kernaghan, "Expropriation Notices on Pan Am Site Shock Landowners; City Offer 'Peanuts,' Homeowner Says," *Spectator*, 17 June 2010; Florence Houirigan, "Stadium Expropriations a Reminder of Van Wagner's Beach in 1960," letter to the editor, *Spectator*, 18 June 2010.

57 Archibald, *A Place to Remember*, 133.

58 Also known as the McMaster Eco-Research Program for Hamilton Harbour, headed by the political scientist Mark Sproule-Jones, the V.K. Copps Chair in Urban Studies. The Canadian Tri-Council (Medical Research Council, Naturals Sciences and Engineering Research Council, and the Social Sciences and Humanities Research Council of Canada) had awarded the program $2.1 millon over three years, before we each came to McMaster and became involved. On this project see Ecowise, *McMaster Eco-Research Program for Hamilton Harbour: Final Report, 1993–1996* (Hamilton, ON: McMaster University, 1996); Mark McNeil, "Eco-Research Program Was Well Worth Effort," *Spectator*, 17 April 1996, B.3; Mark Sproule-Jones, *Restoration of the Great Lakes: Promises, Practices, Performances* (Vancouver: UBC Press, 2002).

59 Historians Craig Heron and Franca Iacovetta, who were at York University when author Ken Cruikshank was there, invited us to present the exhibit. Both of us went on to serve as members of the education and exhibition committees of the centre, and Ken eventually served on its executive. OWAHC has been renamed the Workers Arts and Heritage Centre (WAHC).

60 For the Museum exhibition catalogue, see Nancy B. Bouchier and Ken Cruikshank, *The People and the Bay: A Popular History of Hamilton Harbour* (Hamilton: Ontario Workers Arts and Heritage Centre, 1997); John Mahoney, "On the Beach: Retrospective on Hamilton Bay a Definite Must-See for Everyone"; "Topless? Hey, Cover Your Knees!" *Spectator*, 8 August 1997, B.12.FR; Michael Mercier, "Review," *Urban History Review* 27 (1998): 54–6.

61 Cruikshank and Bouchier, "The Pictures Are Great."

62 Before the article's publication one anonymous reviewer provided us with unexpected insight into the importance of nature, place, and memory, in noting how our paper had evoked good memories of the area; the reviewer's memories were gained not by living there but through the experience of running (presumably in competition) through this nature parkland. See Nancy B. Bouchier and Ken Cruikshank, "The War on the Squatters, 1920–1940: Hamilton's Boathouse Community and the Re-Creation of Recreation on Burlington Bay," *Labour / Le Travail* 51 (Spring, 2003): 9–46.

63 The proposed nature park in the West Harbour area, as envisaged by planners and local boosters, would provide a space of "unsullied nature" to act as "the lungs of the city," protected from the reach of urban and industrial developers. It would also give tourists – such as people attending the Hamilton's 1930 British Empire Games – an aesthetic experience that differed markedly from the not-so-pleasant sights and smells emanating from the city's sewer outlets and waterfront factories. See Nicholas Terpstra, "Local Politics and Local Planning: A Case Study of Hamilton, Ontario, 1915–1930," *Urban History Review / Revue d'Histoire Urbaine* 19, no. 2 (October 1985): 121; and John C. Best, *Thomas Baker McQuesten: Public Works, Politics, and Imagination* (Hamilton, ON: Corinth Press, 1991), especially ch. 5, "A Bachelor ... Whose Bride Is the City Parks System," 51–68.

64 The area's designation as a bird sanctuary and nature preserve protected the hunting rights of some people, for example, bona fide owners of the land adjoining the marsh, but they needed a special permit from authorities in Toronto.

65 For a review of this exhibit, see Jeff Mahoney, "Art Can Turn You Inside Out," *Spectator*, 23 July 2008.

66 Nora Hutchinson, curator, *The Urban Moorings Project* (Hamilton: Hamilton Artists Inc., 2008).

67 John Terpstra, "Connecting with Where We Live: The Urban Moorings Project," in *The Urban Moorings Project Catalogue*, 5. Terpstra's *Falling into Place* (Gaspereau Press, 2002) creatively explores the Iroquois Sandbar (Burlington Heights) through poetry and other means.

68 Tÿs Theÿsmeÿer, foreword to *The Urban Moorings Project Catalogue*. On the RBG–arts community collaboration he states, "Partnerships which meld our landscapes with artistic endeavors and moments of reflection are among our most

preferred"(3). This view echoes Robert Archibald's emphasis about the importance of transcendence in the process of building communities.

69 Quintin Zachary Hewlett, "The Urban Moorings Project," 14 June 2008, Progressive Imposition blogspot, http://progressiveimposition.blogspot.ca/2008/06/urban-moorings-project.html.

70 *The Urban Moorings Project*, 15.

71 Ibid., 30.

72 See http://www.torlukasikfoss.com/.

73 Hewlett, "The Urban Moorings Project." In 2011 seven media and performance artists from Hamilton's Factory Media Arts Centre, some of whom were involved in Urban Moorings, launched a second exhibition inspired by the squatters' story. This "psychogeographic exploration" used new media technologies, installation artwork, and live improvisational performances to create a "distinct form of living archive and landscapes." Shantytown: The Squatters (Projection Installation & Performances)," 9 September–14 October 2011, Factory Media Arts Centre, 228 James Street North, Hamilton, Ontario.

74 *The People and the Bay.*

75 On the Wilson Institute's mission to rethink Canadian history within a globalization framework, see http://www.humanities.mcmaster.ca/~history/wilson/index1.html. In 2008–9 Ken Cruikshank embarked on another form of outreach, using the students of his seminar *History 4K06, The People and the Bay: Environment and Environmentalism in Modern North America* to work on a year-long project with senior high-school multimedia students at nearby Westdale Collegiate Institute. They created a series of multimedia materials to support teachers who use the DVD in their classes. Funding for the set-up of this project generously came from a grant from the Network in Canadian History and Environment Initiative (NiCHE).

76 We handed copies of the DVD free to educational institutions and libraries in the Hamilton Wentworth region. Public demand prompted us to make it available for purchase through the McMaster University bookstore.

77 Mitchell Smyth, "The Battle to Unchain Hamilton Bay," *Spectator*, 25 August 1971.

78 *The People and the Bay*, 43:49.

79 Nancy B. Bouchier and Ken Cruikshank, "Remembering the Struggle for the Environment: Hamilton's Lax Lands / Bayfront Park, 1950s–2008," *Left History* 1, no. 13 (Spring/Summer 2008): 106–28. In 2008 the Bay Area Restoration Council gave us the Recognition Award for *The People and the Bay* documentary.

80 Hamilton has a long tradition of creating parks from garbage and brownfields sites. Eastwood Park, in the north end, was created from filling a polluted inlet with "clean" garbage (free of the rotting vegetable matter that would attract rodents).

The revetment wall at the park was the site of the 1930 British Empire Games' diving competition. See Nancy Bouchier and Ken Cruikshank, "Abandoning Nature: Swimming Pools and Clean, Healthy Recreation in Hamilton, Ontario, c. 1930s–1950s," *Canadian Bulletin of Medical History* 28, no. 2 (2011): 315–37.

81 In September 2011 the Bay Area Restoration Council's Annual Community Workshop focused on the Randle Reef remediation project, with representatives from Environment Canada, McMaster University, and Hamilton Harbour's Remedial Action Plan providing updates on the status of the project, which some people fear will never be carried out in their lifetime. See Howard Elliott (editor), "Randle Reef Quagmire," *Spectator*, 18 February 2010, A08; Howard Elliott (editor), "Randle Reef Frustration," *Spectator*, 26 November 2009, A12; "Learn More about $90m Harbour Cleanup Plan," *Spectator*, 15 November 2008, A04.

82 These plaques were funded by a cash prize from the Dubai International Award for Best Practices to Improve the Living Environment; http://www.hamilton.ca/ProjectsInitiatives/V2020/Awards/Dubai+Waterfront+Trail+Project.htm.

83 Smyth, "The Battle to Unchain Hamilton Bay."

84 Originally produced for the 1992 Reading the Water project, the eighteen-foot painting *Macassa, Hamilton Harbour, Burlington Bay* was re-shown at the You Me Gallery from 11 May to 23 June 2007, 330 James Street North, Hamilton.

85 Cees van Gemerden, *No Trespassing*, the Photography Gallery, Toronto Harbourfront (15 December-28 January 1990). He used seventy-eight photographs of Hamilton's waterfront and text from environmental news stories world-wide, local news on Hamilton's harbour, and personal notes. One of the photographs from the exhibit is reproduced in Alexander Wilson's introduction to his *Culture of Nature: North American Landscape from Disney to Exxon Valdez* (Toronto: University of Toronto Press, 1991), 6; on other activist work by the artist and other activists in Hamilton's arts community, see Elane Hujer, "Artist's Red Hill Photo Elicits Passionate Response," *Spectator*, 3 March 2004, G11; "Mayor Doesn't Speak for Me," letter to the editor, *Spectator*, 10 May 2002, A14; Jeff Mahoney, "The Art of Serving Others; Can I Help You? Deals Frankly with a Group of Workers We Take for Granted," *Spectator*, 18 January 2001, B03; Jeff Mahoney, "Focussing on the Big Picture," *Spectator*, 5 October 2000, D14; Anne Marie Todkill, "Reading the Times," *Canadian Medical Association Journal* 161, no. 10 (16 November 1999): 1299–300.

86 We examine his works in more depth and in the context of other forms of photographic documentation of the bay in "Remembering the Struggle for the Environment."

87 Cees van Gemerden, *Trespassing – More Power Anyone?*, (Bay Area) Photographers Show, Burlington Cultural Centre (24 May–26 July 1992). This exhibit has been re-shown a number of times, most recently at the You Me Gallery, 11 May–23 June 2007, 330 James Street North, Hamilton.

88 Before the Bayfront Park's construction could begin, some twenty thousand tonnes of industrial waste and contaminated soil had first to be removed because the soil was found to contain high levels of lead, cadmium, and other chemical toxins. Ministry of the Environment regulations required that each truckload of toxic fill removed from the Lax land site had to be covered with a tarpaulin to prevent materials from spilling, and truck tires had to be decontaminated before they could leave the area. See Canviro Consultants and Bar Environmental prepared for City of Hamilton, *Remediation Plan for the Former Lax Property*, 17 March 1989, 1.

89 Emilla Casella, "Province Comes Up with Lax Land Cash," *Spectator,* 11 October 1991, A1.

90 Donald L. Hardesty, "Issues in Preserving Toxic Wastes as Heritage Sites," *The Public Historian* 23 (Spring 2001): 20.

12 Where History Meets Biography: Towards a Public Sociology of Sport

PETER DONNELLY AND MICHAEL ATKINSON

To ignore the capacity of sport to assist with social change is not an option, particularly for students, teachers and researchers of sport, all of whom have the capacity and the platform to act as public intellectuals.[1]

In a postscript to *Urban Outcasts*, Löic Wacquant addressed his failure to comment on the riots that occurred in late 2005 in the *banlieues* surrounding major French cities: "the pace of research is not that of media commentary or public action, and … the task of social science is not to surf the wave of current events, but to bring to light the durable mechanisms that produce them."[2] Although Wacquant is, to a great extent, correct, social scientists are increasingly being called upon to engage in research and policy work that directly address current problems and issues. In addition, many social scientists feel a responsibility to provide informed commentary on current events, especially when a lack of critical media coverage results in "news by press release" or a reflexive default to neo-liberal points of view. Bruce Kidd epitomizes the critical social scientist as public intellectual, unfailingly ready to offer informed and thoughtful views to media while he is engaged in academic research and advocacy work. This chapter celebrates his work by exploring the roots of a critical and public sociology of sport – from Marx to Mills to Burawoy. We argue, along with C. Wright Mills,[3] Michael Burawoy, and Alan Ingham, that sociological knowledge is *practical* knowledge, rooted in understanding the connections between history, biography, and social structure. As Bourdieu noted, "surely, Sociology would not be worth an hour's trouble … if it did not give itself the job of restoring to people the meaning of their actions."[4] In reviewing the social changes that have resulted from selected practical sport sociological knowledge, we argue that sociologists of sport have a dual responsibility – "to bring to light the durable mechanisms" *and* "to surf the wave of current events."

In the following, we place public sociology in context by reviewing some old debates and crucial struggles in sociology and the sociology of sport, define public sociology and examine its place in the sociology of sport, and consider some of the contemporary barriers to achieving a public sociology of sport.

Old Debates, Crucial Struggles

Wacquant's concerns regarding the cultivation of practical sociological knowledge are among the most recent iterations of a long-standing debate in the social sciences.[5] The emergence of the sociology of sport in North America in the 1960s and 1970s, for example, coincided with a tempestuous period of debate: should sociology be objective or subjective, value laden or value free, normative or non-normative? The debates were triggered in the United States by the emergence of what Burawoy calls a more "engaged" sociology.[6] While Becker asked, "Whose side are we on?" Gouldner proclaimed "the sociologist as partisan."[7] In the sociology of sport the debate soon morphed into a conflict between basic or pure (a value-laden term) social research and applied social research, the latter implying and being demeaned as an inferior and/or managerialist research approach.

Those debates have re-emerged in new ways at various times during the approximately forty-five-year history of the sociology of sport in North America. For example, in his 1990 presidential address at the North American Society for the Sociology of Sport (NASSS) in Denver, Howard Nixon reviewed the then-current controversies in sociology and the sociology of sport over the issue of relevance when he challenged the audience to engage in a "sport sociology that matters."[8] In the first decades of the twenty-first century sociologists are still struggling to relate the craft of sociology to the even more tenuous field of policy and practice. McDonald asked, in his reflexive essay about research and activism around an anti-racism campaign for the sport of cricket, "Is it possible to reconcile a commitment to progressive political change with sound sociological scholarship, or is the concept of academic integrity itself politically charged?"[9] The struggle implied in this question is reiterated in various ways. For example, St Louis asked, "Is it possible, or even desirable, to build a form of (sport) sociological understanding that combines conceptual precision and analytical rigor with an oppositional value agenda and political commitment?"[10]

McDonald distinguishes two approaches to combining academic research with a political agenda – the moralistic and the radical: "Moralistic research collapses the boundaries between research and activism. Researchers are involved in political struggles using their research as a political weapon to secure political goals. Little attention is paid to the conventions of sound scholarly habits, which are dismissed anyway as elitist and bogus, as the aim of the research is to support the attainment of immediate political goals."[11] Arguing that critical social research maintains those "sound scholarly habits," McDonald notes, "The radical approach is best understood as a politicised application of critical social research ... unlike moralistic social research, the radical approach recognises the distinction between political intervention and political activism."[12]

In an era when few consider any of the sciences to be entirely value free, objective, apolitical, or disinterested, the question becomes one of balance, balance between "socio-political and practical involvement and socio-political and practical detachment."[13] Marxists might contend that the task has always been to achieve "a form of interventionist scholarship capable of coherently combining explanatory and prescriptive commitments."[14] Even where research is specifically *applied*, as Ingham and Donnelly argued some twenty years ago, "to revive old debates about objective/subjective, value laden / value free, normative / non-normative sociology is to miss the point. Practical sociologists recognize that application is an act of political involvement that cannot be performed by either objectivistic or sardonic observers of the human condition."[15]

Given contemporary social, political, and material conditions of knowledge production, the most important question for public and practical sociologists is, we believe, whose knowledge counts? "Whose expertise counts in the political process?"[16] Do we want our knowledge being produced for the highest bidder – tailored to the demands of the highest bidder? The (tenured) university-based scholar is able to provide a relative level of independence that may not be available to consulting firms and others who depend financially on providing requisite answers to those seeking one form of knowledge or another. Jarvie reminds us not only of the range of opportunities available to independent or public scholars to disseminate their work ("the lecture platform, the pamphlet, the radio, the interview, the internet, the research newsletter, the guest lecture, the letter to the newspaper open to us and not others"), but also of the various forms of intervention available ("legislation, policy, writing, investigating, uncovering silences, pressure groups, social forums, campaigns and activism, re-allocation of resources and not accepting injustices in sport").[17]

The most "political" act in knowledge production is interpretation, and an example is instructive. Several academic studies, and studies commissioned by school sport organizations and sometimes by the corporate sector, show that a significant number of business executives had played inter-school sports.[18] The primary interpretation offered is that "the road to the board room leads through the locker room," and that the lessons learned in sports are correlated with occupational attainment and prestige.[19] Only scholars with a relative degree of independence are likely to offer a social reproduction interpretation, pointing out that corporate executives hail predominantly from a social-class position that enjoys both the highest levels of sport participation and the highest levels of occupational prestige; in fact, in many of the better private schools, participation in school sports is a requirement. Such scholars may further point out that the same individuals who advocate reduced taxes and reduced public spending – which often has the consequence of reducing access to parks, playgrounds, and sports facilities and programs and has led to cuts in school sport programs – insist upon access to sports for their own children, through private schools, facilities, lessons, and so on. The road to the boardroom may lead through the locker room, but that does not necessarily democratize access to the boardroom.

For all scientists, from nuclear scientists to social scientists, it is necessary to ask where our academic responsibilities end. "Crafts" of data collection are prescribed in all fields of science, and those who are not engaged in moralistic research or in generating the expedient knowledge of the "consultocracy" will follow the data. Disinterest may apply to data collection (though there is room for much debate on this issue) but certainly not to the consequences of the findings. The craft of public and practical sociology combines rigour, ethics, and honesty in the research process with an ongoing responsibility for the widespread dissemination of findings, and taking responsibility for the consequences of those findings. The emergence or re-emergence of public sociology is just another reminder that this responsibility involves speaking truth to power.

Emergence and Re-emergence of Public Sociology

It is difficult to commence any discussion of public sociology without reference to Karl Marx. Paolucci notes that the very idea of public sociology rings with Marxist tones and sentiments, and Calhoun's review of public sociology clearly acknowledges Marx as the very first public sociologist.[20] Neilson's analysis of the genealogy of public sociology systematically unpacks Marx's influence on the enterprise of public sociology. He quite accurately claims that, following McLung Lee's and Coleman's respective calls for a public sociology in the United States during the 1970s and 1980s, the enterprise became synonymous with Marxism to varying degrees, to the extent that the terms *Marxism* and *public sociology* are now practically interchangeable.[21] Without inspecting the many contours, striations, and flows of Marxist thought in contemporary public sociology, suffice it to say that a Marxist sensitivity to laying bare the structured systems of inequality, the modes of physical exploitation and ideological domination, the need to apply sociological theory for the "public good," and the engagement with real utopias in the research act, all figure prominently in the public sociologist's mind.

While Marx lives on in the spirit of public sociology as a practical matter, genealogical accounts of public sociology cannot ignore the foundational role of C. Wright Mills's thinking on the practice of theorizing private troubles as public issues.[22] From Mills's perspective, public sociologists are people who employ the sociological imagination to think away from the familiar "waves" of daily life and see the larger social forces, patterns, and trends that create possibilities or constraints for, and thus articulate, human existence. Such is the process of conceptualizing everyday life beyond the local, beyond the everyday. Seeing beyond the everyday must also extend, as a matter of self-reflexivity and engaged criticism, with publics – to think ourselves away from our own complacent, and in some cases far more detached and comfortable, roles within our institutions, as "critics without claws."[23] According to Aronowitz, "Mills was aware that to reach beyond the audience of professional social scientists he is obliged to employ a [mindset and] rhetoric that, as much as possible, stays within natural, even colloquial [thinking and] language. Addressing the general reader as well as his diminishing audience of academic colleagues, Mills conveyed often difficult and theoretically sophisticated concepts in plain, but often visual prose, described by one critic as 'muscular.'"[24]

Following former presidents of the American Sociological Association (ASA) Peter Rossi (1980) and William Foote Whyte (1981) in their calls for more relevance in sociology, Herbert Gans arguably coined the term *public sociology* in the late 1980s as part of a burgeoning Marxist-Millsian-inspired movement.[25] While French public intellectuals, including Pierre Bourdieu and Michel Foucault, were enticing sociologists to engage in a brand of critical sociology, and as British sociologist Anthony Giddens moved towards his own version of public intellectualism, the North American collective public-sociology oeuvre was summarized by Gans, who defined a public sociologist as "a public intellectual who applies sociological ideas and findings to social (defined broadly) issues about which sociology (also defined broadly) has something to say." Public sociologists are different from the garden variety of public intellectuals in that the latter "comment on whatever matters show up on the public agenda; public sociologists do so only on issues to which they apply their sociological insights and findings."[26] Gans argues that when sociologists become knowledgeable about social problems, we can be "particularly useful in debunking the conventional wisdom and popular myths (e.g., that teenage pregnancy is a popular cause of poverty)."[27] The subsequent definitional and promotional work of Michael Burawoy would dramatically shift debates about our new role as public intellectuals.

In his personal statement prior to his election as ASA president in 2004, Michael Burawoy defined public sociology:

> As mirror and conscience of society, sociology must define, promote and inform public debate about deepening class and racial inequalities, new gender regimes, environmental degradation, market fundamentalism, state and non-state violence. I believe that the world needs *public sociology* – a sociology that transcends the academy – more than ever. Our potential publics are multiple, ranging from media audiences to policy makers, from silenced minorities to social movements. They are local, global, and national.
>
> As public sociology stimulates debate in all these contexts, it inspires and revitalizes our discipline. In return, theory and research give legitimacy, direction, and substance to public sociology. Teaching is equally central to public sociology: students are our first public for they carry sociology into all walks of life. Finally, the critical imagination, exposing the gap between what is and what could be, infuses values into public sociology to remind us that the world could be different.[28]

Burawoy's view of sociologists as a mirror and conscience of society has them deeply engaged in moral and ethical debates and venturing far beyond a banal and culturally detached sociology of "social facts." His is a humanistic, moral, and democratically socialist vision of sociological research that critically engages with real utopias and promotes understandings of how the world might be a better place. Burawoy argues that a public sociology offers "a vision of socialism that places human society, or social humanity[,] at its organizing center, a vision that was central to Marx but that was too often lost before it was again picked up by Gramsci and Polanyi. If public sociology is to have a progressive impact it will have to hold itself continuously accountable to some such vision of democratic socialism."[29]

Other sociologists' connections with and extensions of public sociology are worth noting. David Riesman's seminal book *The Lonely Crowd* is, to this day, among the most widely celebrated public sociological accounts of lived experience.[30] Robert Blauner's *Racial Oppression in America* and Arlie Hochschild's *The Managed Heart* were both path-breaking public sociological texts illustrating the enduring politics of race and gender in American society.[31] Shortly thereafter, Mark Smith re-investigated debates over the political and interventionist purpose of sociology in *Social Science in the Crucible: The American Debate over Objectivity and Purpose, 1918–1941.*[32] Robert Bellah's *Habits of the Heart* and Ben Agger's *Public Sociology: From Social Facts to Literary Acts* equally call for a sociology that addresses major public issues.[33] Mitch Duneier's *Sidewalk* is perhaps the most critically acclaimed public sociological account of the effects of structural inequality on ethnic minorities, widely praised even by sceptics of the public sociological enterprise.[34] Sudhi Venkatesh's *Gang Leader for a Day: A Rogue Sociologist Crosses the Line* has received similar critical attention for its brashly "public" essence.[35] We might do well to see the public sociological nature of other works, including Dorothy Smith's account of the politics of knowledge production and dissemination in *The Everyday World as Problematic*, Paulo Freire's treatise on informal education in his *Pedagogy of the Oppressed*, and Alain Touraine's research on collective social movements, symbolized by his *Return of the Actor*.[36]

Public Sociology and the Sociology of Sport

Bruce Kidd's personal and professional activism as a sports scholar is indeed dialogical with a recently reinvigorated tradition of engaging in "public sociology." Perhaps more than most colleagues in our field, Bruce Kidd has not only championed the ideology of an interventionist, praxis-oriented, public sociology of sport, but he has translated that ideology into concatenated practice. As such, his work embodies a brand of critical, public sociology for which colleagues in our field have called during the last three decades.[37] For example, Nixon's call for a more relevant sociology of sport was preceded, in 1983, by Gruneau's *Class, Sports, and Social Development*, Whannel's *Blowing the Whistle: The Politics of Sport*, and Morgan's article in the *Journal of Sport and Social Issues* titled "Toward a Critical Theory of Sport"; these authors simultaneously lamented the lack of theoretical diversity, focus, or interventionist thrust of so-called critical or practical sport studies.[38] However, Ben Carrington reminds us that "cultural studies has been engaged in precisely such a project of critical, interventionist, intellectual work [as is being summoned now in calls for a public sociology], grounded in carefully constructed and systematically developed case studies for over 50 years now."[39] Although some of that work has been carried out in the sociology of sport, Carrington was constrained to call for "the renewal of a critical public sociology of sport that draws upon and extends the cultural studies tradition of committed and engaged scholarship."[40]

Nearly three decades later, scores of critical research efforts are evident in journals of sport and physical culture, and contour the situated analyses of the geo-political relevance of sport, exercise, and leisure. Although neither mutually exclusive nor exhaustive, the critical race theories, queer theories, feminist theories, (new) media theories, post-colonial theories, post-structural theories, Marxist or neo-Marxist and other political economic theories, existentialist theories, actor-network theories, critical pedagogy theories, identity-crisis theories, intersectionality theories, globalization and cultural fragmentation theories, risk theories, new social movement theories, environmentalist theories, victimologies, post-modern theories, figurational theory, theories of consumption, and a range of theories loosely collated as cultural studies are woven into so-called interventionist research on sports, leisure and health cultures, and their structures and systems of representation.

Singularly and collectively, scholars working with and through strands of critical research expose the emancipating, constraining, humanistic, frustrating, oppressive, progressive, and connecting aspects of physical culture around the world. Here, there is immense potential to articulate the impacts of inequality and injustice in sport and leisure contexts, and for scholars to help direct inter-institutional policymaking. Consider some of the dominant and emerging topic areas examined within critical sociology of sport research: gender, race, and class inequality in sport; cultural intolerance in sport; exploitation and violence in sport; the hyper-capitalist consumption of sport spectacles; new social movements in sport; sporting neo-liberalisms; critical sports pedagogy; the techno-scientizing of contemporary sport and physical education; bioethics in sport; the economic and cultural impacts of sport mega-events; sport and globalization; sport and trans-national migration; sport for or as international development; human rights in sport; and environmental issues in sport.

At times, however, one must pause to ask whether the critical socio-cultural studies of sport and physical activity (situated in the above contexts) rest on their own intellectual laurels – emerging far too often as an exercise in the philosophical reading of physical culture, power within social formations, or hegemonic representations of moving bodies and identities, and too infrequently as a concerted and unapologetic ritual of transformative praxis. Critical theories, in their most spirited manifestation, attend to and underscore the politics, problems, and possibilities of research as a lever of engaged praxis – as Tomlinson comments, a "praxis in both the sense that human agents are the architects of the world that they inhabit, and the sense that such agents can become the architects of renewal, reform and change."[41] Critical theorizing, from this perspective, is more than the deployment of acerbic thought, proffered discourse on the inequities of cultural domination, a vivisection of structured inequality, or a disembodied rhetoric demanding social change. Critical theory and the research it inspires must be a vehicle of engaged, committed, irreverent, and passionately charged interventionist praxis.

Even critics from outside the academy have identified the failure to launch a public sociology of sport, at least in the United States. For example, Dave Zirin refers to the "frustration, that a variety of people in the field and I share, that the work needs to be more relevant, more accessible, more *public*."[42] Fortunately, for those serious about pursuing a model of engaged, public activism, encouragement abounds in a growing body of literature documenting the history and potential relevance of sociology as praxis. At a time and in a context of reflection on Bruce Kidd's contribution to the public sociology of sport, and being mindful of Luker's comment that sociology risks its future in the academy by continuing to downplay the role of public sociology, we find good reason to review the promises and prospects of public sociology and the pursuit of praxis.[43]

Sociology of Sport: Making a Difference

While there are numerous practical examples of sociologists of sport engaging directly with social issues at local, national, and international levels – ranging from Bruce Kidd's direct interventions with various levels of government, to Alan Ingham's, Bruce Kidd's, George Sage's, and Kim Schimmel's various involvements with regard to municipal stadia construction and/or hosting mega events, to numerous interventions (from Roscoe Brown to Jay Coakley) with regard to race relations in North American sport – the following examples have been organized to capture some of the larger categories in which sociologically informed research has either contributed to or is contributing to larger public debates, or has actually resulted in progressive social changes. These include (1) systematic data collection, (2) combating notions of sport as the "universal panacea," and (3) sport, equity, and social reproduction.[44] The examples also support Ingham and Donnelly's argument that all sociological knowledge is practical knowledge; despite their evident effects on social change, many of the examples of research that follow were carried out without any intent to engage in public debates or provoke social change, and without any attempt to make the data available beyond the classroom and the peer academic community.[45]

1. SYSTEMATIC DATA COLLECTION

As a result of the post-modern shift in the sociology of sport, few graduate students study quantitative methods, journal editors often have difficulty finding reviewers for statistically based research, and numerical data have sometimes been demeaned and dismissed as positivist. However, the application of "normal science" by sociologists of sport – observation, problematization, systematic measurement, and interpretation – has led to some of the most striking insights and social changes, particularly with regard to race, class, and gender relations, and it is encouraging to see a recent increase, at least internationally, in the analysis of publicly available statistical data.

(a) **Quotas, stacking, and leadership positions:** Loy and McElvogue's article, published in the *International Review for the Sociology of Sport*, opened the door to a significant body of research and to systematic monitoring and policy changes.[46] The Civil Rights movement in the United States prodded sociologists of sport and some sport journalists to become aware of racial quotas in popular team sports – how many black players on a team, how many black players in action at any particular time. The growing awareness of quotas prompted Loy and McElvogue to observe that black players in American football and baseball were apparently being "stacked" in non-central playing positions, an observation that was confirmed by systematic measurement. Numerous studies in many countries and in different sports (for example, basketball, CFL football, soccer) have followed the method, and the interpretation outlined by Loy and McElvogue.[47]

We argue that, despite the absence of any formal knowledge translation system, knowledge about stacking and the racial stereotyping and somatotyping that underpin the practice eventually became public knowledge, hastened the integration of team sports, and increasingly opened central positions to minority players. Stacking research also led to the observation that leadership positions in team sports (coaches, managers) were occupied primarily by former central-position players (that is, white players).[48] These observations also lent themselves to systematic measurement and eventually to systematic monitoring of the race of individuals hired to leadership positions in North American professional (and university) team sports, to annual report cards,[49] and to changes in league policies (for example, the National Football League's adoption of the "Rooney Rule") in an attempt to ensure non-discrimination in hiring.

The style of distributive research developed from Loy and McElvogue's work was also applied in other contexts. For example, in Canada it was used to assess representation based on regional and language politics, namely francophone under-representation in the National Hockey League[50] and on Canadian national teams, especially Olympic teams.[51] This series of studies showed the significant under-representation of francophones on Canadian Olympic teams before the Montreal Olympics (1976); the achievement of equity in representation – as a result of planning, target setting, and athlete-development programs in Quebec – at the Montreal Olympics; a decline in under-representation following the Montreal Olympics; and a gradual increase towards equity since the 1980s.[52] It should be recognized that the efforts to achieve equity in representation have been due to political and policy interventions in the Canadian sport development system, based on evidence developed in these studies. More recent research focused specifically on language equity in the Canadian sport system.[53]

(b) Negative effects of Title IX on women's positions: The positive influence of Title IX of the Education Amendments to the Civil Rights Act (1972) on women's sport participation in the United States has been widely acknowledged and celebrated. However, the growing prominence of women's sports in educational institutions had an unintended consequence: it was observed that coaching and administrative positions in university sports, formerly held by women, were increasingly being taken over by men. Again, this observation led to systematic recording and measurement by sociologists of sport,[54] and to regular report cards providing data for the recording of longitudinal trends and for the lobbying efforts of organizations such as the Women's Sports Foundation. As with the Racial Report Cards, the gender of individuals hired to coaching and administrative positions is now closely monitored. Such monitoring extended to Canada, where there have been occasional (although not yet systematic) attempts to determine the number of women in coaching and administrative positions in sport.[55] Following the International Olympic Committee's (1994) proclamation of increasing quotas for women's representation among its own membership, and among the national Olympic committees and international [sport] federations, these are also monitored regularly by researchers in the Centre for Olympic Studies Research at Loughborough University.[56] Although women are far from achieving equity in sport leadership positions, and the IOC quotas have generally not been achieved, it would be a mistake to assume that evidence-based lobbying, regular monitoring, and the establishment of quotas have not led to an increase in women's leadership positions in sport.

(c) **Media representations (such as gender, race or ethnicity, disability, and body image):** With the growth of feminist sociologies of sport during the 1980s an unsettling awareness developed of the role played by sports media in reproducing gender relations. By 1990, sociologists were systematically measuring and cataloguing[57] both the quantity (for example, under-representation and marginalization) of the coverage of women's sports and women athletes in the sports media,[58] and the quality (for example, sexualization and trivialization) of the coverage of women's sports and women athletes in the sports media.[59] During this period, and at least in part because of an evidence-based critique of limited coverage, the quantity of coverage has increased for gender-appropriate sports, and for women athletes and women's sports at major international events such as the Olympics, but male professional sports still command disproportionate amounts of sports media time and space. The quality of coverage has been amenable to change when sports media take note of the criticism of asymmetrical coverage, develop policies regarding more equitable coverage, and train staff accordingly (for example, CBC's television coverage of the Sydney 2000 Olympics).[60] Similar, though far more limited, research attention has been paid to sports media representations of race or ethnicity and disability;[61] there is some evidence of media sensitization to criticism of stereotypical coverage, and, in the United States, several media commentators have lost their positions because of on-air racially inappropriate comments. However, stereo-typical comments about, for example, the "natural athleticism" of athletes of African heritage are still widespread in media coverage of sports such as international soccer, track and field, and distance running.

(d) Sports injuries (frequency and representation): Systematic data collection relating to sports injuries is more recent in the sociology of sport. There are two main, and related, research approaches: the first, associated with the sociology of medicine, concerns the culture of risk in sports, the high frequency of injuries, and the delays in implementing injury-reducing procedures, equipment, and policies; the second concerns masculinity and injury, and the media and cultural representation of sport injuries. It is becoming more and more difficult for football and ice hockey teams, leagues, or federations to ignore research findings relating to, for example, concussion or longevity, or to avoid rule changes to increase the safety of youth participants.[62]

2. COMBATING NOTIONS OF SPORT AS THE UNIVERSAL PANACEA

Athletes and former athletes often hold an unwavering belief in the value of "sport for good." In the early days of the sociology of sport in North America many sociologists of sport were athletes or former athletes who became "evangelist[s] for exercise," using their research to "find support for the so-called social development objectives of physical education."[63] Following the critical and cultural shifts in the field, it became increasingly apparent that "sport" was a social construction, in many ways a tabula rasa upon which a wide range of meanings could be written. For example, there are numerous cases of sport being used to promote social inclusion, but there are probably as many cases in which sport has been used as a basis for social exclusion.

The early functionalist view of sport is still widely prevalent, often outside the academy in sport organizations and non-governmental organizations, and it has an important influence on government policy in many jurisdictions. The list of claims deriving from the notion of "sport for good" is extensive, including the following:

- sport builds character
- sport helps to prevent crime, disease, and illness
- sport helps to overcome social barriers
- sport is a tool for peace building
- sport is a tool for international development
- sport is a tool for the empowerment of girls and women
- sport builds social capital and community

- public subsidies for professional sport stadia and major games have a positive impact on economic, social, and infrastructural development
- the investment of public funds in high-performance sports in order to win medals will inspire increased participation in grassroots sports

Research results regarding the use of sport to achieve these social goals are often equivocal and inconclusive and, while government agencies (in addition to foundations and private sponsors) frequently fund such initiatives and champion the benefits of sport, they do not fund the initiatives well – suggesting that the ideology of "sport for good" is important but not consistently matched well against existing evidence.

In an era of evidence-based government policy some researchers engaged in the public and practical sociology of sport are committed to the evaluation of research and projects relating to "sport for good." In doing so, they manifest Norbert Elias's characterization of "the sociologist as a destroyer of myths."[64] They point out that it is necessary, first, to define what is meant by *sport* in the specific contexts that claims are being made (such as organized sport, recreational play); second, to determine how appropriate the sport-based initiatives are in the specific context (that is, is it possible to achieve the intended goals using such a sport-based initiative?); third, to carry out research that identifies the conditions and circumstances under which sport *may* be involved in accomplishing specific goals, and understanding how sport was involved in achieving those changes; and fourth, to focus funding on the actual goals being sought (for example, infrastructure improvements, increased participation) rather than expecting those goals to be an indirect consequence of funding other initiatives. This work is helping to add a note of caution to policy initiatives and the claims of "sport for good," and it is spurring systematic attempts to understand how, and under what circumstances, sport initiatives may be related to human development and progressive social change.

3. SPORT, EQUITY, AND SOCIAL REPRODUCTION

Over the past thirty years, sociologists of sport have developed a more and more sophisticated understanding of the ways in which sport is involved in reproducing social relations. This has been most evident in terms of gender relations and the ways in which sport has functioned as a "school" for the reproduction of particular forms of masculinity; in the relationships between sport and social class and the involvement of sport in the reproduction of social classes (see the earlier example of school sport, and "locker room" leading to "board room"); and in terms of understanding the ways sport has been implicated in reproducing race relations, and the disturbing implications of the "genetic fallacy." Most recently, this research is becoming more intersectional and, at the level of public sociology, is beginning to be informed by social-determinants approaches. Initially developed with regard to the social determinants of health (anticipated in the sociology of sport by Alan Ingham),[65] such work has now expanded to increase our understanding of the social determinants of educational attainment, life chances, imprisonment, and, for our purposes, sport participation.

Social equity movements, campaigns, initiatives, and policies have increasingly drawn, directly or indirectly, on such research, often using the types of systematic data collection noted in item (1) above, but also drawing on the more sophisticated, theory-driven interpretation of the ways that sport is implicated in reproducing unequal social relations. Sport-for-all campaigns, and various other initiatives to bring about the democratization of participation, have used such research, often in combination with a human rights perspective (various international declarations of the right to participate in sport and physical activity) in order to increase opportunity. These may range from campaigns for more equitable access to facilities and funding, to subsidization of opportunities for low-income individuals to participate, to initiatives to introduce minority participants to formerly exclusively majority sports.

Sociologists of sport have been responsible for initial data collection and interpretation to the point that some of the phenomena described above are now well understood. With the dissemination of their research, the knowledge becomes "public"; the torch is often picked up by others who are able to continue monitoring, reporting, and campaigning for social change (for example, the Canadian Association for the Advancement of Girls and Women in Sport and Physical Activity, or the Institute for Diversity and Ethics in Sport). In the final analysis, such research ideally leads to new policies, regulations, and cultural change.

Barriers to Achieving a Public Sociology of Sport

During an era when socio-cultural researchers of sport, physical activity, and leisure are challenged to justify their place within emerging kinesiological formations and clusters,[66] when they face daunting pressures from the rhizomatic and neo-liberal "audit cultures" within their universities, when they too often quarrel over the relevance of applied or contract-based research, when they are challenged to demonstrate robust empirical "evidence" to legitimate critical thought, and when their academic contributions remain relatively downplayed by colleagues in any number of parent disciplines (for example, sociology, history, philosophy, economics, politics, education, and psychology), the necessity of *doing* critical theory and public sociology as praxis has never been more real.

Barriers within University Space

Any discussion of public sociology must recognize the social, material, and political conditions of knowledge production and that the barriers to its ongoing genesis are not only conceptual but also structural and cultural within universities. Turner claims that "we do not have public intellectuals because we do not have a social role for them; in sociological terms, we need to [first] look at the availability of social space for intellectuals rather than asking questions about possible inhabitants."[67] Bairner further points out how the late-modern university, as "a prison of measured time," allows for little in the way of public intellectual work when it comes to faculty members' annual report cards and review processes.[68] Those interested in public sociological work face internal pressures from "above" to win research grants, must frequently publish in top-tier academic journals, encounter yearly metrics designed to assess traditional academic roles and responsibilities, and socialize with colleagues expressing little respect for public sociology, all the while maintaining subversive and interventionist orientations that jibe tangentially, at best, with the expansionist and neo-liberal climate in our late-modern, corporate universities. Zirin's suggestions that sociologists of sport "should fight to have a sports and society column in their college paper," "should actively seek to intervene in local sports radio," should submit book proposals "to non-academic, commercial presses," and should continue to integrate the art of blogs into the curriculum are admirable[69] and would certainly advance the agenda of a public sociology of sport, but they fail to take into account the constraining conditions of knowledge production now faced by many in the academy.

Barriers within Faculty or Department Space

Within department space, sociologists of sport find little additional refuge. More than twenty-five years ago Hollands noted that, for those in departments of physical education and/or kinesiology, "the very structure of sport study in North America ironically pairs the social critic [sociologist of sport] with those very individuals in sport science whose professional ideology reinforces ahistorical and functionalist approaches to the subject."[70] Andrews in particular is critical of the transformation of the departments of kinesiology, physical activity, sport and health science, and human movement by neo-positivist health agendas, research protocols, and pushes towards traditionally scientific (and often privately funded) research.[71] There is an ongoing constriction, rather than expansion, of the public intellectual's role in such zones.

However, there are hopeful signs emerging initially in the medical and health sciences, much admired by scholars in the kinesiological sciences. Important moves by granting agencies, academic journals, and academic departments towards the democratization of specialist knowledge are leading to a growth of and requirements to publish in open access journals, requirements to engage in knowledge exchange and translation endeavours and publications (including the use of blogs and social media), and requirements to make research results available to media. Research universities are including community engagement and outreach in their mission statements and, while these initiatives are often slow to translate to the departmental level where more traditional means to achieve tenure and promotion may still apply, these traditions are being challenged more and more. A public sociology of sport is easily accommodated under emerging expectations regarding the democratization of knowledge, myth busting, and community engagement.

Disciplinary and Sub-disciplinary Barriers

There is no shortage of critical analyses and theoretical readings of social problems, and scathing dissections of late market capitalism, neo-liberalism, inequality, homophobia, patriarchy, and racism in the sport studies literature, but scholars mostly remain, in Mills's term, "critics without claws." Perhaps these scholars question the form, purpose, legitimacy, content, and explicit mandate of a public sociology, as do Craig Calhoun, François Neilson, or public sociology's most fervent critics Jonathan Turner and Mathieu Deflem.[72] As Carrington points out, "despite the protestations of [a] small and conservatively minded set of sociologists, the 'cultural turn' in sociology can't be reversed merely by [referring to] work inspired by cultural studies as 'decorative.'"[73]

Even more micro-logically, within sub-disciplinary space (the socio-cultural study of sport, sport policy studies, or the sociology of sport more broadly) questions concerning the fetishization of theoretical readings of social life, non-empirically driven accounts of sport and leisure, and mass media research have done little to engender a public sociological zeitgeist among colleagues. A beleaguered focus on identity politics research[74] and the underwritten preoccupation with representational practices over policy- or change-driven research is potentially crippling the sub-discipline. Couple these trends with a general disregard for translational or knowledge-exchange research efforts, a general lack of unique or accessible theory within the sub-discipline, too few connections or dialogues with other disciplines (that is, political science, economics, history, anthropology, philosophy, classics, media studies and communication, human geography, criminology, and others), and a general treatment of public sociology as a specialist enterprise, and a gloomy forecast for the future of praxis or interventionist research within the sociology of sport is easily predicted. However, despite Maguire and Young's warning that involved and engaged research will result in a loss of "the critical and sceptical character of sociology of sport,"[75] there are signs that a practical, and often public sociology increasingly resonates with those in the field. Also, as this chapter has pointed out, engaged research is still dealing with key sociological issues such as social inequity and democratization, abuses of power (for example, sexual harassment in sport), and community studies of, for example, volunteerism, which are concerned with the development of social capital.

Barriers beyond the "Ivory Tower"

A final set of barriers facing those who wish to engage in a public sociology of sport involves access to the relevant publics for whom the research is relevant (such as athletes, participants, and potential participants in sport and physical activity), and engagement with the mediators to those publics including the media itself, as well as coaches, sport administrators, politicians, and policy staff.

The debunking work that is frequently involved in public sociology may not be well received by those with a vested interest in the status quo. Media outlets that depend on presenting a particular image of professional sports may resist evidence that supports, for example, change to produce more healthy working conditions for athletes; and politicians with a neo-liberal agenda may resist evidence that supports greater public spending on participation in sport and physical activity. Tensions may also exist between academics and policy staff, or practitioners who work in various fields of sport, because of a failure by academics to understand the working conditions and constraints under which these people work. Thus it is important for those who are involved in a public sociology of sport to learn to engage with media; to learn to produce sound bites and more accessible ways to disseminate research; and to begin to understand the working conditions and constraints that affect those who will be tasked with effecting the changes that are recommended as a consequence of new research evidence.[76] Perhaps most important, it is necessary for public sociologists of sport to learn, as Zirin suggests, to argue their case in the face of opposition from those who, for various reasons, resist the type of changes that are supported by the research.[77]

Conclusion

In one of two major recent essays on sport and public intellectuals (the other is by Bairner),[78] Jarvie reminds us that "sport's transformative capacity must not be overstated: it is limited, but possibilities do exist within sport to provide some resources of hope in a world that is left wanting on many fronts."[79] While the socio-cultural study of sport is far more critical, investigative, probing, diverse, global, and politically aware than ever before, in the face of less-than-encouraging structural-cultural conditions in our universities and their departments, it is not surprising that only a few of our colleagues have pursued an active, deliberate, or concerted interest in public sociology.[80]

Yet the potential confusion and ambiguity about public, applied, or practical sociology has not detracted colleagues like David Andrews from attempting to breathe new life into the public sociological enterprise. In clear dialogue with Ingham's call for physical cultural studies,[81] Andrews's definitional statement of the University of Maryland's Physical Cultural Studies program is inscribed with an evident ideology of public sociology and intervention:

> Physical Cultural Studies (PCS) advances the critically and theoretically-driven analysis of physical culture, in all its myriad forms. These include sport, exercise, health, dance, and movement related practices. PCS research seeks to locate and understand the expressions and experiences of physical culture in the broader contexts (social, political, economic, and technological) within which they are situated, and which they simultaneously help to (re)produce.
>
> More specifically, PCS is dedicated to the contextually based understanding of the corporeal practices, discourses, and subjectivities through which active bodies become organized, represented, and experienced in relation to the operations of social power. PCS thus identifies the role played by physical culture in reproducing, and sometimes challenging, particular class, ethnic, gender, ability, generational, national, and/or sexual norms and differences. Through the development and strategic dissemination of potentially empowering forms of knowledge and understanding, PCS seeks to illuminate, and intervene into, sites of physical cultural injustice and inequity.[82]

While not every socio-cultural scholar of sport and physical culture might accept or follow Andrews's definitional lead, his attempt to call sociologists of sport to interventionist arms is laudable.

To us, the authors of this chapter, a public sociology of sport must ultimately recognize that existing social problems in sport and physical activity zones are materially based and culturally mediated; it must produce theoretically informed and empirically verified suggestions for policy change; and it must generate models of sport as a site of social integration that celebrates diversity. A public sociology of sport utilizes empirical research to assess if and how physical activity and sport are contexts in which health promotion is evident and human physical, intellectual, artistic, and moral potentials are explored without fear or prejudice. Such a practical sociology of sport involves the deconstruction and destabilization of identities, practices, logics, institutions, and images of power in sport worlds, suggesting concrete policy amendments, rule changes, or progressive cultural adaptations to foster more equitable and pleasurable sport, health, and physical activity environments for all. A public sociology of sport, then, ventures beyond philosophy and critique; it must engage with the process of resolution.[83]

NOTES

1 Grant Jarvie, "Sport, Social Change, and the Public Intellectual," *International Review for the Sociology of Sport* 42, no. 4 (2007): 422.

2 Loïc Wacquant, *Urban Outcasts: A Comparative Sociology of Advanced Marginality* (Cambridge: Polity Press, 2008): 282.

3 Although the title of this chapter carries a clear reference to C. Wright Mills, public sociologist extraordinaire, it is also intended to reference Bruce Kidd's academic training as a political economist and historian, and his life's work as an athlete, academic, and activist – in other words, a public social scientist. See C. Wright Mills, *The Sociological Imagination* (Cambridge: Oxford University Press, 1959).

4 The complete extract reads: "La sociologie ne mériterait peut-être pas une heure de peine si elle avait pour fin seulement de découvrir les ficelles qui font mouvoir les individus qu'elle observe, si elle oubliait qu'elle a affaire à des homes, lors meme que ceux-ci, à la façon des marionettes, jouent un jeux dont ils ignorent les règles, bref, si elle ne se donnait pour tâche de restituer à ces hommes le sens de leur actes." Pierre Bourdieu, "Celibat et Condition Paysanne, *Etudes Rurale* 5–6 (1962): 109. The translation is taken from M. Grenfell, *Pierre Bourdieu: Agent Provocateur* (London: Continuum, 2004).

5 Wacquant, *Urban Outcasts.*

6 Michael Burawoy, "For Public Sociology," *American Sociological Review* 70 (2005): 4–28.

7 Howard Becker, "Whose Side Are We On?" *Social Problems*, 14, no. 3 (1967): 239–47; Alvin Gouldner, "The Sociologist as Partisan: Sociology and the Welfare State," in *For Sociology: Renewal and Critique in Sociology Today* (Harmondsworth, UK: Pelican Books, 1973), 27–68.

8 Howard Nixon, "Sport Sociology that Matters: Imperatives and Challenges for the 1990s," *Sociology of Sport Journal* 8, no. 3 (1991): 281–94.

9 Ian McDonald, "Critical Social Research and Political Intervention: Moralistic versus Radical Approaches," in *Power Games: A Critical Sociology of Sport*, ed. John Sugden and Alan Tomlinson (London: Routledge, 2002), 101.

10 Brett St Louis, "The Vocation of Sport Sociology," *Sociology of Sport Journal* 24, no. 1 (2007): 120.

11 McDonald, "Critical Social Research," 114.

12 Ibid., 115.

13 Eric Dunning, "Sociology of Sport in Balance: Critical Reflections on Some Recent and More Enduring Trends, *Sport in Society* 7, no. 1 (2004): 18.

14 St Louis, "The Vocation," 119.

15 Alan Ingham and Peter Donnelly, "Whose Knowledge Counts? The Production of Knowledge and Issues of Application in the Sociology of Sport," *Sociology of Sport Journal* 7, no. 1 (1990): 62.

16 Ingham and Donnelly, "Whose Knowledge Counts?," go on to utter a note of caution experienced by practical sociologists: "The self-reflexivity of the practical sociologist inevitably results in suspicion about the role of the 'expert' and trepidation about going public / going commercial" (62–3).

17 Jarvie, "Sport, Social Change," 419, 422.

18 Gai Berlage, "Are Children's Competitive Team Sports Socializing Agents for Corporate America?" in Adrian Dunleavy, Andrew Miracle, and Roger Rees (eds.), *Studies in the Sociology of Sport*, 309–24 (Fort Worth: Texas Christian University Press, 1982); Mass Mutual Financial Group, "Press Release: New Nationwide Research Finds Successful Women Business Executives Don't Just Talk a Good Game ... They Played One," New York, 4 February 2003; Oscar Patterson, "Beyond Compassion: Selfish Reasons for Being Unselfish," *Daedalus*, Winter 2002: 26–38; J.R. Seeley, R.A. Sim, and E.W. Loosley, *Crestwood Heights: A Study of the Culture of Suburban Life* (New York: Basic Books, 1956).

19 David Riesman, cited in "The Sexes: Madam Executive," *Time*, 18 February 1974, http://content.time.com/time/magazine/article/0,9171,942783-2,00.html.

20 Paul Paolucci, *Marx's Scientific Dialectics* (Leiden: Brill Academic Publishers, 2008); Craig Calhoun, "The Promise of Public Sociology," *British Journal of Sociology* 56 (2005): 355–63.

21 Francois Nielsen, "The Vacant 'We': Remarks on Public Sociology," *Social Forces* 82 (2004): 1619–27.

22 Mills, *The Sociological Imagination*.

23 Ibid.

24 Stanley Aronowitz, "A Mills Revival?" *Logos* 2 (2003): 49, http://logosjournal.com.

25 Herbert Gans, *Middle American Individualism: The Future of Liberal Democracy* (New York: Free Press, 1988).

26 Ibid., 37.

27 Ibid., 38.

28 Michael Burawoy, "American Sociological Association President-Elect Candidate, Personal Statement," *Footnotes*, March 2002, www.asanet.org/footnotes/mar02/fn11.html.

29 Michael Burawoy, "For a Sociological Marxism: The Complementary Convergence of Antonio Gramsci and Karl Polanyi," *Politics and Society* 31 (2003): 193.

30 David Riesman, *The Lonely Crowd* (New Haven, CT: Yale University Press, 1950).

31 Robert Blauner, *Racial Oppression in America* (New York: Harper & Row, 1972); Arlie Hochschild, *The Managed Heart: Commercialization of Human Feeling* (Berkeley: University of California Press, 1983).

32 Mark Smith, *Social Science in the Crucible: The American Debate over Objectivity and Purpose, 1918–1941* (Durham, NC: Duke University Press, 1985).

33 Robert Bellah, *Habits of the Heart* (Berkeley: University of California Press, 1985); Ben Agger, *Public Sociology: From Social Facts to Literary Acts* (Lanham, MD: Rowman & Littlefield, 2000).

34 Mitch Duneier, *Sidewalk* (New York: Macmillan, 2000).

35 Sudhir Venkatesh, *Gang Leader for a Day: A Rogue Sociologist Crosses the Line* (London: Allen Lane, 2008).

36 Dorothy Smith, *The Everyday World as Problematic: A Feminist Sociology* (Toronto: University of Toronto Press, 1987); Paulo Freire, *Pedagogy of the Oppressed* (New York: Herder & Herder, 1970); Alain Touraine, *Return of the Actor: Social Theory in a Post-Industrial Society* (Minneapolis: University of Minnesota Press, 1988).

37 Alan Bairner, "Sport, Intellectuals, and Public Sociology: Obstacles and Opportunities," *International Review for the Sociology of Sport* 44 (2009): 115–30.

38 Nixon, "Sport Sociology"; Richard Gruneau, *Class, Sport, and Social Development* (Amherst: Massachusetts University Press, 1983); Gary Whannel, *Blowing the Whistle: The Politics of Sport* (London: Pluto, 1983); William Morgan, "Toward a Critical Theory of Sport," *Journal of Sport and Social Issues* 7, no. 1 (1983): 24–34.

39 Ben Carrington, "Rebuttal," *Sociology of Sport Journal* 24, no. 1 (2007): 77.

40 Ben Carrington, "Merely Identity: Cultural Identity and the Politics of Sport," *Sociology of Sport Journal* 24, no. 1 (2007): 49.

41 Alan Tomlinson, "Whose Side Are They On?" *Leisure Studies and Cultural Studies in Britain*, 8 (1989): 97.

42 Dave Zirin, "Calling Sports Sociology Off the Bench," *Contexts* (Summer 2008): 29, emphasis added.

43 Kristin Luker, "Is Academic Sociology Politically Obsolete?" *Contemporary Sociology* 28, no. 1 (1999): 5–10.

44 This is not intended to be a comprehensive review of the ways in which sociology of sport research has become practical and public. Numerous other cases could have been given in which sociologists of sport themselves, and/or their research, have influenced public debates and social policies (for example, research on children's sport, research on sexual harassment and abuse, and research on violence in sports).

45 Ingham and Donnelly, "Who's Knowledge Counts?"

46 John Loy and Joseph McElvogue, "Racial Segregation in American Sport," *International Review for the Sociology of Sport* 5 (1970): 5–24.

47 Donald Ball applied the model to the Canadian Football League and found that positional distribution was not occurring by race but by nationality, with U.S. players (black and white) being "stacked" in the central positions. Mike Cantelon provides an update of the status and distribution of Canadians in the CFL. Donald Ball, "Ascription and Position: A Comparative Analysis of 'Stacking' in Professional Football," *Canadian Review of Sociology and Anthropology* 10 (May 1973): 97–113; Michael Cantelon, "The Canadian Football League: Radically Canadian?" (master's thesis, University of Ottawa, 2001).

48 John Loy, Barrie McPherson, and Gerald Kenyon, *Sport and Social Systems* (Boston: Addison-Wesley, 1978), 133–6.

49 Richard Lapchick's Institute for Diversity and Ethics in Sport at the University of Central Florida produces the most widely circulated Racial Report Cards; the report cards now include graduation rates of U.S. university players (by race and sport) and also gender representation (Racial and Gender Report Cards). www.tidesport.org/racialgenderreportcard.html.

50 S. Coulombe and Marc Lavoie, "Les francophones dans la ligue nationale de hockey: Une analyse economique de la discrimination," *L'Actualité economique* 61, no. 1 (1985): 73–92 ; Marc Lavoie, "Stacking, Performance Differentials, and Salary Discrimination in Professional Ice Hockey: A Survey of the Evidence," *Sociology of Sport Journal* 6, no. 1 (1989): 17–35; Marc Lavoie, G. Grenier, and S. Coulombe, *Why are Performance Differentials and Stacking in Professional Hockey Better Explained by Discrimination than by Style of Play?* Working Papers 9208e (University of Ottawa: Department of Economics, 1992); David Marple, "Analyse de la discrimination que subissent les canadiens français au hockey professionnel," *Mouvement* 10, no. 1 (1975): 7–13.

51 Roger Boileau, Fernand Landry, and Y. Trempe, "Les canadiens français et les grands jeux internationaux," in *Canadian Sport: Sociological Perspectives*, ed. Richard Gruneau and John Albinson (Don Mills, ON: Addison Wesley, 1976), 141–69; Ann Hall, Trevor Slack, Gary Smith, and David Whitson, *Sport in Canadian Society* (Toronto: McClelland & Stewart, 1991); Fernand Landry, C. St-Denis and C. Turgeon, "Les canadiens français et les grands jeux internationaux," *Mouvement* 1, no. 2 (1966): 115–32; Fernand Landry, C. St-Denis, and C. Turgeon, "Les canadiens français et les grands jeux internationaux," *Mouvement* 7, nos. 1–2 (1972): 81–92. The Canadian and U.S. contexts were linked by Kjeldsen, who compared representation or under-representation of francophones on Canadian Olympic teams and that of African Americans on U.S. Olympic teams. Erik Kjeldsen, "Integration of Minorities into Olympic

Sport in Canada and the USA," *Journal of Sport and Social Issues* 8, no. 2 (1984): 29–44.

52 See also Jay Coakley and Peter Donnelly, *Sport in Society: Issues and Controversies*, 2nd Canadian edition (Toronto: McGraw Hill Ryerson, 2009): 276–9.

53 Peter Donnelly, Bruce Kidd, Jean Harvey, Suzanne Laberge, and Geneviéve Rail, "Plus ça change …: Patterns of Association in Canadian Sport," report prepared for the Privy Council Office–initiated / Sport Canada–funded project, "Patterns of Association in Canadian Civil Society: Linguistic Relations in Non-governmental Organizations" (2001); Mira Svoboda and Peter Donnelly, "Linguistic Barriers to Access to High Performance Sport," Sport Canada / TSN Canadian Facts Social Policy Research / Ekos, http://publications.gc.ca/site/eng/298404/publication.html. Coakley and Donnelly, *Sport in Society*, 279–84.There is also a tradition in Canadian research of determining the representation on Canadian national teams by social class, showing a consistent over-representation of athletes from higher social class backgrounds: for example, Rob Beamish, "The Persistence of Inequality: An Analysis of Participation Patterns among Canada's High Performance Athletes," *International Review for the Sociology of Sport* 25, no. 2 (1990): 143–53; Rob Beamish and Jan Borowy, *Q. What Do You Do for a Living? A. I'm an Athlete* (Kingston, ON: Sport Research Group, 1988); Richard Gruneau, "Class or Mass: Notes on the Democratization of Canadian Amateur Sport," in *Canadian Sport: Sociological Perspectives*, ed. Richard Gruneau and John Albinson (Don Mills, ON: Addison Wesley, 1976), 108–41.

54 For example, Vivian Acosta and Linda Carpenter, *Women in Intercollegiate Sport: A Longitudinal National Study 31 Year Update, 1977–2008* (2008), webpages.charter.net/womeninsport. For more recent annual gender reports on U.S. interuniversity sports, see www.acostacarpenter.org/.

55 CIS (Canadian Interuniversity Sport), "Analysis of Male and Female Coaches in CIS Sports," (2005), english.cis-sic.ca/information/members_info/research_stats; Guylaine Demers, "'We Are Coaches': Program Tackles the Under-Representation of Women Coaches," *Canadian Journal of Coaching for Women* 9, no. 2 (2010): 1–8. A series of gender audits of CIS, the Commonwealth Games, and the London (2012) and Sochi (2014) Olympics may be found at www.physical.utoronto.ca/Centre_for_Sport_Policy_Studies/Projects_and_Publications/Research_Reports.aspx.

56 Ian Henry and Leigh Robinson, *Women, Leadership, and the Olympic Movement* (Centre for Olympic Studies and Research, Loughborough University, UK, and the International Olympic Committee, Lausanne, Switzerland, 2010). Following the 2010 Congress of the International Working Group for Women in Sport (IWG), the Sydney Scoreboard was established to keep track of the number of women on the

boards of national and international sport organizations from as many countries as data are available: www.sydneyscoreboard.com/.

57 AAFLA (Amateur Athletic Foundation of Los Angeles), *Gender Stereotyping in Televised Sports* (Los Angeles: Amateur Athletic Foundation of Los Angeles, 1990), www.la84.org/gender-stereotyping-in-televised-sports/; Michael Messner and Cheryl Cooky, *Gender in Televised Sports: News and Highlights Shows, 1989–2009* (Los Angeles: Center for Feminist Research, University of Southern California, 2010).

58 For example, Angela Lumpkin and Linda Williams, "An Analysis of *Sports Illustrated* Feature Articles, 1954–1987," *Sociology of Sport Journal* 8, no. 1 (1991): 16–32.

59 For example, Margaret Duncan, "Sports Photographs and Sexual Difference: Images of Women and Men in the 1984 and 1988 Olympic Games," *Sociology of Sport Journal* 7, no. 1 (1990): 22–43. Although assessments of "quality" involved qualitative methods such as discourse analysis, comparative frequency counts are often made of, for example, gender marking, the framing of camera shots, and commentators' use of athletes' first names. It is unfortunate that the AAFLA studies remain the only ongoing longitudinal database of research on the same media sources; the vast majority of research in this area involves one-off case studies (cf. Peter Donnelly, Margaret MacNeill, and Graham Knight, "Enough Already! A Comment on Gender Representation Research" [unpublished research paper]).

60 Sarah Cluer, Peter Donnelly, Margaret MacNeill, and Graham Knight, "Lessons Learned: A Case Study of CBC Coverage of Men's and Women's Diving at the Sydney Olympics," paper presented at the North American Society for the Sociology of Sport annual conference, San Antonio, Texas, 31 October–3 November 2001).

61 For example, Marie Hardin and Brent Hardin, "The 'Supercrip' in Sport Media: Wheelchair Athletes Discuss Hegemony's Disabled Hero," *SOSOL (Sociology of Sport Online)* (2004); P. David Howe, "From Inside the Newsroom: Paralympic Media and the 'Production' of Elite Disability," *International Review for the Sociology of Sport* 43, no. 2 (2008): 135–50.

62 Michael Atkinson and Kevin Young, *Deviance and Social Control in Sport* (Champaign, IL: Human Kinetics, 2008).

63 Gerald Kenyon, "A Sociology of Sport: On Becoming a Sub-discipline," in R. Brown and Bryant Cratty (eds.), *New Perspectives of Man in Action* (Englewood Cliffs, NJ: Prentice-Hall, 1969). Following the "critical shift" in sociology of sport, many researchers swung to the other extreme, often finding little value in organized sport.

64 For example, Fred Coalter, "Value of Sport Monitor," www.sportengland.org; Fred Coalter, *A Wider Social Role for Sport: Who's Keeping Score?* (London: Routledge, 2007); Bruce Kidd and Peter Donnelly (eds.), *The Benefits of Sport in International Development: Five Literature Reviews* (Geneva: International Working Group for

Sport, Development, and Peace, 2007), www.righttoplay.com/moreinfo/aboutus/ Documents/Literature%20Reviews%20SDP.pdf; Norbert Elias, *What Is Sociology?* (London: Hutchinson, 1978).

65 Alan Ingham, "From Public Issue to Personal Trouble: Well-Being and the Fiscal Crisis of the State," *Sociology of Sport Journal* 2, no. 1 (1985): 43–55.

66 David Andrews, "Kinesiology's 'Inconvenient Truth' and the Physical Cultural Studies Imperative," *Quest* 60 (2008): 45–62.

67 Brian Turner, "British Sociology and Public Intellectuals: Consumer Society and Imperial Decline," *British Journal of Sociology* 57, no. 2 (2006): 170.

68 Bairner, "Sport, Intellectuals, and Public Sociology."

69 Zirin, "Calling Sports Sociology Off the Bench," 31.

70 Robert Hollands, "The Role of Cultural Studies and Social Criticism in the Socio-logical Study of Sports," *Quest* 36 (1984): 73.

71 Andrews, "Kinesiology's 'Inconvenient Truth.'"

72 Calhoun, "The Promise"; Nielsen, "The Vacant 'We'"; Jonathan Turner, "Is Public Sociology Such a Good Idea?" *American Sociologist* 36, nos. 3–4 (2005): 27–45; Mathieu Deflem, "Letter to the Editor – 'The Proper Role of Sociology in the World at Large,'" *Chronicle Review*, 1 October 2004. Deflem was so concerned about inter-est in and the potential influence of a public sociology that he ran a web site, www.savesociology.org; the site was open at the time of writing but was only actively maintained between 2004 and 2006).

73 Carrington, "Rebuttal," 77; Carrington's reference is to Turner, "Is Public Sociology Such a Good Idea?"

74 For example, Mary McDonald, "Beyond the Pale: The Whiteness of Sports Studies and Queer Scholarship," in Jane Caudwell (Ed.), *Sport Sexualities and Queer/Theory* (London: Routledge, 2007), 33–44.

75 Joseph Maguire and Kevin Young (eds.), *Theory, Sport, and Society* (Oxford: Else-vier, 2002), 1.

76 The Sport Participation Research Initiative in Canada specifically creates oppor-tunities for dialogue between researchers, practitioners, and policymakers. Real efforts are made to understand the others' working conditions and job constraints.

77 Zirin, "Calling Sports Sociology Off the Bench."

78 Bairner, "Sport, Intellectuals, and Public Sociology."

79 Jarvie, "Sport, Social Change," 422.

80 For example, Bairner, "Sport, Intellectuals, and Public Sociology"; Carrington, "Merely Identity."

81 Alan Ingham, "Toward a Department of Physical Cultural Studies and an End to Tribal Warfare," in J.-M. Fernandez-Balboa (Ed.), *Critical Postmodernism in Human Movement, Physical Education, and Sport: Rethinking the Profession* (New York: State University of New York Press, 1997), 157–82.

82 David Andrews, *Sport-Commerce-Culture* (New York: Peter Lang, 2006); http://umdknes.com/UMDPCS/UMDPCS/Definition.html.
83 As Ian McDonald, "Critical Social Research," 115, argues, "a radical sociology of sport should be seeking to assist the reconfiguration of the culture of sport by intervening against dominant relations of power. Social researchers working in the privileged spaces of the academy who claim to be radical can be expected to do no more, but no less, than this."

13 Shadow Disciplines, or a Place for Post-Disciplinary Liaisons in the North American Research University: What Are We to Do with Physical Cultural Studies?

PATRICIA VERTINSKY

According to James Chandler in his introduction to a sweeping overview of the disciplines in today's North American research university, if we were to take advice from Descartes to clear the landscape of all residual formations in order to build anew, we would surely design a university system that looked rather different from the one we now inhabit.[1] Whether such a feat is possible or even desirable, the manner in which universities have adapted to intellectual and material change over time, their accommodation to shifting disciplinary arrangements, the critical role of emerging new technologies, and changing protocols in contemporary scholarship have all received intense scrutiny.

Stanley Fish (with tongue in cheek) claims that experts writing about the modern university all have the same plot: a serpent enters a once thriving enterprise of higher education that is dedicated to expanding keen young minds and brings the seeds of corruption and decay, leaving the once great structure in ruins.[2] The identity of the serpent varies from story to story, says Fish, being sometimes ideology, sometimes politics (left or right), sometimes big-time athletics, venture capitalism, political correctness, or the military-industrial complex. As described by Bill Readings in *The University in Ruins,* the serpent has arrived in the form of the market-driven administrator, externally meek and internally menacing, whose techno-bureaucratic notions of excellence have replaced the university's moral or political agenda.[3]

The point I want to take from this is that the influence of the managerial class in setting agendas and defining excellence is indeed critical in today's research university, given the strong sense of a mismatch between developing forms and communities of scholarship and the institutional arrangements that are supposed to advance them. This has been a particularly thorny problem in kinesiology, which has emerged over time as a sort of multidisciplinary organization, transformed from its early focus on physical and health education at the turn of the twentieth century. It was at that time – from about 1880 to 1910 – that the American research university emerged along Humboldt's German model with its unity of teaching and research and a configuration that typically included the organization of arts and science faculties into various discipline-based departments, the development of undergraduate majors (including physical education),[4] graduate programs that increasingly included research, and the emergence of major professional associations that supported journals and conferences and harnessed disciplinary hiring practices.

It is a system that persisted tenaciously through the twentieth century, at least until the late 1960s and 1970s, which brought about some profound disturbances of the disciplinary system and disciplinary cultures, leading to what Clifford Geertz described as the blurring of disciplinary genres into an almost continuous field of interpretation and the emergence of the development of a number of new "fields" or "studies."[5] James Chandler calls these fields "shadow disciplines," including, for example, area studies, cultural studies, women's studies, gender studies, race studies, science studies, performance studies, and media studies, and we can add here emerging forms of socio-cultural and physical cultural studies. "Some address a new or newly important topic (gender, race, performance), some a new body of material (film, television, new media). Some offer a new approach to topics that link existing disciplines (cultural studies). Some are constituted by a high degree of reflexivity with respect to the existing shape of the disciplines (science studies)."[6]

Each of these "studies," suggests Chandler, has offered new approaches to topics that link existing disciplines and has borrowed particular favoured methodologies, but each has also generated new demands on the whole system for different teaching arrangements, new contexts for collegial collaboration, new agendas for research, and so on.[7] Accompanying these arrangements have been new majors, new journals, new ways of doing research (and seeking research funds), and a host of interdisciplinary initiatives arranged in centres, institutes, and collectives. Thus a system of departmental disciplines came to be shadowed by a wide variety of new sub-disciplinary fields potentially requiring "supra-departmental" organization.

Not surprisingly there have been troubling questions about how to manage and locate these variously emerging studies, assess their intellectual viability and sustainability, and repopulate them, or not, through new kinds of hiring practices. Questions have been asked: At what point, if at all, do studies begin to count like, or be incorporated into, existing disciplines? And what might be the criteria for crossing disciplinary thresholds? Does this boundary hopping or disciplinary blurring lead to a change in disciplinary relations or arrangements, to fruitful forms of interdisciplinarity, or to what we might call a new place of post-disciplinary liaisons, and with what effects?

Caught up in these shifting developments has been the case of kinesiology, which (spurred by Franklin Henry's call from Berkeley in the 1960s for a more academic approach to the study of human movement) has developed into a series of multidisciplinary units characterized by the increasing dominance of the sciences. I have told the story of this metamorphosis of the intellectual work in my own academic home at the University of British Columbia over the last two or three decades through an analysis of the spaces of its home, the War Memorial Gymnasium, where, within its changing spaces, the Cartesian divide increasingly intensified its hold upon the academic enterprise.[8] After the abandonment of the academic enterprise that had catered to the athletic needs of the students and to professional training in physical education, the emerging focus on research and technology shifted attention away from the athletic body, and debates raged within the emergent sub-disciplines and studies over laboratory space, curricula, and resources as well as the right name for the school's growing scientific focus (from physical education to human kinetics and now kinesiology). In many respects, groups of faculty members came to inhabit small and different worlds focused increasingly upon applied science and the technical management of sport and the moving body, while those who worked in the social sciences and humanities were given short shrift. It lent credence to Rorty's observation that much of what gets defined as knowledge in a society can be recognized as those beliefs and modes of practice that are successful in helping official groups in that society do what they want to do.[9] Shirl Hoffman, an American leader in the field of physical education or kinesiology expressed the concerns of many over this situation: "I worry about the academic character of some of the PhDs we are graduating, exceptionally narrow people – technicians almost – who lack a scholar's understanding of how their discipline relates to the broader field of physical education and academic life and who studiously avoid anything that looks or sounds too philosophical."[10]

Reflecting Hoffman's anxieties, one of my abiding memories of these transformative years was an administrative leadership that sharpened this push towards, and elevation of, the technical aspects of science and the emphasis on research-measurable outcomes. To encourage research productivity, faculty members were scored and ranked annually on the basis of their research output – eight points for a refereed article in a scientific journal, and six points for an authored book. To a historian, for whom published monographs were in many respects the coin of the realm and could take months if not years to bring to fruition, it told a story louder than words. The use of quantitative tools became mandatory in the graduate curriculum, and, when hiring took place, those who had accumulated the most productivity points had the greater say in determining the nature of the position – and thus the ever-increasing dominance of "objective" science. It was a situation that exemplified the growing cultural divide, articulated by C.P. Snow, between the sciences and humanities and the fact that technicality had become a defining characteristic of science even though a generation of new scholarship had begun to show "with wonderful particularity how the quantitative things we usually think of as technical are bound up with philosophy, labor practices, ... imperialism, ... poverty, ... medical therapeutics, nationalism, criminal law, ... art and objectivity."[11]

The American Academy of Physical Education (and, more recently, Kinesiology) endlessly deplored the fragmentation caused by growing numbers of sub-disciplines and their effects upon the field that they now (mostly) agree should be called kinesiology, but not surprisingly their constituency validated the increasingly strong move to a science-based kinesiology as the field moved into the twenty-first century. This had a number of effects for it tended to rigidify segmented groups with quite distinct cultures and organizational values. The result was often a heady mix of scholarly alienation and disciplinary nationalism, leading to a perceived lack of centrality to the broader academic enterprise. In some universities it caused the dissolution of entire units and, in others, the diversion of specific faculty groups elsewhere, especially those focused on pedagogy, social sciences, and the humanities.[12]

David Andrews spoke passionately about the dominating effects of the sciences in kinesiology at the 2007 meeting of the Academy of Kinesiology and Physical Education, referring to the instantiation of an epistemological hierarchy that continued to privilege positivist over post-positivist, quantitative over qualitative, and predictive over interpretive ways of knowing. He was lamenting his own experience – "in the neo-liberal academic jungle which accords primacy to high-quality science" – of the persistence of C.P. Snow's two solitudes in a faculty that professed a focus on human movement while failing to capitalize on the tremendous opportunities to take advantage of the multiple theoretical and methodological insights available within his unit. "Ways of knowing associated with human movement and the active body are not the exclusive domain of the quantitative data driven logical positivist," he continued. "A true kinesiology program in name and intent requires a complimentary synthesis of epistemologies if it is to realize its diverse and multifaceted empirical project."[13]

I agree with Andrews's points, though it is my experience that our best scientifically minded researchers in kinesiology would not argue with the *principle* (but not necessarily the practice) that science, and the humanities and social sciences, might profitably work side by side to enrich the field and provide important social, cultural, and historical insights into the diverse landscape of physical culture and movement patterns. In health-related, problem-based research on sport and physical activity, for example, most are well aware of the growing efforts of funding agencies to foster stronger interdisciplinary partnerships to bring together models of multilevel "causes of the causes." The growing importance of the health humanities and the introduction of a humanist or social scientist on national research funding panels for scientific research are two of many examples. In some cases scientists are further along the trans-disciplinary path in grasping the potential utility of the emerging field of the science of team science. In an article titled "The Increasing Dominance of Teams in the Production of Knowledge," Wuchty, Jones, and Uzzi evaluated twenty million papers over five decades to demonstrate that, more and more, research is done in teams across nearly all fields (especially in the natural sciences and psychology).[14]

Furthermore it is clear that scientists increasingly pursue knowledge production by working on problems rather than in disciplines, working in clusters that may be too short lived to be institutionalized into departments or programs and that take on the characteristics of networks and assemblages. If these new research configurations hardly fit the traditional taxonomy of disciplines, they have also challenged the organization of academic spaces. As Mario Biagioli points out, the joke that "departments are where scientists go to die" does capture some aspects of a real trend. He further suggests that "the proliferation of disciplinary arrangements and modes of collaboration that escape both Kuhn's holistic group based model and Foucault's notion of discipline has not only rendered the idea of the disciplinary canon or paradigm inapplicable but has expanded the meaning of novelty."[15] These shifting arrangements in the sciences foreground a new and distinct pattern of post-disciplinarity that is gaining broader currency even while the academy struggles to co-ordinate new working arrangements.

By contrast, in the humanities and social sciences there is often pressure to assimilate new domains of knowledge into traditional disciplinary methods (and I see this among some of my own colleagues who hanker to be viewed as "real" sociologists with their dedication to maintain a certain methodism).[16] Robert Post comments that it is genuinely puzzling that it has been so difficult for the humanities to transcend traditional disciplinary methods, while the sciences have more easily adapted to new techniques of knowledge acquisition. In many respects, he suggests, the humanities do not solve problems in the same way as the sciences do, given that what counts as knowledge is far more controversial. As well, questions of expertise and authority render humanities and social science scholars anxious because they contract the sphere of potential political influence, though they also want to maintain the prestige of expert authority.[17] There is a fear that if they subvert the practices of their discipline, not only do they run the danger of repudiating their own disciplinary scholarship, but their academic freedom might also be affected because intellectual authority has inhered in well-established disciplinary communities, and those who move to "in-between" spaces like studies or post-disciplinary assemblages and display charismatic rather than disciplinary authority might disqualify themselves from this protection. Judith Butler points out that if disciplinary innovation were the price that had to be paid to legitimate an argument against unwanted political intrusions, the result would be a conservative academic culture and the suppression of interdisciplinary work in order to preserve academic freedom. In such a case we would need to ask, "For whom is academic freedom preserved, and for what purposes?"[18]

Potential Directions for Physical Cultural Studies: Physical Activity as a Cultural Project

So where is the project of physical cultural studies (PCS) in this complex set of circumstances in the academy, and how can we best analyse its potential contributions in science-dominated kinesiology faculties? As Hargreaves and Vertinsky have demonstrated, the study of physical culture requires an understanding of those cultural practices in which the physical body – the ways it moves, is represented, has meanings assigned to it, and is imbued with power – is central.[19] To achieve this goal, PCS involves advancing the critical and theoretical analysis of physical culture in its many forms through a synthesis of empirical, theoretical, and methodological influences drawn mainly from the sociology and history of sport and physical activity, the sociology of the body, cultural anthropology, cultural geography, and cultural studies. In a discussion of his view of the emerging field of PCS, Andrews draws particular attention to its reliance upon Stuart Hall's interpretation of cultural studies and radical contextualism. Here he borrows from Hall the notion of "a physical culture without guarantees," in which the various dimensions of physical culture are viewed as unavoidably relational, subject to power, and always in the process of becoming constituted.[20] PCS, Andrews continues, is driven by the need to understand the complexities, experiences, and injustices of the physical cultural contexts that the studies confront. Hence PCS is motivated by an unequivocal commitment to progressive social change and a direct challenge to the hegemony of science currently in place within kinesiology, as well as the political economy of the corporate university and the broader political, economic, cultural, and technological contexts in which the process of corporatization exists and operates.[21] Rebecca Goldstein puts this kind of cultural critique in a nutshell. "Culture," she says, "is the pest always sneaking up from behind, clamping its clammy paws over the eyes and shrieking 'guess who.' There is no shaking off culture blocking the path to any ledge in all the ranges of knowledge – the sciences and the social sciences, the humanities and the arts – from which we can look out and see."[22]

In light of these views, a useful question to ask might be whether the most important contributions that PCS can make lie in questioning accepted assumptions about how the sciences in kinesiology operate and the meaning or facts that they produce around physical activity practices, or whether political activism and the desire to expose issues of power and the contradictions and inadequacies of any systems of thought should drive the agenda.[23] Can we usefully analyse the role and potential of PCS for kinesiology from the perspective of Chandler's shadow disciplines, or should we view its potential as an inter- or trans-disciplinary arrangement, a place for constantly shifting problem-specific collaborations, and/or a space for novelty and shifting post-disciplinary liaisons?

Shadow Disciplines and Post-Disciplinary Liaisons

Science Studies

Let me try to address some of these complex questions by examining the fate of some other studies areas over the last two decades that might have useful lessons for PCS and kinesiology generally. Owing to the dominance of science in kinesiology, the history and politics of science studies provide a particularly useful lens through which to examine the work of PCS and its relationship to kinesiology scientists and the work of a kinesiology unit.[24] Science studies comprises a battery of disciplinary perspectives turned upon science and technology – first and foremost sociology but also anthropology, political science, philosophy, gender studies, and history. One of the main tasks of science studies is to demonstrate how science is involved in culture – indeed, how science is culture.[25] (In a number of respects science studies overlaps with science, technology, and society (STS) programs as well as the sociology of scientific knowledge (SSK), and all have a strong focus on the social.)

Scholars in science studies have openly and ardently engaged in political debates about science, technology, and medicine, just as those in physical cultural studies are variously engaged in political and ethical debates around sport and leisure, and an understanding of the cultivation, organization, and reception of embodied practices in various societies. The main idea has been to "tame" science by making it more social (or at least more sociological), using the tools of the sociology of scientific knowledge. Since "science was understood to be shot through with social interests and political struggles[,] it was the job of science studies to lay them bare."[26] Many scholars in science studies thus deliberately adopted a policy of estrangement towards contemporary science, refusing to privilege scientists' own accounts of what they did. Their focus was turned not on what science *is* but how science *works*, by drawing upon a wide range of empirical materials and methods whose development and testing were left to the home disciplines. More often than not, the scientists who are the object of science studies scholars have become puzzled or dismissive of their views.

Science studies has recently lost some of its vigor with the faltering of one of its leading exponents, Bruno Latour, who admitted that critiques of science can at times be useless against objects of some solidity.[27] In *Science in Action* (1986) Latour had championed science studies, departing from Thomas Kuhn's structure of science based on revolution and paradigm shift within the disciplines, to make an all-out assault on the accepted assumptions about how science operates and the meaning or facts that it produces. Studying science, he insisted, requires a close examination of the actors, dynamics, and events that have maintained the packaging of scientific development as well as the need to track the intricate networking of scientific endeavours.[28] His Actor Network Theory was enormously influential; indeed, Latour is one of the most highly cited social scientists working today. It was only when he thought that Jean Baudrillard had taken critique too far by claiming after the events of 11 September 2001 that "the World Trade Towers destroyed themselves under their own weight, so to speak, undermined by the utter nihilism inherent in capitalism itself, as if the terrorism planes were pulled to suicide by the powerful attraction of this black hole of nothingness" that he openly worried that science studies critique had run out of steam. "Is it really our duty to add fresh ruins to fields of ruins?" he asked. "Should we be at war too, we the scholars, the intellectuals?"[29]

History of Science

Could science studies' counterpart, the history of science, provide a model for forming a more productive rapprochement with kinesiology scientists? It appears that, since the 1990s, historians of science have retreated more and more from being a studies or shadow discipline to the discipline of history itself with the stated goal of understanding the science of the past on its own terms. Viewing scientific practices as both constructed and real, they insist that such practices are always contingent to context, just as cultural studies points increasingly to the importance of contextualization. Andrews and Giardina note that contextual cultural studies involves a continuous grappling with theory to see what is useful and appropriate within a particular empirical context, and discarding or reworking that which is not.[30] To historicize what scientific or physical culture practices are and how they work is not thereby to debunk them but is to locate them within the conditions of their creation and organization and attempt to understand them in these terms.

By focusing on what science *is* (and was), in addition to how it *works*, and by retreating back to the discipline of history and its constraints, historians of science have also at times tended to lose the contact that they formerly had with today's scientists. This is unfortunate, says Porter, because "the historical and social study of science is a necessary ally of scientific reason. The contribution of historians is to analyze more richly how the work of science is done and to explore in depth its interactions with the larger culture. It is neither truthful not advantageous to pretend that science by its nature is detached from the world or that it can be sovereign on an island of technicality."[31]

Kindi joins this debate by contending that "an ideal image of science looms over history as both an enforcer of discipline and a motivational ambition."[32] Historians, she believes, are still swayed in their work by traces of an ideal nineteenth-century image of science that sustains the spectre of a crudely empiricist understanding of science. Traces of this ghost remain and continue to affect the history of science despite the critiques of positivist science from the early 1960s on by Thomas Kuhn, Paul Feyerbrand, and others who have insisted that there is no scientific method that all scientific traditions share and that "there are no neutral absolute criteria to distinguish between science and bad science or non-science."[33]

It has also become clear that the history of almost all modern science must be understood as "science in a colonial context," leading to a whole series of issues for science studies around local or indigenous knowledge versus "Western," "global," or "universal science." According to Gayatri Spivak, the academy (including kinesiology) has so far sanctioned ignorance of other than dominant Western epistemes and intellectual traditions.[34] The "ever popular Actor Network Theory requires decolonization and demasculinization," says Suman Seth – an effort supported by Sandra Harding in *The Racial Economy of Science* (1993) and *Sciences from Below* (2008), in which she suggested that feminist and post-colonial theories were strongly complementary and critically important, though neglected, ways of understanding the development and utilization of science and technology.[35] In his extensive work on physical cultures Henning Eichberg has called for a much greater focus upon the interlacement between Western histories of sport and physical culture and non-Western histories, with attention to the political dimensions of body culture. Through body culture, he says, especially in the clash between body cultures, cultural diversity becomes visible.[36]

The various lessons for physical cultural studies from these two sets of "studies that are focused on understanding science and its workings may be that we should neither retreat to our core disciplines of history, sociology, anthropology, and so on (which may or may not stand ready to welcome us), nor avoid the tough disciplinary work of holding up our own methods of inquiry to constant scrutiny. The experiences of science studies suggest that unduly provocative attacks upon the ways in which our scientists work, and the debunking of their methods (while insufficiently critiquing our own methods of inquiry), can push them to avoid or dismiss the more valuable contributions of scientific critique. As Post points out, "criticism of the sciences (in the sense of exposing science's cultural, political, gender, and economic dimensions) has become as predictable as to provide only vanishing intellectual returns."[37] New liaisons between science studies and the humanities are showing promising directions for understanding the practices of science, yet kinesiology units have been reluctant to hire historians, literary theorists, and philosophers, and I know of none that has an artist on staff (the pairing of Leonardo da Vinci and anatomy springs to mind). Lessons from the history of science point to the critical need to show that understandings of science are always contingent to a certain time and place and that new interpretive frameworks are important in helping to reconfigure the relationships between the humanities and the sciences along more productive lines.

Clearly we need to constantly re-examine the nature of our critiques and to rethink more sustainable two-way relationships with our scientists by seeking points of contact or shared problems. Anne Fausto-Sterling, professor of biology and gender studies, highlights the utility of this approach and the value of more serious collaboration. In a meticulous meta-study of the research that has been conducted over time on bone formation, an area in which a number of kinesiology researchers are invested, she explained to scientists the effects of the careless use of racial categories in their research, by demonstrating how claims of racial difference in bone density have historically lacked a theoretical foundation. Showing that specific anatomies and physiologies are not fixed traits, she illustrates precisely the way that, in these studies, the social has produced the biological in a system of constant feedback between body and social experience. Thus we can see, she says, how "individual bone structure emerges from a combination of genetic possibility, diet, exposure to sunlight, skeletal biomechanics, forms of exercise and physical labor, plus other contributors that we have yet to articulate with any clarity." She suggests that "instead of spending our wisdom and dollars on a concept of little scientific use, why not dedicate our brain power and our researchers to studying the biological, cultural and social dynamics of bone development as the interdependent nexus that they are?"[38] The difficulty, as PCS so often finds, lies in creating an environment in which this interdependence can be studied in a full partnership with support from all sides.

Women's Studies

Turning to another set of studies, women's studies, for insight into the potential of PCS, we can see that women's studies flourished during the late 1970s and 1980s with the coming of age of second-wave feminism and affirmative action, and as university administrations were pressed to recognize the need for such programs during what Joan Scott calls the last stand of the liberal university. With the turn away from feminism during the subsequent decades and the increasing corporatization of the research university, however, women's studies programs, with their commitment to the feminist goals of equity and social justice, have become prime targets for reduction or closure. Women's studies advocates have had to respond to tough questions about their reliance on established categories of analysis and to the charge that institutionalization has destroyed their critical edge, and they have offered a variety of new critiques about the production and organization of knowledge. Jacques Derrida warned women's studies early on about the smothering effects of institutionalization upon social activism. Once women's studies became just another cell in the university beehive, he said, with its legitimacy established, its future secured, there would be costs that involved the disciplining of the field, imposition of a certain orthodoxy, and a dulling of its critical edge. Do the women who manage these programs, he suggested, not become in turn the guardians of the law, and do they not risk conducting an institution similar to the institution against which they are fighting?[39] Having been institutionalized on equal footing with other academic and administrative units, adds Biddy Martin, women's studies, plagued by the exclusions entailed by its self-definition, has lost much of its critical and intellectual vigour.[40] (Indeed, graduate students in women's studies programs often find themselves choosing research topics that will win them tenure in their more traditional disciplines.)[41] Wendy Brown argues that the initial impetus for women's studies – the need to end the exclusion of women as objects of knowledge, politics, and policy – has been exhausted. In her view, the proliferation of categories of women by race, ethnicity, sexual preference, and so on has led to an incoherent field organized by social identity rather than genre of inquiry. As long as women's studies programs remain the site of identity politics, she says, their radical influence is doomed to impotence.[42] On the one hand, growing institutional pressures for increasing the measurement of knowledge, with burgeoning corporate concepts of key performance indicators, deliverables, and outcomes, have undermined feminist values and forced a defensiveness around efforts at social activism, while, on the other hand, anxieties over the categorization of women within women's studies – a precondition to any feminist politics – have been impossible to escape, given the problem of exclusion.

The lessons for PCS that we might draw here from women's studies then are that a full-throttled social activist agenda can and often does alienate PCS from the science side of the house in kinesiology as well as the academy generally. Furthermore, there are lessons to be learned from the dangers of category construction that could be helpful to PCS. After all, the act of categorizing is the act of deciding what distinctions matter, and is therefore itself a political act reflecting the positions and interests of the categorizer. Epistemic ignorance, that is the continued exclusion of other than dominant Western intellectual traditions, is a particular arena requiring attention. Nevertheless, the relationship of both women's studies and physical cultural studies to other disciplines in the academy is at base one of critique – an inter- or sometimes anti-disciplinary practice that begins by rejecting the universal subject of disciplinary knowledge and produces new relations to knowledge and new subjects. In the case of PCS, this directly contradicts the positivist emphasis that has sustained kinesiology for so long and challenges the "hidden curriculum" of the disciplines within its programs.[43]

Attending to the Demands of the External Environment

In spite of the disciplinary, post-disciplinary, or interdisciplinary arrangements that have developed within kinesiology units, it is nevertheless the case that universities increasingly support those arrangements of knowledge production for which there is the most external demand – and the nature of this demand is constantly in flux, as we can see from the changing patterns of research funding agencies and the goods to which they are prepared to attach a dollar sign. For this reason we have to be proactive in setting our research agendas, constantly alert to priorities, while working with our colleagues to influence them. A willingness to debate and dialogue, to listen to the ideas, theories, and methods of others, can have the valuable effect of preventing us from being complacent about the conditions of knowledge in our time and encourage a growing awareness that there is validity (and utility) in the insights of both cultural constructivism and the scientific method (and the many things in between). Even those of our science colleagues who still claim to be unrepentant hedgehogs are becoming "foxes with an eye on the henhouse" as research-granting councils offer greater incentives for collaborative ventures and more contextual research projects.[44]

An important impediment to collaborative ventures has been a strong tendency for sociologists, historians, and philosophers in PCS to work alone (sometimes of necessity because there are so few of them) and to ignore pressures to work on problem-oriented and/or interdisciplinary projects, to generate research funds, and to do research with graduate (and undergraduate) students. Whether alone or in groups, however, PCS scholars, by token of their critical interest and broad insights into embodiment, are well primed to pursue research funding that supports their enterprise, practically and ethically.[45] Understanding complex physical-culture patterns includes work on youth health, aging, drugs, technology, fair play, disability, obesity, racial and gender issues, diversity, leisure, and sporting pursuits. We have a range of theoretical and methodological tools to explain how obesity is directly linked to poverty and what might be done to alleviate this; to show why and how aging is often a dismal and inactive as well as a female affair, and to provide strategies to assist; to analyse how the disabled thrive better in some cultural groups than in others; and to show how girls continue to have fewer sporting opportunities than do boys, how technology threatens fair play in all its guises, and in what ways sport and environmental protection do not sit well together. The acknowledgment of the importance of these kinds of topics in a rapidly globalizing world is already encouraging research councils to reprioritize their funding, and supporting these shifts should be one of PCS's priorities – not by anguishing over our unfulfilled legacy but by figuring out how to secure appropriate funding to support our research; getting onto selection committees in funding councils; working with scientific colleagues as well as each other, joining across disciplines, institutions, and internationally; and working to influence policy and pedagogies through our research findings. One might call this colonization, arbitrage, or evangelism, but these are all interdisciplinary tools that can shape the kinesiology of the future.

At the same time, it is important that we not lose our critical edge in pursuing what Andrews boldly calls "politically interventionist obligations." The versatility of our subject matter, and its critical focus upon the body in movement, along with our restlessness with established paradigms and academic dogma, encourage us to push social activist agendas through reflective scholarship along the lines of Chandra Mohanty's "reflective solidarity." But it is also the case that activism – especially if political desire trumps the possibilities of complexity and concreteness – cannot serve as the main justification for maintaining PCS, because it renders disposable the deep and serious intellectual basis that we have developed for our arena of study.[46] If we privilege the political over the intellectual, and the institutionally strategic over the intellectually sound, we provide arguments to distance ourselves from the rest of the university's intellectual mission for research and teaching. In a sense, we still have to decide, as Grossberg points out, where we want to locate the foundations of our ethical and political struggle. How will we define the content of that vision, and, ultimately, how will we decide that culture, and the location of the physical within it, matters? And, of course, we still have to deal with Stanley Fish's newest serpent, the academy's latest incarnation of a managerial class, to be able to pursue the critical edge and emergent value of PCS.

Addendum: A Serpent Deterred

The key is leadership, and, as the dean of a faculty of physical and health education of a leading research university, Bruce Kidd always knew exactly what excellence meant to his unit. He welcomed those within and those without who performed varieties of physical cultural studies, and he brought critique to his science-oriented faculty, indeed all his faculty and students, while supporting putting the active back into activism. Rosa Braidotti suggests that critical theory is about strategies of affirmation – the belief that negative effects can be transformed – and this is the domain in which Bruce Kidd has always shone in his professional and personal life. In Braidotti's words, "the ethical process of transforming negative into positive passions engenders a politics of affirmation in the sense of creating the conditions for a sustainable future ... this results, not in egoism, but in mutually embedded nests of shared interests."[47] I think that the pursuit of these shared interests, the ability to think and act with the times, and in spite of the times, allowed Dean Kidd to build a productive and sustainable unit dedicated to sport, physical culture, and the healthy body, a unit in which shadow disciplines and/or post-disciplinary liaisons such as PCS were among the many potentially valuable modes of knowledge production and critique that could help keep Stanley Fish's serpents at bay and keep kinesiology or physical and health education on the leading edge of the academy and of positive consequence to the communities we serve.

NOTES

1 James Chandler, "Introduction: Doctrines, Disciplines, Discourses, Departments," *Critical Inquiry* 35 (Summer 2009): 729.

2 Stanley Fish, "Take This Job and Do It: Administering the University without an Idea," *Critical Inquiry* 31 (Winter 2005): 271.

3 Bill Readings, *The University in Ruins* (Cambridge, MA: Harvard University Press, 1996).

4 This took some time in Canada. The first university degree program in physical education opened in 1940 at the University of Toronto, followed by others at McGill University (1945), the University of British Columbia and Queen's University (1946), and the University of Western Ontario (1947). Indeed the University of Toronto was the first university in the British Empire to offer a specialized three-year degree program in physical and health education (six men and eleven women constituted the first class).

5 Clifford Geertz, "Blurred Genres: The Refiguration of Social Thought," *American Scholar* 49 (Spring 1980): 166. Geertz remarked on the growing tendency within the social sciences to borrow metaphors from outside their disciplines in order to derive new interpretive frameworks for the study of human behaviour.

6 Chandler, "Introduction," 737.

7 Readings, for example, refers to the emergence of cultural studies as a transdisciplinary movement – "a mixture of Marxism, psychoanalysis and semiotics," promoted by those who are excluded from within, who can neither stay nor leave. *The University in Ruins*, 90–1.

8 Using Walter Benjamin's vision of history as a porous surface whose holes provide windows into discarded memories, I worked with an architect to illuminate meanings and memories of the past and to elicit new understandings about the ideal modern body of architectural discourse and the education of the athletic body in higher education. The memories I chose to record resonated with some of my own (gendered) experiences of the ways in which institutions marginalize minority groups and limit their opportunities – a style that Douglas Booth, in *The Field*, calls reflexive contextualization. Patricia Vertinsky and Sherry McKay, *Disciplining Bodies in the Gymnasium: Memory, Monument, Modernism* (London and New York: Routledge, 2004), 257.

9 Richard Rorty, *Philosophy and the Mirror of Nature* (Princeton, NJ: Princeton University Press, 1979), 10.

10 Shirl J. Hoffman, "Specialization + Fragmentation = Extermination," *Journal of Physical Education, Recreation, and Dance* 56, no. 6 (1985): 20.

11 Theodore M. Porter, "How Science Became Technical," *ISIS* 100 (2009): 297.

12 See a more detailed discussion in Patricia Vertinsky, "Mind the Gap (or Mending it): Qualitative Research and Interdisciplinarity in Kinesiology," *Quest* 61 (2009): 1–14.

13 David L. Andrews, "Kinesiology's 'Inconvenient Truth' and the Physical Cultural Studies Imperative," *Quest* 60 (2008): 50–1.

14 S. Wuchty. B. Jones, and B. Uzzi, "The Increasing Dominance of Teams in Production of Knowledge," *Science* 316 (2007): 1036–9.

15 Mario Biagioli, "Post-Disciplinary Liaisons: Science Studies and the Humanities," *Critical Inquiry* 35 (Summer 2009): 820.

16 Along with this is the danger of the program itself, as Franklin Henry warned decades ago but which still holds true in a number of cases. In 1978 Henry noted that "when a physical education department demonstrates that many of its courses and the research of its students and faculty are in fact possible within the various traditional disciplines, it also signals the university administration that it can be phased out." Franklin M. Henry, "The Academic Discipline of Physical Education," *Quest* 29, no. 2 (1978): 2.

17 Robert Post, "Debating Disciplinarity,"*Critical Inquiry* 35 (Summer 2009): 758. If the sciences must organize themselves to cope with new technological innovations, then so the humanities must organize themselves adequately to react to newly emerging needs to comprehend issues like race or gender where the desire for mutual understanding has grown particularly urgent; in science this has produced the more or less orderly emergence of new disciplines, but this has not been true for the humanities.

18 Judith Butler, "Critique, Dissent, Disciplinarity," *Critical Inquiry* 35 (Summer 2009): 774.

19 Jennifer Hargreaves and Patricia Vertinsky, *Physical Culture, Power, and the Body* (London and New York: Routledge, 2007).

20 Andrews, "Kinesiology's 'Inconvenient Truth,'" 56–7.

21 Ibid., 48.

22 Rebecca Newberger Goldstein, "Theory, Literature, Hoax," *New York Times Book Review* 9 (May 2010): 27.

23 There is the danger of the comfortable equation that cultural studies often makes between its style of intellectual work and its political commitments. Ken Hirschkop, "Cultural Studies and Its Discontents: A Comment on the Sokal Affair," *Social Text* 50, no. 1 (1997): 133.

24 Indeed, although I do not want to discuss here the complex debate around the raison d'être of cultural studies, it is useful to remember that James Carey's theory of culture and invention of cultural studies was in large measure a response to the dominance of science and his demand for a non-positivist understanding of science. Lawrence Grossberg, "The Conversation of Cultural Studies," *Cultural Studies* 23, no. 2 (2009): 178.

25 Thomas F. Gieryn, *Cultural Boundaries of Science: Credibility on the Line* (Chicago: University of Chicago Press, 1999).

26 Lorraine Daston, "Science Studies and the History of Science," *Critical Inquiry* 35 (Summer 2009): 805.

27 Bruno Latour, "Why Has Critique Run Out of Steam? From Matters of Fact to Matters of Concern," *Critical Inquiry* 30 (Winter 2004): 227.

28 Bruno Latour, *Science in Action: How to Follow Scientists and Engineers through Society* (Cambridge, MA: Harvard University Press, 1987).

29 Latour, "Why Has Critique Run Out of Steam?," 227.
30 David L. Andrews and Michael Giardina, "Sport Without Guarantees: Toward a Cultural Studies that Matters," *Cultural Studies~Critical Methodologies* 8 (2008): 395–422.
31 Porter, "How Science Became Technical," 309.
32 Vasso Kindi, "A Spectre Is Haunting History – The Spectre of Science," *Rethinking History* 14, no. 2 (2010): 251.
33 Ibid., 253.
34 Gayatri Spivak, *A Critique of Postcolonial Reason: Toward a History of the Vanishing Present* (Cambridge, MA: Harvard University Press, 1999).
35 Suman Seth, "Putting Knowledge in Its Place: Science, Colonialism, and the Postcolonial," *Postcolonial Studies* 12, no. 4 (2009): 380; Sandra Harding, ed., *The "Racial" Economy of Science: Toward a Democratic Future* (Bloomington: Indiana University Press, 1993).
36 Henning Eichberg, "Body Culture," in *The Routledge Companion to Sport History*, ed. Steve Pope and John Nauright (London and New York: Routledge, 2009).
37 Post, "Debating Disciplinarity," 828.
38 Anne Fausto-Sterling, "The Bare Bones of Race," *Social Studies of Science* 38, no. 5 (2008): 659, 683.
39 See Jacques Derrida, James Adner, Kate Doyle, and Glenn Hendler, "Women in a Beehive: A Seminar with Jacques Derrida," *Differences* 16, no. 3 (2005): 142. This has been a paradox for women's studies since the sustaining of gender as a critical, self-reflexive category rather than a normative one, and the sustaining of women's studies as an intellectually and institutionally radical site rather than a regulatory one, has meant refusing to allow gender and women's studies to be disciplined and thus refusing to affirm women's studies as a coherent field of study.
40 Biddy Martin, "Success and Its Failures," in *Women's Studies on the Edge*, ed. Joan Wallach Scott (Durham, NC, and London: Duke University Press, 2008), 171.
41 Alice Kessler-Harris and Ann Swerdlow, "Pride and Paradox: Despite Success Women's Studies Faces an Uncertain Future," *Chronicle of Higher Education*, 26 April 1996, A64.
42 Wendy Brown, "The Impossibility of Women's Studies," in Scott, *Women's Studies on the Edge*, 17–48.
43 Robyn Wiegman, "Feminism, Institutionalism, and the Idiom of Failure," in Scott, *Women's Studies on the Edge*, 29–153.
44 Gould suggests that neither the fox who cunningly devises many strategies nor the persistent hedgehog who knows one great and effective strategy can work alone. Stephen Jay Gould, *The Hedgehog and the Fox and the Magister's Pox: Mending the Gap between Sciences and the Humanities* (New York: Harmony Books, 2003).
45 Harvard academic Michelle Lamont, in *How Professors Think*, recently studied the decision making of twelve multidisciplinary panels in five U.S. national funding

competitions over a two-year period. One of her main findings was that institutional diversity and disciplinary diversity as criteria were viewed as more important than racial, gender, or ethnic diversity in approving grants. History and economics, she said, tended to do better than others in interdisciplinary panels because historians write well and they write about things that people in other fields can understand; economists have clear views about who among them is above or below the line. Philosophy is a problem discipline because philosophers refuse to believe that non-philosophers can evaluate their work, and English, anthropology, and political science all fare less well because of disagreements within their disciplines about what constitutes excellence (perhaps we can include sociology here). Michelle Lamont, *How Professors Think: Inside the Curious World of Academic Judgment* (Cambridge, MA: Harvard University Press, 2009). See also Kristen Intermann, "Why Diversity Matters: Understanding and Applying the Diversity Component of the National Science Foundations' Broader Impacts Criterion," *Social Epistemology* 23, nos. 3–4 (2009): 249–66.

46 See Lawrence Grossberg, "Does Cultural Studies Have Futures? Should It? (Or What's the Matter with New York?)," *Cultural Studies* 20, no. 1 (2006): 6.

47 Rosa Braidotti, "On Putting the Active Back into Activism," *New Formations*, 68 (Spring 2010): 56.

14 Bruce Kidd, Sport History, and Social Emancipation

DOUGLAS BOOTH

An activist-scholar, Bruce Kidd has devoted his professional life to improving access to sporting opportunities for all, to challenging the commodification of sports people under the impetus of commercialized sport, and to developing an athlete-centred model of sport based on enhancing the "health, education, and social capacities" of sports people in a non-threatening environment.[1] In this chapter I examine Kidd's historical scholarship as an element of his activism; as he puts it, "a shared, critical understanding" of past struggles "can contribute significantly to effective activism."[2] I am especially interested in Kidd's historiography, which I locate in the emancipatory project of late-twentieth-century social history and in the broader context of debates around the empirical-analytical method of professional history.[3]

My chapter comprises three substantive sections. In the first I examine three coterminous subjects: social history as a distinct approach to the study of the past, sport history as a sub-discipline of social history, and Kidd's approach to the social history of sport. Briefly, social historians in the 1960s turned the notion of the dispassionate, detached historian upside down and conceptualized themselves as part of a larger emancipatory project aimed at eliminating class-, gender-, and race-based discrimination. In the 1970s many historians of sport implicitly aligned themselves to the emancipatory project, although Kidd was one of only a handful to openly declare his position. However, if social historians shifted away from ideological and political neutrality, they continued to employ the empirical-analytical methods of traditional modernist history as the basis of their claims to legitimacy. In so doing, they introduced an aporia into their work: historians who prefigure and configure their narratives to conform to their ideas about human suffering, ethical transgressions, and freedom cannot simultaneously claim allegiance to an objective empirical-analytical epistemology. I analyse this aporia in Kidd's historical works in the second section of this chapter. There I focus on the way that Kidd ideologically, politically, and ethically prefigures, and linguistically configures, his narratives. I analyse the content and form of his narratives as (subconscious and conscious) choices that he makes in order to represent his politico-ideological notions of emancipation. In the third section I turn to the ethical dimensions of social history. Emancipation is unquestionably a noble ethical position. Paradoxically, however, the analytical methods and concepts of social history typically ignore the ethical and unethical encounters of everyday social interaction and expose what the moral philosopher Emmanuel Lévinas called the "cruel judgement" of history.[4]

Social History, Sport History, Bruce Kidd

In the 1960s, under the influence of the New Left and its burgeoning interest in cultural politics, social historians began to approach the past from a radically new perspective.[5] For most of the twentieth century, historians took "utmost care" to "refrain from any overt involvement in ideology or moral judgment," which they deemed "inconsistent with serious and disciplined empirical enquiry into what actually happened."[6] Historians generally studied the past for "its own sake," as "an intellectual pursuit, an activity of the reasoning mind."[7] In this approach the reasoning mind pursues the truth about the past through rational investigation of the sources, a process that requires historians to detach themselves from their subjects, contemporary concerns, and social and political conditions.[8] Turning to the lives of ordinary people, social historians increasingly saw the past "as a site of suffering and ethical transgression," and as they incorporated judgments of "politics, morality and propriety in human affairs" into their narratives, so too they reconceptualized themselves as part of a "mission" to empower and emancipate minorities and women.[9]

The history of sport emerged as a new area of study in the 1970s. Many practitioners claimed allegiance to the broader discipline of social history and its emphasis on the lives of ordinary people. Allegiance to social history was intellectually logical and a political strategy. While sport is clearly an integral element of popular culture and the political economy, social history bestowed academic credibility; in some cases it provided a means to counter charges that the study of sport was a trivial intellectual pursuit.[10] Social history also raised deeper questions for historians of sport concerning the structure of society, the place and role of sport in that structure, and the motors of social change. The responses of sport historians to those questions reflected, in part, their political-ideological engagement with issues of emancipation. In the case of social change, for example, those exhibiting little commitment tended to adopt an atheoretical accumulation approach. They viewed the origins and develop-ment of sport as the coalescence of separate quasi-causal chains of sporting and social modifications and the accumulation of their effects.[11] Sporting modifi-cations included the introduction of rules, umpires, and administrative bod-ies, and the construction of specialized and dedicated facilities (for example, pools, gymnasiums, fields); social modifications included the development of transport systems (for example, rail) that facilitated the movement of sport-ing teams and spectators, and new forms of mass production that lowered the costs of sporting equipment and goods, and mass communication that helped popularize sport.[12] Although often rich in details and anecdotes, the accumula-tion approach to social change and the development of modern sport lacked the explanatory power demanded by social historians that they found in the-ory (the advocacy of which concerned traditional historians for whom theory infused predestined meaning and speculation into the discipline).[13] The most influential theories of explanation among early social historians of sport were modernization, Marxism, and feminism. Emancipation was conspicuously absent from the vocabulary of modernization theory, which the Marxists in particular derided as conceptually limited and offering an interpretation of social change only mildly more sophisticated than accumulation.

Bruce Kidd aligned himself with Marxism early in his academic career.[14] He graduated with a bachelor of arts (honours) in political economy from the University of Toronto. Between 1970 and 1973 he taught in the Department of Political Economy at the University of Toronto before crossing to the School of Physical and Health Education where he lectured in the political economy of Canadian sport.[15] Kidd sets out his approach to history in his 1979 mono-graph *The Political Economy of Sport*, which he bases on Karl Marx's theory of historical materialism as formulated in Marx's oft-cited preface to *A Critique of Political Economy*. According to Marx, the "relations of production consti-tutes the economic structure of society, the real foundation on which rises a legal and political superstructure and to which correspond definite forms of social consciousness. The mode of production of material life conditions the social, political, and intellectual life process in general."[16] Extrapolating from Marx, Kidd argues in *The Political Economy of Sport* that the superstructural "forms of government, legal system, educational system, style of family life, political and religious ideas and … forms of sport" in Canada "correspond to the capitalist mode of production" and "express and reinforce the social rela-tions of capitalism." But, critically, Kidd concluded by noting that every super-structure "must be carefully studied in its own context." Affirming this position, he cited the leading Marxist social historians of the time, Paul Baran and Eric Hobsbawm, for whom "historical configurations cannot be dealt with by …

generalization ... but have to be studied *concretely* with the full account of the wealth of factors that participate in the shaping of any particular case."[17]

Marx's metaphor of a determining economic base and structured social totality is the subject of intense debate among Marxists, especially around questions of social change, the effectiveness of the superstructure, and the role of human agents in making society. Indeed, Kidd's 1979 paper "Sport, Dependency, and the Canadian State," which he presented to a conference at Queen's University that was examining the relationship between sport as a cultural production and the modern state, embroiled him in one of these debates. In his paper Kidd engaged dependency theory to highlight exploitative relationships between the United States and Canada. According to Kidd, the subordination of major professional sports in Canada resided in the interests of the United States and in structures of dependency. Referring to hockey, Kidd argued that once city-based teams such as the Toronto Maple Leafs were enmeshed in commercially sponsored competitions, they lost their power to enunciate a sense of Canadian national identity. As part of a commodity market, players represented the highest bidder rather than their local communities, while "generations of Canadian boys grew up wearing (and never taking off) sweaters celebrating the cities of another country, while living in ignorance of their own."[18] By the end of the Second World War the United States–dominated National Hockey League had, Kidd lamented, reduced the amateur Canadian Hockey Association to a "slave farm of hockey," controlling rules, revenues, style of play, player development, and even the national team."[19]

Many historical materialists rejected dependency theory as reductionist and ahistorical Marxism. Responding to Kidd, Colin Leys suggested that dependency derived more from theory than from historical evidence.[20] Elaborating on this point in a related context, sport historian Brian Stoddart later maintained that the socio-political framework of dependency was more complex than generally given credit and must take into account local sporting and economic contexts that often vary from the generalized patterns espoused by dependency theorists.[21] Kidd has grappled with these issues ever since.[22] For example, shortly after Stoddart's commentary, Kidd cited the long campaign against apartheid in sport as evidence of the "scope for human agency" and of the simultaneously "enabling and constraining nature of social structures."[23] In a recent publication Kidd declared that any understanding of social change must recognize both the choices that agents make and the "array of forces" that buffer them and their actions. Reinforcing his point, he cited Marx's time-honoured words: "Men make their own history but they do not make it just as they please; they do not make it under circumstances chosen by themselves, but under circumstances directly encountered, given and transmitted from the past."[24] In many respects,

Marx's epigram, which appeared in his political pamphlet "The Eighteenth Brumaire of Louis Bonaparte,"[25] frames Kidd's historical analyses.

With respect to emancipation, Kidd repeatedly refers to the role of history in mobilizing actors for social change. History, "whether from the oral accounts of forerunners, [or] committed teaching or scholarship, can provide inspiration, instruction and energy," Kidd recently declared. Here he offered the contributions of history to the long struggles against racism as an example, and concluded by citing Lennox Farrell, an African Canadian veteran of some of those campaigns; in Farrell's words, "to remember gives both motivation and tutelage to resist."[26] Consistent with Farrell's words, Kidd urges historians to tell "the full story" of women athletes in Canada who he says have been "systematically annihilated" in public discourse by their absence from sports exhibits, museums, and halls of fame.[27] Following his own advice, Kidd uses his biography of Tom Longboat to remember the full story of the aboriginal runner and to right a past injustice. Kidd's history led to the City of Toronto paying Longboat's heirs $10,000 in compensation; after Longboat had won the Boston Marathon in 1907, Toronto council had promised, but never paid, the runner a $500 civic grant.[28]

In conceptualizing social history as a political tool, Kidd acknowledges that history is contested and frequently appropriated by different groups for their own ends. The olympic movement is one such group.[29] According to Kidd, the olympic movement presents itself as a "universal, trans-historical, and apolitical international sports festival, based on the ancient Games at Olympia and revived in the late nineteenth century by Pierre de Coubertin." In so doing, it "mystif[ies]… the power relations inherent in the ancient and modern Games" and "obliterates the ambitions and achievements of other movements" that have "taken, realised and enjoyed" other "more egalitarian approaches to physical activity." The "naturalisation of Olympic history," Kidd continues, is the olympic movement's principal strategy to "preserve its monopoly over the modern Games."[30] Kidd urges those who are committed to emancipation and truth to "revisit that history," where he claims they will encounter less well-known versions of "struggles for integration, resistance, and alternatives": "The de Coubertin Games were far from inclusive or universal. Women, the working classes, and those from most of the developing world were excluded by explicit prohibitions, the economic barriers created by the amateur code, and the structures of colonialism and, in other cases, alienated by the ideologies of *Citius, Altius, Fortius*, nation-state competition, and corporate celebration."[31] Importantly, in these claims Kidd also reveals his understanding of history as a realist epistemology, and his commitment to careful empirical investigation.[32]

Historians typically present their empirical data from the past in a narrative form. This form raises critical questions about how historians convert raw data into digestible narratives. Traditionally, historians ignored these questions and imagined that their narratives simply "[fell] into shape under the weight of the sheer accumulation of 'the facts.'"[33] Historians committed to emancipation later admitted that their political and ideological positions shaped their narratives. However, social historians still tend to ignore the claims advanced by philosophers of history that they also make linguistic choices that shape both the form and the content of narratives. In the following section I examine Kidd's histories in more detail and particularly his choices as he prefigures and configures his narratives to conform to the emancipation project. These choices, I suggest, also expose an aporia in the claims to truth in social history.

The Aporia of Social History

As well as embracing emancipation as an ethical value, social historians remain committed to the empiricism, logic, and reason of modernist-inspired history. Herein lies a paradox: historians who configure their narratives to convey emancipatory perspectives and positions cannot simultaneously claim total allegiance to an empirical-analytical epistemology and act as if their histories arose from an objective mining of ethical data from the past. Facts and ethics frequently appear together in social history narratives, but modernist-inspired history does not link them conceptually.[34] In this section I focus on Kidd's choices as he constructs his narrative representations of the past and the issues they raise for empirical-analytical social history. I examine these choices under the headings "Narrative Prefiguring" (by which I mean Kidd's explicit political and ideological positions) and "Narrative Configuring" (by which I mean the content and form of his historical narratives).

Narrative Prefiguring

"*All* history is situated, positioned and *for* something or someone," declares Alun Munslow.[35] Even the modernist positivist-inspired principle of avoiding explicit moral judgments constitutes a moral and subjective position.[36] "We apprehend the past and the whole spectacle of history-in-general," says Hayden White, "in terms of felt needs and aspirations that are ultimately personal, having to do with the way we view our own positions in the ongoing social establishment, our hopes and fears for the future, and the image of the kind of humanity we would like to believe we represent."[37] Bruce Kidd makes no bones about his support for critical history (that is, narratives informed by power relations, which respect the dignity of all individuals, and which facilitate social change for the betterment of all) as a strategy for change.[38] Distancing himself from the modernist conceptualization of the detached historian, and echoing Marx's preference for the philosopher who seeks to change the world rather than simply offering an interpretation,[39] Kidd adopts the voice of a left-leaning radical (in White's terminology).[40] In *The Political Economy of Sport* he advocates "protracted struggle" – on sports fields and in workplaces, schools, universities, and homes – as the means to democratize sport and to change the status quo.[41]

History is particularly accommodating of individual perspectives and positions because, as White explains, there are inordinately different and "equally plausible" ways of comprehending the past and organizing historical narratives. Indeed, such are the possibilities that it is "fruitless ... to try to arbitrate among contending conceptions" of the past "on cognitive grounds which purport to be value neutral in essence." Narrative construction, White says, incorporates morally informed positions that he calls "modes of ideological implication," and these frame the historian's *aesthetic* perception (emplotment) and *cognitive* operation (argument), which collectively render "prescriptive statements."[42]

White, in fact, grounds his model of historical narratives in a theory of tropes (that is, the figures of speech – metaphor, metonym, synecdoche, irony – that authors use to create specific effects in the process of modifying or playing with the literal meaning of language). According to White, historians tropologically prefigure their narrative explanations (that is, emplotments, arguments, and ideologies) to conform to their position, viewpoint, or perspective.[43] However, Keith Jenkins believes that White mistakenly inverts the relationship between trope and ideology. Jenkins maintains that ideological or political positions prefigure historical explanations and determine the tropes that historians used to "metaphorically 'figure things out'": "On my reading it is precisely because one is ... a certain type of ... historian that one will be drawn to a particular way of 'figuring things out' in the first place, and that it is therefore the ideological mode which *predetermines* which trope will be used to metaphorically do so."[44] In my view, Kidd's (refreshingly) explicit positioning of himself and his narratives lends weight to Jenkins's argument that White's ideological modes (that is, conservativism, liberalism, radicalism, and anarchism) determine the historian's choices with respect to the ways in which the historian mobilizes evidence from the past and translates it into a narrative representation. In the following sub-section I expound on Kidd's historical representations by examining his narrative configurations.

Narrative Configuring

In examining the ways in which Kidd configures his work to conform to his ideas of emancipation, I delineate between the form and the content of his narratives. Analysis of the form and content of a narrative involves consideration of a multitude of elements, of which I consider six. Under the heading "Narrative Form" I examine Kidd's tropes (that is, metaphors), emplotments (that is, characterizations of his events and actions), arguments, and focalizations (that is, who speaks and who sees within his narratives); under the heading "Narrative Content" I examine his choices of facts and concepts.

NARRATIVE FORM

Discussing the poetic act of troping, Jenkins observes that historians draw upon figurative language "to make the unfamiliar (and ultimately unfathomable) past familiar." According to Jenkins, figurative language "works metaphorically" to transcribe meaning into ordinary language.[45] In other words, through the process of troping, historians "seek to transform the unfamiliar realities of other places or times into metaphors that make the alien world familiar."[46] Kidd employs figurative language to transfer ideas, and create meaning, about the struggles in sport and whether they have succeeded, have failed, or are ongoing. Applying a running analogy to the Amateur Athletic Union of Canada's slow accommodation of women in the 1920s, Kidd refers to "*dawdling*" male officials.[47] Elsewhere in *The Struggle for Canadian Sport* he describes the "*go-for-the-jugular militancy*" of the Workers' Sports Association.[48] In other publications he refers to

- apartheid South Africa as "a *holiday camp* for whites, a *prison camp* for blacks," and the international boycott of South African sport as variously a strategy of "*quarantine*" and a "*cure*";[49]
- the Gay Games as a "*heart-warming* example of how the transitionally abused and marginalized have won sports opportunities for themselves, in ways that powerfully affirm their aspirations to justice and a better life";[50] and
- the "*de Coubertin Olympic Games*" and the "*de Coubertin Olympic Movement*" promoting and celebrating the very problems that bedevil contemporary sport: nation-state competition, elitism, heterosexism, and masculinity.[51]

White believes that figurative language performs a fundamental framing function, enabling historians to contextualize their events by relating them to an imagined totality. According to White, "there are only two ways to relate parts to wholes, by the metaphors of metonymy and synecdoche."[52] Distinguishing between the two forms, Munslow says that "metonymy signifies by reducing an object to a part or parts," and "synecdoche works the other way by integrating objects, emphasising their similarities or essences."[53] In *The Struggle for Canadian Sport* Kidd examines amateur sport and commercial sport as cultural productions that contributed to the nationalization of Canadians. Read as metaphors, amateur and commercial sports defined Canadian national identity at different historical junctures, viz. the 1920s and late-twentieth century respectively. Referring to amateurism, Kidd writes: "The outpouring of Canadianism during the [amateur versus professional] trials of the Canadian Amateur Athletic Union fired the 'nation-building' imagination of both leaders and members alike. In 1910, [amateur stalwart] Norton Crow held discussions about the possibility of a pan-Canadian sports festival along the lines of today's Canada Games. Others dreamed about sports-focused physical education in the schools. Henceforth, the aspirations of Canadian amateurism and English-Canadian nationalism would ever be intertwined."[54]

Reading Canadian sport in the inter-war period as a metonym, Kidd reduces it to four competing forms – amateur sport, professional sport, workers' sport, and women's sport – that "locked horns with each other" and were "rocked by internal conflict, often over basic principles." He wrote:

> It has become commonplace to attribute a broad identity of purpose and meaning to sports. Participants and commentators alike refer to a "community of sport" within which intentions and values are essentially the same. But few observers would have made that assumption during the interwar period. The [professional National Hockey League] NHL challenged [amateur sport] for the top athletes, fans, sponsors, and the largess and leverage of the state. During the Depression, the NHL hired away male amateur stars ... boosting its own legitimacy and audiences ... It was not only the NHL that raided the ranks of the Amateur Athletic Union (AAU). The Workers' Sports Association scored its greatest publicity coup ... when it sent a team of AAU and Women's Amateur Athletic Federation (WAAF) champions to the Peoples' [Games] of 1936 [i.e., the counter-Olympics held in Barcelona]. While the WAAF worked closely with the AAU, there was always tension about the extent of women's activity and who should control it.[55]

Read as a synecdoche, commercial sport captures the essence of Canadian identity during the inter-war period, which "witnessed the triumph of capitalist cultural production over the more avocational or associational forms of cultural activity pursued by the middle and working classes": "Purchased identity replaced the loyalties of roots and self-realization. The public-spirited attempt to develop a pan-Canadian system of sport with organic links to communities across the country was subordinated to the profits of metropolitan and continental interests. The success of the capitalist model was facilitated by and reflected the rapid spread of the 'universal market,' the escalating power of corporate capital generally, and the American take-over of much of Canadian industrial production and popular culture."[56] Kidd needs the two tropes to characterize different phases of Canadian national identity, and thus he moves between metonymical apprehensions of competing groups struggling within a divided nation and synecdochic intimations of national unity.[57]

Historians give their narratives "explanatory affect" by emplotting, or encoding, their histories in culturally resonant forms. White identifies four primary plot structures in Western culture: romance, comedy, tragedy, and satire. In romantic plots agents transcend their circumstances and achieve victory, whereas satirical plots leave agents permanently captivated by harsh circumstances. Comedy and tragedy lie between these two extremes. Comedies hold out hope for "the temporary triumph of man over his world by the prospect of occasional *reconciliations* of the forces at play in the social and natural worlds. Such reconciliations are symbolized in ... festive occasions ... The reconciliations which occur at the end of Comedy are reconciliations of men with men, of men with their world and their society; the condition of society is represented as being purer, saner, and healthier as a result of the conflict among seemingly inalterably opposed elements in the world; these elements are revealed to be, in the long run, harmonizable with one another, unified, at one with themselves and the others." By contrast, "there are no festive occasions" in tragic emplotments "except false and illusory ones," while reconciliations are "more somber" and "more in the nature of resignations of men to the conditions under which they must labor in the world."[58]

Just as Kidd moves between metonymic and synecdoche tropes in *The Struggle for Canadian Sport*, so too he emplots across the modes of tragedy and comedy. He concedes that the romantic utopia of multiple ways of playing in Canada, where each way enjoys respect and space, lies far in the future. For now, the best that Canadians can hope for are temporary reconciliations such as those seen in the 1970s and the 1990s. In the 1970s the federal government, "acting in the interest of pan-Canadian unity," expanded its sporting programs to "help thousands of athletes reach international standards of performance" and to provide an "alternative source of cultural heroes." These programs fuelled the urban middle classes' dreams of a nationalist sports movement. Twenty years later, Canada's "high performance Olympic sector ... revived and updated its developmental ideal" with organizations such as the Professional Coaches Association and the Canadian Athletes Association moving to "implement an 'athlete-centred' model of training and competition" based on improving

the athletes' health, education, and social capacities, as well as their sporting skills, and to provide them with an environment free from sexual harassment and discrimination. In addition, a host of educational institutions, non-governmental bodies such as ParticipAction, new games such as intercrosse, and new ventures like the Special Olympics, the Gay Games, and the North American Indigenous Games keep the spirit of rational recreation alive in other ways, in an effort to inoculate their constituents against the ills and anxieties of postmodern life ... Innovative Outreach programs, such as Toronto's summer softball for the homeless, Ottawa's "On the Move" activities for girls and women, and Halifax's "midnight" basketball league, extend the benefits of physical activity to those long ignored by the mainstream.[59]

But these are merely temporary reconciliations as opposed to the foundations for structural transformation.

Kidd recognizes that powerful structures and forces continually frustrate the ambitions of democratic groups and communities, and he sees new conflicts and challenges ahead for Canadian sport as it moves into the future: "In the scramble to keep programs alive in the face of disappearing resources, amateur sport leaders are ever more preoccupied with the podium and the legitimation, grants and sponsorships that medals are hoped to bring. These pressures intensify the proletarianization and commodification of athletes [and] diminish the possibilities of overcoming the historic inequality of access to sporting opportunity." In addition, "new progressive initiatives ... confront the consumer loyalties, conventional wisdom, economic power, and political clout" of well-established sports corporations, while "continentalist cartels ... with the help of provincial and municipal financial support [and] global pressures threaten the entire material and ideological basis of cultural expression in Canada." Thus, "the effort to create alternatives to commercial sport will continue to be an uphill fight."[60]

As well as emplotting their narratives in culturally resonant forms, historians use different types of formal argument to convey their explanations. White identifies four basic modes of formal argument: formist, mechanistic, organicist, and contextualist. However, according to White, formism (drawing generalizations from descriptions of unique events, actions, and people in the past) and contextualism (explaining events by "setting them within the 'context' of their occurrence") "represent the limits of choice" in Western history; mechanism ("the search for causal laws that determine the outcome of processes discovered in the historical field") and organicism (integration of events, actions, and people in the past as components of a synthetic process that explains historical change) are "heterodoxies" that belong in the nefarious "philosophy of history."[61] In a climate in which many Marxist-influenced scholars in sports studies faced charges of slavishly appropriating mechanistic conceptualizations of the base of society and organicist conceptualizations of the process of the superstructure,[62] it is not surprising that Kidd conformed to mainstream formist and contextualist modes of explanation.

Throughout *The Struggle for Canadian Sport* Kidd contextualizes his four key organizations – the National Hockey League (for example, contextualized with the Canadian economy), the Amateur Athletic Union (for example, the Great Depression), the Workers' Sports Association (for example, class consciousness and the Communist International), and the Women's Amateur Athletic Federation (for example, the international suffrage movement) – as well as the different phases of sport. In the case of the different phases of sport, Kidd places

- the "creation of sports" within the context of "transformations of work, leisure, household life, and notions of self and society that accompanied the expansion of capitalism";[63]
- the rise of commercial sport within the context of the "interrelated transformations of work, urban space, and culture" that "helped create a market for commercial leisure which entrepreneurs eagerly sought to expand and fill";[64] and
- the prophecies and optimism around women's sport in the 1920s in the context of the Great War, which simultaneously undermined traditional male authority and enhanced female agency as shown by "the unstinting contributions of female nurses, munitions and agricultural workers, and … the successful female-led prohibition and suffrage campaigns."[65]

Kidd's contextualization is only moderately integrative, and, like most historians of sport, he privileges formist explanations that "identify the unique, atomistic or dispersive character of events, people and actions," from which he selects "vivid individual events" as the basis of "significant generalisations."[66] For example, "middle-class, English-speaking male Montrealers from the ward of St Antoine" were responsible for "[making] *a* particular way of playing *the* way of playing" in Canada. "Long before they had the means to extend their activities across the full breadth of the new dominion, Montrealers established 'national' regulatory bodies in nine sports – cycling, track and field, rugby, ice hockey, skating, bowling, cricket, and water polo. Eight of these governing bodies were created by a single club, the Montreal Amateur Athletic Association, formed in 1881."[67] A small group of female Torontonians formed the Women's Amateur Athletic Federation in 1925, and they "brought a uniform system of administration and health inspection to seven sports with branches in every region of the country."[68] In 1924 Tom Hill returned to Canada from the Fourth Congress of the Young Communist International and encouraged his comrades in the Young

Communist League to form workers' sports organizations with a view to mobilizing workers "against exploitation, militarism and fascism, and for revolutionary understanding." Within two years a faction within the Young Communist League had established workers' sports associations in seventeen centres.[69] On 22 November 1917 five sports entrepreneurs met in a Montreal hotel to create the National Hockey League with the express purpose to "increase their profits" from the game and to exclude Ed Livingstone, a fellow entrepreneur whom they deemed troublesome and argumentative.[70] Of course, the sheer weight of historical detail in formist argument also creates the illusion of truth.

As noted earlier, Kidd is rare among historians of sport by virtue of his *explicit* political and ideological positioning. He is also unusual in that he intermittently emerges as an agent in the story (that is, a homodiegetic narrator).[71] For example, in *The Struggle for Canadian Sport* Kidd reflects on his experiences as an amateur runner in the 1950s and 1960s, to highlight the benefits of amateurism, which he said "emphasized the pleasures of competition, travel and fraternizing with athletes from other clubs and countries" and which provided "many rewarding opportunities."[72] Similarly, he recalls his empathy for "my sister athletes" who were frustrated by the conservative "protectiveness" of leaders of the Women's Amateur Athletics Federation.[73]

Mostly, however, Kidd assumes the role of an omniscient (that is, heterodiegetic) narrator who offers his readers an (analytical) explanation of what happened.[74] Like most social historians and historians of sport, Kidd uses quotations to shift his focalization from omniscient observer to the perspective of an agent in the story. For example, rejecting claims by "apologists for apartheid" in the late 1980s that the South African state had desegregated sport, Kidd introduces the voice of Ben Kgantsi, president of the Black [Golf] Tournament Players' Association, to explain why his members withdrew from the South African golf tour: "They tell visiting golfers that there is no apartheid in golf, but what they forget to tell them is the lack of facilities in the townships – where our players live. As soon as everything is over, blacks are not allowed to use white courses: it is back to square one of the dusty course in Soweto and other townships."[75]

In *The Struggle for Canadian Sport* Kidd primarily represents the voices of leaders of the Amateur Athletic Union (for example, Thomas Boyd, Norton Crow, William Findlay, John Jackson, A.S. Lamb, Bruce MacDonald, and Henry Roxborough), the Women's Amateur Athletic Federation (for example, Ethel Cartwright, Alexandrine Gibb, Margaret Lord, Mabel Ray, Ann Spalding, and Joyce Plumptre Tyrrell), and the National Hockey League (for example, Frank Calder and Tommy Gorman). In the case of the Workers' Sports Association, Kidd complements the voices of leaders such as Dave Kashtan, Fred Kaczor, and Walter Kaczor with the voice of the *Young Worker*, the official organ of the Young Communist League.[76] Voices from below are thin throughout his text. Even in his biography of Tom Longboat, the voice of the champion aboriginal long-distance runner of the early-twentieth century is sparse. This is somewhat at odds with the general tenor of the social history of sport, which claims to present voices from below.[77]

Although Mike Cronin argues that historians of sport all too often overstate their position with respect to presenting voices from below,[78] the paucity of internal vocalizations in Kidd's narratives is surprising especially in the light of his 1991 title "How Do We Find Our Own Voices in the 'New World Order'? A Commentary of Americanization." In this piece Kidd argues that "francophones, Atlantic and western Canadians, and native people" feel marginalized by the Canadian nationalism of "white, middle-class, central Canadian, English-speaking males." Responding to their situation, the former groups have turned to "American practices in order to improve their chances to play and compete,"[79] but Kidd offers few internal vocalizations of these groups to enrich his narratives. I return to this point in the third section of this chapter where I argue that there is an unfortunate tendency among social historians to diminish the voice of the other by turning the singular and the unique "into an example of an abstract category."[80]

Explaining the past requires historians to make decisions about their narratives. Initially emanating from the historian's ideological political position, those decisions prefigure the narrative and configure its content and form. As noted, Kidd makes clear his political position as a historian, which he explicitly aligns to the emancipation project, and he is candid about his roles in his narratives. "No investigator can expect to be completely independent of her or his data," he writes in *The Struggle for Canadian Sport*, and "I stand closer to my subject than many," also bringing "the experiences and blind spots of someone 'on the inside.'"[81] These words distance Kidd epistemologically from the earlier modernist idea that historians should separate themselves from their subjects and conceal their ideology, politics, and ethics.[82] How much distance? Acknowledging the interactive relationship between himself as an inquiring subject and the past as an external object, Kidd adopts what Joyce Appleby, Lynn Hunt, and Margaret Jacob call a practical realist epistemology.[83] But if practical realism dilutes the primacy of objectivity in historicizing, it does not disrupt the traditional modernist perspective that historical sources are the ultimate arbitrators of the past.[84] Like most historians, Kidd attempts to convey the truth of his content by highlighting the reliability of his sources or facts while remaining silent about his choices of facts and the silences and blind spots in his concepts.

NARRATIVE CONTENT

Social historians ground their claims to truth in their facts (that is, verifiable and corroborated statements in sources) and concepts. Consistent with the modernist craft of empirical history, Kidd maintains vigilance over his sources and those used by his peers. He reminds readers of the importance of checking their sources when he reveals that the *Toronto Daily Star* published fake interviews with Tom Longboat and on one occasion inserted a photograph of a footballer over the runner's name.[85] Kidd also comments that newspaper reports were frequently wrong because they were written hurriedly and were unchecked or because special interests (for example, entrepreneurs, sports organizations) "cultivated reporters [and] publishers, supplying them with prepared copy, photographs and illustrations, treating them with gifts and free lunches, and sometimes bribing them outright."[86] He also draws attention to the reliability of oral sources, when openly questioning the agenda and memory of one leader of the Women's Amateur Athletic Federation.[87] After citing an extract from Michael Ondaatje's *In the Skin of a Lion*, Kidd reassures his readers that the novel is empirically grounded in "interviews and archival photos."[88]

Kidd also invariably comments on the quality and reliability of the sources that his peers use in their texts:

- Alan Metcalfe "draws much of his evidence from … newspapers" in *Canada Learns to Play*;
- Nancy Bouchier employs "an imaginatively wide variety of sources" including sports memorabilia, trophies, and team photographs in *For the Love of the Game*;
- Colin Howell "has done an excellent job of recapturing the major developments and debates from newspapers, archival sources and interviews" in *Northern Sandlots*; and
- Gerald Redmond "provides a competent summary of the secondary literature" in *The Sporting Scots of Nineteenth-Century Canada*.[89]

The insinuation in these statements, of course, is that facts cement truths. While no historians want to get their facts wrong, the factual content in any narrative does not guarantee access to an incontrovertible reality. Analysis of Kidd's historical concepts adds further weight to this view.

In modernist social history a concept derives from examinations of "analogies between historical instances," and it becomes finer and more precise as knowledge expands, until, ultimately, it sets hard, so-to speak, offering an enduring certainty if not an essential truth.[90] Kidd reveals his preference for conceptually grounded history in his book reviews. Texts grounded in atheoretical detail and anecdotes receive harsh criticism;[91] authors who demonstrate conceptual precision receive fulsome praise. Applauding Colin Howell's conceptual sophistication in *Blood, Sweat, and Cheers*, Kidd commends the book as an exemplary "introduction to the way in which social historians approach the history of sport."[92]

While retaining general concepts (for example, class, hegemony, feminism, state, apartheid, non-racialism) in his own work, Kidd generally aligns them with particular descriptions rather than marrying them to theory, as his treatment of the Canadian middle class and the Canadian state illustrates in *The Struggle for Canadian Sport*. Kidd conceptualizes the middle class as the "intellectual workers and self-employed professionals" of the Amateur Athletic Union who were both "conservative in outlook" and sympathetic to business; the nineteenth-century state is simply those dominion, provincial, and local governments that "regulated the use of leisure in the general interests of male hegemony, middle-class morality, and capitalist production."[93] Compared with the rich theoretical discussions of social class and the state in Marxist thought,[94] Kidd's treatment of the Canadian middle class and the Canadian state might seem cavalier (especially against his alertness to the empirical and analytical treatment of the middle classes in his reviews of other historians' work).[95] However, he does elaborate on both concepts in *The Political Economy of Sport*. In a discussion of class, Kidd draws on E.P. Thompson, for whom class is neither a structure nor a category but an experience of human relationships that, "like other relationships, [contains] a fluency which evades analysis if we attempt to stop it dead at any given moment and anatomize its structure. The finest-meshed sociological net cannot give us a pure specimen of class ... The relationship must always be embodied in real people and in real context."[96] In these words Thompson echoes Marx who insisted that the problems of class "will not be resolved by 'the *passé-partout* of a historical-philosophical theory' but by an analysis in each separate case of the 'empirically given circumstances.'"[97]

Few historians completely dispose of their concepts and replace them with the micro-details of constantly changing circumstances and exceptions. Rather, they retain their concepts with their "blind spots and silences."[98] Kidd's use of hegemony is a case in point. Describing the hegemony of amateurism in Canadian sport in the 1920s, Kidd writes that "its rightfulness ... as the basis for sporting morality and governance was widely recognized," and "its contribution to national development universally praised."[99] In short, under this conceptualization of hegemony, amateur leaders persuaded Canadians that the norms and values of their way of playing were, ideologically speaking, "natural, good, and just" while simultaneously concealing its "system of domination."[100] However, identifying the exact moment and spread of amateur hegemony in Canadian sport is more difficult than Kidd suggests here. He quickly admits that "the sanctity of amateurism had been slowly eroding during the 1920s" and that mass unemployment during the Great Depression "dramatically acceler-ated" the process. More precipitously, he acknowledges that amateurism was primarily an English-Canadian idea that largely excluded French-Canadians, First Nations, immigrants, and working-class groups.[101] Thus, it is only at this point that Kidd removes hegemony of its ideological mantle and embraces it, correctly, as a relationship "characterized by conflict and consent, [and] coercion and struggle," and in which "outcomes" are never problem free for either party.[102] Within this framework, dominant groups can never guarantee their ideological aspirations; they must "anticipate challenges" and assess the best "combination of coercion and persuasion." This is "an ongoing process of accommodation and compromise."[103]

Against this background the explanatory power of historical facts and con-cepts resides solely in their insertion into a narrative, that is, in the process of troping and emplotment, which "confers on the facts a significance which a dif-ferent emplotment and troping could take away."[104] In White's words, "when it comes to apprehending the historical record, there are no grounds to be found in the historical record itself for preferring one way of constructing its mean-ing over another."[105] Thus, "in effect the facts are narrative dependent and truth (facticity) is essentially an interpretive matter."[106] It is precisely this freedom to choose an interpretation that leads Jenkins to deem history "promiscuous": "The historical past has gone along with anybody who wanted it – Marxists, Whigs, racists, feminists, structuralists, empiricists, antiquarians, postmod-ernists – anybody can have it … In it we have almost invariably 'found' those origins, roots, teleologies, trajectories, lessons, facts and values we have been looking for."[107] It is this power of the narrative that social historians have over-looked; moreover, they continue to do so.

In selecting his references (that is, facts, concepts) to Canadian sport, and in assigning those references meaning, through his narratives, Kidd reveals his emancipatory and ethical concerns. This is quite different, however, to saying that he legitimizes a version of Canadian sport. Herein is a paradox for social history: historians who configure their narratives to conform to an emancipa-tory mission cannot claim allegiance to an empirical-analytical epistemology and pretend that their histories arise from an objective mining of ethical data from the past.

Ethics and Social History

Social history is replete with ethical references. Bruce Kidd, for example, criti-cizes the olympic movement for insisting that physical cultures "conform to its singular definition." Such a position, Kidd says, "undervalues the rich diversity in humanity" and "lacks ethical grounding."[108] Social historians frequently marry facts and ethics, but modernist-inspired history does not conceptually link the two. While Jenkins says that historians should concede the incommensurability of history and ethics, Munslow suggests that they could encompass ethics by acknowledging "the moral choices they make as they construct the past as a representational narrative."[109] Emphasizing the relationship between ethics and narrative construction, particularly for understanding the present, Munslow says that the way in which historians chose to write about the past allows them to "take up certain political options and uphold preferred moral standards and moral ideals. Moral lessons do not emerge 'from history,'" he argues; rather, historians build moral lessons into their narratives as they create them with the goal of coping with the present.[110]

In his histories (that is, analytical methods and strategies of representation) Kidd presents the voice of Marxism (that is, left radicalism), a voice that comprehends the general direction of social development from the past through to the present and into the future. Kidd also offers his readers "choices between possible alternatives without specifying what [their] decision in a given situation *has to be*." He "places his readers in a position in which, whatever choice they make[,] they … make them in a condition of [profound] self consciousness."[111] In these ways Kidd's ethical stance is beyond reproach. However, for Munslow, the key issue in ethical history is the "mutuality in the relationship between oneself and 'the other' and the process of 'othering.'"[112] In this section I examine Kidd's approach to ethics within this narrower conceptualization.

Discussing the process of othering in history, Munslow defers to the moral philosopher Emmanuel Lévinas for whom ethics constitutes the "first philosophy."[113] Drawing on his thinking about the Holocaust, a subject that saturates his work,[114] Lévinas placed ethics before history and all other philosophies, behaviours, and attitudes. At the heart of Lévinas's ethics are relationships with others that constitute "the core element of intersubjective life: the other person addresses me, calls to me. He does not even have to utter words in order for me to *feel* the summons implicit in his approach."[115] Such a summons invokes an "extensive exploration of the face-to-face relationship" and calls into question issues of human responsibility, social existence, and justice.[116] Critically, rather than locating ethical relations in reason (that is, the empirical-analytical logic of modernist-inspired history), Lévinas situated "reason and truth" in the "ethical relationship between individuals."[117]

Lévinas's idea that "the moment of facing is the moment of ethics" is problematic, however, for social historians who insist on empirically verifying the past. How might they empirically recover the ethical in face-to-face relationships, and how does the ethical relation appear in an absence? "If the ethical moment is only the moment of facing, with the face actually present, then how are we responsible for those who are absent, who have no faces?"[118] Lévinas's answer to these questions lay in what he called the trace. A trace is not "a traditional piece of historical evidence"; it "does not signify a reconstructable past, but the presence of the other as an irrecuperable absence and otherness, and, just as with the face in the present, this leads to an interruption of any possible totalizing system: the other's 'trace does not signify his past ... it is a disturbance imprinting itself' above and beyond the material evidence. The trace, our sense of 'history-ness' [the aura of the past, which is neither the past nor the truth about the past], is the source of our obligation to the past and its call for justice."[119] A trace, what Jacques Derrida subsequently called a cinder (that is, "visible but scarcely readable," "that particular fire and that particular burnt 'thing' can never be recreated, brought back, brought to life"),[120] represents both the "present and absent" mark of the other in the past.[121] It is the remembered and recalled – but never recoverable – moments that disrupt the totalizing systems of the de Coubertin Olympics, Canadian amateur sport, Canadian commercial sport, and apartheid sport.

Kidd occasionally represents the Other and moves towards the lived lives of the Other and their relationships. In *Tom Longboat* he describes a Montreal crowd in 1873 physically trying to stop two aboriginal runners, Keraronwe and Peter Thomas, from completing a two-mile snowshoe race. Subscribing to the popular belief that indigenous Canadians were naturally superior athletes, the crowd launched "hot protests" when the pair took the first two places. Although officials upheld their win, they bowed to public pressure and excluded aboriginals from the race in following years.[122] In *The Struggle for Canadian Sport* Kidd reports police harassment of Dave Kashtan who was arrested for distributing leaflets that condemned "bosses sport" and on another occasion for addressing a meeting of unemployed workers – for which he was charged with sedition, convicted, and jailed.[123]

Kidd's historical accounts rarely capture the affective power of face-to-face moments, the moments of ethical relationships. One interesting exception is his review of Tom Newnham's *By Batons and Barbed Wire*, an account of popular opposition to the South African rugby tour of New Zealand in 1981. Kidd praises Newnham for creating "a chilling book, both inspiring and terrifying (it evoked my own memories of the police riots during the 1968 Democratic Convention in Chicago)."[124] Mostly, Kidd chooses the focalization of the omniscient historian author committed to the cold-blooded distancing of empirical truths and analytical concepts. The effects of this approach appear in Kidd's analysis of the aboriginal athletes Keraronwe and Peter Thomas whom he reduces to victims of "racist restrictions," which in turn are "the result of class prejudice" – the middle classes constructed amateurism to ensure that they played only with their social equals – and a "complex set of beliefs. On the one hand, Aboriginal athletes were regarded as 'natural athletes' and therefore unfair competitors. On the other hand, they were considered savages, which made them unfit for competition against civilized men."[125] Such reductions, such distancing from the face-to-face relationships between the runners and the hostile individuals within the crowd, remove notions of responsibility and, as Lévinas maintained, expose the "cruel … judgement of history [and] of pure reason."[126]

Conclusion

In many respects Bruce Kidd's historical work is an exemplar of the emancipation project in the social history of sport. Kidd is one of a select few to explicitly advocate history as a vehicle to raise political awareness and consciousness in sport with a view to effecting social change. He is also one of the few to explicitly discuss the ethical dimensions of history. In his recent article "The Struggle Must Continue" Kidd concedes the political and ideological foundations of history, noting that no matter how carefully one writes about the past, the words are "always … potentially divisive": "In recent decades, in the former Yugoslavia, in Rwanda, in Iraq and throughout the Middle East, [the past] has been mined selectively to whip up appalling hatred and violence. In Spain, the memories of the civil war and the Franco years have been so painful that public remembrance was outlawed until very recently." For Kidd, ethical history resides in narratives "informed by a respect for the humanity of all" and in narratives that aim to "realize equity and human rights."[127]

What are the mechanisms that Kidd uses to link historical narratives to social change, emancipation, and ethics? A recent citing by Herbert Gutman, a stalwart of the new labour history in the 1960s and 1970s, offers insights into Kidd's thinking. According to Gutman, "historical understanding transforms historical givens into historical contingencies."[128] In other words, reconceptualizing the past as contingent opens the door to seeing alternative experiences and versions of the past; the past does not comprise just one set of constraining structures. The knowledge that history is contingent, Gutman says, frees people to think creatively and critically; contingent history presumably also frees people to consider alternative trajectories between the past and the future.

Gutman's approach, however, seems predicated on two assumptions: that readers bring ideological flexibility to their reception of historical narratives, and that narratives grounded in a realist empirical-analytical epistemology will persuade readers of some or other truth. But if ideology frames the form and content of historical narratives, then logically ideology also frames readers' reception and interpretation of those narratives. As an example, I am more than happy to admit that the ideologically informed tropes in the respective titles of Kidd's *The Struggle for Canadian Sport* and Richard Cashman's *Paradise of Sport: The Rise of Organized Sport in Australia* (that is, radical "struggle" and conservative "paradise") framed both my immediate reception and my subsequent interpretations.[129] The two tropes helped to persuade me of the veracity of Kidd's work and the idealism of Cashman's. As White argues, ideology is the sole basis on which "to arbitrate among the conflicting conceptions of the historical process and of historical knowledge."[130]

Better empiricism, sharper conceptualization, and deeper analysis will not advance the emancipatory mission of history, which can only begin with an understanding of the processes of narrative creation and narrative effects. Paradoxically, in these processes lies the basis for understanding who we are and how we operate. And this understanding is also the basis of ethics, which in its historical forms captures *and* represents instances of suffering in the face-to-face relationships of the past. Ethics, in fact, underpins two forms of truth, truth as an explanation that corresponds to the evidence, and truth as a revelation of the human condition.[131] While Bruce Kidd's histories engage with both forms, his broader career as an activist scholar suggests a preference for truth as a revelation of the human condition.

NOTES

Sincere thanks go to Mark Falcous whose constructive comments improved this chapter.

1 Bruce Kidd, *The Struggle for Canadian Sport* (Toronto: University of Toronto Press, 1996), 268–9. The number of activist-scholars in sport is extremely small. As well as Kidd I would include in their numbers Colin Tatz (Australia), Colin King and Celia Brackenridge (United Kingdom), Trevor Richards (New Zealand), Aswin Desai and Cheryl Roberts (South Africa), and Richard Lapchick and Pat Griffin (United States).

2 See, for example, Bruce Kidd, "Epilogue: The Struggle Must Continue," *Sport in Society* 13, no. 1 (2010): 157; and Bruce Kidd, "The Men's Cultural Centre: Sports and the Dynamic of Women's Oppression / Men's Repression," in Michael Messner and Don Sabo (eds.), *Sport, Men, and the Gender Order* (Champaign, IL: Human Kinetics, 1990), 41–3.

3 In the words of E.P. Thompson, "the modes of historical writing are so diverse; the techniques employed by historians are so various; the themes of historical enquiry are so disparate; and, above all, the conclusions so controversial and so sharply contested within the profession, that it is difficult to adduce any disciplinary coherence." *The Poverty of Theory: Or an Orrery of Errors*, 2nd. ed. (London: Merlin, 1995), 51. Readers should note that much of Kidd's work has been in the sociology of sport and that he was at the vanguard of struggle against conservatives, many of whom manifested as functionalists. See Alan Ingham and Peter Donnelly, "A Sociology of North American Sociology of Sport: Disunity in Unity, 1965 to 1996," *Sociology of Sport Journal* 14, no. 4 (1997): 362–418.

4 Cited in Robert Eaglestone, "The 'Fine Risk' of History: Post-Structuralism, the Past, and the Work of Emmanuel Levinas," *Rethinking History* 2, no. 3 (1998): 317.

5 Grant Farred, *What's My Name? Black Vernacular Intellectuals* (Minneapolis: University of Minnesota Press, 2003).

6 Quotes from Beverly Southgate, "A Pair of White Gloves: Historians and Ethics," *Rethinking History* 10, no. 1 (2006): 49; and David Hackett Fischer, *Historians' Fallacies: Toward a Logic of Historical Thought* (New York: Harper & Row, 1970), 78.

7 Geoffrey Elton, *The Practice of History*, 2nd. ed. (Oxford: Blackwell, 2002), 42 and 44.

8 Geoffrey Elton, *Return to Essentials: Some Reflections on the Present State of Historical Study* (Cambridge: Cambridge University Press, 1991), 52.

9 Quotes from Deborah Posel, "History as Confession: The Case of the South African Truth and Reconciliation Commission," *Public Culture* 20, no. 1 (2008): 122; and Robert Berkhofer, *Beyond the Great Story: History as Text and Discourse* (Cambridge, MA: Harvard University Press, 1995), 146 and 215. See also Keith Jenkins, *Why History? Ethics and Postmodernity* (London: Routledge, 1999), 11; and Michael Cotey Morgan, "The Seventies and the Rebirth of Human Rights," in Niall Ferguson *et al.* (eds.), *The Shock of the Global* (Cambridge: Belknap Press, 2010), 237–50.

10 See, for example, James Walvin, "Sport, Social History, and the Historian," *British Journal of Sports History* 1, no. 1 (1984): 8; and Kidd, *Struggle for Canadian Sport*, 8. On the origins and rise of sport history see Richard Cashman, "The Making of Sporting Traditions," *Bulletin* [of the Australian Society for Sports History], December 1989, 15–28; Alan Metcalfe, "North American Sport History: A Review of North American Sport Historians and Their Works," *Exercise and Sport Sciences Reviews* 2 (1974): 225–38; and Nancy Struna, "Sport History," in John Massengale and Richard Swanson (eds.), *The History of Exercise and Sport Science* (Champaign, IL: Human Kinetics, 1997), 143–79. Kidd offers a nice summary of sport's place in economic, political, social, and cultural life in *The Struggle for Canadian Sport*, 5–8.

11 Tom Bottomore, "Structure and History," in Peter Blau (ed.), *Approaches to the Study of Social Structure* (New York: Free Press, 1975), 164.

12 See, for example, Steven Riess, *Sport in Industrial America, 1850–1920* (Wheeling, WV: Harlan Davidson, 1995), 11–42.

13 See Douglas Booth, "Theory in Sport History," in S.W. Pope and John Nauright (eds.), *The Sports History Reader* (London: Routledge, 2010), 12–33.

14 Bruce Kidd, *The Political Economy of Sport* (Calgary, AB: Canadian Association for Health, Physical Education, and Recreation, 1979), 19–20; Bruce Kidd, "Improvers, Feminists, Capitalists, and Socialists: Shaping Canadian Sport in the 1920s and 1930s," unpublished PhD diss., York University, 1990, 29–30; and Kidd, *Struggle for Canadian Sport*, 186–7.

15 Bruce Kidd, full curriculum vitae, 2009, supplied by the Faculty of Physical Education and Health, University of Toronto.

16 Karl Marx, preface to *A Critique of Political Economy*, in David McLellan, *Karl Marx Selected Writings* (Oxford: Oxford University Press, 1977), 389. Kidd cites this passage in *Political Economy of Sport*, 13.

17 Kidd, *Political Economy of Sport*, 9 and 14.

18 Published as Bruce Kidd, "Sport, Dependency, and the Canadian State," in Hart Cantelon and Richard Gruneau (eds.), *Sport, Culture, and the Modern State* (Toronto: University of Toronto Press, 1982), 281–303; quote from 291–2.

19 Kidd, "Sport, Dependency, and the Canadian State," 291.

20 Colin Leys, "Sport, the State, and Dependency Theory: Response to Kidd," in Cantelon and Gruneau, *Sport, Culture, and the Modern State*, 304–15.

21 Brian Stoddart, "Sport in the Social Construct of the Lesser Developed World: A Commentary," *Sociology of Sport Journal* 6, no. 2 (1989): 125–35.

22 Including in his assessments of other historians' work. Reviewing Colin Howell's analysis of patronage in the Maritimer baseball leagues, for example, Kidd suggests that it would have profited from "a more detailed account of the [local] economic base." Bruce Kidd, "Book Review: Colin Howell, *Northern Sandlots*," *Canadian Historical Review* 78, no. 4 (1997): 648.

23 Bruce Kidd, "From Quarantine to Cure: The New Phase of the Struggle against Apartheid Sport," *Sociology of Sport Journal* 8 (1991): 44–5.

24 Kidd, "The Struggle Must Continue," 159. Kidd also places this quote at the head of chapter 2, "Historical Materialism," in *The Political Economy of Sport*, 5. See also Kidd, "Book Review: Colin Howell, *Blood, Sweat and Cheers*," *University of Toronto Quarterly* 72, no. 1 (Winter 2002/3), 463.

25 In McLellan, *Karl Marx*, 300.

26 Kidd, "The Struggle Must Continue," 157–8.

27 Bruce Kidd, "Missing: Women from Sports Halls of Fame," in Peter Donnelly (ed.), *Taking Sport Seriously: Social Issues in Canadian Sport* (Toronto: Thompson Educational Publishing, 2000), 173.

28 Bruce Kidd, *Tom Longboat* (Markham, ON: Fitzhenry & Whiteside, 2004), 48; Bruce Kidd, "In Defence of Tom Longboat," *Canadian Journal of History of Sport* 14, no. 1 (1983): 34–63; Kidd, curriculum vitae.

29 Sports in general do not warrant the veneration of capital letters. This includes the olympic games, a collection of different sports. Similarly, there is no reason that the philosophy of olympism should have greater claim to a capital letter than do liberalism, humanitarianism, authoritarianism, or utopianism.

30 Bruce Kidd, "'Another World Is Possible': Recapturing Alternative Olympic Histories, Imagining Different Games," in Kevin Young and Kevin Wamsley (eds.), *Global Olympics: Historical and Sociological Studies of the Modern Games* (London: Elsevier, 2005), 143, 144, and 145.

31 Kidd, "Another World Is Possible," 147.

32 Kidd, "Improvers, Feminists, Capitalists, and Socialists," 36.

33 Keith Jenkins, *The Postmodern History Reader* (London: Routledge, 1997), 10.

34 Wulf Kansteiner, "Success, Truth, and Modernism in Holocaust Historiography: Reading Saul Friedländer Thirty-Five Years after the Publication of *Metahistory*," *History and Theory, Theme Issue*, 47 (2009): 30.

35 Alun Munslow, *Narrative and History* (Houndmills, UK: Palgrave Macmillan, 2007), 41.

36 Hayden White, *Metahistory: The Historical Imagination in Nineteenth-Century Europe* (Baltimore, MD: Johns Hopkins University Press, 1973), 26–7; cf. Richard Evans, *In Defence of History* (London: Granta Books, 1997), 51.

37 White, *Metahistory*, 283.

38 Kidd, "The Struggle Must Continue," 164.

39 Kidd, *Political Economy of Sport*, 67; Karl Marx, "Theses on Feuerbach," in McLellan, *Karl Marx*, 158.

40 Following Karl Mannheim, White employs four prime ideological positions: anarchism, conservatism, radicalism, and liberalism. These positions are based on the desirability of maintaining or changing the status quo, the directions that changes in the status quo ought to take, and the means of effecting such changes, and orientations towards time – past, present, or future – as the repository of the ideal social structure or form. Radicals believe in structural transformations in the interests of reconstituting society on new bases, and they envision the possibility of cataclysmic transformations even though they are aware of the power required to effect such transformations. Although they are sensitive to the inertial pull of inherited institutions, radicals concern themselves with the means of effecting change and bringing about utopia. *Metahistory*, 24–5 and 284.

41 Kidd, *Political Economy of Sport*, 67.

42 These statements may, of course, include moral positions. White, *Metahistory*, 27 and 283–4.

43 White, *Metahistory*, 30–1.

44 Keith Jenkins, *On "What Is History?" From Carr and Elton to Rorty and White* (London: Routledge, 1995), 174.

45 Jenkins, *On "What Is History?"* 167. Roland Barthes notes, "It is very rare that [language] imposes at the outset a full meaning which it is impossible to distort. [T]here always remains, around the final meaning, a halo of virtualities where other possible meanings are floating: the meaning can almost always be *interpreted*." *Mythologies*, trans. Annette Lavers (Frogmore, UK: Paladin, 1973), 132.

46 Lloyd Kramer, "Literature, Criticism, and Historical Imagination: The Literary Challenge of Hayden White and Dominick LaCapra," in Lynn Hunt (ed.), *The New Cultural History* (Berkeley: University of California Press, 1989), 109. Interestingly, George Lakoff and Mark Johnson argue that "metaphor is as much a part of our functioning as our sense of touch, and as precious." *Metaphors We Live By* (Chicago: University of Chicago Press, 1980), 4 and 239.

47 Kidd, *The Struggle for Canadian Sport*, 114, emphasis added. Similarly, he likens the olympic movement's sporadic accommodation of women, the working class, third-world nations, persons with disabilities, and LBGTQ to "the runner who takes the lead only to slow down the pace." Kidd, "Another World Is Possible," 155–6.

48 Kidd, *The Struggle for Canadian Sport*, 182, emphasis added.

49 Kidd, "From Quarantine to Cure," 44, emphasis added.

50 Kidd, "Another World Is Possible," 154, emphasis added.

51 Ibid., 147, 154, 155, and 156, emphasis added.

52 Jenkins, *On "What is History?"* 168.

53 Alun Munslow, *Deconstructing History* (London: Routledge, 1997), 156.

54 Kidd, *The Struggle for Canadian Sport*, 37.

55 Kidd, *The Struggle for Canadian Sport*, 262. When the fascist leader Francisco Franco began his war against the Spanish Republic on the morning of the opening ceremonies, he forced the organizers to abandon the games (178).

56 Kidd, *The Struggle for Canadian Sport*, 264.

57 White, *Metahistory*, 285–6.

58 Ibid., 9.

59 Kidd, *The Struggle for Canadian Sport*, 268–9. Other examples of comic emplotments in Kidd's narratives include the defeat of apartheid, equity legislation and policies in government and sports organizations, and the realization of athletes' rights in the Olympic sports (Kidd, "The Struggle Must Continue," 159), and the Paralympic Movement's contribution to transforming "the way most people think about *ability* [and] dramatically reinforcing legislative and other changes that give protection and opportunity to those once cast aside as *disabled*" (Kidd, "Another World Is Possible," 154).

60 Kidd, *The Struggle for Canadian Sport*, 270. Other tragic emplotments in *The Struggle for Canadian Sport* include the "death" of the workers' sports movement

in Canada following the dissolution of the Canadian Amateur Sports Federation (the successor of the Workers' Sport Association of Canada) (179–82) and the "disastrous" collapse of the Women's Amateur Athletic Federation after the Second World War that "eliminated an accepted advocate and a national network and helped marginalize, if not obliterate, sportswomen in newspapers, radio, and television" (144).

61 White, *Metahistory*, 11–20 and 286.

62 See, for example, Richard Gruneau, *Class, Sports, and Social Development* (Amherst: University of Massachusetts Press, 1983), 38–9.

63 Kidd, *The Struggle for Canadian Sport*, 17.

64 Ibid., 188.

65 Ibid., 42–3. In another example worthy of highlighting, Kidd places the "demise of Aboriginal athletes" in the inter-war period in the context of the "gradual economic decline" of aboriginal communities as "'many of the previous kinds of Indian employment came to an end or were permanently reduced … [T]he collapse of small-scale enterprises … seems to have been of exceptional intensity among Indian-owned enterprises, and relatively few appeared after the end of the depression.' Under these circumstances, many Aboriginals returned to the reserves to take the subsistence farming, hunting, fishing and craft production … But in most cases this was not enough to live on, and the government had to step in with welfare payments. Increasingly poverty and despair sometimes turned slurs against Aboriginals into self-fulfilling prophecies." Kidd, *Tom Longboat*, 60–1.

66 Munslow, *Deconstructing History*, 158.

67 Kidd, *The Struggle for Canadian Sport*, 16.

68 Ibid., 97.

69 Ibid., 156–7.

70 Ibid., 184.

71 Munslow, *Narrative and History*, 49.

72 Kidd, *The Struggle for Canadian Sport*, 92.

73 Ibid., 140.

74 Munslow, *Narrative and History*, 49.

75 Kidd, "From Quarantine to Cure," 36.

76 Kidd cites the *Young Worker* nine times in the text of the chapter, and it appears in twenty-four separate references.

77 Kidd, "Improvers, Feminists, Capitalists, and Socialists," 37.

78 Mike Cronin, "Reflections on the Cultural Paradigm," *Sporting Traditions* 27, no. 2 (2010): 1. Cronin singles out the foundational texts in sport history as examples including Tony Mangan's *Athleticism in the Victorian and Edwardian Public School* (a history of schoolmasters and their socially elite charges) and Richard Holt's *Sport and the British* (which examines upper-class administrators and

"gentlemen" alongside working-class professionals). J.A. Mangan, *Athleticism in the Victorian and Edwardian Public School* (Cambridge: Cambridge University Press, 1981); Richard Holt, *Sport and the British* (Oxford: Clarendon Press, 1989). Holt's recognition of the "patchy" coverage of working-class sport in *Sport and the British* led him to edit a collection of essays titled *Sport and the Working Class in Modern Britain* (Manchester, UK: Manchester University Press, 1990). To Cronin's examples I would add Allen Guttmann's *From Ritual to Record*, Mel Adelman's *A Sporting Time*, and Benjamin Rader's *American Sports*; all three privilege the social processes of modernization over the voices of participants – administrators, players, spectators – irrespective of their class affiliations or social position. Allen Guttmann, *From Ritual to Record: The Nature of Modern Sports* (New York: Columbia University Press, 1978); Benjamin Rader, *American Sports: From the Age of Folk Games to the Age of Televised Sports* (Upper Saddle River, NJ: Prentice Hall, 1983); Mel Adelman, *A Sporting Time: New York City and the Rise of Modern Athletics, 1820–70* (Urbana: University of Illinois Press, 1986).

79 Bruce Kidd, "How Do We Find Our Own Voices in the 'New World Order'? A Commentary of Americanization," *Sociology of Sport Journal* 8, no. 2 (1991): 178–80.

80 Robert Eaglestone, *The Holocaust and the Postmodern* (Oxford: Oxford University Press, 2004), 291.

81 Kidd, *The Struggle for Canadian Sport*, x.

82 Joyce Appleby, Lynn Hunt, and Margaret Jacob, *Telling the Truth about History* (New York: W.W. Norton, 1994).

83 Appleby, Hunt, and Jacob, *Telling the Truth about History*, 261.

84 Munslow, *Narrative and History*, 42.

85 Kidd, *Tom Longboat*, 22.

86 Kidd, "In Defence of Tom Longboat," 57n21; Kidd, *Struggle for Canadian Sport*, 262–3.

87 Kidd, *The Struggle for Canadian Sport*, 138.

88 Ibid., 160.

89 Bruce Kidd, "Book Review: Alan Metcalfe, *Canada Learns to Play*," *Journal of Sport History* 16, no. 2 (1989): 197; Bruce Kidd, "Book Review: Nancy Bouchier, *For the Love of the Game: Amateur Sport in Small-Town Ontario, 1838–1895*," *Journal of Interdisciplinary History* 36, no. 1 (2005): 124; Kidd, "Book Review: Colin Howell, *Northern Sandlots*," 648; Bruce Kidd, "Book Review: Gerald Redmond, *The Sporting Scots of Nineteenth-Century Canada*," *Journal of Sport History* 10, no. 3 (1983): 90.

90 Arthur Stinchcombe, *Theoretical Methods in Social History* (New York: Academic Press, 1978), 17; Stanley Fish, "French Theory in America," *New York Times*, 6 April 2008.

91 See, for example, Kidd, "Book Review: Gerald Redmond," 89.

92 See, for example, Kidd, "Book Review: Colin Howell, *Blood, Sweat and Cheers*," 464.

93 Kidd, *The Struggle for Canadian Sport*, 49 and 232–3.

94 See, for example, Erik Olin Wright, "Rethinking, Once Again, the Concept of Class Structure," in John Hall (ed.), *Reworking Class* (Ithaca, NY: Cornell University Press, 1997), 71; and Ralph Miliband, *The State in Capitalist Society* (London: Quartet Books, 1973), 46. In his discussion of the middle class in capitalist societies Wright deals with a store of concepts including "contradictory locations within class relations, mediated class locations, temporally structured class locations, objectively ambiguous class locations, dualistic class locations." Miliband stresses that the state and the government are not synonymous; "'the state' is not a thing [and] does not, as such exist. What 'the state' stands for is a number of particular institutions which, together, constitute its reality, and which interact as parts of what may be called the state system [of power]" (46).

95 Kidd, "Book Review: Alan Metcalfe," 197; Kidd, "Book Review: Nancy Bouchier," 124; Kidd, "Book Review: Colin Howell, *Northern Sandlots*," 647; Kidd, "Book Review: Gerald Redmond," 87.

96 Kidd, *The Political Economy of Sport*, 15–16.

97 Tom Bottomore, "Class Conflict," in *A Dictionary of Marxist Thought* (Oxford: Blackwell, 1983), 77.

98 Alun Munslow, *The Routledge Companion to Historical Studies*, 2nd. ed. (London: Routledge, 2006), 212; Andre Brink, "Stories of History: Reimaging the Past in Post-Apartheid Narrative," in Sarah Nuttall and Carli Coetzee (eds.), *Negotiating the Past: The Making of Memory in South Africa* (Oxford: Oxford University Press, 1998), 37; Goolam Vahed, "Cultural Confrontation: Race, Politics, and Cricket in South Africa in the 1970s and 1980s," *Culture, Sport, Society* 5, no. 2 (2002): 79–107.

99 Kidd, *The Struggle for Canadian Sport*, 74–5 and 90.

100 George Sage, *Power and Ideology in American Sport: A Critical Perspective* (Champaign, IL: Human Kinetics, 1990), 19.

101 Kidd, *The Struggle for Canadian Sport*, 80. See also 75–7, 79, 91, and 262.

102 John Hargreaves, "Sport and Hegemony: Some Theoretical Problems," in Cantelon and Gruneau, *Sport, Culture, and the Modern State*, 134–5.

103 Sage, *Power and Ideology*, 20. The conceptualization of hegemony and its application have been the subjects of long debate in sports studies. See, for example, William Morgan, *Leftist Theories of Sport: A Critique and Reconstruction* (Urbana: University of Illinois Press, 1994), 95; Alan Ingham and Rob Beamish, "Didn't Cyclops Lose His Vision? An Exercise in Sociological Optometry," *Sociology of Sport Journal* 14, no. 2 (1997): 64–75; William Morgan, "Yet Another Critical

Look at Hegemony Theory: A Response to Ingham and Beamish," *Sociology of Sport Journal* 14, no. 2 (1997): 187–95; Richard Holt, *Sport and the British: A Modern History* (Oxford: Claredon Press, 1989), 364.

104 Editor of *History and Theory*, cited in Jenkins, *Postmodern History Reader*, 385.

105 Cited in Jenkins, *Postmodern History Reader*, 389.

106 Editor of *History and Theory*, cited in Jenkins, *Postmodern History Reader*, 385.

107 Jenkins, *Why History?*, 14–15.

108 Kidd, "Another World Is Possible," 156.

109 Jenkins, *Why History?*; Munslow, *Historical Studies*, 95.

110 Munslow, *Historical Studies*, 95.

111 White, *Metahistory*, 329–30.

112 Munslow, *Historical Studies*, 97.

113 Lévinas's key texts are *Totality and Infinity: An Essay on Exteriority*, trans. A. Lingis (Pittsburgh: Duquesne University Press, 1969), and *Otherwise Than Being or Beyond Essence*, trans. A. Lingis (Dordrecht: Kluwer Academic Publishers, 1978). See also Seán Hand, *The Levinas Reader: Emmanuel Levinas* (Oxford: Blackwell, 1989).

114 Eaglestone, *The Holocaust*.

115 Bettina Bergo, "Emmanuel Levinas," in Edward Zalta (ed.), *The Stanford Encyclopedia of Philosophy* (2008), http://plato.stanford.edu/archives/fall2008/entries/levinas/.

116 Bergo, "Emmanuel Levinas," and Eaglestone, *The Holocaust*, 311.

117 Eaglestone, *The Holocaust*, 315.

118 Ibid., 284, and Eaglestone, "The 'Fine Risk' of History," 317.

119 Eaglestone, "The 'Fine Risk' of History," 318.

120 Eaglestone, *The Holocaust*, 288–9.

121 Ibid., 299.

122 Kidd, *Tom Longboat*, 7–8.

123 Kidd, *The Struggle for Canadian Sport*, 173.

124 Bruce Kidd, "Book Reviews: Robert Archer and Antoine Bouillon, *The South African Game*, Tom Newnham, *Batons and Barbed Wire*, and Sam Ramsamy, *Apartheid: The Real Hurdle*," *Journal of Sport and Social Issues* 7, no, 2 (1983): 54.

125 Kidd, *Tom Longboat*, 8.

126 Eaglestone, "The 'Fine Risk' of History," 317. In a recent review essay Willemijn Ruberg usefully discusses the ways historians of emotion grapple with these issues including the fundamental questions of how to define affect and emotion – should historians, for example, incorporate the findings of neuroscience and psychology into their definitions? – and how to "recover or represent (individual/collective) emotions of the past?" "Interdisciplinarity and the History of Emotions," *Cultural and Social History* 6, no. 4 (2009): 507–16.

127 Kidd, "The Struggle Must Continue," 164.
128 Ibid.
129 Richard Cashman, *Paradise of Sport: The Rise of Organised Sport in Australia* (Melbourne: Oxford, 1995).
130 White, *Metahistory*, 22 and 26.
131 Eaglestone, *The Holocaust*, 7.

Acknowledgments

Playing for Change celebrates activism, especially as it is grounded in a critical consideration of the cultural significance of sport and physical activity. It has been inspired by Bruce Kidd, and this collection of essays explores contemporary and historical issues through the lens of the roles that have comprised Bruce's extensive and varied career: athlete, scholar, activist, and administrator. Bruce first came to national prominence as a teenager in the late 1950s and early 1960s, bursting on the scene as one of Canada's most accomplished track stars. In an era before athletic specialization, Bruce was a world-class runner at a variety of distances, setting records in the mile (and making attempts at breaking the legendary four-minute barrier) and at distances of three miles and longer. He won gold and bronze medals at the 1962 Commonwealth Games in Perth, Australia, represented Canada at the 1964 Tokyo Olympic Games, won the Lou Marsh Award in 1961, and was named Canadian male athlete of the year in 1961 and 1962. Such accomplishments, however, were the beginning rather than the culmination of a lifelong engagement with sport.

Bruce brought an activist sensibility to his conception of sport and recreation. In a career too accomplished and varied to summarize justly, he has campaigned for a broad spectrum of human rights within and beyond sport. He was prominent in the anti-apartheid movement, the fight for increased women's and girls' access to sport and recreational opportunities, and a number of arts initiatives that connected with sport. His administrative roles included seventeen years as the director, and later the dean, of what became the Faculty of Physical Education and Health (now named the Faculty of Kinesiology and Physical Education) at the University of Toronto, where his vision of accessible and equitable physical activity influenced both the physical spaces where recreation occurred and the programing that took place within those spaces. Bruce has described himself as a "critical supporter" of the Olympic movement, believing in the positive potential of sport, and is focusing his current efforts on promoting sport for development and peace (SDP).[1] He has recently completed a term as chair of the Commonwealth Advisory Body on Sport, and it is partly in this capacity that he recently proposed a vision of what sport, in this case the Commonwealth Games, can achieve: "It is time I suggest that the Games forge a new common spirit across the Commonwealth by explicitly and practically linking the Games to the goals of democracy, development, and diversity. Just as the Games committed Commonwealth sportspersons to racial justice during the struggle against apartheid, they could contribute to a new standard for social equity by linking high performance sport to sport for all and development through sport."[2]

Such a vision is informed not only by strong personal beliefs and tangible experience from a life within sport but also by a scholarly approach to these issues. Bruce is a leading scholar in the history, sociology, and public policy of sport and physical activity. With a foundation in political economy and history from the University of Toronto, University of Chicago, and York University, he has a unique perspective on the continental sporting landscape (informed also by his decision to compete collegiately for the University of Toronto, while rejecting overtures from American schools). Bruce has written widely on these topics – his monograph, *The Struggle for Canadian Sport*, is an important text in Canadian sport history – informing his activism with empiricism based on a well-articulated theoretical position. An exploration of Kidd's published work is the subject of Douglas Booth's chapter that concludes this volume, but it is worth noting that Booth considers Kidd's scholarship to be "an exemplar of the emancipation project in the social history of sport. Kidd is one of a select few to explicitly advocate history as a vehicle to raise political awareness and consciousness in sport with a view to effecting social change." And Kidd has imbued his teaching and mentorship with a similar commitment to scholarship and activism. He regularly made this connection for undergraduate students in his course on the historical development of Canadian physical activity. On the most recent occasion that Bruce taught this course, he prefaced his syllabus with a quotation from a popular book that encouraged engaged citizenship: "If history shows us anything, it's that the obdurate world *does* yield. Change – surprising, sometimes radical change – *does* happen. The world does turn on its head once in a while. And what seemed almost impossible looking forward seems almost inevitable looking back ... Using insights about *how the world is changed*, we can become active participants in shaping those changes."[3]

All the contributors to this collection share with Bruce Kidd the belief that scholarship is a public act, one that comes with a social responsibility. They represent a cross-section of Canadian and international scholars at varying stages of their careers.[4] Their contributions are an indication of the high esteem in which they hold Bruce Kidd. They include people who have been influenced and mentored by him, as either students or colleagues. They include people who would place themselves within one of the many different academic spheres with which Bruce identifies – sport history, sport sociology, and Olympics studies. Most of all, however, they represent the women and men with whom Bruce has over the years debated the meanings and organization of sport and physical activity. It is to such issues that a group of his friends, comrades, and colleagues turn their attention in this book.

Some of the chapters in this volume were presented at a one-day symposium titled "Scholar, Athlete, Activist: A Celebration in Honour of Bruce Kidd," co-hosted by the Faculty of Physical Education and Health and the Centre for Sport Policy Studies at the University of Toronto on 25 May 2010. The talent and effort exhibited by Nadine McHorgh and Desmond Miller in organizing that event cannot be overstated. The subsequent financial support of the Faculty of Kinesiology and Physical Education and the Centre for Sport Policy Studies at the University of Toronto has been invaluable. And the initiative of Rosanne Lopers-Sweetman, who planted the first seed that sprouted into this book and who has been supportive throughout the entire process, merits special commendation.

NOTES

1 Bruce Kidd, "A New Social Movement: Sport for Development and Peace," *Sport in Society* 11, no. 4 (2008): 370–80.
2 Bruce Kidd, "The Trajectory of the Commonwealth Games: Delhi and Beyond," Keynote Address at the Summit: Delhi 2010 – The Games and the Commonwealth, India Habitat Center, New Delhi, 29 March 2010.
3 Frances Wesley, Brenda Zimmerman, and Michael Quinn Patton, *Getting to Maybe* (Toronto: Random House, 2006), viii, 7.
4 It is with deep sadness that this community lost Jim Riordan during the time that this book was in production. While we are honoured to include his contribution here (co-authored by Hart Cantelon), his absence is felt by all who knew him.

Contributors

Michael Atkinson is Professor in the Faculty of Kinesiology and Physical Education at the University of Toronto. His research interests include the ethnographic study of violence, pain, and suffering in physical cultures, and post-sport physical cultures. His current work focuses on the existential aspects of movement for people with neurological disorders.

Rob Beamish has taught at Queen's University, Kingston, Ontario, for thirty-two years, serving as an associate dean (1995–2002), and is currently head of Sociology (2004–9; 2011 to the present). His research centres on high-performance sport and specific themes in social theory. Rob's work includes *Marx, Method and the Division of Labor*; *Fastest, Highest, Strongest: The Critique of High-Performance Sport* (with Ian Ritchie); *The Promise of Sociology: The Classical Tradition and Contemporary Sociological Thinking*; and *Steroids: A New Look at Performance-Enhancing Drugs*.

Glyn Bissix is Professor in the programs of Community Development and Environmental and Sustainability Studies at Acadia University. His doctorate in resources and environmental management was awarded by the London School of Economics. Glyn's teaching includes community design and active living, parks management, and strategic planning. His publications focus on integrated resource and environmental management, outdoor recreation, health inequalities, active living, and, most recently, the health, environmental, social, and economic impacts of all-terrain-vehicle use.

Douglas Booth is Professor of Sport Studies and Dean of the School of Physical Education at the University of Otago, New Zealand. He is the author of *The Race Game* (1998), *Australian Beach Cultures* (2001), and *The Field* (2005).

Douglas serves on the editorial boards of *Rethinking History*, the *Journal of Sport History*, and *Sport History Review*, and he is an executive member of the Australian Society for Sport History.

Nancy B. Bouchier is Associate Professor of History at McMaster University, Hamilton, Ontario, where she teaches courses in Canadian, sport, and exercise history. She is the author of *For the Love of the Game: Amateur Sport in Small-Town Ontario, 1838–1895*. With Ken Cruikshank she is the author of *The People and the Bay: A Social and Environmental History of Hamilton Harbour* (forthcoming).

Hart Cantelon presently holds professor emeritus status at the University of Lethbridge, Alberta. Prior to his retirement in 2009, he held academic appointments in the School of Physical and Health Education at Queen's University (Kingston, Ontario) and chaired the Department of Kinesiology and Physical Education at the University of Lethbridge. He remains active in sociology of sport research, focusing primarily on the organization of sport in the former Soviet Union and the dynamics of the global ice hockey world.

Ken Cruikshank is Dean of Humanities and Professor of History at McMaster University, Hamilton, Ontario, and past editor of the *Canadian Historical Review*. He teaches courses in Canadian, environmental, and business history. He is the author of *Close Ties: Railways, Government, and the Board of Railway Commissioners, 1851–1933*. Together with Nancy B. Bouchier, he is the author of *The People and the Bay: A Social and Environmental History of Hamilton Harbour* (forthcoming).

Peter Donnelly is Director of the Centre for Sport Policy Studies, and a professor in the Faculty of Kinesiology and Physical Education at the University of Toronto. His research interests include sport politics and policy issues, including the area of children's rights in sport. He has published numerous scholarly works on these and other topics.

Russell Field is Assistant Professor in the Faculty of Kinesiology and Recreation Management at the University of Manitoba. His research focuses on multi-sport events as moments of protest or resistance such as the 1963 Games of the New Emerging Forces. He also studies the cultural representations of sport and physical activity found in both narrative and documentary films and is the founder and executive director of the Canadian Sport Film Festival (www.sportfilmfestival.ca).

Richard Gruneau is Professor of Communication at Simon Fraser University in Burnaby, British Columbia, where he teaches in the areas of political economy, media and ideology, popular cultural studies, histories of communications research, and social theory. His most recent book is *Mega-Events and Globalization: Capital and Spectacle in a Changing World Order* (co-edited with John Horne, 2015).

Stephen Hardy retired in 2014 as Professor of Kinesiology and Affiliate Professor of History at the University of New Hampshire. He played hockey for Bowdoin College, coached at Vermont Academy and Amherst College, and was hockey supervisor for the Eastern College Athletic Conference. He is working with Andrew Holman on a book tentatively titled *Coolest Game: A History of Hockey*. He lives in New Hampshire with his wife, Donna.

Colin Howell is Professor Emeritus in History and Academic Director of the Centre for the Study of Sport and Health at Saint Mary`s University in Halifax, Nova Scotia. A former co-editor of the *Canadian Historical Review*, he is the author of *Blood, Sweat and Cheers: Sport and the Making of Modern Canada* (2001), *Northern Sandlots* (1995), a history of the Victoria General Hospital in Halifax, and numerous edited collections.

John J. MacAloon is Professor of the Social Sciences at the University of Chicago. He is the author of *This Great Symbol*, the classic biography of Pierre de Courbertin, a new edition of which appeared from Routledge in 2008. Professor MacAloon's most recent book is *Bearing Light: Flame Relays and the Struggle for the Olympic Movement* (Routledge, 2013). He holds the Olympic Order for his scholarly and diplomatic contributions to the Olympic movement.

Victoria Paraschak is Professor in Kinesiology at the University of Windsor, Ontario. Her early research focused on the ways that Aboriginal sport and recreation practices and policies have been shaped within unequal power relations in Canada. She has recently been exploring the development of a Strengths and Hope perspective, which focuses first on ascertaining existing strengths of underserved groups and then identifies and accesses available resources to work together with them towards a shared, preferred future.

Robert Pitter is Professor in the School of Kinesiology at Acadia University, Nova Scotia. He teaches about sport, physical culture, and media. His publications have examined sport, physical activity, and society – in the areas of policy, race, pain, and injury – as well as environmental education and organizational theory. They have appeared in *Research in Sport and Exercise Quarterly*, *Quest*, *Sociology of Sport Journal*, *International Review for Sociology of Sport*, and *Journal of Sport and Social Issues*.

William James Riordan (1936–2012) was born in Portsmouth, England, in 1936 and grew up during the Second World War; his war-time memories during those impressionable years serve as a backdrop for several novels written for young adults. While Jim was a prolific writer of children's literature, academic scholars are most familiar with his expansive output of articles and books on contemporary sport. His *Sport and Soviet Society: Development of Sport and Physical Education in Russia and the USSR* (Cambridge University Press, 1977) remains the definitive English-language account of the development of sport in tsarist Russia and the Soviet Union. The co-authored chapter in *Playing for Change* was one of the last academic articles to which Jim contributed prior to his death.

Parissa Safai is Associate Professor in the School of Kinesiology and Health Science in the Faculty of Health at York University, Ontario. Her research interests focus on the critical study of sport at the intersection of risk, health, and health care including the social determinants of athletes' health. Her interests also centre on sport and social inequality with focused attention paid to the impact of gender, socio-economic, and ethnocultural inequities on accessible physical activity for all.

Patricia Vertinsky is a Distinguished University Scholar and Professor of Kinesiology at the University of British Columbia in Vancouver. She is a social and cultural historian working across the fields of women's history, sport history and sociology, physical culture, gender studies, and the history of health and medicine.

Index

Page references in italics refer to illustrations.

Cran, Brad, 70, 88n15
Crane, Charles, 157, 161, 188n47, 192n77
cricket, 5, 10, 11
A Critique of Political Economy (Marx), 409
Cronin, Mike, 420, 432–33n78
Crothers, Bill, 133–4
Cruz, Tomas de la, 230, 238
Cuba and post-war baseball: about, 19, 244;
    American expansionism, 236–9, 244; and
    Castro, 244; and Florida International
    League, 237–8, 244; independence of,
    238, 244; media coverage, 238; players in
    Canada, 242; and Washington Senators,
    234–7
Cuban Winter League (baseball), 19, 238–9,
    242, 244
cultural production processes: assimilation,
    311–12; Bhabha on, 256, 268, 312, 317;
    indigenizing, as term, 316; melting pot vs.
    menudo chowder, 312, 316–17
cultural studies, 397, 403n7, 404n24; and
    contextualization, 396–7; as shadow
    discipline, 23–4, 390. *See also* physical
    cultural studies (PCS)

Daley, Richard, 175, 186n37
Davis, Mike, 33
The Death of Hockey (Kidd and Macfarlane),
    6, 18, 199–200, 222n4
de Coubertin. *See* Coubertin, Pierre de, Baron
Deflem, Mathieu, 378, 387n72
Delhi Commonwealth Games, 2010, 10, 13,
    49, 54
democracy: capitalism and democratic
    pragmatism, 293–4; democratization of
    baseball, 229; democratization of specialist
    knowledge, 378; environmental issues
    and democratic pragmatism, 293–4; and
    public sociology's vision, 368; slums and
    democratic action, 57
Dene Games, 314, 316. *See also* aboriginal
    people; *and entries beginning with* NWT
Denesha, Ruth, 216
Denver, Colorado, rejection of Olympic
    Games, 73, 74
Depression. *See* inter-war years
Deripaska, Oleg, 111
Derrida, Jacques, 399, 405n39, 425

Detroit, Michigan: early history of hockey,
    208, 210, 211
Detwiler, Susan, 342, *343*
development and sport, international. *See*
    international development and sport; sport
    for development and peace (SDP)
Development Program, UN (UNDP), 39, 41,
    55–6, 61n39, 62n55
dirt bikes. *See* off-road motorcycles (ORMs)
disability and sport: Dubin report
    recommendations, 16, 132–3, 140; public
    sociology on, 373–4; Sport Canada policy
    and national sport organizations, 261.
    See also Paralympic Games
discourse analysis: environmental issues,
    292–4; shared-use trails research, 275–6.
    See also race and ethnicity and baseball
Dobson, Andrew, 280, 292
Donnelly, Peter, 261, 266, 271n50, 272n69
doping. *See* banned substances
Dryzek, John, 277, 292–4
Dubin, Hon. Charles, 15–16, 127
Dubin inquiry: about the inquiry, 126–9;
    about the report, 16, 129–33; impact of,
    16, 140–3; and instrumental rationality, 16,
    126, 127, 141–2; issues not considered, 129,
    141; Kidd's views and participation, 131,
    133–4, 137, 355n32; new ethical institutions,
    16; and Olympic principles, 136, 138;
    recommendations, 16, 129, 137–40; trans-
    historical, essentialist notion of sport, 137, 411
Dubin inquiry, issues in sport: athletes as
    ambassadors, 135; banned substances,
    126, 128, 129, 131, 137, 138, 140; broad
    participation vs. elite sport, 16, 133–4,
    136–40, 143; Canadian identity, 130, 132;
    coaches and ethics, 136–7; equality of
    opportunity, 130; ethics and morality, 130,
    133–7, 139, 141, 355n32; full time athletes,
    134; government funding, 132, 139, 141,
    143; government involvement in sport,
    130–3, 136–7, 139; health and fitness, 132;
    inclusion, 16, 131–3, 139–40; internal
    contradictions between sport systems and
    government policies, 128–9, 142; medals
    and money, 132–4, 135, 139, 140–2, 417;
    participation, 131–2, 139; spectator sport and
    entertainment, 136; value of sport, 134–5, 139